'A warts-and-all biography follows John[...] sider, from one drama to the next. It's a[...]
Will Hodgkinson (cl[...]

'Rock biographies can feel like they are ten-a-penny so it is a refreshing change to read a meaty no-holds barred, non-sycophantic record of legendary Man in Black Johnny Cash . . . The wealth of detail on every page, in every incident in Cash's Life (1932–2002) is both impressive and a joy to read. Unlike so many biographies that are reported incidents jigsawed together, this is almost an eyewitness account with not always favourable opinion, perfecting its colour and gravitas'   Nicole Carmichael, *Sunday Express*

'Mr Hilburn got as close to the Cash inner circle as any journalist could. He was the only reporter present at the historic Folsom Prison show in 1968, and he interviewed Cash over the years up to his final days. The result is the most authoritative and revealing portrait to date of the most chronicled figure in country-music history'   Eddie Dean, *Wall Street Journal* (Europe)

'A great story requires great storytelling, and that's exactly what it receives here. Ultimately, Robert Hilburn's biography uncannily resembles its subject: massive and stolid, but with a dangerous glint in its eye'   Charles Shaar Murray, *Literary Review*

'There is madness aplenty in this excellent life of the turbulent Johnny Cash'   Rod Liddle, *Sunday Times*

'Hilburn's biography has the sort of immense scope and tremendous insight that comes from years of interviewing such a truthful, troubling subject'   Rob Fitzpatrick, *Sunday Times*

'How do you write an interesting biography of such a beloved figure? First, hire Robert Hilburn. He is a prodigious researcher, but he keeps a steady hand on the tiller, and never allows his research to swamp his narrative. He knows his music and music history, but unlike far too many music critics, he avoids the temptation to show off'   *Economist*

Robert Hilburn was a music critic and pop-music editor for the *Los Angeles Times* for more than three decades and has worked closely with pop-music legends, including Elton John, Bono, Michael Jackson, John Lennon and Johnny Cash. He hosts a weekly radio show – *Rock 'n' Roll Times with Robert Hilburn* – every Sunday on the Los Angeles-based station KCSN-FM.

By Robert Hilburn

Springsteen
Corn Flakes with John Lennon
Johnny Cash

JOHNNY
CASH
THE LIFE

Robert Hilburn

PHOENIX

A PHOENIX PAPERBACK

First published in Great Britain in 2013
by Weidenfeld & Nicolson
This paperback edition published in 2014
by Phoenix,
an imprint of Orion Books Ltd,
Orion House, 5 Upper St Martin's Lane,
London WC2H 9EA

An Hachette UK company

10 9 8 7 6 5 4 3 2 1

Copyright © Robert Hilburn 2013

A CIP catalogue record for this book
is available from the British Library.

ISBN 978-1-7802-2095-6

Printed and bound by CPI Group (UK) Ltd, Croydon, CR0 4YY

The Orion Publishing Group's policy is to use papers
that are natural, renewable and recyclable products and
made from wood grown in sustainable forests. The logging
and manufacturing processes are expected to conform to
the environmental regulations of the country of origin.

www.orionbooks.co.uk

SONGWRITER, HISTORIAN, FIGHTER OF CAUSES; FRIEND TO THE DEPRIVED AND TROUBLED, FRIEND OF GREAT MEN; A LEADER IN THE TEMPORAL WORLD, AND FOLLOWER IN THE SPIRITUAL WORLD, JOHNNY CASH IS THE TOTAL ENTERTAINER. AN INTERNATION- ALLY FAMOUS PERFORMER, HE CARRIES HIS LOVE FOR HIS COUNTRY AND FOR COUNTRY MUSIC AROUND THE WORLD. THE MAN IN BLACK RETAINS HIS ROOTS IN THE SOIL AS HE GROWS IN CONSCIENCE AND IN- TEGRITY. HE IS ONE OF THE WORLD'S MOST BELOVED AND HONORED STARS.

—Johnny Cash's plaque at
the Country Music Hall of Fame

Contents

PART ONE

CHAPTER 1

DYESS AND THE DREAM

I

THE TWO-AND-A-HALF-MILE walk from the Cash family's five-room, federally assisted farmhouse in rural Dyess, Arkansas, to the town center was just long enough for young J.R. to work up a head full of dreams. For years, the third son of Ray and Carrie Cash walked the narrow gravel road with his schoolboy pals, all of them fantasizing about being cowboy movie stars like Gene Autry and Tex Ritter. But J.R. most enjoyed walking the road alone, especially at night, when the darkness felt like a shield against the rest of the world, leaving him free to pursue a dream that was far more important than he wanted to admit.

On those nights, J.R. would frequently sing to himself, he later told friends when reminiscing about his childhood days, partially to calm his nerves when he heard the rustling of cottonmouth snakes in the grass or the howl of prowling panthers in the woods a few hundred yards away. Years later, some of J.R.'s old chums and even his younger sister Joanne chuckled at the idea of panthers in the woods. Snakes, yes—maybe even an occasional bobcat—but no one knew anything about panthers. "He had a real vivid imagination," says A. J. Henson, who sometimes walked that gravel road with his friend. Even Cash himself often admitted that he never let facts interfere with a good story. But as Joanne put it, there's no doubting one thing about the Dyess years: J.R. loved to sing.

There was something about music that was even more magical to him than movies, a fascination that came naturally. His family, especially his mother, had always turned to songs for comfort and inspiration. Soon after he started grade school, J.R. knew he wanted to be a singer on the radio, and he began to think of that gravel road at night as his own secret stage. When he was feeling especially good, he'd stop after a song, look up at the Arkansas moon, and take a bow.

The first song J.R. remembered hearing was the old hymn "I Am Bound for the Promised Land." He was just three years old, but he joined the chorus— *Oh who will come and go with me? / I am bound for the promised land*—as his mother sang during the 250-mile journey in a flatbed truck that took the family and its little bit of furniture across Arkansas. They had left his birthplace of Kingsland in the hill country of the south-central part of the state to travel to the fertile flat black delta land of Dyess in the northeast corner. Thanks to Franklin Delano Roosevelt's New Deal program, they were about to claim what she told them would be their own promised land on earth.

But for most of the two-day trip in March of 1935, J.R. and his older brothers, Roy (born 1921) and Jack (1929), huddled together under a tarpaulin in the bed of the truck, trying to protect themselves from the punishing cold and rain. The ride along muddy roads was all the more frightening because the vehicle frequently hit potholes with such force that the boys feared the wheels might be knocked loose at any moment. Their mother tried to calm them and her two daughters, Reba (1934) and Louise (1923), with music and the assurance that God was watching over the family.

The story of Dyess had its roots in the Great Depression, when most of the farmers in the state, including J.R.'s father, struggled to survive. As the price of a five-hundred-pound bale of cotton dropped from $125 in 1928 to $35 in 1932, there was panic among farmers over how to provide for their families. President Roosevelt, according to the popular version of a complicated bureaucratic backstory, came to the rescue with a plan to give distraught workers the chance of a more secure future. Through the Federal Emergency Relief Administration, funds were allocated to build small cooperative communities around the country to provide some deserving farmers with homes, twenty acres of land, and a small annual stipend for food and clothing. The social experiment also called for new buildings to house support services, including a cotton gin, general store, restaurant, school, hospital, post office, and gas station.

Officially titled Colonization Project No. 1, Dyess was one of the first cooperatives. In May 1934, more than 1,300 workers taken from Arkansas's welfare rolls had started building houses and roads on a sixteen-thousand-acre spread of land. At the same time, the government began taking applications for Dyess farmers. Only Caucasians were eligible. This wasn't welfare, the applicants were told. The town's new arrivals had to work the land and then use money from the crops, chiefly cotton, to repay the government the cost of the housing, the property, and the stipend before they could receive the deed to the property. When Ray Cash heard about the Dyess project on the radio, he decided in an instant to apply.

Thousands of destitute men lined up at government offices throughout the state to apply for only five hundred homesteads. Ray Cash wasn't intimidated. He presented himself as just the kind of hardworking, industrious family man and fiercely patriotic American that he felt the government administrators were seeking. His paternal roots in North America dated back to 1667, when one of his ancestors, William Cash, came across the Atlantic from Scotland on the ship *Good Intent* and settled in Essex County, Massachusetts. William's descendants then migrated to Virginia in the early 1700s and on to Georgia, where Ray Cash's grandfather Reuben Cash was born.

After Reuben's plantation was destroyed by General William T. Sherman's troops during the Civil War, the former Confederate soldier moved west to Arkansas in 1866. Ray's father, William Henry Cash, was six. He grew up to be a farmer and a Baptist preacher, a circuit rider who served four widely separated counties. Ray, one of twelve children, was born in 1897.

In the interview process for the Dyess land, Ray stressed not only his military service (he had served in France briefly during World War I), but also how hard he had worked to support his family after farming became unprofitable. He'd pursued odd jobs, sometimes walking miles to cut wood at a sawmill or hopping a freight train to Charleston, Mississippi, to help dismantle a chemical plant. Still, there were no guarantees that he would be chosen, and he was desperate to secure some kind of permanent work. After finishing the rigorous interview, he suffered a week of sleepless nights before getting the good news. Ray Cash was one of just five applicants from all of Cleveland County to be accepted for the program.

Following the grueling truck ride from Kingsland, the Cashes arrived at their new home in Dyess, carried in the colony records as house number 226 on Road 3. Years later, photos of early Dyess houses make the residences look primitive and bare-boned, bringing to mind Walker Evans's stark photos of American poverty during the Great Depression. Indeed, the days of rainfall had left the mud so deep and thick on the property that Ray had to leave the truck a hundred yards away from the house and carry J.R. the rest of the way. Still, the new home looked like a mansion to the Cashes. It had been painted white with green trim, and there were glass panes instead of burlap sacks in the windows. The family of seven walked around the house and the barn, admiring them the way farmers might examine a prize cow.

Yet the excitement soon wore off as Ray and his oldest son, Roy, started the arduous work of clearing land. In *Johnny Cash: The Autobiography* in 1997, Cash described the tortured colony land as a "jungle—I mean real jungle. Cottonwood and ash and hickory as well as scrub oak and cypress, the trees and vines and bushes tangled up so thick in places that you couldn't get through, some of it underwater."

According to Cash, his father and brother attacked the land from dawn to nightfall, six days a week, "starting on the highest ground and working their way downward foot by foot, cutting with saws and axes and Kaiser blades—long-handled machetes—and then dynamiting and burning out the stumps." The ordeal was so formidable that by the start of planting season that first spring, the Cashes had been able to clear only about three of the twenty acres.

Dozens of new Dyess residents gave up and moved on, grumbling that the whole program was a sham. There were inevitable whispers about political corruption—and even outsiders began asking questions. Though funds for the colony came from the federal government, the colony owed its existence to a young landowner and county election commissioner in Arkansas more than it did to anyone in Washington, D.C. It was this man that the colony would eventually be named for: William Reynolds Dyess.

Moved by the impact of the Depression on the state's farmers, Dyess had begun campaigning in the early 1930s for a government program to aid farmers and their families. After hearing about the FERA program, W. R. Dyess contacted Harry Hopkins, the program's director in Washington, and came away with more than $3 million. At the same time, Dyess was named FERA representative for Arkansas. He then chose an area about twenty miles from his hometown of Osceola to build the colony. The location and subsequent purchase raised eyebrows. When word got out in 1934 that Dyess was thinking of running for governor or possibly U.S. senator, would-be opponents started asking ticklish questions about the colony.

The acreage in question was part of a three-county stretch in Arkansas known as the "sunken lands"—territory redesigned by a series of earthquakes in 1811 and 1812. The shifts in the ground caused by the quakes, centered just thirty miles northeast of the future site of Dyess, caused various stretches of land to sink up to fifty feet in places. Water rushed in, turning much of the area into swampland overrun with tangled vegetation and the mushy soil that locals referred to as "gumbo."

Why, Dyess's detractors wanted to know, did the program director pick this particular land—land that no farmer in his right mind would have chosen? Was the purchase a favor for Lee Wilson, a family friend who owned the sodden acreage? Backers of the project countered that there was desperation in the air in Arkansas in the 1930s and the colony property was dirt cheap. The state would really have been under fire, they maintained, if Dyess had used federal funds to buy top-grade farmland. By buying property that, in essence, no one else wanted, he made sure that the colony got more land for its money. That was the view ultimately accepted by most Dyess residents, who dismissed the small group of dissenters in the colony as a "radical" or "troublemaking" fringe.

Still, there was enough of a stir that, in 1934, the Federal Emergency Relief Administration sent three men to investigate the complaints against W. R. Dyess. One member of the team did accuse Dyess of indiscretion in spending some of the money to improve roads on noncolony property that he and Wilson owned. Otherwise, the trio found no evidence of criminal acts. In Washington, Harry Hopkins made no attempt to remove or penalize Dyess. Additional complaints surfaced later about check fraud and payroll irregularities, but Dyess's supporters dismissed them as smears by political opponents, and formal investigations revealed no serious problems.

On January 24, 1936, just months before the formal incorporation of the colony, the issue of W. R. Dyess became history; the man behind the dream was killed in a plane crash. But the residents of the new colony had always thought of President Roosevelt—not their neighbor—as their savior. FDR's comforting voice on the radio and his New Deal policies were giving millions of people hope. The president was beloved by the people of Dyess, and he took on saintly qualities to young J.R. Roosevelt never visited the colony, but his wife, Eleanor, was present on June 9, 1936, for the dedication of the new administration building.

Mrs. Roosevelt, who had vigorously encouraged Harry Hopkins's work in providing emergency relief around the country, arrived with a car and driver, accompanied by four state troopers on motorcycles. After delivering a short speech from the porch of the two-story building, she spent hours shaking hands with all of the 2,500 or so folks who turned out, including J.R. At least that's the way he remembered it. His boyhood friend J. E. Huff later maintained that Mrs. Roosevelt patted them both on the head. Either way, J.R. talked his mother and father into staying in the town center so he could watch through the Dyess Café window as she ate dinner.

The fact that the government was responsible for giving his family and neighbors a second chance left the youngster with a deep patriotism and a profound respect for the American presidency.

II

J.R. wasn't expected to pick cotton until he was six, but he started carrying water to the rest of the family in the fields by his fourth birthday, and he'd often linger just to sing gospel songs with them. He'd also sit at his mother's feet at night in the family living room as she played the same songs on an acoustic guitar or the family's $37 upright piano. The tunes all came from an old Baptist hymn book, and they became ingrained in him; J.R. would sing at least one, often "I'll Fly Away" or "Softly and Tenderly," to himself almost every day for much of his life. In future years when overwhelmed by drugs and other pressures, he would often isolate himself and turn to music as a refuge; the purity of music was a place of comfort and affirmation.

Carrie Cash loved gospel music and listened to it on the battery-powered Sears radio that Ray bought for the family, a luxury in their struggling farm community. J.R. sat with his mother and listened to the gospel singers, but he was also drawn to the country music singers his brother Roy favored. As he sat by the radio, J.R. was fascinated to see how Roy listened to the country singers with the same devotion that his mother showed toward her gospel singers. Though it took him years to put it into words, he found something warmly satisfying in the way music brought people together and lifted their spirits. Each moment with the radio was especially valued because playing time was limited; it was expensive to get the battery charged.

J.R. soon followed the singers he heard on the radio the way other boys in Dyess would later collect baseball cards; he was enthralled by them, learning their names and individual vocal styles, and he had an uncanny memory for lyrics. He'd often challenge Roy to see who knew the most words to various country hits of the day, and J.R. invariably won. He also came to know where the country music stations were on the dial—whether it was WLW in Cincinnati or a border station in Mexico, or WSM in Nashville—and when his favorite shows aired so he could make the most of his precious listening minutes.

The youngster didn't just listen to country and gospel, however.

Some stations played country and pop, and the music-hungry boy looked forward to hearing anything by Bing Crosby or, later, the early rhythm and blues of the Ink Spots. As he got older, J.R. would expand his listening habits to include the fifteen-minute mystery dramas, such as *I Love a Mystery* and *Inner Sanctum.* He also followed comedy and quiz shows such as the Jack Benny show and *Truth or Consequences.* But his first loves remained country and gospel music.

As it happened, the first country singer J.R. recalled hearing was Jimmie Rodgers, who was known to millions of fans in the South and Southwest in the late 1920s and early 1930s as the "Singing Brakeman," because he had worked on and frequently sang about the railroads. Thanks to an appealing bluesy-country approach and songs about a wanderlust lifestyle that stirred the imagination of his mostly rural audience, Rodgers was the first country music superstar. The first Rodgers song J.R. heard was "Hobo Bill's Last Ride," a melancholy tale of a lonely man dying in a boxcar on a freezing night far away from home. J.R. was about five, and the record reminded him of his own anxious journey from Kingsland as well as the times he'd watched his father hop off a freight when returning from one of his job hunts.

Rodgers's music felt so intimate and immediate that J.R. actually believed Rodgers was singing live through the radio speaker just to him. The family didn't have a phonograph, so he didn't understand that he had been listening to a record—something that could be played again and again. He was thrilled a few days later when he heard that magical Rodgers voice again on the radio. He raced around the house, trying to get everyone to sit with him and listen to this story about the lonely, dying man. So impressed was he with the singer that years later, J.R. would tell some of his schoolmates that he was named after Jimmie Rodgers. In truth, the initials had grown out of a stalemate between his parents over a name. Cash's mother wanted to name him John after her father, John Rivers. His father said it should be Ray. So they just settled on the initials. (In some childhood writings Cash signed them simply JR, but J.R. was more common.) The youngster was also especially fond of the mostly sunny, sing-along styles of the Carter Family and Gene

Autry. But the other radio tune from childhood that touched him the most was Vernon Dalhart's "The Prisoner's Song," which was the first million-selling country recording. Like "Hobo Bill's Last Ride," Dalhart's 1924 hit was a lonesome underdog tale. Both songs reflected the themes of heartache and strife that would play a prominent part in many of Cash's own compositions. He later told me he found something uplifting in songs about hard times, speculating that maybe he got that feeling just because someone cared enough about troubled people to write songs about them.

Ray, always a serious-minded man, picked up early on his son's fascination with music and tried to quash what he considered a frivolous pastime. Cash remembered his father often saying, "You ought to turn that stuff off."

The first real crisis for Dyess residents came early in 1937. Torrential rain pelted much of the delta for days, swelling the Mississippi and other rivers in the region and flooding many of the surrounding farms and towns. It began to look like their dreams of a better life were going to be literally washed away. Adding to the trauma, the rain didn't just keep coming, but sometimes gave way to clear skies, raising momentary hopes in the colony that the town would be spared. Then the rains returned harder than ever on January 21, and emergency workers began leading families to higher ground. By nightfall, some seven or eight hundred people were housed at the community center. But it wasn't water from the Mississippi that threatened the residents of Dyess, as Cash often said later. It was the water of the less-well-known Tyronza River, which ran through the heart of the colony.

By noon the next day, the number of people at the community center had doubled. As conditions worsened—it was so cold that the rain froze as it hit the ground, making it difficult to operate trucks and tractors—residents who could stay with relatives elsewhere in the state began leaving Dyess by train. The water began rising during the night more rapidly than before, and by the morning of the twenty-third it was clear that a near-complete evacuation was necessary; there hadn't been any electricity for three days.

Carrie and the younger Cash children were among the first to leave, returning by train to Kingsland to stay with relatives, not knowing if they would ever return. Ray Cash stayed in Dyess with Roy in hopes of safeguarding the house and to help in rescue work. Despite all the fear and upheaval, only two deaths were reported in the area—and the water soon started receding. By February 3 the roads were dry, and the word went out that it was safe to return. The Cashes were back home within two weeks—in plenty of time to celebrate J.R.'s fifth birthday on February 26.

The drama of the time was still vivid in J.R.'s mind nearly a quarter century later when he wrote a song about the flood, "Five Feet High and Rising," that became one of his signature tunes. Looking back on the song, which appeared on a 1959 album titled *Songs of Our Soil,* Cash saw the struggle of the flood as another example of the power of faith and a community working together.

"My mama always taught me that good things come from adversity if we put our faith in the Lord," he said, explaining the genesis of the song. "We couldn't see much good in the flood waters when they were causing us to leave home. But when the water went down, we found that it had washed a load of rich black bottom dirt across our land. The following year we had the best crop we'd ever had."

Thanks to the rich new layer of soil, on February 8, 1938, Ray was able to repay the government $2,183.60 to cover the cost of the land and the cash advances. The twenty acres of delta land were now his, and life in Dyess started to feel good. The whole family thanked God for His blessings three days a week at the First Baptist Church near the town center. That two-story building was as important in young J.R.'s life as the radio.

III

J.R. was taught to believe the literal message of heaven and hell, salvation and eternal damnation. He was also warned to be suspicious of other religions. Catholics, he was told, didn't answer to God but to a mysterious tyrant in Rome, and the Jews killed Christ. Cash later rejected that backward thinking, showing enough tolerance for others' beliefs that he married a Catholic, Vivian Liberto, and agreed to raise his daughters in that faith. When one of his daughters, Rosanne, married a Jew, record producer and guitarist John Leventhal, her father warmly welcomed him into the family. Racism was also rampant in Dyess, and it took a while before he was able to shake its venom.

J.R. joined the rest of his family at the church every Sunday morning, Sunday evening, and Wednesday night. Unlike other kids, who complained about having to go to church, he looked forward to the music, the sermons, and the sense of community. Just as music had warmed his home, church was an early comfort. By the time J.R. was nine, he had two more siblings—a sister, Joanne, born in 1938, and a brother, Tommy, born two years later. Nothing in all he heard about the Bible and God's Commandments struck him as more important than honoring thy father and mother—and he prayed that he'd have a loving wife and family someday. He even pictured the kind of wife he wanted and the way he would raise his children. She would have to be as sweet and loyal as his mother, and he wanted to give his sons and daughters the same affection she showered on him. When he thought about the man he'd like to be, though, he thought of his older brother Jack, and never his father.

Everyone in the family looked upon Jack, who was named after heavyweight boxing champ Jack Dempsey, as the golden child. Handsome, intelligent, outgoing, and generous, Jack made up his mind early that he would serve the Lord by joining the ministry. Even other residents of Dyess spoke about his inspiring spirit and message, and how he had seemed, even at the age of eleven, to behave like a preacher. Jack was especially thoughtful to people in need, counseling adults who drank too much and comforting anyone facing illness or a death in the family. J.R. marveled at how his brother, who was just over two years older, could make adults three times his age feel better about themselves.

J.R. noticed that his friends' older brothers discouraged their younger siblings from hanging out with them in town or at school, but Jack always welcomed J.R. Even Jack's positive influence, however, couldn't keep J.R. from developing a rebellious streak as he approached his teens, when he began to show what his father branded an "attitude." He was moody, sometimes snapping back at his father and his teachers. He started smoking cigarettes at the age of ten—an ultimate act of rebellion at the time. He didn't have money to buy any, so he would sneak some of his father's tobacco and roll his own, or he would bum them from other kids.

"Looking back, that was the first sign of John's addictive personality," his sister Joanne says. "The other boys might smoke an occasional cigarette, but John smoked all the time—except when he was at home." There's no way he would have worried his mother by smoking in front of her.

Jack, who didn't smoke, learned about J.R.'s habit, yet he wasn't judgmental. That was one of the things that J.R. liked best about his brother. J.R. felt such a tight bond with Jack that he even delighted in going fishing with him, which surprised everyone else in the family because J.R. usually preferred fishing alone. He liked his solitude. As he did on the gravel road, the youngster would sometimes lie at the water's edge, staring at the sky and singing his favorite songs—though most often silently to himself to avoid disturbing the fish.

On Saturday, May 13, 1944, J.R. was planning to go to his favorite fishing spot in one of the colony's drainage ditches just off the two-and-a-half-mile route to the town center. Most of the time, fourteen-year-old Jack was too busy to spend the day fishing. If he wasn't helping someone in the community, he was trying to raise money for his family—delivering the *Memphis Press-Scimitar* or doing odd jobs. On this day, too, he planned to earn money by making some fence posts at the high school agricultural building. He knew the family could use the extra $3.

Years later, Cash remembered an exchange in the family living room that would haunt him for the rest of his life.

"[Jack] said he felt like something was going to happen and my mother said, 'Well, don't go,'" Cash said. "Jack stared at the door when an expression of death came over his face."

J.R. pleaded with Jack, "Come, go fishing." But Jack felt a duty to the family.

As Jack headed toward town, J.R. went to the fishing hole, but his heart wasn't in it. He felt restless. Instead of staying most of the day, he stood up after a couple of hours and headed home. That's when he saw the mailman's car coming toward him with his father in it. As soon as he saw his father's ashen face, he knew something bad had happened.

Jack had been cutting the fence posts out of oak logs at the school workshop on a table saw without a guard on it, and the blade had ripped into the boy's stomach. Stunned and bleeding, Jack tried to push his intestines back into his abdomen as he staggered from the shop building. He was spotted by a school official, who rushed him to the hospital. The teenager was alive but unconscious when J.R. and his father arrived. The family gathered around the golden child, their world cruelly and instantly shattered. Though the doctors held out little hope, Jack remained alive, but barely.

Neighbors who had been helped over the years by Jack stopped by the hospital to join the family in prayer. The outpouring overwhelmed J.R. All these people loved his brother as much as he did. It taught him a lot about compassion, he said later. He hoped someday that people would care for him like they cared about Jack.

When the boy's condition worsened on Wednesday, a special service was held at the Baptist church, drawing people from all over Dyess. Learning the next morning that Jack's condition had improved dramatically, Ray and Carrie Cash believed it was a miracle. But the euphoria was short-lived. The family was told on Friday morning that the end was imminent, and they crowded into the hospital room.

"[Jack] started to groan and asked Mama to hold his hand," Cash said, remembering the farewell scene late in life. He said his brother closed his eyes and told Carrie he was at a river. "One way goes to the bad place; the other way goes to the light. I'm going to the light." Then he said, "Can you hear the angels singing? Look at this city, this beautiful city, the gold and all the jewels, the angels. Listen, Mama, can you hear them?"

He died Saturday morning.

Pretty much the whole town came to the funeral on Sunday and joined the family in singing favorite hymns. Jack was buried in a cemetery in nearby Wilson; the words on the gravestone read "Meet

Me in Heaven," Years later, Cash would use the phrase in a song. At the height of his stardom in 1970, Cash would also dedicate his songbook, *Songs of Johnny Cash,* to his brother.

> We lost you one sad day in May 1944.
> Though the songs that we sang
> Are gone from the cotton fields
> I can hear the sound of your voice
> As they are sung far and wide
>
> In loving memory
> Your brother, J.R.

Still reeling, the Cash family was back in the fields on Monday picking cotton. The crops wouldn't wait. The loss of her son, however, was too much for Carrie.

"I watched as my mother fell to her knees and let her head drop onto her chest," Cash recalled in his 1997 autobiography. "My poor daddy came up to her and took her arm, but she brushed him away. 'I'll get up when *God* pushes me up!'"

Finally, slowly and painfully, she got back to her feet and resumed picking cotton. She still had a husband to care for and children to raise.

Through the week, J.R. kept thinking about his brother's words—about a crossroads between the lightness and the dark. "I made my choice after his death which way I was going to go," Cash decades later told a friend, producer-director James Keach. "I answered a call to come down the aisle [in church] and shook the preacher's hand and I accepted Jesus Christ as savior that next Sunday.

"[Jack's] been with me all these years, and sometimes when I [was] so messed up, in such bad trouble, in jail somewhere, I would say, 'I know you're really ashamed of me.' I'm still talking to him. A lot of things might have been different if it weren't for him. He knew about the entertainment world. He knew about the trash that went on. My father would always talk about the evil stage, the evil show business. But Jack didn't. He encouraged me."

J.R. tried to avoid his father's eyes in the months after Jack's death because he didn't want to see the disappointment and the blame. His father had told J.R. the accident would never have happened if he had kept his brother from going to the school shop that day, but really, what could he have done?

During this time, J.R. became increasingly distant, showing little interest in school or hanging out with his pals. More than ever, he treasured his time alone, whether it was at the fishing pond or the school library. Even when he was around friends, they'd often notice a lonely, melancholy quality about him. Rosanne, his daughter, believes a part of that sense of sadness never left her father. "Dad was wounded so profoundly by Jack's death, and by his father's reaction—the blame and recrimination and bitterness," she says. "If someone survives that kind of damage, either great evil or great art can come out of it. And my dad had the seed of great art in him."

It was around this time that J.R. saw a movie that left a lasting impression on him. For most kids, *Frankenstein,* the 1931 film about a mad scientist who creates a monster by putting a criminal's brain into his man-made being, was simply a scary horror story. But Cash felt sorry for the monster, who was killed by a mob that thought he'd murdered a young girl, when in fact the monster had tried to befriend her. Explaining his sympathy for the monster, Cash said he was someone "made up of bad parts but was trying to do good."

James Mangold, who directed *Walk the Line,* the 2005 film about the relationship between Cash and June Carter in the 1960s, talked to Cash about *Frankenstein* and came away from the conversation with the belief that Cash identified so strongly with the movie because he worried, in the aftermath of Jack's death and his father's reaction, that he, too, might have bad parts. "He certainly felt terribly misunderstood by his father."

In his increasing loneliness and grief, J.R. started writing down his thoughts, sometimes in the form of a poem, a short story, or even a song. He found he loved to express himself in words. "I'd never known death either in the family or among friends, and suddenly I realized that I wasn't immortal—that I too could die someday," he said. The writings reflected a darkness that would reappear in Cash's music throughout the years.

J.R. also tried to lose himself in books, showing a particular fondness for American history and the Old West. The stories and accounts stimulated his increasingly active mind, and he often took them with him to the fishing hole. He also developed a great appetite for poetry that never left him.

Like many kids, he loved the work of Edgar Allan Poe as he got older, but he responded most to poets who, like his beloved gospel music, offered inspiring messages. He especially prized one poem—Joaquin Miller's "Columbus." His face would still light up years later when he described the story of Columbus crossing the ocean and facing a series of seemingly impossible hurdles, only to respond each time with the words "Sail on!"

"Some people might think that's corny stuff...how Columbus says, 'Sail on,'" Cash acknowledged late in life. "But it always thrilled me to death. I love that stuff."

Through all this, however, nothing comforted him more than those solitary late-night walks on the gravel road, though he was now singing hymns along with Jimmie Rodgers and Ernest Tubb songs.

It was on one of those walks that J.R. had a revelation that caused him to race home to share it with his mother. For months he had been trying to figure out how to keep Jack's spirit alive and, perhaps, gain some smidgen of affection from his father. He even thought briefly about the ministry, but he couldn't convince himself, even at age twelve, that it was the right choice. The breakthrough came as he walked down the road singing gospel tunes. That was it. He could spread Jack's message through music; he would be a gospel singer.

Joanne Cash remembers her brother running into the house to tell his mother the news. Carrie smiled and hugged her son. When she told Ray about the boy's latest dream, he scoffed. The reaction hurt J.R., but the youngster was used to being disappointed by his father.

J.R.'s demeanor differed greatly from that of his more outgoing brothers and sisters, and his parents interpreted it in opposing ways. J.R.'s father saw the boy's daydreaming and love of music as lazy and unfocused. Ray Cash later explained, "I wanted him to start preparing for the day when he'd be on his own and have to take care of his family." Ray even complained about J.R.'s facial expression or lack of it. Whereas he'd seen enthusiasm and warmth in Jack's face, Ray found it hard to tell what his younger son was thinking—or if the boy was even listening to him—because his eyes didn't reveal any emotion. Carrie Cash thought her son's daydreaming and quiet demeanor were signs that he was thoughtful and sensitive. "He hardly ever said anything," she said years later. "But he listened. He was drinking it all in."

The boy tried hard to be loyal to his father; it was the Commandment that meant the most to him, and he did appreciate the way his father worked tirelessly to provide for the family. Yet, he said later, there was no getting around it: Ray Cash could be cruel, especially when he drank too much. Many of J.R.'s relatives and schoolboy chums would challenge that description of Ray. They said old man Cash was simply gruff, like most hardworking men in Depression-ravaged rural America. But J.R.'s list of complaints against his father went further than not hearing "I love you" regularly.

J.R. was forever wounded when he came home from grade school and found his dog lying dead in the woods near the house. To J.R.'s horror, he learned that his father had shot the animal after it broke into the chicken coop and killed a half-dozen chickens. Most of their neighbors would have done the same thing, but other farmers would have found a more humane way to tell their youngsters, perhaps simply saying the animal had run away. J.R. sensed that his father almost felt glee in telling him about the shooting.

Years later, Ray Cash said he wished he had handled the incident differently. "I wouldn't have killed that dog if I had thought about it," he told Christopher S. Wren for a biography, *The Life of Johnny Cash: Winners Got Scars Too,* in the early 1970s. "I dragged the dog back into the woods. I hated the killing, but it was done. J.R. found the dog and he came and asked me why I shot him. I told him. He never said anything about it to this day."

Though the elder Cash never said anything on the record about his thoughts regarding J.R. and Jack, there remained a lingering resentment over the tragedy.

"Grandpa always kind of blamed Dad for Jack's death," says Cash's daughter Kathy. "And Dad had this real sad guilt thing about him his whole life. You could just see it in his eyes. You can look at almost any picture and see this dark sadness thing going on. Dad even told me...that one time when his daddy had been drinking, he said something like, 'Too bad it wasn't you instead of Jack.' I said, 'Oh, my God, Dad. What a horrible thing to say.' And he said, 'Yeah, I think about that every time I see him.'"

IV

J.R. was walking down a colony road one day more than a year after Jack's death when he was surprised to hear music coming from one of the wooden houses. He didn't know at first if the voice and guitar strumming were from a record or someone inside. Curious, he walked up to the door, where he saw a boy about his age singing and playing an old Ernest Tubb hit called "Drivin' Nails in My Coffin."

The boy, Jesse Barnhill, invited J.R. inside; he was delighted someone else was interested in music. J.R. had seen the teenager around school, but he had never spent any time with him. Jesse suffered from polio, which made walking difficult and clumsy. His paralyzed right arm was only half as long as his left, and his right hand was withered. J.R. marveled that the boy could play the guitar.

Jesse tried to teach J.R. how to play, but J.R. didn't catch on. Even so, J.R. longed for one of the guitars he saw in the Sears Roebuck catalog, especially the Gene Autry model, thinking it would be fun to hold while he was singing. But the family couldn't afford it, so he mostly just sang along while Jesse copied the guitar parts from the records.

Not only did J.R. start spending a lot of time with Jesse, but also he helped his friend overcome his hesitancy and brave the outside world—ignoring the kids who made fun of him. With J.R. leading the way, they'd go to the town center, usually to see a movie or listen to the jukebox in the tiny café. They'd often be joined by Harry Clanton, who was in J.R.'s class. J.R. liked Harry because he had a wonderful sense of humor, and J.R. loved a good joke. Together, J.R. and Harry became known as cutups and pranksters in class—going to elaborate means to entertain the other students with such antics as leaving a dead squirrel in the teacher's desk drawer or causing havoc in the library by pulling out scores of books and putting them back in the wrong places.

When J.R. was feeling especially aggressive, the pranks would take on a harder edge. He loved, for instance, to break bottles he'd find stacked up behind stores in town or sneak into a field at night and set fire to a farmer's haystack. In the Dyess High School annual at the end of his junior year, Cash was called "historian" for his interest in the subject, while Clanton, who was known throughout the school as the mastermind behind all the pranks, was simply "The Schemer."

After his weekly trip to the movies, Cash never had enough money to play the jukebox, but he did a good job of talking others into pushing the button next to the name of Eddy Arnold, who had become a new favorite. Arnold was the hottest thing in country music in the mid-1940s, thanks to such records as "I'll Hold You in My Heart (Till I Can Hold You in My Arms)." Unlike the rawer honky-tonk style that J.R. usually preferred, Arnold sang with a crooning, pop-flavored approach that made him sort of the Bing Crosby of country.

One day in the summer of 1947, J.R. heard on the radio that the cast of one of his favorite radio shows, the *High Noon Roundup,* was coming to Dyess for a concert. The whole Cash family listened to the show, which was broadcast live over Memphis station WMPS, during their lunch breaks from the fields. J.R. arrived at the school for the concert two hours early with Jesse and Harry. He puffed anxiously on a cigarette, hoping to figure out a way to meet the Louvin Brothers, who were the stars of the weekday program.

J.R. recognized Charlie Louvin when he got out of a black Cadillac, and the teenager's knees shook as Louvin walked toward him. All Louvin wanted was directions to the restroom, but J.R. took advantage of the request to escort the radio star there. He wanted to ask Louvin how he could get into the music business, but he didn't have the nerve. Just walking alongside Louvin, however, made the whole idea of being a professional singer seem more possible.

After the show, J.R. and his friends watched as the musicians put their equipment into their car and headed back to Memphis. J.R. would have given anything to be in the car with them. When Louvin waved at him as they pulled away, it was his biggest thrill since Eleanor Roosevelt shook his hand. In the weeks after the concert, J.R. started thinking of country singers and the Roosevelts in the same light. They both brought people together and made them feel good, and people cheered them. He assumed, of course, they must all be Baptists.

V

As J.R. moved through high school, he began to feel increasingly anxious about his future. For all the time he had spent thinking about being on the radio, he realized he didn't have any idea how to make that happen. There was no station in Dyess where he might try to persuade someone to give a local boy the chance to show what he could do. J.R. still talked to his family and a few friends about being on the radio someday, but privately he was starting to worry.

Truth be known, Ray wasn't the only one in the Cash family who had doubts about J.R.'s musical dreams. Carrie wanted to support her son, but his voice was high-pitched, not at all husky and deep-rooted like the singers on the radio. Besides, he was shy. How could he be a singer if he couldn't stand before an audience? Carrie had tried to help J.R. with his insecurity by arranging for him to sing in front of the church congregation. Cash later called it the "most horrible experience of my life." It might have been all right in church if his mother had been onstage with him, but he found himself standing next to the preacher and a stranger on piano. He felt as if he "totally bombed," but his mother didn't give up; she kept pushing him to sing before the congregation, and every time J.R. felt embarrassed. It wasn't the singing—it was the people watching him.

That wall of shyness began to crack one afternoon in the summer of 1947. Carrie and Joanne were doing the dishes in the kitchen when they heard a voice through the open window singing a new gospel song that had been sweeping the country, "Everybody's Gonna Have a Wonderful Time Up There."

Carrie looked out the window and saw fifteen-year-old J.R. pumping water into a bucket.

"Is that you singing, J.R.?"

He spun around and smiled, "Yes, Mama. My voice has gotten a little lower."

Carrie called her son into the kitchen and she cried as she hugged him.

"You've got a gift, J.R. You are going to sing," she told him. "God's got his hand on you. You're going to carry the message of Jesus Christ."

Carrie was so caught up in J.R.'s "gift" that she vowed to do what she could to nurture him. She wanted J.R. to take singing lessons, but he resisted for almost two years. Finally, Carrie insisted. She was making $5 to $6 a week using the family's new washing machine to launder the clothes of some of the schoolteachers. She set aside $3 for once-a-week lessons with a young teacher in Lepanto, a larger town eight miles away. J.R. went along grudgingly each week to see LaVanda Mae Fielder. It might have been okay if she had let him sing songs he knew, but he had to sing songs the teacher thought were good vocal exercises, such as the Irish ballad "I'll Take You Home Again, Kathleen."

After just three lessons, Fielder was frustrated by the teenager's lack of progress. To make him more comfortable, she changed her strategy. She asked him to pick a song. He thought immediately of Hank Williams, whose "Lovesick Blues" was all over the radio in the early months of 1949. The chance to sing one of his favorite new songs freed J.R., and his voice was so engaging, the teacher closed the lid on her piano and told him the lessons were over. He shouldn't ever let anyone change his style, *"ever,"* she repeated forcefully.

These words gave J.R. enough confidence finally to stand in front of the church congregation without quivering. He started becoming more active at school, too, widening his group of friends and even showing his poems and other writings to some of his classmates. He gained such a good reputation as a writer that several of his friends paid him—usually about fifty cents—to write their homework poems or essays. "He was good with words," recalls J. E. Huff. "He was smarter than we were. That's for sure." Classmate A. J. Henson liked a poem that J.R. wrote for him so much that he could still recite it more than five decades later:

> *The top hand mounted his trusty steed*
> *And rode across the plain.*
> *He said, "I'll ride until setting sun*
> *Unless I lose my rein."*
> *The top hand gave a jerk*
> *And Bob drew up the slack.*
> *He rode his trail until setting sun*
> *Then rode a freight train back.*

A.J. got an A on the assignment.

Still, J.R. couldn't shake the pressure of needing to find a job after high school. All the years his father told him he was foolish to waste his energy on music had left an impression.

VI

As their senior year approached, J.R. and his friends spent many an evening trying to figure out how to escape the toilsome life their parents led. "The only thing we knew for sure was we weren't going to be farmers," Huff says. The government program in Dyess had given people like Ray Cash the chance to survive, but never to flourish. The land was worked so hard that it had already lost what richness it had had, making it almost impossible for families to break even. Many of the long-timers left the delta settlement for Memphis, just fifty miles away, or other parts of the country where they could find better pay and easier work. Ray Cash began taking odd jobs in nearby towns to supplement his income.

With his pals, J.R. weighed the merits of the main career paths that young men from poor families in the South often chose in the

1940s: head north to the auto plants in Michigan or join the military. There was also a third option—head to California in hopes of claiming agriculture jobs—but no one in Dyess wanted anything further to do with harvesting crops. Henson was the first of the three to make the break. While J.R. and J.E. returned to school, A.J. joined the Army.

On the outside, things were good at school during J.R.'s last year, though his grades, as usual, were only a little above average in most classes, even his favorites, English and history. He was elected class vice president, appeared in school plays, and was chosen to sing at the commencement exercises—not a country song, but "Drink to Me Only with Thine Eyes," an expression of faith with lyrics from a seventeenth-century poem by Ben Jonson. In the yearbook, the editors made a special mention of him: "It was in this year that one of our number showed so much talent on the stage, both as an actor and with his voice, that we think he should be publically recognized: this boy was J.R. Cash."

But the good feelings of his final school year didn't last long. Deep inside, J.R. couldn't shake the fact that he had no idea how to break into the music business. He thought about heading to Nashville, the home of country music, but he knew he didn't have the courage to do it, and that left him despondent. By graduation day, even the joys of his solitary walks had faded.

Desperate to demonstrate his independence from his father, J.R. heard there were some jobs available in west Arkansas picking strawberries, and, despite all his years of dreading picking cotton, he headed for the town of Bald Knob. The trip proved a bust; the strawberry crop was too small for him to make any money, so he headed home after three days. Not knowing what to do next, he happened to bump into Frank McKinney, a barber in Dyess. McKinney was thinking about taking the bus to Michigan to try to find a job in the auto industry, and he invited J.R. to go along. J.R. agreed so quickly that he spent much of the bus ride wondering if he was making a mistake.

In Michigan, J.R. got a job the first day as a punch press operator at the Fisher body plant in Pontiac. He walked a mile and a half to work each morning, but this wasn't like the gravel road in Dyess.

He couldn't sing on the city streets, and he didn't have enough spirit left to daydream. He felt trapped. The only thing to keep him company was his chain-smoking. From the first day, he found the work tedious and repetitious—far worse than picking cotton back home, because he wasn't surrounded by the love of his family and community. For the first time, he also felt the sting of being branded an outsider, someone who was considered inferior—and this experience led him to begin to question some of the racist attitudes prevalent in Dyess.

While J.R. was working on a Pontiac one day, the fender slipped and cut his arm. When he went to the medical office, a doctor looked at his file card and smirked when he saw the words "Dyess, Ark." "All you Southern hicks are always just looking for a way to get off work," he said. J.R. tried to explain that it was an accident, but the doctor was unbending. Cash recalled the doctor's response: "How long you gonna work here? You gonna get yourself a good paycheck or two and then split like they all do?"

A few days later, Cash came down with stomach flu, but he wouldn't go back to the doctor; he didn't want any further abuse. The landlady at his boardinghouse gave him a big glass of wine and told him to get some sleep—he'd feel better in the morning. He did feel better the next day, but he decided he was going home. Between the monotony of the work and the anti-Southern bias, after a couple of weeks he'd had enough of the car factory. He hitchhiked back to Dyess.

His mother was thrilled to see her son, but she was also alarmed by how skinny J.R. was. He had always been slender, which is why he hadn't joined the sports teams at school with most of his pals. But he was now down to 140 pounds, low for a six-foot teenager. Carrie did her best to stuff him with home cooking around the clock.

Despite his craving for independence, J.R. was so desperate to get a job that he accepted his father's offer to try to get him taken on at the oleomargarine plant near Dyess, where Ray was working. Predictably, J.R. hated the regimentation and he quit after a few days. Ray just shook his head once again. J.R. wondered if his father wasn't right after all. Maybe he wouldn't amount to anything. Maybe he was lazy and unfocused.

With nowhere else to turn, he decided to follow his father's lead one last time and do what Ray had done three decades earlier. He would join the military. J.R. always enjoyed hearing his father talk about his adventures in World War I and about such appealing perks as going to Paris and seeing the Eiffel Tower. Besides, this was one way to finally please Ray. He first thought of joining the Army, like the elder Cash, but the Air Force seemed more glamorous and probably safer in case all the talk about war in Korea proved true.

On July 7, 1950, J.R. drove the family's 1945 Ford to Blytheville and enlisted in the Air Force. Because regulations required a first name rather than initials, J.R. wrote down John, though no one had ever called him that. When asked for a middle name, he wrote simply R. He was just six weeks past high school and, after many false starts, he was finally saying good-bye to Dyess.

In his mind, however, J.R. would return to his hometown frequently—not just the house on Road 3 and his family, but also the wider community and all that it had meant to him. He'd sometimes imagine himself walking out of the movie theater in the town center and turning to the right, where he could see the porch of the administration building where Eleanor Roosevelt had stood. He would turn left, walk one block down Main Street, and see the old Baptist church, head another block down Main and picture the school library and the assembly hall where he'd seen the Louvins. A little farther along Main and J.R. could imagine the spot on the riverbank where he often fished and another spot on the river where he was baptized. It was a short stretch of land, just 250 yards, but he knew that the lesson of Dyess was one of inspiration and hope.

As J.R. said good-bye to his family at the station in Memphis and boarded the train for Lackland Air Force Base in San Antonio, Texas, the initial excitement of joining the service quickly gave way to nervousness. He found himself staring out the window, avoiding conversation with the other enlistees, some of whom seemed to relish the adventures ahead. One of his worries when he'd signed up had been getting sent into battle in Korea. He was now fretting over another kind of survival.

As with the trip to Michigan, he soon began asking himself if he hadn't made a mistake. If anything, the failure of the Pontiac experience made him even more apprehensive. Would this trip, too, end in disaster? Was he smart enough to compete with the boys from the big city? Would the recruits from the North treat him with contempt like the doctor in Pontiac?

What about his spiritual values? He wasn't used to being around alcohol, and he had never had a serious relationship with a girl. Would he be able to stay on the right path, or would he let Jack and his mother down? Could he actually flunk out? Would the Air Force send him home if he didn't measure up?

The thought of that possible humiliation numbed him. He couldn't shake his fear of what lay ahead. J.R. finally just laid his head against the seat and hoped, as he often did in moments of stress, to find that comfort in the escape of sleep.

Chapter 2

VIVIAN AND THE AIR FORCE

I

JOHN R. CASH, as he was now starting to think of himself, was one of thousands of men rushed through the revolving door of basic training at Lackland in the late summer of 1950, the normal thirteen-week training schedule cut to seven as the country mobilized for war in Korea. For someone whose high school class had numbered just twenty-two, the size of the operation was overwhelming.

After being trucked from the train station to Lackland, the new arrivals were quickly introduced to Air Force routine. They were given GI haircuts and issued dog tags, clothing, and supplies, then taken to the mess hall for dinner. Afterward, they were assigned places among the double-deck bunks that lined the main section of the two-story wooden barracks. Most of the recruits stayed up late memorizing their Air Force serial numbers, learning how to make their beds military-style, and getting to know one another. They didn't get to sleep until shortly before being roused for a six a.m. roll call.

In rapid order that week, John and the others were administered typhoid and smallpox vaccinations. They were ordered to ship all their civilian clothes and shoes home, then given explicit instructions on just how to arrange their belongings in the footlockers by their bunks. The regimentation reminded him of the auto factory. He asked himself, *Four years of this?*

Even so, his immersion into Air Force life proved a blessing. Between the grueling physical training, intense classroom sessions, and battery of aptitude tests, Cash didn't have time to brood over possible rejection or failure. He was so exhausted after the long, demanding days that he spent much of his Sundays, his only time off, sleeping. He rarely ventured out of the barracks except to go to church or pick up necessities from the PX.

While others in his training squadron grumbled about the lack of free time, John embraced the nonstop schedule. Though he hadn't shown much interest in sports in school, he proved to be fairly athletic, mastering the various exercises designed to turn young men into soldiers. He did so well on the classroom instruction that others turned to him for help, just like the students had done at Dyess High.

Near the end of the stay at Lackland, John's squadron took yet another round of aptitude tests, and he showed potential in several areas, including air police, aircraft mechanic, and radio operator. He didn't know exactly what the last entailed, but he liked the sound of "radio." When his application for that school was accepted, John was overjoyed. He had stood up against the big city boys and, in most cases, outshone them.

When he went home to Dyess for a few days before reporting to Keesler Air Force Base in Biloxi, Mississippi, for more training, he felt like he belonged in his blue Air Force uniform. Even his father offered a rare handshake. During the third week of September, John R. Cash's family again said good-bye to him in Memphis, but this time his mood was entirely different. John's earlier nervousness was gone. On this trip, he didn't stare anxiously out the window. When he finally went to sleep, he wasn't looking for escape. He was looking forward to the six months in Biloxi. He was eager to get to know his classmates better, maybe play some music, and maybe even meet some girls.

Located on the shore of the Gulf of Mexico, Keesler was popular among the airmen because it was just ninety miles from the bright lights and good times of New Orleans. Where better to spend a weekend pass than the most party-minded city in the South? Soon after he arrived at the base, John started hearing about the great bars and fast women in the Big Easy. Many in his barracks spent their first free weekend exploring both. But John stayed in Biloxi. Despite his excellent showing at Lackland, he wasn't about to take his class work for granted. It felt good to excel. He even found himself doing something he had rarely done in high school: during his off hours, he actually studied. Besides, his Baptist upbringing raised a red flag about New Orleans.

John's dedication to his studies increased as he learned about the important role radio intercept operators played in the Air Force. He wasn't studying something mundane like repairing radios or constructing relay towers; he was learning how to eavesdrop on enemy radio transmissions. This was the Cold War, and the threat of Communism was being felt across America. It was challenging work, as foreign military strategists went to elaborate lengths to prevent their messages from being intercepted. They frequently sent out meaningless, distracting noises on the same frequencies before slipping in the real Morse code signals.

If eventually accepted as an intercept operator, John would have to listen to the competing signals through headphones for up to eight hours at a stretch, trying to distinguish the real transmissions from the decoys. Once the Morse code was isolated, he would then jot down the letters and pass them along to a group of translators who would try to decode them. The more John learned about the intercept mission, the more motivated he was by the touch of glamour and adventure associated with it. He even imagined himself living out some of the World War II spy movies he had enjoyed back in Dyess. He liked the thought of being a hero. Wait until he told his dad about *this*.

John finished the Morse code course weeks ahead of schedule, which made him the envy of many of the others in his training group. Ben Perea, a New Mexico native who was in the same class at Keesler, had heard of John but wouldn't get to know him until they traveled on the same ship to Germany. "He stood out at Keesler," Perea recalls. "He was the model—the one the instructors would point to. Everyone knew he was very smart." It was a word—*smart*—that many of his fellow airmen would use in describing Cash.

As rumors of his accomplishments spread around the base, other airmen began searching out the young man from Dyess. They wanted to hang out with him, and he enjoyed the attention. They invited him to go with them to New Orleans, telling him again about the music, the food, and, mostly, the women. Confident about his progress, John surprised himself by actually toying with the idea of joining them.

II

John had been so focused on basic training at Lackland that he couldn't remember even listening to the radio for the seven weeks he spent there, so it felt good finally to be able to relax enough to tune in the popular country stations at Keesler. He even found a new favorite singer, Hank Snow, whose rollicking "I'm Moving On" topped the country charts for five months in 1950.

Like Cash, Snow was a huge Jimmie Rodgers fan, and he was at his best on story songs—as much reciting the lyrics as singing them. Both qualities were later typical of Cash's recordings. He was enamored by "I'm Moving On" because the lyrics employed railroad imagery ("That big eight-wheeler rollin' down the track") to express feelings of wanderlust and independence, the same sentiments Cash would turn to years later when writing the song that helped him get his first record contract, "Hey, Porter."

It wasn't, however, the only record John would later recall from his days at Keesler. He also favored Ernest Tubb's "(Remember Me) I'm the One Who Loves You." Hank Williams's "Long Gone Lonesome Blues," Red Foley's good-natured "Chattanoogie Shoe Shine Boy," and a pair of Eddy Arnold hits, "Anytime" and "Bouquet of Roses." He especially admired the pure romanticism in Arnold's singing, how his crooning delivery made love seem natural and uncomplicated—just the kind of relationship John wanted.

By mid-October, John had met a couple of Southern boys who

also enjoyed singing what they referred to as "hillbilly" songs. The three often got together in the barracks and took turns singing lead on hits of the day. Others teased them about all the fun they were missing by not going with them to New Orleans. Increasingly, the tales of sexual conquests began to tempt John. Finally, he headed off with them on a trip to Bourbon Street.

Caught up in all the boasting on the ride down, John bragged about his own experiences with women. From the way he talked, you'd think he was a real ladies' man. In truth, John had dated a few girls in Dyess, even gone steady with a couple of them for a spell. But he hadn't come close to a serious relationship, much less sexual intimacy with any of them.

Still, he was no virgin.

When he was fifteen, J.R. and some other boys hooked up one night with a girl who was known around the small town as "easy to get." At her urging, Cash insisted, they took her to a riverbank, where she lay on a blanket in the moonlight and had sex with each of them. Even though the girl seemed eager, the experience was unsettling and left John with such a deep sense of shame that he never referred to the incident in either of his autobiographies or in any of his formal interviews.

But he did speak of the night to a friend in the late 1990s. From the way he described the girl, it was possible she was at least somewhat mentally challenged, and John was still so sensitive about that night that he apparently changed the girl's name to avoid embarrassing her or her family as he discussed it with the friend. According to A.J. Henson, J.R. never mentioned the name or the incident to him.

The only other time J.R. tried to have sex in Dyess, he told the same friend, was with a "nice young girl" he met while working at the roller rink in town. He somehow talked her into going to bed with him, but he was so nervous that he "couldn't get it up." The girl thought that was hilarious, leaving J.R. too embarrassed even to try to get intimate with any other girls during high school.

Now on the way to New Orleans, he listened to the other trainees talk about all the women who would be waiting for them—just like John had seen in so many of the war movies. He wanted a girlfriend, even if only so he could show off her picture to the other guys and look forward to her letters. Expecting to go to a dance or perhaps the local USO social club, he was shocked when his pals took him to a brothel. All the stories about "conquests" in New Orleans had really just been trips to houses of ill repute.

John's first instinct was to walk away, but hormones took over. He went to a room with one of the prostitutes, and the experience reminded him of the night on the riverbank. It wasn't just that it was against his Baptist teachings; the encounter was cold and clinical. He wanted to have sex again. He wanted it badly. He was still only nineteen, after all. But he realized what he wanted most of all was sex with a genuine connection. John returned to New Orleans a few times, but there is no indication that he visited another brothel. Mostly he stayed on the base, reading and singing country songs.

During his final weeks at Keesler, John was rewarded for his hard work when he was approached about joining a new, elite group of radio intercept operators. The USAF Security Service was set up in the fall of 1948 in response to the increasing complexity of enemy communication techniques. Security Service bases were located in Alaska and several foreign countries, including Japan, Korea, and Germany.

After interviews and a detailed security check, John was formally invited to join the unit and given his choice of duty in remote Adak, Alaska, or Landsberg, West Germany. They were choice outposts, reserved for the most promising intercept operators. The selection process didn't focus just on test performance, but also weighed character, intelligence, and emotional stability. John opted for Landsberg because he wanted to see the sights of Europe.

To his great frustration, the security operation was so top secret that he was prohibited from telling anybody, including his family, about the delicate nature of his assignment. All he could say was that he was going to be stationed in Landsberg. But first he had to go through four more months of intense training to sharpen his intercept skills. On April 27, he headed back to San Antonio, this time to Brooks Air Force Base.

III

By late May, John was settled enough to begin thinking about life overseas, and again, he daydreamed about having someone special back home. Six months earlier he would not have had the nerve even to approach a girl he didn't know. But his success in the training classes emboldened him—to a point. He began looking for a girl of his own everywhere he went in San Antonio, from movie theaters to cafés. It was easier said than done.

While his Air Force blues caught the eye of young girls, his shyness and his insecurity over his dirt farm roots resurfaced, making it hard for him to introduce himself to them. How, he kept asking himself, could anyone from Dyess stand up to a sophisticated big city girl? Even if he got a girl's attention, John found himself unable to keep the conversation going for long. "Surely," he kept thinking, "she'll see right through this Air Force uniform and dismiss me as some hillbilly."

After all the setbacks, John had little reason to believe that July 18, 1951, a Wednesday, would be any different. He and a friend were heading back to Brooks after a movie when John spotted the St. Mary's roller rink, and it reminded him of the good times he'd had skating in Dyess. Specifically, he remembered the way girls used to show up eager to meet boys.

Dragging his friend along, John headed for the rink. It was near closing time, but he rented a pair of skates anyway and watched groups of young girls skating by. That's when he spotted someone he would later describe as the prettiest girl he had ever seen. She was petite—no more than five feet, ninety-five pounds—and she was skating with a girlfriend. He watched her for a few minutes, hoping she'd stop so he could introduce himself. But the pretty brunette kept circling the rink. The pressure on him increased when the announcement came over the loudspeaker that the rink was closing in fifteen minutes.

Almost before he knew what was happening, John started skating slowly toward the girl, not stopping until he actually bumped into her. To anyone watching, it would have looked like a scene from a screwball comedy. When the girl fell to the ground, John reached down to help her up, apologizing profusely. Though he wouldn't find out until later, Vivian Liberto had been watching him, too, hoping he would come over and say hello. She might even have exaggerated the impact of their encounter and fallen on purpose.

Rather than J.R. or even John, he told her to call him "Johnny," the first time anyone could recall his using that name. It was as if he wanted something new and more personal, a sign perhaps of just how fast and hard he'd fallen for this young beauty. Johnny stared into her hazel eyes and at her light bronze skin, trying to figure out what to say. Finally he blurted out, "Would you like to skate with me?"

When she replied yes, Johnny felt his heart racing. Crazily enough, the shy boy from Dyess started singing to her, but not one of his country favorites. Probably fearing she might have no interest in country music, he chose a pop song, "I Still Feel the Same about You," which was a current hit by Georgia Gibbs. It was perhaps an odd selection, because the song wasn't a tale of romantic bliss but an apology for having broken a girl's heart.

Vivian was flattered. It was the first time anyone had sung to her. As they continued to skate, Johnny told her that he was from Arkansas and was going to be sailing to West Germany soon. She in turn said she was seventeen and a senior at an all-girls Catholic high school. Johnny was so dazzled by her that the Catholic part didn't even faze him, despite all the whispering he'd heard in Dyess about the mysterious religion.

As they circled the rink, Johnny pretended he was a novice skater, which encouraged Vivian to hold onto him frequently because she thought he was about to fall. When the house lights flickered, indicating closing time, John felt himself panic. He didn't want to let this girl go. "Can I take you home?" he blurted out, and his spirits soared when she answered, "Sure."

Because he didn't have a car, John had to accompany Vivian home on the bus. On the way, he learned that her family had deep roots in San Antonio. There was a popular market named Liberto's, and one of her uncles had started the first Spanish-speaking radio station in town. Her father, Tom, owned an insurance agency and her mother was a homemaker. She had a younger sister and an older brother. When they arrived at her front door, he asked if he could see her again. After she said she'd like that, he leaned over and tried to kiss her. Stepping back, she said, "I don't kiss boys on the first date."

It may not have been the reaction John hoped for at the time, but it was, in fact, the perfect answer.

Cash was attracted by Vivian's beauty, but he also quickly decided that Vivian was a "good" girl and that she'd make a faithful, loving wife and a caring mother. And, he would soon learn, she was even a fan of country music. If he had known that, he joked years later, he would have sung her an Eddy Arnold song. Within a week, he was thinking he would someday marry her.

In her room that night, Vivian retraced every moment of the evening. She told herself she had found her Prince Charming. She spent much of the night tossing and turning, wondering if he'd really call. Her answer came early the next morning. John called not just that day but every other day until he left Brooks in early August. The pair also went out every time he could get away. They went to movies. They went to the malt shop. They went window-shopping. They held hands and strolled along the city's picturesque River Walk in the moonlight. It wasn't long before Johnny got that first kiss while they sat on the roof of a car at a drive-in. Soon after, he carved *J.C. Loves V.L.* on one of the wooden benches along the River Walk. They daydreamed about the future. They were collecting a remarkable number of memories for just three weeks together.

Even though Vivian's father was concerned about his "baby" dating an Air Force man, Vivian's younger sister, Sylvia, remembers that her parents couldn't help but like this polite, respectful young man who said "Yes, ma'am" and "No, sir" without fail. Still, Sylvia recalls, her father was relieved when he learned Johnny was finally leaving for his new assignment in Germany. There was no way, he figured, that the relationship would last.

But Johnny convinced himself that it would. He told Vivian—or "Viv," as he began calling her—that he loved her, would always love her, and wanted to spend his life with her. He told her he would write a letter every day—and he made her promise to do the same.

It was heady stuff for a nineteen-year-old boy, but it was even more of a fairy tale for a seventeen-year-old girl. He seemed so mature in his uniform. She also thought he was smart, caring, a man of faith, and, of course, very, very sexy.

Johnny wanted to make love to her, but she refused. In reality, he probably didn't try that hard, because he didn't want to jeopardize his new dream by giving her the wrong impression of his intentions. One day, he told himself over and over, Vivian Liberto would be Mrs. Johnny Cash and he'd be a singer on the radio. This vision gave him immense comfort as he returned to Dyess in the final days of August. He had promised Viv he would call her before the ship left Brooklyn for West Germany, but he couldn't wait.

On the morning of September 4 he called from Dyess, and she was thrilled to hear his voice. In a letter he wrote her later that same day, he asked her to send him a large photo so he could put it over his bed in Germany and look at it every morning and night. He enclosed a photo he'd had taken at the base. He ended by urging, "Write, honey." Seven days later, he wrote her the first of several letters from Camp Kilmer in New Jersey, where he and other members of what would eventually be named the 6912th Security Squadron were being assembled before they left for Germany. He signed it "Love, Johnny."

While they were waiting to be shipped out, Bob Moodie, whom John had met at Brooks, invited him to spend the weekend at his folks' place in Rhode Island. On the way, they stopped off in New York City, and John took an immediate liking to the place. He especially loved all the bookshops and movie theaters, but the most notable thing was seeing his first Broadway play. A stranger, noticing the two young men in uniform, gave them free tickets to the musical comedy *Two on the Aisle*. John loved the experience and became a lifelong fan of Broadway theater.

Cash's group left the Brooklyn Navy Yard on September 20, 1951, for Germany aboard the USNS *General W. G. Haan,* a seventeen-thousand-ton ship capable of carrying just under four thousand troops. Writing to Vivian once they were under way, he signed his note "Oceans and oceans of love and devotion, Johnny."

* * *

On the first day at sea, Cash was walking back to his double-deck berth when he noticed the guy on the bunk beneath his was reading the Bible. When he looked closer, he saw it was Ben Perea, whom he recognized from Keesler Air Force Base.

"Do you read the Bible often?" Cash asked.

When Perea nodded yes, John replied, "Me too."

The next day Perea caught John's attention again, this time sitting on his bunk singing "Beautiful Brown Eyes," an old country song revived earlier in the year in a recording by Jimmy Wakely. John stopped and sat alongside Perea. It was the start of a friendship that lasted throughout their Air Force days and beyond. Ben was a shy, deeply religious young man who would avoid the excesses of German nightlife, and John admired him. John was also drawn to Perea because his father was a railroad man. Plus, Ben was Catholic, and John had a new desire to learn all he could about the religion.

The pair spent hours and hours on the ship and in the barracks in Landsberg singing songs. Ben didn't think John was much of a singer in their early days together, but it was fun having someone to sing with. During the trip, they pretty much sang popular country hits, which meant a lot of Hank Williams and Eddy Arnold. Ben remembers they probably sang Jimmie Davis's "You Are My Sunshine" most of all because it was such a simple but moving song.

When he wasn't singing, John was lying on his bunk writing letters to Vivian. In one, he mentioned that Vic Damone, who was a well-known pop singer at the time, was aboard the ship and had organized a choir that met every night.

"How do you like that?" he wrote. "Pretty big time, huh? Me singing with Vic Damone." John may actually have worked up enough nerve to sit in with the choir on a couple of numbers, but he didn't have any contact with Damone. His only singing partner on the ship was Perea. But again, he wasn't inclined to let the facts get in the way of a good story.

IV

It was the first week in October when the giant transport ship arrived at the port city of Bremerhaven on the North Sea coast of West Germany. Cash and the other new members of the security team boarded a train for the long ride south to Landsberg, near Munich. The air base was a former outpost for the Luftwaffe, the German Air Force, and it was notorious in Germany because Adolf Hitler wrote *Mein Kampf* while imprisoned there in 1924. The surrounding area was a breathtaking mix of rivers, lakes, park grounds, and mountains. It was ideal for fishing, sailing, and skiing—all of which Cash pursued over the next three years.

Before he could explore those attractions, though, John spent time checking out the amenities on the base itself and was delighted to find a movie theater. During that first week, on October 13, he and Ben Perea saw a gritty low-budget Warner Bros. film titled *Inside the Walls of Folsom Prison.* John liked the movie and mentioned it in a letter that night to Vivian. In later interviews, Cash always said he wrote "Folsom Prison Blues" after seeing it. In truth, he would write it *long* after seeing the film.

During the long high-pressure hours in the radio intercept room, he started feeling like a prisoner himself. He did begin to toy with a song about Folsom Prison, but nothing came of it at the time. As much as he loved music, John didn't know much about songwriting yet.

Ben remembers that John often jotted down musical ideas in a spiral notebook, but they were usually spin-offs of existing songs—either parodies or blatant copies. Over the next few months, John forgot about Folsom Prison. He didn't return to the idea until he happened to hear a song in the barracks two years later—a song that gave him the blueprint for his first signature hit.

In his early letters to Vivian, John noted that the locals treated Americans like gods. "I don't know why, but they do," he declared. "They would even get out in the street to let one of us pass. They must think we are over here to protect them. I can just see me protecting them. All I want is a nice fox hole." The playful reference to a foxhole was as close as he could come under the strict Security Service rules to explaining the tense, anxious atmosphere around the base.

Massive numbers of Russian troops were stationed in the Soviet zone of Austria less than a hundred miles away, directly across the Danube River from Linz, Austria, where more U.S. Air Force units were based. "The Russians were talking big and making lots of military noises all along the line dividing them and U.S. forces," says Bob Mehaffey, the supervisor of Cash's forty-man unit. "This was just after the Berlin Airlift, and the Russian military was still very upset about that. We knew that the Russian armor along the border was far greater in numbers than ours, and the Russians could be deep into West Germany before our military could sufficiently react. They could overrun us in twenty minutes—and there was constant tension. Air Force people were rarely assigned weapons, but everybody in our unit, including John, was assigned a carbine."

This tension added greatly to the strain of already grueling monitoring sessions for members of the 6912th squadron. Typically, Cash and others worked in eight-hour shifts, but they were sometimes increased to twelve hours or more during emergency conditions or when the team was short-staffed. Every effort was made to keep the shifts to eight hours, Mehaffey says, because "we lost a bunch of operators who couldn't handle the pressure and went bonkers. Some returned to the unit pretty soon, but some never did."

An operator might get so fatigued that his body couldn't tolerate it and he'd lose control emotionally. Mehaffey recalls one especially tense twelve-hour session in 1951 when one of his most stable operators suddenly got up from his chair and walked full speed right into the wall and just kept pounding his head against it and crying. Mehaffey rushed over and asked what was wrong, and the operator said helplessly, "I can't find the door." Mehaffey took the man to the medical offices, where doctors medicated him and sent him to bed for twenty-four hours. In this case, the operator did return to work.

Years later, Cash told an interviewer about a meltdown of his own at Landsberg. "One night, after I had been in Germany for about a year, I just got fed up," he said. "We were working the second floor and, before I knew it, I picked up my typewriter and threw it plumb through the window. I started crying. They sent me to the dispensary and gave me a couple of aspirins. I got the rest of the night off."

Mehaffey doesn't recall any such incident. Most likely Cash was severely worn down, and he made up the story to convey his feeling of confinement. Cash did feel alienated in his new environment to such a degree that he sometimes felt he was himself at war—against the system, authority, the regimentation, and, increasingly, the temptations. Thousands of miles from home, he was in a typical military culture in which everyone around him, it seemed, was beginning to sample what for him was forbidden fruit—women and booze.

Once again John stood out among the operators. While most others monitored transmissions from other Iron Curtain countries, including East Germany, Hungary, and Romania, John was one of those given the most challenging assignment. He had to monitor the transmissions of the Russians themselves, who sent Morse code signals with such speed that most U.S. operators simply couldn't keep up with them.

Chuck Riley, an airman who later earned a degree in economics at the University of Toledo, was impressed by Cash's mind. "John was no hillbilly stereotype. He had a tremendous level of intelligence. We had lots of interesting and drawn-out conversations on world affairs and historical things. He had a remarkable vocabulary and a quick wit. As great as his musical talent, I always thought his intelligence might have been an even greater gift."

Almost immediately after arriving in Landsberg, airmen began receiving "Dear John" letters from their girls back home saying they were sorry, but they had found somebody new. To make matters worse, one of the biggest country hits at the time was Jean Shepard and Ferlin Husky's "A Dear John Letter." Even the non–country fans at Landsberg remembered it playing on radios and phonographs throughout the barracks.

According to Mehaffey, the reaction to the letters was so traumatic that the soldiers in his unit developed a ritual to help one another cope with the news. "When someone got a 'Dear John' let-ter, we'd have him stand on top of his footlocker and read the letter to everybody in the barracks. Not everyone did it, but a lot of them did. It somehow took the pressure off."

For months, John privately feared bad news whenever he picked up his mail. Constantly trying to reassure himself of her love, he wrote to Vivian every day—sometimes two or three times a day—and he complained when she was even a day late writing back. He was frantic during the times when he didn't hear from her for a week or more. In a letter to Vivian soon after his arrival in Landsberg, John was already scolding her for not writing.

"I still didn't get a letter from you honey, and I'm getting pretty desperate," he wrote on October 16. "The mail clerk is scared of me now, I give him such mean looks every time I go to check my mail, which is twice a day....The boys have been telling me that you didn't love me anymore. That's why you don't write, but I don't believe that. You do love me don't you my darling? I love you. Yours, Johnny."

Cash was relieved when Vivian's letters finally started arriving regularly, but any break in the chain would set him off again. Over the course of his deployment, the letter count between them easily passed the one-thousand mark.

When he soon received an eight-by-ten photo of Vivian, John rushed to the PX and bought a frame for it. He put the picture on the wall above his bunk—a "Hands Off" note attached. The others in the barracks reminded him of all the "Dear John" letters, predict-ing it wouldn't be long before he got his heart broken. One airman even dared him to bet $10. John took the bet, promising, "Viv is dif-ferent."

Noticing the photo was still on the wall months later, the airman paid up.

Cash was convinced that Vivian was the girl of his dreams, and that made it only natural for him to share one of his dreams with her—the one about being a singer on the radio. In a letter that first fall, he told Vivian that he had just bought a harmonica to keep himself occupied in the barracks, and he spoke about hav-ing his own band once he got back to the States. He also wrote about getting together regularly with some guys in the barracks to play guitar and sing. While Perea sometimes joined them, the lineup consisted mostly of Cash, Ted Freeman from West Virginia, Orville (Wayne) Rigdon from Louisiana, and Reid Cummins and Bill Carnahan from Missouri. They called themselves the Landsberg Barbarians.

When John saw how well Rigdon played guitar, he bought himself a German model for $5 and asked Rigdon to teach him how to play. But John still had trouble getting the hang of the chords and gave up trying to master the instrument; he merely strummed along while singing. Over the next three years, he would update Vivian on records he had heard or repeat that he was going to have his own band one day. He was especially proud of the time he bought a set of albums containing several Jimmie Rodgers songs he hadn't heard before—and the purchase late in his stay of a tape recorder so he could gauge the progress in his singing by making recordings of his voice.

On days off, the airmen frequented one of two clubs in Landsberg. Though the base was integrated, the white airmen tended to go to Der Goggle, while the African Americans favored Der Ziederbrau. On the nights when the squadron filled the places, there weren't many German patrons. Not many men, anyway. Women were always there.

"Remember, this was so close after World War II that the German populace was still having problems with hunger, real poverty," Mehaffey explains. "Buying somebody a meal was a big gift. If you wanted a woman, there was no problem. You could pick one up on the street or in a club and she'd take you home with her if you bought her a meal."

When they had three days free, the Americans, often as many as fifty to one hundred of them, headed by train to Munich or the smaller town of Starnberg, where they would take over a hotel and turn the bar into their own private club. The guys would play music, drink, and look for women. Unlike in the barracks with the Barbarians, John was not the center of attention during these parties. In photos from one of those early nights out he looks fairly anonymous, except for one in which he, obviously a bit tipsy, leans toward the camera while fooling around with a fiddle.

In Cash's 1975 autobiography, *Man in Black*, he wrote about the dark side of his German experience: "As the long weeks and months went by, Dyess, Arkansas, and that little church, and the things I had learned there, and the life I had lived there became more and more distant. From beer, I graduated to German cognac and having more wild times.... The booze and the profanity began launching me into all kinds of other habits which soon became second nature."

Mehaffey, who was responsible for keeping tabs on all his unit members, suggests that Cash acted pretty much like the rest of the security team in his early months in Landsberg. "Johnny wasn't much different from the rest of us," he says. "Like all of us, he was young, foolish, looking for adventure. Women, drinking, gambling, fighting, and freedom like we had never had before. Johnny was right in there, no worse, no better. Understand, we didn't think we were wild—and by the standards of the time, we were pretty mild. Our fights were, for the most part, a blow or two and over."

One thing that did strike Mehaffey about the young airman was how certain he was about his career goals.

"We were all kids," he says. "None of us knew what we wanted to do—except Johnny. From the beginning, he knew he was going to be a singer. I can still see him sitting on a metal GI cot with the mattress rolled up, strumming that guitar."

In the endless letters to Vivian, Cash chronicled in detail his coming-of-age experiences—focusing on the conflict between his religious beliefs and his prurient desires. Oddly, he alluded to his transgressions, including the drinking and veiled references to womanizing, in several of these letters—all the time encouraging her to be faithful and to wait for him. The letters are an absorbing mixture of guilt and restraint, devotion and confession, trust and accusation. Mehaffey sensed Cash's emotional tug-of-war. There were times, he says, when the guys would all be whooping it up in a club and he'd notice John sitting off by himself, glum and staring into space, looking lost and alone.

In a letter to Vivian early in 1952, Cash confessed that he had been with a girl once in Augsburg and another in Munich. "Darling, those girls don't mean a thing to me," he reassured her. "You should know that. I just see them one night, and never see them again....Baby, I'd trade 100 of girls like that for one kiss from you."

To his daughter Kathy, the hints of infidelity were a sign of his insecurity "about her finding somebody better than him. I think his remarks were a test to see how she would react. He wanted to see if she'd stay by his side—and she always did. She never seriously dated anybody while he was gone, and that was important to him." She adds, "The sense I got from all those letters was that he was also horribly lonely. He was trying to give himself pep talks all the time, telling my mom how great everything was going to be."

The earliest known mention of marriage came in a letter dated July 18, 1952—apparently in response to something Vivian had written. John began the handwritten note by telling her, "Yes, I wish we could be married soon too honey." Shortly after, he replaced his usual greeting—"My Darling Viv" or "Hello Sweet Darling"—with "My Wife to Be."

Cash didn't hide his feelings from his pals in Landsberg. William Harrell, one of the other interceptor operators, remembered John saying he wanted to marry Vivian so much that he was thinking about converting to Catholicism, even though the religion seemed a bit mysterious and foreign to him. From time to time in letters, especially the early ones, he'd just throw in a question to Vivian. Out of the blue, he'd ask something like, "Honey, what is Catechism?"

Another time he asked, "Darling, if a Protestant marries a Catholic girl, the wedding has to be Catholic and their children have to be brought up Catholics, don't they? And they can't name their own kids. Someone else names their kids, don't they? Maybe that's not right, but that's what I've heard."

In February 1953, two days after turning twenty-one, he bought Viv an engagement ring and mailed it to her.

Still, he continued to wrestle with the issue of her Catholicism. In a letter that May, he said he had read something "very disgusting and disappointing" in a book about "mixed" marriage. "It's urging Catholics not to marry Protestants and Protestants not to marry

Catholics," he wrote her. "If my life were going to be like this book says, I'd be in misery all my life living with you. I don't believe it even though it's a Catholic publication and I know you wouldn't."

With that, the issue passed for a while, and Cash's letters were back to simple "love and kisses."

Women, religion, and alcohol weren't the only issues that Cash grappled with at Landsberg. According to a story that circulated among some of his Landsberg cohorts, John and a couple of friends had drunk too much during a weekend in Augsburg, just northwest of Munich, when Cash saw a black airman walking with a white woman. He yelled at the soldier, saying he shouldn't be going with a white woman. The argument got so heated that a military police-man had to restrain the men, the story went. It shocked his mates, because there were lots of African Americans on the base and John had gotten along well with them, especially C. V. White, an outgo-ing guy with a love for flashy clothes. It was White's wardrobe, in fact, that gave John the germ of an idea that his friend Carl Perkins would turn into "Blue Suede Shoes."

Also, writing to Vivian in early May of 1953, Cash apparently re-ferred to the same drunken incident which he described as an argu-ment at a train station, not mentioning any interracial component. "I called him every name anyone has ever given a Negro," he wrote. "The further he walked away, the louder I yelled, calling him 'Coon,' 'Nigger,' 'Jig-a-boo,' and a few others." He continued, "This morn-ing I was so sick I wanted to die. I drank a lot of coffee and threw it back up." Cash later maintained that the episode in Germany was an irrational drunken outburst. He acknowledged that he had grown up around much racial prejudice, admitting to a friend in the late 1990s that a relative had been a member of the Ku Klux Klan and had committed acts of violence against blacks. But that was long before his family moved to Dyess, he said. Like millions of other whites of his generation in the South, he felt that he eventually dis-tanced himself from the earlier bigotry of the region, and for him that process began in Germany. Despite the Landsberg incidents, Cash told James Keach, who would eventually co-produce the film *Walk the Line* with Cathy Konrad, "I never, ever disliked blacks."

Cash's high school classmate A. J. Henson supports that view. "I would say that there was racism in Dyess," Henson confirms. "Since there were no blacks there, we didn't have many incidents. But the talk was no one wanted much to do with blacks. A group of us were in Wilson and we were walking on the sidewalk when we met a black man. I stepped to the side so he could get past. One of the boys got on me for that and said that whites didn't get out of the way like that. I think most of us have changed since then. I have three adopted black grandchildren."

Cash's daughter Rosanne believes the time in Landsberg helped her father become a more tolerant person. "I think Dad took the prejudices of his upbringing with him to Germany," she says. "He had never seen the wider world; didn't know anything else. His mind quickly began to open. The little travel journals he kept were just so rich and wonderful—he wrote about mountains and monuments, how much things cost, how old they were, histories of places, train rides and boat trips, and of seeing the queen travel through the streets of London. He was clearly enamored with the world, and reveled in a new sense of sophistication and worldliness. Along with that new sense of worldliness came a much greater tolerance and understanding of the evils of racism. Once that was dissolved in him, it never appeared again. He was, in adulthood, the most tolerant person I knew."

To underscore the point, Rosanne relates a moment when she was nineteen and lying on her bed reading a book on astrology when her dad walked in and asked what she was reading. "I showed him and he nodded. I said, 'You don't believe in this, do you?' He said, 'No, but I think you should find out everything you can about it.' Once his mind started to open, there was no stopping it. It was huge. He 'contained multitudes.'"

During the summer of 1953, Cash was well past running with the crowd in German bars. He asked Vivian to come to Germany and live with him in an apartment in Munich. Because she was still under twenty-one, the Air Force required written permission from her parents before she could join him. So he wrote to Vivian's father on July 17 asking for his daughter's hand, but Tom Liberto turned him down. "Dear John," Liberto wrote on August 8. "I know I have taken more time than I needed in order to properly answer your letter which I have thoroughly read and understood. Mrs. Liberto and I did not try to find the answer that would be best for you and Vivian by our own judgment, but rather we spent a few days in prayer asking Divine Guidance."

In the letter, Vivian's father went even further in discouraging an immediate marriage. Pointing out how little time the couple had known each other before Cash went off to Germany, Liberto recommended they "extend this courtship at least a reasonable time after your arrival in the States" to make sure they were right for each other.

Cash was crushed, and he continued to pour out his love for Vivian in letters.

With his return home only a few months away now, Cash spent his off-hours fishing and sightseeing in Europe, including a spin through London and Paris that fall. Perea enjoyed traveling with Cash because he knew they would be seeing historical sites, not bar-hopping in search of women.

There was a disarming innocence in the letters Cash wrote to Vivian during that trip—the letters Rosanne had found so illuminating.

From Paris, on October 18, he wrote: "After a long ride, we reached a cold, foggy Paris at 8:30 a.m....We took a taxi through Pigalle and finally stopped at 'the Arch of Triumph.' It was really a beautiful thing. About 3 times as big as I thought it would be and a lot prettier. We walked around there, taking pictures, etc., and then we went on to the Eiffel Tower....We couldn't see it from very far off because of the fog and we didn't go to the top because we were plenty cold on the ground...and it sure looked a lot colder up there.

"We fooled around the Eiffel Tower awhile taking pictures, then walked down the waterfront. The Eiffel Tower is just a few yards from the Seine River. We sat down on the riverside and watched the people fish for a while. Then we walked down the riverside and came up on the streets and took a subway back to the main part of town. We window shopped for a while, then ate dinner at a swank restaurant. At 1:30 p.m., we returned to the hotel and got some much needed sleep."

Three days later he wrote Vivian from London: "Today we really saw a lot of London. We ate breakfast at 9 o'clock (lazy), then for a while we walked the streets. We took a bus to Buckingham Palace and got there just in time to see the 11 o'clock guard changing ceremony. After taking pictures and seeing as much of the Palace as possible, we walked on down to the Thames River and walked out on Westminster Bridge just as Big Ben was striking twelve. We had a meal of 'fish & chips' near the bridge, then walked up to Picadilly Circus. Times-Square sure hasn't got much on this place."

There were still occasional rough spots in John and Vivian's long-distance relationship, most of them involving religion or alcohol or both. When in January 1954 Vivian confessed that she had become ill after taking a drink at a Christmas party, Cash was furious and threatened to end the relationship: "Now, darling, what do you want to do? Do you want to choose a life of drinking and running around with those drunkards and filthy talking people, or do you want our marriage, our happiness? I want to know now Vivian. It's either our love, or your social drinks."

The following day, he continued to press the issue. Whatever Vivian wrote in response, Cash was satisfied—and he started talking again about their life together. Once more the note was signed "Your husband, Your Johnny for life."

It was when John began to think more and more about the wedding and going home that he resumed going to church, at least occasionally.

He also carved out time on base to work on his music.

In the early months of 1954, Johnny told Vivian about hearing a bunch of new Hank Snow songs and mentioned that he felt his singing was getting better. "I think I've improved my voice since I've gotten this recorder," he wrote. "I guess it's only natural. When I'm not working or sleeping, that's about all I do, is listen to music or play it."

But the most important piece of music he heard the whole time he was in Germany he stumbled upon by accident.

Walking through the barracks one day, he heard a strangely seductive piece of pop-blues about a railroad train and a lonely woman's grief over a lost love. He walked over to Chuck Riley's bunk to listen more closely to this moody track. The song was "Crescent City Blues," part of a concept album, *Seven Dreams*, by composer-arranger Gordon Jenkins, who worked with such pop stars as Nat "King" Cole, Frank Sinatra, and the Andrews Sisters.

Riley had just bought the album at the PX, and he remembers Cash asking him to play it again. John was fascinated by the words and the gently haunting tune:

When I was just a baby, my mama told me, "Sue,
When you're grown up I want that you should go and see and do."
But I'm stuck in Crescent City just watching life mosey by
When I hear that whistle blowin', I hang my head and cry.

A few days later, Cash came back and borrowed the record from Riley to write down the lyrics or perhaps copy it on his tape recorder. As much as any song he heard in Landsberg, "Crescent City Blues" captured the recurring loneliness Cash felt. Remembering the Folsom Prison film, he almost immediately began trying to incorporate some of the feeling of "Crescent City Blues" into a song about the despair of prison confinement, but it would be months before he would finish it. Riley, a jazz fan, had bought the pop album only on a whim. He couldn't find any new jazz albums in the bins, and he liked its cover.

This was the second of a remarkable pair of coincidences that would pay enormous dividends. If John's unit had arrived in Landsberg just two weeks later, he probably would never have seen the Folsom Prison film, and if Riley hadn't bought the Jenkins album, Cash might never have heard the recording and been inspired to write the song that would prove to be so pivotal for him.

Cash also had a minor operation in late March to remove a cyst on his chin, and it left a scar. In coming years, rumors would circulate that the scar came from a knife fight, adding to his rugged, he-man image in the early days of his career.

In April he was promoted to staff sergeant and was asked by the Air Force to reenlist. No way. He wanted to go home.

As eager as he was to see Vivian and begin his civilian life, in his final weeks in Germany John began to realize just how much he missed Dyess and his family. "I had such grief about being away from home for almost three years," he later said. "I missed the fields, I missed the land, the woods, the river, the swimming hole."

It was that homesickness that led him to write the poem "Hey, Porter" on the train as he began his journey home from Landsberg. The song was also a victory statement of sorts. Just twenty-two, Cash felt he had emerged from the challenges and temptations of Landsberg in relatively good shape. He could now look forward to everything that really mattered to him. He'd be back with Vivian, his family, his faith, and his music. The joy of that moment was what "Hey, Porter" was all about. Johnny Cash was returning to his personal promised land:

> Hey, porter, hey, porter,
> would you tell me the time?
> How much longer will it be 'til we cross
> that Mason Dixon Line?
> At daylight would you tell that engineer
> to slow it down,
> or better still, just stop the train
> 'cause I wanna look around?
>
> Hey, porter, hey, porter,
> what time did you say?
> How much longer will it be 'til I can
> see the light of day?
> When we hit Dixie, would you tell that engineer
> to ring his bell,
> and ask everybody that ain't asleep
> to stand right up and yell?
>
> Hey, porter, hey, porter,
> it's getting light outside.
> This ol' train is puffin' smoke,
> and I have to strain my eyes.
> But ask that engineer if he will

blow his whistle, please,
'cause I smell frost on cotton leaves
and I feel that southern breeze.

Hey, porter, hey, porter,
please get my bags for me.
I need nobody to tell me now
that we're in Tennessee.
Go tell that engineer to make that
lonesome whistle scream.
We're not so far from home,
so take it easy on the steam.

Hey, porter, hey, porter,
please open up the door.
When they stop the train, I'm gonna get off first
'cause I can't wait no more.
Tell that engineer I said thanks a lot
and I didn't mind the fare.
I'm gonna set my feet on southern soil
and breathe that southern air.

"Hey, Porter" was an excellent piece of writing—filled with warmth and disarming nuance, and it would forever serve as a reminder to Cash that he was at his best as a writer when he wrote about something from his own experience—songs about the cotton fields, the flood of 1937, and hard times of every sort. The only thing he regretted was that he'd written it about returning to Tennessee rather than Arkansas. He later joked, "The problem is I just couldn't think of enough words that rhymed with Arkansas."

But maybe Tennessee was more appropriate. Arkansas was John R. Cash's past. Tennessee would be his future. The young man from Dyess was dreaming again.

CHAPTER 3

MEMPHIS AND SAM PHILLIPS

I

FOR SOMEONE AS RAW and independent as Johnny Cash, there wasn't a better place to try to enter the music business than Memphis in the summer of 1954. On July 4, Cash's American Airlines flight returned him to Memphis to see his fiancée and family for the first time in three years; and the very next day, Elvis Presley would walk into Sam Phillips's fledgling Sun Records studio to make the record that arguably would define both the attitude and sound of rock 'n' roll.

It was easy in the years following that July 5 Elvis session for young people to think that rock 'n' roll had always been around, like school bells and the World Series. For all practical purposes, however, rock as we came to know it was born that night. Almost by accident, Phillips and three musicians tapped into the volatile social currents of the time and unleashed a force so mighty that it would unite a generation.

In attempting to explain the magic of that summer night, music fans and critics have tended to focus on Presley the charismatic teenage singer who went on to be the music's biggest star. Yet Phillips played an equally important—if not more important—role. As much a rebel as any long-haired musician who would follow in his footsteps on the rock trail, the thirty-one-year-old Alabama native didn't invent rock 'n' roll, but he knew it when he heard it. Unlike some of the big-name Nashville producers, Phillips didn't believe in forcing a certain style or sound on his artists. Sam's genius was in encouraging independent artists to be themselves and recognizing when a record had the human quality that would make it resonate with listeners.

When Phillips, a largely unknown radio announcer and engineer, first opened his storefront recording studio near downtown Memphis in 1950, even his best friends thought it was a good thing Sam was keeping his day job at WREC. How could he ever compete with the major labels in New York and Los Angeles that boasted pop stars like Perry Como and Patti Page? But there was something the doubters didn't know about this ambitious young man: his unshakable faith in the power and appeal of the roots country and blues he had loved growing up in the South. He didn't plan to compete with the pop sounds; he intended to replace them.

Perhaps the sound that caught Phillips's ear that night could only have been forged in Memphis. The city is less than three hours by car from the country music recording center of Nashville, but they are so different that it's hard to believe you haven't crossed a state boundary when driving between them on Interstate 40. There's even an old saying: Nashville may be the capital of Tennessee, but Memphis is the capital of Mississippi. The city's Beale Street had already been a showplace for black music for half a century. "I had grown up in the South, and I felt a definite kinship between the white Southern country artists and the black Southern blues or spiritual artists," Phillips said years later. "Our ties were too close for the two not to overlap. It was a natural thing. It's just that the record business in those days looked at the music as totally separate. They didn't realize that it was a natural exchange and that the public would eventually accept it."

To that end, Phillips opened his storefront recording studio at 706 Union Avenue, hoping to record the city's deep pool of gifted black musicians. He started by making singles with local blues and R&B artists, including B. B. King and Howlin' Wolf, on assignment from indie record companies such as Chess in Chicago and

Modern in Los Angeles. After one of those singles, a lively novelty song titled "Rocket 88" that he made with Ike Turner and Jackie Brenston, became a number-one R&B hit for Chess, Phillips started his own Sun Records. With just one employee, a receptionist-secretary who handled most of the books, Phillips worked like a man possessed. Besides recording the artists, he drove hundreds of miles a week in his 1947 DeSoto, hoping to persuade DJs in the region to play the recordings on the radio and talk record shops into stocking them.

Phillips's early recordings with white artists tended toward straight country, and he may have had the same thing in mind for Presley. He had been impressed when the teenager stopped by Sun Studios in 1953 to make a record for his mother, a sideline business that helped Phillips pay the bills. Phillips wasn't knocked out by Presley's tentative vocal on an old pop tune called "My Happiness," but there was something about the singer's tone that stuck with him.

When he went into the studio with Elvis on July 5, Sam put him together with two musicians who had worked on some of Phillips's earlier recordings, guitarist Scotty Moore and bassist Bill Black. To help the youngster relax, Phillips suggested he just sing some of his favorite tunes. When Elvis responded with lots of pop stuff, including a slow, hesitant version of "Harbor Lights," a Top 10 hit for Bing Crosby four years before, Phillips's heart sank. The night looked like a lost cause. Eventually, he turned off the tape recorder and told the guys to take a break.

He was startled moments later when Presley began strumming playfully on his acoustic guitar and singing "That's All Right," a blues tune by Arthur "Big Boy" Crudup. Phillips quickly turned the tape machine back on and encouraged the musicians to play the tune a few times.

The moment was as close to a "big bang" as can be found in pop music. There's a raw sex appeal and authority in Presley's vocal, and Moore's memorable guitar break, influenced by the thumb and finger style of country guitarists Chet Atkins and Merle Travis, adds energy and color. With the release of that record, the guitar took its place as the essential rock 'n' roll instrument. Legions of players, including Eric Clapton, Jimmy Page, and John Lennon, have spoken with awe about the impact of hearing Elvis's voice and Scotty's guitar on those early Sun singles.

The record caused such a stir in the South that young singers from all around the region, including Louisiana, Texas, and Mississippi, began lining up outside Phillips's door, each wanting to be the next Elvis.

John R. Cash would eventually take his place in that line. But, from a career perspective, the choice of Memphis as his new home was pure luck.

As Cash's plane began its descent over Memphis, he didn't know anything about Sam Phillips, Elvis Presley, or Sun Records. He had decided to move to Memphis because his older brother, Roy, lived there and had promised to help him find a job. The Air Force—and years of his father's taunts—had taught Cash to be a practical man.

II

Even though most of his family would also be waiting at the Memphis airport to greet him, Johnny only had eyes for one person. He and Vivian were too excited for words as he took her in his arms and gave her a kiss that went on long enough that his family broke into nervous laughter. Even the normally taciturn Ray chipped in. "Vivian," he joked, "you're going to eat him up."

The joviality finally caused the pair to break their embrace and John to turn his attention to the rest of his family. With Vivian at his side, he shook hands with or hugged Carrie and Ray, his brothers Roy and Tommy, his sisters Reba, Louise, and Joanne, plus some nieces and nephews. Even though they could see how much the now six-foot-two, 165-pound Cash had grown, they were surprised by his added muscles when he held them close.

The whole group headed for Dyess, where Carrie and Ray had sold the farmhouse and bought a new place near the town center, but John still felt at home, and he couldn't wait to give Vivian a tour of the school, the fishing hole, and other favorite haunts of his youth.

He was disappointed during the visit home that he couldn't introduce Vivian to all of his high school friends, but most had already joined the exodus out of town. He left photos of her with the parents of some of them to make sure they could see how lovely she was. There was another major disappointment, too: Vivian had promised her father that she wouldn't have sex with John before their marriage, and she didn't relent.

After a few days, John was restless. He wanted to head to San Antonio to ask Vivian's father formally for her hand in marriage. Vivian was touched by the sweet, old-fashioned gesture; she knew it would mean a lot to her parents. Borrowing Ray and Carrie's car, he and Vivian drove to San Antonio, where, for old times' sake, they returned the first evening to the River Walk and found the bench where John had carved their initials.

Despite his original skepticism, Tom Liberto was charmed by his future son-in-law. It still troubled him that the couple had spent less than thirty days in each other's company. But Vivian was twenty-one, and he was impressed by John's willingness to be married in the Catholic Church and his pledge to raise the children in the faith. This, he felt, was indeed a model young man, and he finally gave his consent.

While Vivian worked on the wedding plans, John returned to Dyess to drop off his folks' car and then caught the bus to Memphis. Roy picked him up at the station and took him to the large DeSoto-Plymouth dealership where he worked as a mechanic. Roy wanted him to meet Marshall Grant and Luther Perkins, a couple of fellow mechanics who often played old country and gospel songs on their guitars during lunch breaks. Maybe, Roy figured, they could start a band together.

Marshall, who had moved to Memphis from his native North Carolina, was immediately struck by Cash's charisma. "He didn't even have his Air Force suit on," Grant said. "He was in regular clothes, but something drew you to him. By the time Roy introduced us, it felt like the hair on the back of my head was sticking straight out. It startled me a little bit. But it also gave me the sense that I wanted to get to know this guy. He looked like a star.

"When Roy introduced us, John said, 'I hear you pick a little bit,' and I said, 'Very little,' and he chuckled, 'Well, that's me, too.'" Grant took Cash over to meet Perkins, a poker-faced Mississippi native who was working on a broken car radio, and John said the same thing to Luther, "I hear you pick a little." They agreed to get together to play some music after John returned from San Antonio.

Next, Roy took his brother to the Memphis Police Department, where Roy had a friend on the force. There was no position open, but the friend recommended that he talk to George Bates at the Home Equipment Company. It was a popular appliance store in town, and Bates was known to go out of his way to help out ex-servicemen.

Roy drove Cash to Home Equipment at 2529 Summer Avenue, where they introduced themselves to George Bates. When Bates asked John if he thought he could be a good salesman, John told him the truth. He said he really wanted to be a singer, but he had just returned from Germany and was going to be married in a few weeks, so he needed a job. Undaunted, Bates replied, "Well, we'll give you a job and see if you can [sell]. I really like your self-confidence. That's one thing a salesman has to have."

Relieved, John shook Bates's hand and set out with Roy to find an apartment. The best he could afford was a small second-floor place at 1624 Eastmoreland Avenue. John wasn't happy with it, later calling the apartment "hot and horrible." The newlyweds wouldn't even have their own kitchen; they had to share one on the third floor with other tenants. But it was cheap at $55 a month, and it was a start. The next thing Cash needed was a car, and Roy helped him get a good deal on a new green Plymouth, using money John had saved from Germany for a down payment.

With all the practical things taken care of, John decided to explore a job at a radio station—a way, he figured, to help him eventually get a chance to sing on the air. One of the guys in Germany had been an announcer on station WMCA in Corinth, Mississippi, about a hundred miles from Memphis, and he told John to look up the station's manager, John Bell; maybe he could get hired as an announcer.

Bell wasn't impressed by Cash. He told him to enroll in a radio school, where he could get some training. John heeded Bell's advice and enrolled in Keegan's School of Broadcasting on Madison Avenue, using his GI Bill benefits to cover costs. He took announcing classes, which he'd attend two mornings a week before work.

On the drive back to San Antonio, John listened to the radio, searching for something by his heroes, and sure enough, there was a huge new Hank Snow hit, "I Don't Hurt Anymore," that was just starting a twenty-week reign at number one on the country charts. He sang along with the radio, and he thought about school and how it was going to lead to his own radio show someday. He couldn't wait to tell Vivian.

After their long-distance courtship, John and Vivian were finally able to say "I do" before Vivian's uncle, Father Vincent Liberto, in a ceremony held at St. Ann's Catholic Church on Sunday, August 7, 1954. After a reception at the St. Anthony Hotel, the Cashes headed for Palestine, Texas, where they spent their wedding night. It was at just about the halfway point of the 440 miles to Memphis. They had five days before John started work.

It was during their first week in Memphis that John first heard Elvis Presley's "That's All Right" on the radio. Like many, he didn't know at first if it was a country record or a blues record. But he liked it a lot, and he took notice when the DJ kept saying it was the hottest record in town. One other thing caught John's ear on that first hearing: this exciting new record wasn't on RCA or Decca or one of the other big Nashville labels. As the DJ put it, "That's All Right" was on Memphis's *own* Sun Records.

Sun Records?

The country boy in Cash instinctively liked the name. It took him back to the start of the day in the cotton fields—which was the exact same image Sam Phillips had in mind when he thought of the name in the first place. Cash would have bought the record, but his budget was too tight. He had to settle for listening to it on the radio. He thought about going to Sun Records, but he didn't kid himself; he wasn't good enough yet to make a record. He didn't even have a band. That reminded him of the two guys Roy had introduced him to a couple of weeks before. He headed back to Automobile Sales at

309 Union Avenue, a major commercial street in midtown Memphis.

Marshall Grant was delighted to see Cash again, and they made arrangements to get together at Marshall's house at 4199 Nakomis the following weekend; John and Vivian needed their first weekend in town to get things in shape at their apartment. Marshall said he'd invite Luther Perkins, Roy, and another employee, a steel guitar player named A. W. "Red" Kernodle. John then got into his car, turned right on Union Avenue, and headed home. Four blocks later, he passed a nondescript single-story building. Little did he suspect that it was the home of Sun Records.

III

John felt he was on a roll as he drove his new Plymouth to the Home Equipment Company headquarters on Thursday morning to begin the store's version of basic training. Owner George Bates wanted new employees to spend time in each department so they would know how to respond to any customer question. Whether it was roofing, new flooring, aluminum siding, air conditioning, fiberglass, wrought iron rails, or appliances, Home Equipment was ready to help—complete with easy-payment plans.

Bates also wanted his new employee to get some experience working the store floor before sending him out to solicit customers door-to-door. John tried to pitch refrigerators, vacuum cleaners, and other household appliances, but after two days, he still had no sales. Bates told him not to worry; he'd eventually get the knack. John liked Bates and tried to believe him.

Meanwhile, John was looking forward to getting together with the guys to play some music. Marshall and Luther were both born in 1928, which made them closer to Roy Cash's age than John's, but they formed an immediate rapport with the young man. While they gathered at Marshall's house, the wives played cards in the kitchen.

Marshall described Vivian as "one of the most beautiful women I had seen in my life...lovely skin and gorgeous eyes. She and my wife fell in love in a matter of minutes, and that helped her start to get over some of her homesickness because she didn't know anybody around here except John and Roy."

For their first get-together, John brought along his cheap German guitar. He quickly emerged as the group's unofficial leader. As they strummed their guitars, John sang lead and Marshall took over harmony, trying to sound as much as they could like the Louvin Brothers. Marshall admitted they were pretty rough. None of them was even good enough on the guitar to play lead, so they all had to play rhythm. Every so often, John would venture off and start singing a Hank Snow or Hank Williams song, but it was mostly gospel.

Roy never joined in the playing, despite an early interest in music when he and little J.R. would devote themselves to learning all the singers on the family radio. He just sat on the sofa, encouraging everyone. He saved his greatest praise, of course, for his brother.

Each time the guys got together on a Friday or Saturday night (sometimes both), the music sounded a touch better. Marshall and Luther just saw it as recreation; John was the only one who was serious about a music career. But something happened during one of their early get-togethers that started Marshall believing that all this fooling around might actually lead to something. Just before the end of the night, John, somewhat timidly, said he wanted to play a gospel song he had written in Germany. Titled "Belshazzar," the song was drawn from the Old Testament and told the story of a king with false values.

Marshall was impressed that John could actually write a song. Roy, too, hearing about his brother's writing, was even more certain that John was going to be a star.

As Grant recalled, John was excited a few days later to learn that Elvis Presley was going to do a free show at the opening of a new Katz Drug Store. John and Vivian went to the opening and watched Elvis, Scotty Moore, and Bill Black perform on the back of a flatbed truck parked outside the store. Because Elvis had only the one record out, they kept playing "That's All Right" and "Blue Moon of Kentucky" over and over.

John was mesmerized by what he saw and heard, from the sensual energy of the music to the enthusiasm of the group of young, mostly female fans. He also was struck by how young Elvis looked. He was just a kid, he told Marshall later. In fact, John, Marshall, and Luther all began calling Elvis "the Kid." Though only three years Elvis's senior, at twenty-two, John suddenly felt old. He told himself he'd better get started if he was ever going to make it in the music business.

After Elvis stepped down from the truck, John went over and told him how much he liked his music. Elvis was flattered and invited John and Vivian to come see him again the next night at the Eagle's Nest, a 350-capacity nightclub/dance hall located at the edge of the city limits at Highway 78 and Winchester Road.

Once again, Cash marveled at Elvis's smooth delivery and the trio's tightness. Afterward he said hello again, but he didn't mention what was really on his mind: how to get in to Sun Records. John did bring up Sun when talking to Scotty Moore, and Scotty advised him just to call Sam Phillips and make an appointment. He told John, "He's lookin' for new talent."

During a break at work the following week, John looked up Sun Records in the phone directory and dialed the number. When a woman answered, he asked to speak to Sam Phillips, but was told he was out of town. Oddly, John felt relieved. Always a realist, he knew he wasn't anywhere near good enough to make a record yet. He wrote the Sun number on a piece of paper, though, and stuck it in his pocket.

When John showed up at Marshall's house the following Friday, Marshall sensed something different about him. Instead of joking around between and even during songs, he was serious. He kept going over the same two or three numbers rather than shifting from one to the next as he had done on previous nights. One of the songs, "I Was There When It Happened," was a gospel tune popularized by Jimmie Davis, the former Louisiana governor. Another was his own "Belshazzar." John wanted their group to play as confidently as Elvis and his guys played.

That attitude turned their meetings from relaxed free-for-alls into real rehearsals—and the other guys picked up on it. Marshall was starting to see a future for the group, and he made a key suggestion: to be really good onstage, they needed a much fuller sound. It wasn't enough for them all just to play acoustic guitars—and steel guitar on the occasional nights when Red Kernodle stopped by. Luther said he knew where he could borrow an electric guitar, and Marshall agreed to get a standup bass, even though he didn't know how to play one. Because John was the singer, it was agreed that he would continue playing rhythm guitar. And sure enough, Luther showed up the following weekend with a Fender Telecaster and Marshall had a bass he'd bought for $25. Both instruments were pretty worn out. The Telecaster didn't even have a volume control, so Luther had to place his hands across the strings to muffle them when he wanted to soften the tone. Trying to learn to play the bass, Marshall had written the names of the notes on adhesive and placed the tape by the respective strings. But their sound was already more commanding.

In his struggle to find and hold notes, Luther played a very slow, steady rhythm on his guitar. Marshall tried to follow along, playing the same notes as best he could, in the same deliberate manner. They were literally going from one note to the next like someone typing in a halting hunt-and-peck style.

They kept it up the next weekend, but they just couldn't get beyond that simple, primitive sound—the humble beginnings of what they began to refer to as the *tick-tack-tick-tack* sound, the style others would someday label *boom-chicka-boom*. It wasn't that they thought they had discovered something; it was just about the only way they could play. Oh, well, they told themselves, it's a start. They'd get better.

When John went into the kitchen to tell Vivian about the progress they were making, he got some news of his own.

She was pregnant.

The other wives cheered as he took Vivian in his arms and gave her a hug. He had been home only three months, but his dreams were starting to come true. About that time Cash would later say, "I was full of joy every morning."

And by mid-October, he was ready to go see Sam Phillips.

Chapter 4

SUN RECORDS, THE TENNESSEE TWO, AND *BOOM CHICKA BOOM*

I

CASH STARTED HIS NEW CAMPAIGN to reach Phillips by phoning Sun Records, only to be told again that Phillips was out of town. After three or four attempts, Cash assumed that Phillips was flooded by audition requests and was simply not taking calls. As he later learned, Phillips was indeed on the road constantly, hoping to get more airplay and better sales distribution for Elvis's records. Phillips was so focused on his young star that he released only two singles by other artists in the entire second half of 1954—and he didn't devote much promotion time to any of them.

As soon as "That's All Right" and "Blue Moon of Kentucky" hit in July, Phillips knew he had to rush out another single to convince radio stations and retailers that Sun's new star wasn't just a one-hit wonder. Phillips released Elvis's second single, "Good Rockin' Tonight" and "I Don't Care If the Sun Don't Shine," the last week of September, and he spent most of October on the road promoting it throughout the South. He also accompanied Elvis to Nashville for his Grand Ole Opry debut on October 2. The Opry, of course, was the goal of every country singer. Not only was it the most respected of many of the country music showcases around the country, but also it offered the most exposure, thanks to a national NBC radio hookup every Saturday night.

Phillips likely knew from the beginning that Elvis and the Opry weren't going to be a good fit. For all its storied history, the Opry, in the rapidly shifting culture of the mid-1950s, was definitely the old guard. Elvis, Sam liked to think, was the future. When Opry manager Jim Denny proved cool to Elvis's performance, Phillips thought immediately of the next-best country showcase—the Louisiana Hayride in Shreveport, Louisiana.

The Hayride, which had played a major role in the launching of Hank Williams, was less formal than the Opry, more open to change and experimentation. Though its radio show didn't have as big an audience, it blanketed the Southern and Southwest regions, which were the heart of Sun's market. Phillips headed to Shreveport to watch Elvis make his Hayride debut on October 16. Management was delighted by what they saw and signed him to a one-year contract.

Back in Memphis, John Cash was getting impatient.

When he phoned Sun in late October or early November, he got some good news: Sam was supposed to be back in the office on Monday. That was all John needed to know. On Monday, he stopped by Sun on his way to work and waited by the front door for Phillips to arrive. His aggressiveness paid off; Phillips was impressed by Cash's enterprise. When John told him he wanted to make a record, Sam invited him into the studio.

There was something about this young singer that appealed to Phillips. He wasn't like most of the other young singers who had been coming by Sun since Elvis's success; there seemed to be a certain depth to him. When Phillips finally asked him to sing something, Cash picked up his guitar and launched into some of the songs he'd been doing in Germany, which meant a lot of Hank Snow, Eddy Arnold, and Jimmie Rodgers, as well as "Belshazzar."

He sang for two or three hours, just going from one song to the next at random, even throwing in "I'll Take You Home Again, Kathleen" when it popped into his head. Phillips heard something in Cash that he liked—a certain authority. It was virtually a replay of his first reaction to Elvis. Phillips also noticed that Cash, like Elvis, had a charisma about him. He was tall and commanding—he looked like a star. Phillips asked about his band. Actually, Cash replied, it was just three guys, and they weren't real experienced. Looking back, Phillips recalled that it wasn't clear if Cash was auditioning for himself or for the group. No matter, Phillips said; he'd like to meet the other musicians. Sam wasn't big on polish. He was into feeling. He told Cash that if he could find the right song, he might be interested in recording him.

Cash got into his car and drove the four blocks to Automobile Sales, where he told Marshall, Luther, and Red about meeting Sam. In hopes of catching Phillips before he left town again, the four of them went back to Sun the next morning. "It was just to say hello," Grant recalled. "We didn't even bring our instruments, but we could see that he liked John and we all got along pretty good." Once again, Phillips invited Cash to come back if he came up with a good song.

Feeling they had a mandate, the foursome went back to work on "I Was There When It Happened," the song they thought best showcased them. Cash knew Sam didn't want gospel music, but figured maybe he could change his mind if the song was good enough. The musicians spent a couple of weeks rehearsing and then went back for an informal audition. As Phillips set up microphones in the studio, the musicians began tuning their instruments. Suddenly, Kernodle started shaking so badly he couldn't tune the pegs on the steel guitar. He kept going over or under the desired marks. This in turn made everyone else more nervous. After a few minutes of this, he stood up, walked over to Marshall, and whispered, "Grant, I can't do anything but hold y'all back." With that he left.

Embarrassed, Cash took Phillips into the control booth, where he explained what had happened. "John apologized to me for not having a professional band, but I said that he should let me hear what they could do and I would be able to tell whether they had a style I would be able to work with," Phillips recalled.

At Phillips's signal, John, Marshall, and Luther started playing "I Was There When It Happened," but they were so ragged—Marshall swore that John was shaking almost as badly as Red had been, perspiration pouring down his face—that they feared the worst.

Sam came back into the studio and adjusted the microphones again to improve the sound balance. He then asked them to play the song again. This time they were more relaxed. and the music came together nicely. They felt they had nailed it.

Marshall didn't know what to make of it when Sam's first words to them as he walked out of the control booth were "There's something really squirrely about you guys."

Squirrely?

What he meant, it turned out, was that there was something different about them—which was high praise in the Sun owner's mind.

"I've never heard anything like it before, it's different," he told them. "I like that. But I'm not going to record a gospel song. I can't sell 'em. I've tried and it didn't work."

Though he didn't spell it out for them, Phillips was fond of the trio's spare but insistent rhythm, and he especially liked the understated force in Cash's voice. When listening to most want-to-be singers, Phillips could tell exactly who they were trying to sound like—in most cases recently, Elvis Presley.

When Cash sang, the only person Phillips heard was Cash himself. Not only was he different from Elvis; he was different from the Nashville singers. Phillips was privately pleased, too, that the steel guitarist had left. He felt that the instrument would have taken away from the trio's uniqueness; it would have made the music sound too much like all those conventional country records coming out of Nashville.

At the end of the audition Phillips told Cash, "If you come up with something original, something that's not gospel, I'd like to hear you again."

The solution came quickly.

When they next gathered at the house on Nakomis, John pulled out a piece of paper with the "Hey, Porter" poem written on it.

"What do you think of this?"

II

It was a good thing Cash's country music dream was driving him on, because it kept him from brooding about his problems at Home Equipment. Actually, it was just one problem: he couldn't sell anything door-to-door. Maybe it would have been different if his route had covered the wealthiest families, but he was the new guy, so he had to spend his days in the poorest neighborhoods.

John had seen people struggle too many years in Dyess to ever forget what it was like. He knew that many of the people who answered his knock had barely enough money to feed and clothe their families. Some depended on the charity of their church, family members, and neighbors. So in most stops on his route, John just made a half-hearted pitch.

John's low-key selling style worked in his favor one day at the store. Vivian was suffering from severe morning sickness, and John wanted to find an apartment closer to Home Equipment than the one on Eastmoreland, which was a good fifteen minutes away, so he could rush home if she needed him. He also wanted to get a first-floor place so his wife wouldn't have to climb stairs and risk the chance of falling. But he couldn't find anything he could afford.

Just before closing time one evening, a woman came into the store to look at used refrigerators. When John walked over to her, she asked him the price of a nondescript unit. Before looking at the tag, John guessed, "About thirty dollars." After seeing the tag, he shrugged. "They want sixty-five dollars for that, and it only has a thirty-day guarantee."

The woman was Pat Isom, and she was understandably surprised. Was this nice young salesman trying to talk her out of buying the refrigerator? She asked if he enjoyed working at the store and John said yes, except that he was having trouble finding an apartment nearby for $55. He then explained Vivian's pregnancy and the run-down apartment on Eastmoreland.

Isom and her husband owned a duplex just three blocks away, and they were trying to rent one of the units. Cash followed her over to 2553 Tutwiler Avenue and thought the place was perfect, but he didn't think he could afford it. When Isom said he could have it for

$55, John wanted to hug her. As the months went by, he could rarely pay the Isoms even that much, but he paid as much as he could, and the couple was nice enough to let this "real quiet and bashful boy" run a tab.

Vivian was overjoyed by the new, cleaner apartment, but she was also worried about finances and the upcoming baby. Gently she brought up the possibility of moving back to San Antonio so they could be close to her family. Unknown to Johnny, her father was sending her a small check periodically to help them get by.

The Isoms weren't the only ones whose generosity greatly benefited John and Vivian. George Bates was proving to be an even bigger help to his new employee. Cash did sell an occasional washing machine or some ornamental fencing, but it wasn't adding up. All he was making from commissions was about $12 to $15 a week, which simply was not enough to live on, especially with a baby on the way.

He went to Bates to talk about his future. He thanked his boss again for believing in him. But he said he just couldn't make it on his commission. Bates told Cash that if he'd keep trying to sell, he would receive a weekly advance—as long as the young man agreed to pay it back eventually. John thanked Bates profusely, but he couldn't help feeling he was some kind of guinea pig—"like a pet project to see how far I would go on taking draws and not producing anything."

But the support meant a lot to Cash. He was glad to see that the world outside Dyess had some kindness in it, too.

The residents of Memphis's poorest black neighborhoods reminded Cash of a lot of the people in Dyess. He noticed particularly how they remained hopeful in the face of overwhelming economic odds and how music seemed to help lift their spirits. In almost every house he heard music coming from the radio—usually blues and gospel artists. He enjoyed the sounds, and he began listening to more black music on the radio. It was another significant step in building his musical vision. He was starting to weave together lots of rootsy influences. One of his favorites was Sister Rosetta Tharpe, a black gospel singer who'd grown up only about fifty miles from

Dyess. John had been loosely following Tharpe's career for years, admiring the way she mixed gospel themes with a rollicking, high-energy blues style—as on "Strange Things Happening Every Day." In time, he learned that she took spiritual music into nightclubs and dance halls, not just churches and stately auditoriums—something he hoped to do one day.

On one of his daily sales rounds, he came across an elderly man strumming his guitar on his front porch. Cash walked up to him and said he sure liked the music. The man invited John to sit down, and he kept on playing blues tunes for the better part of an hour. He even boasted about how they carried his records at the Home of the Blues shop on Beale Street. At first Cash didn't believe him, but the man went into the house and came back with a 78-rpm single with his name on it: Gus Cannon.

Born in the Mississippi Delta, Cannon was in his early twenties when he moved to Memphis around 1907. He began recording in the late 1920s and fronted a jug band for years. One of the group's songs, "Walk Right In," would become a folk-pop hit in the 1960s when recorded by the Rooftop Singers. Cannon had been retired since the late 1930s. Cash came back a few days later with his guitar, and the men played a few tunes together. Then John resumed his door-knocking for Home Equipment. Because of that black music, Cash started going to the Home of the Blues himself, looking for records by Sister Tharpe and others. On his tight budget, he couldn't afford actually to buy anything, but he enjoyed being around the records, and he liked to listen to the customers talk about their favorite artists.

Most days, he spent much of his time at home listening to the radio to keep up with what his favorite singers were doing. He and Vivian also took walks in the park and drove to Roy's house, where they were always welcome. Roy knew how difficult it was to get going financially, so he helped John and Vivian in lots of subtle ways. He and his wife had them over for dinner often, and when he went to buy clothes, he took John along, making sure to buy his younger brother at least a shirt or some socks.

On Sundays, John and Vivian frequently traveled to Dyess for some of Carrie's country cooking, which was one thing John had missed greatly in Germany. Years later he would still speak about a "craving in his bones" for that Southern food. The one thing he did develop a taste for in Germany was large wiener sausages, which in turn left him a lifelong fan of hot dogs. Over the years, he developed a private list of favorite hot dog stands or shops around the country and invariably stopped by for a dog or two when he was in the area. At one point, after the money was flowing in, he even thought of opening his own hot dog chain, but calmer heads prevailed. Johnny Cash would never be known as a good businessman.

III

Marshall liked the "Hey, Porter" poem, but it was just a poem. How were they going to turn it into a song? They thought about taking the melody of some old song and putting the words to it, which was a common practice in country, folk, and blues music. John had done it on the songs he fiddled with in Germany. But they couldn't think of anything that worked with "Hey, Porter," so they tried to make up a tune themselves. They just started hitting the strings to see where it would take them. Roy was still a regular, cheering them on.

They all looked to Luther's guitar as the heart of their sound; but he was unable to move beyond that simple *tick-tack-tick-tack*—or hunt-and-peck—style. "John played the first note and the second one and asked Luther if he could do that. Luther worked and worked on it…must have been an hour or two, and he finally got it," Marshall said. "That's about all we achieved that first night."

Over the years, rather than apologize for their limitations as musicians, Marshall saw those limitations as a secret weapon. "Our inability had a lot more to do with our success than our ability," he said. "If we had done what we wanted to do in those days—which was play like all those great musicians in Nashville—we would have sounded like everyone else, and that would have taken away from the character in John's voice."

Though long embarrassed by his lack of range on the guitar, Luther, too, grew to be proud of the sound he brought to the group.

"You know how all those hot-shot guitarists race their fingers all over the strings?" he'd say time and again. "Well, they're looking for the right sound. I found it."

By the time they were comfortable with "Hey, Porter," it was December and everyone was caught up in the holidays. Sam Phillips was rushing to release Elvis's third single. John had been telling Vivian that a Sun contract would be the best Christmas present of all, but it wasn't going to happen.

There was one milestone for the group that month, though. A neighbor heard them rehearsing and asked if they would play some spiritual music at her church one evening. It would just be for a few ladies, and they wouldn't be able to pay them. But the guys jumped at the chance. Setting aside "Hey, Porter," they worked up a half-dozen or so gospel tunes for the church performance, including "I Was There When It Happened" and "Belshazzar." Soon, they realized their band needed a name.

"You're the best with words, John, you come up with something," Marshall told him.

In almost no time, Cash had a playful name. "Well, let's see, you're from North Carolina [Marshall], you're from Mississippi [Luther], and I'm from Arkansas...how about the Tennessee Three?"

He offered Tennessee Trio as an alternative, but Luther and Marshall liked the sound of the Tennessee Three. After all, they did live in Memphis now, and they liked the Southern connection.

The church show wasn't a glamorous affair, but it was a start. The Tennessee Three played for about twenty minutes to about a dozen elderly ladies in the basement of the Galloway United Methodist Church.

John couldn't wait to tell his mother about the performance when the family got together for Christmas. Roy, ever the cheerleader, told everyone that John was going to make a record for the Sun label. John then sang "Hey, Porter." Carrie was surprised it wasn't a gospel song, but she loved it anyway—particularly the part about coming home.

John wasted no time in getting back to Sam Phillips in the new year, and Sam gave "Hey, Porter" a thumbs-up. He said he'd record the song as soon as John came up with another original song for the back of the single. John again brought up "Belshazzar," but Sam reminded him of the no-gospel rule. Once again, the Tennessee Three returned to the drawing board.

John had wanted Vivian to come to the audition, but she was five months pregnant and still feeling the effects of morning sickness. Instead, she paced the floor while he was gone. Despite all John's hopes, she couldn't quite imagine how a band could jump from Marshall's home rehearsal garage to a record contract. So she was all the more excited when Cash raced up the walk with a big smile on his face and told her, "Baby, we're cuttin' a record."

In contrast to the anxiety he'd felt over finding a job after high school and his entrance into the Air Force, John was absolutely certain that he was on his way to a life in country music once Phillips said he liked "Hey, Porter."

As George Bates had done, Phillips was fast becoming something of a father figure to Cash, one of several who would serve in that role over the years. In time, he'd speak of both men as his "angels." There was something about Phillips that made Cash trust him implicitly—at least in the beginning—whether he was talking about music or giving advice on money matters. Though the record company owner was only nine years older, John called him "Mr. Phillips," even after he left Sun. "I've got a lot of respect for him," Cash declared. "He's really a man of vision....[H]e can see something happening that nobody else could."

Never one to shy away from hard work, Cash threw himself into following through on Phillips's career suggestions in the early months of 1955—including trying to book some live shows so that he'd be comfortable when he started touring behind "Hey, Porter." Phillips said it didn't matter where he played—schoolhouses, town socials, rural roadhouses—just as long as he got some experience in "hooking" a crowd.

Most of all, though, Phillips kept reminding John about the need for new songs. Sam had opened his own publishing company, Hi-Lo Music, and he made sure that all the Sun artists signed with it. By owning the publishing rights, he made a few more cents per record—and every penny counted in those early fledgling days. But Phillips also believed that Cash's ability to write would give him a big advantage against the Nashville singers, most of whom depended on a network of songwriters for material. Cash began working on lining up live shows and songwriting—all the while trying to honor his responsibilities to Home Equipment. George Bates sensed that John would be giving up his job soon, but he was so fond of the young man that he would regularly ask for updates about the band's progress.

Ever the dreamer, Cash was already feeling so much a part of the music business that he was bringing home copies of the magazines and trade publications, including *Billboard* and *Cash Box*. He loved seeing photos of the new artists so he could picture them when he heard them on the radio. Luther and Marshall, by contrast, still couldn't imagine giving up their mechanic jobs. This was fun, they told each other, but you couldn't count on getting your weekly $60.

Progress was slow on the live show front. John didn't turn out to be any better at selling his music than at selling aluminum siding. On his days off, he—sometimes with Marshall or Luther or both—would drive his green Plymouth through small towns outside Memphis, hoping to find places that would let them set up a show. They stopped at movie theaters, social halls, schools, food markets, and roadhouses. No place was too small.

Hoping to impress the various businessmen, John always mentioned that he was going to have a release on Sun Records. The problem was that most of the merchants hadn't heard of Sun Records, and the ones who had told him to come back when he had the record. He became so frustrated that he even started offering to do shows for free—and he still couldn't find any takers. Finally, he gave up and just concentrated on his songwriting.

* * *

In looking for song ideas, John rummaged back over the pieces of songs he had been trying to put together ever since Landsberg. He also replayed in his head many of his favorite records—all the way back to Dyess days—in hopes of finding something to trigger his imagination.

That meant a lot of Jimmie Rodgers recordings. Rodgers was still Cash's main inspiration—and he wasn't alone in his feeling for the man's music. As Rodgers's plaque in the Country Music Hall of Fame declares, he "stands foremost in the country music field as 'the man who started it all.' His songs told the great stories of the singing rails, the powerful steam locomotives and the wonderful railroad people that he loved so well. Although small in stature, he was a giant among men, starting a trend in the musical taste of millions."

Just as Sam Phillips often used the word "different" when dishing out praise, John employed the word "authentic," and his model, in many ways, was Rodgers, who started making records in 1927 at the age of twenty-nine. Partly because Rodgers's millions of fans knew about his life as a railroad brakeman, but mostly because he sang with natural, almost storytelling intimacy, those fans believed he was singing about himself and his experiences. Though commonplace in the rock world of the 1960s and beyond, this idea of "personal singing and songwriting" was revolutionary in Rodgers's era, especially among best-selling music makers, who depended on Tin Pan Alley compositions.

Even in the blues and country fields, where songs tended to be more conversational and anecdotal, the recordings were less autobiographical than one might now assume. They were usually reflections on common experiences rather than the consistent chronicling of a writer's or singer's own life. Rodgers blurred the distinction between common experience and personal testimony because he sounded so convincing, whether he'd actually written the song he was singing or not.

In 1931 Rodgers wrote one of his most evocative tunes, "T.B. Blues"—at a time when he was actually battling tuberculosis, which would kill him two years later. During his final recording sessions in New York City, the story went, Rodgers was so ill that he had to sit in a chair or, sometimes, lie on a cot between songs.

"When Jimmie Rodgers sang 'T.B. Blues,' his audiences knew that he meant it—and that was one of the things, amid all the hillbilly hokum of the day that distinguished him....It was what country music fans mean today when they bestow their highest accolade on an artist by calling him 'sincere,'" writes Nolan Porterfield in his biography *Jimmie Rodgers.*

Cash could have used "sincere" as well to describe what he prized in an artist, but he wasn't talking just about how convincing a record sounded; he wanted to know that something in the singer's background showed he was singing from his heart about experiences he had lived. To him, that was the greatest test of an artist—and that's what made him so proud of "Hey, Porter." He was being authentic to himself and his own life.

As Cash listened to Rodgers's records, he identified with the man who had grown up in hard times and found in music both a comfort and a personal salvation. It was those records that also instilled in Cash much of his fascination with railroads and their imagery in song. Whenever Cash reached deep inside for his best songs, whether it was in 1955 or decades later, he was usually reaching back to that Jimmie Rodgers tradition.

But Cash was still learning how to write songs. He spent hour after hour listening to country music on the radio, hoping to hear a theme or lyric that would inspire him to create a song of his own. As he listened, he kept a pencil and a pad nearby so he could jot down his thoughts. Many a night Vivian sat with him, listening to the music, until she would fall asleep, but John would go on for several more hours. He'd bring some of the scribbled notes with him when he got together with Marshall and Luther, but most of the pages ended up in the trash.

John's and Marshall's accounts of this period often differed when it came to the order in which the songs were written, but it appears that one of the first serious songs after "Hey, Porter" was one that Cash had been thinking about ever since Landsberg: "Folsom Prison Blues."

IV

The genesis of what would become one of Cash's signature compositions was "Crescent City Blues," the Gordon Jenkins song that

Cash had heard in the barracks at Landsberg. According to Marshall, John first mentioned "Crescent City Blues" at one of the rehearsals soon after Phillips agreed to make a record with them. "Just before he played it for us for the first time, he told about how he wanted to write a song about a prison ever since seeing the Folsom Prison movie, but he didn't figure out a way to do it until he heard the Jenkins song."

The concept of "Folsom Prison Blues" appealed to Cash on several levels. First, there was a long history of prison songs in country music. As a writer, too, he was drawn to melancholy themes.

What caught Cash's ear in the "Crescent City Blues" recording was the desperation in the female singer's voice as she longed for the man who had gotten away. Jenkins's line about a lonesome train whistle reminded him of so many country tunes, notably Hank Williams's "I'm So Lonesome I Could Cry," and he loved the bit about wanting the train whistle to blow her blues away. It gave Cash the blueprint he needed—even if it took more than a year after he first heard Jenkins's song for him to turn it into his song.

First the Jenkins version:

I hear the train a-comin', it's rolling 'round the bend
And I ain't been kissed, Lord, since I don't know when
The boys in Crescent City don't seem to know I'm here
That lonesome whistle seems to tell me, Sue, disappear.

When I was just a baby, my mama told me, Sue,
When you're grown up, I want that you should go and see and do.
But I'm stuck in Crescent City just watching life mosey by
When I hear that whistle blowing, I hang my head and cry.

I see rich folks eating in that fancy dining car
They're probably having pheasant breast and Eastern caviar.
Now I ain't crying envy and I ain't crying me
It's just that they get to see things I've never seen.

If I owned that lonesome whistle, if that railroad train was mine.
I bet I'd find a man a little farther down the line.

Far from Crescent City is where I'd like to stay.
And I'd let that lonesome whistle blow my blues away.

And here's how Cash turned "Crescent City Blues" into "Folsom Prison Blues":

I hear the train a comin'
It's rolling round the bend
And I ain't seen the sunshine since I don't know when,
I'm stuck in Folsom prison, and time keeps draggin' on
But that train keeps a rollin' on down to San Antone.

When I was just a baby my mama told me, Son,
Always be a good boy, don't ever play with guns.
But I shot a man in Reno just to watch him die
When I hear that whistle blowing, I hang my head and cry.

I bet there's rich folks eating from a fancy dining car
They're probably drinkin' coffee and smoking big cigars.
Well I know I had it coming, I know I can't be free
But those people keep a movin'
And that's what tortures me....

Well if they freed me from this prison,
If that railroad train was mine
I bet I'd move it on a little farther down the line
Far from Folsom prison, that's where I want to stay
And I'd let that lonesome whistle blow my blues away.

"He will tell you in a minute that he stole the song, but he made it a more interesting song," Grant said. "Everybody sang about love; not everyone sang about shooting a man 'just to watch him die.' I didn't know if you could even put that in a song. As soon as I heard it, I remember asking, 'John, are you sure they'll play something like that on the radio?'"

When you compare the lyrics of "Crescent City Blues" and "Folsom Prison Blues," it's easy to see where he substituted the Folsom

Prison setting and the reference to San Antonio. You can also understand the changing of "pheasant breast and Eastern caviar" to "drinkin' coffee and smoking big cigars" to give the song a more blue-collar sensibility.

Still, the crucial change is the one Marshall's comment addressed. Cash wanted to capture the ultimate loneliness, which he had sometimes felt during those long, grueling days in the monitoring room at Landsberg. He wanted to write not just about someone who was lonely for his girl, but about someone so empty inside that he felt cut off from both his family and his faith—someone so numb spiritually that he could take pleasure in killing a man just to watch him die.

The trigger to the line came from the song "T for Texas," which was on a Jimmie Rodgers album Cash had bought in Landsberg. He'd been so excited to find it that he wrote Vivian at length about it. It's tempting to imagine he might even have listened to "Crescent City Blues" and "T for Texas" back-to-back and realized how the startling Rodgers line, *"I'm gonna shoot poor Thelma / Just to see her jump and fall,"* could bring a real sense of desperation to the "Crescent City Blues" model. It was the heartlessness of shooting a man just to watch him die that was the central breakthrough of Cash's "Folsom Prison Blues."

It took about three weeks for the musicians to work up a version of the song. As with "Hey, Porter," Luther had the hardest time, so John ended up teaching it to him virtually note by note.

Everyone—John, Luther, Marshall, Roy—was knocked out by the song, but Cash didn't want to go back to Phillips with just one song. He wanted to hedge his bets by playing several different types of songs for Phillips. The guys had been playing Lead Belly's "Goodnight Irene" just for fun, and it sounded good, so they could do that, even though it didn't meet Phillips's request for an original song. There was also "Wide Open Road," the song John had written, or at least started, in Germany with Hank Snow in mind.

John's brother Roy thought "Wide Open Road" was John's best song yet, but John himself wasn't so sure. He thought it was pretty standard country stuff, but in the early months of 1955 Sam had seemed at least a little interested in it, so that gave them two possible B-sides for the Sun session. The guys also worked up arrangements of two other songs John had written—"Port of Lonely Hearts" and "My Treasure"—as well as "My Two-Timin' Woman," a Snow song that Sam also had seemed to like when John sang it for him at the first audition.

Personally, the only new song Cash felt strongly about was "Folsom Prison Blues." "John was a little nervous about the song because he had taken so much of the song from Jenkins, so he told Sam about the two songs," Marshall said. "But Sam didn't seem to care at all. Everyone was taking stuff from old songs, he said. He didn't even ask to hear the Jenkins song."

Though Sun's logs don't confirm the date, Marshall believed they went into the studio in late February or early March for their first formal session. There is a tape in the Sun vaults that includes at least part of what they recorded that day. It begins with four limp, unconvincing attempts at "Folsom Prison Blues," two reasonable but not knockout versions of "Hey, Porter," as well as one or two takes on the other songs they had rehearsed.

At the end of the day, the only song that Phillips accepted was "Hey, Porter." and he wanted to set up another session to get a stronger version of it. Cash was disappointed that Phillips didn't respond to "Folsom Prison Blues," but he was thrilled about "Hey, Porter." Plus, Phillips had given Cash a starting point on another song when he said he'd like a love song, a "weeper," because country fans and DJs couldn't resist them.

During the drive home, Cash kept thinking about the term "weeper," and he thought of a catchy phrase that he had heard Eddie Hill, a local disc jockey, use countless times on the air: "We've got some good songs, love songs, sweet songs, happy songs, and sad songs that'll make you cry, cry, cry."

At home, John sat on the living room couch and started sketching a song built around the words "cry, cry, cry." Vivian was astonished when he said it was finished fifteen minutes later.

Again there was no music, but the words sounded to Cash like something you'd hear on the radio. Vivian thought it was wonderful. By the time he showed it to Marshall and Luther a few days later, he had made only a couple of revisions. It was pretty much a first-draft song.

It wasn't as personal or distinctive as "Hey, Porter," but it sounded more radio-friendly, like a melding together of every heartbreak song he had ever heard on the air. Very much in the tradition of such Hank Williams songs as "Your Cheatin' Heart," the song put all the blame for the breakup on the other party and warned that she'd be sorry she'd been so cruel. It was just what Phillips had requested: a real weeper.

It began:

> *Everybody knows where you go when the sun goes down.*
> *I think you only live to see the lights up town.*
> *I wasted my time when I would try, try, try,*
> *'Cause when the lights have lost their glow, you'll cry, cry, cry.*

It took only a few nights with Grant and Perkins for Cash to put the music to the words of the song, which he originally called "You're Gonna Cry, Cry, Cry." It was easier for Luther to play than "Hey, Porter" because the song's lead guitar run was much simpler. The threesome rushed back to Sun Records and played the song for Phillips, who liked it immediately. Again he used the words "different" and "unique."

Cash was expecting to record both songs right away, but Phillips told them it would be a few weeks before they could get into the studio because he was still tied up with Elvis. Just keep working on the songs, Phillips advised, so they'd be "red hot" in the studio.

This time, Cash left Sun so excited that he went straight over to Home Equipment Company.

"I'm on my way," he told Bates. "I'm gonna make records and I'm gonna pay back all that money." The store owner came back with a good-natured "Well, you gotta make a lot of records to pay back all that money." Cash's debt was mounting, probably nearing $500, an intimidating amount for someone earning—not counting Bates's advances—only about $60 a month in commissions.

John then stopped by Marshall's home and went on and on about how "Hey, Porter" could be a hit all over the South, like Elvis's records. The bass player found John's enthusiasm "endearing" but also "pie-in-the-sky." All Marshall hoped was for a few copies of the actual record to hang on the walls around the house and at the dealership.

V

Though Phillips had warned John and the others that it would be several weeks before he'd be able to work with them, John started trying to get a date from Phillips within days. Usually John had to leave a message with the office assistant, Marion Keisker. It got to the point where all he had to do was stick his head in the door and Marion would just shake her head no. To help reassure Cash that they really were going to make a record together, Phillips had a recording contract drafted. Notably, Sam wanted to sign only Cash, not the Tennessee Three.

Cash sat down with Marshall and Luther to relay Phillips's decision. He promised they would still divide the royalties three ways, and Marshall and Luther were fine with that arrangement. John had one other thing to clear with them: Sam had also suggested putting John's name on the record rather than just the Tennessee Three because he thought it sounded more personal. He also preferred the more youthful "Johnny." Thus, the label would read "Johnny Cash and the Tennessee Two."

Luther and Marshall were also fine with that.

Johnny Cash signed the Sun contract on April 1. It was a pretty standard deal—a one-year pact calling for a royalty rate of about three cents per record, with Sun having the right to extend the agreement via two one-year options.

One of John's favorite stories for years after was that he walked out of Sun that morning with just fifteen cents in his pocket and gave the change to a hobo on the street. No one remembered any hobos around Sun Studios, but Cash did give money to needy people throughout his life. The story was probably just another opportunity for Cash to encourage others to "help thy neighbor."

When John got to Home Equipment after the signing, some

of the employees ribbed him. One tried to convince John that no contract signed on April Fools' Day was valid. After all the joking, Cash bounced an idea off Bates. He believed he could get his own weekly fifteen-minute show on radio station KWEM if Bates would sponsor the program. For years, KWEM had presented some of the region's most talented artists, including B. B. King, Junior Parker, and Howlin' Wolf, from its studio in West Memphis, just across the state line in Arkansas. They all had to pay for the airtime or get sponsors to pay for it. The performers used the exposure to plug local club appearances.

Once again, Bates came through.

In May, Cash got word from Sam Phillips that he was finally ready to record "Hey, Porter." The session went surprisingly well; Phillips was satisfied after just three takes. "Hey, Porter" was a superior piece of work on every level. The song conveys convincingly the feeling of someone in love with his regional roots. Unlike most of the singers on the radio at the time, he didn't just sing along with the beat. He treated every line as if it mattered. And that spare but steady rhythm by Grant and Perkins also stood out from the copycat instrumental format of most records.

"You're Gonna Cry, Cry, Cry," recorded a few days later, was more troublesome.

"We had to do thirty-five takes before we got 'Cry, Cry, Cry' right," Cash recalled, surely engaging in his characteristic embellishment. But the session did drag on. The problem, once again, was Luther's lead guitar part. "I kept changing the arrangement on him and he kept messing it up," said Cash. "It was a comedy of errors until I finally told him to forget about the guitar break we were trying for and just [work] his way through it. That worked out fine, I thought."

Perkins once again relied on the *boom-chicka-boom* sound.

After they had the songs on tape, Cash kept after Phillips to tell him when the record would be released. Phillips was working on Elvis, but he assured Cash that he wanted the record out as soon as possible. It sounded like a hit to him.

Soon after the "Cry" session, John wrote a letter to one of his best pals among the Landsberg Barbarians, Ted Freeman. As usual, he wrote in a playful style. He didn't want to sound like he was bragging.

"We finally made the other side of my record," he wrote. "We worked two and a half hours Thursday night. Finally got it perfected. Sounds like hell. No, I believe it will be purty good. The name of it is 'You're Gonna Cry, Cry, Cry.' It's a flat romping job. That ole' clickety-clack rhythm....It's going to be out in two to three weeks. Can't say when 'cause I don't know. It all depends on when the market is right. When they start making the record here, I'll send you a copy."

He signed it "Johnny Cash of Johnny Cash and the Tennessee Two."

A few days later, more good news: KWEM called. The station had an opening at four p.m., beginning Saturday, May 21. Cash contacted his mother and asked her to spread the word to everyone in Dyess: J.R. had done it. He had his own radio show.

CHAPTER 5

"HEY, PORTER," "FOLSOM PRISON BLUES," AND A BABY GIRL

I

To anyone in Memphis who was listening to KWEM while mowing the lawn or driving home from work on that Saturday afternoon in late May 1955, the new Johnny Cash show probably sounded even more amateurish than the other pay-to-play musical quarter hours on the station. Cash kept a tape of the show, and it is endearing, in retrospect, to hear the twenty-three-year-old finally get the chance to step behind the microphone and try to act like one of the real country music stars he had heard on the radio in Dyess.

After a thirty-second instrumental, he addressed the audience in a halting, nervous voice. Clearly the radio school hadn't fully prepared him for the real thing: "Ah, hello folks, this is Johnny Cash and I'd like to introduce you to the other two boys here," he said. "This is Luther Perkins over here hitting all those hard notes on guitar" (Luther actually played a couple of quick notes as if to say hello), "and, ah, Marshall Grant hitting the low notes on the bass fiddle over here."

Even more clumsily, he told the "folks" that this was their first appearance "by way of radio" and he "sincerely" hoped that everyone would enjoy the show. He then invited listeners to write in requesting a song—assuring them that if he and "the boys" didn't know it, they'd try to learn it. The few seconds it took to read a commercial surely seemed like an eternity, and he must have felt a huge sense of relief when he could stop talking and kick off "Wide Open Road," one of the songs he had played for Phillips. He also sang "One More Ride," a Sons of the Pioneers tune that he used to sing in Germany, and "Belshazzar."

Cash didn't play "Hey, Porter" or "You're Gonna Cry, Cry, Cry," since, as Grant explained years later, Phillips had asked them not to play either song because he wanted some of the city's top DJs to be the first to air them. That form of flattery reliably led the DJs to play the song more frequently than they normally would. As usual, Cash took Sam's advice to heart; he didn't even mention he had been signed to Sun. He did play "Luther Played the Boogie," a mostly instrumental tune that had come about largely by accident. During one of the endless evenings devoted to getting Luther to learn a few more licks, an exhausted Cash just sat back and laughed, saying, "Luther, you sure play the boogie strange."

"Everybody laughed and forgot it until the next week when John came in with this song about Luther playing the boogie woogie," Marshall recalled. "We thought it was just a joke until we started playing it, and we all liked the feel of the song. We ended up recording it and using it in the shows, but it wasn't something Sam ever seemed to care about."

That was the first radio show: fifteen minutes and out. Listening to the tape years later makes you respect Phillips all the more for being able to see the potential in these three novices. John hoped Home Equipment would get some business from the show to reward Bates's faith in him, but at least at first, it didn't generate any new customers.

Three days after the broadcast, Vivian checked in to St. Joseph's Hospital to give birth to the couple's first child. A few weeks before, her doctor had told the couple they were going to have twins, but he had mistaken Vivian's heartbeat for the heartbeat of a second baby. There was only one new addition to the Cash household: Rosanne. To create her name, Vivian said, they combined Johnny's pet names for her breasts: Rose and Anne.

When they got home with their new daughter, John and Vivian

were so happy that they told each other they'd love to have eight children someday. Vivian's younger sister, Sylvia, who came over from San Antonio to help her with the baby, found that the couple had so little money, she had to use her graduation money to buy groceries and diapers, which she washed by hand. The Cash family came over from Dyess to see Rosanne, and Carrie pulled her son aside. She wanted to thank him for carrying on Jack's message in the radio show. "I loved it that you did a gospel song, son."

Even though he hadn't released "Hey, Porter" yet, Phillips brought Cash to the studio to talk about the next single. While he was there, John noticed a note on Phillips's appointment calendar about sending "Folsom Prison Blues" to Tennessee Ernie Ford, whose folksy storytelling approach Phillips figured might be more suitable for the song than Cash's style.

John asked him why, and Phillips, thinking about potential publishing royalties, pointed out diplomatically that Ford was hot, with his version of "The Ballad of Davy Crockett." When Cash pressed him, Phillips finally admitted that he didn't think John and the guys were going to be able to capture the song on record.

"Give us another chance," Cash pleaded, explaining how much the song meant to him. Listening to him, Phillips wavered. He admired Cash's spirit, and he didn't want to do anything to harm the confidence of this budding star. Besides, if Cash and the Tennessee Two couldn't get it a second time around, he could always send it to Ford then.

So Cash and the guys went back to Grant's garage and worked on "Folsom Prison Blues." After a couple of weeks, the trio moved the song into a quicker tempo than the languid pace of "Crescent City Blues." It wasn't exactly a happy beat, the kind that Phillips favored, but the rhythm was becoming infectious. Before going back to Sun, Cash knew he'd need another song for the back side of the single. Marshall brought up "Luther Played the Boogie," but John smirked. He wanted something better than that—maybe another "weeper." In fact, he had already been working on a song called "So Doggone Lonesome" with Ernest Tubb in mind ever since Landsberg, and he was finally satisfied with it. Marshall thought the song was perfect for the group's minimal *boom-chicka-boom* style.

By now even Marshall and Luther were beginning to tell the difference between songs Cash cared about and the ones he was just cranking out. They didn't know precisely what it was that made John almost caress some of the tunes, but they could spot it as soon as he started playing. And clearly, the bassist thought, Cash cared about "So Doggone Lonesome."

For his part, Cash would eventually separate his compositions whimsically between songs written by J. R. Cash and those written by Johnny Cash. The difference was between songs that he felt were in the personal, Jimmie Rodgers tradition, like "Hey, Porter" and "Folsom Prison Blues," and those that were simply commercial ditties, like "You're Gonna Cry, Cry, Cry" and "Wide Open Road."

To a neutral observer, "So Doggone Lonesome" might sound like a fairly generic country tale—and there is the undeniable feel of a commercial sensibility to it. Cash had to know it was going to sound great on a barroom jukebox. Yet there was also something compelling about the lyrics once Cash began singing them. His performance was essential in bringing out the ache of the song—an early sign of Cash's ability, like Rodgers's, to make his best songs feel like they came straight from the heart, totally unvarnished or unfiltered. The song is about his longing for Vivian while he was in Germany.

It begins:

I do my best to hide this low-down feelin';
I try to make believe there's nothing wrong.
But they're always asking me about you, darlin',
and it hurts me so to tell 'em that you're gone.
If they ask me, I guess I'd be denyin'
that I've been unhappy all alone.
But if they heard my heart, they'd hear it cryin',
"Where's my darlin, when's she coming home?"
I ask myself a million times what's right for me to do,
to try to lose my blues alone or hang around with you.

*But I think it's pretty good until that moon comes shinin' through,
and then I get so doggone lonesome.*

As expected, Sam showed little enthusiasm for "Luther Played
the Boogie," but he liked "So Doggone Lonesome" and thought the
new arrangement of "Folsom Prison Blues" was much improved. "I
didn't know that it would have real mass appeal," Phillips remembered. "But we got such a dynamic cut on that damn thing. And
I got to thinking about it, that we all, in a way, are in prison, you
know? I had to stretch my imagination, but I didn't expect the public to do that." Still, Phillips was willing to take a chance on the
song. The two tracks would be Cash's next single, but there was no
need to rush into the studio. They had to get "Hey, Porter" out first.

Phillips received the first shipment of "Hey, Porter" in mid-June,
and he asked Marion to call John and tell him it had arrived. She
located him at Home Equipment, and he phoned Marshall and
Luther so they could meet him at Sun.

Once there, John held the record in his hands and went over every
word on the yellow label. He noticed that Phillips had shortened the
title of "You're Gonna Cry, Cry, Cry" to "Cry! Cry! Cry!" and had put exclamation points in both titles. Most of all, he saw the names "Johnny
Cash" and, in much smaller type, "the Tennessee Two" and asked
Sam to please make "the Tennessee Two" bigger in the future. Cash
also saw that his songwriter credit was given as J. Cash under "Hey,
Porter!" and only Cash under "Cry! Cry! Cry!" Just a mistake, Phillips
said, but he continued, strangely, to go back and forth between J.
Cash, Cash, and Johnny Cash on future Sun releases.

Phillips told them the record wouldn't be officially released for
another week—on June 21—but he asked John to take early copies
around to some of the Memphis DJs, including Bob Neal at WMPS.

To encourage artists to bring them early copies of a record, DJs
would usually interrupt their show and put the new record directly on the turntable, and that's exactly what Neal did when Cash
brought him his single. He played "Hey, Porter." He then turned
the record over and played "Cry, Cry, Cry." Then, if it's not just the
storyteller in Cash at work, Neal dropped the fragile shellac 78-rpm
record and it shattered on the floor.

Cash gasped, but Neal told him not to worry. He'd call Sam and get another copy. He shook Cash's hand and said, "You're going to be hearing a lot more of those songs on WMPS."

Soon after, Marshall was driving to work, listening to DJ Sleepy Eyed John on WHHM, when he heard "Hey, Porter" for the first time.

"It was unbelievable," Grant said. "I thought that was it. The next day about five stations in Memphis played it. The day after that, all of them were playing it. By the end of the week, they were all playing both sides."

II

Despite all Cash's efforts, it was Grant who found the first couple of bookings, even though one was just a free show for a benefit sponsored by a boat club of which he was a member. The other engagement was more memorable: their first paid gig. Marshall heard from a mechanic buddy that a Ford dealership just down Union Avenue was going to hold a gala all-day sales celebration. Marshall walked over to Hull-Dobbs and asked the manager if he had any musical entertainment lined up.

When the manager said no, Marshall said he had a band and he would love to play for the customers. The manager agreed to pay the group $50 to play on a flatbed truck for two hours. Marshall was so excited to get the paying gig that he would probably have agreed to stand on his head on the truck. John and Luther were also delighted by the booking, and they spent an evening trying to work up two dozen songs, figuring that would get them through a half hour, and they could then just repeat the set as new customers came onto the lot. They would play "Hey, Porter" and "Cry, Cry, Cry," of course, as well as several of their gospel favorites and some numbers by Hank Snow and Hank Williams.

At the dealership, they learned they would be playing on the truck while it was being driven up and down Union Avenue with a huge banner advertising the sale. Oh, well, $50 was $50. So they got up on the truck and started playing "Hey, Porter" as soon as the vehicle moved out onto the street. Right away they realized that no one on the sidewalk could hear them for more than a few seconds before the truck moved on. So the guys threw out their half-hour repertoire and just played "Hey, Porter" and "Cry, Cry, Cry" over and over and over again.

To celebrate, the three bandmates took their wives to dinner and the movies. John, in particular, was up in the clouds. When "Hey, Porter" was released, he resumed the search for some live dates, but he found little interest among club owners in Memphis. When he bragged to one that he was on the same label as Elvis Presley, the club owner said he'd book him if he brought Elvis, too.

Hoping the hometown boy angle might help, Cash drove around northeastern Arkansas, and sure enough, he found takers in many of the towns of his youth, including Osceola, Wilson, and Lepanto, where he had spent many a night during high school at the pool hall and movie theater. The wives sold tickets at the door at various schools and theaters, usually for fifty cents, and the trio divided the profits with the venue. The conditions were often primitive; some of the facilities didn't even have a sound system. But the experience taught Cash and the Tennessee Two how to reach out to an audience in all kinds of situations.

John's family spread the word in Dyess, and John saw lots of familiar faces in the audiences; in fact, it wasn't uncommon for John to know half the people in the room personally. If Cash didn't have time to stop by his parents' house on the way to the show, Carrie would often bring some food along to the venue. They would sit on the lawn outside the building and eat, adding an even more informal touch to the evening. This really was the bottom rung of the show business ladder. For all the energy that went into setting themselves up and then driving to the facility, the shows drew small audiences, between fifty and one hundred most nights, which meant John, Luther, and Marshall usually made between $12 and $25 collectively.

The first step toward the big time occurred a couple of weeks after the record came out. Sonny James, a self-effacing young singer who'd had a couple of hits on Capitol Records, heard "Cry, Cry, Cry" on the radio and called Phillips to see if he could get John to play a show that James's manager had put together for that night in nearby Covington. Cash jumped at the chance, even though he hadn't checked with Marshall and Luther to see if they were free. How could anything be more important than this? It was going to be a real show, not a "pretend" one like most of those in Arkansas. When Cash wasn't able to reach Marshall, he and Luther headed to Covington, figuring they'd work out something. They were relieved when James's bass player volunteered to take Grant's part.

Backstage, Cash was more excited than Vivian had ever seen him, even more than on the day he came home from his first recording session. Actually, there were only a few hundred people in the audience, but it must have seemed like thousands after all the intimate shows in Arkansas. Years later Cash would talk about the show as if it had been a blur—and it probably was. By show-time, he and Luther were so nervous they played their two songs at super-speed.

Later that night, Cash thanked James profusely for the opportunity, and James in turn complimented Cash on a "great sound" and told him he thought he had a big future in country music. John also had a question. He noticed that James had included a hymn in his set. John told Sonny he had originally wanted to be a gospel singer and asked whether someone could hold on to his Christian values despite all the wild stories he'd heard about life in country music. James assured Cash that it was possible to avoid temptations if he worked at it, but it wasn't always easy. By late July, two things were apparent: the single was going to be big, at least by Sun standards, and "Cry, Cry, Cry" was the hit side. Cash was too happy to fret about it. To him, "Hey, Porter" would always be his first hit.

III

Cash and the guys had done a dozen or so shows when John got a message he couldn't believe. Bob Neal, the local DJ who also managed Elvis, invited John to join a short tour he was putting together for early August starring Webb Pierce and Presley. Best of all, the tour would end with a big show at the outdoor, four-thousand-capacity Overton Park band shell in Memphis.

Touring with the red-hot Elvis was cool, but the real thrill for Cash was being onstage with Webb Pierce, who was the show's official headliner. With his robust yet high-pitched voice, Pierce had so dominated country music radio ever since his first hit in early 1952 that he'd held the number-one spot on the charts for more than eighty weeks—an average of twenty-five weeks a year. He had also been one of the favorites among the country fans in the Landsberg barracks.

This was such a major step that Cash talked Marshall and Luther into taking a couple of days off work so they could rehearse. He always thought that Elvis was responsible for getting them on the package show, but it is more likely that Sam Phillips asked Neal to do him a favor and add his new singer to the lineup. Sam had arranged for Neal to handle the concert bookings for all the Sun acts; eventually they would become partners in a talent agency called Stars, Inc.

Two days before the tour started, Phillips returned to the studio with Cash to record the next single so he'd have something ready when "Cry, Cry, Cry" started to peak. Again, the idea with a new act was to keep the momentum going. At the session, John, Luther, and Marshall sang "Luther Played the Boogie" and "Mean Eyed Cat," a ditty by Cash in the mock-angry style of Hank Snow's "My Two Timin' Woman." But Phillips had little interest in either of them. He still wanted to stay focused on "Folsom Prison Blues" and, secondarily, "So Doggone Lonesome."

More than he had with the first single, Phillips worked on making sure Cash was out in front of the music on "Folsom" so the voice and words caught the listener's full attention. That required him to fiddle a lot with microphone placement to guarantee the right distance between Cash and the Tennessee Two. More than with most other recording artists, Phillips later maintained, people listened to Johnny Cash records to listen to Cash, not the band. The Tennessee Two's role was to accentuate his vocals, not compete with them.

Afterward, Cash waited around for a verdict. Was "Folsom Prison

Blues" good enough this time? What did Sam think of "So Doggone Lonesome"? All he heard was "I think we're okay." The next day Phillips was on the phone to Cash. He seemed a little unsure about which of the new songs to push with the DJs. To test "Folsom Prison Blues," he asked John to play it on the tour, maybe the closing show in Memphis.

As one of the supporting acts, Cash didn't have much time onstage during the brief tour, but he went over well in the opener on Monday, August 1, in Tupelo, Mississippi, which happened to be Elvis's birthplace. Even Pierce came up to John backstage and said he'd enjoyed his set. John couldn't believe he was talking to the biggest star in country music, or that Pierce invited him to stop by the motel after the show so they could get to know each other.

After what happened during the show that night, however, Pierce didn't even go to the motel. He was so rattled by the way the fans reacted to Presley—his *support* act—that he left town as soon as his performance was over. Though Elvis had only four singles out, much of the crowd had come to see him, and they kept yelling for more long after the twenty-year-old had left the stage. When it was clear that Elvis wasn't coming back, most of his fans left—before Pierce even got to the microphone.

Webb tried to brush it all off when he saw Cash the next day in Sheffield, Alabama. Tupelo, after all, was Elvis's town. But Presley upstaged Pierce again in Sheffield and the next two nights in Little Rock and Camden, Arkansas. It was a major embarrassment for Webb, who was known around Nashville to have an ego as big as his booming voice. While Cash didn't get nearly as big a reaction as his Sun label mate in those cities, he got respectable responses—and he got loud cheers from many of the fans on Friday when the mini-tour hit the Overton Park Shell amphitheater. Befitting their hometown status, Elvis and John got their photos in one Memphis newspaper's write-up of the show, but not Pierce.

All this further convinced Phillips that the country music old guard in Nashville was vulnerable. Pierce was only thirty-four, but the young artists from Sun had made him look fifty. And it wasn't just Pierce who was being pushed aside. Country radio either had to embrace these new young acts fully or see young country fans follow the artists to pop and rock 'n' roll stations, which was what eventually happened. As Sam watched Presley and Cash onstage at the Overton, he knew that *Billboard* was reporting strong sales for "Cry, Cry, Cry" throughout the South and Southwest. He also liked the crowd's reaction to "Folsom Prison Blues."

Marshall remembered Vivian's being a bit overwhelmed by all the screaming young girls at the shows, even if they were mostly going crazy over Elvis. This wasn't the fun-loving, relatively tame family crowd she had seen at country shows in San Antonio. This was something much more intense and sexual.

After the triumph at Overton, John shook hands and signed autographs with fans. His parents had come in for the show, and he made sure to introduce both Sam Phillips and George Bates to his father, praising both men so lavishly that Marshall got the idea John was trying to send a message to Ray that these two successful businessmen believed in his son. Why didn't he?

Ray, in turn, was quiet as usual. The only thing Cash remembered about his father's reaction was that he asked him—perhaps innocently—if he still had his day job.

John also took Vivian around to meet the other musicians in the show. He was so affectionate, he made her blush. "Here's my wife," he would say. "Isn't she the prettiest thing you ever saw?" His sweetness almost allowed her to recover from the sight of all those screaming girls.

Johnny and Vivian celebrated their first anniversary two days later, about as content as they could be. Johnny Cash was a happy husband, father, and recording artist as he waited for Sam to release his second single—and Vivian was happy because Johnny was happy. Naively, she thought that if he could make enough money in music, he would be able to quit his job at Home Equipment Company and spend more time at home. So a few days later she was as excited as he was when he rushed through the door with a copy of *Billboard* magazine. Turning to page forty-six, he pointed to the country music singles charts for the Memphis area. "Look, honey, we're number three! That's just two spots behind Webb Pierce!"

Still, Vivian couldn't help asking how he felt about the screaming girls. It wasn't, at this early stage, so much fear as simply curiosity.

"No, baby, I am never tempted," he replied over the breakfast table. "Do you know why? When those women come up to me, I think of them as mannequins....Just phony, plastic mannequins. You don't ever need to worry, baby. You're on my mind every minute, day and night."

Vivian believed in her husband. If their relationship could survive the three years when John was in Germany, it could survive anything. She was so proud of him that she didn't even mind that he was starting to spend more and more time off by himself around the house trying to come up with some new songs. It was his work. Besides, she had plenty to do herself. The couple had learned there was another baby on the way.

Bob Neal was lining up tour dates for her husband, which meant he'd probably be hitting the road again soon, but Vivian tried not to think about it, and John was especially affectionate. He'd take her out roller-skating or to the movies, but the most fun was sitting around the house playing with Rosanne.

Waiting for Neal to act, Cash became restless and resumed seeking out whatever minor club dates he could find around Memphis and northeast Arkansas—to polish his performance skills and to make a few dollars. To help bring in extra money, Grant arranged with a photographer-friend to print up eight-by-ten photos of Cash and the Tennessee Two, which he sold for twenty-five cents at the shows. Cash later insisted he could have made a lot more money in those days by playing honky-tonks, but he refused for religious reasons. As Marshall said, however, he and John did play a few, but they were so rowdy that John worried about Vivian's safety, especially now that she was pregnant. At some of the places, Marshall joked, you saw more guns and knives than fans.

Soon Neal did line up a few dates. This time Elvis would headline and John would be a special guest attraction. The tour would start in Texarkana, Arkansas, on September 2 and continue in Forest City and Bono, Arkansas; Sikeston, Missouri; and Clarksdale, Mississippi. Again, the crowds in Arkansas were dotted with family and friends. Even though Elvis was the star, Cash was starting to get his share of the attention.

"I could see the momentum already there," Marshall said. "John was becoming popular, with that little different sound we had. His big gigantic voice was cutting through something fierce. You could see it grow day by day."

After another few weeks off, they went back on the road with Elvis, this time to dates in Texas—Cherry Spring, Midland, Amarillo, Lubbock (where a teenage Buddy Holly was the opening act)—that were too far from Memphis for the band members to return home after each show. That meant wives stayed home.

When John, Marshall, and Luther first talked about touring, the plan was for them all to go in the same car—alternating among their cars—and to take turns behind the wheel, but John proved to be such a terrible driver that Marshall and Luther soon decided they would do all the driving. "Oh my God," Cash's daughter Kathy says about his driving. "The thing is he'd push the gas pedal to the floor and the car would swerve forward, then he'd slam on the brakes, and it was like that mile after mile, this sudden jerking, and it didn't help that he would be looking at you and talking rather than watching the road."

The boredom of the road caused John to revive his teenage love of pranks. It started off pretty tamely—simply something to liven up those long hours on the road or in hotel rooms as they waited for the next show. One of Grant's favorite pranks of his own came on the Texas tour, when Elvis and many of the musicians pulled in to a truck stop around three a.m. to eat. At the time, the artists would travel caravan-style, partly for the companionship and partly to help out in case someone had car trouble on those long, often desolate Southern highways. The caravan system also provided some security in the event they ran into a few locals who wanted to impress their friends by roughing up a bunch of hillbilly singers.

On this occasion, John, Elvis, and Marshall went to pay their bills, but the cashier was in the kitchen. While they waited, Marshall noticed some slices of pie in the round glass display case. When he spotted a piece of pumpkin pie without the usual whipped cream on it, he reached into his toiletry bag for a can of shaving cream, which he sprayed on top of the pie. Elvis thought it was so funny that he decided to wait in the truck stop in hopes of seeing someone take a bite of the pie.

Marshall never learned if Elvis actually saw anyone get a soapy bite, but he could tell that the incident struck a chord with Cash. From that point on, John, Marshall, and Luther would try to out-prank one another.

Around this time, Cash started to hear rumors that RCA Records was trying to buy Presley's contract. When he brought it up, Phillips told him he didn't want to sell the contract, but that Elvis and Colonel Tom Parker, who had taken over the young phenom's management contract from Neal, were determined to move to a bigger label. By the time Cash returned from the brief West Texas swing with Presley in mid-November, the deal was done. RCA paid Sun $35,000 for the rights to Presley and everything he had recorded for the label; it was one of the largest amounts ever paid at that point for a recording artist's contract.

Phillips told Cash that as much as he hated to see Elvis go, he was excited about the future. Thanks to the RCA deal, Phillips had more money to spend promoting Sun Records and expanding dis-tribution around the country. He also had good news for Cash: "Cry, Cry, Cry" was number fourteen on *Billboard*'s latest list of the best-selling country records in the nation—the *nation,* Phillips stressed, not just the South.

During the meeting with Phillips, Cash got the feeling he had just received a promotion. From what he could tell, Phillips was now going to be putting as much energy into his career as he had once done for Elvis: he was now Sun's number-one artist. Phillips told Cash his top priority was to get him on the Louisiana Hayride's radio show in Shreveport because of the crucial role the Hayride had played in building Elvis's popularity.

Vivian tried to share Johnny's joy, but the time apart—even though it was only a few days here and there—troubled her more than she had expected. She knew that the traveling was necessary and that Johnny was just trying to take care of his family. But it didn't make her any less lonesome in the duplex on Tutwiler.

IV

The Louisiana Hayride, which was broadcast from Shreveport throughout the South, meant a lot to Cash. Airing on KWKH every Saturday night from the downtown three-thousand-seat Municipal Auditorium, a lavish art deco structure opened in 1929, the Hayride was launched in April 1948. Though the opening lineup wasn't exactly star-studded, it was only a few months before Hank Williams started a residency there—moving rapidly from fifth on the bill to the wildly popular headliner. Williams's spectacular rise gave the Hayride a reputation throughout the country music world of a star-maker, and Elvis took the Hayride similarly by storm in 1954.

The importance of the Hayride wasn't its pay scale. Most of the performers were paid union scale, $12 a night, which barely covered their gas and food. The value was the exposure. With its potent fifty-thousand-watt station, KWKH's signal alone provided invaluable reach, but the Hayride show was also carried by some two hundred other stations, from as far west as El Paso, north to St. Louis, east to Jacksonville, and down the coast to Miami. That meant a lot of potential record buyers.

Phillips started lobbying Horace "Hoss" Logan, who was both program director at KWKH and emcee of the Hayride, about Cash in November. He sent Logan a copy of Cash's single along with a note saying the record was outselling Elvis's latest release in Memphis. Logan was impressed by both the record and the sales, so he told Phillips he'd find a guest spot on the show for him as soon as he could. The debut turned out to be on December 3, when Cash and the Tennessee Two were billed as "special guests" at the bottom of a bill featuring Jimmy Newman, Johnny Horton, David Houston, and others. John couldn't have been more thrilled. To him, the Hayride meant one thing: he'd be standing on the same stage as Hank Williams.

"I have to admit he was pretty rough around the edges—rougher even than Elvis was when he'd debuted just over a year earlier," Logan later maintained. "But the raw talent was there. So were the sincerity and style that would soon make Johnny famous, and the crowd reacted warmly."

Logan approached Cash as soon as his short set was over and asked him to become a Hayride regular. The 350-mile drive along two-lane roads from Memphis was arduous, but the opportunity was great. Phillips advised Cash to accept immediately.

John spent most of the month at home with Vivian, trying his best to concentrate on his job at Home Equipment but finding it increasingly difficult. Marshall and Luther, too, were getting worn out by having to drive home from out-of-town gigs late at night and then be at the auto dealership early the next morning. But they weren't thinking about quitting their day jobs. Cash thought about it, though, every day.

He closed out the year in style, returning to Shreveport for a gala New Year's Eve concert at the Hayride. He was still one of the "special guests" on a bill that was topped by Elvis and also featured Johnny Horton and George Jones, but he felt like a star. After all, he was now a regular. Following the show, he and Vivian celebrated New Year's with many of the members of the Hayride cast. No doubt about it, 1955 had been a great year.

Believing he had a "monster" on his hands with "Folsom Prison Blues" and "So Doggone Lonesome," Phillips took out a half-page ad in the January 21, 1956, issue of *Billboard* to announce the record's release. It included a reprint of the *Billboard* review from two weeks earlier: "Cash delivers two solid, sincere and very genuine country blues sides. There is a great melancholy, minor key flavor and the definitely above-par lyrics for both get a wonderfully expressive treatment....Both could break out."

Next to a studio portrait of Cash were the words "handsome and young," part of Phillips's continuing effort to link Cash with the new wave in country and rock. In a wry slap at the country establishment in Nashville, Phillips identified Sun Records as "America's No. 1 Country & Western Label."

Two weeks later, the single was number fourteen among country records across the nation—a sales position that had taken "Cry, Cry, Cry" months to reach. Ernest Tubb rushed out his version of "So Doggone Lonesome" a few days later. Though Cash had actually written the song with Tubb in mind, he played no part in getting the veteran country star to record it. Tubb simply heard it on the radio. Veteran artists in the 1950s often re-recorded promising songs by new or unknown artists because they knew DJs would tend to play the known artist over the unknown. But things were happening too fast for Tubb.

The Cash single was already number ten across the country by the time *Billboard* announced the Tubb version. Disc jockeys weren't about to drop Cash's record, which was getting strong radio response, to play Tubb's. As a result, the remake never made the charts. Cash's two-sided hit, meanwhile, went all the way to number four.

It was during this period that Cash finally quit his job at Home Equipment Company. His first sizable royalty check from Sun was for around $2,000 and he and Vivian drove to San Antonio to pay her parents back part of the nearly $800 they had given them over the months. Soon after, he started repaying George Bates back for the $1,200 he had advanced him. It was an emotional moment for both men. "He got up and hugged me and he had tears in his eyes," Cash said years later. "He was proud of me."

Cash also followed through on a longtime pledge to himself: he started pressing his father to retire from his job at the oleomargarine plant in Wilson and move to Memphis. Cash wanted to help his parents buy a nice place so they could have modern utilities and be closer to the rest of the Cash clan. Besides John and Roy, Reba and Louise were now living in Memphis too. But not wanting to make his folks feel pressured, Cash just planted the seed and waited for them to make a decision. More cautiously, Grant and Perkins took extended leaves of absence, thus keeping the door open in case things didn't work out.

Throughout this period, Phillips was urging Cash to come up with some new songs. Thinking of Vivian's mounting insecurity about all the female fans on the road, he composed his most personal song yet.

Chapter 6

LOUISIANA HAYRIDE AND "I WALK THE LINE"

I

GLADEWATER AND LONGVIEW would be just two more names on the list of the hundreds of towns in which Cash performed over five decades—except that he most likely wrote "I Walk the Line" in one of the two neighboring East Texas locales. Cash usually said Gladewater; Marshall Grant always claimed it was Longview. There was even sharp disagreement over the distinctive hum at the start of the record. John himself had two explanations. Usually he said it was inspired by a haunting sound he'd heard one time when he accidentally played a tape backward on the reel-to-reel recorder he bought in Germany. But he also spoke of having wanted to open a record with a hum ever since childhood, when he'd delighted in the way the town doctor always went around humming. Grant thought the humming was simply designed to help Luther get the right feel on the song.

"I Walk the Line" is a heartfelt, straightforward love song in the tradition of Jimmie Davis's "You Are My Sunshine" or Don Gibson's "I Can't Stop Loving You." And as usual, Cash's authoritative vocal made the declaration all the more human and believable:

> *I keep a close watch on this heart of mine.*
> *I keep my eyes wide open all the time.*

I keep the ends out for the tie that binds.
Because you're mine I walk the line.

I find it very, very easy to be true.
I find myself alone when each day is through.
Yes, I'll admit that I'm a fool for you.
Because you're mine I walk the line.

As sure as night is dark and day is light,
I keep you on my mind both day and night.
And happiness I've known proves that it's right.
Because you're mine I walk the line.

You've got a way to keep me on your side.
You give me cause for love that I can't hide.
For you I know I'd even try to turn the tide.
Because you're mine I walk the line.

I keep a close watch on this heart of mine.
I keep my eyes wide open all the time.
I keep the ends out for the tie that binds.
Because you're mine I walk the line.

While it was undeniably inspired by his love for Vivian, Cash sometimes spoke of a second meaning. Though he never confronted Phillips about it, Cash missed his gospel side, and he designed "I Walk the Line" as an expression of spiritual as well as romantic allegiance.

In his 1975 autobiography, *Man in Black,* Cash pointed out that he was intending to "say" something in the song, writing lyrics "that will have a lot of meaning not only for me, but for everybody who hears it—that says I'm going to be true not only to those who believe in me and depend on me, but to myself and God—a song that might give courage to others as well as myself." During an interview just months before his death, he smiled and told me, "Sam never knew it, but 'I Walk the Line' was my first gospel hit."

Cash recalled Phillips being more excited about "I Walk the Line" than any other song he had brought him. That's one of the things Cash loved about Phillips—his enthusiasm. "He was excitable, not at all laid-back," Cash said. "When we'd put something on tape he liked, he'd come bursting out of the control room into the studio, laughing and clapping his hands, yelling and hollering, 'That was great! That was wonderful!'"

Once again, however, Phillips thought the arrangement was too slow and mournful. As always, he wanted a more lively rhythm.

"Do me a favor," he told Cash. "Just do one more take for me, and let's move the tempo up quite a bit."

Cash didn't like what he heard. This song was his baby. He wanted the record to reflect the tender sentiments he felt.

"We don't want to make a rock 'n' roll song out of this," he told Phillips. "I wrote this song for my wife and I want to keep it as a real slow ballad."

Phillips tried to soothe Cash.

"I don't have a problem with that, John," he said. "I just want to hear it one time for my own personal view. Just move the tempo up to a good flow and record it for me just one time."

Cash obliged, but he left the studio believing that Phillips would release the original, slow version.

Even before "I Walk the Line," Cash had heard Phillips talk about the importance of rhythm in a record so often that he thought it would be funny to write a song that was, in essence, all about rhythm. He came up with the story line from watching an energetic shoeshine boy at work. By the time he finished the song, which he called "Get Rhythm," Cash really liked it. It wasn't just a throwaway after all. He wasn't sure the song was right for him because it edged closer to rock than anything he had done previously, but Phillips liked it and put it on the flip side of the "I Walk the Line" single.

Cash heard "I Walk the Line" on the radio for the first time when he was in Shreveport for the Hayride—and he was shocked. It wasn't the slow version that he'd wanted; it was the slightly faster recording that Phillips had coaxed him into doing. Cash confronted Phillips as soon as he got back to Memphis. Sam explained that he'd released the faster version only because he'd played it for some of his DJ friends and they all liked that version better.

"Give me just two weeks," he said. "If it doesn't do what I think it's going to do, I promise you right here, I'll pull the record and we'll release the slow ballad."

Cash was reluctant, but he agreed.

After those two weeks, the record was a smash, and Cash rarely mentioned the slow version again.

Typical of the country music industry's reaction to "I Walk the Line" was *Billboard's* glowing review: "'Mr. Folsom Prison Blues' has a top-notch pairing on this wax. First, he generates a load of excitement with his special kind of melancholy sound on a superior piece of slow-paced 'love and devotion' material. On the flip, there's a wonderful swinging blues job with the great 'down' guitar trademark."

Phillips must have been feeling invincible by then. His Sun discoveries were dominating *Billboard's* national country sales chart in early May 1956. Elvis Presley was at number one with "Heartbreak Hotel," his formal RCA debut, followed by Carl Perkins's "Blue Suede Shoes" at number two, Elvis's "I Forgot to Remember to Forget," which had been Presley's last Sun single before he went to RCA, at number three, and "Folsom Prison Blues" at number six. Take that, Nashville! Even more spectacularly, "Heartbreak Hotel" and "Blue Suede Shoes" were number one and number three, respectively, on the list of national pop best-sellers. Take that, New York, Chicago, and Los Angeles! To add to the celebration around Sun Records, *Billboard* also had lavish praise for the label's first Roy Orbison single. The young Texan had been steered to Phillips after Orbison met Cash in Odessa, Texas, and asked for some career advice.

To celebrate their good fortune, Phillips and Bob Neal took out two ads in the May 12 issue of *Billboard.* In the first, they showcased "Blue Suede Shoes" in the top half and Cash's new record in the bottom half. Alongside Cash's photo, the copy read, "Another two-sider by one of the truly great talent finds." Perkins, who was signed just before Cash, may have been outselling Cash at the moment, but Phillips still saw Cash as his special talent. Elsewhere in the same issue, Phillips and Neal celebrated their new Stars, Inc. joint venture with photos of their growing roster.

That ad further aligned Sun and Stars, Inc.—and, in turn, Cash—with rock 'n' roll. Above photos of Perkins, Cash, Warren Smith, Eddie Bond, Orbison, and Jack Earls, the ad proclaimed boldly, "These are the biggest drawing stars in the rock 'n' roll business." This early marketing of Cash to the rock market would prove to be of major significance in his career. Even if he had made the same records in Nashville, he might simply have been viewed as another hillbilly star—like Webb Pierce or Ray Price. But his ties to Elvis and Phillips and Sun Records would forever give Cash credibility in the wider, more culturally important rock 'n' roll market.

II

For all the talk about Cash's being Sun's number-one artist after Elvis left, the sudden emergence of Carl Perkins could have caused some strained feelings, but Cash felt an immediate identification with Perkins when they first met at Sun in early 1955.

Cash admired Elvis's talent, and they had good times on the road, but they didn't really have that much in common beyond grand ambitions and the Sun label. Elvis was going after a teen audience. Cash aimed for an adult country crowd. More important, Cash was married and trying to remain faithful to Vivian. Elvis was single and eager to take advantage of it. He pursued the young female fans with such abandon that Cash found it a bit distasteful. About one of Elvis's shows on the Hayride, Cash said he saw Elvis pick out three or four girls in the audience and motion to them to follow along as he left the stage. "And they would fight each other to get to the stage door," Cash said. "He took 'em into the dressing room. One night we counted nine girls that he had sex with in the dressing room."

Cash also saw Elvis, despite the poverty of his youth, as a city boy. He hadn't worked the cotton fields or walked those long, lonely country roads the way Cash and, it turned out, Perkins had. Carl was also Cash's age and married. He was raised in west Tennessee, just across the Mississippi River from Dyess. They even had identical scars on their fingers from the sharp needles of the cotton bolls. When they were booked on the same tour, Cash and Perkins often rode in the same car and used the time to bounce song ideas off each other. Just as Cash said Perkins helped him pick "I Walk the Line" as the title of his song, Cash gave Perkins the idea for "Blue Suede Shoes" in the fall of 1955; C. V. White, the sharp-dressing airman in Landsberg, had playfully warned John one night, "Don't step on my blue suede shoes."

So Cash was cheering Perkins on as "Blue Suede Shoes" became a massive hit in the country, pop, and R&B fields in early 1956. In fact, the record shot up the charts so fast that Steve Sholes, the RCA executive who signed Elvis, started having second thoughts about his decision when Presley's first single, "Heartbreak Hotel," got off to a slow start. Because of "Blue Suede Shoes," Carl's band was booked as a guest on Perry Como's highly rated national TV show on March 24, but they never made it to New York. On the day before the show, the car in which Perkins and his band were riding crashed at high speed into the back of a pickup truck near Dover, Delaware, in the early morning hours. Perkins suffered three fractured vertebrae in his neck, a concussion, and a broken collarbone. He was taken to a nearby hospital, where he lay unconscious for nearly twenty-four hours. His brother Jay was even worse off, with a fractured neck and serious internal injuries.

Remarkably, Carl was back on tour within a month, joining Cash for a few West Texas shows starting April 21 in Beaumont. The accident brought the two singers even closer. Though Jay hadn't died in the crash, Carl understood what it must have felt like for Cash to lose his brother. They grew even closer two years later when Jay died of cancer.

Once Carl joined the tour, Cash had lots to tell his friend. He had bought a house at 4492 Sandy Cove Circle in northeast Memphis and had a new daughter, Kathy, who had been born the previous week.

Vivian was another reason why Cash welcomed Perkins back to the road. Carl's refusal to get involved with the women who threw themselves at country singers made it easier for Cash to resist what he had already admitted to Perkins was a temptation he was finding harder and harder to ignore. Carl was a teenager when he met his future wife, Valda, but the relationship was threatened early on by

Carl's fooling around. When he almost lost her, he pledged that he would change his ways, and they were married on January 24, 1953. Perkins worked hard on the road to live up to his pledge.

Perkins, who had three children by this time, had even put down rules for himself. He and Jay, who played bass in the band, would return to the motel room after the show and call home. "I took my marriage vows very seriously," he told Cash. "I knew if I wasn't true to them that Valda wouldn't stay with me for a second." Carl's friendship and example helped Cash live up to his own vow to walk the line—at least initially.

Despite the active touring schedule, the Saturday night Hayride appearances were the centerpiece of Cash's week. Elvis topped the bill when Cash made his first appearance of the year on January 21, and a Hayride old-timer sensed a bit of a rivalry between the two young men.

"I think they knew they were different from everyone else on the show," says Norm Bale, one of the Hayride announcers. "They were from Memphis and they both had hot records on the radio. Lots of people on the show would be regulars for years, but these two felt they were just passing through. They'd both come out to a corner of the stage and watch the other's show, to see how they were going over. Johnny never got the reaction Elvis did because of all the screaming girls, but he had a lot of charisma and became a favorite of the older Hayride regulars."

Cash was going over so well that he was moved into the headline spot on January 28, filling in for Elvis, who was in New York making his first TV guest appearance on CBS's weekly *Stage Show,* hosted by Jimmy and Tommy Dorsey. With Elvis still away, Cash continued to headline the Hayride on February 11 and 18, but Elvis returned triumphantly on February 25 to reclaim his top spot. Cash, however, had become such a force on the show that his name was in the same size type as that of the emerging king of rock 'n' roll. He played the Hayride seven more times that spring, many of the dates with Johnny Horton.

Claude King, a Shreveport native who would later have a long run of modest country hits as well as one Top 10 pop hit, "Wolverton

Mountain," felt that "Johnny tended to keep to himself a lot back-stage. He wasn't snooty or anything, he was just shy. But he hit it off with Johnny Horton, but then again everybody got along with Johnny Horton. He was the most natural, down-to-earth fellow you ever met."

John LaGale "Johnny" Horton was born in Los Angeles in April 1925, but his father—a construction worker with Texas roots who had taken his family west in search of a job—returned to Texas a few years later, and young Johnny was raised in Tyler, Texas, half-way between Shreveport and Dallas. Horton loved the area and continued to make Shreveport his home even after he started hav-ing hit records on Columbia. He was a big fellow, just over six foot two, and handsome in a good ole boy sort of way.

There was a lot Cash liked about Horton. He didn't drink or fool around on the road. Most of all, perhaps, Horton was a fisherman. He would rather go fishing than walk onstage any day. One of the best-known tales in Hayride annals is about the way Horton would stand on one side of the stage with a fishing reel and sail a lure into a coffee cup all the way across on the other side. It was as popular with the Hayride regulars as any song in the show.

Horton invited Cash to spend the night at his house after one early Hayride show, and Cash immediately felt at home. Horton's wife, Billie Jean, was the widow of Hank Williams and by all ac-counts the prettiest woman in country music. Claude King's wife, Barbara, describes her as "beyond Elizabeth Taylor."

What Cash liked about her was that she was funny, self-assured, and ready to jump into the conversation whether the topic was country music or bass fishing. "Horton had a lot of friends but nobody bonded with him like Cash," Billie Jean says. "They were inseparable."

III

Things couldn't have been brighter when Cash came home to Memphis on June 1 to play the Overton Park Shell, this time as the headliner, joined on the bill by Carl Perkins and Roy Orbison. It was a heady time because "I Walk the Line" was number one in Memphis and it had just entered *Billboard's* list of national country best-sellers at number eight. To make it even better, "Rock 'n' Roll Ruby," a song Cash had written backstage at the Hayride, was number four in Memphis, thanks to a version recorded by Warren Smith. Cash didn't feel that the song, with its rock imagery, was quite right for him, but he thought Sam might want it for one of his new horde of rockabilly-minded singers.

This was the first time Johnny had been able to spend more than a week at the house since the family moved in. Except for three shows, he would be at Sandy Cove through the month, and he was relaxed. He already had written his next Sun single, a mid-tempo song called "Train of Love" that was a good-natured mix of Cash's favorite country song image (trains) and country music's most commercial topic (romance).

Vivian was thrilled that Johnny was home and in such good spirits. This is what she had always envisioned their marriage to be. According to her sister Sylvia, they walked around like high school sweethearts, holding hands and giving each other quick kisses. But nothing could stop Cash from listening to music. One song that fascinated him was Tennessee Ernie Ford's recording of "Sixteen Tons," a folk-country tale about a coal miner who works through intense pain only to get "another day older and deeper in debt." The song was played on the radio so often during the winter of 1955 that Marshall got to the point where he'd turn it off on their long car drives, only to have Johnny turn the knob back to the station. Cash never mentioned the connection, but one key line in the song is worth noting: *"Cain't no-a high-toned woman make me walk the line."*

Initially Cash thought "Sixteen Tons" was an old folk song, but he noticed one day in a music magazine that the writer was Merle Travis and the song first appeared in the late 1940s on Travis's concept album *Folk Songs of the Hills.* Cash was familiar with Travis's lively hits, including "So Round, So Firm, So Fully Packed," but he knew him primarily as a brilliant guitar player, not a songwriter. "Sixteen Tons" made him look at Travis in an entirely different light.

From then on, Travis was another of his heroes; he had little further interest in the Ernie Ford record.

"I think John recognized that the difference between Merle and Ernie was the purity of soul and genuine 'coal mining, Kentucky mountain man' folk musician in Merle, whereas Ernie was, in many ways, too smooth and canned, like a studio performer," says Roy Cash Jr., John's nephew.

Folk Songs was built around a series of original and traditional songs about workers on the railroad and in the coal mines. Travis himself had been raised in Muhlenberg County, Kentucky, and his family worked in the coal mines there. Listening to the album, Cash started thinking about making more music that was rooted in the soil and the struggle of the people he knew in Dyess. He was especially fascinated by the way each of the songs on the album was preceded by a short narrative that set up the lyrics. But the idea of actually making an album like that seemed a long way off. If Phillips didn't want gospel music, he wasn't going to be any more open to old-time folk music.

But there was lots of good news, too. Cash's parents were ready to retire and move to Memphis, and he used money from his second royalty check to make the down payment on a place a couple of miles from his own house. Ray and Carrie were already spending most weekends in Memphis to be with the family, and it was at one of those gatherings that Cash proudly declared he had graduated from the Louisiana Hayride. He was now going to be singing at the Grand Ole Opry.

Despite the them-versus-us nature of the Nashville-Memphis relationship, the brain trust at the Opry couldn't ignore the change going on with the arrival of rock 'n' roll, and they felt they needed to embrace one of the young mavericks in the Sun stable. They had already lost out on Elvis, and they didn't want to make the same mistake twice.

Once "I Walk the Line" started breaking out in the country and pop fields, the Opry booked Cash and the Tennessee Two for its July 7 broadcast. While excited to appear on country music's premier show, Cash was sad to leave the rival Hayride, which had given him his start, and he would return occasionally for old time's sake.

Cash wasn't the only one who was nervous on the night of his Opry debut. The Opry folks, too, were hoping this new partnership would work. A write-up on the show in the *Nashville Banner* focused on the anticipation in the Ryman Auditorium as Cash prepared to go onstage to sing "I Walk the Line": "All the Opry people were pulling for this newest member of their family to score big with those 3,800 folks looking on and folks listening to the network show from coast-to-coast."

There was no need to worry. As the *Banner* reported, Cash was a smash. After the opening lines of "I Walk the Line," there was a veritable tornado of applause. "As his last words filtered into the farthermost corners, many in the crowd were on their feet, cheering, waving and clapping."

Most significantly, the paper quoted "one of America's foremost authorities on country music" as saying, "Cash will be every bit as good as Elvis Presley. Probably better and he'll last a whole lot longer. He has sincerity, he has bombast, he has tone, and he carries to the rafters, the top row hears him."

Asked that night about his feelings after the show, Cash said, "I am grateful, happy and humble. It is the ambition of every hillbilly singer to reach the Opry in his lifetime. It's the top for us. I feel mighty lucky to be here tonight...and I thank everyone."

The article was so glowing that Phillips couldn't have written it better, but the *Banner,* a big booster of Nashville's country music industry, was reaching out to Cash on behalf of the entire industry, saying: Enough of this Nashville-Memphis war, enough of this country–rock 'n' roll war! Join us!

Cash was deeply proud of making the Opry stage, but he didn't feel as comfortable there as he had at the Hayride. He played the Opry only twice more in 1956. He was too busy doing higher-paying shows around the country. Nashville wasn't alone in reaching out to him.

In mid-July he was about to embark on his most ambitious tour yet, a series of Opry package shows that would take him as far north as Toronto and as far west as New Mexico. But first Phillips wanted to record a new single so that he'd have something ready when "I Walk the Line" started to slow down. They entered the studio on August 8 with just two songs, and no one seemed all that sure about either one. In fact, Cash was surprised that Phillips hadn't asked him to go back and write something else.

"Train of Love" had a playful sing-along side, but it wasn't going to make anyone take notice the way "I Walk the Line," "Folsom Prison Blues," and "Hey, Porter" had. Cash even said as much in a letter to one of his old Landsberg buddies. The song was so routine that country DJs ended up devoting more airtime to the record's flip side, "There You Go," a more upbeat tune, though still lacking the character and personal tone of the earlier singles. Both songs were a reminder that Cash, for all his early flashes of brilliance, was still trying to figure out what he wanted to say in his music and how to say it.

Privately, Cash also wondered if Phillips wasn't spreading himself too thin by taking on so many new artists. He felt that Sam had begun to accept pretty much any song he brought in, rather than insisting on something stronger. And Phillips may finally have been feeling the strain. He hired an assistant to help him in the studio.

Jack Clement had served as a member of the U.S. Marine Corps's ceremonial band in Washington, D.C., before returning to his native Memphis in hopes of getting into the music business. He had recorded a couple of songs with a young rockabilly singer named Billy Lee Riley, and Phillips was so impressed he hired Clement on the spot. He paid immediate dividends by discovering Jerry Lee Lewis, who showed up at the Sun studio one day just as Cash had. Clement made a test recording with Lewis and played it for Sam, who decided to sign Lewis after hearing less than thirty seconds.

There was an old joke among road-weary country artists that agents must plan a tour by throwing darts at a wall map. Everyone had stories about playing a show in, say, Memphis and then having to drive 280 miles to Atlanta, then turn around and drive 250 miles back to Nashville for a show the next night, then drive back east 286 miles to Montgomery, Alabama, rather than having the shows booked more sensibly, so they could simply drive straight from Memphis to Nashville to Montgomery to Atlanta.

It was this need for grueling all-night trips that caused so many musicians to rely on uppers or other fatigue-battling drugs to help them stay awake. They would even speak of the distance between towns by the number of pills they'd need for the drive:

How far is it from Memphis to Dallas?

Two pills.

But there weren't any drugs in the Cash car in the summer of 1956, and John, Luther, and Marshall would frequently arrive in a city exhausted just hours before a show. To save money, they'd often change clothes and freshen up in a gas station restroom or backstage dressing room rather than check in to a motel. After the show, they'd be back on the road, where it's a wonder that—without some kind of chemical stimulant—Perkins and Grant didn't doze off. The trips were made all the longer and more dangerous by the narrow two-lane highways that were common at the time. Cash was still not allowed to get near the wheel. The road was so hard on the cars that Marshall and Luther had to take them into the shop constantly to work on them when they got back to Memphis. "If we hadn't been mechanics," said Marshall, "we couldn't have afforded to go on the road."

Booked on multi-act package shows, Cash was making $100 a performance, but it still had to be divided three ways, and the travel expenses continued to mount. On nights when the distance to the next city wasn't too great, they would check in to a cheap motel. Where there was only one double bed, they'd flip a coin to see which two got to share the bed and who had to sleep on a rollaway bed or, more likely, the floor. Their diet was ridiculous—mostly baloney sandwiches and candy bars. Eventually they splurged and bought a small portable grill, which enabled them to cook themselves some steaks or pork chops. They even started carrying shotguns so they could stop the car if they spotted a rabbit or some other potential meal on rural back roads.

The compensation for all this work, of course, was the promise of bigger audiences, bigger paychecks, and, for someone with Cash's deep-rooted wanderlust, the chance to see all those new cities. During that fall alone, they rolled into El Paso, Toronto, and Detroit. They also got to see a wide range of honky-tonks, ballrooms, auditoriums, and fairgrounds: Danceland in Cedar Rapids, Iowa; the Ice Arena in Albuquerque, New Mexico; Fair Park Auditorium in Abilene, Texas; and the Independence Memorial Hall in Iola, Kansas. To battle the fatigue, Cash became adept at taking naps, either in the car outside the venue or in whatever quiet space he could find in the club or auditorium.

It was all so new and exciting that no one was really complaining. During these tours, the friendship between Cash and Johnny Horton deepened. "Cash could talk to you for hours about any subject, and it was hard to find someone like that in that world," Horton's wife, Billie Jean, says. "He was smart, and he wasn't just interested in chasing girls and getting drunk."

IV

Cash was home for a week in early December before heading west for his first series of shows in California, something he was looking forward to with great expectations. What kid didn't grow up wanting to go to Hollywood, where all those movies were made and, by the 1950s, where the TV stars lived?

While in Memphis, Cash visited Phillips the morning of December 4 to talk about the trouble he was having coming up with new songs, and Phillips reassured him. Sam knew it was hard to write on the road, and he told Cash not to worry; ideas would eventually start flowing again. That afternoon Cash got a call from Phillips. Elvis had stopped by unexpectedly, and Sam wanted Cash to come down to the studio so they could get a photo of the two for the local paper. Cash brought Vivian with him, and when they got to the studio, they found a crowded room.

Carl Perkins had been working on a new record when Elvis stopped by, and they'd started fooling around on some songs in an informal jam session. The material included Bill Monroe bluegrass tunes, some Chuck Berry rockers, a Gene Autry number, a Hank Snow hit, and lots of gospel—"Just a Little Talk with Jesus," "Peace in the Valley," and "Blessed Jesus (Hold My Hand)." And there was this loudmouthed piano player, Jerry Lee Lewis, joining in and acting as if he were the real star of the day even though his first Sun single, "Crazy Arms," had just been released. Phillips was standing behind his soundboard, happily recording the session. Cash claimed he sang on the session, but if so, he must have been standing too far from the mike for it to pick up his voice, because it's not audible on the tape that was made that day.

The photo of the foursome ran in the *Memphis Press Scimitar* along with a story declaring that this "quartet could sell a million." The story of that afternoon session grew into legend as years went by, and rockabilly fans around the world dreamed of hearing the "Million Dollar Quartet," as it became known. They got their wish in 1981, when part of the December 4 session was released in bootleg form and became an underground best-seller. Other bootleg editions were also released before RCA finally put out an authorized version in 1990.

The next day, Cash kissed Vivian and the girls good-bye and headed for California.

Bob Neal, who was still feeling the pain of having lost Elvis's contract to Tom Parker, had been talking to Cash a lot about California. Parker had taken Elvis there to get him into the movies, because movies, Parker believed, were here to stay, while this rock 'n' roll fad could evaporate overnight. So, Neal figured, what's good for Elvis was good for Cash, too. He told Johnny that he ought to be in the movies, and the idea appealed to Cash. Neal pledged he would set up some meetings with studio heads, with an eye toward signing a multi-picture deal like Elvis had. But that would take time. Cash's first trip was strictly musical.

The California tour started at the Red Barn in Salinas, which was one of the roughest spots on the country music landscape; fistfights on the dance floor and hurled beer bottles were commonplace. It was also Cash's introduction to Stewart Carnall, who came from a wealthy Southern California family and prep school background, but was determined to make it on his own money, much of which he'd spend partying or betting on horses. After a stint in the Army, Carnall began booking some country music shows. When he heard "Hey, Porter" on the jukebox, he fell in love with Cash's voice. Carnall called Bob Neal in Memphis and booked Cash for $300 a night for some California dates. The Red Barn was the first stop.

Because he was such a fan, Carnall personally drove Cash and the Tennessee Two to all the California dates in his brand-new Cadillac. Cash and the guys got the false impression that Carnall was this straitlaced rich kid, and they started having fun with him. During their travels through the rural parts of the state, Cash would ask Carnall to stop at roadside fruit stands, and he and Marshall and Luther delighted in leaving the peelings all over Carnall's shiny El Dorado. They'd also try to embarrass Carnall at restaurants by picking up the food with their hands. Eventually, Carnall realized what was happening and upped the stakes. At a restaurant in Modesto, he ordered breaded veal cutlet and mashed potatoes, all of it covered with thick brown gravy. As soon as the food appeared, Carnall picked up the cutlet, tore it in two, and stuffed a piece in his mouth. As Cash and the guys watched the gravy drip down Carnall's hand and onto his fancy shirt, they broke into a cheer. The friendship was on.

The tour was fun, but the date Cash was looking forward to most was Town Hall Party, a Saturday night show in a three-thousand-capacity ballroom in the Los Angeles suburb of Compton that was broadcast live for three hours on KTTV, Channel 11. One reason the show appealed to Cash was that some movie or TV exec just might catch his act on KTTV and jump-start his acting career. But he also wanted to meet some of the cast, especially Merle Travis and Tex Ritter. He felt immediately at home. The atmosphere was far closer to that of the informal, open-minded Louisiana Hayride than the more regimented Opry. Plus, he felt like part of the show's musical family. He enjoyed sitting around backstage talking to his two heroes during the three-hour telecast as much as going out onstage. But once he was there, the crowd response was wondrous.

"He stood out onstage from the start," recalls Larry Collins, the guitar-playing, hopscotching, hyperactive half of the Collins Kids, one of the Party's key attractions. "He had a physical presence that was commanding, plus this great, authentic voice, and he meant it when he sang. His music wasn't any casual, showbiz thing. When he sang, it came from the guts of his soul."

Larry was only twelve at the time, and Lorrie, his pretty sister and the duo's main singer, was just two years older—and Cash enjoyed their act, which combined a bit of rock energy and country twang into a sound not unlike what was being created back at Sun. He spent a long time that night talking to them and their parents, who invited him to join some other Party cast members for a barbecue the next afternoon at their home in the San Fernando Valley. "He was just very down to earth," Larry says. "But you could tell there was something about him that was different from most of the musicians on the show. He wasn't content with what he had. He was aiming high."

Two other nights also stood out on the California tour. Fred Maddox, part of the colorful, high-spirited Maddox Brothers and Rose family act, had a club in Ontario, just east of Los Angeles, called Fred Maddox's Playhouse. Maddox proved to be as flamboyant a promoter as he was a performer. He wanted to take advantage of Cash's Elvis-Sun connection, so the poster for the show read "Johnny Cash—The Memphis Flash," and a good-natured Cash took it as a challenge. He wore the bright red jacket his mother had made for him as well as black pants and two-tone black and white shoes. He gave as rockin' a show as he could, supplementing his own tunes with "Blue Suede Shoes," "That's All Right," and Chuck Berry's "30 Days," as well as "Sixteen Tons." Still, even the young fans liked "I Walk the Line" best.

Maddox wasn't alone in linking Cash with Elvis.

There was also the show in Northern California that was attended by Ralph Gleason, the celebrated music critic of the *San Francisco Chronicle*. It was Cash's first big-time review and it was a rave. The headline read: "It Looks as Though Elvis Has a Rival—From Arkansas."

Though Cash carried a copy of the review all the way back to Memphis, he didn't recognize its significance. Gleason wasn't just a sympathetic country music writer, eager to boost a new act; he was a respected jazz and rock critic who would eventually serve as co-founder of *Rolling Stone* magazine. He was an early champion of the idea that pop music could be more than simply light entertainment; it could be a serious art form. Gleason's early stamp of approval reinforced Cash's connection to rock culture first established by his place on the Sun roster.

Cash was looking forward to being home for the holidays when the tour ended, but he had enjoyed himself so much in California that he couldn't wait to come back. It seemed like one big party, and in a way, it was. Carnall and Cash agreed it'd be fun to work together again, and Carnall phoned Neal to arrange for some more dates in California. The young promoter was so enthusiastic that he went much further than simply booking more shows. It was the start of a process in which Carnall would become Cash's co-manager.

Neal was hesitant at first. Was the fast-talking Carnall another operator who would try to lure Cash away from him the way Colonel Parker had done with Presley? *Naw,* Neal must have figured. What are the chances of lightning striking him twice? He took Carnall's offer—which included $5,000 in cash—and the partnership was set.

There was something else that Cash liked about his trip to California: the Collins Kids. Larry was smart, funny, and talented, and Cash enjoyed his youthful innocence. Johnny was discouraged by the way the road had seemed to wear down so many of the musicians he had met over the past year. They were for the most part cynical and sarcastic. They didn't seem to care about music as much as they did a bottle of Jack Daniels and the women who followed them back to their motels. Larry reminded John of his own wide-eyed days in Dyess, when the music and lights all seemed thrilling. He also liked the fact that Lorrie loved music and was so confident at the microphone. There was something about her smile, too—not quite adoring, but certainly admiring.

"My impression of Johnny was that he was very, very shy and quiet," Lorrie Collins says. "When we first saw him onstage, you could tell he was kind of uncomfortable, maybe a bit unsure of himself in front of people. He had come a long way in a short time. Suddenly, 'I Walk the Line' was a huge hit, but his mother was still making his clothes."

Cash found himself spending time with the two youngsters, both backstage at Town Hall Party and on the few shows they did together that month. "There was this solitude about him," Larry remembers. "There could be a hundred people backstage and Johnny would be over in the corner with Lorrie and I. That was our space. He could relax. The same thing at the Sunday afternoon gatherings at our house. It was like we were his family away from home."

Cash was thankful when his own family gathered for Christmas dinner at his parents' house in Memphis. "I Walk the Line" had made him a star everywhere. He was even named the most promising country singer of the year by the nation's country DJs, and requests for concert dates were coming in from all over the country and Canada.

The image of all those screaming girls kept coming back to Vivian. As much as she tried to be supportive, she would find herself wishing he didn't have to go away all the time.

"I'm doing this for us, baby," he told her whenever the issue came up.

Even so, there were times at night when she would stare across the room at her husband, sitting on the sofa working on his songwriting, and feel alone. There was something about the way he was throwing himself into his work that alarmed her. She'd find herself talking to him at times and realize he wasn't really listening. She was starting to learn that there was no way the young man from Arkansas was going to let anything interfere with his dream of being a country music star.

Cash was confused by her growing disenchantment.

He had worked hard to give his family a comfortable home and someone to be proud of.

He loved making music and singing to all those fans. In fact, he felt he had to devote even more of his time to it.

He couldn't just stay home.

The hit song that he had written to assure her that he'd always be by her side was threatening to push them apart.

CHAPTER 7

COLUMBIA RECORDS, "BIG RIVER," AND PILLS

I

ADDICTION, AS COMMONLY DEFINED in the 1950s, was simply the act of giving in to "habit-forming pursuits"—which meant Johnny Cash was an addict many times over. By the start of 1957, several habit-forming pursuits had already made their presence known in Cash's life or were about to do so. Not all were bad.

Everyone who knew Cash in those days agreed he was devoted to music and the scriptures. He may have moved into secular music without a moment's hesitation and lost the habit of regular church-going once he started spending most of his time on the road, yet he read the Bible almost every day, and he rarely went twenty-four hours without singing those old Baptist hymns in his head. In his later years, Cash would say those hymns were his favorite form of prayer, his church of choice.

Marshall Grant also saw early in Cash a compulsion to help others, a behavior he attributed to Cash's spiritual values and modest roots. He was always going out of his way, Grant wrote in his 2006 book, *I Was There When It Happened: My Life with Johnny Cash*, to help people in need—family, friends, or strangers—regardless of his own finances. "There were many times on tour when we'd stop at a grocery store to buy food and supplies and John would see...someone who seemed to be struggling," and would try to help out.

Grant also told of Cash learning about fans who had traveled long distances to see his concerts, and he'd pay not only for their meals in town but also for their lodging. "He'd give you the shirt off his back, and if he was straight, everything else he had in his possession."

In fact, Grant believed, the thing Johnny Cash was most addicted to was "trying to do good."

As Cash was also discovering, he was becoming addicted to the road. After years of the isolation of Dyess and the restrictions of the Air Force, Cash appeared forever restless, eager to move on to the next town and the next experience. He would eventually quote a line from a Billy Joe Shaver song: "Moving's the closest thing to being free." He also realized that it was intoxicating to have thousands of people cheering the very sight of him each night as he walked onstage. Fame, like music, was another way to strike down his insecurities.

But there were more troubling pursuits—classic addictions, some might say—only a few months away, and they would ignite a pattern of guilt and torment in his personal life that sometimes brought him to his knees. Once away from Memphis and family, he would become drawn to a particular type of woman, though it would take a while before he came to the point of setting aside his values, as a married Christian, and actively pursued the temptation. Sensing a slowly growing void at home, he tended to be attracted to women who were pretty, smart, spiritual, and, most of all, supportive of his music in ways that helped him in his struggle for self-worth. "John was not just looking to get laid," says songwriter Tom T. Hall, a longtime friend. "He was searching for love."

Also looming just ahead were drugs, especially amphetamines, and they would cause dramatic mood fluctuations and extreme behavior patterns, influences that would both interfere with and yet sometimes deepen his art.

In describing Cash's drug use, his friend James Keach quoted a remark by Lenny Bruce, the cutting-edge comedian and social observer, who had his own drug issues: "I take a hit and I feel like a new man, and the new man wants a hit." About Cash, Keach says, "John said one pill was too many and a thousand wasn't enough. And so it was like once he got into it, he couldn't stop."

While continuing to smoke cigarettes, Cash was still months away from his first amphetamine when he and the Tennessee Two left Memphis for New York in mid-January 1957 in a brand-new black Cadillac. He and other country musicians didn't favor the fancy cars merely for their prestige. They were also a practical choice—built well enough to stand up to the rigors of the road better than any other make. The guys were motoring north for what they expected to be one of the high points of their young career: a January 19 guest appearance on the hugely popular Jackie Gleason TV variety show on CBS.

Though Bob Neal could have gone after one of several other shows, such as Milton Berle or Steve Allen, he had a special reason for wanting Gleason. It was on another Gleason-produced program, *Stage Show*, that Elvis had made his national TV debut almost one year earlier. To make his Gleason booking even sweeter, Neal arranged for Cash to appear on up to ten shows—four more than Colonel Tom Parker had secured for Elvis.

Cash looked at Elvis's spectacular rise in 1956 as an encouraging sign that he might enjoy a similar career trajectory. After all, Sam Phillips and the folks in Nashville were telling him his songwriting and his maturity could make him even bigger than Presley. And the success of "I Walk the Line" made him feel that Sam might be right. On the night of the Gleason taping, "I Walk the Line" was in its eighth month on the national country charts, and the new "Train of Love"/"There You Go" single was in the country Top 10. It wasn't coming close to matching the pop success of "I Walk the Line," but that's what the Gleason show was designed to do: increase Cash's mainstream exposure.

After the taping, Gleason thanked Cash and said he was looking forward to seeing him again soon. But that program—which was aired a week later—proved to be Cash's only appearance. Gleason experimented from week to week with the show's format, sometimes devoting the entire hour to a musical special or a reprise of a popular *Honeymooners* segment. If Cash had created a buzz like Elvis, Gleason might have found time for him on another show, but as it was, the options weren't exercised. The Gleason show went off the air in late June.

Once touring began in earnest in early February, the cities came so fast that Cash had trouble keeping up with all the names: Akron, Pittsburgh, Cincinnati, Austin, Tucson, San Diego. When Cash first heard Hank Snow's travelogue toast "I've Been Everywhere" a few years later, he laughed out loud. Boy, could he identify with that. Sometimes he'd substitute his own tour itinerary for the cities mentioned in Snow's hyper-paced song and sing them out loud. On those long, endless trips Grant evolved as the man in charge—doing most of the driving, booking travel arrangements—while John and Luther just concentrated on the shows. The two men both had an easygoing, nonjudgmental style that led them to form a deep friendship. While everyone else was calling Cash either Johnny or John, Luther good-naturedly called him J.R., and Cash responded by calling Perkins L.M. (for Luther Monroe).

By now, John was headlining most of the multi-act package shows, but he still felt the need to prove himself. He didn't want to be one of those guys in country music who spent his whole life riding one or two old hits. But the miles in the car at night left him constantly exhausted. He often arrived just before showtime and was usually back in the car and on the highway again right after the show.

When he and Marshall and Luther did get a room for the night, Cash was usually too keyed up to take advantage of it. He often spent the night staring at the ceiling or sitting in a chair, smoking cigarettes and trying to come up with those elusive song ideas. With so much time on his hands, Cash was eager to find ways to fill it. Slowly he found himself slipping back into his Landsberg ways. Once in a while the boredom, the loneliness, and a few beers combined, and Cash ended up in bed with one of the girls who knew their way around the country music dressing rooms and motels. Marshall gently tried to remind Cash that he was married, but John didn't see it as a problem; these occasional trysts didn't mean anything.

Nephew Roy Cash Jr., who often stayed with Vivian at night, remembers being routinely awakened at ungodly hours—often three or four in the morning—when Cash would call as he arrived in another city. These weren't brief "I love you" check-ins. He would often keep Vivian on the phone for an hour or more, describing what was happening at the shows, bouncing song ideas off her, and telling her over and over how much he missed her and the girls. Sometimes the calls would be so long that Vivian would play Rook with Roy while listening to her husband. On top of the calls, there was a constant stream of postcards and letters.

As crowds across the country were still cheering mightily night after night, Neal was getting feelers from Hollywood, or so he told Cash. They'd both been envious when Elvis's multiyear movie contract got off to an impressive box office start the previous November, as *Love Me Tender* earned its entire $1 million production costs in a single week: $540,000 in the United States, the rest overseas. Those figures convinced Hollywood doubters that this young rock 'n' roller was indeed a red-hot film property. Within the next twelve months, Elvis would be back in theaters with two more song-heavy films, *Loving You* and *Jailhouse Rock*.

Neal believed that Elvis's success meant the studios would be lining up to sign Cash. There must have been talk about the movies around the Cash house, because Vivian told a columnist from the *San Antonio Light* who called later in 1957 that Johnny was in Hollywood making a screen test. But that appears to have been wishful thinking on Cash's part.

Grant didn't think all the movie talk was good for his friend. He felt it distracted Cash from his most important challenge—songwriting. But that may be too harsh a judgment. The strain of the road made it hard for Cash to find the energy and the time to think about composing new material. At the same time, Phillips was starting to worry that the Tennessee Two's sound was too narrow. Part of the appeal of "I Walk the Line" was its unique tone. "Train of Love" and "There You Go" came across to DJs, especially in pop, as too simple.

Even though "There You Go" reached number one on the country chart, Phillips was savvy enough to know the success was due more to the DJs' interest in Cash spurred by "I Walk the Line" than to any audience enthusiasm for the new record. Plus, the Gleason show exposure had not noticeably helped expand Cash's appeal in the pop field. At the same time, Carl Perkins hadn't come close to the sales bonanza of "Blue Suede Shoes" with his follow-up, the rollicking but less dynamic "Boppin' the Blues." Roy Orbison, too, hadn't been able to build on the modest success of "Ooby Dooby." None of Sun's other young hopefuls had caused much of a stir outside Memphis.

Remarkably, Phillips, the man whose judgment had produced the Presley record that helped change pop culture around the world just two years earlier, feared he was losing his touch. He had no idea how to help Cash regain his momentum in the studio.

II

During his second trip to California, Cash hoped to meet with movie or TV executives, but Neal thought that was premature. He told Cash he was still "fielding offers," though there is no indication that there was any genuine interest in Cash among studios.

Then when Cash headed back south in March, he learned that he was going to have a new tour mate: none other than Sun's new shining star, Jerry Lee Lewis. In fact, Lewis—along with Carl Perkins and the Collins Kids—would be on the road with him a lot during March, April, and early May, including an extensive swing through Canada. Because concert promoters were trying to lure both country and rock fans, ads frequently boasted that the tour package was "the biggest country rock 'n' roll show ever" to come to the area.

Cash tried to make Lewis feel welcome, which wasn't always easy, given Lewis's raging cockiness. Carl Perkins got so upset over Lewis's overbearing manner that he challenged him to a fight early in the tour and almost got into another one after Lewis demanded one night that he go on after Perkins, even though, as the bigger star, Perkins had the right to follow the newcomer.

On the tour, Cash teamed up with Carl's wild-child younger brother Clayton to put together some memorable pranks. After one show, they decided they didn't like the peach color scheme in their hotel rooms, so they went to a nearby hardware store, bought a can of black paint, and stayed up most of the night painting the walls. To make sure other guests would remember them, Clayton also bought several strands of rope, and he and John tied one end of a rope to a hotel room doorknob, then stretched the rope across the hall and tied the other end tautly to the opposite doorknob. They repeated the process up and down the hallway, then bent over laughing the next morning in the lobby when the front desk clerk started receiving calls from disgruntled guests who claimed they'd been locked in their rooms.

At a show in the Midwest, Cash and the troupe came up with one of their most ambitious stunts. Staying at a hotel that was filled with members of a female bowling league, they got the idea of taking the bed, chairs, and lamps from John's room and setting them up in the hallway outside an elevator on the fifth floor. Cash, the gang leader, got under the covers with a sleeping cap on his head. When the elevator doors opened, a group of women saw this strange man in bed in the middle of the hall. As the story came down over the years, the women screamed and rode the elevator back to the main floor, where they related what they had seen. The desk clerk and house detective rode the elevator back to the fifth floor, only to find the hallway empty. Cash and the guys had, of course, pushed the furniture back into his room as soon as the women took off.

On another night during this period, Cash and Rose Maddox, who was one of the featured singers on the tour, decide to shake things up. Pretending to be having a violent argument in his hotel room, they sent young Larry Collins into the hall, knocking on doors and screaming for help. Just as some of the guests stuck their heads out, Larry ran back toward Cash's room, hollering, "Daddy, Daddy, don't shoot Mommy." At that moment, Cash fired a starter's pistol that he had picked up somewhere. The hotel staff didn't think it was funny, and police questioned Cash and Maddox the next day. There was some concern the show would be canceled, but the police finally relented and let the two off with just a warning.

It was only April.

Cash returned to Memphis early in the month for a concert at the Ellis Auditorium, and Phillips took advantage of his brief time in town to bring Cash and the Tennessee Two into the studio to put the next single on tape. Phillips thought Cash's sound needed shaking up, and he asked his production assistant Jack Clement, who had been having success with Jerry Lee Lewis in the studio, to help him think of ways to dress up Cash's minimalist approach. But Clement held back; he had so much respect for anyone who could write a song as iconic as "I Walk the Line" that he felt a bit intimidated as Cash recorded "Don't Make Me Go" and "Next in Line," a pair of melancholy love songs.

Cash's vocal was unusually lifeless on "Next in Line," and Grant and Perkins seemed equally colorless on "Don't Make Me Go," the stronger of the two tunes. Phillips had plenty of material after three tries at "Next in Line," but he apparently thought enough of "Don't Make Me Go" to get Cash to run through it ten times in hopes of injecting more pulse into it. Clement's input was so minimal that he didn't even mention it years later when he spoke of Cash and the Sun era. Record buyers didn't show much more interest in the single. "Next in Line" stalled at number nine on the country chart—Cash's lowest position since "Cry, Cry, Cry"—and made it only to number ninety-nine in the pop field. Meanwhile, Cash and Perkins watched Jerry Lee Lewis's second single, "Whole Lotta Shakin' Goin' On," race into the Top 10 on both the pop and country charts. It was Sun's biggest hit since "Blue Suede Shoes," and its success gave Clement the confidence to take more of a leadership role the next time out with Cash—if Phillips asked again.

Phillips went him one better. Rather than asking Clement to assist in the studio, Phillips had him take over as Cash's producer. If Cash wasn't coming up with new hits himself, maybe Clement could help him find some good songs by other writers. Cash was hurt when he learned that Phillips was turning him over to Clement; he wrongly assumed Phillips had lost faith in him. Around the same time, he also heard from artists on other labels that his three-cent royalty rate was too low; they were getting four and five cents a record. The difference in a million-seller like "Blue Suede Shoes" could be up to $20,000, a huge amount in 1957.

Cash suddenly felt underappreciated and underpaid. Seeing Elvis's success, he asked his manager, "Do you think RCA Victor might be interested in me, too?" Because of his ties to Phillips, Neal tried to assure Cash that things were fine with Sun. He said he'd talk to Sam about getting a higher royalty rate.

Clement felt that Cash misunderstood the dynamics at Sun. "He was the last one of his artists that Sam let me work with," he says. "John was his fair-haired boy. [Sam] loved his music. He respected him and enjoyed working with him, but he thought John needed a new voice with him in the studio. Maybe Sam should have explained the situation better to John."

On the long car rides, Cash thought hard about his writing, trying to figure out what was different between some of his best early songs and the ones he'd been writing recently. He realized he had drifted away from writing from his personal experience. Wanting to get back to that approach, Cash recalled the time a stranger came up to him backstage during his first trip to California. The man had just been released from prison and was looking forward to going home to Shreveport to see his wife. But he didn't know how or when he could get there because he was broke and jobless. He knew that Cash was a regular on the Louisiana Hayride and asked him to say hello to his wife if he got to Shreveport first.

The story reminded Cash of his own bouts with loneliness, and he liked the idea of telling a different kind of prisoner story. In writing it, he tried to include the kind of sentimental undercurrents that Jimmie Rodgers would have put into it. He even wrote some railroad imagery into the opening line of "Give My Love to Rose":

> I found him by the railroad track this mornin,
> I could see that he was nearly dead.
> I knelt down beside him and I listened
> just to hear the words the dyin' fellow said.

He said: They let me out of prison out in Frisco
for ten long years I paid for what I'd done.
I was tryin' to get back to Louisiana,
to see my Rose and get to know my son.
Give my love to Rose, please won't you mister?
Take her all my money; tell her, buy some pretty clothes.
Tell my boy that Daddy's so proud of him
and don't forget to give my love to Rose.

Won't-cha tell them I said thanks for waiting for me.
Tell my boy to help his mom at home.
Tell my Rose to try to find another,
'Cause it ain't right that she should live alone.
Mister, here's a bag with all my money.
It won't last them long the way it goes.
God bless you for findin' me this morning.
Now don't forget to give my love to Rose.

This wasn't just a weeper for Phillips or a generic song for the jukebox. This was a song Cash felt deeply, a real J.R. number. He liked the idea of casting a prisoner in a tender light because it meshed with his Baptist values of forgiveness. He liked the song so much, he used his older daughter's nickname in it.

When Cash got back to Memphis in late June, he played it for Clement, who shared Cash's fondness for the song, though he privately wondered whether DJs would find it too slow-paced. Clement was more enthusiastic about the chances of another song Cash played for him, an upbeat bluesy number that fit Phillips's recipe for a hit: a sad song with a happy beat. It was "Home of the Blues," and Clement knew right away that this was going to be the time to give Cash some studio flash.

On the record credits, Cash was joined for the first time by two co-writers, Vic McAlpin and Glenn Douglas Tubb. In truth Cash didn't write it at all, except for perhaps a couple of words. Grant says McAlpin had brought the song to Cash and offered him part of the songwriting rights if he'd record it. That was a fairly common practice in Nashville at the time, as songwriters competed against one another to get hit singers to record their songs. In addition, some songwriters were so desperate for rent money that they'd sell the rights to their songs to singers or other writers for as little as $50 to $100.

None of that was Clement's concern. He just wanted a hit as they headed into the studio on July 1. It's easy to see how the song would appeal to Cash's and Clement's sense of drama and despair. When read aloud, the lyrics almost sound like a parody of a barroom lament. Yet Cash told the story with empathy, and Clement instilled in it an emotional resolve that made "Home of the Blues" one of the most striking country singles of that year. The record opens with a series of lonely guitar notes, each deliberately descending the musical scale. After the final note, Cash's voice begins amid some rollicking blues and country piano strains. It was a major overhaul of the Cash sound.

Cash didn't quite know what to think of "Home of the Blues." The emphasis was on the production, not on him or the Tennessee Two. Looking back, Grant said the switch from Sam Phillips to Jack Clement was uncomfortable for everyone. "When Jack came along, everything changed," he said. "With Sam, he pretty much let us do our thing. Everything you hear on those early songs came from the heart. Jack had his own ideas about how the record should sound. He wanted to add things. I think John felt like he was losing control of his own music."

When Clement played "Home of the Blues" for Phillips, the Sun owner rushed the single to DJs. Cash was thankful for a few days off in August so that he could spend time with the family, and photos show them happily at play. Yet Cash was still concerned about his status at Sun as he headed back to California, where a top Nashville record executive with perfect timing asked, "How would you feel about joining Columbia Records?"

III

Don Law came to the United States from his native England in the early 1920s and got started in the record business a decade later after meeting a fellow Brit who was a legendary figure in the music world. Uncle Art Satherley had discovered, signed, or recorded such landmark artists as Gene Autry, Bob Wills and His Texas Playboys, Lefty Frizzell, and Roy Acuff. After learning his way around the recording studio from Satherley, working with such seminal blues artists as Robert Johnson and Ma Rainey, Law was named head of Columbia Records' country division in 1953. He produced giant hits, including Ray Price's "Crazy Arms" and Marty Robbins's "Singing the Blues."

Law was drawn to the sincerity and straightforwardness of Cash's voice as soon as he heard "Hey, Porter." He felt that this Memphis newcomer's future looked even brighter after hearing "Folsom Prison Blues" and "I Walk the Line." When Cash's name came up during a conversation in Nashville with the Collins Kids, who were Columbia artists, Law told Larry and Lorrie that he'd like to meet the singer. They said Cash was going to be on Town Hall Party on August 31 and suggested Law come to Los Angeles and meet him. "He's a really nice guy," they told him.

The Columbia executive was at Town Hall Party that night to see Cash and Carl Perkins, whom he was also interested in signing. Larry and Lorrie introduced Law and Cash backstage. It wasn't a good place to talk business, so Law was delighted to learn that Cash was planning to attend a barbecue the next day at the Collinses' home. After seeing Cash convey such authority onstage, Law was surprised to find how "sensitive, warm—and very nervous" Cash was offstage. It's understandable that Cash was anxious. He knew about Law's standing in the music industry, and after feeling he'd been cut loose by Phillips, he was eager for validation.

Law was aware that Cash's Sun contract didn't expire until July 31, 1958, but he wanted to sign him early because he believed that other labels would also be after him. Law even had terms ready. He offered Cash five cents per record in royalties, two cents more than Sun, plus a $50,000 signing bonus. He also promised Cash total freedom in the studio. "Even gospel music, Mr. Law?" Cash asked. Law nodded. "Even gospel music." Knowing what an important decision it would be for Cash, Law urged him to go home and talk it over with his wife. He said he'd call in a few weeks.

Meeting Law wasn't the only noteworthy thing about Cash's return to California. Johnny was surprised to find how glad he was to see Lorrie Collins. She was still only fifteen, but she was so poised that she seemed closer to nineteen or twenty. Lorrie was both flattered and confused by his obvious interest.

"We'd talk backstage and he told me he liked me," she says. "He was still real shy, kinda looking at his shoes rather than me. I was nervous because he was married and had kids." Cash was also puzzled by the sudden attraction. It was the first time he'd felt truly drawn to someone since meeting Vivian. In the coming months, he kept asking himself what it was about Lorrie that so appealed to him.

After remaining in Los Angeles a few days to have his tonsils removed, Cash returned to Memphis, where he had a month off before starting another tour in Georgia. He spent the first week wrestling with the implications of the move to Columbia. On the one hand, there was the matter of loyalty to Phillips. He also trusted Sam's judgment. On the other hand, Phillips had turned him over to Clement. Columbia, meanwhile, was the big time. He'd be on the same label as Ray Price and Marty Robbins and Carl Smith. He'd have the chance to record gospel music and maybe even a concept album like *Folk Songs of the Hills*.

Vivian said she'd be happy whatever his decision. Marshall had mixed feelings. He thought it would be a gamble going to Columbia and Nashville, but he also could see that things were beginning to wind down at Sun. "As soon as Jack Clement came in, Sam started turning his attention elsewhere," Grant said, as well as "spending a lot of time by his pool." Luther left the decision to John and Marshall. After all, they'd be going to Columbia together and would continue to share in the record royalties.

Still uncertain, Cash went to see Phillips. Without telling him about the Columbia offer, he pointed out the three-cent royalty rate in his contract and asked Phillips to raise it. He would have stayed if Phillips had offered him even a penny increase, Cash later said, but Phillips refused. Cash had his answer. When Law phoned him soon after the meeting with Phillips, Cash didn't even wait for Law to ask if he wanted to sign with the label. He said, "If you still want me, Mr. Law, I want to sign with you."

*   *   *

It was just a week after the Columbia decision that Cash's life would take another seismic shift: he would take his first amphetamine.

Gordon Terry, a champion fiddler from Alabama with a wide, disarming smile and a good word for everybody, was performing with Cash in the fall of 1957 when he heard Johnny complain that he was so tired he didn't know if he'd be able to do the show the next night. (Some later said that the incident took place in Jacksonville; others thought it was somewhere in Georgia.) Eager to help, Terry, who regularly took pills to keep alert on the road, reached into his pocket and pulled out some little tablets.

The pill was amphetamine, and it worked wonders. Cash not only felt energized but also felt more confident onstage that night. He started to feel the shyness melt away; this is what he always thought performing should be like.

The next day he tracked Terry down and asked where he could get some more of those pills. Were they legal? Oh, sure, Terry told him. Any doctor would prescribe them. Terry then reached into his pocket and gave Cash a dozen or so of the pills.

When the two ran into each other a couple of days later, Terry was surprised to hear Cash ask if he had some more pills.

But Cash was not a man for moderation. He was soon craving more pills, and to his delight, he found them easy to get. When he ran low on the road, he would just pick up the yellow pages and find the number of a local doctor. "I'd just say something like, 'Doc, this is Johnny Cash. I've got a long tour comin' up and I gotta do a lot of night drivin'. I need some of those diet pills to keep me awake.'"

No problem.

Cash, however, soon sensed there was something wrong in his growing need for the pills, and he did a good job of not letting those close to him—especially Vivian—know about the drugs. It would be months before even Marshall realized that this newfound energy and vitality weresn't natural. By that time, Cash was taking five or ten pills a day—and before long, he and Grant would both look back on that number as the innocent days.

IV

As royalty checks continued to roll in, with the prospects of bigger ones soon from Columbia, Cash celebrated by buying another new house—a 3,300-square-foot ranch-style house at 5676 Walnut Grove Place. Not coincidentally, it was in one of the city's most exclusive areas, not far from where Sam Phillips and George Bates lived. The move showed that Cash, for all his concern about coming up with another pop hit, was feeling pretty confident about his future. Shortly afterward, Vivian learned she was pregnant again.

It was in the midst of all this that Phillips started hearing rumors about Cash and Perkins leaving Sun. Losing Elvis was bad, but he at least got some money in return. In the case of Cash and Perkins, he wouldn't get anything. On top of that, Phillips prized Cash, he felt he had the talent to be a star for years and years. Who was going next? Jerry Lee? Phillips tracked Cash down to see if the rumors were true. Knowing he had to work with Phillips for several more months, Cash didn't want to anger his boss. He assured Phillips that he hadn't signed with Columbia.

"I looked Johnny right in the eye and I said, 'John, I understand that you have signed an option to go to another label at the expiration of your contract with Sun,'" Phillips said. "'I want you to look me straight in the eye and tell me, have you or have you not?' I knew when he opened his mouth he was lying. The only damn lie Johnny Cash ever told me that I'm aware of. That hurt. That *hurt.*"

Phillips went straight from Cash to Perkins, who admitted he had signed an option to go to Columbia as soon as the Sun deal expired. Hoping he could still change Perkins's mind, Phillips made a long, impassioned plea to stay with Sun, David McGee recorded in *Go, Cat, Go!,* a book he wrote with Perkins.

"I think you're makin' a bad mistake," Phillips said. "You're gonna get up there and get lost. I understand John's leavin' too."

After Perkins confirmed that Cash had indeed signed, Phillips told Perkins that Cash would be okay at the larger label, but warned that Perkins needed more personalized treatment. "I know what you do, and they don't understand in Nashville," he said. "If anybody does, it's Chet Atkins, and you're not going on RCA Victor.

There ain't nobody over at Columbia Records that knows anything about rockabilly music."

Perkins, perhaps offended by Phillips's suggestion that he wasn't as strong-minded and talented as Cash, struck back.

"Mr. Phillips," he said. "It ain't gonna do me no good to stay down here."

When Phillips asked what he meant, Perkins expressed the frustrations he shared with Cash.

"You got Jerry Lee on the brain," he snapped. "That's all you talk about when I'm in here and it has been that way for the last year. Every time I come in here you wanna play me something he's done. All you're bragging on is him. I'm sure he's making you a lotta money. I know he's got hit records. But you put on his records, 'Jerry Lee Lewis and His Pumping Piano.' You ain't never said nothin' about me and my guitar."

Clearly pleading, Phillips offered to start calling Perkins the "Rockin' Guitar Man."

But it was too late.

Angrily, he called Cash to ask why he had lied to him.

"Well, I don't think you've been all that truthful to me about a lot of things," Cash told him. "I thought I'd just kinda pay you back."

Phillips felt betrayed.

When asked about their relationship over the years, Phillips and Cash would go back and forth between expressing great respect for each other and restating their separate versions of how the relationship deteriorated.

Phillips often argued that Cash and Perkins were immature. He felt that he had given both of them the same kind of special attention he was now giving Lewis back when they were both getting started. But "they saw it as if we were petting Jerry Lee," he said. "They had forgotten that we had brought them along in the same way. They were young people and there was an awful lot of jealousy."

Clement blamed Phillips for letting Cash get away.

"Sam was stupid," Clement says. "Sam was willing to give John an extra penny or two in his royalty, but he wanted John to have to come back and plead for it. That was Sam's way of showing John who was boss. But John didn't want to argue. When Sam said no that first time, John never asked again."

Now that he was leaving, Cash was becoming more comfortable with Clement. They had gone into the studio a couple of times over the summer to cut some tracks for what would be Cash's first full-length album. The title, *Johnny Cash with His Red, Hot and Blue Guitar*, was a nod to Sam Phillips's radio buddy Dewey Phillips's show, *Red, Hot and Blue*. Much to Cash's mother's delight, the collection contained the gospel song he'd first sung for Phillips, "I Was There When It Happened."

During a tour break in mid-November, Cash went to Clement with a song that he'd written after reading a magazine article about the Mississippi: "Big River." In some ways it is his most richly poetic song—the one that Bob Dylan often mentioned when talking about how much he admired Cash as a writer. "There are so many ways you can go at something in a song," Dylan says. "One thing is to give life to inanimate objects. Johnny Cash is good at that. He's got the line that goes, 'A freighter said, "She's been here, but she's gone, boy, she's gone."'" That's great. That's high art. If you do that once in a song, you usually turn it on its head right then and there."

Now, I taught the weeping willow how to cry,
and I showed the clouds how to cover up a clear, blue sky.
And the tears that I cried for that woman are gonna flood you, big river.
Then I'm gonna sit right here until I die.

I met her accidentally in St. Paul Minnesota,
And it tore me up every time I heard her drawl, Southern drawl.
Then I heard my dream was back Downstream cavortin' in Davenport,
And I followed you, big river, when you called.

Then you took me to St. Louis later on down the river.
A freighter said she's been here, but she's gone, boy, she's gone.
I found her trail in Memphis, but she just walked up the block.
She raised a few eyebrows and then she went on down alone.

Now, won't you batter down by Baton Rouge; River Queen, roll it on.
Take that woman on down to New Orleans, New Orleans.
Go on, I've had enough; dump my blues down in the gulf.
She loves you, big river, more than me.

Now I taught the weeping willow how to cry, cry, cry
And I showed the clouds how to cover up a clear blue sky.
And the tears that I cried for that woman are gonna flood you Big River.
Then I'm gonna sit right here until I die.

Clement was enthusiastic; he even contributed some striking guitar licks to the recording. Cash felt it was the best thing by far he had done since "I Walk the Line." It even had rhythm. But he still needed something for the other side of the single. The answer was the most unlikely of Cash recordings on Sun, the song he would somewhat apologetically describe as this "teenage thing."

Sitting around the studio a few weeks before the November session, Clement mentioned to Cash that he'd like to make records himself, either for Sun or for another label. When Cash asked him if he had recorded anything, Clement played a song that was so teen-oriented that Cash couldn't believe what he was hearing.

With its corny pop vocal backing and clichéd lyrics about a young starlet who gives up everything for the love of the boy who works at a candy store, "Ballad of a Teenage Queen" had almost nothing in common with the best of Cash's music. Besides, Cash later pointed out playfully, the melody sounded like it was lifted from "Twinkle, Twinkle, Little Star." Still, he admitted it was catchy. Maybe, he thought, it could be another smash like "Whole Lotta Shakin'." Clement couldn't have been more surprised when Cash said he'd like to record it. He certainly wasn't going to refuse Cash the song, so they recorded both the marvelous "Big River" and the flimsy "Queen" the same day.

Billboard predicted big things for "Ballad of a Teenage Queen" and "Big River" when the single was released a month later. Its review read: "This is the most popish try for Cash in a while. 'Queen' tells a cute story that can appeal to teens, and the artist's approach is highly attractive. Flip has more of a traditional c&w flavor, but the rhythmic presentation can also appeal in pop marts. A dual-market contender."

To help promote "Ballad" in that market, Sun's Canadian label partner sponsored a series of contests to name a local "teenage queen" in each stop of a fifteen-day December tour of Canada. Cash made personal appearances at record stores, and a drawing was held to name a winner who would be announced at the concert each night. Teens packed the stores.

Cash ended the year with a couple of shows in California. Again, he was looking forward to going back to Town Hall Party on December 28. He wanted to see Lorrie Collins to find out if what he had heard from some of the Party cast members was true: Was she really engaged to teen idol Ricky Nelson?

Nelson, whose exposure on the weekly TV show *The Adventures of Ozzie and Harriet* had led to a successful recording contract, had seen the Collins Kids one night on the Town Hall Party telecast, and he loved their high-energy rockabilly style. He asked a mutual friend, Glen Larson of the pop vocal group the Four Preps, if he would go with him to Town Hall Party and introduce him to Lorrie.

"I thought he was cute on the TV show, just like any other teenage girl," Lorrie recalls. "When he walked into the room backstage, everyone was speechless. No one could imagine Ricky Nelson coming to Town Hall Party, but he was really into the music. He was like Johnny a little, very shy, wearing a white leather coat, black and white shoes—a real fifties outfit. He mumbled a little about how much he liked what Larry and I did. At the end of the evening, he asked if he could have my phone number and I said sure."

Ricky, who was a huge fan of the Sun Records roster, was so enamored with Lorrie that he eventually persuaded his father, Ozzie Nelson, to bring her on the TV show, where they dueted on "Just Because," an old country song that the Collins Kids and Elvis had each recorded. They were soon engaged.

When Lorrie confirmed the engagement to Cash backstage at Town Hall Party, he just walked away, she says. Later that evening, Lorrie felt Cash glaring across the room at her. Finally he went over to her and whispered, "Lorrie, don't ever send a boy to do a man's job." It sounded like a joke, but Johnny wasn't smiling.

Cash backed off, but not far enough so that Lorrie didn't continue to sense an interest on his part. "Johnny was still there watching during our engagement," she remembers. "I could feel that."

PART
TWO

CHAPTER 8

HOLLYWOOD, TOWN HALL PARTY, AND LORRIE COLLINS

I

JOHNNY CASH KNEW HE WAS at a crossroads at the start of 1958, much of the uncertainty growing out of his move to Columbia Records. Even though the new contract wouldn't take effect until August 1, he was already thinking about other changes in his life. By the time he would actually go into the studio for the first session with Don Law, he would also have said good-bye to Memphis and the Grand Ole Opry and be looking forward to Hollywood, his dream of making it in the movies, and seeing more of Lorrie Collins.

It was both a tense and a celebratory time, made all the more disorienting because the popularity of "Teenage Queen" led to an increasingly hectic tour schedule. The first six months of the year would be a haze of traveling to shows that stretched all over California, Texas, the Midwest, the Northwest, and Canada—and sometimes back again. He also did more television, including the Lawrence Welk show in Los Angeles, a guest appearance at the Grand Ole Opry, and even a return visit to the Louisiana Hayride. To cope, he began slowly upping his reliance on amphetamines.

The Hayride stop on January 25 gave him a break from the stress by allowing him to spend a few days fishing with Johnny and Billie

Jean Horton. It felt good to unwind, making him think at least fleetingly of moving his family to Shreveport to be near his two special
friends.

"We were three buddies who went hunting together, and you
never tired of talking to each other," Billie Jean says. "We were as
close as three feet in the same sock."

One thing he didn't talk about was the growing strain in his relationship with Vivian.

"He didn't have to," Billie Jean continues. "She didn't like the
music. She was a homebound person. He wasn't. I could see from
the very beginning that...it was a marriage that wasn't meant to
be. They stayed in my house, and Vivian wouldn't sit around the
breakfast table and talk music with us. She would wander around
the house. It was very clear that she didn't have any interest in the
music."

Cash kept his drug use secret. "As far as we could tell, Johnny
was not on drugs," she adds. "Horton wouldn't have let him get
away with it. Horton didn't even drink, and Cash respected that."

Similarly, Vivian hadn't yet suspected that her husband was becoming addicted to pills. He had always been restless and moody.
Besides, she felt such joy having him home from one of his length-
ening absences that she probably wouldn't have noticed anyway. At
that time in their marriage, Cash tried whenever he was at home to
be the caring, loving husband and father he had always intended to
be. In family photos, his eyes are as clear as can be.

"I don't think any of us really knew it at that time," Roy Cash Jr.
says about his uncle's drug use. "Even after he moved to California
that summer, I visited them a couple of times and I didn't see anything unusual. He might have been a little out of it once, but I just
thought he must have had a rough time on the road."

Cash's road was expanding to include a new kind of TV exposure.
Thanks to the appeal of "Teenage Queen," Dick Clark booked Cash
for appearances on both *American Bandstand* and later the new,
more formal concert-style *Dick Clark Show.* Though eager for the
exposure, Cash had mixed feelings about both programs.

When he went on Jackie Gleason's and Paul Winchell's TV
shows to plug "I Walk the Line," he was singing to adults mostly,

both in the studio and in living rooms across the country. Going on Dick Clark's shows, he was singing—sometimes lip-synching—to kids. He felt a little foolish, Grant remembered, but Cash kept comforting himself with the fact that "Big River" was a Top 10 hit in the country field. That record, he told himself, showed what he was really about.

The popularity of "Teenage Queen" was bittersweet to Sam Phillips, too. It was great to have another pop hit, but it reminded him of what he was losing in this young man. Not that it was all losses for Sam: Cash stopped by Sun Studios during a tour break in February just as Clement was enjoying success again with a new Jerry Lee Lewis single, "Great Balls of Fire." It was another knockout slice of full-throttle rock 'n' roll, establishing Lewis to many industry observers as the leading challenger to Elvis's rock crown.

Even Hollywood was clamoring for Lewis, who headed to California to film a cameo for a major studio release (from MGM, no less) titled *High School Confidential.* The film, a tale of juvenile delinquency no doubt inspired by the earlier success of *Blackboard Jungle,* starred bombshell Mamie Van Doren. Though Lewis's only time on screen was performing the title song, he created most of the buzz among the teens who bought tickets to see the movie when it was released in June.

Elvis's old Sun label mate was doing so spectacularly well that you could almost picture Colonel Tom Parker asking himself whether he should cover his bet and try to pick up this youngster's management contract too. But Lewis would prove to be no Elvis. He was too headstrong for anyone to know quite what to do with him. He wasn't good at listening to advice, either in the studio or in his personal life. Clement was wise enough just to sit back and let Lewis rock out when it came time to do another record. From a distance, all Cash could see was that Clement kept coming up with hits.

As soon as he met with Clement on that February visit, he asked good-naturedly, "Got any more hits for me?" As it happened, Clement had just written a song patterned after the seductive lilt of one of Cash's favorite pop recordings, Dean Martin's "Memories Are Made of This." Clement played a rough demo of his tune, "Guess

Things Happen That Way," and Cash said he'd love to record it. The problem was, Clement had already promised the song to Marty Robbins.

"Marty Robbins!" Cash responded.

Cash liked Robbins, but he was on Columbia Records. What was his producer doing writing songs for someone on another label? As it turned out, Robbins was one of several recordings artists who had come to Clement after the success of "Teenage Queen," asking if he had a song for them. The producer played Robbins a couple of songs, and Robbins jumped on "Guess Things Happen." Not about to turn down such a hot artist, Clement said sure. There was just one hurdle.

Though based in Nashville, Robbins had been under the wing of Columbia's pop division ever since his single "A White Sport Coat (and a Pink Carnation)" became such a huge pop teen hit in 1957. That meant Columbia's New York's pop boss, Mitch Miller, had to approve Robbins's song choices, not Don Law. To Cash's good fortune, Miller didn't like "Guess Things Happen That Way," allowing the song to fall into Cash's hands. He and the Tennessee Two were joined in the studio on April 9 by drummer James Van Eaton and pianist Jimmy Wilson to cut the track.

It took six attempts before Clement was comfortable with the prized mix of sad lyrics and happy beat. This record wasn't in the heartfelt tradition of Cash's best compositions, but Cash was far more satisfied with it than with "Teenage Queen." Despite the added instrumentation, the arrangement returned to their original *boom-chicka-boom* style.

For the back side of the single, Clement turned to "Come In Stranger," a Cash song they had recorded before "Teenage Queen." Cash called it his "life-on-the-road song," but it's better seen as his second "Vivian song," this time focusing on his long road trips from her point of view. With more dates coming all the time, he had gone from fewer than 75 days on the road in 1956 to more than 140 in 1957. If his songs can be considered either personal J.R. songs or purely commercial songs, this was a J.R. song. The closing verse goes:

She said "Come in, stranger,
and won't you listen to my plea?
Stay long enough, so that the one I love
is not a stranger to me."

Together, "Guess Things Happen That Way" and "Come In Stranger" made easily the most appealing Cash single since "I Walk the Line" and "Get Rhythm." Cash was especially pleased because the record appealed to an older audience than the Dick Clark fans.

The success of "Guess Things Happen" meant money in Phillips's pocket, but it also caused Sam to fret again about Cash's leaving the label. He sent Cash an angry letter demanding that the singer record twenty more songs to fulfill the sixty-five-song requirement of his contract. When Cash flatly refused, Phillips threatened to sue. Carnall and Neal told Cash not to worry—that Phillips would never sue him over the contract provisions because he wouldn't want anyone to go through his business records in case Cash challenged his royalty statements.

Seeing he was getting nowhere, Phillips asked Clement to use his friendship with Cash to get the singer into the studio. Cash again refused, but Clement asked him to reconsider, saying he was afraid that Phillips would fire him if he couldn't come up with the additional recordings, which Phillips wanted for future singles or albums. Clement was as big a storyteller as Cash, so he may have made up the threat, but it worked. "I pretty quickly realized that Jack was one of us," Cash said, meaning a "worker" at Sun rather than the boss. "He was just doing his job, and I saw right away that he was really good at it."

Cash agreed to go into the studio, but he told Clement that he'd have to get everything he needed in one day. That was as much as he was willing to do for Phillips. The result was a mad scramble on May 15 when they got together at nine a.m. for the first of three three-hour sessions, the Tennessee Two again supplemented by drummer James Van Eaton and pianist Jimmy Wilson. Cash kicked things off with two of his own songs, including a ballad titled "You're the Nearest Thing to Heaven," which Cash co-wrote with Hoyt Johnson and Jimmy Atkins.

None of the four songs they laid down at the two p.m. session were noteworthy. Searching around for something to record at the five p.m. session, Cash noticed a Hank Williams songbook in the studio. "Let's do some of these," he told Clement, and they recorded five songs, including one that Williams had written for his second wife, the future Billie Jean Horton. Cash knew about the song because Billie Jean had told him about the day Williams sang "I Could Never Be Ashamed of You" to her while driving from Nashville to Shreveport.

Despite the busy day, Cash and Clement finished with only twelve songs, so Clement asked Cash to come back to the studio again. Sensing Cash's fondness for "Nearest Thing," Clement said he'd talk Phillips into releasing it as a single if Cash would cut another song for the back side of the record. Clement even had a couple of songs in mind, both written by Charlie Rich, a marvelous singer, songwriter, and pianist who would become a major pop and country star after joining Epic Records in the late 1960s. The song Clement especially liked was "The Ways of a Woman in Love," a tale of romantic infatuation with a sing-along feel that was reminiscent of "Ballad of a Teenage Queen," though far less syrupy lyrically. In the end, Clement was able to get Cash to record eight more songs, which pleased Phillips.

Billboard predicted a big future for "Guess Things Happen That Way" and gave it a coveted spotlight position in its pop section. But the publication gave it less favorable attention than a new Jerry Lee Lewis recording, "High School Confidential." In addition, Sun Records' half-page ad in the same issue featured only the Lewis record. Imagine the surprise, then, when "Guess Things Happen" climbed higher on the pop charts. The reasons weren't strictly musical.

While Cash went on the road again in West Texas, Lewis headed to England on what was billed as the biggest tour ever by an American rock 'n' roller. But the trip turned into a nightmare as soon as Lewis's plane landed at London's Heathrow Airport on May 22. A reporter for the *Daily Mail* noticed a young girl traveling with the twenty-three-year-old Lewis. Looking for quotes for his story, the reporter asked her if she was related to the singer. The girl, Myra Gale Lewis, replied proudly, "I'm Myra, Jerry's wife."

When the reporter asked Lewis how old Myra was, he answered "fifteen," adding two years to her real age to avoid raising eyebrows. But reporters still sensed a scandal in the making. By the end of the day, the press learned that Myra was Jerry Lee's first cousin and the couple had been married several months before Lewis's divorce from his second wife was finalized. The headlines caused a backlash even among Lewis fans. Instead of sellouts, Lewis found himself performing to half-empty houses, his onetime fans booing him ferociously.

The tour was canceled after a few dates, and Lewis returned to the States, only to learn that the scandal had caused DJs around the country to boycott his records. "High School Confidential" stalled at number twenty-one on the pop charts, which was higher than Lewis would ever climb again in the pop world. Cash was again Sun Records' number-one attraction.

II

The lure of Hollywood was strong for Cash. Stew Carnall kept telling him about the good times they could have there, and Neal was still dangling the prospect of a TV and movie career in front of him. California also appealed to Cash because it would distance him even further from the country music scene in Nashville. He didn't want to be identified with what he saw was the provincial thinking there, and he liked to think of himself as an outsider—someone like the characters played by Marlon Brando in *The Wild One* and James Dean in *Rebel Without a Cause,* two films that Cash loved. Even onstage, Cash tried to stand apart. He didn't indulge in the rhinestone suits and "aw-shucks" demeanor of so many country stars. He wasn't overtly rebellious like Elvis or Jerry Lee, but in his mind he saw himself standing alongside Brando and Dean rather than Roy Acuff and Webb Pierce. When he wore black shirts and pants, because he liked the way they looked and they didn't show dirt, some of the other entertainers took a look at his colorless appearance and nicknamed him "The Undertaker."

Marshall and Luther were both against the move west because it didn't make sense logistically. Living near the center of the country made driving around the States and Canada a lot easier than trying to route everything through the West Coast. Plus, they'd be far from Columbia's recording studios in Nashville. When Cash mentioned the complaints to Carnall, his friend just smiled and said, "Johnny, that's what airplanes are for."

Vivian, who had already moved to one new city for Johnny, dreaded the prospect of having to relocate again, especially to a city even farther from her folks in San Antonio. The timing was also bad because the couple's third child was due in late July. But Vivian wanted to be supportive, so she said it was Johnny's decision. Marshall and Luther similarly put their fate in his hands. And his decision was: go.

Before heading west, Cash went into the studio in Nashville with Law for his first Columbia session on July 24, a week before the new contract took effect. Cash had held most of his new songs back from Sun so that he wouldn't start off at Columbia empty-handed.

For all his talk about wanting to do things his way, however, Cash unveiled no bold blueprint. As at Sun, he was simply a gifted young man who swung back and forth between commercial and creative impulses—only no longer with someone like Phillips, at least early in their relationship, around to help point out the good and the bad. He soon found that working with Don Law was going to be far different from going into the studio with Phillips and Clement.

According to Grant, "even though they respected what John wanted to do, there was always the feeling at Sun that Sam and Jack made the final decision about the recordings." At Columbia, Law didn't even screen the songs ahead of time. Law had promised Cash full creative control, and he wanted to stay as far away as possible from the decision-making process to ensure that Cash didn't feel confined.

When W. S. Holland later joined Cash as his drummer, he noticed the difference right away. "John would come in with a song and John would play it and Don would say, 'Oh, that's good,'" says Holland, who played on Carl Perkins's records at Sun. "I don't remember Don ever telling anybody what to do the way Sam had done."

There was, however, some forward movement. Now free to record gospel music, Cash went into the session with two spiritual-minded tunes, his own "It Was Jesus" and Ira Stanphill's "Suppertime," which Cash first heard in a recording by Jimmie Davis. The other four songs recorded that day were all secular Cash originals. Of them, Law was most impressed by "What Do I Care," a modest love song that would become one side of Cash's first Columbia single. It wasn't, however, a great Cash song—not even close to the convincing, personal vein of "I Walk the Line" or "Come In Stranger." The only other song from the session that Law would put on the first Columbia album was "Suppertime," whose old-time country feel was accentuated by the steel guitar styling of Don Helms, who had been a member of Hank Williams's band.

Needing enough material for an album and two singles, Cash and Law went back in the studio on August 8, when they recorded not only a song for the other side of the single, the sprightly "All Over Again," but also four songs that would appear on Cash's first Columbia album. The most notable of the tunes was "Run Softly, Blue River," a Cash song with some of the same imagery and lilt of "Big River." The other key song that Law earmarked for the album was a reworking of the old folk song "Frankie and Johnny" (retitled in this case "Frankie's Man Johnny").

The third session, on August 13, was even more promising as Cash brought in three songs, each of which would remain part of his concert repertoire for years. The first was "I Still Miss Someone," a sweet love song with the simple but devotional feel of "I Walk the Line." Surprisingly, the song was mostly written by Cash's nephew Roy Jr., who was by then a student at Memphis State University. Roy wrote it in class as a poem, and then put a melody to it while strumming a guitar his uncle had given him. Cash helped him rework the lyrics, and the two shared credit on the song, which begins:

> At my door the leaves are falling,
> the cold, wild wind will come
> Sweethearts walk by together,
> and I still miss someone.

The other songs in that session reflected Cash's fondness for storytelling, one drawing upon his love of the Old West, the other his own Dyess memories. The narrative of "Don't Take Your Guns to Town" wasn't original; it could have been drawn from any of a number of western movies Cash saw as a boy. and it fit into the tradition of such earlier country hits as "Streets of Laredo" and "High Noon." Still, Cash's vocal authority brought a freshness and appeal to the story of a young man who ignores his mother's warnings and ends up dead on a saloon floor after a gunfight. "Pickin' Time" has a more personal edge, a sentimental tale of a family on the farm thanking God for their blessings.

At the end of the three sessions, Cash and Law were both pleased. Law felt that "Don't Take Your Guns to Town" was the best song, but "All Over Again" and "What Do I Care" were safer commercial choices. He put them back-to-back on the first single, which they rushed out in September even though both Sun releases—"Guess Things Happen That Way" and "The Ways of a Woman in Love"—were both still in the Top 10 in the country field.

Columbia celebrated with a *Billboard* ad that proclaimed the "First Columbia Smash from Johnny Cash," replacing all the "S's" with "$'s." The ad also noted, "Johnny, who's been on the charts for over a year now, records exclusively on high-fidelity records by Columbia."

Cash was feeling good about his decision to go to Columbia. When he performed that month at the label's national sales convention in Estes Park, Colorado, he received an enthusiastic standing ovation and a warm welcome from Goddard Lieberson, the debonair president of the label. Though his background was mostly in classical and Broadway cast albums, Lieberson was a big supporter who saw Cash more as a folksinger than a country singer.

To underscore the point, he later gave Cash some folk and blues recordings, including folklorist Alan Lomax's 1947 *Blues in the Mississippi Night.* That album was tailor-made for Cash: a series of songs by Big Bill Broonzy, Memphis Slim, and Sonny Boy Williams that spoke about brutal racism in the South—including levee camps and prison farms—with such candor that the musicians were given false names in the liner notes to protect themselves and their families. Cash listened to it endlessly for months.

Back in Memphis, Phillips was not rolling over for Columbia. He put out his own trade ad, which was, in effect, an open letter to record store owners and DJs that declared, "Sun has patiently recorded Johnny Cash with always potent material, first in the country category and gradually manipulating his material and approach to songs to gain him a fantastic following in the pop field, yet not losing his earthy country feel. However, Johnny Cash has signed with Columbia Records as of Aug. 1, 1958. Upon learning that he was anticipating this move, we spent the next five months producing some of the finest sides for future Sun releases on Cash that we have ever had the pleasures of cutting. Please believe us when we say you are in for some tremendous releases on Cash on SUN for at least the next two years."

The ad was signed "Appreciatively, Sam C. Phillips."

To follow through, Sun released four of the Hank Williams songs that Cash recorded that May 15 evening with Clement in a mini-album (or EP) titled *Johnny Cash Sings Hank Williams*. By October, it was the third-best-selling pop EP in the country, trailing only volumes one and two of Elvis Presley's *King Creole*. Aggressively, Phillips came back less than two months later with another EP, this one titled *Country Boy*, again drawing from material recorded with Clement in May. Thanks to his large backlog of Cash recordings, Phillips was able to keep releasing new Cash singles well into 1961.

But Columbia had reason to celebrate as well. "All Over Again" went to number four on the country chart and number thirty-eight on the pop. With the album due to ship in December, Cash felt relieved. Some music critics over the years have suggested that Cash and Law weren't all that pleased with the album because it had been recorded so quickly, but most country acts in the 1950s worked that fast. Few groups would even spend much time rehearsing the material; they'd often just slap the arrangements together during the session.

In fact, Cash felt he had passed the first test in a move toward creative control. The album, *The Fabulous Johnny Cash*, contained three songs with spiritual themes. He also looked forward to the second single, "Don't Take Your Guns to Town"/"I Still Miss Someone."

As long as Columbia and Sun were taking out ads in *Billboard,* Carnall and Neal decided to take one out as well. In a play on the popular TV show *Have Gun—Will Travel,* Carnall came up with a line that they featured at the top of the ad: "Have Guitar Will Pick." The purpose of the ad was to announce that Cash Enterprises was now based in the center of Hollywood in a strip of business offices on Sunset Boulevard named "Crossroads of the World."

The move was happening. Around September 1, following the wrap of his first recording sessions with Law in Nashville, Cash said good-bye to Memphis. He, Vivian, Rosanne, Kathy, and month-old Cindy moved across the country and into a house on Coldwater Canyon Avenue in Studio City, just blocks from Republic and Universal studios. And within days, as Vivian was trying to get the place in order, Cash was back on the road.

III

On September 18, Cash headlined the West Texas Fair in Abilene, where he performed two evening shows before a total of 10,700 fans. Reporting on the event, the *Abilene Reporter-News* noted the next day that Cash played mostly his hits. Then near the end of the story was a throwaway line that probably caught the eye of more than a few members of the Cash entourage: "Between the two shows, Johnny Cash and Lorrie Collins managed to tour the carnival as well as sign hundreds of autographs."

There had been growing concern among some of Cash's inner circle that the twenty-six-year-old Cash and the now sixteen-year-old Collins were spending a lot of time together. But no one knew quite what to make of it—or do about it. At a time when Jerry Lee Lewis's downfall was on everyone's mind, the biggest fear was the potential for scandal. Yet that was a huge leap—from occasional handholding to Jerry Lee Lewis. Certainly, they told themselves, Johnny had too much at stake to go any further.

But Cash remained smitten with Lorrie, and he needed to talk to someone about his feelings. Marshall was too judgmental, and Cash didn't feel comfortable confiding in Carnall or Neal. He chose Johnny Western, a singer-songwriter who co-wrote the theme song for *Have Gun—Will Travel.* A featured performer for years with Gene Autry, Western was a good-natured guy who loved country and folk music. Cash had brought him on tour to emcee the show and sing a few songs. He trusted Western enough to open up to him about Lorrie during a drive in the desert outside Los Angeles.

"There was something different to Johnny about this little Oklahoma girl," Western says. "She had the figure, fresh face—beautiful, very photogenic onstage—and John told me how crazy he was about her. I just knew it was a total disaster for him, and I came up with the metaphor of the cowboy in the movies who has to ride away into the sunset. I told him he's got to ride away and that if he doesn't, he's going to lose everything—his family, his career. He said, 'You're right. I know you're right. But damn, I'm just crazy about her. I feel like a schoolboy around her.'"

As signs of the relationship grew, there was increasing alarm in the Cash camp, but Western resisted any further efforts to caution him. Thanks to the income from touring and the two record labels, Johnny was feeling on top of the world. After struggling to make ends meet on $50 a week in 1954, he was on track just four years later to make a quarter of a million dollars.

When Johnny Carson told Cash he was selling his Encino house to move to New York, Cash bought it on the spot for $75,000. Encino was a trophy-house suburb of Los Angeles, just minutes from Hollywood and a favorite of film stars, notably John Wayne and Clark Gable. The house, at 4259 Hayvenhurst Avenue, was just up the street from where Michael Jackson's family would later make their home. Cash also used his new wealth to indulge himself by buying everything that had ever interested him—from Civil War artifacts to vintage guns—and he began combing antique stores and junkyards on the road as one way to combat the boredom of touring. Typical of his excessive nature, Cash—who had enjoyed firing guns ever since his Dyess days—wouldn't buy just a couple of guns; he'd purchase a half dozen or more at a time.

On tour, he and the guys would find some isolated spot along the highway and fire at tin cans or whatever else they could find. In their most crazed moments, Cash and Gordon Terry would put blanks in their guns and even stage mock gunfights in hotel hallways or lobbies.

Through the touring and the relationship with Lorrie Collins, Cash continued to hone his musical direction. In an interview with the *Los Angeles Times,* Cash seemed to be wrestling with that very question. "Personally, I like a song with a story and a meaning," he said. "Much of the so-called country-western music that I sing is actually folk music." After weighing his options, Cash decided it was finally time to do a full gospel album. At various times, he gave different reasons for the decision. He sometimes spoke of a gospel album as a way of making up for having gotten away from gospel music at Sun. At other times he mentioned it as part of his pledge to carry on his brother Jack's work. He almost always said he did it for his mother.

The move wasn't unprecedented, because gospel had deep ties to country music, but it was a daring move at a time when Cash was on such a commercial roll. The record company and his fans would have much greater interest in a collection of pop-country hits, but Cash took a big step toward defining his artistic independence in moving forward with the album. When he told Law of his plans, Cash was relieved to hear "That'd be fine."

After a tour that took him to Colorado, Oklahoma, Missouri, Texas, Alabama, Florida, and Tennessee, Cash was back in Los Angeles in time to headline the Town Hall Party, sharing the bill again with the Collins Kids on November 15.

Thanks to *Johnny Cash at Town Hall Party,* a DVD released in 2002 by Bear Family Records, it's possible to see Cash's performance that night. He did two short sets, dividing his time between some of his favorite Sun material—including "Get Rhythm" and "I Walk the Line"—and some of the songs on his just-released Columbia album. Notably, three of the eleven songs were spiritual, including his early favorite, "I Was There When It Happened."

Cash, clear-eyed and comfortable in the Town Hall setting, joked with the audience about how he and the Tennessee Two had just moved to California and were trying to reestablish themselves in the music business. Then he slipped in a plug for his new album, *The Fabulous Johnny Cash.* "We've got a whole variety of songs in it," he said. "Some slow ones, some fast ones. Some old ones, some new ones. Little bit of everything."

After the show, he was back on the road, including a stop in Shreveport to visit the Hortons and appear at the Louisiana Hayride. Billie Jean says he told them then about his feelings for Lorrie, and Billie Jean wondered, "Was he really going to leave Vivian?" She didn't have to wait long for an answer.

Four days after he and the Collins Kids closed the year with a New Year's Eve show at Town Hall Party, Lorrie, still sixteen, eloped with Carnall, who was thirty-five, to Las Vegas, where they were married by a Lutheran minister before returning home the same night. According to one account, Cash accompanied them.

Everyone in the Cash camp was shocked—not just because of the age difference but because no one could remember Collins and Carnall being at all close. Everyone had been watching Collins and Cash. To make things even more puzzling, Lorrie returned to the family home in Van Nuys the night of the wedding and didn't tell anyone about the marriage for several days. The news was broken publicly in a Harrison Carroll showbiz column in the *Los Angeles Herald-Examiner,* apparently on a tip from Carnall, who conveniently added a year to Lorrie's age and took nine years off his own.

The column read in part: "One of the idols of the rock 'n' roll set, 17-year-old singer Lorrie Collins, has been secretly married since Jan. 4 to Stewart Carnall, 26." It identified Carnall as Johnny Cash's manager and said even Lorrie's parents didn't know about the elopement until "a few days ago." Someone else who didn't know about the wedding until then was Ricky Nelson, who thought he and Lorrie were still engaged. The suspicion among some of the Cash musical family was that Carnall married Collins to prevent a full-blown scandal with Cash, one that could even involve criminal action because of Lorrie's age.

Years later, Lorrie told me she didn't think Carnall married her to protect Cash; if anything, she felt Stew, a fiercely competitive man, may have been trying to "outdo" Cash by wooing her. She loved Cash and believes Cash loved her, and they even talked vaguely about marriage. But the relationship frightened her because of her age, Cash's marriage, and their respective careers. In fact, she says she refused to be intimate with Cash for those reasons. "We had situations where we were alone, but I was scared to death. It could ruin both our careers…a lot of lives…and I loved his kids."

Unknown to the Cash camp, Carnall spent a lot of time with the Collins Kids when Cash was on the road because he also booked the duo. "After a while, he started teasing me about getting married and the great life he could give me," Lorrie told me. "It was very impulsive."

The couple stayed together some twenty years, but she looks back with mixed feelings on the relationship, particularly because of the pain it caused her family, including Larry. He went on to become a successful songwriter (his credits include cowriting the Tanya Tucker hit, "Delta Dawn"), but he would always blame the marriage—and Carnall—for taking away the Collins Kids' trajectory.

"I have two beautiful daughters that I love more than life, but the way that I did it…the people I hurt and why? It was rough at first, but I eventually learned to love Stew. He could be funny, caring and loving." But, she says, Carnall's drinking problems eventually led to their divorce.

Larry Collins says he spoke with Cash several years later and Lorrie's name came up. Cash told him, "You know Larry, I really loved Lorrie."

CHAPTER 9

"RIDE THIS TRAIN" AND THE HUNTSVILLE PRISON RODEO

I

BEFORE ENTERING THE STUDIO on January 23, 1959, Cash spent weeks going back and forth over the songs for his long-awaited gospel album. At first he thought about focusing on the hymns he'd heard during all those hours in church in Dyess. He also considered doing something like Elvis had done in an EP—a collection of mostly contemporary gospel songs that were proven favorites in the late 1950s, songs such as Thomas A. Dorsey's "Peace in the Valley" and the Frankie Laine hit "I Believe." Cash eventually dismissed both options as too predictable. He wanted to make his own statement; he most certainly didn't want to look like he was copying Elvis.

To start, Cash, always conscious of his role as a songwriter, wrote four songs, most notably "I Call Him," which he co-wrote with his nephew Roy Jr. Reaching back, he also chose two public domain tunes, "Swing Low, Sweet Chariot" and "The Old Account." To fill the remaining six slots on the album, Cash turned to a couple of new songs from Nashville publishers and a few that he had heard on records, including "Lead Me Gently Home" from a Sons of the Pioneers album.

With the songs gathered, Cash and the Tennessee Two went

into the studio with a few extra musicians and a vocal group and recorded eleven of the songs in the one day. The twelfth song, Cash's "It Was Jesus," was left over from the *Fabulous Johnny Cash* sessions. Everyone was in high spirits because *Fabulous* was shaping up as a big pop success. It had already entered the pop Top 20 and would eventually spend nearly three months on the national sales charts.

There was a tendency in Nashville, especially, to do what Cash would call "showbiz gospel," but Cash brought a reverence to the vocals during the session that bordered on somberness. This wasn't the boisterous call-and-response jubilation that was commonly found at the time in black gospel or the rolling-thunder drama of the popular white gospel groups of the day. Instead, Cash brought his Sunday morning churchgoing voice. He sang with a deliberateness and sincerity that suggested he was singing right to his biggest fan, his mother.

But Law had trouble framing Cash's voice on the album. On some tracks, the Tennessee Two step forward with a touch of *boom-chicka-boom,* while on others it's Marvin Hughes's piano that shapes the arrangement; elsewhere the background vocalists come alarmingly close to the corny pop punctuation that Cash found so objectionable on "Teenage Queen." Despite the shortcomings, *Hymns* was a step forward in Cash's slow but steady search for his own voice and direction.

On the day after the session, Cash headed to Kansas City for the start of a tour that would keep him on the road in the Midwest until he headed to New York for his first appearance on the Ed Sullivan show. As usual, he called home every night to speak to Vivian and the girls. He also sent them letters and postcards regularly. Cash may have been uncertain about his marriage, but he did his best to keep anyone in Encino—the girls especially—from knowing. He was trying to make it work.

The Cashes lived in the Hayvenhurst house for only three years, but Rosanne and Kathy, the two oldest daughters, have sweet memories of the place. They remember their dad being around a lot when they were preschoolers and turning the house into a combination zoo and cotton patch: to liven things up, Cash bought a monkey and a parrot, which he named after the country comedy duo Homer and Jethro; he also planted a few rows of cotton on the front lawn to remind him of Dyess. Vivian felt reassured. She even tried to reach out to his musician friends by hosting weekend barbecues. "Vivian was lovely," Johnny Western says. "She made all of us welcome at her home. Some of my fondest memories of Johnny were at the Encino house." Kathy Cash recalls how her folks went around holding hands and hugging each other. "It was so sweet," she says.

Vivian's sister Sylvia envied their marriage at the time. "It was just something special to watch, like if Johnny was writing and Vivian was tired, she would not go to bed without him," she says. "She might lie on the couch and fall asleep while he sat in the chair."

Marshall Grant didn't have such good memories of the Hollywood years. His wife was homesick, and he hated the long, long drives to the East Coast dates. The extra distance didn't bother Cash, because he was flying to the start of each tour and then flying home at the end. To save money, Marshall and Luther continued to drive. After a few months, Luther's wife, Bertie, gave her husband an ultimatum: she was going home to Memphis with or without him. Perkins stayed in Los Angeles—a sign that Cash took as confirmation of their deep friendship. The decision did lead to the end of Perkins's marriage.

Grant was also troubled by Cash's increasingly erratic drug-fueled behavior away from his family. "You never could tell when John was going to be straight or when he wasn't because he could change at the drop of his hat," he recalled. Cash could stay straight for days at a time. It was when the demands of the road or the pressures of his personal life built up that he would turn to amphetamines.

The one person Cash could consistently relax with was Johnny Horton, which is why Cash headed to Shreveport a couple of days before their joint Louisiana Hayride appearance on March 7. There was much to celebrate. Cash's "Don't Take Your Guns to Town" single was number one on the country charts and number thirty-three on the pop charts. Horton's "When It's Springtime in Alaska," meanwhile, was number three on the country charts. Plus, it was good fishing weather.

Like many country singers from poor backgrounds, Cash kept asking himself whether he deserved all the fame and attention. Had he been singled out by God, as his mother once told him? Or had he just been lucky, and it was all going to fade away tomorrow? Horton's was a good shoulder to lean on because he wasn't nearly as ambitious as Cash. Horton was so laid-back that Billie Jean had to remind him he needed to go out and make some money.

One other thing Cash liked about Horton was the singer's deep-rooted fascination with spiritualism. Cash loved to listen to Horton's theories about the afterlife and reincarnation. He also appreciated that Horton didn't pass judgment on the Lorrie Collins affair. Cash found himself depending more and more on Horton's friendship. The downside of his visits to Shreveport was that he would be reminded by Horton and Billie Jean of the kind of relationship he wished he had with Vivian.

II

Cash set aside only one day in Nashville—March 12—to record his third Columbia album, which he wanted to build around a song that was a breakthrough in his writing. "Five Feet High and Rising" was Cash at his pure storytelling best—the depiction of the Dyess flood that sent the family rushing for higher ground. While written in the same general style of "Don't Take Your Guns to Town," it was more original and better crafted. The song sounded like a folk song that had been handed down for generations, but it was totally Cash's vision.

How high is the water, Mama? Two feet high and rising.
How high is the water, Papa? She said it's two feet high and rising.
But we can make it to the road in a homemade boat,
'cause that's the only thing we got left that'll float.
It's already over all the wheat and the oats. Two feet high and rising.

How high is the water, Mama? Three feet high and rising.
How high is the water, Papa? She said it's three feet high and rising.
Well, the hives are gone; I lost my bees; chickens are sleepin' in the
willow trees;
cows in water up past their knees; three feet high and rising.

How high is the water, Mama? Four feet high and rising.
How high is the water, Papa? She said it's four feet high and rising.
Hey, come look through the window pane; the bus is comin' gonna
take us to the train.
Looks like we'll be blessed with a little more rain. Four feet high
and rising.

How high is the water, Mama? Five feet high and rising.
How high is the water, Papa? She said it's five feet high and rising.
Well, the rails are washed out north of town; we gotta head for
higher ground.
We can't come back till the water comes down. Five feet high and
rising;
Well, it's five feet high and rising.

Law loved "Five Feet High and Rising," and he paired it with an-other song Cash recorded at the same session as a future single, "I Got Stripes," a raucous prison tale Cash wrote with Los Angeles disc jockey and friend Charlie Williams after listening to Lead Belly's "On a Monday."

Though Cash once felt uneasy borrowing freely from existing songs, he now realized it was common practice. Even with the songs he considered his original compositions, he often leaned on melodies he had heard over the years. More than ever after "Five Feet High and Rising," he told himself his specialty was words and stories.

Cash's other songs at the session weren't up to the creative level of "Five Feet," but "Old Apache Squaw" was noteworthy because it was Cash's first step into reflections on the struggles of Native Americans. Cash had been intrigued by their plight ever since read-ing about the Old West in high school. He had even been telling people for years that he was part Cherokee, though there was no evidence to support the claim, and he eventually quit making it. Johnny Western saw the song as part of a larger sympathy: "Because of his poor background, Johnny had this underlying feeling for the underdog, and there was nobody more an underdog than the American Indian."

Despite some weak material, Law was satisfied with the album, which John titled *Songs of Our Soil* to draw attention to its folk sensibilities. But it would have to wait its turn. First, Columbia had to release *Hymns by Johnny Cash,* which didn't make the pop charts. On the singles front, Columbia and Sun were both making the country best-seller list with Cash records—the old faithful "Luther Played the Boogie," and another Jack Clement–written tune, "Katy Too," from Sun; "Frankie's Man Johnny" and "I Got Stripes"/"Five Feet High" from Columbia.

All these singles helped make Cash an even hotter property on the road, and Carnall tried to fill every booking request, even if it meant a numbing schedule that stretched from Nashville to Jacksonville to Grand Rapids to Yuma, to a festival in Australia—all in just six weeks. He and Cash were having too much fun to want to slow down.

In early April, Cash, the Tennessee Two, and Carnall were driving to a show in Michigan when they spotted a hatchery. Someone came up with the bright idea of stopping and buying some baby chicks to take along on the tour and then bring home. For his part, Cash thought they'd be fun for the girls, and they could have fresh eggs every day. So Cash and the others loaded a few dozen of the little critters, along with food and water, and headed on down the road. The guys left the chicks in dresser drawers in the hotel while they did their shows.

When Cash went to the Detroit airport with a box full of chicks, however, an airline agent said he couldn't bring poultry on board.

Not one to be denied, Cash made up an elaborate story about how these weren't just ordinary chicks but expensive chickens imported from France.

After several minutes, the beleaguered agent turned to the

flight's captain for a ruling. Cash went through his story again. The captain finally agreed, but only on the condition that Cash keep them in the box on his lap. Cash thanked the man profusely and proceeded to his seat. Just after the plane took off, however, he opened the box—either by accident or from sheer mischievousness—and the chickens wriggled out and started racing around the plane, causing some women, who apparently thought there were mice running around at their feet, to start screaming. When the captain appeared, threatening to land the plane, Cash told him the chicks got out by accident and promised to round them up and put them back into the box. He spent several minutes going up and down the aisles, trying to gather them all.

Cash took the chicks home, where he raised them in his backyard. They were a big hit with the girls, though there was one problem. A couple of them turned out to be roosters, which meant they welcomed the break of day with loud crowing. The neighbors weren't happy. Cash and Carnall loved it all the more.

Carnall had grown up near the Santa Anita racetrack, and he loved playing the horses almost as much as he loved being around show business—maybe more. He combined his passions that spring, telling a publicist buddy while at Hollywood Park, a rival track across town from Santa Anita, that Cash had written a song for Silky Sullivan, one of the most popular racehorses of the 1950s in Southern California because of his colorful racing style.

Silky would start off slowly, falling twenty, thirty, even forty lengths behind. Just when it appeared he had no chance, he'd suddenly take off—as if the big red horse had rocket boosters attached—and seemingly fly down the track, often catching the leader at the wire. It made for thrilling watching—and betting. The publicist told Carnall that if he'd bring Cash to the track, he'd have a photographer take his picture with the horse and invite some newspaper reporters to attend.

Carnall returned to the track a few days later with Cash to pose with Silky Sullivan for the photographer. As Cash stood next to the horse at Stall 50 in the track stables, the photographer asked him to sing to the horse. Surprising everyone, Cash nodded and started singing "Guess Things Happen That Way"—not the Silky Sullivan song. When he finished, one of the reporters asked, "What about the Silky Sullivan song?" Sheepishly, Cash said he didn't remember the words.

While it's not clear whether he had really written a song about the horse before Carnall told him about the publicity opportunity or not until afterward, Cash did write something called "The Ballad of Silky Sullivan," which included the line "Silky came up for the kill / passed 'em all like standing still."

III

By summer, Grant and Perkins had had enough of California and the extra traveling it required and moved back to Memphis. As loath as he was to admit it, Grant welcomed the distance from Cash. He hated to see what the pills were doing to his friend.

Soon after returning to Memphis, Grant and Perkins drove 2,200 miles to Calgary, Alberta, where they were scheduled to play two days at the world-famous Calgary Stampede. When they got to their hotel the morning of the first concert, they were surprised to find that Cash, who was supposed to have flown in from Los Angeles the night before, hadn't checked in. Marshall spent two hours tracking down Carnall on the phone. When he finally reached him, Carnall calmly informed him that Cash wasn't going to perform for the twelve thousand fans at the Stampede. Grant and Perkins had no choice but to drive the 2,200 miles back to Memphis.

That summer was a turning point in Cash's drug use. As his guilt about his marriage and the pressures of his career both mounted, he was now approaching fifteen or more pills some days, and he was having trouble getting enough prescriptions to cover that number. Grant in time came to believe that one of the reasons Cash remained in Los Angeles was that it was easier to get pills there than in Memphis or Nashville. But his main supply came from Mexico. After hearing you could get all the drugs you wanted on the black market there, Cash took advantage of a June 20 appearance in El Paso to go across the border into Juárez and buy a couple of hundred pills. He found the experience so easy that he would sometimes fly to El Paso even when he didn't have a show.

Back in Los Angeles, Don Law had good news. When Columbia signed Cash in 1958, it had been a one-year contract with four one-year options. In other words, Columbia could drop him after the first year. Instead, the record company was so pleased with Cash's sales that it gave him a new contract on July 1 that extended the deal until Decembr 31, 1963, and provided a $10,000 bonus.

The effect of Cash's growing pill use, meanwhile, had become obvious to anyone who bought a ticket to his show with the Tennessee Two at the Town Hall Party on August 8. As shown in the Bear Family DVD, not only had Cash lost considerable weight since his November appearance, but also he had an almost glassy stare onstage and was consumed now by nervous energy. At the same time, he was reaching out aggressively to the audience with his gestures and comments, as well as doing an over-the-top parody of Elvis Presley singing "Heartbreak Hotel." During the number, he pretended to throw his back out while burlesquing Elvis's famous hip twists. He also feverishly combed his hair into Elvis's ducktail. It may have been amusing to the casual observer, but in the stark lens of the camera and in hindsight, it looks as though Cash was quickly spiraling out of control.

His career, though, was moving at increasing speed. The producers of a new TV series, *The Rebel,* asked him to sing the theme song and even signed him to appear on the show. Cash was elated, because the show's theme appealed to both his fascination with the Civil War era and his fondness for anyone championing the rights of the underdog. In *The Rebel,* the show's main character, Johnny Yuma, was a disillusioned Civil War veteran roaming through the West, lending a helping hand to settlers battling oppressive forces. Cash also signed for a small nonsinging role in the hit series *Wagon Train.*

The week after the Town Hall Party appearance, Cash was off to Nashville to record the *Rebel* song, which Columbia would release as part of a four-song mini-album to coincide with the start of the TV series, and another song that would be released as a holiday single, Katherine K. Davis's "Little Drummer Boy."

On the day after the "Drummer Boy" session, Cash appeared at the Terre Haute Fair in Indiana, and then played additional fair dates in Illinois, New York, and Tennessee before what seemed like an otherwise insignificant date in London, Ontario. But that's where he met Saul Holiff, a young, ambitious concert promoter who was impressed by Cash's charisma and made a note to book him for more shows in the region.

Cash always tried to boost Vivian's spirits by bringing home presents for her and the kids, from stuffed animals to fancy dresses and expensive jewelry. But he had a big surprise for her on their fifth anniversary. Columbia wanted him to go to Europe for a couple of promotional appearances in late September—a music festival in Frankfurt and a TV show in London—and he wanted Vivian to come along, to give them the honeymoon they'd never had.

One of the highlights of the tour was a visit to Landsberg, where Cash gave her a tour of the old Air Force base and introduced her to a few people he had known there. She was charmed when some seemed to remember how much he'd talked about her. He even showed her his favorite fishing spot and a tree on which he had carved their initials. To make the trip all the more memorable, he bought her a new diamond. Cash may have felt a huge void in his relationship with Vivian, but he still loved her, and the visit to Landsberg reminded him of all the loving and passionate letters they wrote each other.

Back in the States, Cash headed to Huntsville, Texas, to appear at the annual prison rodeo on October 4, 1969. The rodeo, originally conceived as entertainment for inmates and prison employees, dated from the 1930s and had been featuring country stars—along with the bull-riding and cow-milking contests—since Eddy Arnold performed there in 1951. Besides Cash, James Arness of *Gunsmoke* would be part of the day's entertainment lineup. Cash approached the afternoon as just another date on the concert trail until he stepped onstage and felt the waves of emotion from the inmates in the audience as he and the Tennessee Two launched into "Folsom Prison Blues." The reaction gave Cash chills—the cheers, the whistling, and the gratitude in the inmates' eyes.

To make the day even more unforgettable, a thunderstorm hit during Cash's set, and the rain caused a power failure onstage. The prisoners had been told to remain in their seats during the show, but hundreds came down to the edge of the stage so they could hear Cash, now playing and singing without amplification. When he finished "Folsom," they asked him to sing it again. "We all got soaking wet, but we had a great time," Cash recalled. He had never felt that much affection from an audience, even on his best nights at the Opry and the Louisiana Hayride. After the show, he asked Carnall to book him at another prison. Within days, Carnall had a 1960 New Year's Day date at San Quentin State Prison in California.

Around the same time, Columbia released *Songs of Our Soil,* and the label's promotion department did all it could to connect the album to the folk boom in pop. The *Billboard* review fell right into line, describing the release as a collection of folk ballads and predicting it would be a big seller. The forecast didn't prove accurate. *Songs of Our Soil* failed to make the pop charts.

Columbia had high hopes for "The Little Drummer Boy" as a holiday season hit. The label took out four half-page ads in the October 12 issue of *Billboard* touting a new single from Cash with the words "Johnny Cash Sings the Most Stirring and Inspirational Song of Our Time." Despite the push, the single was not a big seller. But Cash barely seemed to notice. He was moving at a disorienting speed on several different fronts.

Before heading back to California, Cash again spent time with Horton, whose high-spirited, almost cartoonish rendition of "The Battle of New Orleans," a historical narrative written and recorded in 1957 by Jimmie Driftwood, spent six weeks at number one on the pop charts—a bigger hit than any of Cash's records. But Horton couldn't have cared less. He just wanted to go fishing.

Cash had had a great time on the European trip, but he worried that Vivian's resentment would eventually resurface. As much as he loved her, that anxiety made it difficult for him to unwind at home. When in L.A., he felt more comfortable with Johnny Western or Merle Travis or Stew Carnall.

Western was like Horton in many ways, a great storyteller who had a soothing aura of wisdom and who never seemed to pass judgment on Cash's erratic behavior. Cash once borrowed Western's brand-new Cadillac, only to phone him the next morning to say he'd lost the car. The last thing Cash could remember about the previous night was taking it to the Farmers Market shopping center just south of Hollywood. Western raced over to the center and found his car, the doors unlocked and the keys in plain sight on the seat.

As for Travis, Cash looked on him as a mentor and spent dozens of hours at his house talking to him about *Folk Songs of the Hills.* It was during this time that Cash started slowly patching together his own concept album, in which he wanted to tell about life in the Old West.

For Carnall's part, his marriage to Lorrie Collins hadn't uprooted his relationship with Cash. The booking agent appealed to Cash's rebellious side, and his entertaining antics helped Cash forget the tensions engulfing him—strains that had grown to include even making music. Law was pressuring Cash to record another album quickly, but he was working on the concept album, and that was going to take a lot more time. He was also having trouble once again finding new song ideas. During a lunch stop on the road one time, Carnall told Cash to relax. He pointed out that most Nashville singers didn't write their own material; they depended on others for their songs. He took Cash over to the café's jukebox and said, "Take a look at the songs on there and pick some that you like and record them." Cash loved the idea. He could feel some of the pressure already melting away.

One reason for the men's mutual attraction was their love of the outrageous. When Carnall mentioned one day in 1958 that he had offers for Cash to do New Year's Eve shows in three different cities in California, Cash said, "Let's do them all." Carnall thought it was a great idea. He booked the shows in San Diego, Los Angeles (at Town Hall Party), and Northern California and chartered a plane to hop up the coast.

Given the close ties between Cash and Carnall, it was only natural that Bob Neal began to feel left out. Neal had gotten Johnny some TV roles, but television wasn't what Cash wanted. He wanted the big screen. The writing was on the wall when all Neal could deliver was a part in a film that was so low budget it's a wonder that Cash even took the role. While Elvis was making movies for MGM, Paramount, and 20th Century–Fox, Cash's film would be released by unheralded Sutton Pictures. Neal was also tired of California. So he quit as Cash's manager, effective November 1. In just four years, the former DJ had let two superstars slip through his hands.

Cash eventually went ahead with the Sutton film. Titled *Five Minutes to Live,* it aimed for the taut, hard-edged "film noir" genre. Cash was cast in the lead role of a crazed thug in the story about a bank robbery gone wrong. The director was Bill Karn, whose credits included some TV crime shows and a C-budget film, *Ma Barker's Killer Brood.* The high note for trivia fans, however, is that the banker's young son was played by Ron Howard, the future actor and director.

Initially, Cash and Carnall must have had second thoughts about the project. At any rate, the film, due to begin filming in December, got pushed back into the new year because of money problems.

With time on their hands after the postponement, Cash and Carnall decided to drive up to Ventura County, about forty-five miles north of Los Angeles. It was a peaceful, laid-back area where Carnall had gone to prep school. As he drove Cash along the back roads and through quaint small towns, the area spoke to Cash, who was homesick for country living. Since he had just bought the big house in Encino, he wasn't thinking so much of moving to Ventura County himself, but he thought it might be an ideal spot for his parents. Maybe he could find a way to talk them into moving out west. Maybe he could even entice his brother Roy to join them. Cash seemed to be looking to family as a way to reduce the tension that was starting to consume him. Having relatives so close might also make it easier for Vivian when he was away on the road.

Once Carnall helped him understand that it was acceptable to do a collection of other people's songs, Cash went to work on that idea, and it felt like a vacation after all the time and energy he was putting into the larger concept album. He actually used two numbers that he spotted on the jukebox that day—Ray Price's "My Shoes Keep Walking Back to You" and George Jones's "Just One Day"—but most were from records he loved from hearing on the radio, including Hank Williams's "I'm So Lonesome I Could Cry" and Bob Wills's "Time Changes Everything."

The album, which would be called *Now, There Was a Song!* was clearly secondary to the Old West project. Cash wanted that album to be a loving portrait of a region of America that he treasured, a theme that grew out of the admiration he had for the unheralded working people in small towns like Dyess. Specifically, he wanted the songs to address the "voices that weren't commonly heard at the time—voices that were ignored or even suppressed in the entertainment media, not to mention the political and education establishments." Meticulously Cash drafted a list of songs for the album and, crucially, a narrative that would run between the songs and put them into a dramatic context.

Cash was still working his way through the album's content in December when he went to Nashville to record another Johnny Yuma song for the *Rebel* TV series. He used the remaining time in the three-hour session to record three songs he was considering for the concept album, including "Going to Memphis," a tale of a convict on a chain gang. Even without any narrative attached, the traditional song—to which Cash added some of his own lyrics—impressed Law, and they agreed to get together again after the first of the year to do some more work on the album.

The only person more excited than Johnny Cash about his 1960 New Year's Day concert at San Quentin was a twenty-two-year-old convict named Merle Ronald Haggard. After a rebellious youth and years of reform school, Haggard was arrested in 1957 during an attempted burglary one night at a Bakersfield café during which he and his buddy were so drunk, they didn't realize the place was still open while they were trying to break in the back door. He then aggravated the situation by fleeing the jail, though he maintains he was encouraged by guards to think he was free to go. Because of Haggard's history of lawbreaking, the judge sentenced him to San Quentin for a maximum of fifteen years.

While there, Haggard realized he was going to spend his entire life behind bars if he didn't change his ways. He found his direction at that New Year's Day concert. When he saw how the inmates went wild for Cash, Haggard reconnected with his own dreams of a music career and vowed to turn his life around. Paroled a few months later, he went back to Bakersfield and began playing country music clubs.

Haggard remembers that Cash looked terrible onstage at San Quentin. "He was hung over from the night before, and his voice was almost gone, but he came out on that stage and just blew everybody away," he says. "He ripped down the walls with his music and he touched us with his songs. For a little while, he'd accomplished the impossible. He had replaced our misery with music. He'd made us forget where we were."

Already a Cash fan, Haggard had been awaiting the New Year's Day show with the same sense of awe that Cash had brought to the Louvin Brothers' appearance in Dyess. He found out where Cash's party would be arriving and waited there. He went up to young Larry Collins, who had reunited with Lorrie by then, and asked if he could help carry his guitar into the stage area. He also introduced himself to Johnny Western and told him he wanted to be a singer too one day.

Cash didn't meet Haggard that time, but he was again moved by the deep affection of the prison audience. For reasons he didn't try to figure out, he could identify with these men's lust for freedom and redemption. On the way out of the prison, the warden invited Cash to come back any time he wanted. Cash turned to the warden and said, "Can't think of any better place to spend next New Year's Day." Carnall, who was standing nearby, marked the date on his schedule.

IV

After spending most of January and early February on the road in the Midwest, Cash was still raving about that San Quentin audience when he went into the studio with Law on February 15 and 16 to record more tracks for his concept album, which he planned to call *Ride This Train*. Law was eager to get the album done as quickly as possible because Columbia execs were now avid for more concept albums in the wake of Marty Robbins's *Gunfighter Ballads and Trail Songs*. That set of cowboy songs, built around the huge pop-country hit "El Paso," was already in the Top 10 on the pop charts.

Cash was nervous when he first heard about Robbins's album because he thought it might look like he was trying to copy him with his own concept package. Once he heard *Gunfighter*, however, he was relieved. The songs on the album were similar in style to his, but there was no deeper concept involved. Robbins's album felt to Cash like a random group of songs, not the kind of cohesive work he was aiming to put together.

As on Travis's *Folk Songs,* Cash had intended to introduce each song with a little piece of narration, but he soon came up with a far more ambitious plan. In the narration, he brought the listener along on an imaginary train ride across the country, stopping at various spots outlined in the songs—from coal mining territory in Kentucky (for Merle Travis's "Loading Coal") to lumberjack country in Oregon (Leon Payne's "Lumberjack") to the swamps of Louisiana (Cash's own "Dorraine of Ponchartrain").

Though the songs wouldn't seem to have much in common when considered individually, the narration brought them together in a way that enabled Cash to address various elements he saw in the American character. The brilliance of the album was in that narration, where he celebrated the land, its people, its history, and, crucially, its diversity. There is no musical backing during the narrative segments, just the occasional sound of a locomotive and its sometimes triumphant, sometimes lonely whistle.

Cash recorded the narration after all the album's songs had been recorded. Listening to it now, we might think that Cash is tipping his hat to the Hank Snow hit "I've Been Everywhere" when he rattles off city names and Native American tribes at auctioneer speed, but this session was recorded two years before Snow's hit was released.

In the songs that followed, Cash sang about the "heart and muscle" of the country. The album was a bold step toward defining the theme of underdogs and working-class heroes that would characterize his music for nearly fifty years. In "Loading Coal," Cash sang about a boy seeing how hard his father works every day in the mines and anticipating his turn to take his father's place. In "When Papa Played the Dobro," Cash relayed once again his belief in the power of music to lift one's spirits. "Boss Jack" dealt with slave workers on a cotton plantation and their dreams of freedom.

Throwing out his trademark *boom-chicka-boom* sound, Cash instead tailored the arrangements to reflect the spirit and historical tone of the songs. Johnny Western, who played guitar on the sessions, marveled at what he described as Cash's "creative explosion."

"Most of the singers in Nashville ask themselves, 'Will this song be a hit?'" Western says. "John wanted to sell records too, but the question he asked himself was 'Do I really want to do this song?' That's what made him unique. He'd come across a song and he'd go, 'People ought to know about this.' For whatever reason, he had this mission to share things with his audience.

"Johnny wasn't willing to compromise on anything when he was making that album. He even did a version of Edna St. Vincent Millay's poem 'The Ballad of the Harp Weaver' because he felt it was such an inspirational story. The problem is the track ran five or six or seven minutes, which meant no one was going to ever play it on the radio. But John didn't care. He wanted his fans to hear the song."

Ultimately, "Harp Weaver" didn't make it onto *Ride This Train* because Cash couldn't find a way to tie it in with the other songs in the collection, but he performed it often in concert, and it was a huge favorite.

It took Cash just two days in the studio to record the concept project, and then he returned to the studio the following day to record *Now, There Was a Song!*—the collection of country favorites he had conceived with Carnall. The problem was that Cash had exhausted all his inspiration on the *Ride This Train* project. The new rhythm tracks were timid, and Cash didn't connect with the songs vocally. No one was ever going to think of, say, Cash's version of "My Shoes Keep Walking Back to You" over Ray Price's earlier hit rendition.

To Cash's mind, the *Song* album was just for fun; the album that mattered was *Ride This Train.* More than anything else he had done, *Ride This Train* made Cash feel as if he had forged a connection with Jimmie Rodgers and the rest of his greatest musical heroes. He felt authentic. It was the most ambitious album country music had ever seen from a star of his stature.

"Johnny was in great spirits on those sessions," Western says. "He was straight as a string. Some of my best memories of John are from that time, which is why it broke my heart in later sessions when his voice started to go because of all the drugs."

CHAPTER 10

BILLIE JEAN AND THE MARRIAGE PROPOSAL

I

CASH TOOK ADVANTAGE OF FREE time at home early in 1960 to take another ride through Ventura County, which he had been eager to do ever since the visit with Carnall. This time he wanted to see a 9,200-square-foot strip mall that his friend, actor and recording artist Sheb Wooley, owned in the quiet little community of Oak View, next door to the upscale resort town of Ojai. It was named the Purple People Mall after Wooley's 1958 pop hit "The Purple People Eater." During the drive, Cash noticed a small trailer park for sale on the highway that led from Oak View to Ojai. He liked the idea of owning a business, but more important, he saw the park as a way to lure his parents out west. After getting assurances that his parents would manage the park for him, Cash bought the Mountain View Trailer Court, which he renamed the Johnny Cash Trailer Rancho. He offered free albums to the first fifteen people who signed up for space.

When it came time to release another single, Cash and Law both agreed that "Seasons in My Heart," from the forthcoming *Now, There Was a Song!* sessions, made sense, but Cash caught Law by surprise with his choice for the other side of the record: "Smiling Bill McCall."

Marshall Grant had never heard the song before Cash played it in the studio. The bassist knew Cash loved to fool around with novelty songs and parodies to entertain himself on the road, but this one was just stupid. The song was a rambling account of a singer whose deep, sexy voice on the radio made men envious and women swoon, but who lived in fear of someone finding out that he was really four feet tall and bald. Though the song was fictional, some folks in Nashville would later think Cash was making fun of Hank Snow, who was five foot four and wore some of the worst toupees in the history of show business. But Cash would never make fun of one of his musical heroes.

In the song, he was poking fun at a man actually named Bill McCall, the head of Four Star Records in Los Angeles, who was accused by many musicians, including Patsy Cline, of exploiting them. The song was Cash's way of sticking it to the exec. As usual, Law went along with Cash, and the record was released in March. "Seasons" gained attention mostly on country radio stations, but to Law's amazement, pop DJs started picking up on "McCall."

Smelling one of those offbeat hits that every so often capture the radio audience's interest, Columbia put a tongue-in-cheek full-page ad in *Billboard* to promote the record. Despite the early signals, however, "McCall" failed to make the Top 100 on the pop charts. "Seasons" stalled at number ten on the country charts, followed by "McCall" at number thirteen. Cash brushed off the disappointing results; he had done what he wanted.

Law was totally supportive of both *Ride This Train* and *Now, There Was a Song!* but he didn't hear another potential single in either album. That meant it could be a long time before Cash had another hit on the radio. He gently encouraged Cash to come up with something they might release as a single.

By the time Cash returned to the road on March 4 in Winnipeg, he had a song idea, albeit a slim one—a story about a guy longing to get home to the girl of his dreams in Saskatoon, somewhat the reverse of "Ballad of a Teenage Queen." He figured he needed to get back on the pop charts, and "The Girl in Saskatoon," which he co-wrote with Horton, was certainly closer to a teen pop song than anything he had recorded since leaving Sun. Eager to get Cash back into the studio, Law went to Los Angeles in mid-May to record. Cash was in Los Angeles to guest on the Tennessee Ernie Ford TV show, which aired on May 12. Normally Ford's show, which came on opposite Frank Sinatra's, did well in the ratings, but Cash's appearance happened to come the night Sinatra welcomed Elvis Presley home from the Army.

In the studio with Law to record "Saskatoon" on May 10, he brought another song that was apparently left over from his *Ride This Train* period. "Locomotive Man" tapped into the folk and blues tradition of boasting about a woman in every port—or in this case at every train stop. Cash's voice wasn't in good shape, though, and Law felt they'd have to get together again in Nashville to redo both songs. Without "Saskatoon" ready, they were left short of a single, so Cash and Law again sorted through tracks they had already recorded. They settled on a song from the upcoming *Now, There Was a Song!* album, an old Hank Thompson hit titled "Honky-Tonk Girl," and another non-Cash composition, "Second Honeymoon." Those were slim pickings, and the single did even worse than "Bill McCall." His next two, "Going to Memphis" in September and "Saskatoon" in December, wouldn't make the country charts at all—a first for a new Cash single. Columbia's golden boy was floundering. Back in New York, executives grew increasingly concerned.

To Cash's everlasting regret, *Five Minutes to Live,* which he finally began filming in Hollywood in June, was low-budget even by low-budget standards—under $100,000 for everything, from cast to crew to film costs. Cash's contract called for just two weeks' work at $700 a week, less than he'd make in one night on the concert trail. Though Cash had no training or real experience as an actor, Bill Karn, the director, took the same approach with Cash as Law: "Whatever you want to do is fine with me, Johnny." Just released from jail, Cash's character gets involved in a bank heist with a hard-boiled criminal played by Vic Tayback (best known later on for his role as the diner owner in the TV series *Alice*). The Tayback character demands that the bank vice president cash a phony $70,000 check within five minutes or else Cash will kill the banker's wife. Terrorizing the wife, Cash tried to project the menace and tension of all the bad guys he'd seen in the movies, but his acting is over the top.

Before filming was finished, Cash got word that the picture was being shut down because the production company had run out of money. That might have been a blessing, considering how badly it was shaping up, but Cash was so thoroughly wedded to the idea of a Hollywood career that he agreed to put up some $20,000 of his own money to get the film back on track. But filming didn't resume until September because it took time to clear everyone's schedule. When the movie was finally wrapped, Cash looked eagerly to hitting the road again, including a few dates in Canada that November.

He was greeted in Canada by Saul Holiff, who had booked him a few times by now and was looking for a way to become permanently attached to a man he saw as a rising star. To impress Cash, Holiff handed him a list of the dates, the promotion he had done for each, and how ticket sales were doing in each city. Cash, who was becoming increasingly frustrated by all the time Carnall was spending partying and playing the horses, indeed took notice. It would be nice, he thought, to have someone with this guy's determination and drive watching out for him.

Holiff had operated a men's clothing store and a restaurant before he turned to putting on music shows. "He was all about marketing," says Holiff's son Jonathan. "He lived and breathed advertising and slogans. He loved puns to the point where, as a child, it would make me cringe because he would pun [on] everything."

The slogan for his clothing store: "If your clothes aren't becoming to you, you should be coming to us."

The puns and slogans shouldn't mislead anyone into thinking Holiff was a hack. He was a serious and sophisticated man who was given to nicely tailored clothes and fine wines. But he wasn't afraid of hard work or of taking chances. After making money in the clothing business, Holiff opened Sol's Square Boy, the first drive-in restaurant in London, Ontario, to feature electronic ordering at your car window. It served square rather than round hamburgers, and that led to the slogan "Four extra bites for your money." He started putting on concerts in town as a way to boost business at the restaurant. He'd book someone—Bill Haley and His Comets, the

Everly Brothers, the Ink Spots—and require them under the contract to swing by the drive-in after the show to sign autographs.

Holiff didn't know anything about pop music; he was a jazz and classical fan. To keep up with what was hot in pop, he went to a local record store every week to find out what the kids were listening to, and then he'd book that act. That's how he had originally heard of Cash. When Holilff realized he could make more money promoting shows than he could with the restaurant and clothing businesses, he began producing concerts all around the region. All the while, though, he was looking for a singer with whom he could team up and make a splash in the United States—and to Holiff's mind they would be a team. He saw himself as Colonel Tom Parker and eventually decided that Cash could be his Elvis Presley. Years later, in fact, he was able to finagle a Kentucky colonelcy so he wouldn't be outranked by Parker. His goal, simply put, was to make a million dollars. In the words of Jonathan Holiff, his father "had a big ego and he loved to dress in fine clothes. Whatever John got, Saul got the same thing, whether it was a [hotel] room or a limousine with a chauffeur."

By the time of this 1960 tour, Holiff had checked into every aspect of Cash's career, from his itineraries to his weekly position on the charts, and one thing struck him: How come this talented, charismatic recording artist was still toiling on the country music circuit? Why were he and the people around him thinking so small? Holiff broached the subject gently, telling Cash he was a folksinger like Burl Ives and Harry Belafonte, and he ought to be playing more sophisticated venues, such as Carnegie Hall in New York and the Hollywood Bowl in Los Angeles. Cash listened intently; those prestigious rooms sounded good to him. Holiff also wondered why Cash didn't add a drummer to his group to get a bigger sound. At the end of the tour, they agreed to keep in touch.

There had been talk of adding a drummer to the Tennessee Two ever since the Sun days, but Cash kept putting it off; he didn't want to go through the trouble of breaking in a new band member, and none of them wanted to spend the extra money. But Holiff's suggestion made Cash reconsider. After all, he was already using a drummer on some of his recordings, and it made sense to have the live show sound as close as possible to the records. He even began to think about adding some backup singers, but Grant convinced him that, too, was an unnecessary expense.

Cash finally decided to move ahead when he was booked in to the world-famous Steel Pier amusement park in Atlantic City for six days in mid-August. He had seen newsreel footage of the Pier, which proudly billed itself as the "Nation's Showplace," thanks to such flamboyant attractions as a horse that dove into a pool of water and a high-wire motorcyclist. Besides the circus-like attractions, the park included four theaters that could seat up to twelve thousand people. When Cash brought up the issue of a drummer again, Grant suggested W. S. "Fluke" Holland, a big teddy bear of a man, whom they both knew from Carl Perkins's band. Everyone got along with him, which was important when you consider all the hours they'd be spending together on the road. Grant also knew that Holland was available because he had left Perkins's band in 1959 as Carl's mounting drinking problems caused him to lose interest in touring. The drummer was just about to go back to his old job at an air-conditioning company when Grant called with an offer to play the Steel Pier.

Holland agreed, and everything went well. Holland pretty much knew the songs, and he just followed Grant's lead on the bass strings when he got lost. The four bonded quickly. Holland, too, was a born prankster. When Cash and Grant heard that Fabian, the pretty-boy singer from Philadelphia who was being promoted as the new Elvis, was going to follow them at the Steel Pier, the group decided to leave him a present. They got a couple of cartons of eggs, broke them open, and poured the contents all over the lighting rigs backstage, which meant there'd be a foul odor in the theater as soon as the lights were turned on for Fabian's show. That sealed the deal with Holland. On those early shows, Cash, out of loyalty to Perkins and Grant, introduced the threesome as the Tennessee Two Plus One. In time, however, they became the Tennessee Three.

II

Whereas he once tried desperately to keep his addiction private, Cash was now walking around with so many amphetamines in his pockets that they would sometimes spill out onto the floor. Gordon Terry, who'd given him his first pill three years earlier, did a double take one morning in the Midwest when he saw Cash take a handful out of his pocket and offer them to another musician.

Cash was feeling pressure from many areas. His film was a fiasco, surely shaking any lingering belief he had that movies were ever going to play a significant role in his career. As proud as he was of *Ride This Train,* he couldn't ignore the fact that he wasn't turning out hit singles. Though he didn't know it at the time, Columbia executives had brought up Cash's sales slump with Law and asked if anything was wrong. Law did his best to cover for Cash, saying there was some good stuff on the way.

On a personal level, Cash's relationship with Vivian was edging toward a crisis point, and he added to his torment by falling in love with women who were off-limits. First it had been Lorrie Collins. And now, he was slowly admitting to himself, he was thinking more and more about his best friend's wife.

Months before, Johnny Horton, who had been experiencing premonitions about his death, had asked Cash to watch over Billie Jean and their daughters in case anything happened to him. In turn, Horton agreed he'd take care of Vivian and the girls if anything happened to Cash.

Ever since, Cash had been plagued by thoughts of what he'd do if Billie Jean were suddenly free. Would he want to be with her? What about his marriage? He had always been taught that divorce was wrong, but there was divorce all around him in country music. Luther and his wife were breaking up, and he could see how much happier the guitarist was with the woman he was now dating. Didn't people have a right to be happy?

With the pressure coming in waves, Cash kept reaching into his pocket for more pills. He offered no excuses for them as his habit neared twenty a day, and the strain was starting to show in his gaunt face and in his frequently glazed eyes. The dramatic physical transformation in Cash is obvious even in the contrast between the scenes of *Five Minutes to Live* that were filmed in June and the ones filmed when shooting resumed in Los Angeles in September.

Cash was likely high on pills the night of September 29 in Beverly Hills when he picked up a container of propane gas and threw it in the trunk of his car without making sure the lid was secure. As Cash headed home at around 30 mph on a residential street, the container fell over and the gas leaked into the passenger compartment, where it suddenly exploded—perhaps from the spark of Cash's ever-present cigarette. Remarkably, Cash was able to leap from the rolling car and suffered only minor bruises and burns on his face and arms. The car continued on down the hill until it struck a lamppost. The fire was put out before the can of propane or the gas tank could catch fire. Cash declined medical attention at the scene.

Five Minutes to Live, meanwhile, was being hastily edited for release before the end of the year. To get advance reaction to the film, producers held a sneak preview that fall in Los Angeles. "They asked people to write their feelings about the film on cards on tables in the lobby," Lorrie Collins recalls. "Johnny didn't even want to read them. He knew the film was pretty bad. One card even read 'The movie should have been called *Five Minutes to Die.*' Johnny was devastated."

The filmmakers also screened the film again at the Melrose Theatre in Nashville during the annual country music DJ convention the weekend of November 4. Cash was looking forward to the convention because the country DJs had just voted *Ride This Train* and *Now, There Was a Song!* third and fifth, respectively, on the list of favorite country albums of the year. But the screening ruined any sense of celebration. Cash, who had come into town with Vivian, had to sit through another public humiliation. All the talk about his being the next Elvis, a movie star, evaporated before the final credits rolled. Not only was his acting horrible, but also he looked sick—or stoned.

The drying agent in amphetamines, especially when compounded by cigarettes and alcohol, led to bouts of chronic laryngitis, which could reduce Cash's voice to a near-whisper for a few hours or even weeks at a time. He was feeling the effects of the pills when he went into the studio in Nashville on Wednesday, November 2, to record the theme to *Five Minutes to Live,* so Law gave up after a few tries and rescheduled the session for the following Saturday. Cash promised to take it easy, but he seemed determined to party around the clock once the disc jockey convention started.

That was enough for Vivian to finally lash out at him, even though they were in public at the Hermitage Hotel. Hoping for some time together on Friday night, she screamed at Cash when he told her in the lobby he wanted to visit with some of his musician friends. Cash yelled back, then walked away.

It was well past the midnight hour when Cash returned to their room, and he fell into such a deep sleep that when the phone rang just after five a.m., he merely took the receiver off the hook and dropped it on the floor, Vivian recorded in her memoir. She quickly picked it up and heard the shocking news that Johnny Horton had been killed in a car crash, a head-on collision at 1:35 a.m. on Highway 79 near Cameron, Texas.

She sat on the bed for several minutes, trying to figure out how to break the news to John. Just then, there was a loud knock on the hotel room door. It was Dewey Phillips, the Memphis disc jockey. When Vivian opened the door, Phillips stepped into the room and shouted at the still sleeping Cash, "Hey, man, did you hear Johnny Horton died?"

As Cash slowly opened his eyes, Phillips shouted again, "He got killed by a drunk driver, man! He's dead!"

Cash sat straight up in bed, then put his head in his hands and let out a mournful cry: "Nooooooooooo! Nooooo!"

Cash tried to call Billie Jean, but he couldn't get through. Then he phoned Grant and said he wanted to buy a ticket on the next plane to Shreveport. But Grant reminded him that he had to record "Five Minutes to Live" that afternoon; he was already late in getting it to the film company. He also mentioned that Cash was supposed to perform at the Columbia Record convention luncheon and make his first appearance at the Grand Ole Opry in more than a year. Finally, Cash relented. He would do all that before going to Shreveport.

Vivian would later say that for Cash, Horton's death brought back "all the horror" of his brother Jack's death—and that he again wondered if he wasn't partially responsible. A week before the crash, Horton had called Cash's home in Los Angeles. Cash wasn't home, but Vivian gave the message to her husband. But he was "busy with this and that" and never returned the call.

In fact, Horton had tried to get hold of Cash several times in the days before his death, and Cash avoided the calls. That led to speculation among some in the Cash camp that Horton had discovered his friend and Billie Jean were having an affair—and that Cash didn't know what to say. But the more likely story was that Cash was going through a bad drug period and he didn't want Horton to find out.

After Horton's death, Cash anguished for months over whether he might have been able to help his friend if he had spoken to him on the phone. Others later told Cash that Horton, who had often talked to Cash about his premonitions, feared so strongly in the final week of his life that he was going to die in a car crash that he tried to cancel his appearance at the Skyline Club in Austin. But his manager, Tillman Franks, told him it was too late, that he would get a bad name among bookers if he started canceling at the last minute.

One reason for Horton's premonition about the Skyline, eerily enough, was that the club was also the last place Billie Jean's ex, Hank Williams, had played before dying of a heart attack in the backseat of his Cadillac. Hearing about that, Cash blamed himself even more strongly. He would have told his friend to go ahead and cancel the Skyline date.

As promised, Cash showed up at the Columbia Records luncheon, then the 4 p.m. recording session, and finally at the Opry, where he sang "Going to Memphis." Along the way, a *Nashville Tennessean* reporter asked him about Horton. "He was my best friend," Cash responded. "I worked with Johnny more than anybody else. I've tried to copy his personal habits, his clean living. Johnny was in constant communication with God. No matter what happened he was always smiling."

Before catching a plane to Shreveport, Cash asked his DJ buddy

Charlie Williams to get Vivian to the airport Sunday in time for her early morning flight to Los Angeles. But Williams spent the night partying and slept through his wake-up call, causing Vivian to take a later plane. Weeks later, Cash told Western that the flight Vivian had missed crashed into the Gulf of Mexico, killing everyone on board. He seemed genuinely shaken, Western remembered. Curious, Western tried to find out the details of the crash, but he discovered that the only crash in the Gulf of Mexico occurred a few days later—a plane from Miami. It was another of Johnny's stories, he realized, but as usual, there was a point to it. Cash felt as if his whole world was coming down around him.

III

As soon as Billie Jean saw Cash's cab pull up to the curb outside her house, she raced across the lawn with her three children. Together, the five stood in a long embrace—trying desperately to comfort one another. Billie Jean had been married to Horton for seven years, and Cash knew how much she loved him. At the same time, Billie Jean knew how much her husband meant to Cash.

While Billie Jean stayed in seclusion, Cash greeted the parade of neighbors and friends who stopped by the house to express their sympathies. He also arranged for the final rites to be held the following Tuesday at the Bossier City Rose-Neath Funeral Home chapel. He sat with Billie Jean and the children at the services and, at her request, read a passage from the Bible. David Kamich, a Columbia Records executive, thought Cash's reading and subsequent eulogy were deeply moving. But others found Cash embarrassing—rambling and disheveled. More than one asked themselves if he was drunk.

Some of Horton's friends also thought it was inappropriate for Cash to be staying at the house rather than checking in to a hotel. Eyebrows were raised at a reception at the house following the service when Cash and Billie Jean sat outside on a swing instead of joining the mourners in the living room. Later Billie Jean says she'd felt too fragile to mingle with the guests, and that all Cash was doing was trying to support her. "I don't know what I would have done if Johnny hadn't been with me," she says. "He was distraught, but he took care of me and my babies."

Through it all, they both knew there was another dynamic at work. While no words were spoken, Billie Jean had known for months that Cash was falling in love with her, and she could easily have fallen into his arms if she hadn't been married. "From the time I met Johnny Cash," she adds, "I wanted him, but I was married to a man that I loved and I had three kids and Johnny had three."

Now that Horton was gone, Johnny and Billie Jean finally confessed that they loved each other, but just what did that mean? They were both too distressed even to begin to think clearly. Gradually, over days, they began to talk about the future. Slowly, too, they became lovers. Cash told her how he had promised to watch out for her in case of Horton's death. He also suggested that he go with her to New York to look over Horton's royalty account at Columbia. There should be enough money in it for Billie Jean to live comfortably, because Horton had had three Top 10 pop hits in the last eighteen months, but Cash wanted to make sure; record companies could be notoriously slow in crediting royalties to an account. If she needed money until the royalties arrived, Cash said he'd transfer funds from his royalty account to provide for her.

The Louisiana Hayride wanted to hold a fund-raising memorial concert in Horton's honor in early December, but it was delayed until the seventeenth because Cash was scheduled to begin a brief tour of Germany on December 2. He wanted to take Billie Jean with him, but she needed to stay with her children. The break was good for both of them. They had to think about just where this relationship was heading.

On the German tour, Cash was pretty much out of it. The trigger this time was clearly the combination of Horton's death and his longing for Billie Jean. Cash tried to look at the relationship from every angle—his own, Billie Jean's, Johnny Horton's, Vivian's, the children's. He knew he was playing with fire again. Just as the Jerry Lee Lewis scandal should have warned him away from any relationship with Lorrie Collins, Eddie Fisher's leaving his wife, Debbie Reynolds, in favor of his best friend's widow, Elizabeth Taylor, led to a backlash among fans that pretty much derailed Fisher's singing career. Cash's fans, too, could be repelled if he decided to leave Vivian for Billie Jean. But he was too consumed by the prospect of a future with Billie Jean to worry about what such a decision would mean to his fans.

At one of the last stops on the tour, Cash noticed Luther Perkins sitting in the hotel lobby writing what Cash thought was a letter.

"Writing to Margie?" Cash asked.

Luther had met Margie Higgins at a taping of the Jimmy Dean TV show in Washington, D.C., in 1957, when he was still married to Bertie. It was the start of a relationship that meant so much to Perkins that he would drive hundreds of miles between tours to see her. After months of separation, Luther was now looking forward to marrying Margie.

"I'm writing her a song," Perkins replied with a big smile. It caught Cash off guard because he had never known Perkins to write a song.

"Let me take a look at it," Cash said. Perkins handed him the sheet of paper, and Cash was touched by the sweetness of the words. He told Perkins it was a beautiful song.

Cash thought about Luther and Margie a lot in the following days, searching their story for an answer to his own feelings about Billie Jean. On the flight back to the United States, Cash told himself he was going to ask Billie Jean to marry him.

Besides Cash, the lineup for the Horton memorial show at the Municipal Auditorium in Shreveport included Marty Robbins, Sheb Wooley, Johnny Western, and Gordon Terry. Afterward, Billie Jean wrote a letter to Cash, thanking him for putting on the show.

Billie Jean felt she had a soul mate in Cash, but she also saw some warning signs, especially the amphetamines.

"There was a little bit of drugs before, I think, but when Johnny Horton died, that put him over the top," she says. "I lived with Hank Williams, the king of the dope, and I was afraid Johnny was going to destroy himself if he didn't get off those pills."

Their time in New York made her feel like a princess. Cash

took her to Broadway shows, bought her a trunkful of clothes and other gifts. His affection made her forget momentarily her concerns about his drug use.

When Cash asked her to marry him, she wanted to say yes, but she was still confused. She thought about her children, and it worried her that Cash was willing to walk away from his own. She also felt she needed some time; it was so soon after Johnny Horton's death. Cash told her he understood and to take all the time she needed.

It wasn't an easy period for either of them.

When Cash sang "I Walk the Line" each night onstage, he was reminded of his deep conflict. He didn't want to hurt Vivian or, especially, the girls, but he thought about Billie Jean constantly. The band members knew something was going on, but they didn't ask.

"Because of all the pills, we never knew from one day to the next how he would react," says Western. "After what I told him he should do about Lorrie Collins, maybe he didn't want to confide in me again about something that serious. If he had asked, I would have told him the same thing: 'John, you have to ride away.'"

Early in the new year, Cash got some surprising news. During his trip home over the holidays, Vivian had gotten pregnant again. How thrilling that had always sounded in the past. This time, though, it left him even more confused. It seemed that the only escape was in pills.

Anxious, he began to press Billie Jean for an answer, perhaps pushing too hard. In time, Billie Jean might have accepted the proposal, but she wasn't ready. Unable to stall any longer, she told him no.

Billie Jean tried to break the news gently. She explained it was too soon after Johnny Horton's death, and she also mentioned, almost in passing, that she didn't want to be tied down because she wanted to pursue a career in music herself. Cash told her he'd love for her to have a career; they could even tour together.

What she didn't reveal were the real reasons: the drugs and his willingness to leave his family.

Cash wanted to be understanding. He told her to take more time.

He called her almost daily for weeks, but he finally gave up and became bitter. He was fixated on the notion that the only reason she turned him down was that she wanted to be a singer, and he channeled that hurt into a song. To his mind, she was now the villain. Without any reference to Billie Jean, "Sing It Pretty, Sue" would appear on an album in 1962.

> *So you gave up all between us for a glamorous career*
> *And with all your talent you should be the big star of the year*
> *Then you'll be public property so I release my claim to you*
> *Go on and give 'em all you've got, sing it pretty, Sue.*

Cash was also depressed in the early months of 1961 by the *Five Minutes to Live* disaster. Carnall continued to look high and low for more roles, but he knew the word-of-mouth on the first film was going to make that difficult. Predictably, reviews were brutal, especially about the acting.

Even before *Five Minutes to Live* hit the theaters (usually as the bottom half of a drive-in double bill), Carnall started doing damage control. In May he told *Los Angeles Times* film critic and columnist Philip K. Scheuer that Cash's film dream had just come true: he'd acquired the movie rights to the story of Jimmie Rodgers's life from Rodgers's widow. This was a film he really cared about.

Given all the turmoil, Cash felt a desperate need for a new start. For one thing, he wanted to get out of Los Angeles—but not back to Tennessee. He liked the independence of living in California rather than in the tight Nashville music community. He thought immediately of the quiet, rural open spaces of the Ojai area. He was still hoping his brother Roy and his wife would move there. Meanwhile, Cash told a local building contractor, Curly Lewis, that he was interested in finding a parcel of land for himself.

Lewis found the perfect property for a new house in Casitas Springs, less than five miles from the trailer park. The eleven-acre site was on the side of a hill (Cash often described it as a mountain) with no neighbors above and valleys on either side. With land for crops and horses, this was about as rural and isolated as you could get and still be only an hour outside Los Angeles.

Casitas Springs was founded in the 1940s as a bedroom community to serve the nearby oil field workers. By 1961, the collection of
modest homes, the handful of mom and pop shops, and a couple of
bars might have struck the average visitor as pretty trailer park–like
itself, and that downscale setting must have been part of its appeal
to Cash.

For Cash, who was bruised and battered emotionally, Casitas
Springs was a way to say good-bye to Hollywood and get back to his
roots. Lewis, who became a close friend to Cash, knew just what
John wanted. During one of their visits to the site, Lewis said, "Here
at the end of Tobacco Road, you get heaven."

In mid-June, Cash did a concert in San Antonio and told a
reporter for the *San Antonio Light,* which closely monitored the
Cashes' doings because of Vivian's hometown connection, that he
was building a new home on a site he had just purchased. He said
one reason for the move was that the L.A. smog was bad for his
throat and sinuses, but the main reason was that he wanted the isolation and what he felt was the freedom of rural life. "In the country,
it's more peaceful and you have more room."

Working with Lewis, Cash designed his dream house, a sprawl-
ing, five-thousand-square-foot single-story ranch-style structure
with four bedrooms, including a large master bedroom with the
ceiling painted black with gold sparkles to resemble the sky at
night. In its isolated mountain setting, the house was a private retreat from the rest of the world.

Even Vivian got caught up in her husband's enthusiasm, especially when he became so excited walking around the property with
Lewis that he fell to the ground and smiled as he stretched out and
told the contractor, "I want the master bathtub this big and right
here." Always trying to put a positive spin on things, she thought
the baby and the house would encourage her husband to settle
down and recommit himself to the marriage; no more late-night
partying, no more drinking, no more pills, no more rumors of other
women. Maybe, she told herself, the worst was over.

CHAPTER 11

CASITAS SPRINGS AND SAUL HOLIFF

I

GIVEN CASH'S DESIRE FOR a new start, it was only a matter of time before he cut his ties to Carnall. The rise and fall of that relationship, in fact, was mirrored by the ups and downs of a thoroughbred horse they had bought with high hopes in 1959. They had pictured themselves rooting Walk the Line to victory at glamorous Santa Anita, Hollywood Park, or Del Mar, then stepping into the winner's circle for photos and, not least of all, cashing those $100 win tickets. But Walk the Line encountered physical problems almost immediately, bringing unexpected vet bills. By the time the horse was finally cleared to run in late 1960, he showed little speed or spirit in morning workouts.

The horse's handlers advised Carnall and Cash they'd just be wasting their money to race him at one of the Southern California tracks; there was no way he would be even remotely competitive. Not one to give up easily, Carnall suggested running him across the border at the Agua Caliente track in Tijuana, where the caliber of horses was much lower. Gamely, Cash agreed to ship the horse south; the purses would be lower, but still it'd be fun to stand in the winner's circle.

Carnall and Cash led a large party of friends, including their wives, to Caliente on November 26, during Cash's brief time at home before flying to Germany. Wearing the silks of Cash-Carnall, Walk the Line was entered in a $2,500 claiming race that was limited to horses that had never won—which wasn't exactly the bottom of the barrel at Caliente, but close enough to see it.

Bettors thought so little of Walk the Line that he went off at 10–1 odds in the twelve-horse field. And they were right. The *Racing Form*'s summary of the race said it all: "Walk the Line was no threat."

Hoping the race was a fluke, Carnall entered Walk the Line in another claiming race at Caliente two weeks later, and this time there was so little betting interest that he went off at a staggering 72–1. Predictably, Walk the Line finished far back. The horse raced fourteen times in 1961, all in Mexico, and the closest he came to winning was a second-place finish on May 5 in a $1,000 claiming-maiden race. His payoff that day was just $215. The horse was a money pit.

Cash, meanwhile, was finding Carnall increasingly difficult to track down, and he became increasingly frustrated with their relationship. He knew that Carnall was either at the track or out partying—all of which made that Saul Holiff guy look even more attractive.

On May 10, 1961, Cash started another Canadian tour, and Holiff was again by his side—complete with facts and figures about the tour and more talk about how Cash wasn't maximizing his potential. Holiff's professionalism made Cash more furious every time he was unable to reach Carnall in Los Angeles. The end came eight days later before a show at a hockey rink in North Bay, Ontario.

"I stood right next to Johnny when he fired Stew over the telephone," Western remembers. "Johnny had been trying to get him all day because of some important contract negotiation, but Stew was at the racetrack. When we got to the show, Johnny found a pay phone backstage and he called Stew again. This time he reached him. He said, 'Stew, I've done this for the last time. You're fired.' Stew put Lorrie on the phone, hoping she could save his job, but Johnny said, 'Lorrie, I love you, kid, but this is the end. There's nothing you can say or do. Stew is finished as of right this minute.' And Johnny hung up. It was over."

Stepping in quickly, Holiff went to Columbia Records in New York as Cash's representative to urge the executives to treat Cash more like a pop act, knowing the label spent far, far more on promoting its pop acts than its country ones. Columbia staffers remember that Holiff was loud and insistent. He acted as if Cash was the biggest act on the label, when in fact the Columbia brass—from Goddard Lieberson on down—wondered if they should even resign him when his contract expired. Holiff then flew to the Far East to help promote an October USO tour he had booked for Cash.

To further his growing relationship with Holiff, Cash sent him a letter containing what he called "top secret" information that would give Holiff an edge in booking two other acts that Carnall represented, Rose Maddox and Bob Luman.

"Hint #1," Cash wrote.

"I never paid Rose Maddox more than $150 per day and usually $125 per day and she was constantly available.

"Hint #2.

"Bob Luman has never worked a tour with anyone but me and we paid him $150 to $200 per day."

Finally, he warned Holiff, "Stew will try to 'snow' you."

Not ready to commit fully to a new management pact, however, Cash started scheduling his own dates. Because of his aversion to confrontation, it was a role for which he was ill equipped; he tended to accept whatever offer was given him, regardless of how low. When Western walked into Cash's office one day in Los Angeles, he found him selling the whole show—including himself, the Tennessee Three, Gordon Terry, Rose Maddox, and Western—to a promoter for $1,250, which was less than Cash should have been getting for himself and the Tennessee Three alone.

Western wrote a blunt, pleading letter to Holiff.

"I hope on the next trip that you can reach some sort of management thing with Johnny as he is wandering in a fog, so to speak, now," the July 1 letter read. "He is trying to keep his business affairs together and is also booking himself, neither of which is even a little bit successful. He is not a good businessman nor should he be on the phone when the bookers call for a Cash show. He is in serious need of expert advice on what to record and what to release,

Saul, and if there was ever a big star on the brink of disaster, it's Johnny right now unless he has some qualified help immediately."

In addition to his stressing the need for management help, Western's plea about Cash also needing advice on what to record and what to release underscored the feeling within the Cash camp that John needed stronger direction than Don Law was providing—and Holiff got the point. Over the coming months, Holiff would tell both Cash and Columbia executives that not only did Cash need bigger play, but also he needed a new producer.

II

Marshall Grant pored over music sales charts the way Carnall devoured the *Racing Form.* Back when Cash was hot, the bass player loved to check out all the various charts—the pop album chart, the pop singles chart, the EP chart, the country best-seller list, the regional charts—and he delighted every time he found Cash's name. During the early months of 1961, however, Grant was resigned to not seeing Cash on any chart. There hadn't been a Columbia album or single on the country singles charts since the previous October.

The reason was Cash himself. "With the drugs and his personal problems, we were having a hard time getting him into the studio," said Grant. "Even when Law would schedule a session, we never knew if he'd show up or what condition he'd be in."

All of this caused considerable soul-searching among everyone except Cash. Johnny Western felt that Cash was pretty much oblivious to his declining condition; he kept seeing fans packing the venues and cheering everything he did. "I don't think he was alarmed," Western says. "He was being his own creative person. When something didn't sell, it gave him an excuse to go ahead in another direction."

Western, however, was also alarmed about Cash's drift. He kept in touch with disc jockeys and promoters around the country, and the feedback about Cash's singles was increasingly negative. "When the amphetamines started to cause problems with his voice, the DJs noticed," Western says. "Smokey Smith, who was on the radio in

Des Moines, was really disappointed by Johnny's performance on 'The Girl from Saskatoon' and 'Locomotive Man.' He told me, 'I want you to tell Johnny Cash that if he ever makes another record as bad as those two, don't even send it to me because I'm not going to play it.' And Smokey was one of Johnny's biggest fans.

"It put me in a terrible position. I couldn't go to Johnny and tell him the songs were okay but his voice was awful. He didn't want to hear it. He didn't think anything was wrong. He kept telling himself, 'I'm doing what I want to do and one of the records is going to click and the sales will be there.' It was a tough time. Gordon Terry and I used to room together, and we'd say all the time that we can't talk to Johnny anymore about the music, because you never knew what mood he was going to be in."

To help accommodate Cash's moods and vocal problems, Law booked a studio at Radio Recorders in Los Angeles for an entire week in late February instead of just the usual one day, hoping John would show up at some point in working shape. Before flying to California, Law spoke with Cash by phone, eager for some hint about what he wanted to record. Looking for any sign of a turn-around, Law was encouraged when Cash said he had two new songs—an Irish ballad called "Forty Shades of Green," which he'd written after seeing the Irish countryside during a brief visit there, and "The Big Battle," a recitation-type song that he claimed was one of the best things he had ever done. Cash was even thinking that the song, which was set in Civil War times, could become part of another concept album.

Cash felt especially good about "The Big Battle." Even when he could find the time and the focus amid everything going on with Billie Jean, the drugs, and the constant touring, he worried that he had fallen into the trap of trying to write jukebox singles. Everything he wrote was starting to sound like something he had heard on jukeboxes or the radio. He told himself there was no meaning in most of what he was writing. He wanted to get back to songs that lifted people—the kinds of songs that had drawn people to him in the first place.

To regain his purpose as a writer, he searched through a stack of poems and story ideas he had written down over the years, looking for anything that "said something" the way "I Walk the Line" and "Five Feet High and Rising" had. He found the outline of a story about the casualties of war. Despite its Civil War ties, the story could apply to any military battle. The original impulse came from the many hours he'd spent in the Air Force watching all the young airmen at the base and thinking of how many millions of men like them had been sent into battle over the centuries. He also remembered all the stories he had read about how the horrors of war live on, both in the emotional scars suffered by the survivors and in the pain of dead men's loved ones. About the song, he later said, "The big battle comes after the killing...in the conscience, in the hearts and grief of the people that suffered the loss." He felt as deeply about it as about anything he had ever written.

He didn't know if it would be a hit, but he wanted it to be his next single. That was the kind of music he wanted to stake his career on. "The Big Battle" and *Ride This Train* would be standards by which he would measure his work for years.

In the phone conversation with Law, Cash mentioned another idea that gave the producer pause. Even though Cash had just done a gospel album, he wanted to record another one—a collection of old-time gospel numbers. What he didn't tell Law, however, was that a gospel album had an additional appeal to him: it would help ease the pressure to write new material. Rather than point out the urgency of building sales, Law again—for good or ill—left the decision in Cash's hands. First they'd record "Forty Shades of Green" and "The Big Battle."

Cash's enthusiasm for the two songs gave Law hope that he would show up in good voice for the February sessions at Radio Recorders. To capture the lush feel that Cash wanted for "Forty Shades of Green," Law assembled a large cast of singers and musicians—including a string section—for the session. Just before the session was to start at eight p.m., however, Law got a phone call from Vivian saying that Cash had a 103-degree temperature and couldn't make it that first night. Rather than send all the musicians home, Law went ahead and recorded "Forty Shades of Green" and "The Big Battle" with Johnny Western doing the vocals. Law could then have Cash record the vocals on both songs later and substitute

Cash's vocals for Western's. This was a common practice for salvaging part of a session.

When Cash laid down the vocals on the songs a month later in Los Angeles, he brought up another album idea to Law. He was still trying to outline what he was calling his new concept albums—collections of prison and battlefield songs. But this was something else, and it too wasn't dependent on new Cash songs. The album would be called *The Sound of Sun* and would be built around songs by other writers as well as his own older material. Ever since he left Sun, Cash had been hearing from his fans and even other musicians that they preferred those records to the Columbia ones. They weren't talking about the songs, Cash stressed to Law, but the *sound* of the stark, echo-driven Sun studio.

Law had tried to capture that sound at the Bradley recording facility in Nashville, but its ambience lacked Sun's crucial dynamics. Cash suggested moving from the larger, better-known Studio A at Bradley, where they had worked until that point, to the smaller Studio B to see if it might better replicate the desired sound. As usual, Law nodded. He booked Studio B for the last week in April, hoping to record both the gospel album and the Sun project.

Perhaps to remind everyone of the feel he wanted, Cash kicked things off by playing a few of his early Sun releases. He then played various songs by other artists that he had enjoyed over the years. When recording for the album resumed on July 19, Cash included a couple of his own songs, "Play It Pretty, Sue" and "Tennessee Flat-Top Box." The latter was reminiscent of the spirit of "Luther Plays the Boogie." Much like Chuck Berry's "Johnny B. Goode," it was the story of a boy who played the guitar so pretty that people would come from all around just to hear him.

A third song he introduced in that session was an old blues-folk song, "Delia's Gone," which Johnny Western had recorded two years earlier. The story was based on the murder of a fourteen-year-old African American girl, Delia Green, on Christmas Eve 1900 in Savannah, Georgia, but the accounts took many different forms in song over the years, most of them told from the killer's point of view. There was a placid, sing-along feel to Western's version and a Pat Boone pop treatment in 1960, but Cash wanted a more threatening song in keeping with the line from Jimmie Rodgers— *I'm gonna shoot poor Thelma, / Just to see her jump and fall*—that had inspired Cash's similar striking line in "Folsom Prison Blues." In his hands, the folk tune became something immediate and menacing. Cash liked the way this album was shaping up.

III

Days after the birth of their fourth daughter, Tara, on August 24, 1961, the Cashes moved into their new home on Nye Road in Casitas Springs, and the neighbors turned out to welcome the famous new resident. One of the well-wishers, who arrived carrying a bouquet of flowers, was the Reverend Floyd Gressett, pastor of the Avenue Community Church in Ventura. Despite his continued longing for Billie Jean, Cash hoped that this move to the country could be a turning point with Vivian.

Within weeks, however, he was back on the road, and the tour got off to a unsettling start on September 21 in Boston. Rose Maddox, who had been the featured female singer with the group for much of the year, was badly shaken when the landing gear on her plane malfunctioned on the approach to Logan Airport that day, causing the plane to slide into the waters of Boston Harbor. The accident made Cash feel protective toward Maddox, who was four years older and married. To help her overcome her sudden fear of flying, Cash encouraged her to fly with him to shows rather than ride in the car with the guys. He also stepped in when she complained that promoters were making passes at her. She would soon leave the tour, partly because Cash was having to reschedule so many shows on account of his drug problems; the cancellations played havoc with her other concert obligations.

Around this time, Cash decided to name Holiff his manager. Cash wrote notes on a yellow legal pad, outlining all the things he expected Holiff to do for him. He wanted a disciplined operation this time, not a repeat of the part-time job, part-time party approach of the Carnall years. But he ended up just giving the pages to Holiff and they sealed the deal with a handshake. Though he would always maintain a Canadian residence, Holiff moved to California to open an office for Cash, and he traveled with him on tour.

For the first time since Sam Phillips, Cash felt he was in good hands. Holiff promised Cash he'd be onstage at Carnegie Hall and the Hollywood Bowl within a year. To celebrate the signing, Cash took Holiff to Columbia Records and introduced him as his new manager. The introduction caught much of the staff by surprise; the fast-talking Canadian had raised such a fuss during his New York visit in May that people had assumed for months that he already had the job.

Another topic among Columbia staffers was how strange Cash acted during his visit. "He'd come into an office and just keep walking around the room," one label executive told Marshall Grant. "He would mumble something and then keep pacing while you answered, even going out into the hall and returning and ask something else."

During the tour, Cash spent a week in the cold of Newfoundland and Nova Scotia, doing shows as well as taking time off to hunt moose with a reporter and a photographer who were going to do a spread on the hunt for *Field and Stream* magazine. To make a party out of it, John invited Johnny Western to go along. He was already in Newfoundland when he got a frantic phone call from Vivian. She told him snakes were slithering around the yard and fans were knocking on the door at all hours wanting to see him. She begged him to come home. Cash, who had a lifelong fear of snakes himself, flew back to California, where he tried to calm his wife's fears. He'd have someone come in and get rid of the snakes, he promised, and he'd put up a "Private Property" sign to help discourage fans from coming up the driveway. The next day, he headed back to the moose hunt.

The erratic behavior continued. While in Nashville a month later—November 15, 1961—he and Glenn Douglas Tubb, one of the writers of "Home of the Blues," were arrested one morning on a drunkenness charge and spent four hours in jail before being released on bond. Cash identified himself on the police blotter as an "actor." Two weeks later in California, Cash made the news again when Ventura police clocked him going 90 mph on the Ojai

Freeway at one a.m. They stopped him after a six-mile chase. He explained to the officers, "I just wanted to find out if I could still outrun a police car." He was cited for speeding and driving without a driver's license in his possession.

Though Cash had gone to great lengths to hide his increasingly unruly lifestyle from his parents, Carrie Cash had begun to notice his drawn appearance and strange, restless behavior even before the latest news reports. Vivian, too, had been turning to her mother-in-law, hoping she could help persuade her son to spend more time with his family and to take better care of himself. As Roy Cash Jr. recalls, "I can distinctly remember my grandmother at the trailer park wondering out loud if J.R. was 'becoming a dope addict.'"

It was during this period that Holiff got a vivid demonstration of Cash's unstable behavior. During an engagement at the Cave supper club in Vancouver, Cash learned that Billie Jean Horton, who had followed up on pursuing a singing career, was appearing in town as part of a tour featuring Wanda Jackson and Buck Owens. To stretch the coincidence even further, Cash and Horton ended up staying at the same hotel.

Billie Jean says that Cash showed up at her concert, wanting to talk to her again about a future together. But any slim chance that she might change her mind about marrying him was ruined when Cash arrived at the hotel later that night and pounded loudly on her door, clearly under the influence of drugs. Furious at yet another rejection, he later stormed out of her room and smashed every crystal chandelier in the hallway. After being called by the hotel manager, Holiff agreed to pay for the damage, but it wasn't enough to keep Cash from being banned from the hotel.

Though Holiff was absolutely convinced that Cash could be a far bigger star, drug problems and all, it was hard to find much outside support for that belief. Expectations in the industry had fallen to such an extent that Cash's new single—"Tennessee Flat-Top Box"—wasn't even one of the twelve "spotlight" singles in *Billboard* magazine when it was released in the late fall.

In talking to Columbia about Cash's disappointing figures, Holiff continued to blame the label for inadequate promotion. His persistent message: You need to market Cash as a pop act, not just a country one. The label's equally consistent response: The promotion staff has limited time and money, and it has to focus its attention on records that are showing the most pop sales potential. Give us a record with that potential and we'll be glad to get behind it.

To make things worse for Holiff, Cash was losing career momentum even in the country field. In *Billboard*'s annual poll of country DJs, Cash had fallen from fourth most popular performer in 1960 to a tie for tenth in 1961, and he wasn't represented at all on the lists of favorite albums or single records. Cash was especially discouraged when he didn't even make the list of favorite songwriters.

On the tour front, Holiff now had to replace Rose Maddox, and he was delighted to learn that Patsy Cline had some open dates. Cline had two of the most memorable country hits that year in "Crazy" and "She's Got You," which made her a powerful addition to the Cash cast. Cline was as popular backstage as she was with the audience—a real tomboy who fit in well with all the male musicians. "She was a great road buddy," Johnny Western says. "She loved hearing jokes and loved telling them. She had the biggest laugh in the world."

Unfortunately, Cline's deal was just for the month of January, and Holiff knew that she would eventually want to headline her own shows, so he started searching for another female singer. Partly because she charged less than Cline, Holiff came up with a new name: June Carter.

Like everybody his age who loved country music, Cash grew up listening to the Carter Family's music. One of the most fascinating chapters in all of pop music, the Carter Family—Alvin Pleasant Delaney Carter, his wife, Sara, and his brother's wife, Maybelle, who was Sara's cousin—emerged from the isolated foothills of Clinch Mountain in Virginia to help lay much of the foundation of commercial country music.

The Carters not only changed the emphasis from old-time instrumentals to smooth intimate vocals, but also brought a certain class and style to what had been wild, untamed country music, opening the door to a much wider audience. Sara sang lead vocals and played autoharp, while Maybelle sang harmony and chiefly played the guitar. Maybelle had a distinctive style—playing the melody lines with her thumb while scratching out the rhythm with her fingers—which gave the group a softer, more contemporary sound than the traditional banjo or fiddle accompaniment. A.P. sang backup vocals and sometimes took over the lead.

Most important, the Carter Family showcased, on records and radio shows, hundreds of mostly British and Appalachian folk songs that A.P. had learned on his travels throughout the region while looking for work or just rambling about. Though he didn't write such classics as "Keep on the Sunny Side," "Wildwood Flower," and "Will the Circle Be Unbroken," Carter arranged and popularized them. Altogether, the Carters' impact on the evolution of country music in the first half of the twentieth century was rivaled only by that of Cash's main hero, Jimmie Rodgers.

A. P. Carter was the leader of the trio. Born in 1891 in Virginia in an area then known as Poor Valley, Carter worked at various jobs, from sawmills to construction sites. For years, music was just a personal passion. He and Sara and Maybelle would play and sing at gatherings around Maces Springs, the valley town in which they all lived. Slowly, he began thinking about trying to make some money with the trio. He was already in his late thirties in the summer of 1927 when he took a skeptical Sara and Maybelle to Bristol, Tennessee, to audition for Ralph Peer, hoping to get a recording contract with the Victor Company. He wasn't alone at Peer's door. When a newspaper article reported that acts could make $200 a day plus royalties cutting records with Peer, there was a rush of hopeful musicians and singers from around the region.

The Carters stood out, though, because Peer, above all things, wanted record makers who performed their own material. His reasoning was twofold. In most cases, a good new song had more commercial potential than another version of a song that had already been a hit. In addition, new songs meant that Peer could assign copyright in the material to his publishing company, which meant more money for him. An old traditional song was just as valuable if it was in the public domain because Peer could still get publishing rights. Peer liked the Carters' sound and the prospect of all those great public domain songs that A.P. had collected. The Carters were soon in New York making a record—and on their way to making country music history.

All Cash knew of the Carter story was that as a boy he had loved the music, and he still held the Carter Family in great esteem. Cash also knew that June was Maybelle's daughter and that she sang professionally with her mother and her sisters. Cash had first met her during an Opry appearance in 1956, and there is a famous photo with him down on one knee as if proposing to her. They both later claimed he'd told June then that he was going to marry her someday, though no one around Cash believed that the story was anything more than another one of his manufactured tales. In 1956 his "I Walk the Line" was riding the charts, and he was still deeply in love with Vivian.

Though Cash and Carter had met from time to time on the country circuit, they were pretty much strangers when Holiff arranged for her to join the show for a December 9 date at the Big D Jamboree, which was Dallas's equivalent of the Louisiana Hayride. It was in essence a tryout to see how they would get along. Cash had been playing the Jamboree since 1955, and the audiences had always been enthusiastic. Cash was looking forward to seeing Carter, but he arrived late at the barnlike Sportatorium arena—its main attraction each week was professional wrestling matches—and didn't see her before he had to go onstage for the first of two shows.

At the intermission, June, who was then married to her second husband, Edwin "Rip" Nix, looked for Cash, but she couldn't find him. So she tracked down Grant. "Hey, big buddy, someone told me I needed to talk to you about a little problem I've got," she said in the cornball character of her stage persona. "I'm in Oklahoma City tomorrow afternoon with y'all and I need a ride. I ain't got no ride up there and I was wondering if I could ride with you."

Knowing that Cash, Perkins, Western, Terry, and he were already going to be in the car, Grant said he didn't think he could squeeze anyone else in.

"Well, I'll sit on somebody's lap," she replied perkily.

Fair enough, Grant said, as long as Cash approved.

When Grant relayed Carter's request, Cash said no problem—adding with a sly grin, "As long as mine is the lap she sits on."

The trip proved especially cozy because they ran into sleet and snow, causing the Oklahoma City show to be canceled. June made a big impression on Cash. He told the other guys in the group that she was off-limits to them, the inference being that he had his eye on her.

For a man with a bruised ego after the Billie Jean affair, a still tense home life, and a continuing slide in record sales, June Carter came along at just the right time. She was fun, she was flirtatious, she made Cash feel special, and, crucially, she was part of the history of country music. June Carter and the Carter Family were "authentic." They had even recorded with Jimmie Rodgers. For June, there was a need to reestablish her solo career. She had recently signed a contract, but it was with tiny Liberty Records in Los Angeles, a sign that none of the country labels in Nashville saw any potential in her. Within two months, she was added permanently to the Cash touring show. It wouldn't be long before John, now twenty-nine, and June, thirty-two, would look across the stage at each other and ask themselves if this could be the one.

CHAPTER 12

JUNE CARTER

I

VALERIE JUNE CARTER was known to the people of Poor Valley as Daddy's girl. Ezra "Eck" Carter, a fascinating character himself, taught her to be driven, independent, and resilient. One of her early memories was of the time she jumped on the back of his Harley-Davidson and held on for dear life as he raced the country roads. Eck, who was known to have a bit of a wild streak, had crashed through many fences and skidded off roads while taking the turns too fast in a car or on his bike. And sure enough, Eck drove the Harley into a ditch on this day with June, hurling her into a nearby cornfield. Undaunted, the youngster jumped back on the bike and the pair continued their journey. She was five.

Another trait that Eck passed along was a thirst for the world outside the remote valley in southwest Virginia. As a boy, he loved nothing better than going to the general store and waiting for the train to roll into town. On some days the train wouldn't even stop because there was no one who wanted to get on or off in tiny Maces Springs, but even then he counted on the train slowing so that someone could throw off the mail sack. From then on, Eck's dream was to ride that train and to handle the mail—and the industrious young man eventually got that very job.

As a railroad mail clerk, Eck was the envy of Maces Springs while still only in his twenties, not just because he made more money than anyone else, but because he would return home with all sorts of little treasures, including phonograph records and books, both of which were rare in the valley. Eck loved to read: history, religion, and especially technical manuals that explained how things worked, whether it was cars or electrical current. He also enjoyed building things, particularly projects that benefited his neighbors. Eck's most ambitious undertaking was bringing electrical power to the region. He started by building a homemade generator to provide current for his own house; then he dammed up the local Holston River to increase the unit's power so that he could share the electricity with others. The Appalachian Power Company eventually bought the system from him.

All of this made Ezra Carter heroic in young June's eyes—even with his occasional drinking problems—and she admired her mother for marrying him. Indeed, one lesson June learned from her mother was this: Once you find the right man, go after him.

Maybelle Addington was sixteen in December of 1925 when she came to Maces Springs from a neighboring valley to sing and play guitar with Sara and A.P. in a special musical program at the school. It was there that she met A.P.'s brother Ezra, and she thought he was the most beautiful man she had ever seen. Maybelle soon said good-bye to her boyfriend; Ezra, who was twenty-seven, just as quickly broke his engagement with a local schoolteacher. The couple was married three months later.

By the time June, the second of three daughters, was born on June 23, 1929, the Carter Family trio was on its way to becoming a country music institution. A.P., Sara, and Maybelle had recorded many of their most celebrated tunes for the Victor Recording Company, but only A.P. thought this could really lead somewhere. On June's birth certificate, Maybelle listed her occupation as "homemaker," not "recording artist." Yet the record deal was bringing in money. At a historic session in Camden, New Jersey, in early May 1928, they recorded twelve songs, including what would become one of their signature tunes, "Wildwood Flower." They were paid $600, enough money for A.P. and Sara to move to a much fancier home, but he chose to remain in Bristol, in his beloved valley.

As the Carters' popularity grew, A.P. spent more and more time traveling through the region, searching for new songs and booking shows for the group, though it was a constant struggle to get Sara to go on the road. In a parallel to the distance between Johnny Cash and Vivian, A.P.'s obsession with music ultimately drove the couple apart. As the friction increased, Sara turned to A.P.'s cousin Coy Bays for comfort and, as it turned out, love. But the affair was short-lived. Bays moved to New Mexico early in 1933 with relatives who were looking both for better income opportunities and for a way to put an end to the scandalous affair. Whether because she was ashamed or because she could no longer stand living with her husband, Sara moved to the neighboring Rich Valley, where she had been raised. In 1936 she filed for divorce, and the decree was granted on October 15. But even that didn't break up the Carter Family trio. With A.P. leading the way, the group continued to make occasional records. For one thing, they all needed the money.

Two years later, just when it didn't look as if even A.P.'s determination could keep the Carter Family together, the trio was offered—out of the blue—its own radio show on XERA near Del Rio, Texas. Boasting the most powerful signal of any station in North America (more than half a million watts), XERA evaded U.S. radio restrictions (normally limiting stations to fifty thousand watts) by planting its transmitter across the border in Mexico. Under the six-month deal, the Carters would each be paid $75 a week. It was enough for Eck to give up his job with the railroad and move with Maybelle and their youngest daughter, five-year-old Anita, to Texas. June, age nine, and Helen, eleven, remained in Maces Springs with Maybelle's mother so they wouldn't have to change schools. On XERA, the Carters' music could be heard on virtually any radio in America, including the one in the Cash home in Dyess. According to reports at the time, XERA's signal was so strong that ranchers could listen to the station via their wire fences.

The Carter Family owed their sudden good fortune to the clever marketing and medical hocus-pocus of John R. Brinkley. He was a Kansas doctor who was making millions using the airways to advertise products and medical procedures that promised to cure a variety of ills, the most outlandish of which was transplanting goat glands into humans, supposedly to cure a lack of sexual prowess. He leased time on XERA and decided to hire the Carter Family because country music singers had proved effective in reaching potential customers. XERA had showcased so many country stars, including Gene Autry, Jimmie Rodgers, and Patsy Montana, that Del Rio picked up the nickname "the hillbilly Hollywood."

Back home in Maces Springs, June and Helen missed their parents and Anita, but at least they could hear their mama's voice on XERA every morning and night. They were surprised one evening in February to hear Aunt Sara suddenly speak up between songs, something they couldn't remember her doing before. She dedicated one of the Carters' most popular love songs, "I'm Thinking Tonight of My Blue Eyes," to her former lover, Coy Bays, whom she hadn't seen in six years.

June was too young to understand the significance of the dedication, but she would later point to the story of Sara and Coy as reaffirming her mother's lesson of not giving up on the man of your dreams. During their six years apart, Sara had not stopped loving Bays, but she didn't know if he felt the same way. When she noticed the radio show getting mail from every corner of the nation, she thought that maybe, just maybe, Bays was out west somewhere listening and that he still cared for her. Amazingly, Bays was listening that night with his mother. He soon drove to Del Rio. Eventually he and Sara were married.

After the final broadcast, Sara headed to California with Bays, while the others returned to Maces Springs. Sara and Maybelle both assumed they were saying good-bye to XERA, but Brinkley's staff made them an offer that not even Sara could refuse. The station wanted the Carters back for another year, and this time they wanted the whole family—including Helen and June, and A.P. and Sara's two children. To make the offer even harder to resist, the children would each be paid $15 a week.

For June, this step into the spotlight was scary. Daddy's girl had learned in Maces Springs that she could do almost anything—except sing. When she was called on to join her sisters in a musical program, she would turn to comedy or dancing as a diversion. "When you don't have much of a voice and harmony is all around you, you reach out and pick something you can use," she wrote in her first autobiography. "In my case, it was just plain guts. Since I couldn't sing, I talked a lot and tried to cover all the bad notes with laughter."

II

After the Mexican government shut down XERA following an agreement with U.S. officials regarding radio bandwidth standards, the Carters' radio career seemed to be over, until Harry O'Neill, the Chicago adman who had hired the Carters for Brinkley, bought airtime on WBT, a fifty-thousand-watt station in Charlotte, North Carolina, and in 1942 asked the Carters to follow him there. But Sara, wanting to be with her husband, soon returned to California, marking the end of the original Carter Family.

From time to time A.P. would talk about getting everyone back together, but it never amounted to anything. Deeply disheartened, this towering musical influence settled for running a general store in Maces Springs—his place in music history largely buried for years until folk and country historians began to appreciate his vast contributions to American musical culture.

That left Ezra as the keeper of the Carter musical flame in the form of Maybelle and the girls. Ezra wasn't all that interested in the Carters' musical heritage; he saw the group primarily as a means for his family to get out of Poor Valley. He lined up a daily show on a station in nearby Richmond and also arranged live shows for the group throughout the area, performing at courthouses, movie theaters, and schools. The newly named Carter Sisters and Mother Maybelle gradually built enough of a following that WRVA, a larger station in Richmond, lured them to the Old Dominion Barn Dance, a country music stage show.

It was an ideal workshop for the Carter sisters. Anita's strong voice made her a favorite with the crowd, who especially enjoyed her yodeling and the way she'd tease the audience by holding a note so long that they would burst into applause. But it was June who made the greatest strides in Richmond, slowly developing a humorous persona that leaned heavily on the sort of folksy, golly-gee backwoods humor of Minnie Pearl, who delighted Opry audiences with her trademark greeting, "How—dee!" Despite their illustrious musical heritage, the Carter girls' act was much closer to vaudeville than to folk music purity.

Teenaged June, who was naturally outgoing, became hostess of a morning show on the station. Her ambition was so obvious that Sunshine Sue, the Barn Dance's star, worried about the Carters upstaging her. Ultimately, Sue made things uncomfortable for Eck and the group, and they quit the Old Dominion in 1948, ending the stay in Richmond, during which June graduated from high school.

After all his hard work, Eck uncharacteristically became discouraged enough to take the family back to Maces Springs, asking himself if he shouldn't give up this music venture. But fate stepped in again. The Carters soon got an offer to appear regularly on WNOX, a small but influential radio station in Knoxville that liked to bill itself as the "stepping stone to the Grand Ole Opry," the major league of country music. The station was also known for having some top-notch young musicians, including a shy young guitar player named Chester "Chet" Atkins. Eck wasn't sure he wanted to get involved in show business again, but June pushed him—the only one in the family to do so. *Yes, yes, yes,* she told her daddy. *Let's go to Knoxville.* It was as if she was the one driving the Harley now and everyone else was holding on.

While his wife and daughters settled in at the station, Eck started working on ways to make the act more marketable. Hearing all the talk about the twenty-four-year-old Atkins, he asked the guitarist to join the Carter quartet, and Chet accepted. His stylish guitar playing and keen musical ideas spruced up the Carter Family material. Soon, Atkins was such an integral part of the group that the name was changed to the Carter Sisters and Mother Maybelle, Chet Atkins and His Famous Guitar.

June's charisma and ease in the spotlight weren't lost on Steve Sholes, the RCA Victor executive who later brought Elvis Presley to the label. After signing Maybelle and the sisters to a contract, he signed June to a separate solo deal and took her to New York in early 1949 to cut a single, "Country Girl," and to guest on some Homer and Jethro records, including the comedy duo's novelty version of "Baby, It's Cold Outside," a Frank Loesser composition that had won an Academy Award for best original song earlier that year. Their parody went to number twenty-two in the pop field. The duo wanted June to go with them on tour and were surprised when she refused. Daddy's girl may have been ambitious, but she was also loyal.

The Carters stepped up the radio station ladder when KWTO in Springfield, Missouri, came calling. They were making good money again, and June took quickly to the high life. "They spent money like there was no tomorrow," Atkins related. "Cars, clothes, anything they wanted." In Springfield, the Carters were sharing the stage regularly with big-name country attractions, including a promising new singer named Carl Smith, who everyone thought was the handsomest man in all of country music.

The Carters were on such a roll that the Grand Ole Opry approached Eck about having them join the Opry cast. The Carters made their debut early in 1950 on the Opry stage at the famed Ryman Auditorium. They were an immediate hit. "The roof came offa that building," as June declared later. It was easy to see why. When they stepped up to the microphone at center stage, the Carters brought with them the history of their years on the radio, the great Carter Family songs, plus youthful vitality, humor, and even a touch of sexuality. At the Opry, June continued to blossom as a comedienne, even stepping away from the group at the start of their weekly appearance to joke around with whichever country star happened to be emceeing that section of the program. Typical of her frequently flirtatious humor was this exchange, which she would repeat in various forms in city after city on tour:

Emcee: How you doing tonight, June?
June: Well, I just got back from entertaining the troops at [the name of a nearby military base] and I had to jump into this wolf hole.

Emcee: You mean "foxhole," June.

June [looking innocent and confused]: Well, a fox may have dug it, but it was sure full of wolves when I jumped in.

Before the audience had a chance to stop laughing, she and the group would go into a song.

By now, Helen was married and pregnant, but Anita and June were the center of considerable male attention in a country music world known for its romantic entanglements as much as for its heartbreak songs. Because she was the prettier one, Anita had the most stars chasing after her, including such A-level names as Hank Williams and Elvis Presley. Her voice, too, caught a lot of ears. At the very time when Johnny Cash was listening to Hank Snow records in Landsberg, Snow was asking Anita to sing with him at a recording session in New York that led to a Top 5 country hit.

Williams had more than singing on his mind when he took Anita with him to New York a year later to sing "I Can't Help It (If I'm Still in Love With You)" on TV on the *Kate Smith Evening Hour*. In the April 23 segment, the budding sexual electricity between them was obvious. If Anita looked a little anxious, she was. Men were drawn to her—and Williams was no exception. She had already married, at seventeen, a Nashville fiddler named Dale Potter, a move so impulsive she didn't even tell her parents ahead of time. The marriage was short-lived. On her twentieth birthday in 1953, she married another musician, steel guitarist Don Davis, who had previously dated June. The couple had a daughter, Lorrie, in 1959, then divorced, then remarried and had a son, Jay, before divorcing again in the mid-1960s.

June also found no shortage of admirers. The one who caught her eye was Carl Smith, who had moved from Springfield to become a popular member of the Opry cast and chalk up a series of number-one singles. Because of Smith's movie star good looks (he reminded many in Nashville of the actor Rory Calhoun), June knew that women would always be throwing themselves at Smith, but there was a lot she liked about him, including the idea of being a country music royal couple. They wed on July 9, 1952, and they indeed became a popular team onstage, where June would sometimes do parodies of Smith's hits, for instance, turning his "Just Wait Till I Get You Alone" into "You Flopped When You Got Me Alone."

With the family's musical career going so well, Eck started spending more and more time at home in Maces Springs. But he left the Carters in good hands. Through his connection with Hank Snow, he had met Colonel Tom Parker, who began booking their shows, eventually teaming them up with his newest find, Elvis Presley.

Years later, Cash tended to be defensive about June's relationship with Elvis, suspecting they might have been intimate. June did like Elvis immensely, but more in the role of a big sister who was always there to listen to his problems and even iron his pants and shirts. Like Cash, June tended to look at Elvis as something of a kid; she was six years older and more sophisticated. She also saw that line outside his dressing room each night and knew he was not her future. Besides, Elvis, like so many, was more interested in Anita. He pursued her like a giddy schoolboy, even faking a heart attack backstage in Florida to get her attention and sympathy.

For all their charm onstage together, June and Carl Smith soon discovered that their marriage was going to be a rocky one, largely because Smith wanted June to give up her career and be a stay-at-home wife—the same role Vivian was playing in Cash's life. Gradually, too, June started hearing reports about Smith's fooling around. She tried to write it off as just country music shenanigans until it became apparent to her that he had fallen in love with someone else—a pretty young country singer named Goldie Hill. When June learned in the early months of 1955 that she was pregnant, she hoped it would cause her husband to recommit himself to their marriage, but it was too late; the new relationship was too far along. The Smiths' separation was still a secret to country music fans when their daughter, Rebecca Carlene Smith (who later embarked on a singing career as Carlene Carter), was born on September 26. For the sake of their image, the couple even got together for photos with the baby. But there was no turning back. The divorce became final in December 1956. Smith married Goldie Hill the following year, and she gave up her promising career to be the full-time Mrs.

Carl Smith on a five-hundred-acre horse farm outside Nashville. The Smiths had three children and remained married until her death in 2005.

Always sensitive about not being as pretty as her sister, June felt humiliated that her husband had left her for another woman. The last thing she wanted was to see her friends and fans; for once, she needed to be out of the spotlight—at least in Nashville. In her autobiography she was brutally candid: "When your heart has been broken, you gather the pieces together, take your little girl and catch a plane to New York....I thought I was the ugliest girl who ever lived. You feel that way when your marriage has failed."

III

June found a natural out from her divorce embarrassment when director Elia Kazan, best known for *A Streetcar Named Desire* and *On the Waterfront,* encouraged her to go to New York to study acting. He had seen her on an Opry show and thought she was a natural.

She was twenty-seven when she arrived in New York with Carlene in late 1956 and enrolled in the Neighborhood Playhouse School of the Theatre, known for a demanding series of workshops and boasting a group of students that included over the years such names as Robert Duvall, Gregory Peck, and Joanne Woodward. After a few weeks, June realized it was going to be hard to find paying jobs, so she decided to leave Carlene in Nashville with her mother. She shared an apartment in New York with Rosemary Edelman, the daughter of Hollywood TV and film producer Louis F. Edelman, and the two remained lifelong friends.

In New York, June hoped to reinvent herself as a serious actress. She was tired of being the clown. Not wanting to cut her ties to country music completely, however, she returned to Nashville on weekends to appear on the Opry with the family. She made a few appearances on TV variety shows and had small acting jobs in a couple of dramatic shows, but it didn't add up to much.

On one of her trips back to Nashville, she met a handsome young man named Edwin Lee Nix, who had been a popular football player in the area in both high school and college. Known by everyone as Rip, a nickname he'd picked up as a boy because he loved to sleep so much, Nix worked in his father's auto shop as a teenager and eventually opened his own body shop. He used his profits to race boats and to support his dreams of becoming an inventor.

Given Nix's low-key nature and June's high-energy drive, it seemed an unlikely match, but something about Nix caught June's eye when he showed up to fix the motor on Ezra's boat. About three weeks later she invited him to the house for supper. But Nix was so involved in getting his boat ready for a race in Alabama that he forgot until June called to ask why he hadn't shown up. He apologized and asked her to go to Alabama with him. It felt good for June to be seeing someone who wasn't part of the tawdry melodrama of country music. Maybe, she told herself, it was time to find a more normal relationship. They continued dating on what seemed to be a relatively casual basis until they learned in the fall of 1957 that June was pregnant. They were wed on November 11. A daughter, Rosanna Lea—or Rosie, as they called her—was born July 13.

Almost immediately, Nix and Carter realized how different their lives were—and neither had much interest in changing. Rip loved his boats (he held a world speed record at one point), while June wanted to be on the stage. Rip moved into the house that June received from the divorce with Smith, and he kept an eye on Carlene and Rosie—with help from Maybelle—while June spent three weeks out of every month on the road. Early on, he accompanied her to some fair dates, but he didn't like all the traveling. "I drove 2,500 miles in a week and it just wore you out," he says. As to the larger picture, "things were fine at first between us, but we eventually grew further and further apart because we very seldom got to see each other."

June had one advantage when looking for live gigs in that many female singers at the time stayed home with their husband or children. Still, it was hard going back on the road—always being the "extra" on the bill, never the headliner—and having to put up with the travel and sexual rites of the lifestyle. June did a pretty good job of being one of the guys, but it was a tough life, and she developed an especially strong relationship with Don Gibson, who was one of the biggest country stars of the late 1950s and early 1960s thanks to such hits as "I Can't Stop Loving You" and "Oh Lonesome Me."

Despite his immense talent, Gibson was a tragic figure who suffered from depression and intense stage fright, both of which fueled a drinking problem. Some who knew June at the time suggest she was simply trying to help him get his life together. Tom T. Hall's wife, Dixie, maintains there was a bit of Florence Nightingale in June. But others felt that June was once again hoping to become part of another country music royal couple. She and Gibson, though both married at the time, were still seeing each other when June first shared the stage with Cash in Dallas.

CHAPTER 13

THE DRUGS AND CARNEGIE HALL

I

JOHNNY CASH'S LIFE was moving so fast, and in so many conflicting directions, that each year felt pivotal to him—and the start of 1962 proved no exception. It was the year of June Carter, Carnegie Hall, and the Hollywood Bowl, and those three came together in a dramatic six-week period that affected Cash's life more than anything else since meeting Sam Phillips. It was a period of extraordinary joy and deep humiliation.

June joined the Cash tour on January 28, 1962, in Des Moines, sharing the bill with Patsy Cline and George Jones. Cash had been playing the 4,100-seat KRNT Theater in Des Moines since 1957, and he filled the place for three shows. It was a sign that however shaky Cash's record sales, he was still a red-hot live attraction. He had been looking forward to seeing June again ever since the car ride to Oklahoma City, and he went searching for her as soon as he got to the theater for the one thirty p.m. show. To impress her, he had put on his flashiest shirt, which was purple and black. He was somewhat deflated when June took one look at the shirt and pointed out that it was all wrinkled.

When Cash told her he didn't care, she replied, "Well, I do. You don't wanna go out there with a shirt like that."

Unused to being ordered around, Cash responded, "You telling me to take off my shirt?"

"Yes, go on in the dressing room and take it off and give it to me."

That night Cash stopped by Carter's room at the hotel, ostensibly to thank her for ironing his shirt, but she had been around country singers too long not to suspect something more was on his mind. For her part, she was certainly attracted to him; she thought he had a tremendous charisma onstage, and she respected him as an artist. She had been following his recordings ever since "Cry, Cry, Cry." She was expecting him to come in and try to sweep her off her feet, but he wanted to talk about the Carter Family and Jimmie Rodgers, and the conversation continued to their respective childhoods and their parents. Johnny was especially interested when June said her father loved to read about history and religion. Eventually that first night Cash leaned over and tried to kiss Carter, but she resisted. As she later put it, "I kind of chummed him out of the room, very gracefully."

The next day he headed back to California, but they both knew that for them it was only a matter of time. She called him "John" from the start, switching later to "Cash" only in those moments when she wanted to point out to him that he wasn't being himself—when he was high on drugs or on ego. "I was enthralled," he said. "Here was this vivacious, exuberant, funny, happy girl, as talented and spirited and strong-willed as they come, and she was bringing out the best in me. It felt wonderful."

Before the start of the next tour in Miami, Cash spent February 10, 11, and 12 in Nashville, recording more tracks for the album that was going to salute the old Sun Records sound. It was a carelessly assembled collection of songs, including "Cotton Fields," the old folk-blues song popularized by Lead Belly, and "In the Jailhouse Now," a Jimmie Rodgers tune that was revived in the 1950s by Webb Pierce. Cash also took another crack at "Sing It Pretty, Sue" and "Delia's Gone." That gave him and Law a lot of material to choose from. As it turned out, none of it was a bona fide hit. Columbia didn't see enough potential in "Delia's Gone" even to release it as a single.

The Sound of Johnny Cash didn't crack the pop sales charts when it was released later in the year. Not only did the Nashville studio fail to reproduce the stark seduction of the old Sun studio, but also Cash's vocals were mostly indifferent. He later told me, "I remember where my head was at the time I was singing those songs. I wasn't too with it on some of them." About "Cotton Fields," specifically, he said, "I had no business recording that song in the first place. Kind of showbiz cotton-patch song. Ledbetter [Lead Belly's real name, Huddie Ledbetter] didn't mean it that way."

In the wave of failure, there was one consolation. *Billboard*'s staff was enthusiastic about "The Big Battle," including the single in their "spotlight" section. "A fine saga song of a soldier on a Civil War battlefield," they called it. "One of his best recent outings and the tune, of his own cliffing, is right up his alley. It can make it big."

Cash read the review on the way to Miami for the next tour, and the words allowed him to hold on to his belief in his own artistic heart. Despite the disappointing sales, he was in good spirits. He was going to see June again, and Carnegie Hall was only three months away.

While hoping that June would be more receptive this time, Cash recognized that she was trying to keep a civil distance, and he toned down his advances. He sensed something special about her, and he didn't want her to think he was just another country star on the make. He was happy that she'd be on the bill at Carnegie Hall, and he delighted in sharing his dreams for the show with her.

They continued their friendship as the tour moved to Houston and then Shreveport, where they performed on a revamped edition of the Louisiana Hayride (the original format had ended in 1960). There's no evidence of his seeing Billie Jean, who, it turned out, was no fan of June Carter, whom she had met during her days as Mrs. Hank Williams. "He was desperate for someone in his life, and June was on the road and June was a hustler," Billie Jean says. "That's her reputation. She was a longtime hustler."

It's easy to dismiss her comments as jealousy, but Billie Jean wasn't alone in seeing June as trying to "nab" Johnny Cash. In fact, June's entry into Cash's life caused so much suspicion—among Vivian, John's parents, band members, and gossipers in

Nashville—that she was in many ways an early country equivalent of Yoko Ono in John Lennon's world. The gist of the grumbling that went on for years was that she was out to break up Cash's marriage and use him as a springboard for her own career. As the years went by, she, again like Yoko, would be considered a villain by many of Cash's old friends when she blocked their access to him, fearing they would contribute to his drug use. It wasn't an easy role, but June was determined to play it.

If her goal was strictly career advancement, she might have looked elsewhere. Cash's commercial prospects were shaky by the end of 1961. He hadn't had a knockout country hit since "Don't Take Your Guns to Town" two years earlier, and the mounting drug use made his future appear increasingly uncertain. Billie Jean had already rejected a place in Cash's life because of those drugs. June, however, was immediately attracted to this troubled artist—and true to her Carter genes, she was ready to fight for this man.

The rumors started flying as soon as she arrived on the scene. In her memoir, Vivian, after mentioning her husband's drug use in the early 1960s, writes: "And worse yet, some of Johnny's band members began dropping not-so-subtle hints to me that June was after Johnny on the road, and that I should really do something about it.

"When I confronted Johnny with the reports, he insisted June had done none of those things I had been told. He said I was letting my imagination get the better of me, and not to listen to gossip. I chose to believe Johnny, but I couldn't shake the uncomfortable feelings I had about her."

Cash and Carter were together constantly on the road. Several members of the troupe, including Marshall Grant, were very fond of Vivian, and it's easy to see how they could assume there was more going on than there actually was at that point. But after Shreveport Cash returned home to California, where he continued to work on the plans for the Carnegie Hall date. He was back in Nashville on March 19 and 20 for a recording session whose only interesting feature is that Anita Carter contributed vocals on two tunes, one of Cash's favorite gospel numbers, "Were You There (When They Crucified My Lord)," and "Johnny Reb," a song written by Merle Kilgore, whom he knew from the Louisiana Hayride. Neither track was released; Cash's voice sounded fried. But he did mention to Marshall after the session that Anita was "one beautiful woman." Marshall asked himself if Vivian was now going to have to worry about two Carter sisters.

After some Midwestern shows that month, Cash returned to Los Angeles and recorded in late April a version of "Bonanza!" the title song from one of the nation's hottest TV shows. Al Caiola had a hit instrumental version in the spring of 1961, but no one had done a vocal version. After the exposure of "Johnny Yuma," it seemed a logical commercial move—but first Cash and Johnny Western wrote new lyrics. In addition, that month Cash and *Bonanza* star Lorne Greene planned to do a duet on "The Shifting Whispering Sands," an Old West ballad that had been a Top 10 hit in 1956 for western-pop singer Rusty Draper. But Cash was sick and didn't make the session. He later overdubbed his vocal on the tape that Greene and the musicians made that day; but that recording, too, was never released.

With recording out of the way, he headed to Spartanburg, South Carolina, on May 3 for a short series of shows leading up to the date at Carnegie Hall on May 10. Two days later in Columbia, South Carolina, Cash was feeling nervous about the New York showcase and took a walk with June, hoping to relax. When they got back to the hotel, they went to her room, where she told him to lie on the bed so she could rub his back and try to ease a sudden series of spasms. Cash recalled years later the tension in the room.

"It got real quiet, neither one of us said anything. Finally I said, 'I wish I weren't feeling the way I am.' She asked what I meant and I said, 'About you.' And she said she was 'feeling the same way, 'cause there's only trouble if we keep feeling this way.'"

With that Cash stood up and said, "We won't, then. We'll just work together." Cash insisted they were only trying to be sensible. "We both had that attitude," he said. "We weren't gonna start anything."

II

Carnegie Hall and the Hollywood Bowl were part of Holiff's master plan to reposition Cash, in the eyes of disc jockeys and talent bookers, from a country music singer to a folksinger with strong mainstream appeal. If he could do that, Holiff figured he'd have a much better chance of getting his client booked on primetime TV shows and into the more lucrative pop market.

The industry had been talking about a coming folk boom ever since the Weavers and Harry Belafonte became so popular in the early and mid-1950s respectively, but it was the success of the Kingston Trio late in the decade that made execs look to folk as the next rock 'n' roll—or, more precisely, the musical choice of those teenagers who had embraced rock in the 1950s and were hungry for more substantial fare as they reached college age.

The Trio was still hugely popular in 1962, but the artist who contributed even more to the growing enthusiasm for folk was a young woman whose angelic voice and purist approach struck a deep emotional chord in young people. Joan Baez was only nineteen in 1960 when she released her debut album on the folk-centered Vanguard label and started building enough of a national following for that album to stay on the charts for more than two years, earning her the cover of *Time* magazine. At the same time, dozens of young folk artists were playing the clubs and coffeehouses of New York's Greenwich Village, just a subway ride away from the headquarters of the big record companies.

Cash's label had already signed one of the most promising of those artists, Bob Dylan. Producer John Hammond was excited enough about Dylan to send Cash an advance copy of his self-titled first album in the fall of 1961. Cash was greatly impressed and sent Hammond a note of thanks. When Dylan's album failed to sell well, the young songwriter became known around the label as "Hammond's Folly." The producer was forever thankful to Cash for expressing his support to Columbia bigwigs.

Columbia executives all the way up to Lieberson understood the commercial advantages of promoting Cash as a folk artist, but they didn't see it as an easy sell. Cash was thirty, which could make it hard for him to become accepted as one of the voices of this new generation. Holiff countered by pointing out that many of Cash's original fans were rock 'n' rollers, and they had already responded to the singer's folk side, as demonstrated by such hits as "Five Feet High and Rising." Besides, he noted, Cash was five years younger than Belafonte, whose folk sensibilities had contributed greatly to making him one of the industry's biggest sellers since 1956. Two of Belafonte's live albums had even been recorded at Carnegie Hall.

To add to Cash's folk credentials, Holiff put together a package for New York that also included June Carter and the Carter Family—making this the first time Cash would share the stage with June's mother and sisters.

In booking Carnegie Hall, Holiff wanted to show that Cash could sell tickets in New York, the nation's biggest record sales market—one not known for country music shows—and he wanted Columbia to tap into the Carnegie Hall live album tradition. Despite some concerns about Cash's unpredictable behavior, Columbia executives gave Don Law the okay to record the event. Holiff, in turn, stressed to Cash the importance of the moment: no disappearing act.

In the days leading up to the performance, Cash thought about the show's format with the same energy and drive with which he approached his concept albums. He wanted to take advantage of this prestigious spotlight to show who he was musically, including his roots—and anytime he talked about roots, he turned to Jimmie Rodgers. He even called the cast members together the day of the show to rehearse. To the shock of everyone present, however, Cash was so wasted from drugs, worry, and lack of sleep that his voice was reduced to a mere whisper.

"Johnny had been getting steadily worse, but things really hit bottom at Carnegie Hall," says Johnny Western. "He could sometimes pull himself together for important moments, but I think the Dutch courage left him that day. He knew this was a major event for him. The show was sold out in advance. The record company was recording it. I think the pressure just got to him and he turned even more to the pills.

"Johnny's voice was so shot he gave his secretary handwritten notes with instructions to all of us. He couldn't sing a note. He had been taking diet pills to lose weight so he could get into that Jimmie Rodgers outfit [which Rodgers's daughter had given Cash to wear at the show]. He was as skinny as rain."

To add to the anxiety, Cash disappeared after the rehearsal and didn't return until just in time for the show. "It was literally a minute before we had to go on and John finally shows up," Grant later said. "He was just downright filthy, dirty, really nasty. It was embarrassing for all of us. I knew that this was going to be a bad night for us."

When he walked onstage, Cash was intending to sing chiefly Rodgers's songs, something that must have made Holiff and Columbia executives frantic. They wanted a Johnny Cash album, not a Jimmie Rodgers album. He even designed a dramatic entrance for his set. He lit one of Rodgers's own railroad lanterns backstage and ordered the house lights turned off so that the only light on him would be from the lantern flame. He then walked through the dark to a chair at the center of the stage, put his knee on the chair—a signature move by Rodgers—planning to open with one of Rodgers's most famous compositions, "Waiting for a Train."

Cash expected an immediate wave of enthusiastic applause, but the audience was confused. Always nervous at the start of shows, he panicked.

"If there were any people out there who knew about Jimmie Rodgers (and I'm sure there were at least a few), they were slow to make the visual connection," he wrote thirty-five years later in his second autobiography. "I thought they were going to be in awe — *this must be something special, what's he going to do* — but they weren't. They were yelling out for 'Folsom Prison Blues' before I even got to the microphone.

"So I turned around and handed the lantern to somebody and I went into my regular opening number, whatever it was at the time. Which would have been fine, I guess, if I'd been able to sing. But I couldn't. I was mouthing the words. All the people were hearing from me was my guitar."

Aghast, Don Law signaled for the crew to turn off the recording equipment. Not knowing what else to do, Cash plowed on desperately, hoping to salvage something of the evening.

"I kept asking for glasses of water to ease my dry throat," he wrote. "I kept hoping the pills I'd taken would boost me up to where I didn't care anymore, but they didn't. It was just a nightmare and I remember it all with perfect clarity. June came out dressed in a beautiful white robe with a heart sewn into it when I did 'Ballad of the Heart Weaver.' I whispered my way through 'Give My Love to Rose,' hoping to pull it all together somehow, but I failed. It was awful, start to finish."

The mood backstage was near funereal.

June tried to encourage Cash, but he would have none of it. He snapped at her, then sat glumly in a corner of his dressing room, sending out such bad vibes that none of the regulars dared go near him. It took an outsider—Ed McCurdy, a folksinger best known for the antiwar anthem "Last Night I Had the Strangest Dream"—to finally bridge the gap.

Johnny Western and Gordon Terry had made the rounds of the Greenwich Village folk clubs the night before and had run into McCurdy at the Bitter End. McCurdy said he knew who they both were and that he was looking forward to the show. They ended up spending much of the night together, and Western invited McCurdy to come backstage after the show to meet Cash.

At Carnegie Hall, McCurdy sat in disbelief as he watched Cash unravel onstage, but he sensed early on the reason for the problem. After the show, he followed Western into the dressing room and noticed Cash sitting by himself, his head down. He walked over to him.

"It's called Dexedrine, isn't it?" he said.

Cash looked up, wondering who this stranger was.

"What is?" he finally replied.

"What you're taking," McCurdy continued.

"Yeah. Why?"

"I just kind of recognized it," McCurdy said. "I'm a kindred spirit. I've been into all that stuff myself. I'm in a program right now and don't do anything, but I recognize Dexedrine. That stuff will kill you, y'know."

Cash didn't like people questioning him about his drugs and he snapped back, "Yeah? Well, so will a car wreck."

But he loosened up when McCurdy introduced himself. He knew some of McCurdy's songs, especially "Strangest Dream." The talk helped distract Cash from the disappointment of the night sufficiently for him to go to a club with McCurdy, where he met a young folksinger named Peter LaFarge, who had recorded an album on Columbia.

Cash already knew of LaFarge because Gene Ferguson, a promotion man at Columbia and a Cash crony, had given him a copy of LaFarge's "The Ballad of Ira Hayes," a dramatic account of the life of Ira Hamilton Hayes, a Pima Indian who was one of six Marines featured in the historic photo of the flag raising on Iwo Jima during World War II. The photo was a powerful symbol of American courage and determination, one of the most celebrated images of the war. Never comfortable with the attention, Hayes returned to his native Arizona and tried to lead a normal life, but he couldn't escape fame. People would even seek him out on the reservation to thank him for his heroism. He re-created the famous moment in the John Wayne movie *Sands of Iwo Jima.*

But Hayes's life proved tragic. Feeling unworthy of the attention because other soldiers had given their lives in battle, the ex-Marine sank deeper and deeper into alcoholism. He was arrested fifty-two times for public drunkenness before he was found dead in an abandoned adobe hut. The county coroner labeled the death the result of exposure and alcohol poisoning. Hayes's story was told in *The Outsider,* a 1961 film starring Tony Curtis as the ill-fated war hero.

The meeting with LaFarge reminded Cash of the song, and he told the songwriter he was going to record it someday.

Though the damage to Cash's reputation from the Carnegie Hall fiasco was severe in the industry, the fallout could have been even worse if Robert Shelton, the *New York Times* music critic, hadn't treated the episode with restraint. He wrote, "Although the star, Johnny Cash, was suffering from a throat ailment, which made it difficult to judge his performance, the evening afforded several divergent moments."

When Cash read it the next morning, he was relieved. He was pleased that Shelton went to great lengths to pay respect to Maybelle Carter and the Carter Family tradition and declared that Cash was a singer and songwriter in the vein of country greats such as the late Jimmie Rodgers and the late Hank Williams. That, after all, was what he had hoped the concert would demonstrate.

It was a sign of Cash's lifted spirits that morning that he went around to the musicians on the Carnegie bill to thank them for sticking by him. "That made a big impression on us because he often would blame everyone else when things went wrong during those drug years," Western says. "He'd also stay away from everyone. There were many, many times when Gordon and I didn't know if he was going to speak to us all day. Sometimes we never saw him until showtime. But this time he was very sheepish. He took responsibility. He said, 'This was my fault, that mess last night. I apologize.'"

No one would ever mistake the Mint Hotel in downtown Las Vegas for one of the world's most prestigious concert stops, but Cash welcomed the chance to check in on May 17 for an eight-night engagement in the hotel's two-hundred-seat lounge. After the pressure cooker of Carnegie Hall, this was a chance to relax. He also didn't have to get into the car after the show and drive hundreds of miles to the next venue. Most of all, he was looking forward to spending time with June Carter.

Though he'd barked at her at Carnegie Hall, he was touched by her show of concern. As he looked back, he also valued the way she seemed to understand his need for time by himself to regroup emotionally. Yes, he was thinking, there is a lot to like about June Carter, and he knew he was kidding himself when he said he would settle for friendship. During a brief East Coast tour between the New York and Las Vegas dates, John told June of his deepening feelings. They stuck to their pledge of friendship only, but he did kiss her for the first time. Other commitments prevented June from joining him for the first three shows at the Mint, but they spoke by phone every day, sometimes twice a day.

As soon as she arrived on May 20, Cash went to her room and

kissed her for the second time. It was clear the pledge was over. No longer trying to keep up her guard, June asked John to give her some time to unpack and get into something comfortable. He returned to his room and drank a half pint of brandy and three or four beers to get up his courage. Then he went back to June's room.

By the end of the Mint run, everyone attached to the show knew the affair was under way. Because he had witnessed Cash's flings with other singers on the road, Marshall Grant wasn't too surprised until Cash started talking about how this time was different.

"I'm the last person in the world to get onstage and try to be a jokester, never was my thing," Cash wrote in one of his autobiographies. "She's an outgoing, exuberant personality and I'm very reserved when I'm around people I don't know.... I can walk into a room with 12 people and I'm more nervous than I would be in front of an auditorium filled with 10,000 people. She's not. If I've got to meet a lot of people backstage and she's there, I'll grab her and say, 'You'll go with me, speak to them.' She starts conversations with them and I can never think of anything to say."

Over the next few months he began to think of June as his new Billie Jean, and he didn't want to lose her, too. Because Billie Jean had been frightened off, in part, by his drug use, Cash tried to keep that side of him from June, but he was fooling only himself. If she didn't know about Cash's drug dependence, she would have been the only one in the country music industry who didn't.

June felt equally strongly about Cash. With Cash, she could picture having the life she wanted. But they both had tempers and strong wills, and she knew the relationship could be more stormy than storybook.

Rather than return home after the Mint shows, Cash flew to Nashville for some recording sessions and to be with June. After spending June 6 working on a Christmas album, he devoted the next evening to an ambitious idea that grew out of the weeks he had spent planning his Carnegie Hall concert.

While working on "Waiting for a Train" and other Jimmie Rodgers songs, Cash began imagining an album that would fea-

1934 Jack

The contrasting expressions of Cash and his brother Jack mirror the differences the boys' parents saw in their sons. Where Ray thought of Jack as enthusiastic and focused, he looked upon J.R. as lazy and unresponsive. Carrie viewed J.R. more sympathetically. She believed his quiet demeanor suggested a thoughtful and sensitive child. (John Carter Cash collection)

Below: The Cash family around 1950. Back row, from left: Roy, Carrie, Louise, Ray, Reba, and J.R. In front: Tommy and Joanne. (Rosanne Cash collection)

Left: Fiddling around at far left with Air Force buddies in a club in Germany. About Cash, his squad supervisor said, "We were all kids. None of us knew what we wanted to do—except Johnny. From the beginning, he knew he was going to be a singer. I can still see him sitting on a metal GI cot with the mattress rolled up, strumming that guitar." (Bob Mehaffey collection)

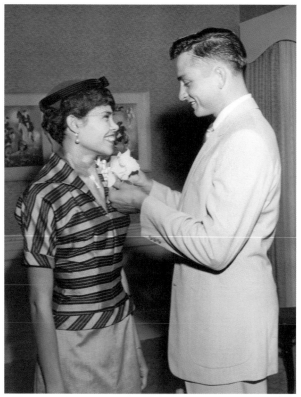

Cash spent nearly three years in Germany dreaming of the day he could return home and marry Vivian Liberto—and that dream finally came true in the summer of 1954. (Rosanne Cash collection)

Cash and the Tennessee Two— Marshall Grant, left, and Luther Perkins— on the concert trail after signing with Sun Records in 1955. (Rosanne Cash collection)

Sam Phillips and Cash celebrate the national success of Johnny's breakthrough hit, "I Walk the Line," in 1956. (Knox Phillips collection)

The family at home in Encino, California, after signing with giant Columbia Records in 1958—from left: Kathy, Vivian, Rosanne, and Cindy in John's lap. "Those were great times," Kathy said. "We never went anywhere without my folks holding hands or their arms around each other." (Don Hunstein, courtesy of Sony Music Entertainment)

Cash wrote "I Walk the Line" to help assure Vivian that he wouldn't be tempted by all the adoring female fans that inevitably showed up backstage on the road. (Don Hunstein, courtesy of Sony Music Entertainment)

Vivian and Johnny at a Los Angeles nightclub with manager Stew Carnall and his wife, Lorrie Collins, across from Carnall. To the right of Lorrie are her mother, Irene, and sister, Sylvia. Many in the Cash camp believed Carnall married the teenage Lorrie to prevent a potential scandal over her relationship with Cash. (Rosanne Cash collection)

Publicity still from the ill-fated 1961 film *Five Minutes to Live* starring Cash and Cay Forrester. (Silver Screen Collection/Getty Images)

Billie Jean Horton, with her husband, Johnny Horton, at her side, was known as the prettiest woman in country music, and Cash, next to Vivian, was so captivated by Billie Jean that he asked her to marry him weeks after Horton's death in a 1960 car crash. Fearful of his drug use, Billie Jean turned him down. (Billie Jean Horton collection)

Cash with Frank Wakefield, left, and Bob Dylan, right, after his triumphant performance at the Newport Folk Festival in 1964. (Estate of David Gahr/Getty Images)

The tension in the Cash household was evident on the faces by the time of daughter Tara's birth in the summer of 1961. (Rosanne Cash collection)

In a photo that appeared in hundreds of newspapers around the world, Cash is headed to a federal courthouse in El Paso in October 1965 after being arrested for possession of more than a thousand pills. (Associated Press)

Cash on the day of his landmark concert at Folsom Prison in January 1968. "I knew this was it, my chance to make up for all the times when I had messed up," he said. (© Dan Poush)

Moments before going onstage at Folsom, Cash suddenly felt calm. "There was something in their eyes that made me realize everything was going to be OK," he said of the audience. "I felt I had something they needed." Robert Hilburn, at Cash's side, covered the concert for the *Los Angeles Times*. (© Jim Marshall Photography LLC)

Cash's relationship with his longtime manager Saul Holiff, right, was a delicate balance of huge career strides and tumultuous confrontation. (Photograph by Jorgan Halling/ Saul Holiff Collection)

ture traditional folk songs about railroads and working people, songs like "John Henry" and "Casey Jones." The problem was that those songs were too familiar, even to schoolchildren. He needed to redesign them to give them fresh identity and impact. The easy thing would have been to repeat the narration-song, narration-song format of *Ride This Train;* but Cash wanted to move beyond that. To supply backing vocals and, no doubt, encouragement, he brought June, Maybelle, Anita, and Helen into the studio with him.

During the session, which stretched from seven p.m. to two thirty a.m., Cash created an expanded eight-and-a-half-minute version of "John Henry." He turned the tale of a steel-driving man trying to beat a steam drill in laying railroad tracks into an epic expression of a workingman's courage and will—and the belief that a machine can never take the place of a human heart.

Besides customizing the lyrics, Cash employed several special techniques, including narration, spoken dialogue, and sound effects (a hammer striking steel rails among them), as well as variations in tempo to accentuate the drama of the heroic struggle. Cash had been experimenting with the song live, and the strong audience response inspired him to keep expanding it until he felt it was ready for the studio. For her encouragement and input, he gave June half the songwriting credit on the track, which he titled "The Legend of John Henry's Hammer." He was pleased with how the music turned out, and he began to think of it as the centerpiece of another concept album, this one about the constant struggle of the workingman in America.

While in Nashville, June introduced Cash to her father. Cash had worried that Eck Carter would look with disfavor upon him because of the drug rumors; and, after all, he was a married man having an affair with Carter's married daughter. But Eck welcomed the singer into the family home in Madison, a Nashville suburb, and said he should feel free to stay there whenever he was in town. At that first meeting they went off by themselves for much of the evening, caught up in their mutual passion for books and their shared interest in religion. It was especially stimulating to Cash, because books had been a solitary pursuit for him over the years; he often wanted to talk about the latest history or religious book he had read, but no one in his circle seemed the least interested.

Dixie Dean, who later married songwriter Tom T. Hall and edited the Nashville country music weekly *Music City News,* was living with Maybelle and Eck at the time, and she remembers Cash's early visits to the house. Maybelle was still appearing on the Opry on weekends and doing an odd live date elsewhere, but it wasn't enough to live on, so she worked at hospitals, watching over ill patients, earning about $10 to $12 a night. Eck was no longer working and was dividing his time between Madison and a second home in Florida.

"Maybelle and I were co-writing songs, and I was sitting at the kitchen table working on a lyric on a yellow pad when John came in," Dixie says. "The first thing he did was take off his boots, the ankle-high kind they had back then, and he had these big holes in his socks and I thought it was so funny.

"Then he came over to the table and looked over my shoulder at my notepad. He asked if I wrote that song and I said I did, and he just looked at it and finally said, 'You're halfway smart.' He was always joking like that. Later, when he was getting ready to leave, he walked back over and said, 'I'd like to record that song if I may.'"

Dixie knew that he was trying to get together with June and that June was nervous because of the drugs. "He was in bad shape at the time," Dixie remembers. "He was gaunt and very thin, and when he'd stay over in the spare room, we'd find pills all over the floor the next day. But we were pulling for him. He was warm and he treated me like a big sister. In those days there were always two camps—the people who were in John's camp and the people in June's camp. I was in both camps. I cared about them both."

After a couple of vacation days, John and June headed for Los Angeles and the Hollywood Bowl—and the inevitable encounter with Vivian. "Saul told me I should not be with June anymore," Cash related. "He said, 'You're going to go through a living hell.' I said, 'I know, but I'm not gonna live without June.'"

IV

Just as great athletes are able to shake off a disappointing performance, Cash showed in the "John Henry" session that he too was able to put the embarrassing Carnegie Hall show behind him quickly and look forward to the next challenge, the eighteen-thousand-seat Hollywood Bowl. Not so with Holiff. He was worried about a relapse at the Bowl, the summer home of the Los Angeles Philharmonic. The Beatles would play there in both 1964 and 1965, but country was a rare presence. The only previous show listed in the Bowl archives featured Hank Snow, Lefty Frizzell, the Collins Kids, and the L.A. Philharmonic on "Western and Country Music Night," way back in the summer of 1955.

In bringing Cash to the Bowl, Holiff went to great lengths to make sure there would be a full house. He teamed up with a local radio station, KFOX, to guarantee that the concert would receive heavy promotion among the city's country music fans. He also packed the bill with enough stars for two shows: Marty Robbins, Don Gibson, Patsy Cline, Flatt and Scruggs, George Jones, Mother Maybelle and the Carter Family, Sheb Wooley, Johnny Western, Gordon Terry, Tompall and the Glaser Brothers, the Hollywood Square Dancers, and Roger Miller. To emphasize Cash's folk connection, Holiff titled the evening the "1ST GIANT FOLK WESTERN BLUEGRASS MUSICAL SPECTACULAR."

He also took steps to minimize the damage in case Cash's voice was anything close to the Carnegie Hall nightmare. Instead of having Cash—who was, after all, the headliner—close the show with a lengthy set, he restricted him to thirty minutes. Holiff wasn't just worried about Cash's voice. He also knew Vivian would be attending the concert, and the pressure of putting his wife and his new girlfriend together could send Cash reaching for even more pills.

To everyone's relief, Cash showed up at the Bowl that afternoon in relatively decent shape. He may have taken pills, but he was in good spirits, and his voice sounded at least passable. Holiff and other members of Cash's inner circle celebrated backstage, but not everyone would go away happy.

At the end of the show, Vivian took the girls and John's parents to the artists' parking area, as instructed, to say good-bye to John before he headed for Phoenix, where another concert was scheduled for the following night. Accounts vary as to what happened next. Some remember John greeting the family, but he was distracted, constantly looking over his shoulder for June. When he finally saw her, he quickly said good night to the family and led June to a Cadillac. Others recall John and June both just rushing by on their way to the car.

Whichever version is true, the result was the same: Vivian was humiliated and his parents were furious.

"I remember him in the backseat of the car when all of a sudden—out of nowhere—June races up and jumps right in the middle of the backseat, not at the other end of the backseat, but right next to him," relates Kathy Cash. "Then she goes, 'Bye-bye, Vivian. Bye-bye, girls.'"

Johnny Western, who drove the Cadillac to Phoenix that night, also watched the drama unfold. "As soon as Vivian saw him get into that car," says Western, "a lightbulb came on. Maybe it was the way he looked at June. Maybe it was the way they sat together so close in the backseat. The look on Vivian's face was pure anguish."

The scene troubled many in Cash's circle, including Grant, who thought the world of Vivian. But Patsy Cline apparently was the only one who spoke directly to June about it. The two singers were part of a small sorority of female stars in country music, and they found they had a lot in common when they met around the time June's marriage with Carl Smith was ending.

They were both from Virginia, had sung on the radio as teenagers, and had rocky marriages. Beneath her brassy, cocky persona, Cline had deep feelings of insecurity, especially when it came to men. Three years older, June became something of a big sister. She listened to Patsy's problems, offered advice, and even let Patsy use her house as a retreat when she needed quiet time.

One persistent message from June to Patsy was to stop her fooling around with so many men. She even had a name for it: "running, jumping, and playing."

Shortly after the Bowl incident, big sister June went into another one of her lectures: "Patsy, you've got to quit your running and jumping. You're married."

Cline responded angrily, "Who are you to talk? You're doing the same thing to Vivian that Goldie Hill did to you."

The words hit June hard. But it was too late. She was in love with John, and she remembered her mother's lesson of never giving up on the man you love.

Chapter 14

"RING OF FIRE," "UNDERSTAND YOUR MAN," AND THE TROOPS IN THE FAR EAST

I

CASH WANTED TO BE WITH JUNE as much as possible, and he went often to Nashville, both to see her and to do more recording sessions. He was eager to proceed with the album inspired by "John Henry." Don Law, too, was desperate for some new music, hoping for something to put Cash back on the charts in a big way. He was deeply impressed by "The Legend of John Henry's Hammer," but he couldn't release an eight-and-a-half-minute single when DJs rarely played anything more than three minutes long in order to squeeze in more commercials and talk.

During July 30 and 31 sessions in 1962, Cash recorded a version of "Casey Jones," the traditional song about a courageous train engineer, and "Waiting for a Train," the Jimmie Rodgers song. Again he had the Carters sing backup vocals. Returning to the studio four weeks later, Cash recorded another one of his longtime favorites, Merle Travis's tale of coal mining life, "Nine Pound Hammer," as well as his first formal duet when Anita joined him on the gospel-type call-and-response of the traditional tune "Another Man Done Gone."

But the song that most interested Cash, it turned out, was one that fit perfectly with his plans for the album, which he had decided to call *Blood, Sweat and Tears.* "Busted" was written by Harlan Howard, one of Nashville's hottest writers thanks to such honky-tonk gems as "Heartaches by the Number" and "I Fall to Pieces." Howard and his wife, a pretty young singer named Jan, had known John and June separately for years. Howard was born in Detroit, but his parents were from coal mining country in Kentucky, and he was fascinated by their tales of poverty and hard times back home. To honor that tradition, he took a break from his more commercial compositions and wrote "Busted," never imagining anyone would want to record it.

Cash heard the song on a Burl Ives album and redesigned it, changing the setting from coal mines to cotton country. In addition, Cash changed the arrangement in the studio, throwing out the bright, sparkly tone of the Ives recording to a starker, more plaintive tone that seemed to better reflect the theme of the song and the album.

Law thought "Busted" had big commercial potential, and he told Cash he'd like to release it as a single as soon as possible, which meant at the end of the year. Columbia had just released "In the Jailhouse Now," off the *Sound of Johnny Cash* album, and it climbed to number eight on the country charts, but it never made its way onto the pop charts at all. Columbia then planned to release "Bonanza!" in September, hoping fans of the TV show would be eager to buy it.

With June by his side, Cash resumed touring after the *Blood, Sweat and Tears* sessions, doing shows chiefly in the Midwest. He dreaded returning home because it would mean another confrontation with Vivian.

When he got back to Casitas Springs, the atmosphere was unbearable—and for all the couple's hopes of shielding their problems from the children, it impacted everyone in the Cash household. It was as if darkness suddenly fell on what had been a picture-perfect time for the youngsters.

Unable to face Vivian, and not wanting to frighten the girls, Cash would bolt out of the house at all hours of the day and night, get into his car, and, he wrote later, "drive recklessly for hours through the streets and into the hills and deserts of California until either I wrecked the car or finally stopped from exhaustion."

Frantic from worry, Vivian would wait at home for some kind of word—often from a policeman or a neighbor—so that she could go pick him up in another car and bring him home, only to have him race back out the door a few hours later and start the wait all over again. What kind of life was this?

The USO Far East tour came at an ideal time for Cash because it gave him a chance to get away from his problems at home. There was such a demand to see him that he sometimes played six shows a day, to as many as eight thousand soldiers each, on a tour that ran from October 28 to November 12. Cash, also joined by the Tennessee Three, spent countless hours meeting with soldiers, both in hospital wards and on the military outposts. By the end of the Korean leg, he came down with a severe case of laryngitis and had to spend time in the hospital himself before heading to Japan for the remaining shows. The mood among the soldiers in the Far East was anxious because the United States appeared to be on the brink of another war, this time sending troops to South Vietnam to defend the American ally against attack from Communist North Vietnam.

As on that day at San Quentin in 1960, Cash sensed in the overwhelming response that there was more at stake than simply playing to an audience starved for entertainment. He believed that these men and women saw in him a piece of home, and in the coming months that helped him greatly to further his identity in the music world. Looking into the faces of the sometimes smiling, sometimes downcast young soldiers, Cash felt he was summarizing in his music the things they both believed in, in terms of shared heritage and personal aspirations. He knew he would always have to answer to the commercial demands of a music career—he had to sell records and draw crowds—but he also began to accept that his personal destiny was tied to something more challenging and rewarding.

On the most exhilarating days, he told himself, in his naiveté and grand ambition, that he was celebrating the best of America. Cash volunteered to take messages from some of the soldiers to their loved ones back home. He then delivered them personally backstage after inviting the parents, girlfriends, or wives to be his guests when he did a concert near the soldier's hometown. Cash, who often worried about his failure to live in accordance with his religious beliefs, felt reassured that God was blessing him after all. He discussed this with June, who also took their good fortune as a sign that God was watching over them, that they were going through a form of redemption.

Still, these moments of joy couldn't erase all the unrest that had built up between the couple. John and June were already talking about spending their lives together, but there was the matter of their marriages. Privately, Cash was conflicted. How could he justify leaving his wife and the children? But then again, didn't he have a right to be happy? For June, whose marriage was already unraveling, his drug habit remained a concern. On some nights she felt gloriously happy about her relationship with John, while on others she felt helpless.

When June returned to Nashville after the tour, she got a call from Anita, who needed a song to finish an album she was making for Mercury Records. She was already planning to record one song June had written with Merle Kilgore, "As the Sparrow Goes," and she wondered if June had another.

Kilgore frequently got together with June in Nashville to write songs. Hank Snow and Anita recorded a duet of one of the early Carter-Kilgore compositions, "Promised to John" (not a reference to Cash), and June also recorded a couple of their songs for Liberty Records, but none captured much attention.

When Anita phoned this time, June thought immediately of "(Love's) Ring of Fire," the song she and Kilgore had written about her increasingly tumultuous affair with Cash. June got the idea for the song after seeing an underlined phrase in a book of Elizabethan poetry—about love being a burning ring of fire (or something to that effect; the exact wording changed over the years).

It was a simple song, but producer Jerry Kennedy liked the conflicting sense of lust and torment in the song, and Anita recorded it for a single. When he heard the song, Cash, too, wanted to record it, but he held back because he didn't want to do anything to hurt Anita's chances with the song.

*　　*　　*

The USO tour may have done wonders for Cash's psyche, but he still had to deal with the challenge of selling more records. When he got back from the Far East, Cash learned that Columbia had told Law point-blank to stop wasting money and time on this drug addict. Law could proceed with the release of "Busted," but he couldn't record anything else. Unless the situation changed dramatically, Cash was going to be dropped when his contract expired at the end of the year.

Still believing in his artist, Law lobbied hard. He told his bosses that Cash was growing steadily as an artist and the new *Blood, Sweat and Tears* album would demonstrate it. Cash's best years, Law argued, were still ahead; no one else in country music was showing the daring and imagination of Cash. He pointed to the rave notices about the Far East tour. The New York powers agreed to let Law and Cash go into the studio one more time. The date was set for the first week in March 1963.

Law, Cash, and Holiff were encouraged when *Billboard* magazine named the "Busted" single a "spotlight pick" in its January 12 issue, declaring, "Here is the old Johnny Cash on one of his best offerings in a long time.... Could go both country and pop." The trade publication, however, was even more enthusiastic about another "spotlight pick" in that issue: "A most sensual tune is sold in winning fashion by the thrush who shows off her own individual and exciting singing style." The single being praised by *Billboard* was Anita Carter's "(Love's) Ring of Fire." In the end, neither record was a hit. "Busted" spent only three weeks on the country charts, and "(Love's) Ring of Fire" didn't make the charts at all. Cash couldn't believe it. How could he fail with a song as great as "Busted"?

As the March recording date neared, Cash was frantic. According to a much-repeated Cash legend, the answer to his search for a hit came to him in a dream, when he imagined a version of "(Love's) Ring of Fire" featuring a blast of mariachi horns. That would get everyone's ear, he told Law the next day.

Cash may indeed have dreamed that horn arrangement, but it's more likely that he heard a similar mariachi outburst on Bob Moore's recording of "Mexico," which had been a Top 10 pop hit the previous summer. Law even hired Bill McElhiney and Karl Garvin, the two Nashville trumpet players on Moore's record, to play on Cash's session.

Cash was betting everything on that song and arrangement. When Law scheduled the fateful session in Nashville, he planned to devote the entire three hours to the one song. There was no Plan B. Holiff had already begun canvassing other labels in case Columbia did drop his artist.

On March 5 the Nashville music community was shocked to learn Patsy Cline had been killed in a plane crash just outside Nashville. She was thirty. June was too shaken to go to the funeral, so she babysat for Patsy's children. The "Fire" session that week was postponed. Law set a new date of March 25.

In the meantime, there was some good news. The *Blood, Sweat and Tears* album, which had been given up for dead after "Busted" stalled on the charts, started selling enough to break onto the pop charts, even if it was just a wobbly number 134. But Cash and Law were too nervous about Cash's future on the label to rest their case on that showing.

Cash was so jittery on the eve of the session that he turned to an old friend. Whatever Cash thought of "Teenage Queen," he believed that Jack Clement knew how to make hits. No one was more surprised than Clement, who had moved from Nashville to Beaumont, Texas, where he ran a recording studio and a publishing business, when Cash gave him a call.

"I was taking a bath one night when the phone rang and it was Cash," Clement says. "He told me about this song and how he had a dream about using mariachi horns on the intro. To some people, it probably sounded like a crazy idea, but I think he knew it would sound normal to me. Besides, he wanted someone in his corner."

Though he told Law that he just wanted Clement to sit in on the session, it was clear to everyone that Clement was in charge. Cash wasn't in great shape vocally; the stress had led to the usual uptick in his consumption of pills, but he put everything he had into the song.

Whereas Anita's vocal, as lovely as it was, had failed to capture the song's underlying drama, Cash's approach truly made him sound like a man caught in a tangled romantic web. He also massaged the words a bit and shortened the title to "Ring of Fire."

This was no casual undertaking. The session had the desperate feel of a last chance as the musicians worked on the song again and again. In the end, everyone was elated. Clement had done a great job on the record, not just overseeing the horn parts, but also showcasing the classic *boom-chick-a-boom* rhythm more dynamically than anything Cash had done since leaving Sun. Clement later said he was surprised how excited everyone was that day. He had no idea what was at stake.

When Bob Moore heard the single on the radio, he figured Cash had gotten the idea for the horns from "Mexico" and he took it as a compliment. "To me," he said, "it was like a wink and a nod, as if to say, 'Job well done, Bob.'" Years later, Cash would repay the favor by hiring Moore to produce one of his albums.

The executives in New York were as excited as the musicians in Nashville. Holiff didn't have to browbeat them to promote the record in the pop market. Even *Billboard* went along for the ride. In its May 4 edition the publication declared that in "a real enthusiastic performance, Cash sings this story saga emotionally over a sharp backing that has a Tex-Mex trumpet sound."

"Ring of Fire" entered the pop charts at number seventy-two on June 1 and rapidly climbed to number seventeen. In the country field, the single spent seven weeks at number one. To take advantage of the momentum, Law and Cash quickly put together an album of selected recordings that hadn't appeared on LPs before, including "The Big Battle" and "Tennessee Flat-Top Box." Cash also slipped in two gospel numbers, "Were You There (When They Crucified My Lord)" and "Peace in the Valley." Thanks to the massive radio airplay for the single, the album, titled *Ring of Fire: The Best of Johnny Cash,* spent more than a year on the pop charts, giving Cash his first gold record, signifying at least 500,000 sales.

Cash was again Columbia Records' golden boy. Holiff went back to other labels with a much stronger hand, but he couldn't get a better deal than Columbia was offering: a five-year pact that guaranteed Cash $500,000. The promotion-minded Holiff also got the label to throw in six full-page ads a year in the music trades to support Cash's releases. To the outside world, Cash was back on top of his game. To those close to him, however, his personal life was still alarming.

George Jones, who had quite a reputation himself for erratic behavior on the road, said that Cash far surpassed him in terms of trashing hotel rooms. In fact, he wrote in his 1996 autobiography, he learned during a stop at a Midwest Holiday Inn in the early 1960s that Cash had broken so many pieces of furniture in the chain's motels that he knew exactly what each item cost.

Jones got into an argument with Cash at the motel and accidentally broke a lamp. Cash noted matter-of-factly, "One broken lamp. That'll be forty-five dollars."

Jones then pulled down some drapes. Cash said, "That'll be three hundred dollars."

The singer then ran into the bathroom, took the porcelain top off the toilet tank, and smashed it in the bathtub: "One commode top, a hundred seventy-five dollars," John said.

When Saul Holiff confronted Jones with a bill for the room damages, Jones was amazed that all of Cash's predicted costs were accurate right down to the penny.

II

"Ring of Fire" could be heard on jukeboxes, on the radio, and on home record players almost everywhere in America—except one hillside home in Casitas Springs. Vivian had once stood by the radio for hours hoping to hear one of John's records, but she now avoided music stations. The pain of this single was even greater than usual. During one of his rare visits home, Vivian maintained, John told her that he had written a song while drunk and on pills, called "Ring of Fire," which was about "a certain female body part." What really riled Vivian, according to her account, was that he said he wrote it while fishing with Merle Kilgore on Lake Casitas but gave his songwriting credit to June Carter because "she needs the money and I feel sorry for her." The authorship of the song, however, was resolved when Kilgore later confirmed that he and Carter wrote it.

There was one place where Vivian couldn't avoid the song: Cash's return date at the Hollywood Bowl on June 22, 1963. Once again, Holiff teamed with radio station KFOX to send out a star-packed lineup in support of Cash. While the fans at the Bowl cheered "Ring of Fire," Vivian wished she could be anywhere else, but it was one of her rare chances to see her husband. "If she had not been such a devoted mother and had gone on the road with him, then the marriage would not have failed," her sister Sylvia says. "But she wasn't going to have somebody else raise her children back at home. Besides, she kept holding to the dream that Johnny would eventually realize what he was giving up and come back to his family."

At the end of the night, Vivian's actions were more telling than words. She didn't even go backstage. She didn't want to risk another humiliation. To make matters worse, Cash was in horrible shape that night, his voice little more than a rasp. She headed back to Casitas Springs with the children.

Cash's drug addiction was becoming dangerous enough that Marshall Grant felt especially anxious. It was tough enough trying to cover for Cash when he failed to show up for a concert, but it was even more draining to see the destruction Cash was causing in his personal life, and he felt horrible when Vivian would call him on the road, begging him to do anything he could to make sure Johnny came home during tour breaks.

"I asked him countless times at the end of a tour, 'John, why don't you go home and see the kids and spend some time with Vivian?' Most times," Marshall remembered, "he wouldn't go home, but even when he did, he seldom stayed long. He might stay overnight for a day or two, but then he'd jump into whatever vehicle was available and head into the desert, sometimes for three or four days at a stretch."

Rosanne Cash shared Marshall's despair. "When I was six years old [in Encino], it was like my daddy had always come home," she says. "But when I was eight [in Casitas Springs], somebody else came home. He was distracted and depressed and antsy. He had this little office in the house. He'd go in there, close the door, and put on records all the time. He'd stay up all night."

Because of the suffering of Cash's family, Grant found himself resenting June Carter, especially after she began demanding that Cash get a divorce. But he knew Vivian was wrong when she claimed that June encouraged Johnny's drug-taking so that he wouldn't feel guilty about leaving his family.

In fact, Grant's view of June had changed dramatically by the time they played the Hollywood Bowl in 1963. She had come to him weeks earlier to ask how they could work together in fighting the pills. Grant had already been telling hotel desk clerks to forward to him packages addressed to Cash so he could intercept pill shipments. He and June eventually became allies in that effort, and Grant admired her for it because he knew how angry Cash could get when anyone came between him and his drugs.

Marshall began to realize the depth of June's growing devotion when he saw that she was willing to risk her place in John's life by forcing him to confront his addiction. He would later say, "June is the hero in any story you want to write about Johnny Cash."

The turning point in June's relationship with Marshall had been the previous December in Albuquerque, when no one could get John to leave his hotel room to head to El Paso for the next show. As everyone else stood around, June stormed into Cash's room and shouted, "Lay there, star!"

"He came out of that bed madder than I'd ever seen anyone," she said later. "I was embarrassed, scared, and expecting to be fired, but we were on our way to the airport."

Thinking her days with the Cash troupe were over, Carter sat at the airport wondering what to do next in terms of her career. Just then, Cash walked up to her and handed her an Indian peace pipe he had bought for her in the souvenir shop.

Grant was impressed again when June took the lead in searching Cash's room for drugs. One reason Cash and Carter had separate rooms on the road was for the sake of appearances, but another was that Cash didn't want anyone going through his hiding places, which ranged from his guitar case to old socks to the insides of toilet tanks. If June found any pills, she'd flush them down the toilet, and then had the nerve to tell Cash what she had done. According to Marshall, on occasion June would even encourage Johnny to go home between tours to see his children. She thought it would help lighten his sometimes dark moods.

Despite Vivian's suspicions, Cash was not always in June's arms between tours. Often he would just go off on his own, trying to escape. There were also times when the tension between John and June got so intense that they needed to take a break from each other, and John would sometimes turn to other women for comfort. There was constant uncertainty.

"It was tough not knowing where he was, what he was doing, whether he was hurt, or if he'd hooked up with some of the undesirable people he sometimes ran with and was lying dead in the gutter somewhere," said Grant. "We couldn't help him if we couldn't find him."

Don and Harold Reid, who would later tour with Cash as members of the Statler Brothers vocal quartet, recall that Cash felt so much torment about his family and June that he once went to the airport ticket counter at the end of a tour and asked for a ticket on the next flight. When asked where he wanted to go, he said, "Wherever the next plane will take me." Harold Reid felt sorry for him. "You could see his head and his heart were fighting inside."

III

At the center of all this turmoil, Cash continued to find a refuge in his music; it was the one part of his life he felt he could control. On the endless nights between tours when he would often drive out in the desert or simply crash in a town where he knew no one could track him down, he'd think about his music, searching for themes that fit his interests and beliefs. Even though it was "Ring of Fire" that had saved his Columbia contract, he returned again and again to the music that most pleased him—especially *Ride This Train* and the gospel collections.

In his moments of isolation, he continued to draw comfort and strength from the underdogs of the past, the characters in movies and books about the Old West, both the heroes and the outlaws. Like them, he felt happiest when there were no boundaries to fence him in. As his addiction deepened, he went back to piecing together the concept album celebrating the Old West.

Even when he was touring, Cash often tried to lose himself in his records. By now he had moved on from *Folk Songs of the Hills* and *Blues in the Mississippi Night* to other folk and blues collections. He carried a portable record player with him so he could listen to music backstage or at the hotel. Among the albums that he played repeatedly was the seven-volume Southern Heritage series which was released by Atlantic Records in 1960. It was further, invaluable documentation of the diverse music of the rural South— recordings put together by Alan Lomax, who had also been responsible for *Blues in the Mississippi Night.* Each volume was devoted to another genre of Southern folk music, from Blue Ridge Mountain music and white spirituals to folk songs for children and black gospel. Cash played the set so often that he could recite the titles of all the songs on each album—in order. He was especially pleased to see a Carter Family song, "Lonesome Valley," in the collection.

Another album that captured Cash's imagination during this period was the second Bob Dylan LP. Cash had been playing *The Freewheelin' Bob Dylan* ever since producer John Hammond sent him a copy in the spring, and Cash marveled at the brilliance of Dylan's writing. He had liked Dylan's eponymous first album, but it was mainly the honesty and conviction of Dylan's approach to folk standards that appealed to him; Dylan had written only two of its thirteen songs.

When he saw Dylan's credit as the writer of the new album's opening song, "Blowin' in the Wind," Cash's first thought was that Dylan had simply arranged some folk classic; the song was so good, Cash figured it had been handed down through the ages. Seeing Dylan identified as writer on song after song, however, he realized that this promising folksinger had blossomed into a profoundly gifted songwriter. Cash loved how Dylan would move from the romantic complexity of "Girl from the North Country" to the wry putdown of "Don't Think Twice, It's All Right," and then segue to the urgent political commentary of "Masters of War."

Cash felt an immediate kinship with Dylan and was pleased to see *Freewheelin'* attract enough of an audience to reach number twenty-two on the pop charts. Its success—along with the Top 10 popularity of Peter, Paul and Mary's cover version of "Blowin' in the Wind"—gave Cash hope that his serious music, too, could eventually reach that same audience.

Eager to express his admiration, Cash wrote Dylan a letter soon after hearing *Freewheelin'*, and Dylan wrote back, saying he had been a fan since "I Walk the Line." Cash invited Dylan to visit him the next time he was in California. Dylan later told him he'd tried but couldn't find the house in Casitas Springs. When Dylan then wrote Cash from Carmel, Cash thought about taking the five-hour drive north, but Dylan had already left for New York. It was the start of a lifelong friendship, built mostly on respect rather than time spent together, because both men were essentially loners. They looked to each other not for companionship but for inspiration.

When asked in the early 1970s if he shared the widespread view that Dylan tended to be aloof and withdrawn, Cash told me, "We never did really talk that much. There was a mutual understanding between us. I never did try to dig into his personal life and he didn't try to dig into mine. If he's aloof and hard to get to, I can understand why. So many people have taken advantage of him, tried to do him in when they did get to him that I wouldn't blame him for being aloof and hard to get to. Everybody tells him what he should write, how to think, what to sing. That's really his business."

While the lucrative new record deal gave Cash the confidence to pursue his own instincts even more boldly, it also reminded him of the need to sell records.

As soon as it was apparent that "Ring of Fire" was going to be his biggest seller yet, he returned to the Columbia recording studio in Nashville in a shameless attempt to duplicate the single's success, all the way down to another mariachi horn intro. He even brought his good luck charm, Jack Clement, back from Beaumont to stand by his side. But nothing could make "The Matador" sparkle. The song was a slight, melodramatic tale of a once great but aging matador facing the bull for the last time, while his lost love watches with her new flame from the stands.

To judge from the *Billboard* charts alone, "The Matador" was a big success. After all, it went to number one on the country charts and number forty-four on the pop charts. But as had been the case with his early hits, there was such demand for a new Cash single after "Ring of Fire" that virtually anything would have done well—at least initially. But though "Ring of Fire" had stayed on the country charts for twenty-six weeks, "The Matador" dropped off after thirteen. In the end, Cash was embarrassed by the calculation involved. He rarely performed the song live and never bothered to include it on any of his "greatest hits" albums.

Columbia Records, however, was delighted, and Don Law felt vindicated in his decision to let Cash set his own agenda in the studio. To honor Sara and Maybelle Carter, Cash talked Law into doing a Carter Family "reunion" album with them in July.

John and June had become so comfortable together that they began to flaunt their relationship. Whereas even weeks earlier they'd tried to avoid any publicity away from the stage, they were now willing to pose for a photo when a newspaper reporter spotted them in a restaurant on July 24 in Kingston, Tennessee, just across the state line from Maces Springs.

The reporter didn't know, or at least chose not to mention, that they were married to other people; they came across in the story as a couple, taking a break from the concert trail while June showed John around her old teenage stomping grounds. The article noted that the two famous singers had "enjoyed relaxation in the traditional East Tennessee manner by spending a quiet day fishing on Holston River," and that the mood was so relaxed at breakfast the next morning that John asked June to throw him a bite of her ham.

Holiff had not slowed in his efforts to link Cash with the evolving folk movement. He got Cash a role in a low-budget MGM film, *Hootenanny Hoot,* which tried to capitalize on the folk boom the same way that films like *Rock Around the Clock* had used a parade of rock stars to lure teens into theaters in the late 1950s. Cash's appearance to sing "Frankie's Man Johnny" was the only interesting thing about the film, even though he looks miserably out of place amid the mostly pop-folk acts.

Johnny fared better in an appearance that fall on an episode of the *Hootenanny* series on ABC, singing "Busted" and "Five Feet High and Rising." The show was taped at SMU in Dallas on September 30 and aired on October 5. But the performance failed to help Cash's reputation among the folk purists, because Joan Baez and other important folk artists were refusing to go on the show after the *Hootenanny* producers rejected Pete Seeger over his "left-wing views."

Ironically, the most effective thing Cash did to connect with the folk audience had nothing to do with Holiff's strategy. On November 12 he went into the studio in Nashville to record a song that had clearly been influenced by his hours of listening to Dylan's music. Not only did "Understand Your Man" carry much of the melodic feel of "Don't Think Twice, It's All Right," but also the lyrics reflected a similar mix of confrontation and wit. The theme, however, was all Cash's. The number was a not so thinly veiled message to Vivian.

Don't call my name out your window, "I'm leavin'!" I won't even turn my head.
Don't send your kinfolks to give me no talkin'; I'll be gone like I said.
You'd say the same old things that you been saying all along,
lay there in your bed, keep your mouth shut till I'm gone.
Don't give me that old familiar cryin' cussin' moan.
Understand your man.

As soon as the Columbia brass in New York heard the record, they made plans to give it a heavy pop promotion push—and they congratulated themselves for keeping Cash in the Columbia family.

As Kathy Cash recalls, her mom was worried to death when her dad wasn't at home and even more worried when he was. "He would do stupid, bizarre things, like get in the camper and disappear without saying he was leaving," she says. "Or he'd scream or just say, 'Don't talk to me, I'm writing.' When I'd hear them yelling, I'd go to my room and close the door. I had this little record player, so I'd put on a record, anything to drown it out. But it never worked. Then we'd all go to bed, and we'd get up the next day and he'd be gone."

Over several months, Vivian had put together a list of people and places to call when looking for her husband. The trail often led to Curly Lewis, the contractor who had built their house, and Floyd Gressett, the minister who had walked up the driveway to welcome them when they first moved to Casitas Springs. She detested both men for not standing up to Cash when he was in a drugged or drunken state.

Cash continued to flee the confrontations by driving to remote desert areas either to go hunting or simply to lie on the ground at night and let the drugs go to work. Death Valley was a favorite destination because he was fascinated by the name of the place. On occasion, however, he brought Lewis along, and the contractor seemed to delight in Cash's often foolish daredevil antics, such as the time John drove his camper into the Mojave Desert and came across the fenced-off Naval Air Weapons Station. The land seemed isolated enough that Cash ignored the "No Trespassing" sign and drove through a gate. The camper bounced along a rough dirt road for several miles before they reached a curious sight: a paved highway that was marred by occasional bomb craters and burned-out remains of military vehicles.

Soon they were approached by someone in a military vehicle, who explained they were lucky to still be alive because the area was littered with thousands of dud bombs and land mines.

After that, although Lewis continued to spend time with Cash, he let Cash go on the all-night explorations by himself. When Cash returned from the desert, he was usually too wasted to go home, so he'd spend a day or two at a ranch owned by Gressett.

While Vivian and the girls attended Catholic services, Cash had joined Gressett's nondenominational congregation in the spring of 1963; it was the first time he had gone to church regularly since Dyess. The church's adopted slogan was "No law but love; no creed but Christ."

Cash felt comfortable with Gressett because he, like Ezra Carter, didn't judge him. "Floyd Gressett was always kind to me, even when I was at my worst," Cash wrote in his first autobiography.

"But he was wise enough to know from having preached for 13 years in the prisons of California that a man taking drugs isn't going to listen to you."

One of the prisons that Gressett visited regularly was Folsom, and he told Cash the prisoners would love to see him if he ever had time. Singing "Folsom Prison Blues" at Folsom Prison obviously appealed to Cash, and he passed the idea along to Holiff, who eventually worked out a date with Gressett for November 11, 1966.

To make their silent pact work, Cash said, he pretended that the pastor didn't know he was hooked on drugs, and Gressett had to act as if he didn't know. "He came looking for me more than once and found me at the point of death from days without food," Cash wrote. "He'd take me back to the ranch and give me food and a bed."

Sometimes Gressett joined Cash at the ranch, which was in the Cuyuma Valley about ninety miles north of Ventura. At other times Cash was alone or with his nephew Damon Fielder, the son of his older sister Louise. Cash was only ten years older than Damon, and he enjoyed his nephew's company. Like Cash himself, Damon was a man of few words, and he loved to go camping, hunting (usually just for jackrabbits), and fishing. He also treated Cash like an uncle, not a star.

"Gressett provided a place for us to hide for two or three days when J.R. didn't want to be home," says Fielder. "Over time, J.R. must have burned every piece of wood on that ranch, because there wasn't any firewood. He'd rip the boards and doors off the barn and shed and put them in a fire because he couldn't find any firewood."

On some days, when he wasn't in any condition to drive ninety miles, or was found by a neighbor simply wandering around in a daze, Cash ended up at Fielder's apartment in Oak View.

"He'd be so spaced out that he wasn't making any sense, so of course he didn't want to go home," Fielder says. "He was really changing physically during this period. It got to the point where he looked like a drug addict. We wore the same kind of clothes, so he gave me a lot of his clothes after he lost all that weight. He'd sometimes call me from the airport in Los Angeles and say, 'I don't have any clothes,' so I'd go to my closet and get his clothes and take them to him."

Fielder had known Vivian since Memphis, which caused him frequently to end up in the middle of their arguments.

"Vivian would call and say, 'Are you with Johnny?' and it would be hard because I didn't want to be disloyal to J.R.," he says. "But Vivian was like my second mother, the sweetest lady that ever was, and all of a sudden, she is the jilted wife who thought she had done everything right and wanted to stay in the marriage. So I'd tell her the truth: 'I have talked to him and he asked me not to tell you where he is. He'll be home soon; he's just messed up.'"

Cash went home to Vivian for Christmas, but it was a painful time. After the strain of the holidays, he looked forward to being back on the road and seeing June. They opened a week's engagement at the Mint Hotel in Las Vegas on January 2, 1964, and it didn't take long for the friction over his behavior to resurface. In their time apart, June had hoped that Cash would act on their lengthy, sometimes nightly talks—"bouts," some would say—regarding his drug use and the marriage. But she could tell that nothing had changed.

Back in California, things took another bad turn for Vivian when she heard her husband's "Understand Your Man," his open letter to her. Now she had two reasons to avoid the music stations.

Don Law was pleased to see that *Billboard* magazine in its January 25 issue praised the single of "Understand Your Man" and Cash's version of Merle Travis's "Dark as a Dungeon," calling the release so appealing that the only problem DJs were going to have was "deciding which of these sides is to be played first." As it turned out, they had no trouble determining which song to play: "Understand Your Man" spent six weeks at number one on the country charts, while "Dungeon" made it only to number forty-nine. "Understand Your Man" also went to number thirty-five on the pop charts.

Meanwhile, Holiff continued to push on the television front. Cash not only made repeat musical appearances on *Hootenanny* but also was penciled in as a key guest on several TV pilots aimed at the networks or syndication. In its January 18 issue, *Billboard* ran a roundup on the various efforts. *Star Route,* hosted by actor Rod Cameron, was a sort of country version of *This Is Your Life.*

Another project, hosted by Houston DJ Bill Bailey, was designed to be a "pop country" variety show with a live audience. The third show was called *Shindig,* and it was also a variety show, featuring Cash and artists from across the pop, country, and rock spectrum. Only *Shindig* would prove noteworthy, but the show had been completely redesigned by the time it aired that fall. Instead of the original country format, it focused on rock 'n' roll, highlighting such major emerging stars as the Beatles, the Rolling Stones, and James Brown, along with Cash and Sun alums Jerry Lee Lewis and Roy Orbison.

The relationship between Cash and Carter was not all romance and cheering crowds. What Cash would look back on as his first real showdown with June came in early March while they were in Toronto, where as usual they had adjoining rooms. He had been up for days and seemed drained, physically and emotionally. Suddenly June walked into his room and said flatly, "I'm going. I can't handle this anymore. I'm going to tell Saul that I can't work with you anymore. It's over."

Writing about the incident in his second autobiography, Cash said he didn't know exactly what had prompted her outburst—though it's easy to assume it was her exasperation with the drug and divorce issues.

Rather than apologize, he lashed out verbally and grabbed her so that she couldn't leave the room. When June struggled, he slapped her with the back of his hand. Realizing what he had done, he let her go, and she went back to her room. While she was in the shower Cash went into her room, gathered up her suitcase and all her clothes, including her shoes, and took them back to his room and locked the door. *Now let's see her go!*

Soon, June, covering herself with a towel, knocked on the door and demanded her clothes, but Cash refused until she promised not to leave. After tempers cooled, she gave in. The relationship was salvaged—for the moment. But the stress between them would resurface throughout the tour.

Johnny Western was driving John and June to the airport in Detroit a few weeks after the Toronto incident when they got into a screaming match in the backseat of the rental car. "They were go-ing on and on about why his divorce was not happening," he says. "And Johnny challenged her about her marriage. They called each other liars and just about every other name you could think of. But by the time we got to the airport, they had kissed and made up. It was surreal. It was not a fun time for anyone."

In the first week in March, Cash went into the studio in Nashville to record songs for an album Columbia planned to rush out in order to capitalize on the success of the "Understand Your Man" single. The emphasis of the album, titled *I Walk the Line,* would be on six Cash favorites from his Sun days. To round out the collection, Cash threw in a song that Maybelle and Dixie Dean had written, "Troublesome Waters." When he had all the material he needed for the album, he decided finally to record that Peter LaFarge song he had been thinking about for so long, the forceful commentary of "The Ballad of Ira Hayes." He wanted it to be his next single—and it would be one of his finest moments on record.

Around the same time, Holiff came up with a booking coup—a showcase appearance at the prestigious Newport Folk Festival, where Cash would be introduced by Pete Seeger, no less, and share the bill with Dylan. This was, Holiff hoped, Cash's chance to make up for the Carnegie Hall fiasco.

Once again, those around Cash were hoping that a corner had been turned. Less than six weeks later, however, he was in Cali-fornia during a tour break when he apparently fell asleep at the wheel of his camper, flipping the vehicle over on a highway near his house. He was cited for not having his driver's license with him. Newport wasn't until July 24, four months away, which left Holiff and Grant and the others with plenty of time to worry: Which Cash would show up?

CHAPTER 15

NEWPORT, BOB DYLAN, "IRA HAYES," AND *BALLADS OF THE TRUE WEST*

I

UNLIKE CARNEGIE HALL and the Hollywood Bowl, where all you had to do was rent the facility for the night, musicians had to be invited to play Newport. George Wein, a jazz pianist turned concert promoter, had operated the popular Newport Jazz Festival for years before starting the folk spinoff in 1959. In both ventures he was widely admired for choosing performers for their artistic credentials, not simply their record sales. Pete Seeger was a member of the original board of directors of the festival, which quickly became a crown jewel of the folk circuit.

While Holiff looked at Newport as part of his commercial strategy, Cash saw it as another chance to define his musical identity, and he spent days drafting set lists, searching for the right combination of songs. Considering all the time he spent with June, it's understandable that he opted for a Carter Family song. When it came to his own recordings, the last thing he wanted was a greatest hits package; there'd be no "Teenage Queen" on a bill with Dylan. In the end, he didn't even include "Ring of Fire." The titles that were penciled in and erased from his worksheet leaned toward songs he felt strongly about, such as "I Still Miss Someone," "Busted," and "I Walk the Line." He wouldn't finalize the exact list until the day of the show. For the most part, the more than 225 musicians appearing at Newport, many of them amateur or semiprofessional, had grown up in the Southern folk culture. In putting together his set, he wanted to demonstrate his musical kinship with them.

In his overview of the 1964 festival, *New York Times* critic Robert Shelton stressed the populist spirit of the affair: "Prison-born work songs or blues were not merely interpreted this weekend, but were also brought here by singers who had been in the jails of Louisiana and Texas. Many of the performers had waged their personal war on poverty long before it became national policy. An effort was made throughout the festival to show the meaning of folk music in the lives and milieus of the people to whom it was not just a diverting intellectual game, but a vital form of cultural expression as well."

For all the daring of *Ride This Train* and *Blood, Sweat and Tears,* Cash's best work on the Columbia label had gone largely unnoticed by the cultural elite, as represented by such tastemakers as the *New York Times* and *Time* magazine, and aside from Shelton, there had been little media interest in the Carnegie Hall show.

But Newport was different. In the media's eyes, there was a seriousness and historical measurement at work that deserved attention. Even if key publications chose not to send their own critics or correspondents to the festival, editors and critics would all read Shelton's review of it and often base their future coverage of the artists on his recommendations. Thanks largely to Dylan's appearance, there was so much interest in the bill that Newport smashed its 1958 attendance record of 57,000 fans when over 70,000 paid to see one or more of the weekend shows.

With all that at stake, Cash's nerves started getting the best of him, which meant taking pills. He was scheduled to perform the night of Friday, July 24, on a bill with Joan Baez, the Chad Mitchell Trio, and Phil Ochs, but he was in such wobbly shape, he missed his flight from the West Coast. Holiff must have thought, *Here we go again!* Fortunately, Holiff was able to talk Wein into moving Cash's spot to Saturday night, when he'd share the stage with Peter, Paul and Mary, who had replaced the Kingston Trio as the most successful folk group in the country.

Some of the festival veterans—aware of Cash's history of missing shows—were miffed at Cash's lack of professionalism, and Pete Seeger reflected this in his sarcastic introduction.

"Ladies and gentlemen, the next performer was supposed to be on the program last night, but he couldn't get here," Seeger told the audience. "He was way out on the West Coast and he found that, somehow, you can't get from Nevada to Newport, Rhode Island, in one day. But he did get here tonight." Cash wasn't apologetic for his no-show on Friday. Without a word to the audience, he opened with two songs from his Sun Records roots—"Big River" and "Folsom Prison Blues"—before turning to "I Still Miss Someone."

He didn't look good. With his drawn face and his unfocused manner, he resembled a man on a wanted poster, and his tenacious gum chewing suggested a casualness that struck some as downright rude. As much as he wanted the folk audience endorsement, he was so doped up that he came across as distant, almost condescending, as he looked out at a sea of mostly college kids no older than twenty-two.

However prickly his manner, Cash's voice was in good shape, rugged and authoritative.

According to observers, the crowd was caught up from the beginning. These college students had been listening to Cash's songs for years—especially the Sun ones—and they welcomed a bit of rock 'n' roll flash and aggression into the show. When he asked for a glass of water after his customized version of the folk standard "Rock Island Line," someone in the audience asked if he didn't want something stronger. "No," he replied. "I don't drink anymore." Pausing, he added, "I don't drink any *less*, but I don't drink any *more*."

Then he got serious.

"Got a special request from a friend of ours to do a song tonight and I'm very honored," he said. "I ain't never been so honored in my life. I'm so honored I can't [inaudible]. Hey, Bob. My good friend, Bob Dylan. I'd like to do one of his songs....We've been doing it on our shows all over the country...and trying to tell the folks about Bob. We think he's the best songwriter of the age since Pete Seeger."

He then launched into "Don't Think Twice, It's All Right," changing Dylan's "babe" to "gal" and adding his own tagline to the song: "I said just forget it from now on, Sugar, it's okay." After reaching back for "I Walk the Line," Cash got to the centerpiece of his set: "The Ballad of Ira Hayes."

"Ira Hayes was a great hero," he told the audience. "The song was written by Peter LaFarge. It's my latest recording on Columbia. We don't try to be overly commercial with our records, but if you like it, it's Columbia CL 1283."

The order number was just made up, but Cash sang the song with a commitment and purpose that transformed his set. It was the moment he had been waiting for. This was his message for Newport. This was who he was and what he believed in. Cash closed with the Carter Family's "Keep on the Sunny Side," toning down the sing-along feel of the tune to emphasize its original spiritual foundation. Then he was gone—just twenty minutes, but charismatic and inspiring.

"Ira Hayes" was a revelation for an audience that knew Cash chiefly for his hits, as good as "I Walk the Line" and others were. Again, his early days at Sun helped him here. He was to this young audience a link to rock's magical beginnings—the larger-than-life figure who once stood with Elvis and Jerry Lee. It was thrilling to discover him still relevant and dynamic.

Some of the old-line folkies were skeptical when Wein added this country star to the Newport bill, but the musicians embraced him warmly. Performers came from all over the festival grounds to watch his set. Afterward, they rushed up to congratulate him backstage. "No matter where you were or what you were doing, every musician that was there came to watch Johnny perform," folksinger Tom Paxton said. "Just a magnificent performance," George Wein declared.

For Grant, the concert was another example of Cash's ability to reach out and connect with audiences, however diverse. Whether he was singing to soldiers in Korea or convicts in California, blue-collar workers in the Midwest or now college-age folk fans, Cash was welcomed as a comrade. "People believed in Johnny Cash,"

Grant said. "They didn't just like his music. They believed in him."

Cash's chief memory of the post-show activities was a gathering in a hotel room with Dylan and Joan Baez, who were so happy they "were jumping on the bed like little kids." They traded songs for hours. At one point, Baez turned on a tape recorder and Dylan played two songs for Cash, "It Ain't Me, Babe" and "Mama, You've Been on My Mind." In return, Cash gave Dylan a guitar.

In his *Times* review of the Newport festival, Robert Shelton singled Cash out: "The Nashville star closed the gap between commercial country and folk music with a masterly set of story-telling songs."

The cultural elite had spoken: Johnny Cash was a major artist. He was on his way to becoming the most important figure in country music since Hank Williams.

II

Cash wasn't testing "Ira Hayes" at Newport. He had such faith in the song and its message that he had already finished a concept album about the treatment of Native Americans. Folk music had already adopted the civil rights movement as a cause: Dylan and Baez sang at the historic March on Washington in the summer of 1963, during which the Reverend Martin Luther King Jr. gave his landmark "I Have a Dream" speech.

There was, however, little outcry about Indian rights. Cash had already written one sympathetic song about Native Americans, and he found in "Ira Hayes" a song that didn't merely touch on the Indians' plight but exposed it in modern times. Bigotry wasn't just an eighteenth- or nineteenth-century problem, he felt; it was a twentieth-century disgrace. The more he thought about the song, the more he saw it as the foundation of an entire album.

Eager for additional inspiration, he visited Ira Hayes's mother on the Pima reservation in Arizona. The woman was so touched that she gave Cash a small black stone that became translucent when put under a light. Known as an "Apache tear," the stone held deep symbolism in the Pima culture, and Cash had it mounted in a gold chain and hung it around his neck. He wore it on the day he recorded "Ira Hayes" in the first week in March.

Cash invited Peter LaFarge to attend the session. Like Dylan, the songwriter had been a fan of Cash's since the Sun days, and he was flattered that Cash was recording the song. While LaFarge was in Nashville, Cash spent hours with him, going over other songs with even more tenacity than he had shown during the *Ride This Train* period.

It was easy to see why Cash and LaFarge would connect. They were about the same age (LaFarge was a year older), shared an empathy with Native Americans, and they viewed music as their life's mission, a validation. They also shared a restless, illicit-substance-fueled wild streak that made observers fear they could both self-destruct.

Yet there were differences. Compared to Cash, LaFarge was born with a silver spoon in his mouth. His father, Oliver LaFarge, was an anthropologist who was educated at Harvard and whose roots in America went back to the *Mayflower.* He won a Pulitzer Prize in 1930 for a novel, *Laughing Boy,* a trailblazing love story that treated Native Americans with dignity rather than depicting them as villainous or backward. He eventually served as head of the Association on American Indian Affairs.

After his parents divorced in 1935, Peter's mother, who was independently wealthy, moved with him and his sister to Colorado, where she bought a four-thousand-acre ranch and remarried. Restless and independent as a teenager, Peter joined the rodeo circuit and then went into the Navy. Returning to civilian life, he tried to build a career as an actor and playwright in New York City. He was in his late thirties when he finally got turned on to the burgeoning folk scene, finding in the music of Cisco Houston and Woody Guthrie a focus on history and social purpose that enabled him to put into song his feelings about life in the West and about Native Americans.

Not fully understanding LaFarge's history, Cash saw him as an authentic voice of the Indian people, someone who had experienced much of the discrimination he wrote about. "Peter was very proud of his heritage and he was adamant about the wrongs that his people had suffered over the years," Cash mistakenly said of him. In return, LaFarge would salute Cash in an essay for the May 1965 issue of the folk magazine *Sing Out!* He declared that Cash had the "heart of a folksinger in the purest sense."

In putting together the album he titled *Bitter Tears: Ballads of the American Indian,* Cash turned to four other LaFarge compositions: "As Long As the Grass Shall Grow," which criticizes American presidents through history for breaking treaties time and again; "Drums," a proud salute to American Indian culture over the years; "White Girl," a look at the prejudice that thwarts a relationship between an American Indian and an Anglo; and "Custer," a savage portrait of the general who was treated in school textbooks as a hero for his slaughter of Native Americans.

To that foundation Cash added two of his own songs, "The Talking Leaves," another look at government betrayal, and "Apache Tears," a tale of suffering which likely was inspired by the stone he received from Ira Hayes's mother. The final song, "The Vanishing Race," was credited on the album to Johnny Horton.

When it came time to go into the studio, Grant and the others were on edge. They knew how much this album meant to Cash, but they had seen him blow off so many sessions that they wondered if he could pull himself together this time. Grant feared the worst when Cash entered the studio on June 29. He still looked gaunt and pale, his eyes sunken. "You can see it all in that cover," the bass player said, referring to the photo on the *Bitter Tears* jacket. "Look at it closely. Look at his face, skin, bones, his elbow; that's what we're dealing with."

Despite his appearance, Cash was ready for the test. He had arranged his schedule so that he would have three days free before the session—just to rest. It worked. Grant would later marvel at how focused his friend was. "Sometimes when we went into the studio, he was still searching for what he wanted to do," Grant said. "He'd try one thing, then just the opposite. He'd come up with a song, and then go on to another. But this time, he knew what he wanted. It was John at his best."

III

After the runaway success of "Ring of Fire," Cash believed that he'd be on the charts with every new release. "The Matador" and "Understand Your Man" were solid hits, so he couldn't believe the feedback from Columbia promotion men in mid-June 1964: DJs weren't playing "The Ballad of Ira Hayes." *Billboard* expected so little of the record that the magazine didn't write about it all—the first time that had happened to Cash.

He was angry, not just at the DJs but at his record company. Likely egged on by Holiff, he didn't feel that the company was promoting the record hard enough. He still believed that if Columbia had done more for "Busted," he might have had the Top 10 hit in 1963 rather than Ray Charles, whose highly orchestrated version came out a few months later. He didn't want to miss out again with "Ira Hayes."

When Holiff pressed Columbia, the radio promotion staff told him the song was too long; for programming reasons, DJs preferred records that ran two to three minutes, and "Ira Hayes" ran just over four. But Cash didn't accept that excuse; Marty Robbins's "El Paso" ran more than four and a half minutes, and DJs jumped all over it.

Cash's single did show up on the *Billboard* country chart—which was based on sales and radio airplay—on July 11, but at an unspectacular number forty-two. By contrast, "The Matador" and "Understand Your Man" had entered the same chart at number twenty and number thirty, respectively. "Hayes" climbed to number eighteen two weeks later before falling to number twenty. To reverse the slide, more radio airplay was deemed essential.

Hugh Cherry, a veteran country DJ with a maverick spirit to match Cash's, shared Cash's fury. Cherry, who wrote the liner notes for the *Bitter Tears* album, believed that the Columbia promotion staff was, in essence, missing in action. "They were gutless," he said. "They found a lot of resentment from country DJs over the subject matter; they feared their conservative listeners would tune out, so they buried the record, and Columbia just rolled over. They could have pressured them in all sorts of ways, but ultimately they decided against it because they didn't want to alienate the program directors."

While Holiff vowed to keep working on the label, Cash struck out on his own by contacting Johnny Western, who, with partner Pat Shields, had set up a radio promotion company called Great Western Associates in Los Angeles.

"Johnny wanted us to do what the record company should have done—going back to the disc jockeys and fighting for the airplay," Western says. "We sent another copy of the single to every DJ we had in our address file, regardless if it was a big station or a little station. Johnny felt so strongly about the song he came over to the office and signed dozens and dozens of personal notes to disc jockeys, saying things like 'I really need your help on this one, pal,' and 'Give it a shot. Love, Johnny.'"

Included in every packet was a four-page brochure with the photo of the flag being raised on Iwo Jima and lines from the songs on the front and the slogan "NOBODY BUT NOBODY MORE ORIGINAL THAN JOHNNY CASH" on the back. Inside, the brochure contained a transcript of an editorial that ran on country radio station KHAT in Phoenix, praising Cash for doing a "magnificent job in recreating" the tragic story of Ira Hayes: "We wonder if, in years to come, people from all over this great nation of ours, when they visit Washington D.C. and pause before the statue of the Marines raising the flag on Iwo Jima, won't softly start humming 'The Ballad of Ira Hayes.'"

The mailings were tied to a full-page ad Cash took out in the August 22 issue of *Billboard* magazine attacking radio's resistance to the record. During what he admitted was a substance-induced rage, he drafted an open letter to all the disc jockeys who weren't playing the record, especially those at pop stations.

Its key line: "Where are your guts?"

In the lengthy, rambling diatribe, he criticized the DJs for shying away from the record's controversial theme. He appealed to their conscience by including American Indian rights among other headline-making social issues: "'Ballad of Ira Hayes' is strong medicine. So is Rochester—Harlem, Birmingham, Vietnam."

He also argued that pop DJs were avoiding the record because of his country roots. Addressing this issue, he pointed to his appearance at the Newport Folk Festival, where "Ira Hayes" had stolen his portion of the show: "And we all know that the audience (of near 20,000) were not 'country' or hillbillies. They were an intelligent cross-section of American youth—and middle age."

In closing, he added, "I've blown my horn now, just this once, then no more. Since I've said these things now, I find myself not caring if the record is programmed or not. I won't ask you to cram it down their throats. But as an American who is almost a half-breed Cherokee-Mohawk (and who knows what else?)—I had to fight back when I realized that so many stations are afraid of 'Ira Hayes.'

"Just one question: WHY?"

Hugh Cherry urged Cash to place the ad in *Billboard,* even though the label had warned him about a backlash. "What backlash?" Cherry asked years later. "If they were offended, what could they do—stop playing the record? They weren't playing it anyway; that was the whole point of the ad."

Because the ad appeared in the country section of *Billboard,* many in Nashville thought it was only aimed at them rather than also at pop radio. People in the industry, especially in broadcasting, as Cherry told it, "were going, 'Fuck him!' and 'Who does he think he is?'" There was even talk about boycotting his records. But the experience taught both Cash and Nashville something.

It showed broadcasters that "they couldn't stop playing his records because the listeners wanted to hear them," Cherry said. "The people who listened to the radio and bought records didn't know anything about some ad in *Billboard.* It showed Johnny Cash was more important than any individual disc jockey."

Despite the odds, the "Ira Hayes" campaign—much to the surprise of Columbia executives—worked. By mid-September, the single was number three on the country charts. Cash was so thrilled, he took the Apache tear stone from around his neck and gave it to Western in appreciation. Now he hoped the "Ira Hayes" momentum would carry over to the *Bitter Tears* album, but he soon learned there were still some bruised feelings in Nashville.

Ignoring the success of "Ira Hayes" on its own charts, *Billboard* gave *Bitter Tears* a lukewarm mention. Although most of the publication's reviews of albums went on for several sentences, complete with generous praise, the text of the *Bitter Tears* review was a one-sentence kiss-off: "Cash, in narrative and song, documents the tragic history of the American Indian."

To add to the insult, Cash's own label ran a full-page ad in the same issue, but it didn't mention *Bitter Tears.* The ad saluted Cash's new single, a duet with June on Dylan's "It Ain't Me, Babe." Despite the success of "Ira Hayes," Columbia didn't see much commercial potential in *Bitter Tears*—or perhaps, as Cherry suggested, the label still feared arousing any underlying hostility among country DJs over the "Hayes" *Billboard* ad controversy.

Columbia preferred to concentrate on "It Ain't Me, Babe," a record that had more obvious pop and country potential—and one that helped raise the profile of two of its artists. The single would be a smash on country and pop charts, but *Bitter Tears*—even with minimal marketing—also found an audience. It climbed to number forty-seven on the pop charts and all the way to number three on the country charts.

This experience strengthened Cash's determination. His faith in "Ira Hayes" and *Bitter Tears* separated him even further from the relatively timid creative stances of his fellow country stars. Increasingly, he was building a national following that believed in him as a musician and an artist.

As 1964 came to an end, Cash had ties to the rock world (through Sun Records), the folk world, the country world, and even the pop world. At thirty-two, Cash was on his way to becoming a musical institution—and he could take pride in the fact that he had done it largely on his own terms. He was not the creation of a producer, a record company, or a manager. For better or worse, he had called the shots.

It was an enormously important period for him—and he wasn't through.

His creative instincts heightened, Cash looked forward to doing an album of modern and traditional folk songs, largely because he wanted to record more Dylan. After spending most of November on the road, he went into the studio for a series of sessions in mid-December in Nashville. In the end, he recorded only two more Dylan songs—a second attempt at "Mama, You've Been on My Mind" and his longtime favorite, "Don't Think Twice, It's All Right." To add some of Dylan's harmonica flavor, he brought in Charlie McCoy, who would later play on Dylan's Nashville recordings.

IV

The news that Cash was following up "It Ain't Me, Babe" by recording more Dylan songs caused grumbling around Nashville that Cash was selling out—jumping on the Dylan folk music bandwagon as a way to make greater inroads into the more lucrative pop world. His detractors failed to recognize the creative similarities between Cash and Dylan.

Dylan has frequently said he didn't set out to change songwriting or society, but he was clearly filled with the high purpose of living up to the ideals he saw expressed in Woody Guthrie's work. "I always admired true artists who were dedicated, so I learned from them," Dylan says. "Popular culture usually comes to an end very quickly. It gets thrown in the grave. I wanted to do something that stood alongside Rembrandt's paintings."

Like Cash, Dylan found his musical heroes in the past—not just the legendary names like Guthrie, Jimmie Rodgers, the Carter Family, and Robert Johnson, but scores of Irish, Scottish, and English balladeers. Cash and Dylan delighted in talking about and playing those traditional ballads.

In advising young songwriters how to develop their craft, Dylan stresses the roots of today's music. "It's only natural to pattern yourself after someone," he says. "If I wanted to be a painter, I might think about trying to be like Van Gogh, or if I was an actor, act like Laurence Olivier.

"But you can't just copy somebody. If you like somebody's work, the important thing is to be exposed to everything that person has been exposed to. Anyone who wants to be a songwriter should listen to as much folk music as they can and study the form and structure of stuff that has been around 100 years. I go back to Stephen Foster."

Beyond their mutual respect for tradition and purposeful themes, both men believed it was essential not to let anyone else set their agendas. They wanted to be free to move in any direction at any time. For all his love of country music, there were few artists in Nashville who inspired Cash at all. He did admire Marty Robbins for moving from teen hits to honky-tonk to Old West themes. But he was discouraged by the way most of his peers played it so safe.

For all the speculation that Cash was recording an entire album of Dylan songs (maybe even calling it, some joked, *Johnny Cash Sings Bob Dylan*), he used only the three Dylan compositions. When it was released, Nashville was surprised to find that the album—which he'd called *Orange Blossom Special*—wasn't any more folk-based than some of his earlier efforts. However much he identified with the commentary and spirit of folk music, he was still, at heart, a country artist. Once again, those around Cash marveled at his ability to step away, even if only temporarily, from the instability of his personal life and rise to the occasion—not that they appreciated what struck many of them as unusual, if not downright weird, twists and turns in his musical direction. Grant measured Cash's success almost exclusively by chart position. Though he rarely said it to Cash directly, Grant thought the drugs were responsible for many of Cash's seemingly erratic artistic decisions.

As the two headed to their respective homes for Christmas, Grant asked, "Well, John, what you going to do next?" It was just a casual question, but Cash took it seriously. He sat with Grant and outlined in detail a long series of possibilities, including an album about the Old West, a gospel album recorded in Israel, and that album of prison songs that he had been thinking about for years. Grant just hoped there were some hits in there.

Columbia execs and Nashville DJs were relieved when they heard the *Orange Blossom Special* album; this was something they all could feel comfortable with. When the album was released early in 1965, the label took out a full-page ad in *Billboard*.

The trade publication, too, embraced it: "Cash is in fine form here and he has been coupled with a great choice of material. There are train songs like 'Orange Blossom Special,' country songs like 'The Long Black Veil,' revival-type material such as 'Amen' and his hit 'It Ain't Me, Babe.' Cash displays a sense of drama and wit." By the end of March, both the single and the album were in the country Top 5. They also made the Top 50 on the pop charts.

As he had told Grant, Cash had already moved on. When *Orange Blossom Special* was beginning its chart rise, Cash was back in the studio in Nashville working on the album about the Old West. He had enough songs after two days for an entire LP, but he was on such a roll, he kept recording for five more days in March and one more in April, ending up with enough material for two albums.

Because Cash viewed the collection as a unified work, complete with a few linking narratives à la *Ride This Train,* he wanted to release the songs in a double album, which was a bit much even for the obliging Law. A double album? How could Law get his bosses at Columbia to agree to such a risky commercial move? It was hard enough to get people to buy a full album, much less shell out the added bucks for a double one. But Cash was so hot that everyone signed off on the project. It sounded crazy, but maybe Cash would pull off another surprise.

Almost as remarkable as the music were the liner notes that Cash wrote for the album. As if tired of having everyone, including his own bandmates, question his motives and direction as an artist, he recounted the history of the album in considerable detail. The result countered the notion that he was stumbling blindly from one concept to another, or that he was following the pop charts for inspiration.

In the notes for the collection, *Johnny Cash Sings Ballads of the True West,* Cash explained that he got the idea from Law, who even gave him some books on Western lore. As he read more on the subject, he came across a magazine called *True West* and began reading it religiously. He even looked up Joe Small, the publisher of *True West,* as well as *Frontier Times* and *Old West,* and visited his office in Austin, Texas. He eventually dedicated the album to Small, among others.

After reading all he could find about the period, Cash turned to his friend Tex Ritter to put together a list of traditional songs—and Cash used several of them, including "I Ride an Old Paint," "Bury Me Not on the Lone Prairie," and "Streets of Laredo." Another key song was "Mister Garfield," an old folk song he learned from Ramblin' Jack Elliott about the shock of an earlier presidential assassination. But Cash wrote a few himself, most notably "Mean as Hell," a vivid portrait of the spirit and challenges facing the outsiders Cash so identified with in the Old West. In the song, the Devil, after being confined in God's hell for thousands of years, asks the Lord if he can find a hell of his own, and God points him to the desert wasteland of the Rio Grande in the American Southwest.

Cash's liner notes also chronicle what amounted, collectively, to weeks he spent alone on personal journeys in the desert, trying to get as close as he could to the spirit of the Old West figures. He became so engrossed in the project that he put in countless more hours on the road and at home in California, going to antique and junk stores to search for items from the period.

"I followed trails in my Jeep and on foot, and I slept under the mesquite bushes and in gullies," he wrote, possibly taking poetic license in places, but weaving a mostly convincing narrative. "I heard the timber wolves, looked for golden nuggets in old creek beds, sat for hours beneath a manzanita bush in an ancient Indian burial ground, breathed the West wind and heard the tales it tells only to those who listen."

Grant and others assumed that Cash was wandering around aimlessly those many days and nights when he was nowhere to be found, and indeed he was on the night of May 11, when he was arrested for public drunkenness at five a.m. after a concert in Starkville, Mississippi, and spent three hours in jail before being released. But Cash himself characterized much of his "missing" time as a lonely but obsessive quest for his next song.

While Cash was following his own musical path, Hollywood kept after him to do songs for movies. Just after the Starkville arrest, he recorded a song he wrote on spec for the latest James Bond film,

Thunderball, but the producers chose Tom Jones's version of a song written by John Barry and Don Black—and it's easy to see why. Cash's "Thunderball" has one of the clumsiest sets of lyrics he ever wrote, and the musical arrangement—which leaned toward a sort of rambling, Old West "Ghost Riders in the Sky" feel—lacked the contemporary edge needed for a Bond thriller. A month later Cash applied the same "Ghost Rider" undercurrents to the title track of a John Wayne western, *The Sons of Katie Elder,* and it worked better. The song was used over the film's opening credits.

Looking ahead, Cash decided to forget about his long-standing goal of recording an album of prison songs in favor of doing a live album taped at a prison. This is where he belonged, he told Law, not Carnegie Hall. After the embarrassing foul-up in New York and all the times Cash hadn't shown up for recording sessions, Law was wary. But once again, he went along with his star. Cash and Holiff decided on the Kansas State Reformatory because they'd already set up a date there for July 6. It would be, Law believed, the first time a big-name singer had ever cut an album inside a prison.

Bob Dylan once said that ideas for songs were coming to him so fast in the 1960s, he didn't want to go to sleep because he was afraid he might miss them. Cash was moving at the same speed. Some of those around him—especially Grant—continued to shake their heads at many of Cash's ideas. Others were crossing their fingers as Cash's private life continued to spiral out of control.

"The farther we got into the mid-1960s, the more worried we were," Johnny Western says. "There were times we'd find him when we thought he was dead, like the morning in Waterloo [Iowa] in 1965. It was a week before the *True West* sessions and it was colder than hell. John had the window wide open in the hotel and he was passed out on top of the covers with just his boxers on...cold as ice. Marshall called the doctor, who gave him some shots and got him under some warm blankets. And you know what? He gets up and does the show that night. It was touch and go like that for years."

Those on the road with Cash weren't the only ones who felt at times like they were on constant alert. In California, Vivian was in such bad shape—from worry and depression, lack of sleep, and little interest in food—that her oldest daughter, Rosanne, feared the worst. She says, "It got so bad that I remember coming home from school every day, wondering if my mother was going to be alive."

CHAPTER 16

THE LOS PADRES FIRE AND THE EL PASO DRUG BUST

I

ONE OF ROSANNE AND KATHY CASH's most vivid childhood memories was watching their mother puffing anxiously on a cigarette as she stared through the living room window of their Casitas Springs house on those rare nights in the mid-1960s when she thought her husband might actually be coming home. Vivian imagined him in the arms of June Carter, or dead somewhere, and she prayed to see the headlights in the driveway that would prove her wrong. On most nights, Vivian gave up around one a.m. and tried to grab a few hours' sleep before getting the girls ready for class at St. Catherine-by-the-Sea elementary school.

Though Cash was showing up less and less often, she held out hope that he would be home one night in mid-June 1965 after Saul Holiff phoned from the airport in Los Angeles to say that Johnny was on the way. Vivian took her familiar place at the window and let the girls stay up late to greet their father, whom they hadn't seen in months. By two a.m., she knew she was going to be alone with the children again. As she headed for the bedroom, she figured that Johnny was at Reverend Gressett's ranch, where no one would yell at him for taking pills. The next day she was too embarrassed to call

Gressett or anyone else to ask about her husband's whereabouts, so she just waited again.

It was nearly a week of day-and-night vigils for Vivian before Cash's camper—which he named "Jesse" after the outlaw Jesse James—headed up the driveway. Despite all the pain he had caused her, she wanted to run to him just like the day he arrived home from Germany at the airport in Memphis eleven years earlier. As he approached the front door, her nostalgia gave way to resentment. Why was he doing this to her? Why was he abandoning his family? Cash, feeling guilty and defensive, sensed her fury, and an argument broke out immediately. Finally, he shouted that he wanted a divorce. He had broached the subject before, but only fleetingly, never so angrily, and it was always quickly dropped. This time he tried to force the issue.

Johnny Western says Cash told him that he offered Vivian a half-million-dollar settlement if she'd give him the divorce, though his finances remained in such bad shape, he must have been kidding himself if he thought he could put that much money together. Most of the new Columbia contract income was going to pay off old loans. Vivian shouted back, refusing even to consider a divorce, and he stormed off to his sanctuary, an office at one end of the house.

Rosanne thinks her mother would have given up on the marriage earlier except for her Catholicism. "Her father was such a devout Catholic that a divorce would have been one of the worst possible things for his daughter, and I know my mother felt the weight of that."

As her sister Kathy recalls, "Dad would try so hard to stay positive, to make light of things, to always have a great sense of humor, but he would get into these moods where he just seemed to shut down and didn't want to talk or really do much of anything except spend time by himself in his office.

"The office became a symbol for us when we were little. There was a time when we were always welcome in the office. He might be working on a song or reading one of his magazines about the Old West, but the door was open and he'd stop everything and we'd have a good time. After a while, however, the door was shut. You'd have to knock and sometimes he'd go, 'WHAT?' and you'd think 'Why does he have to talk like that?' This wasn't always because of drugs; he was like that up until the day he died, but it was worse—more highs and lows—when he was using."

Kathy feels that her mother was easier to read.

"My mom was an incredible person," she says. "They were fire and water. She was very open and very honest. If she didn't like something, you knew it in a heartbeat. She was the disciplinarian in our house. I think that's one thing that appealed to him about her—that and her high religious morals. He got a lot of his strength from Mom, especially in the early days. I think he was so lonely and felt so out of his element during the Air Force. He had never been out of Arkansas, and she was his attachment to the States. She gave him something to hold onto during those hours he was stuck in that room, trying to listen to that Morse code.

"He told me the reason he wrote 'Folsom Prison' was it captured the loneliness he felt in that room night after night. He told me, 'I felt terrified sometimes because I knew the door was locked for security reasons and I couldn't get out. It was like being in prison.' My mother was his light at the end of the tunnel. That's what was so hard on him later, when he found out they had different goals—that she wasn't happy just sitting at home without him."

It wasn't just the increasing conflict that made Kathy realize things had changed. After that night in the parking lot at the Hollywood Bowl, she gradually noticed that her dad not only wasn't coming home but also wasn't carrying an armful of presents every time he did make it. "I thought, 'How could he forget our presents?' because it used to be a big deal when he would have a bag and there would be presents for everybody and we'd sit on the floor and he would always give Mom hers first and then he'd give us our presents. So we got to where we would go, 'Where's our presents, Daddy?' He'd say, 'I didn't have time...I had to do this-or-that.' He had never said that before. He'd even tell us about the times he almost missed his flight because he was in the gift shop looking for something extra for us."

Rosanne remembers the period as frightening and heartbreaking.

"It just got to where it was like somebody else was coming home, not my daddy," she says. "The drugs were at work. He'd stay up all night. He and my mom would fight. It was so sad. He would always be having accidents. He turned the tractor over one day and almost killed himself, and we had to call the fire department after he set fire to the hillside. One time he took me on his lap and put his arms around me and said, 'I'm glad to be alive,' because the tractor could have rolled over on him. He held me so tightly. I felt so close to him. I wished it could always be like that. But then he'd be gone again."

The girls finally got to see their dad before they left for school the next morning, but he was gone by the time they returned home. As he had so often, he needed to escape. He drove his camper to the nearby home of his nephew Damon Fielder.

Damon slid in beside Johnny in the camper on the morning of June 27, and the pair started out on the half-hour drive to the Sespe Creek entrance of the Los Padres National Forest watershed. The Los Padres forest is one of the many natural wonders of California and one reason why Cash was drawn to Casitas Springs. Covering nearly 1.8 million acres in all, it stretched from the breathtaking Big Sur coastline south of Monterey to lakes and mountain ranges to the south, and was home to many protected species, including the American condor.

Getting into the passenger seat was Damon's first regret of the day. Cash was a terrible driver under the best of circum-stances—and it was clear from his dazed look that he had already been into the pills. The resulting series of starts and stops made the camper feel like something from a slapstick comedy.

As Damon crashed against the door time and again while the camper careened along the rugged dirt road, his patience was also taking a beating. Watching Cash take a swig of whiskey and down a few more pills on the ride, Damon couldn't hold his tongue any longer.

"Why do you take those things?"

"I like to control my moods and they help me do that," Cash replied unapologetically.

"Well, you're an idiot."

Cash just scooped up more pills from an old fruit jar on the floor as the camper bounced along a rugged dirt road.

Finally, Damon reached over and turned off the ignition, bringing the camper to a halt. Before Cash could react, Damon pulled out the key, walked around to the driver's side of the vehicle, and demanded that Cash let him drive. Surprisingly, Cash obliged—and the camper resumed its journey, much more smoothly this time.

Damon was so upset, though, he didn't even want to sit near Cash as he stopped the camper near a promising fishing spot at the end of one canyon. "I'm going to fish over there. I don't want anything to do with you," he told Cash, who replied, "That's fine. I don't want to be by you, either." Damon headed to a secluded stretch of water, cast his line, and closed his eyes, trying to brush away his anger.

His tranquility was broken around four thirty p.m. by a strong smell in the usually pure Los Padres air. It was smoke, and it was coming from the direction of the camper. He rushed back to find Cash on his knees in front of the truck, fanning a fast-spreading blaze. There was a spent package of matches on the ground by his side. Damon figured his uncle had started the fire to keep warm and in his drugged state had let it get out of control.

As flames swept through the nearby brush, he realized they needed to get out fast. He called for Cash to come along, but the belligerent singer said he wasn't going anywhere. Damon tried to grab his uncle, but Cash resisted, and he was too strong to budge. In a panic, as the fire surrounded them, Damon grabbed a thick tree branch about three feet long and swung at Cash's head as hard as he could. The blow brought Cash to his knees, but it didn't knock him out as Damon had hoped. Cash got up and stumbled over to the shallow creek, where he sat down, thinking he'd be safe.

Fearing the worst, Damon raced for help, warning other campers along the trail and eventually hooking up with a fire helicopter crew who flew him to the fire site to rescue Cash. Damon's heart was racing until the helicopter landed and he saw his uncle was still alive in the creek. This time he had no trouble persuading Cash to vacate the area. The pills and whiskey had begun to wear off, and the water was cold.

Watching Cash get into the helicopter, Damon knew he'd helped save his uncle's life. He was crushed a few days later, however, to hear that Cash—whose near-death experience did nothing to curb his pill intake—told Carrie that Damon had left him in the forest to die.

Cash was equally disingenuous when asked by forestry officials, investigating the cause of the 508-acre burn, how the fire got started. He blamed it on sparks from a defective exhaust system on his camper. When a judge later questioned Cash about the fire, he was equally defiant: "I didn't do it, my truck did and it's dead, so you can't question it." Asked during a deposition about the loss of forty-nine of the region's fifty-three condors in the blaze, he certainly didn't make any friends when he snapped, "I don't care about your damn yellow buzzards."

Cash was in such bad shape after the fire that Law had to cancel plans for the live recording on July 6 at the prison in Kansas, causing the mild-mannered producer to vow not even to think of doing any more live album projects with Cash.

Touring resumed in mid-July and continued steadily into the fall, breaking only for a couple of recording sessions, until a fateful Texas swing that ended in Dallas the first week in October. Things had improved enough that Grant, who normally handled tour receipts, wasn't on guard when Cash volunteered to take the receipts with him to California and deposit them in the group's joint business bank account.

Grant dropped Cash off at the airport and then continued on to Memphis in the mobile home the group used on the road. When he got home that afternoon, he called Vivian to see if everything was okay, and she all but laughed. She hadn't even heard from her husband. Grant's heart sank.

II

The origins of amphetamines can be traced back to the late 1880s, but their effects weren't widely known until a 1935 study showed that the drug gave people incredible energy and enhanced their mood—qualities that led to its being widely distributed to soldiers during World War II to combat fatigue. In 1965 the Federal Drug Administration tightened prescription requirements, making it harder for heavy users to get the virtually unlimited amounts they were accustomed to. This made it increasingly difficult for Cash to satisfy his craving for pills, especially when he was on the road.

After the Dallas show, he flew to El Paso, one of his favorite supply points, where he asked a cab driver to take him to Juárez and get him some pills. The driver assured him that it would be no problem, so Cash waited—feeling like an outlaw, he said—as the driver went into a Juárez bar to buy the drugs. "I slid down a little lower in the backseat each time someone looked my way," he wrote in *Man in Black*. "I had never done it this way before."

Back at his hotel, Cash popped a few pills and killed time before the evening flight to Los Angeles by searching for antique guns in some downtown pawnshops. He was looking at a Colt .44 Army pistol, which had long been one of his favorites, when he was approached by a man he immediately suspected was a plainclothes policeman. Cash assumed he was curious about the gun in his hand.

"I collect antique pistols," Cash volunteered, holding the weapon out to the man.

"It's a nice one," the man replied, in what Cash described as a friendly manner.

After some more small talk, the man asked Cash what time his plane was leaving, and Cash told him nine p.m.

On the way back to the hotel, he started worrying about the flight, worrying that the policeman might intercept him. But why, he asked himself? The gun was an antique, which meant it was legal. And he had hidden all his pills in two socks, one of which he'd put inside his guitar and one in the lining of his suitcase.

By the time Cash got to his seat on the plane, he figured he was home free, that he was just feeling a bit paranoid.

Then he saw two men walking down the aisle toward him. One was the man from the pawnshop.

The man asked Cash if he had a gun, and when he nodded that he did, he was ordered off the plane. In an empty room in the terminal, the men went through both his luggage and his guitar case. They found the pills, but they still didn't seem satisfied. They went through the suitcase and the guitar again.

Finally, one asked, "Where's the heroin?"

When he heard that, Cash became angry. He told them he had never taken heroin. The men explained they had assumed he was into heroin because they had seen the cab driver huddling with a known heroin dealer in the Juárez bar.

Cash was relieved, but the officers pointed out that he had still broken the law. He was taken to the El Paso county jail until a bond hearing the next day.

Grant learned of the arrest the next day and hired a former El Paso County judge, Woodrow Wilson Bean, to represent Cash. Hoping to minimize publicity, Bean—whom Cash proudly pointed out was believed to be a distant relative of Judge Roy Bean, a legendary figure in Old West lore—asked that newsmen be barred from the hearing, but the request was rejected by U.S. Commissioner Colbert Coldwell.

Cash, dressed in a business suit, was on edge during the hearing. He cursed at one of the reporters and threatened to kick a photographer's camera. In the end, Cash posted a $1,500 bond and was released pending an arraignment on December 28. He was given permission to leave town but not the continental United States.

As he headed home to Casitas Springs, Cash felt as if a mask had been ripped off, leaving him looking like a hypocrite for singing all those gospel songs and telling people they could overcome their problems. He'd been in minor scrapes with the law before, but until now, knowledge of his drug use had been limited to country music insiders. Now his fans knew the truth. Not only did newspapers around the country report on the arrest, but also hundreds carried a photo of him being escorted out of the courthouse in handcuffs by a U.S. marshal, his face grim, looking all the more sinister behind dark glasses.

This time, at least, Vivian's wait wasn't in vain. Cash went straight home to Casitas Springs, and he was contrite. Humiliated and fearing the effect of the arrest on his career, he reached out to both Vivian and his parents, talking more openly than before about his addiction and vowing to turn himself around. While at home, he learned that Peter LaFarge had been found dead from a probable overdose in his apartment in New York. LaFarge's death made him feel that it was even more urgent to clean up. After years of disappointment, Vivian wanted to believe. She wanted to take his pledge to straighten up as a sign that he also was going to give up June Carter and rededicate himself to his family. But it was too late. She couldn't erase his insecurity and pain.

Vivian angrily showed him the newspaper photo of him in handcuffs and his daughters told him that kids were saying bad things about him in school. For the first time in his life, he said, "I felt real shame."

Grant was encouraged when Cash showed up "straight as an arrow and ten pounds heavier" two weeks later for his first post-arrest concert in Charlotte, North Carolina. Grant told himself that the arrest might have been the best thing that could have happened to Cash, thinking, "This might shake him up enough to where he'll get off those things."

In Nashville, June Carter wondered about her place in Cash's life; he had gone home to Vivian, not to her, in a time of trouble. She had already told Rip Nix that she wanted a divorce, hoping that would encourage Cash finally to leave Vivian. Cash tried to reassure June. He said it would have looked bad in the judge's eyes if he hadn't gone home to his family, and he told her he still wanted to be with her.

Meanwhile, Holiff was working tirelessly to persuade promoters around the country not to give up on Cash. Most did continue to book him, but there was one highly publicized exception. Officials at Texas A&M University canceled plans for a Cash show scheduled for November 24 on campus, citing the El Paso arrest. "The administration didn't feel it was wise to present an entertainer with a cloud hanging over him," said the dean of students. "We try to provide a clean, Christian atmosphere for our students."

But some students came to Cash's rescue. Not only did more than two thousand of them sign petitions protesting the cancellation, but also a student committee worked out a deal with Holiff for Cash to perform on the scheduled date at a nearby off-campus club.

Through all the headlines, Cash continued to be a strong presence on the radio and sales charts. The *Orange Blossom Special* album spent thirteen weeks on *Billboard*'s pop charts, and four of his singles made the Top 15 on the country charts: "Orange Blossom Special," "Mr. Garfield" from the *True West* album, "The Sons of Katie Elder," and "Happy to Be with You," a ballad that Cash co-wrote with June and Merle Kilgore.

The only disappointment commercially had nothing to do with adverse publicity. As label execs feared, a double album was too expensive for most Cash fans. *True West* didn't make the national sales charts. Still, Cash and Law believed in the music and they made a bold decision: they reshaped the material into a single album, which they titled *Mean as Hell!* and scheduled for release early in the new year. (It would do well, but not spectacularly, on the country charts.)

The variation in quality between the *Orange Blossom Special* and *True West* albums and the "Katie Elder" and "Happy to Be with You" singles reveals the difference between the personal music that Cash felt most comfortable playing and the records he made solely with the charts in mind. The albums had been heartfelt projects for Cash, and he'd focused his care and attention on them. The singles were another story.

"Happy to Be with You" was a particularly disappointing attempt to recapture the commercial bounce of "Ring of Fire." Though this new song was a statement of contentment, it employed the trumpets and lyric structure of the earlier hit. Even though "Elder" and "Happy" sold well, Cash rarely sang them in concert.

Experiencing another dry spell in his songwriting, Cash was at a strange point in his career; for perhaps the first time since *Ride This Train,* he didn't have another concept album in mind. The solution came in the fall of 1965 from a familiar source. Jack Clement told Cash he had a new song that would be perfect for him—a playful slap at all the protest music that seemed to be growing increasingly strident and humorless. It was called "The One on the Right Is on the Left" and Cash loved it.

The sociopolitical climate in America in 1965 was at an extreme of bitterness, with young people becoming increasingly aggressive in their opposition to government policies and practices both at home—only two years earlier, Martin Luther King Jr. had delivered his famous "I Have a Dream" speech—and overseas, where the United States had finally joined the ground war in South Vietnam. Many adults dismissed the protesters as traitors and cowards.

For all the commentary of "Ira Hayes," Cash didn't think of himself as a protest singer. He considered his music squarely in the folk tradition that he so admired. "My thing was never protest music," he said. "I was into documenting life in our country and in our times and in earlier times. That's what I was doing in *Ride This Train* and in *Bitter Tears* and even the prison songs. I was trying to write about history so that people could understand what was going on. To me protest music was like politics, and that was never my bag."

Cash began to think about doing a whole album of comic songs. He didn't think of them as novelties so much as another way to look at the human condition. He saw in songs like "Dirty Old Egg Sucking Dog" and "One on the Right" a way to laugh at himself at a time when it seemed everyone was taking themselves too seriously. He recorded "One on the Right" on November 29 and asked Clement to come up with some more tunes so that he could construct an album around them. After all, there was nothing else on his agenda now that the prison album had been scrapped.

Columbia was excited about the pop potential of "One on the Right" and rushed out the single as fast as possible. It was a hit in both country and pop markets.

Given the somberness of Cash's life after the El Paso arrest, it seemed a strange time to do a novelty album, but maybe that was the point.

III

When Cash returned to El Paso for the arraignment on December 28, he pled no contest to the charges before a U.S. District Court judge. The next day, newspapers throughout the country and Canada carried photos of Cash walking from the courthouse, Vivian at his side. But there was no hiding the damage. Vivian told friends it was the most embarrassing moment of her life. In Nashville,

June Carter, too, was distraught. After all her warnings, Cash was still out of control—and it didn't make her feel any better that he had chosen once again to lean on Vivian, even if it did make sense as an effort to burnish his image.

Cash was soon to learn that the photo had had even worse consequences than he imagined. Leaders of the National States' Rights Party, a white supremacist group in Alabama, seized on the photo, which, when reproduced in grainy newsprint, made Vivian look dark-skinned and possessed of facial features some considered African American. Whether outraged by the apparent miscegenation or eager to get back at Cash for his "Ira Hayes" protest stance (Native Americans were also a target of white supremacists), the group reprinted the photo in its newspaper the *Thunderbolt* and undertook an aggressive campaign against Cash.

In the publication, the States' Rights Party alluded to the El Paso arrest and urged its readers to boycott Cash's recordings, claiming, "Money from the sale of [Cash's] records goes to scum like Johnny Cash to keep them supplied with drugs and negro women." The article even referred to Cash's "mongrelized" children. Reprints were widely circulated.

Fearing a backlash among fans, especially those in the South, Holiff launched a counteroffensive in the media. "That meant contacting newspapers to get the story out about what was correct to offset articles that were repeating these hate things," he said.

While Cash publicly threatened to sue the *Thunderbolt* for $12 million, Holiff was working behind the scenes. He contacted Vivian's father, asking for a copy of Vivian's marriage certificate—which would state her race as Caucasian—and a history of Vivian's bloodlines. On October 17, Liberto sent him the marriage certificate and a letter in which he detailed Vivian's Italian, Dutch, and English heritage. The material, including a list of the whites-only schools Vivian attended, was sent to the editor of the *Thunderbolt*. The accompanying letter read, "We feel sure that the members of your organization are capable of being fair-minded when faced with evidence such as the enclosed. To refuse to correct this situation would suggest that you are not adhering to many of the Christian principles that you advocate."

During this period Cash received a few death threats, and a handful of protesters showed up at some dates in the South, but there was no sign that Cash's record sales or concert attendance figures were suffering. Eventually the issue faded away.

In her 2007 memoir Vivian wrote that the stress she felt at the time was "almost unbearable. I wanted to die." She added that she tried to persuade Cash not to speak publicly about the *Thunderbolt* charges. "To this day," she said, "I hate when accusations and threats from people like that are dignified with any response at all."

At least there was good news from El Paso. In March 1966 Cash appeared before U.S. District Judge D. W. Suttle, who gave him a thirty-day suspended sentence and a $1,000 fine rather than the maximum penalty of a year in jail. Before the sentencing, Cash had pleaded for leniency: "I know that I have made a terrible mistake and would like to go back to rebuilding the image I had before this happened." Suttle was handed a folder containing numerous testimonials, including one from the U.S. Department of Justice praising Cash for entertaining the troops, and one from Reverend Gressett.

Despite standing by her man in El Paso, Vivian realized by early 1966 that divorce was probably the only answer. The brief hint of reconciliation after El Paso was already a distant memory. "Johnny refused to talk to me anymore," she wrote. "I'd say, 'Can we please talk?' and he'd say, 'I don't want to argue,' and he'd leave....That was our big problem in the end: he didn't want to be confrontational or questioned."

More than ever, Vivian's "contact" with her husband continued to be Marshall Grant. Luther Perkins and Fluke Holland didn't want to get involved with what had become a state of full-scale warfare between the couple. Grant was the only one who would even try to fight for her. At the same time, Vivian admitted to herself that she couldn't compete with June. For one thing, she couldn't be on the road with Johnny and share his love of music. But she also came to understand that June was simply tougher than she was.

In her book she pointed to a traumatic meeting with June in the mid-1960s, a "tense five minutes of angry words, posturing and June punctuating her position with five devastating words that rendered me speechless: 'Vivian, he *will* be mine.' With that she turned and walked away."

The breaking point came during a routine physical early in the year.

"I know I looked pathetic," Vivian wrote. "I was down to weighing 95 pounds, and I was weak and sickly and crying (my permanent state behind closed doors). I knew I needed help but I didn't know how to ask. I was rapidly deteriorating. My doctor's face grew serious as he...looked me straight in the eyes: 'Vivian, you need to do something. If you don't, somebody else will be raising your girls.'"

The remarks struck Vivian's most tender nerve. "This wasn't meant to be a slap at June," Sylvia says. "The doctor didn't know about her. It was just that he could see how nervousness and smoking and drinking coffee had worn [Vivian] down, but when she heard that, everything changed. She wanted to be with her kids even if it meant [ending] her marriage, even if it meant going against our church's teachings. From that day on, it was just a matter of time."

Cash began to sense a change on Vivian's part and it frightened him. For all his talk about wanting a divorce, he was torn inside. Chief among his concerns was the children.

"I knew I was going to leave Vivian, but then I'd look at those four little girls," he recalled. "I said, 'Man, I'm gonna give up something that's gonna break my heart, but my heart will be broken more if I don't marry June.' When I was in California, my big reason for staying stoned all the time was her. I wanted to be somewhere else in my mind."

With Vivian on the way out of his life, Cash reached out to other members of his family, most of whom sided with his wife. He even tried to repair his relationship with his nephew Damon, who'd stopped talking to him after learning about Cash's accusation of leaving him in the forest to die.

Damon was puttering around the house in Oak View one day when a limousine pulled up out front. The driver handed him a note from Cash, inviting him to a concert John was doing in Southern California. It read, "Please join me." But the hurt was still too deep. Damon loved Cash the man and admired Cash the artist, but he couldn't tolerate any more of his uncle's behavior. Neither Cash's celebrity nor his blood ties were enough for Damon to forgive all that had happened.

Without pause, he picked up a pencil, turned the note over, and wrote two words. They were to him a cry of rage on behalf of all those who had been victimized by his uncle's drug use—including Cash's parents, his bandmates, and the thousands of concert fans who had been disappointed by all the "no show" nights. But mostly Damon was thinking about his own pain and the abuse Vivian and the children had suffered, abuse he had seen firsthand year after year.

Damon handed the note to the limo driver and asked him to deliver it to his uncle.

It read: *"FUCK YOU."*

PART
THREE

CHAPTER 17

THE DEATHWATCH

I

IF THE SHAME OF EL PASO wasn't enough to turn Cash's life around, Marshall Grant wondered if anything was. Within days of the arraignment, Cash was back on pills. After the closeness of the early days, Grant felt their relationship growing increasingly distant; instead of a partner, he felt more like an employee with a job description that stretched from playing bass to taking care of hotel and flight arrangements to, above all, helping keep Cash alive.

Overdoses and near overdoses had become so common that everyone in the touring party cited various times and places: Johnny Western mentioned Waterloo, June Carter named Des Moines, Grant alluded to a string of towns. In addition, there were the near-fatal drug-induced accidents, including the time in the summer of 1965 when Cash borrowed June's Cadillac in Nashville and crashed it into a telephone pole, breaking his nose and knocking out four upper front teeth. To break the tension, Luther Perkins came up with a piece of advice people in Cash's camp would repeat for years: "Let him sleep for twenty-four hours. If he wakes up, he's alive, if he doesn't, he's dead."

The experience that everyone in the Cash camp recalled most vividly happened at the Four Seasons Motor Hotel in Toronto on the morning after a March 19, 1966, show at the city's prestigious new O'Keefe Centre—just five months after the El Paso arrest. The concert hall had opened in 1960 with the pre-Broadway premiere of *Camelot,* starring Richard Burton and Julie Andrews. Playing there was another step in Holiff's campaign to upgrade Cash's image.

There were signs of trouble even before the show, Holiff said, when Cash showed up "very, very, very strung out—terribly so. Johnny had smashed a bottle [and] he came out onstage in bare feet." Watching a wobbly Cash try to step around the pieces of glass, the theater manager decided to cancel the afternoon show even though the audience was already in place. The evening concert went on as scheduled, but Cash's performance was shaky at best.

Things would get worse.

Because the group had to leave at seven the next morning to make it to Rochester in time for an afternoon show, Grant went to bed as soon as he got back to the hotel, he detailed in his memoir. But he was awakened around two a.m. by June, who said John had left the hotel with Ronnie Hawkins, an American rock 'n' roller who owned a club in Toronto. Knowing Cash's tendency to stay out all night, she was worried that he wouldn't be back in time for the trip.

Grant went to Hawkins's club on Yonge Street, but it was closed. Hearing noise from a second-floor window, he hollered until he got someone's attention. He was told that Cash had gone to a nearby Chinese restaurant. When that proved a dead end, Grant returned to the club and yelled again until another head popped out the second-floor window. To make sure he got to Cash this time, he said he needed to talk to him because of some problems at home in California.

The gambit worked, and Cash soon appeared in the window. Grant told him that he needed to come with him and call Vivian because there was a problem with the girls. It was now three a.m., and Cash said he'd be along shortly. An hour later, finally back at the hotel, Grant explained to Cash that he had lied, that the real reason he wanted him back at the hotel was the seven a.m. departure. Cash was unhappy, but he assured Grant he'd be ready.

At six thirty, Grant knocked on Cash's door to make sure he was up. When Cash didn't answer, Grant used his key to enter the room, where he found clothes and dishes spread all over the bed and the floor, but no sign of John.

Hoping that Cash had already gone to the motor home for the drive to Rochester, Grant rushed to the parking lot, where he found the singer slumped over in the vehicle's dinette area. Grant grabbed a hand mirror from the counter and stuck it under Cash's nose, hoping for a sign that he was breathing. There was none. Grant feared Cash's luck had finally run out, only to be relieved a few seconds later when a slight wisp appeared on the mirror.

There wasn't time to go back to the hotel for help, so he tried to blow air into the singer's lungs. After what seemed like several minutes, Cash uttered a faint grunt. June soon arrived with other members of the tour party, and they helped move Cash to a bed in the rear of the motor home. Grant's first thought was to cancel the show in Rochester, but he had seen Cash recover rapidly from past incidents like this, so he decided to press on.

Not wanting customs agents to see Cash in such bad shape, Marshall and June hid him under a pile of blankets at the border crossing. It worked; the troupe made it to Rochester on time. As the motor home pulled up to the venue, Cash was finally sitting up. Marshall and June gave him several cups of coffee and helped him change clothes.

Cash appeared deathly ill as he headed to the microphone to begin the show with "Folsom Prison Blues." Why, Grant wondered, didn't Cash's fans recognize how sick he was—not just this time but over the last few years? All the crowd saw, however, was their hero. When the final song ended an hour later, flashbulbs popped throughout the room as fans yelled for more. Cash had been near death only hours before, but he had just given what Grant called one of the best performances of his career.

While Cash headed for the dressing room, Grant asked himself how a man blessed with such talent could also be so screwed up. How could someone inspire millions yet inflict such pain on himself and those closest to him? But there wasn't time to dwell on those questions. The only thing he cared about as he walked back to the motor home was finding Cash alive the next time he knocked on his hotel room door.

II

To replace Johnny Western, Gordon Terry, and Tex Ritter, who had dropped off the tour or started doing fewer dates for various reasons, Cash and Holiff put together a new lineup to go along with June and the Tennessee Three. They had already added the Statler Brothers, a personable and talented male vocal group they spotted at a show in Virginia in 1964, who would remain a popular part of the package for years. The team of brothers Don and Harold Reid, Lew DeWitt, and Phil Balsley had a gospel background that appealed to Cash, plus they had a strong feel for secular material, too, and even a flair for comedy.

Cash also offered a hand to Carl Perkins. The rockabilly star had fallen into relative obscurity, sabotaged chiefly by his alcoholism. As Sam Phillips had predicted, Don Law didn't know how to bring out Perkins's unique blend of country and rock, and Carl was dropped from the label in 1963. He then was signed by Decca Records, but he did no better there.

Cash had been keeping tabs on Perkins, and he took advantage of a Southern tour swing in January 1966 to stop by Carl's house in Jackson, Tennessee, to invite his friend to join him on the next show, in Chattanooga—just for old times' sake, he said. But Cash was hoping to make Carl a regular part of his show if things went well, and they did. Perkins's rockabilly zest added some flash, and Cash enjoyed spending time with him offstage.

Of all the performers he would describe as his brothers over the years, no one was quite as close to Cash as Carl. It wasn't just that they shared poor rural roots; they also understood each other's substance abuse problems. Except for June, no one spent more time on the road with Cash than Perkins. At times they seemed almost to cling to each other for dear life. Perkins would later tell of going into the back of the motor home where they could be alone, and they'd "get so drunk—me on my whiskey and he on his pills—that we couldn't see each other and we'd start crying. We'd sit there and talk about our dead brothers and get to feeling sorry for ourselves."

The only one who could step into their private sanctuary was June.

"June was taking it and praying and crying and hoping that someday we'd stand up and be men," Perkins told Christopher S. Wren in the early 1970s. "She preached at both of us...our heads hanging down so bad we couldn't eat. 'John,' I said. 'One of these days we're going to have to get off it.' And he said, 'I know it.'"

With Carl and the Statlers in place, Cash turned to the Carter Family. June had been pushing the idea for some time because she wanted to see her family working again after a long period of inactivity. But Cash didn't add Mother Maybelle, Helen, and Anita just to please his girlfriend. He loved sharing the stage with the Carters. On those few occasions when he had brought them on the road, he'd felt proud to be part of that great Carter Family legacy. He had grown so close to Maybelle and Eck that he often spent time at their house when he was in Nashville.

Cash especially looked forward to talking about spiritual matters with Eck. They read the Bible together, and Cash would experience moments of peace. Unfortunately, the feeling wouldn't last. He'd get back on the road and start popping the pills. What he found most comforting about Eck was that no matter how many times he fell, Eck never lectured him. Eck just tried to tell him that he had a choice in life. He didn't have to keep turning to drugs; he could turn to God. It'd take until mid-September for the Carters to get all their affairs in order and officially join the tour, but when they did, the final piece in his touring family was in place.

Because he was no longer going home to California, Cash had to find a place to stay in Nashville. He couldn't move in with June because her divorce wasn't final, so he and Waylon Jennings, an exciting young singer with a maverick Cash-like attitude, rented a modest one-bedroom apartment in Madison, the town where both June and her parents lived. Waylon, who was born in 1937, was still a teenager in West Texas when he first heard "Cry, Cry, Cry" on the radio; he loved Cash's voice so much that he later said he had to work hard at not imitating Cash when he started singing in talent contests.

Farcically, they both acted as if each had no knowledge that the other was deeply into pills, even though Waylon, too, was taking them a fistful at a time. They certainly didn't share their drugs. Waylon kept his in back of the air conditioner; John often hid his behind the television set.

"It was like a sitcom; we were the original 'Odd Couple,'" Waylon wrote with Lenny Kaye in *Waylon: An Autobiography*. "I was supposed to clean up, and John was the one doing the cooking. If I'd be in one room polishing, he'd be in the other room making a mess...making himself a mess. He'd be stirring biscuits and gravy, dressed in one of his thin black gabardine suits, and the flour rising in clouds of white dust all over him."

For all the great stories that grew out of their time in the apartment, they were rarely there together, as they were usually on separate tours. Besides, Cash preferred to be with Maybelle and Eck. "He came to my house when he was ready and he left when he was ready," Maybelle said of Cash. She and Eck didn't even mind when he'd show up late at night, so high on drugs that he didn't bother to knock on the door. He'd either kick it in or break a window, climb in, and pass out on the living room sofa. When he awoke the next morning, he'd find Eck fixing the door or window and Maybelle asking, "Would you like some breakfast, John?"

III

Though Vivian, June, and Marshall seemed to be battling Johnny's dark side constantly, no one likely had a more stormy relationship with Cash than Saul Holiff. From the time he first saw Cash in Canada, Holiff had delivered on his promise to upgrade Cash's image—billing him as "America's Singing Storyteller." In trade ads, however, Holiff wasn't above employing wordplay, promoting Cash as "The Song-Singin', Gun-Slingin', Cash Register–Ringin' Entertainer." Holiff would lash out at Columbia execs whenever sales and airplay fell below expectations and then turn around and scold Cash just as sternly when he would miss recording sessions or cancel concert dates. As he found more and more concert promoters unwilling to take a chance after having been burned in the past, Holiff started booking concerts himself, knowing he would lose money every time Cash didn't show up. He also decided to focus more on overseas dates, figuring foreign promoters would be eager to get an American star of Cash's stature and might not be aware of the cancellation issues.

Most people thought that Holiff named his management company—Volatile Attractions—as a wry admission of his and Cash's explosive temperaments, though in fact the name was a reference to the unpredictability of the stock market, in which Holiff invested heavily. Inevitably, Cash's drug-driven impatience and Holiff's gruff personality began to clash soon after they formally started working together.

Holiff's son Jonathan, who studied his father's life in detail while making an award-winning documentary film titled *My Father and the Man in Black,* believes that the first time Cash fired Saul was shortly after the Hollywood Bowl concert in 1963, which would have been less than two years after the pair shook hands on the deal. The issue apparently was Holiff's decision to start managing George Jones, too. Jonathan says, "I found a letter in which Saul said to Johnny, 'You approved of my idea of handling George Jones out of your office, under your auspices. You know he pays all his own bills....You're not covering any of his costs. You remain my one and only focus."

But, the younger Holiff believes, Cash still feared that Saul's attention would be divided by working with Jones. After two months, however, Cash learned that Holiff was no longer handling Jones, and he asked Holiff to be his manager again.

Johnny Western called Holiff a "very smart guy, a visionary," and Marshall Grant acknowledged that he "took us to another level," but no one saw a lot of personal warmth between Saul and John. "Saul told us one time that he was there because Cash got him more money than anyone else he ever worked with," Harold Reid says. "I don't think he and John had any other relationship than business."

Studying both men's lives, Jonathan was intrigued by the similarities between Cash and his father. They both lost siblings at an early age, both served in the Air Force (Holiff in the Royal Canadian Air Force), both auditioned to be disc jockeys, and both sold door-to-door. "Ultimately, however," he says, "they were as different as oil and water.

"Saul was a guy who was raised in the middle of the Depression. His father went bankrupt and Saul had to drop out of school, and it was a great source of embarrassment for him for his entire life. Among Jews, education is considered very, very important, and Saul always felt inferior as a consequence. But he was truly a self-made man."

Despite recurring conflicts, the team stayed together—until Holiff reached a breaking point in 1966. In an effort to expand Cash's concert horizons further, Holiff worked hard to put together an ambitious two-week tour of Europe. The highlight for Holiff was getting Cash onto one of the world's most prestigious stages, the famous Olympia theater in Paris, which was known for presenting such stylish figures as Edith Piaf, Charles Aznavour, and Josephine Baker. Cash would be the first country artist ever to perform on the Olympia stage. The show was scheduled for May 11.

Again, Cash let Holiff down.

As soon as he arrived in England on May 5, John learned that Dylan was going to be doing a show in Cardiff, also on May 11. So he decided to hook up again with Bob and hired a driver to take him to Wales. Film footage exists of the two of them backstage before the show, where they played "I Still Miss Someone" with Dylan at the piano singing lead, as Cash, clearly stoned, tries to keep up. The scene was captured in *Eat the Document,* a Dylan tour documentary by D. A. Pennebaker. Though never formally released, the film has been available over the years in bootleg editions, and the footage offers an unsettling glimpse of Cash's drugged state at the time.

"Saul worked on that Paris show for a very long time, and everyone was gathered at Heathrow that day to fly over to Paris—the band, Saul, June, my mother," says Jonathan Holiff. "But Johnny did not show up. He went on what Saul called a 'wild escapade' with Bob Dylan.... Saul was so pissed off that he said, 'That's it.' He walked around Hyde Park about eight times, drank a bottle of scotch, and flew home to Ontario."

Even after the long flight, Holiff was adamant. He had worked with this madman long enough. In a defiant letter, he told Cash that he didn't want any commission for the English tour despite everything he had done: "62 letters, countless calls, wires, notes and three months of preparation—manifests, work permits, etc.—so things would go smooth."

He also apparently responded to a claim by Cash that Holiff had browbeaten the tour's English promoter: "Browbeat? The incident you refer to according to Merv [Conn, the promoter] was after your call from Newcastle, when you complained bitterly about your treatment, the poor promotion, etc. and requested cancellation of the last date. I called Merv to advise him accordingly. He was not browbeaten. However, you are more of an authority on the subject than I am."

Finally, he wrote, "As agreed five years ago, I resign and give one month's notice. I intend to be in Buffalo on the last day there [June 25] to collect my commission and to come to what I hope is a peaceful arrangement for the balance of monies owed."

Once again Cash sought relief from the turmoil in his music. After the English dates, he and June made their first trip to the Holy Land, and they were enthralled. On the flight back to the States after the vacation, he talked again about doing a gospel album in Israel.

When Cash returned to Nashville, Don Law was waiting with good news. The *Everybody Loves a Nut* album had just entered the country chart at number twenty-two, joining *Mean as Hell!* which was number fourteen in its tenth week. But Law, in his usual unthreatening way, also pointed out to John that the cupboard was bare. He had scheduled several sessions during the year, but Cash had either canceled them or shown up too wasted to record. The last successful date was January 29, when they wrapped up the *Nut* album. Otherwise, all they had were tracks recorded at various points during the closing months of 1965, when Cash was continuing to have difficulty writing good new songs of his own.

Amid the drought, he decided to crank out versions of such varied material as "Wabash Cannonball," another classic old train song; "You Comb Her Hair," a love song by his buddies Harlan Howard and Hank Cochran that had already been recorded by

George Jones; and even "Guess Things Happen That Way," his old Sun hit.

The jewel among the field was a song that had "hit" written all over it. "For Lovin' Me," a dynamic bit of male bravado, was composed by Gordon Lightfoot, a young Canadian who shared a publisher with Dylan. If Cash had been in good enough shape to fill the song with the right sensual tension, Law would have rushed it out as soon as possible as a single. Unfortunately, the arrangement on the recording was listless and Cash wasn't convincing in the role of a love 'em and leave 'em kinda guy.

Besides, Law told Cash, Waylon had already recorded the song, and DJs were jumping all over it. Jennings's version captured the song's strong sexual undercurrents and went a long way toward making Nashville realize it had a budding superstar on its hands.

In talking to Cash, Law was hoping to hear he had some new songs or ideas, but there was no sign that his dry spell was over. Cash did mention a live prison album again, but the memory of the second botched live recording remained too strong for Law even to consider it. Cash was so unfocused that Law found it hard to know if Cash was even listening to him during the conversation. Cash would sometimes stay at Law's apartment in Nashville, which enabled Law to observe his behavior even more closely than in the studio. "He was a very complex and a very tortured person," he said. "He'd come in and go through every drawer. I don't know what he was looking for."

With Cash offering no alternative and Columbia needing a follow-up album for *Nut,* Law suggested the only option he could think of. He put the best of the tracks on hand into an album aimed at fans who'd liked "Happy to Be with You." In no shape to go into the studio, Cash gave the okay to release the album, titled *Happiness Is You.* It was his weakest yet.

IV

There would be no showdown in Buffalo after all. After a brief cooling-off period, it was as if Holiff had never quit. Without a word of explanation, he and Cash just picked up where they'd left off. Holiff knew that Cash was still his best chance to make a million dollars—and Cash told himself he'd probably never find anyone else who would take such abuse yet show such determination and ambition. Some Cash observers have suggested that Holiff was another father figure, though Cash, in later years, didn't refer to Holiff with the same deep affection he showed for George Bates, Sam Phillips, or Eck Carter.

Back in the fold, Holiff turned his attention to Don Law. For all of Law's distinguished history at Columbia, Holiff felt that Cash needed a stronger voice in the company, someone who would fight for promotional dollars in a way the laid-back Law didn't. Though he never told Cash, Holiff also felt that a stronger producer would challenge him more when he didn't come up with songs or album concepts that had commercial appeal.

The producer Holiff began focusing on was Bob Johnston, a young, free-spirited Texan who had been championed at Columbia by the greatly respected John Hammond and who was working in the pop division with such high-profile acts as Simon & Garfunkel and Bob Dylan. Cash was impressed, but he wanted to be loyal to Law. He told Holiff to give him some time to think about it.

Around the time of the Buffalo date, John and June guested on *Rainbow Quest,* an informal TV talk show devoted to traditional American music. Hosted by Pete Seeger, it was broadcast by WNJU in Newark, New Jersey, a UHF station, which meant limited viewership. To underscore the old-time concept, Seeger and his guests sat around a kitchen table (complete with coffeepot) and talked about the history of the songs they sang. Other guests in the series included the Stanley Brothers, Buffy Sainte-Marie, Doc Watson, and Mississippi John Hurt.

The *Rainbow Quest* episode, which can be seen on DVD, offers a telling portrait of Cash's depth as an artist and his destructiveness. In a future time of more careful image control, Cash wouldn't have been allowed anywhere near a TV camera in his condition.

From the opening moments of the show, Cash exhibited the squirming, twitching mannerisms of an addict. As the camera panned to him after June sang "Worried Man Blues" early in the show, Cash took off his shoes and did the rest of the program in his stockinged feet. It's no wonder Seeger seemed more at ease talking to June. Then again, Seeger respected Cash. He looked on admiringly as Cash sang some tunes from his childhood—"I Am a Pilgrim" and "There's a Mother Always Waiting"—and, especially, when he sang Peter LaFarge's "As Long As the Grass Shall Grow."

The broadcast was another example of Cash's ability to tailor his performance to his audience—in this case folk bard Seeger. It wasn't a stretch. Cash loved this music. But he also knew what would work in that setting. It's a point Don Reid picked up on early in the Statler Brothers' tenure with Cash. "We saw him perform differently for different crowds," he says. "There was the big city John, the rural John, the college John, the convict John, the White House John. I was struck by how much he was attuned to the audience and their feelings and [would] try to find something in his own experience that enabled them to come together."

Out in Casitas Springs, Vivian continued to agonize over her future. Since the doctor's warning, she had been trying to imagine life without Johnny Cash. What would be the effect of a divorce on her and her kids? She even asked Ray and Carrie Cash what she should do, and her mother-in-law advised her to file for divorce, saying, "That'll shake him up, and he'll come back home." The remark showed how little even his mother knew about Cash's thinking and condition at the time.

All Vivian knew was that she couldn't take it anymore.

On a Friday afternoon in June, Vivian signed the divorce papers in her attorney's office in Ventura. She charged extreme mental cruelty and asked for alimony and custody of the girls. Cash was served with the divorce notice on August 14 in Denver, and the papers were formally filed at the courthouse on August 17. The news hit the headlines the next day.

"When my mom said 'divorce,' I didn't know what it meant," says Kathy, who was ten in 1966. "She held me in her arms and said, 'It means his clothes won't be hanging in the closet.' I said,

'Okay, can I go play?' I loved my dad, but it wasn't like it was going to be any different. We never saw him anymore anyway."

Cash tried to downplay the issue. He told Marshall that Vivian was bluffing. But he was frantic. Though he stated in his first autobiography that he didn't contest the divorce, he sent Holiff a telegram instructing him, "Fight this." Holiff hired an attorney, and both sides dug in.

Some close to Cash at the time said he didn't want a divorce. That's not the same as saying he wanted to go back to Vivian. At best, he wanted the status quo, which meant he would still have his family—and he wouldn't have to give Vivian half of everything he owned. The correspondence with Holiff centered mostly on minimizing the latter. Even in later years, his daughters Rosanne and Kathy say he never even hinted that he had wanted to go back to their mother.

The battle over settlement terms would go on for months.

Meanwhile, June's marriage to Nix was history. Nix didn't contest it. "I didn't want to drag the kids in front of all those people and make a big case out of it," he says. "I'm not upset about it. It's just something that happens."

Years later, he expressed no hard feelings toward either June or Johnny. "Anyone could see we weren't meant for each other," he notes of June. "She'd be home for about five days, then gone for twenty. Even in that five days, she'd be nervous and restless, and I'd say, 'June, you're ready to go back on the road, ain't you?' and she'd say, 'I guess so.' It was the same with her mother. That was their life. They grew up that way. You can't expect them to be any other way."

The hardest thing about Cash's fractured relationship with Vivian was how little time he had with his girls. One of the strongest tenets from his Dyess youth was the importance of family, and he had seen so many other country entertainers throw their families away; he was haunted by the idea of doing the same thing. After he gave up Casitas Springs for Nashville in 1965, he repeatedly begged Vivian to let the children visit him—but there was no way she could trust him when he didn't even have a proper home. For most of his life, either in letters or in conversation, Cash would express guilt over his relationship with his children. He spent much of his life trying to repair the void that was created during that time, but the damage was immense.

As soon as Vivian filed for divorce, Cash renewed his requests to see the girls, but she still demanded that he have a suitable place for them to stay. Cash started looking in Nashville for a house to buy.

V

Cash kept to himself a lot, both on tour and in Nashville, in the weeks after the divorce filing. Grant, Holiff, and Law hoped he was using the time to write new songs; they knew of his tendency to turn to music in moments of great stress. If so, Cash didn't have much to show for it when he met with Law in the fall. Hoping to speed things along, Law tried to get Cash into the studio, but it took until November 1 before they finally made it.

One of the two songs recorded that day was impressive. "You Beat All I Ever Saw" was a love song with some of the simple lyrical conviction and melodic ease of "I Walk the Line." As with "For Lovin' Me," however, something misfired during the session. The musical backing was uninspired, and Cash's vocals failed to convey the heartfelt words, especially when he delivered the title line in a low, gruff, gimmicky manner.

The other song was the ill-conceived "Put the Sugar to Bed," which listed Maybelle Carter as co-writer. It sounded like a mix of Cash's usual wordplay and a night of too many drugs. It even opened with another burst of the "Ring of Fire" trumpets. Once more, Marshall Grant shook his head at what he was hearing.

With nothing else at hand, Law released "You Beat All I Ever Saw" and "Put the Sugar to Bed" as a single, and "You Beat" became a modest hit. But the session reinforced Holiff's belief that Cash needed a new producer. He couldn't understand why Law wasn't able to get better work out of an artist of Cash's stature—regardless of drug problems.

In a letter to Cash days after "You Beat All I Ever Saw" went out to disc jockeys, Holiff wrote: "I urge you to declare yourself immediately and go with Bob Johnson [*sic*]. Contrary to the various malicious rumors about him—he is too smart to treat you in a high-handed manner or come on strong in any way with you. But he is man enough to stand up to you and take a stand."

He then challenged Cash himself. "Although you've never been exactly undernourished in the area of good material or the ability to come up with same, no one is infallible and sometimes your good judgment has wavered," he wrote, adding that Johnston "is musically knowledgeable and creative enough [to offer] at least palatable and exciting ideas for your consideration. That's more than anyone has done in recent years."

Holilff urged Cash to speak up on behalf of Johnston, but offered to do so himself—"tactfully"—if Cash felt reluctant for any reason, assuring his client, "Columbia quite naturally will abide by your decision." Clearly, Holiff had already been twisting the label's arm. He sent a blind carbon copy of the letter to Bill Gallagher, the vice president and general manager of Columbia Records, who was in a position to decide Law's fate.

Johnston himself had already been working internally to take over Nashville's country operations. He had been lobbying Gallagher for months, but how could he get rid of Law or Frank Jones, whom Law had brought in as his second in command with the understanding he'd eventually take over?

The answer came from Clive Davis, the shrewd, ambitious attorney who was being groomed to replace Goddard Lieberson as head of CBS Records, which ran the Columbia and Epic labels. As an attorney rather than a "music man," Davis was a controversial choice within the company, and many shook their heads when he started making musical decisions.

Though a fan of Broadway musicals and mainstream pop, Davis saw that times were changing, and he was alarmed that rival labels were doing a much better job of signing artists who were attractive to the young rock generation. He also felt that Nashville was too content selling to the country audience rather than trying to pick up additional sales in the far larger pop market. Because of Johnston's work with Dylan and Simon & Garfunkel and his feel for country music, Davis saw him as an ideal replacement for Law, who would reach the mandatory retirement age of sixty-five the following February 27.

Columbia had routinely waived that requirement for top executives, including Lieberson himself, but Davis made it clear to Law that he would have to exit. He felt that Law and Jones were both too timid about adding pop appeal to their records because they were afraid of alienating country music DJs. To make the decision less harsh, Davis agreed to Law's request that he be allowed to keep working, as an independent producer, with four of his artists—as long as those artists wanted to keep working with him. The ones on his list: Cash, Ray Price, Carl Smith, and the duo Flatt and Scruggs.

Insiders at the label and in Nashville knew about the pending changes by the end of the year, and Columbia let everyone else in on the news in January. *Billboard* reported that Johnston was moving to Nashville shortly to take over from Law and that he was bringing some of his New York acts, including Dylan, to Nashville to record. Despite Holiff's urgings, Cash, out of loyalty, stuck with Law for a few more sessions. Cash just didn't like to be rushed when it came to decision making. June Carter could attest to that.

CHAPTER 18

THE DIVORCE, BOB JOHNSTON, AND A SUICIDE TALE

I

EVER SINCE THE "It Ain't Me, Babe" duet, John and June's teamings were an increasingly popular part of the live show. One reason was the chemistry; they looked like a real couple, and they were having fun. Even more popular than "Babe" in the show was "Jackson," a song written by Billy "Edd" Wheeler, a budding songwriter and playwright who had the idea for the song after reading Edward Albee's play *Who's Afraid of Virginia Woolf?* and admiring the savage verbal skirmishes between the college professor and his wife. He wrote "Jackson" as a good-natured folksy tale of domestic sarcasm.

John thought it'd sound great live because he and June could act out the song's raucous spirit. They had been singing it in concert for some time before finally recording it on January 11, 1967. With the added punch of Carl Perkins's guitar, the music on "Jackson" sounded snappier than on any Cash single since "Ring of Fire." In the song, the fire has gone out of a relationship, and John's character boasts about the sexual conquests ahead when he visits the city of Jackson. June, in turn, knows it's all bluster and that he's just a big-talking man everyone can see through. Law penciled it in as a potential single.

Encouraged, Cash sat down with Law a few weeks later to play some songs he had been writing, as well as a few older ones he had been too uncertain about to show him. It was an odd assortment, but Law liked a couple of them enough to schedule a session for the first week in March. Many of the stories touched on familiar Cash themes. Two stood out: "Another Song to Sing" and "The Masterpiece," both of which spoke to the heart of Cash's love for music with an inspirational edge.

As usual after *Ride This Train,* Cash spent some time figuring out how to tie the songs together. Once again he saw them as snapshots of people and beliefs from the American past; but he knew that he couldn't turn them into another series of stops on a train ride, and some of them were too contemporary to fit into another chronicle of the Old West. So he settled on the timeless imagery of "The Star-Spangled Banner." He wanted the music to be simple, often nothing more elaborate than what you'd hear around a campfire. Cash began the album, *From Sea to Shining Sea,* with the opening notes of the national anthem, giving way to a narration that featured another of his favorite devices—a shout-out of actual towns, including, in a nod to Bob Dylan, Hibbing, Minnesota.

The wild card in the sessions was another playful duet along the lines of "Jackson." Using an idea from Marshall Grant, Cash reworked the lyrics of "Long-Legged Guitar Pickin' Man" for him and June. There was no way the song would fit into the collection, but Cash and Law were thinking about a duet album to capitalize on "Jackson," which had already entered the country sales chart. They called the album *Carryin' On with Johnny Cash & June Carter,* which surely caused snickers among the Cash entourage.

II

Tired of his nomadic existence in Nashville and wanting a home for the girls to visit during the summer, Cash looked in the early spring at some lots along Old Hickory Lake in Hendersonville, a small town just north of Nashville. He asked Braxton Dixon, a successful architect-builder, to help him in his search. On a tour of the area, Dixon drove Cash past a house that he was building for himself—a house built of stone and carefully chosen hand-hewn timber. Set on a cliff, the house offered lovely views of the lake. Cash didn't want to see anything else. "Name your price," Cash said.

Wanting to keep the house for himself, Dixon set a figure he thought was high enough—$150,000—to cause Cash to back off. But Cash refused to blink. Even though he had to borrow money from Columbia Records to make the down payment, Cash had to have that house.

"It just looked like what I'd like to live in, the rough timbers and the stones, on the lake," he said. "It was quiet and peaceful. It was also big and roomy and rugged. I don't think he ever expected me to pay him for that house. I expected he thought I would have to give it back to him. If I'd stayed in the shape I was in, I'd never pay for it. But I knew all along that someday I'd pay him back...because I knew I'd straighten up."

If Cash really believed he would someday straighten up, he may have been the only one.

Cash's behavior, especially when it came to missing shows, continued to infuriate Holiff, who was having so much trouble securing bookings that he turned to the head of the largest talent-booking agency in Nashville in hopes of lining up lucrative county and state fair appearances for Cash. But Cash's reputation prevented even the agency's head, Lucky Moeller, from finding many takers—just four dates from among the hundreds of fairs around the country that year.

Holiff continued to believe that Cash's future rested with Bob Johnston, and he hoped to take advantage of a brief Canadian tour in early April to persuade Cash finally to request a change of producers. But John was in no shape even to listen; he was becoming increasingly unreliable on the road. Instead of making progress on the Johnston matter, Holiff had to deal just with getting Cash to the next town. Cash made it only as far as Edmonton, the fourth stop.

"He was on a rampage of pills, and he had a Martin, an expensive guitar, very expensive guitar," Holiff recalled. "And he was in a darkened room, and he hadn't slept for a couple of days, and he's already missed one of the dates. And they're all my dates that I had to set up because nobody wanted to book him. You know, they couldn't trust that he would be there. He took the guitar and smashed it against the wall. I had said things to provoke him. And I guess he just didn't have the nerve to hit me with the guitar, so he hit it against the wall and smashed it."

Just weeks after the Edmonton incident, Holiff sent Cash a scolding telegram: "YOUR PROFESSIONAL BEHAVIOR IS TOTALLY REPREHENSIBLE, SHOWING A COMPLETE DISREGARD FOR THE RIGHTS AND FEELINGS OF EVERYONE AROUND YOU."

Still, Holiff continued to represent Cash—and he continued to push for Johnston. Gradually, Cash weakened. Maybe Holiff was right. After all, Johnston was working with Bob Dylan. But Cash didn't want to make a move until he and Law finished the duets album. He thought he owed Don that much.

Eager to show off his new house and mark the twenty-third anniversary of his brother Jack's death, Cash invited his family members to join him in Hendersonville on May 20, even though only the kitchen and one bedroom were finished. Since his parents didn't want to fly alone from California, Cash flew to Los Angeles to accompany them on the flight back to Tennessee. While in California, Cash picked up some more drugs, and he was as high as the plane on the return trip.

"I'd been up for about three days and nights straight with no sleep, and I was told later that when we landed in Memphis, I got up out of my seat and fell on my face on the floor of the plane," he said. "I had taken barbiturates, thinking I would sleep until Memphis, but evidently I had taken far too many.

"The pilot told Mother and Daddy, 'You'll have to get him out of here. He can't fly on to Nashville on this plane.' They had me carried off, called Roy, who hadn't yet left Memphis, and took me to a motel. The next thing I remember was the following day on the plane going to Nashville. I stumbled off the plane, still groggy from the barbiturates."

Tommy Cash was waiting at the Nashville airport, and he was furious about the embarrassment his brother had caused their mother and father. Tommy, who'd been hired by John to represent him on various projects in Nashville, was heartbroken over the collapse of his brother's marriage and his continued drug abuse.

"During those years, I saw his personality change," says Tommy Cash. "He became filled with paranoia and anger. When I'd talk to him about it, he'd say, 'Mind your own business. I'm all right, I'm fine.' He wasn't mean to me, but he was mean to a lot of people. I saw a lot of that."

But Tommy couldn't restrain himself that night at the airport.

"You scared Mama and Daddy half to death and you're high and you're out of your mind!" he shouted.

Cash responded by sucker-punching his brother in the face, knocking him to the ground.

"I got up, and I was in real good physical condition," Tommy adds, "because I was always a good athlete. Daddy stepped in between us and said, 'Boys you shouldn't fight in front of your mother.' The next day John was all apologetic, and I accepted his apology. He gave me one of his prized Indian head coins. But it showed why we were all scared to death about what was going to happen to him and what the drugs did to him."

Two days after the anniversary gathering, Cash was in the studio with June working on the duet album.

Cash didn't spend night after night trying to choose the right songs for the package, as he had done with the concept albums. He already had three numbers: "Jackson," "Long-Legged," and "It Ain't Me, Babe." Beyond that, he and June were open to suggestions. Someone brought up Ray Charles, and Cash thought it'd be fun to do some of the songs that Charles had recorded before he made his foray into the country field in the 1960s with heavily orchestrated versions of hits such as "I Can't Stop Loving You" and "Crying Time." That led to John and June teaming up on "I Got a Woman" and "What'd I Say." Charles may have had an affinity for country music, but John and June showed little feel for R&B. The rest of the album was a sort of family affair—and it wasn't very good. Even Cash realized he needed fresh ideas. It was time for this fellow Johnston.

*   *   *

As soon as Cash bought the new house, he started lobbying Vivian to let the girls spend some time with him—and she finally relented that summer.

To have time at home with the girls, Cash limited his touring during those six weeks in 1967 to fewer than a half-dozen shows. The house still wasn't finished when the girls arrived; the only furniture was a dining room table, a bed, and a few chairs. He bought a twin bed for each of the girls and placed them head to head in a cross shape in the center of the house's large second bedroom. Rosanne was now twelve, Kathy eleven, and Cindy and Tara turning eight and six, respectively.

"It was so cute, because the headboards all came together so that we could talk at night and feel so close," Kathy remembers. "Mom, of course, was worried. I'd call at least once a week to let her know we missed her but we were fine—and we *were* fine; we had a blast. He was so much fun, and we'd all laugh so much. Those summers in Hendersonville were some of the best times of my life."

One of her favorite memories was of Cash teaching them to water-ski.

"I mean, you're talking about four girls in the boat at once and trying to teach all four of us, and he did a great job," she says. "He also taught us all how to drive and how to cast a fishing pole. It had been so long since Dad had any real time with us, and it seemed like he was trying to cram everything he ever wanted to do into that summer."

Though Cash was still deep into pills, he seemed more upbeat and loving than he had in years. "He was still very shaky and gaunt, but you got the sense he was trying to get better," Rosanne recalls. "I could see him trying. I don't think my mom was being mean by not letting us visit him earlier. She always encouraged us to have a relationship with our father. She was a strong woman. She was just worried about how he'd be. She sent him a laundry list of things he had to follow. One of them was to take us to mass every Sunday, and he did."

Cash's oldest daughter also remembers how he would pick peaches and wild blackberries from his orchard and make ice cream, lighting firecrackers to kill the time while he was cranking the ice-cream churn. He'd also take the girls to the movies, some-times three a day, and rent a local roller rink so they and other family members could have the place to themselves.

June and her daughters were frequent visitors at the house that first summer, but they went home in the evenings; John and June still weren't admitting to anyone, especially Cash's daughters, that they had been sleeping together for years. The California girls had no idea they were meeting their future stepmother and stepsis-ters. Meanwhile, June's girls had been accumulating stories about Cash's odd behavior well before he married their mother, since he was a frequent guest at June's house in Madison and at their grand-parents' house.

"We'd wake up and find the kitchen was on fire because he had done something wrong while making breakfast, or he'd show up without his key and take an axe to the front door," Carlene says. "Mama wasn't scared of him, but she was scared *for* him. The mar-riage only happened because he made a change."

III

A gruff but quick-thinking maverick, Bob Johnston was born in Hillsboro, Texas, in 1932, which made him the same age as Cash. His father was a chiropractor and his mother, Diane Johnston, was a songwriter whose tunes were recorded by Gene Autry and Asleep at the Wheel. After a tour in the Navy, Bob recorded a few rockabilly-type songs under the name Don Johnston, but nothing much happened, and he turned to producing.

After a brief stay at Kapp Records, he found his way to Columbia Records in the mid-sixties where, thanks to a combination of talent and fast talking, he got to work with Dylan on the *Highway 61 Re-visited* album and with Simon & Garfunkel on their breakthrough collection *Sounds of Silence.* It was an extraordinary one-two punch that landed him the Nashville job.

Out of respect for Don Law, Johnston didn't plan to go after Cash right away, but Cash was quick to invite him to the house in the summer of 1967. "I went out to see him, and he told me to jump in the boat and go for a ride on the lake, but I told him, 'I wouldn't get on a bicycle with you,'" Johnston remembers. "I could see he was in pretty bad shape. So we eventually sat on the ground and he asked, 'Can you tell me what's going to happen to me? What do I need to do with my music?'

"I said, 'You need to build a mausoleum in your head with big iron doors so that nobody can get in there except you. You don't let me in there, you don't let June in there, you don't let your manager in there, you don't let the record company people in there. You have to decide for yourself what you want to do with your music—and not let anyone else tell you. If you do that, you're going to be one of the biggest stars in the world.'"

In his spaced-out state, Cash just stared at Johnston, leaving the producer with no inkling whether Cash was going to start working with him or stay with Law, but John immediately knew he wanted this Texan by his side in the studio. He liked Johnston's spirit; here was a man who talked about the record executives as if they were the enemy. Cash notified Holiff that he wanted to start working with Johnston.

Shortly after the meeting at the house, Johnston was sitting in his office at Columbia Records on Music Row when Cash stopped by.

"He walked in and said, 'I've got an idea for an album, but I don't guess you'll like it either,'" Johnston recalls. "He said, 'I've always wanted to go to a prison and record the show, but no one would let me do it.'" Clearly he had conveniently forgotten his no-show at the Kansas prison date two years earlier.

Seizing the moment, Johnston picked up the phone and called San Quentin, but he couldn't get through to the warden, so he just left a message that Johnny Cash wanted to record an album there. "I called San Quentin because that was the one I thought of first," Johnston says. "Then, I thought of Folsom and called there. If I couldn't get through there, I would have called Sing-Sing."

Johnston had no idea that Cash had played Folsom the year before, so he was surprised when the warden told him right away that he'd love to have John come back. When Johnston hung up, he warned Cash not to tell anyone at Columbia about their plan because someone might veto the idea. Sure enough, Johnston maintained years later, Cash returned to his office a few weeks later, shaken because somebody at Columbia had found out about the prison plans and told him they'd drop him if he proceeded. Johnston said not to worry; he'd find a way to get the album done—despite the "goddamn record company."

Clive Davis didn't deny Johnston's key role in finally getting the Folsom project started, but he rejected the idea that anyone at Columbia wanted to kill the project or was thinking about dropping Cash from the roster.

"I appointed Bob Johnston to the position in Nashville and he reported to me," Davis says. "I remember discussions with him about the album and I supported it—or it would have never happened. I could have stopped it, but why would I? We believed in Johnny Cash. Why else would we have re-signed him to a very lucrative contract just before Folsom? The *Greatest Hits* album was huge. No way would we drop an artist the stature of Johnny Cash."

Indeed, Cash was having a good year sales-wise. "Jackson" went to number two in the country field. To keep the momentum going, Columbia released "Long-Legged Guitar Pickin' Man" as a single in late May, and it reached number six on the country charts, but, like "Jackson," it failed to crack the pop market.

Johnny Cash's Greatest Hits, Volume 1 lit up the summer album charts. Columbia celebrated the release with a full-page ad in *Billboard* that featured the line "The only thing greater than one Johnny Cash hit is a lot of Johnny Cash hits. Johnny's new album is Cash all the way with 11 of his all-time country classics."

The album went to number one on the country charts and broke the Top 100 on the pop charts. It was enough to persuade Davis to tear up Cash's 1964 contract and order his staff to draft a new one that would increase Cash's royalty rate from five cents to nine. If an album sold for four dollars, he would get thirty-six cents from every copy plus any writing royalties.

Cash went into the studio with Johnston for the first time on October 2 to record a song, "Rosanna's Going Wild," that was written by June and her sisters. The song was the story of a sexy young thing who raised eyebrows with her air of abandon. It wasn't one of

Cash's great records, but it packed a wallop on the radio even if it, once again, shamelessly echoed the trumpet blare of "Ring of Fire."

For their first session together, Johnston spent hours in the studio before the musicians arrived, making sure the microphones and speakers were linked up correctly. For all the trouble Law had had re-creating the dynamics of Cash's Sun recordings, Johnston's attention to sonic detail paid off right away. The Statler Brothers' Don Reid says the difference between Law and Johnston was enormous. "I don't think Don had a lot of creativity, whereas Bob was a big bag of energy and always ready to work. His sessions were creative and loose where Don Law just walked through the motions." The single went to number two on the country charts.

There was more good news in the Cash camp. A date had been set for the live Folsom recording: January 13, 1968.

IV

Grant and others feared there was no way Cash would be in any kind of shape to do the live album. Between the divorce and his mounting financial problems, Cash was deeper into drugs than anyone could remember. Grant felt as if he was on twenty-four-hour vigil at this point. June gave up—again—in early October. She told Cash it was over.

Suddenly alone, without either his family or the woman he loved, on October 21 Cash poured out his heart to Holiff in a rambling ten-page letter about his relationship with June. Cash still saw Holiff as the only one in his world who could get things done.

In the letter, Cash wove back and forth, like a drunken driver crossing lanes, between an almost childlike helplessness and full-fledged rage. He recounted how he had given up his family for June and accused her of having a long history of heartlessly chewing men up and spitting them out. Desperate, he pledged he would seek treatment for his addiction if Holiff could stop June from leaving him.

It wasn't the only angry letter the drugged-out Cash sent Holiff that month.

In researching the film about his father, Jonathan Holiff found a trail of canceled dates in 1967 and a letter his father sent Cash on October 27 that year in response to Cash's demand that Holiff lower his commission rate to help Cash get over his financial woes. "Johnny was missing more shows than he was doing at this time, and my father pointed that out in his letter," Jonathan says.

Saul wrote: "You missed $40,000 worth of dates in one year! If you continue like this, it will lead to disaster. Your solution is to cut back my commissions. I am willing to do that, but I want your co-operation in cutting your own expenses and in missing no more dates."

The debts were wide-ranging—from money he owed his family, including his parents, out in California, to a whopping $125,000 government fine (reduced in 1969 to $82,000) for his part in the Los Padres National Forest fire, to payments on the new house and the potential divorce settlement.

With the attorney bills piling up, Cash finally instructed his lawyers to go ahead with the latest offer from Vivian. Under the agreement, she received the Casitas Springs house, alimony of $1,000 a month, and child support payments of $1,600 a month, as well as half the royalties forever on Cash's musical works made during the marriage. That meant she would collect money on both the songs he'd written, such as "I Walk the Line," and the ones he had simply recorded, such as—and this must have been bitter-sweet—"Ring of Fire" and "It Ain't Me, Babe." For his part, Cash got chiefly the trailer park and the remaining 50 percent of his writing and recording royalties. He would control 100 percent of the royalties on any new records or songs.

For much of the rest of his life, he would speak of that fall of 1967 as some of his darkest days.

"If you looked in his eyes, you never saw happy, smiling eyes even if he was having a good time," says Bill Miller, who grew over the years from being a boyhood fan to a friend who put together a line of fan merchandise with Cash, and who opened a Johnny Cash museum in Nashville in 2013. "There was always this deep inten-sity, this profound sadness. I saw it, and we talked about it."

Miller attributes part of the sadness to Cash's continuing guilt over his failure to be a better father in the 1960s. Miller feels it was that guilt, and his religious upbringing, that contributed to Cash's refusal to judge others.

When recounting the darkness of the fall of 1967, Cash invariably told three stories that have been repeated time and again in books and articles—one of which involves an alleged suicide attempt. The first step in his march toward regaining his will to live supposedly occurred in early October, when, as he later explained it, he went into the historic Nickajack Cave on the Tennessee River, just north of Chattanooga. He had often explored the massive system of caves looking for souvenirs from the Civil War or early Native American relics, sometimes with buddies, but usually alone.

On this occasion, Cash, buried under remorse over the breakup of his marriage, decided it was too painful to keep on living. Nickajack contained the remains of "many spelunkers and amateur adventurers who'd lost their lives in the caves over the years, usually by losing their way, and it was my hope and intention to join that company," he wrote in his second autobiography. "If I crawled far enough in, I thought, I'd never be able to find my way back out, and nobody would be able to locate me until I was dead, if indeed they ever could."

According to his account, he parked his Jeep outside and crawled through the cave for two or three hours until the batteries gave out in his flashlight and he lay down in the darkness, preparing to die. "The absolute lack of light was appropriate," he wrote, "for at that moment, I was as far from God as I have ever been. My separation from Him, the deepest and most ravaging of the various kinds of loneliness I'd felt over the years, seemed finally complete."

But then something came over him. "I thought I'd left Him, but He hadn't left me," Cash continued. "I felt something very powerful start to happen to me, a sensation of utter peace, clarity, and sobriety. I didn't believe it at first. I couldn't understand it. How, after being awake for so long and driving my body so hard and taking so many pills—dozens of them, scores, even hundreds—could I possibly feel all right? There in Nickajack Cave I became conscious of a very clear, simple idea: I was going to die at God's time, not mine.

I hadn't prayed over my decision to seek death in the cave, but that hadn't stopped God from intervening."

Cash made his way out of the cave, aided by a wisp of air that guided him to an exit, where he found June and his mother waiting with a basket of food and drink. "I knew there was something wrong," his mother told him, he wrote. "I had to come and find you."

He supposedly decided then and there to quit drugs.

In all his drugged days and nights, Cash likely did sometimes feel sufficiently trapped and devoid of hope that he wanted to give up on life, and the story dramatized the feelings of helplessness and recovery.

Nevertheless, the problem with the story and the way Cash told it is twofold.

First, Nickaback Cave was underwater in the fall of 1967, as a Cash historian discovered after an extensive check of weather records.

Second, Cash did not quit drugs that day.

Cash was on a tour break a month after the supposed Nickaback adventure when he somehow ended up in LaFayette, Georgia, a tiny burg just across the state line from Chattanooga. He was arrested for public drunkenness on the afternoon of Thursday, November 2, and spent the night in jail. He was taken from the cell the next morning to see Sheriff Ralph Jones, who surprised him by saying he was free to go.

Recalled Cash, "He was sitting behind the counter and he looked up at me and he said, 'My wife is such a big fan of yours that she's got every record you got and watches you every chance she can on the television. When I told her I had you in my jail, she cried.'"

Jones then placed Cash's pills, money, and pocketknife on the counter and continued, "But I'm not gonna cry. You wanna kill yourself? I'm gonna give you your God-given right to go ahead and do that, so take your pills and go."

This story was true. Sheriff Jones confirmed this account in 1970.

Deeply touched, Cash resolved again he would give up drugs—
which leads to the final story in the trilogy.

Whether because of Sheriff Jones's lecture, his pledge to seek treatment if June would stick with him, or the upcoming Folsom date,
Cash returned home on Saturday and, through June, turned the following day to a psychiatrist, Dr. Nat Winston. Winston agreed to see
Cash on Monday.

In his first autobiography, Cash wrote that he made it through
Sunday without any pills, but Monday he found a bottle of amphetamines he had hidden in the bathroom, and he swallowed a handful.
He spent most of the day in the house in a daze, but just before
dark he raced outside for some air. Suddenly "craving excitement,"
he drove his tractor along the cliff that overlooked the lake, daring
himself to get closer and closer to the edge—until the earth gave
way and Cash tumbled into the lake with the tractor right behind
him, barely missing him. He tried to pull himself out of the freezing water, but he didn't have the strength.

Just when he thought he was going to drown, Braxton Dixon,
who had apparently seen the whole thing from his adjacent property, came rushing down to the lake and pulled him to safety. When
he awoke around four a.m., Dr. Winston was sitting beside the
bed. With June and her parents by his side, Cash spent the next
three weeks (or, by some accounts, thirty days) in the house, kicking drugs.

That story is partly true.

Dr. Winston confirmed years later that he did help Cash, though
he remembered the time of his arrival that night as ten p.m. and
the detox period closer to ten days.

"When I got to the house, Johnny was lying on this huge round
bed, and he didn't weigh more than 125 pounds," the psychiatrist
told me. "He was just a skeleton, and he was out of it. When he
woke up, I recommended he see someone in private practice who
could devote more time with him, but June was more comfortable
with me, so I agreed. I stopped by to see him every day. He was very
polite. He wanted to get off the drugs, and he knew he couldn't do
it himself."

Things progressed so well over the next week and a half that Cash was in good enough shape to follow through on a promise he had made months before, to perform November 18 at a benefit concert to raise money for the local high school band. Cash wrote in his memoir that he had never felt stronger onstage. He was finally off drugs for good.

Well, not really.

Cash was getting more rest and healthier meals, thanks to June's and Maybelle's cooking, than he had in ages, and his pattern of recovery continued throughout the month. The gaunt addict look went away. Cash gained at least thirty pounds. A thrilled Marshall Grant proclaimed, "Old John is back."

Cash ended the year with a brief California tour that included a November 28 stop at the 6,300-seat Shrine Auditorium in Los Angeles. He looked great with the extra weight, and his voice sounded stronger than it had in ages. Carl Perkins was so inspired by what he saw in his friend that he walked onto the beach north of L.A. the day after the Shrine show and threw a bottle of bourbon into the ocean. He made a pledge to God that he would never take another drink.

As the musicians headed home for Christmas shows, everyone hoped for the best, but Grant knew the moment of truth was at hand when he learned on December 22 that the divorce from Vivian had become final. Even though John had signed off on it, Grant feared the worst—and sure enough he heard from June that Cash, deeply depressed, was off to Chattanooga, where he again turned to drugs, telling a musician friend, "This is the worst day of my life."

Folsom was just twenty-two days away.

CHAPTER 19

FOLSOM PRISON AND MARRYING JUNE

I

As far back as his Air Force days, Cash had paused each New Year's Eve to go over the highs and lows of the year and to set a few goals. He would eventually commit those thoughts to paper, but he was still keeping them in his head in 1967—and he was badly shaken by the way things had been going. Even when his personal life was hopelessly messed up, he had usually been proud of his music. No longer. He realized that he hadn't felt good about an album since the *True West* package. *Everybody Loves a Nut* was fun, but a side step. *Carryin' On* was lazy, and with *Shining Sea* he had mostly just gone through the motions.

With the Folsom date nearing, he asked himself if he could regain the discipline and drive. Even the question frightened him. As he put it much later, "If I couldn't pull myself together for an album I had been wanting to make for years, I didn't know if I could ever find my way again."

Cash credited Bob Johnston with helping him overcome his fears.

"Bob kept telling me I was an artist," Cash told me. "He would sit me down and say, 'Cash, you and Bob Dylan are different. You're "fuckin' artists." You don't just make records. You make records that mean something to you and the people who hear them.' I liked the sound of the word 'artist,' and he helped me understand I needed to put everything I had into the Folsom album."

Typically, concert albums in the 1960s were stocking stuffers to a large extent, just another way of packaging a singer's greatest hits. But Cash and Johnston had no interest in anything so conventional. Johnston wanted to capture Cash's dynamics in a way that hadn't been done since the Sun days. Cash wanted to reestablish his creative passion.

In the early days of January 1968, Cash was searching for songs that would speak to the men in Folsom, the maximum-security prison near Sacramento. Because the date was so close, he had to rely on songs he knew or had already recorded rather than search for tunes the way he had for his earlier concept albums.

During the process, Cash once again demonstrated his ability to immerse himself in his subject matter, a sensitivity so strong he could virtually take on the personality of the people he was singing about. When recording *Ride This Train,* he'd transformed the hard work and determination he saw in the people in Dyess into a series of songs which reflected that same spirit in the country at large. In *Bitter Tears,* he related to the underdog plight of Native Americans. But he had never empathized with his themes as completely as he would at Folsom.

Cash knew what it was like to be in jail, to stand before his loved ones in handcuffs, and to walk through the seedy parts of town in search of drugs. He knew the deep pain of breaking his mother's heart and the numbing ache of facing a future without hope. He identified with the lingering anti-authority rage of someone who felt he had been treated unfairly by the legal system. He believed he had been set up in El Paso—targeted because of his fame—and he'd felt helpless against the courts during the divorce proceedings.

Marshall Grant realized Cash was serious about the album when he arranged for everyone, including the Tennessee Three and the Statler Brothers, to arrive in Sacramento a day early so they could rehearse in a banquet room at the El Rancho motel. "It made a big impression on us all because John usually had no patience for rehearsals," Grant said.

As it happened, Governor Ronald Reagan was holding a $500-a-plate fund-raising dinner at the motel, and many of the guests peered into the La Fiesta Room to see what all the noise was about. When Reagan himself stopped by to say hello, Cash took advantage of the moment to introduce his father. He was still trying to show Ray that he had amounted to something.

When Grant saw the set list Cash had put together, he was surprised not to find a lot of hits. He couldn't imagine John not doing "I Walk the Line"—which he had performed at every show since 1956—or "Ring of Fire." The bassist was even more surprised when Cash pulled out a tape, given to him a few hours earlier by Reverend Gressett, and played a song called "Greystone Chapel," a spiritual about God's mercy in reaching out to even the forsaken sinners in Folsom. Cash was especially intrigued because it was written by a Folsom inmate, Glen Sherley.

"I'm gonna sing this tomorrow," Cash announced to the group. "Let's go through it." Turning to Gressett, he added that he'd like to meet the writer.

Though the rehearsal lasted until nearly midnight, Cash was up by six the next morning and back in the banquet room, going over the lyrics to a couple of songs, including "Greystone Chapel." He was taken not just with the song but with the idea that an inmate had turned his trials into something so uplifting.

When Cash arrived at Folsom that morning, the prison looked as still as a cemetery. Its massive stone walls appeared capable of preventing any sound from escaping to the outside world. "Coach" Lloyd Kelley, the superintendent of recreation, ushered Cash and his touring party—all dressed in stylish black suits—through a series of gates into a large courtyard, where long lines of inmates, dressed in their blue denim shirts and pants, were waiting. Several nodded or waved as Cash headed to a temporary dressing room. On the way, he peeked into the cafeteria where the show would be held. The room looked like an aircraft hangar, with its slanted ceiling and concrete floor. Instead of long dining tables commonly shown in prison films, prisoners sat at tables for four secured to the floor. A banner across the front of the stage read *"Welcome Johnny Cash."*

The first of two concerts—which would begin at 9:40 a.m.—was still two hours away.

In the dressing area, Kelley thoughtfully warned Cash not to worry that the prisoners weren't enjoying the show if they didn't stand up or rush the stage. Conditions at Folsom were tense because some inmates had held a guard at knifepoint just two weeks before, and the convicts had been told that the concert would be stopped if anyone left his seat. Guards with shotguns would watch the concert from an overhead ramp.

Just before showtime, Cash huddled with Johnston and with his DJ friend Hugh Cherry, who was going to emcee the concert, about how to introduce Cash. Cherry assumed he'd give John a big welcome, but Johnston vetoed that idea. He told Cash just to walk out onstage and introduce himself to kick things off on a more personal level.

As Carl Perkins warmed up the audience a few minutes later with "Blue Suede Shoes," Cash stood against one of the cafeteria walls, where he could watch Perkins while getting a feel for the crowd's mood.

"I knew this was it, my chance to make up for all the times when I had messed up," he told me later. "I kept hoping my voice wouldn't give out again. Then I suddenly felt calm. I could see the men looking over at me. There was something in their eyes that made me realize everything was going to be okay. I felt I had something they needed."

Cash's sense of well-being wasn't entirely spontaneous—it was also chemically induced.

As he waited onstage for Cash, Marshall Grant was apprehensive because he knew that amid the pressure, John had again turned to drugs before leaving the El Rancho. He could see it in the distant look in Cash's eyes. It wasn't as bad as on his worst days, but it was troubling.

Johnston saw it too as they drove to the prison together.

"Just as we turned off the highway," he recalls, "we passed this sign that said something to the effect of all visitors being subject to searches, and I looked over and John was frantically going through his pockets, so I knew he had been carrying some [pills]. When I later asked him, he said, 'I took more pills that morning than I ever had in my life.' He was scared."

II

"Hello, I'm Johnny Cash."

The roar was chilling as Cash uttered the opening line that would become a concert trademark.

Instantly, Perkins and the Tennessee Three began to play "Folsom Prison Blues," and many in the audience moved their lips as they sang along silently. Several howls and shouts saluted the song's most dramatic line: *I shot a man in Reno, just to watch him die.*

In this setting, the changes Cash had made years before to Gordon Jenkins's lyrics were especially striking. Members of the audience nodded when he sang about how time keeps dragging on and about the torture of being stuck in prison while that train keeps moving down the line.

Sensing the crowd's enthusiasm, Cash threw himself into the performance. Grant would describe what followed as Cash's most captivating performance to date. He put such intensity into his vocals that his voice became strained at times, but the atmosphere was electric as Cash prowled the stage between verses with the pent-up tension of a caged panther.

In a bold bit of sequencing, he moved from one of his best-known numbers to two tales of blue-collar struggle that hadn't been hits for him: Harlan Howard's "Busted" and Merle Travis's "Dark as a Dungeon." The audience knew "Busted" from the Ray Charles hit, but Cash's stripped-down treatment felt truer to the desperation of a man struggling to put food on his family's table. He followed with a lovely, intimate treatment of "I Still Miss Someone," the ballad that was such a favorite of his that it would be appearing on one of his albums for the fourth time.

After showing his tender side, Cash injected the show with the raw, rowdy humor that he figured the prisoners must employ themselves to combat the hard prison life; he had certainly turned to it a lot in his own dark times. Besides, he knew the men wanted to be entertained as well as touched by somber themes. Cash had included "Cocaine Blues" on *Now, There Was a Song!* but in a sanitized version that carried the title "Transfusion Blues," because the record company warned that DJs wouldn't play any song with "cocaine" in it. This time Cash didn't hold anything back in the story about a man who shot his unfaithful woman dead while under the influence of whiskey and cocaine.

Every Cash fan in the crowd knew about the El Paso arrest, and most assumed he had written "Cocaine Blues," because of the references to "takin' the pill," running into trouble in Juárez, and being sentenced to the Folsom pen. Yet the original song—written in the 1940s by T. J. "Red" Arnall—also contained references to both "the pill" and Juárez. Cash changed only the prison locale, but not by much; Arnall had used nearby San Quentin. To add to the song's hard-boiled tone, Cash altered a line about shooting a woman down to shooting "that bad bitch down."

It was that "bitch" line, which Cash delivered with particular relish, that signaled to the inmates that Cash was as unruly and crazy as they were—and they whooped and hollered. He pushed things even further with the gallows humor of "25 Minutes to Go," and the response again was roaring. Next came a ballad titled "I'm Here to Get My Baby Out of Jail." Written in the 1930s, the tune appealed to Cash because of a narrative twist: the "baby" of the title referred not to a girlfriend or wife but to a son who had gone astray. He forgot some of the song's words near the end and turned to "Orange Blossom Special" to regain his momentum.

To establish a more personal mood, Cash let the band leave the stage while he sat on a stool and sang three ballads, accompanied only by his acoustic guitar—"Long Black Veil," "Send a Picture of Mother," and "The Wall." Then he returned to what he called the "entertainment portion" of the show: "Dirty Old Egg Sucking Dog," "Flushed from the Bathroom of Your Heart," and "Joe Bean."

June then joined him, bringing an immediate touch of sexual tension to the show. Despite her modest black dress that came down to the top of her knees, the prisoners let loose some catcalls. They sang "I Got a Woman," which was followed by "The Legend of John Henry." In one of the show's few miscues, June then tried to lighten the mood again by reading one of the comedy bits that worked well on the country circuit, but it was a waste of time.

Cash tried to rebound with "Green, Green Grass of Home," the most popular prison song in country music in the 1960s, but his version was curiously timid, possibly because he was thinking ahead to the morning's wild card, "Greystone Chapel."

"This next song was written by a man right here in Folsom Prison, and last night was the first time I've ever sung this song," Cash told the crowd. "We may be a little rough on it today. We'll definitely do it again on our next show…because…it may be released as a single. I'm not sure. Anyway, this song was written by our friend Glen Sherley."

As the convicts whooped it up, Cash looked down at Sherley, who had been given a seat in the front row of tables.

"Hope we do your song justice, Glen."

As he expected, the crowd was delighted to hear a song written by one of their own. The moment took Cash back to his Baptist roots, when he first heard about the saving grace of God. When he finished, Cash reached down and shook Sherley's hand, then headed backstage. Johnston was already mapping out the second show, which they had scheduled in case anything went wrong during the first one. The program had run long, Johnston explained, so there was no need to do everything again. Cash decided to drop a few songs, but he said he'd also like to try a couple of new ones. They were still talking when Reverend Gressett interrupted them. He wanted to introduce Glen Sherley.

Cash shook Sherley's hand again and the pair chatted for several minutes. Cash wanted to know about the man's background. Why was he in Folsom? (Armed robbery.) Had he written a lot of songs? (Hundreds.) How long was his sentence? (Five years to life.) Cash promised to keep in touch.

At the second show, Cash dropped a few numbers, as planned, while adding "Give My Love to Rose," "I Got Stripes," and "Long-Legged Guitar Picking Man." The performance ran smoothly, and everyone was in high spirits as they all left the grounds. Cash was still fixated on Sherley. He told Gressett that he'd like to help get the inmate paroled.

Not everyone, however, had fallen for Sherley. Hugh Cherry and Marshall Grant both sensed he was a hustler who had found the perfect mark. "John always tried to see the best in people, especially an underdog," Grant said. "Hustlers could pick up on that miles away and they would always hit on John, and he'd fall for it every time." Al Qualls, a Florida banker and friend, once told Cash he had a speech defect: "You can't say, 'no.'"

Any remaining hopes that the "month-long" Winston treatment had cured Cash's drug use were shattered a week later in Baltimore.

Holiff had been trying to get CBC television in Canada to do a special for four years, and he found a sympathetic ear in Stan Jacobson, a producer at the network. It wasn't until early 1968, however, that Jacobson could find an opening in the schedule for a one-hour music special featuring Cash and members of his troupe. To discuss the show with Cash, Jacobson flew to Baltimore, and he was worried by what he found.

"[Cash] was playing this small theater, maybe two thousand people tops, and his performance was all over the place, really ragged," Jacobson says. "After the show, I rode the bus with him and June to the Howard Johnson, and he was slapping his face, time after time, as if there were bugs there. I was a huge fan, but I wondered what I was getting myself into. I ran into more problems because we wanted the O'Keefe Centre to sponsor the show, and a representative of the Centre said no way because Cash and the band painted all the dressing room mirrors black when they played there [before]. But we eventually made a deal, and the show went great. It finished number one in the ratings, which was remarkable because the Stanley Cup playoffs were the same week and nothing ever tops the Stanley Cup ratings." Holiff then set his sights on U.S. television, using the CBC tape as part of his sales pitch.

Three days later, Cash asked June to marry him.

John and June were onstage at the Gardens hockey arena in Holiff's hometown of London, Ontario, when Cash popped the question. June acted all flustered—and maybe she was caught off guard by the timing, but the two had been talking for weeks about getting married, even discussing specific dates. Excited to be part of such a special moment, the crowd showered the couple with affection when June accepted his proposal.

One person who wasn't happy was Marshall Grant.

"When she walked off the stage that night, I said, 'June, you've made a hell of a mistake. What about all the times you told me he'd have to get straight before you'd marry him? That was the only thing we had to get him off [drugs]...the promise that you'd marry him. Now what are we going to do?' Because we both knew he was still on the pills."

Others thought Marshall was being naive. The consensus among Cash's musical family was that the only reason she hadn't already married him was that he was still married to Vivian. They shared Vivian's view that all June wanted was to be Mrs. Johnny Cash, period.

Talking about that night years later, Grant suspected that Cash's proposal was simply a bit of showbiz flash. Country music entertainers had a history of getting married onstage (Hank Williams and Billie Jean Horton repeated their vows twice at the New Orleans Municipal Auditorium in front of five thousand paying fans at each show). But it's also possible that Cash, fresh from the Folsom triumph and being honored at "Johnny Cash Day" celebrations in both Memphis and Dyess, was grateful for the way his life had rebounded from just months before, and he wanted to share the marriage news with his fans.

The couple returned to Nashville and attended the Grammy Awards dinner on February 29, where "Jackson" was named best country recording by a group or duo. Holding the statuette that night, June told a reporter, "What a nice wedding gift this is!"

With their obligations out of the way, John and June drove the following day to nearby Franklin, Kentucky, where they were married in the First Methodist Church in front of a few dozen family members and friends. It was an unusually modest event, hastily planned and without any fanfare. Merle Kilgore was best man and Micki Brooks, a longtime friend of June's, was matron of honor. The couple returned to Cash's house on Old Hickory Lake after the ceremony and hosted a reception for around 150 people. Nine days later they were on tour again.

III

Back in Nashville, Bob Johnston got a scare when he returned to the studio and listened to the Folsom tapes.

"I knew John had done a great show, but you never really know what you have on tape until you listen to it, and the one thing that bothered me was the high ceilings in the cafeteria," Johnston recalls. "That could cause all sorts of problems—and sure enough there was this rumble in the tape that could have ruined the record if we didn't get rid of it. We spent three weeks in the studio trying all sorts of things to get rid of that sound.

"Finally, I went into the studio with my engineer on a Saturday so we could go over every step to see if we could figure out what was causing the rumble. Just as we sat down, I saw him turn a knob on the speaker and I asked what he was doing. He said, 'Nothing, man, just putting a little Nashville on it.' Well, that was the problem. He was putting an echo on it. I walked over and turned it off and there went the rumble. I hadn't noticed what he was doing until that day. With that fixed, I mixed the entire album that night."

Johnston captured the spirit of the concert brilliantly, not only picking the final song list but also supplementing the music with actual sounds from the prison, including loudspeaker announcements to the convicts. Cash couldn't have been happier.

One reason why New York was optimistic about the album's pop potential was that the *Los Angeles Times* had devoted an entire page in its Sunday entertainment section to the Folsom concert—largely unprecedented attention from a mainstream newspaper for a Nashville project. The execs were further encouraged when other publications endorsed the album. In *Cosmopolitan*, noted jazz critic Nat Hentoff defined Cash's new place in the music spectrum: "He started as a country-and-western storyteller, but he's gone on to make so strong an impact on the folk and pop fields that now there's no hemming Johnny Cash into any one category."

Time magazine, the biggest national journalistic platform of all in the 1960s, added its own rave, calling the collection one of "the most original and compelling pop albums of the year."

Johnny Cash at Folsom Prison was also embraced strongly by the underground rock radio and press, especially a new national rock journal named *Rolling Stone*. Aware of the biweekly magazine's growing cultural impact on the careers of Dylan, Janis Joplin, and other Columbia rock acts, Clive Davis took out a flashy ad for the Folsom Prison album. More significantly, *Rolling Stone* co-founder Jann Wenner saluted Cash in a passionate and thoughtful essay praising the singer's profound artistry and his role in the rapidly growing merger of country and rock. At the same time, Tom Donahue, a San Francisco FM disc jockey who helped pioneer underground rock radio in America, started playing the album, which led scores of other FM stations to follow suit.

In building an audience for the live album, Cash benefited greatly from his ties to the rock 'n' roll legacy of Sun Records. If any other Nashville country artist, including someone as gifted as Marty Robbins, had made *Folsom,* it wouldn't have been embraced by rock tastemakers in the same way; Cash was the only country star (apart from other members of the Sun stable) viewed by rock critics and DJs as one of them. These writers and commentators had grown up adoring Elvis Presley, Jerry Lee Lewis—and Johnny Cash. *Folsom Prison* reintroduced him. Wenner's *Rolling Stone* essay outlined the case.

"Cash, more than any other contemporary [country] performer, is meaningful in a rock and roll context," he wrote, placing Cash in a time line that stretched from Presley (and Sun Records) to Dylan. Underscoring that rock foundation, Wenner pointed out that Cash's backup group included Carl Perkins, "the man who wrote 'Blue Suede Shoes.'"

He stressed the link between Dylan and Cash: "They are both master singers, master story-tellers and master bluesmen. They share the same tradition, they are good friends and the work of each can tell you about the work of the other."

In both its influence and its insight, *Rolling Stone* was proclaiming Cash an artist for the times—someone equally relevant to rock, pop, and country audiences. The essay provided an enormous sales boost for Cash, because the young rock audience was beginning to control the national sales charts. Wenner's words also helped increase respect for country music among the cultural elite, which in turn helped open the eyes and ears of people at network radio and television.

Cash's reputation as a maverick who'd done jail time, and the El Paso drug bust, too, strengthened his link to rock 'n' roll; it was his music as well as his image that paved the way for the country-rock coalition that Willie Nelson and Waylon Jennings would tap into with their outlaw movement in the late 1970s.

Folsom Prison would have been a major country seller regardless, but it took the rock 'n' roll connection to turn it into a cultural and commercial breakthrough. The single, "Folsom Prison Blues," eventually spent eighteen weeks on the country charts, including four at number one. The album stayed on the pop charts for 122 weeks. The album eventually sold more than 3 million copies in the United States alone.

On the Folsom stage, Cash combined the raw charisma and creative vitality of his Sun days with the artistic discipline and ambition of the Columbia years in an explosive package. Among those who stepped forward to congratulate him was his old mentor Sam Phillips. "From our first record together, I knew he was a talent and he could be a star," Phillips said years later. "But he went even further than I imagined. With that album, he became a great talent and a superstar. I told him how proud I was of him because I know what he went through to get there."

IV

After years of wariness caused by the singer's many no-shows, concert promoters were again scrambling to book Johnny Cash. The success of *Folsom* built upon that frenzy. Sensing this was Cash's moment, Holiff booked as many dates as possible, from the Midwest in March and April to Britain in May. Amid this euphoria, Cash told Johnston he wanted to do another gospel album, but not like before. He wanted to produce the most ambitious gospel album ever in country music—and record it live in Israel.

"He said it was something he'd always wanted to do, like the prison album, but that he couldn't talk anyone into it," Johnston says. Columbia hadn't trusted Cash enough after Carnegie Hall to spend money on a live album in the United States, much less Israel. But that was before *Folsom*.

According to the producer, Cash asked him to put aside a couple of weeks and go with him and June to Israel, where they would walk the streets together to get inspiration for the live album.

But Johnston had a counter-proposal. He remembers telling Cash, "'That's a great idea, but you don't need me. You and June go. Walk around and write songs. I'll give you a camera and a tape recorder and you just put down what you see and feel. Then bring it back here and we'll do the album.' He was quiet for a second, then he winked at me and I knew we were all right, because that's what he always did when he liked something. He winked.

"The label had reservations when I told them about it, but they had reservations about everything. Hell, they told me to take the guitars off Dylan's album. I didn't care what the hell the label thought. If Johnny Cash wanted to stand under an elm tree and sing 'Jingle Bells,' I would have been all for it. You've got to believe in your artists."

John and June headed back to Israel at the end of the British tour, carrying a tape recorder to capture their thoughts as they visited the historic sites they knew from the Bible. They were deeply moved, and the passion showed in the narrations Cash taped on the trip.

After a few weeks touring in the States, John returned home and spent most of July going over plans for the album, which he titled *Holy Land*. Unlike with previous theme albums, he wasn't looking for traditional material. He wanted everything in this album to be his personal statement.

One key exception was "Daddy Sang Bass," a song Carl Perkins wrote backstage one night. He had been humming the melody to "Will the Circle Be Unbroken," the gospel standard popularized by the Carter Family, when he started reflecting on the family sing-alongs of his childhood days. He played the opening verse for Cash, who thought it would be perfect for the album.

When Cash got together again with Johnston in mid-July, he outlined his grand plans for the album. He was working off the same narration-plus-song blueprint he used on *Ride This Train,* but he wanted to mix several of the narrations that he taped in Israel with studio recordings of new songs. It was a daunting task, but the always upbeat Johnston said, "Well, let's get started."

The two men went into the studio on July 19 and recorded the prologue for the album. Cash recited the words in a reverential tone that couldn't have been more different from the raucous, occasionally four-letter-word spirit of *Folsom.* If Cash understood the soul of a convict, he also knew the faith of a believer.

Before bringing in the musicians, Cash went to Los Angeles to tape a guest appearance on *The Summer Brothers Smothers Show,* hosted by Glen Campbell, a sign that TV execs were noticing the growing popularity of country music. Back in the studio July 29 to 31, he recorded most of the songs for the album.

"John was very absorbed with that album," the Statlers' Don Reid says. "I think he felt he was doing something he would be remembered for. Like most sessions, he was still arranging as we were recording. Whatever crossed his mind, he would just stop and say, 'You guys come in on the second line and then we'll all hit it big on the last chorus' or some such instruction. He arranged by feel and always on the spot."

When Johnston finished piecing the *Holy Land* album together, Cash felt he had another major work, and he was ecstatic, but Johnston knew it wasn't what Columbia wanted to follow *Folsom.* Sure enough, the promotion department in New York looked at *Holy Land* as just another concept album that the public was bound to ignore. There was some thought about not even bothering to release a single. The fans seemed to like the rough-edged Cash image. Why confuse everybody with this choirboy stuff?

Cash and Johnston resisted and pushed "Daddy Sang Bass" as a single. It was an ultra-catchy tune, and Johnston had captured its nostalgic sing-along spirit. Not wanting to alienate the man who was rapidly becoming its hottest artist, Columbia agreed. But the executives wanted to wait until December to take advantage of its Christmas season appeal.

The flip side of the single was "He Turned the Water into Wine," a song Cash wrote for the album and was so well-crafted that it sounded like a gospel standard that had been handed down for generations. Cash felt it was one of the cornerstones of the album, but the tune would always have a bittersweet edge to it.

The July 31 session was the last time he'd ever be in the studio with Luther Perkins.

Luther's second wife, Margie, had hoped her husband would go with her and their three-year-old adopted daughter, Kathy, to a friend's house for a poker party the night of August 2, but Luther was ill. Margie phoned a couple of times to check on him, but stopped calling after he said he was going to have a cigarette and then try and get some sleep. Marshall Grant had often seen Luther fall asleep in a hotel bed or in the car with a lit cigarette in his hand, and he marveled at Luther's luck at never having started a fire, though Grant often picked up the dropped cigarette butts and extinguished them just in case. That night, Luther's luck finally gave out.

Margie returned to the house on Old Hickory Lake, not far from the Cash home, to find Luther passed out on the floor. The fire department rushed him to the hospital at Vanderbilt University, where doctors found that he had suffered third-degree burns to 50 percent of his body. Cash, too, sped to the hospital, but his friend never regained consciousness. Luther died two days later and was buried in the same Hendersonville cemetery where Cash had bought a series of plots for his own family.

Grant always looked back on the death as almost merciful. Doctors told him that if Luther had lived, they probably would have been forced to amputate both his hands. He would never have played the guitar again.

Perkins's widow says Cash blamed himself. "Johnny told me, 'Margie, I really believe I caused Luther's death.' He said he was the one who gave Luther pills years before because Luther used to get so tired traveling between shows," she adds. "He never took as many pills as Johnny, but Johnny felt bad because he had gotten him into pills and would even go to Luther sometimes to get more for himself. He was worried that Luther took the pills the night he died."

Cash had good reason to feel guilty. Luther had called Cash earlier the night of the fire, in an apparently drugged or drunken state, and asked him to come over and talk. But Cash didn't pick up the warning signal. It was late, and he figured he could check in on him the next morning. Besides, he assumed that Margie was there to take care of him. In the days after Luther's death, John and June insisted that Margie and her daughter stay with them until she could find a new place to live. Cash also contributed to the building of a $2 million burn center in Luther's name at Vanderbilt.

Decades later, Dr. Nat Winston would recall Cash telling him that two of the events in his life that had had the greatest impact were the day his brother Jack was killed and Luther Perkins's death. More than once, too, Cash said, "A part of me died with Luther."

When Rosanne, Kathy, Cindy, and Tara returned to Hendersonville for their second summer visit, everything had changed. John and June were married, and the room the Cash girls shared the year before had been divided into separate spaces for Carlene and Rosie. Though the girls all got along well personally, the sleeping arrangements were the first in a series of slights that made the Cash kids think Carlene and Rosie were getting preferential treatment.

"We'd get here as teenagers," Kathy Cash says, "and Rosie and Carlene would have a Porsche and an MG in the driveway. Then I'd go in their room and they'd have so many clothes and so much makeup that I was really jealous."

In her 2007 memoir *I Walked the Line: My Life with Johnny Cash,* Vivian blamed June for the perceived slights, but she acknowledged they were really due to a difference of philosophy regarding parenting. Her girls "saw June's two daughters living it up....Meanwhile back in California, Rosanne, Kathy, Cindy and Tara's wardrobes consisted of their school uniforms and maybe two or three other outfits. No extras. No luxury items. I didn't believe in spoiling them. So compared to June's daughters, I know the girls felt second rate."

Carlene and Rosie recognized that they were being treated royally.

"At our old home with Daddy Rip, when Mom was on the road, Rosie and I had chores," Carlene says. "We mowed the lawn, did the dishes, dusted and vacuumed. When we moved in with Big John, which is what I called [Cash], those chores stopped. We had people cleaning up for us hand and foot. Mom said now that we had full-time staff and lawn workers, life would be different."

But even when money was scarce for the Carters in the 1950s and early 1960s, June had made sure to put enough aside so she could show her daughters some of the high life that she craved. "Mom used to take us to New York religiously, at least twice a year all through our lives," Carlene adds. "We would stay at the Sherry-Netherland, go out to eat at Delmonico's, go for a ride in a buggy in Central Park, and see Broadway shows or the Rockettes at Radio City Music Hall. It was just me and Mama and Rosie, usually for a long weekend."

Back in Tennessee, Cash, for all his misadventures, tried to be a strict parent to June's daughters. It was a big deal, Carlene remembers, when she asked permission to go on her first date.

"I had just turned fourteen and we wanted to see the rock band Steppenwolf in Nashville and Big John was in a tizzy about the whole thing. He thought he should set a curfew, but he didn't know what time it should be. He finally asked me what time the curfew should be. I figured the show would be over around ten thirty, so I told him, 'What about this: I'll see the band, then go to Shoney's with the others for a hamburger and be home by eleven.' He said, 'That sounds good. Go ahead.'

"Well, I get home around eleven thirty and he was waiting at the door, smoking cigarettes like there was no tomorrow. He grounded me for three months. The next day he runs into Braxton Dixon, who went to the same show, and Braxton told him he was being too harsh. Braxton had gone out to dinner too, and he didn't get home until midnight."

To everyone's surprise, Steppenwolf's tour bus pulled up outside the house the next day. The band's leader, John Kay, was a big fan and wanted to meet Cash. "They just fawned all over him," Carlene recalls. "I think it made him feel even guiltier about grounding me, but he held me to it. The whole thing showed me how little experience he had as a father. I mean, Vivian handled all the discipline in that family. It was totally new to him."

* * *

Tragedy hit Cash's world again on September 16 when the neighboring home of Roy Orbison burned down, killing two of the singer's sons. Orbison, who was on tour in England, rushed home. It was the second horrific loss for him. His wife, Claudette, had been killed in front of his eyes when her motorcycle was struck by a semi-trailer truck in 1966. When Orbison told Cash after the fire that he could never live on the site again, Cash bought the property and planted an orchard so no one else could build there either. Orbison was forever grateful.

With the shock of Luther's and the Orbison boys' deaths, Cash started cutting back on his drug use, according to Grant. "I think those deaths reminded him of how close he had come to death himself. In the months after Luther's death, he'd still slip up," Grant noted. "But he was definitely better."

Reluctant to look for a replacement for Luther, Cash asked Carl Perkins to take over Luther's part, but even though Perkins was a far superior guitarist, he couldn't duplicate the steady, unbending rhythm which maximized that signature sound. Cash also thought it was unfair to set such narrow limits on Perkins's talent. So he put out the word in Nashville that he was looking for a new guitarist—and he got lots of applicants. Everyone knew Cash paid his band members handsomely.

Cash was in Fayetteville on September 17 for a show in support of the reelection campaign of Arkansas governor Winthrop Rockefeller when he found his new guitarist. Marshall and Carl were scheduled to fly in from Memphis, but their flight was canceled because of bad weather. Cash was getting ready to do the show when June introduced him to a young woman who said her boyfriend knew all his songs and could play just like Luther. Cash invited the young truck driver backstage, where he played "Folsom Prison Blues" and "I Walk the Line" almost exactly like Luther. His name was Bob Wootton, and Cash brought him onstage that same day. He soon became the newest member of the Tennessee Three. Though he'd remain an important part of the group for almost two decades, and was even married to Anita Carter for a while, Wootton never became as close to Cash as Luther had been.

One of Wootton's first dates was at Carnegie Hall on October 23, Cash's first engagement there since his embarrassment six years earlier. Cash faced a star-studded crowd that included Bob Dylan and Janis Joplin, and he triumphed. In a rave *New York Times* review, Robert Shelton contrasted the new Cash with the one he'd seen in 1962.

He wrote: "Soul music of a rare kind—country soul from the concerned and sensitive white South that Northerners tend to forget—was heard Wednesday night at Carnegie Hall as Johnny Cash made a stirring comeback to New York....His performance was testimony that his own personal bouts with illness and control have been resolved, putting him at as strong a level as he has had since the middle nineteen-fifties."

By now there were more offers coming in for concerts and TV shows than Holiff could handle. Cash moved on from Carnegie Hall to England for a tour, during which he recorded the *Holy Land* songs for a radio special that would air after the album was released in December. He then returned to the Midwest for a series of dates that concluded with a benefit for Native Americans.

Because of *Bitter Tears,* Cash had been approached even before the *Folsom* success to do a benefit that was scheduled for December 9 at the St. Francis Mission on the Rosebud Reservation in South Dakota. On the following day he visited the site of the Wounded Knee Massacre, where in 1890 some 150 men, women, and children of the Lakota Sioux were killed and 51 wounded by members of the U.S. Seventh Cavalry. During this and other selected dates during the year, he was accompanied by a film crew who were gathering footage for a public television documentary, *Johnny Cash: The Man, His World, His Music,* by director Robert Elfstrom.

When Cash sat down for his annual New Year's Eve reflections, he was too close to the situation to appreciate fully that he had just finished one of the most remarkable years in pop history. He'd not only made what is perhaps the greatest country album ever—a work so powerful and rich that *Rolling Stone* magazine would one day name it one of the hundred best albums regardless of genre—but also recorded a gospel album that was light-years away from the conventional collection of hymns. Country music is filled with tales of Saturday night sin and Sunday morning salvation, but no country artist had ever addressed the subjects so forcefully in back-to-back packages.

Cash didn't forget the dark times—the death of Luther and of family friend Jimmy Howard, and the Orbison fire—but he felt that he had finally turned a corner in his life. Holiff was telling him he might get movie offers, and maybe even his own TV show. He was slowly emerging from the long nightmare of pills. And he had June. He decided he wanted to write down his New Year's Eve thoughts for the first time.

In a six-page note addressed "To myself" on the stationery of his House of Cash publishing company, he began: "I feel that this year, 1968, has been, in many ways, the best year of my 36 years of life. It has been a sober, serious year. And probably the busiest year of my life, as well as the most fulfilling."

He cited several significant moments, from his marriage to June and the Holy Land trip to the Folsom concert and the sold-out shows at Carnegie Hall and the London Palladium. He even mentioned that his concert fee had shot up from $4,000 to $12,000. He cited Wounded Knee and fishing on Old Hickory Lake, Ezra Carter, and the documentary as high points in his year.

What the letter didn't convey was his personal hunger and his fears—a craving in his own life for the redemption he outlined in his music. Looking back in 1972 on that note and others he wrote in 1969, 1970, and 1971, Cash dismissed most of them as superficial, too focused on material matters rather than on spiritual health.

"Yes, congratulations John Cash on your superstardom. Big deal," he wrote in 1972.

"True you must be grateful for God's showers of blessings, but regardless of all you have been quoted as saying to the contrary, you are too excited over your personal wealth, career successes and other vain, fleeting things.

"OK.

"I hereby resolve, asking God's help, that I shall court wisdom more and more in this my 41st year. Especially heavenly wisdom."

The shift in his emphasis was profound. He highlighted the

change in thinking in his 1975 autobiography, *Man in Black,* where he focused on his spiritual rededication. In it he referred to New Year's Eve 1968 as a turning point in his life. Once again, he took poetic license. Rather than reprint the actual 1968 letter, he wrote a new letter expressing what he felt he should have written the first time, and he passed it off as the original.

It read: "Dear Cash, Let's look at 1968. You did all right in a lot of ways. You blew it in others....You stayed off pills but you're still awfully carnal. You know what those little vices of yours are. Get to work on them before they multiply and lower your resistance to other temptations, like pills for instance. You still think about them from time to time. You need to pray more. You hardly ever pray. Big deals ahead in 1969, possibly a network TV show, but the biggest deal you've got is your family and home. You'd better hang with God if you want the other deals to work out....Your friend, Cash."

The "carnal" reference was surprisingly revealing. Despite the image that John and June painted in public, he was acknowledging the rockiness of their courtship and the fact that he had sometimes turned to other women. Some of those relationships had been serious enough, according to one Cash confidant, that four women were shocked when he asked June to marry him. They each thought he was going to ask them. One of the women was reportedly Anita.

Even if the 1968 letter lingered mainly over his career accomplishments, he was starting to realize that it wasn't enough simply to express his faith in his music and his frequent good deeds. He wanted to live up to his spiritual obligations. For years, his gospel recordings and even his spiritual statements were made in part out of a sense of duty; he was doing it for his mother and his brother Jack. But Ezra Carter did much to kindle his true spirituality through the hours and hours he spent reading the Bible with Cash and trying to explain how to reconcile the conflicts Cash felt between his personal ambition and his Christian humility.

That process intensified near the end of another tour of Far East military bases with the USO. Cash was greatly troubled by the Vietnam War. His natural instinct was to support his country at all costs, but his visits to hospitals and talks with soldiers hit him hard, and he admitted his doubts to his brother Tommy. "Maybe," he said, "they may be dying for a cause that isn't just."

The soul-searching made him further question his own behavior. He was in bad shape physically by the end of the Asian tour. June told reporters he was ill; others feared he had relapsed. Just then, he bumped into an old friend, the Reverend Jimmie Snow, the son of Hank Snow and a onetime country singer himself.

"We were in Vietnam and we got together and reminisced for a while," Snow says. "It was pretty casual, but I could see something was troubling him. When he turned to go, he stopped and looked at me and asked if I'd call him when we got back home. He said, 'I need to talk to you.'"

Two weeks later, Snow went to see Cash at his house.

"We talked about God for probably four or five hours," Snow recalls. "He said he had slipped away from his faith over the years and he wanted to get back in touch with it, but didn't know how. I took his hand and I said, 'Let's pray.'"

CHAPTER 20

THE JOHNNY CASH SHOW AND SUPERSTARDOM

I

FOR THE FIRST TIME in a decade, Cash was waking up most mornings without feeling the need to reach for pills. The Far East trip reminded him how vulnerable he was and how much was at stake if he had another relapse. With the validation of the *Folsom* success and his relationship with June finally stabilizing, Cash wanted to embrace the moment, not escape from it. He felt reborn creatively in February 1969. During those four weeks he went into the recording studio with Dylan, recorded a second prison concert, and signed to host a weekly TV show. The last two projects had been in the works for months.

Cash had no interest in returning to Folsom for a sequel even though there were several high-profile examples of successful live album sequels, including *Belafonte Returns to Carnegie Hall* in 1960 and Johnny Rivers's *Meanwhile Back at the Whisky à Go Go* in 1965. Bob Johnston didn't push the idea. He wanted Cash to feel free to explore his own creative instincts.

The trail to San Quentin began in an office at Granada Television, an independent TV network in England. Geoffrey Cannon, who was also rock critic for the *Guardian* newspaper, was part of an ambitious "think tank" charged with coming up with "far out" programming ideas. The group, including Jonathan Cott, who was also serving as *Rolling Stone*'s first European editor, had a special affinity for documentaries that placed music in a provocative cultural context. They had already contributed to *The Doors Are Open*, an acclaimed 1968 TV documentary that interspersed footage of a Doors concert in London with scenes from Vietnam and rioting in the United States to underscore the music's reflection of the decade's social upheaval.

After hearing the *Folsom* album, Cannon thought of exploring the sociological ties between country music and prison life, but hopes to get Cash to return to Folsom for another concert were sidetracked when Holiff told the production team in late December 1968 that Cash had no interest in the idea. Even so, Cannon remained intrigued. "Nothing like a concert where a jailbird sang songs about desperation to no-hopers and lifers in prison had ever been transmitted on national network television, and this was one of our touchstones," he says.

Meanwhile, Holiff, always eager for more television exposure, began thinking about how the Granada project could build fans for Cash in England and, presumably, throughout Europe. When Cannon contacted Holiff a second time later that month, Holiff repeated that Cash had no interest in going back to Folsom. Just as Cannon was about to hang up, Holiff added, "But Johnny is going to San Quentin. He'd be happy to make a film with you there."

As Holiff worked hard to convince Columbia execs in New York that they should record the show for another album, the Granada team rushed to prepare for the February 24 performance. Things were moving so fast that Granada reps didn't actually meet with Cash until two days before San Quentin.

From his earliest days with Cash, Holiff felt that television was the key to gaining a wider audience, believing that seeing Cash was more compelling than just listening to him. In July 1965 Holiff pitched a TV series to CBS, hinting that Cash might be playing the lead in a new Edward Padula production on Broadway. (There were talks with Padula, who had produced *Bye Bye Birdie*, but nothing materialized.) Holiff had concentrated on CBS because it was the dominant U.S. network.

ABC, however, was a distant third in the ratings and was looking for a way up. The network saw Cash as a way to piggyback on the success of CBS's brightest new star, Glen Campbell, who hosted a weekly county music–leaning variety show. Not only were both male country singers with pop potential, but also they were both from Arkansas and about the same age. Even more important in ABC's eyes, Cash, thanks to *Folsom,* was starting to create the same buzz in pop circles that Campbell had months earlier thanks to such crossover hits as "Gentle on My Mind" and "By the Time I Get to Phoenix."

Having no relationship with Holiff, Bill Carruthers, a director and producer who got his start in television directing the zany Soupy Sales show, approached Cash directly soon after *Folsom* hit the charts about doing a weekly variety show for ABC. Cash was torn. All the way back to *American Bandstand* and "Ballad of a Teenage Queen," he knew how uncomfortable he could be if he wasn't presented in the right setting and surrounded by compatible acts. But Holiff had done a good job convincing him of the importance of television to his career, so Cash decided to give it a try—if Screen Gems, the production company that would develop the show for ABC, agreed to some terms. Cash told Holiff he wanted to choose his own musical guests, and he didn't want to move back to Los Angeles, where the Campbell show was taped. He insisted on the Ryman Auditorium in Nashville.

Screen Gems was fine with the Ryman and assured Cash that his input on guests would be welcome, which, in the adrenaline rush of putting a show together, must have sounded like more of a commitment to Cash than it proved to be. The contracts were drawn up and the series was announced the first week in February. Cash would be the summer replacement for the Saturday night variety show *Hollywood Palace.*

Two weeks later, Cash met with Carruthers to go over preliminary plans. When Cash then spoke to the press, his remarks seemed directed as much to Screen Gems as to his fans; in fact, his remarks sometimes conflicted with ABC's own description of the show. According to a network press release, the show would draw guests from all fields, even rock, which was referred to as "Now Generation" music. In Los Angeles, Carruthers suggested that the show would be "85 percent music and some comedy too."

In Nashville, Cash told local reporters, "We will have three or four guests on each weekly show and although many will come from the popular field, the show will not be a major departure from the country music that we came from. If there is a theme to the show, it is to illustrate the contemporary nature of modern country music. So the integral part of each week's show will be country music." He made no mention of comedians, even though they were a component of most variety shows at the time.

Though Cash's success with *Folsom* swept away most of the strained feelings along Music Row left over from the 1964 "Ira Hayes" *Billboard* ad flap, there were still pockets of resentment among Nashville's elite, and there was considerable grumbling about all this talk of non-country artists being featured, including Bob Dylan.

II

Dylan began recording his albums in Nashville with the *Blonde on Blonde* sessions in February 1966 at Bob Johnston's suggestion, but his love of country music dated back to his childhood in Hibbing, Minnesota. He would listen to many of the same recording stars that Cash enjoyed in Dyess and in the Air Force, especially Jimmie Rodgers. During his teens, he was also spellbound by the music of Cash and other Sun artists. "Of course, I knew of him before he ever heard of me," Dylan wrote years later about Cash. "In '55 or '56, 'I Walk the Line' played all summer on the radio, and it was different from anything else you had ever heard. It was profound, and so was the tone of it, every line: deep and rich, awesome and mysterious all at once."

Given their restless curiosity as artists, Cash and Dylan might have made shifts into folk and country, respectively, in the 1960s quite independent of each other. Just as Cash's admiration for Dylan added enthusiasm to his embrace of folk music in the early 1960s, however, Dylan's respect for Cash made Dylan's transition from rock to country easier.

Dylan's move began in the fall of 1968, when he recorded the *John Wesley Harding* album not with the rock 'n' roll crew who had joined him on *Highway 61 Revisited* but with two of the Nashville musicians Johnston had recruited for the *Blonde on Blonde* sessions, drummer Kenneth Buttrey and bassist Charlie McCoy. Except for "I'll Be Your Baby Tonight," the album wasn't full-blown country, but it was a softer and more rural sound than Dylan fans had come to expect. Dylan was ready to move even deeper into country when he returned to Nashville in February 1969 to record *Nashville Skyline*.

While Dylan was in town, Johnston set up a separate session at the Columbia Studios for Cash, mainly, a conspiracy theorist might suggest, so that he could lure Cash and Dylan into a studio to cut some tracks together—and that's what happened. After recording two songs on February 17, Cash was back in the studio the next evening when Dylan stopped by to say hello. Cash was delighted to see him, and they went to dinner. When they returned, they found that Johnston had rearranged the microphones and brought in some chairs and a table to give the room the informal feel of a music club. As Johnston remembers it, "When they came back and saw the little café setup, I knew they were going to sing together. They looked at each other and went out and got their guitars and started singing. People started yelling out song titles ... 'How about this one or that one?' I even yelled out songs too, and they came up with some. They were laughing and having fun."

It wasn't a repeat of the "Million Dollar Quartet" sessions at Sun, where the artists just sang bits and pieces of old favorites, but it was close. Backed by Cash's musicians, they opened with Dylan's 1964 composition "One Too Many Mornings" and later traded verses on the even earlier "Girl from the North Country." They followed with numbers identified with Cash, including "Big River," "I Still Miss Someone," and perhaps a bit playfully "Understand Your Man," the song Cash wrote after stealing a Dylan melody.

Then they turned to two Sun favorites, Elvis's "That's All Right" and Carl Perkins's "Matchbox," before reaching into their country memory bank for two Jimmie Rodgers tunes as well as the country standards "You Are My Sunshine" and "Careless Love," plus the gospel favorite "Just a Closer Walk with Thee."

When they finished, Johnston knew that the music was ragged; Dylan and Cash had messed up lyrics in places and lost track of the melody in others. But he felt that what he had was a wonderful piece of history. Here were two great figures in music having fun in an unguarded moment. It was magical, and Johnston was proud of being the catalyst that made it happen. To his immense disappointment, the only track to emerge officially from the session would be "Girl from the North County," which Dylan used on *Nashville Skyline.*

"Columbia didn't want to put the sessions out," Johnston says. "They cringed. The only thing they could hear was [that Cash and Dylan] were laughing in the middle of some songs or didn't come out exactly together at the end of others. Maybe Columbia was just trying to protect their stars; they didn't want to let people hear them like this—which was typical of how stupid record companies are. This was history!"

It's also possible that Columbia execs, without Johnston's knowledge, had learned that even Cash and Dylan were uncertain about the album. Years later Cash referred to it as "musically inferior," adding, "It's not up to par for either one of us. I think [Bob] was embarrassed over that and I don't blame him." As with the "Million Dollar Quartet" sessions, however, tapes of the Dylan-Cash recordings eventually found their way onto bootlegs and became prized underground possessions for decades.

Johnston didn't have more clout in the decision because he was on shaky ground at Columbia. He had butted heads with the New York brass too often, and his announcement in the spring of 1967 that the label planned to drop half its sixty-artist roster caused enormous resentment among Nashville traditionalists. When Clive Davis went to Nashville that fall for an industry dinner, he was surprised when the comedienne Minnie Pearl, a beloved figure in country music, cornered him. "We have a way of doing things in Nashville," she told the Columbia president. "Although we compete, we do it with civility and respect. I've got to tell you that your man Bob Johnston is conducting business with neither of those adjectives. He is creating such an image problem for Columbia Records. On behalf of the Nashville community, we don't like him."

Adding this to what he was hearing from his own executives, Davis took action: he replaced Johnston as head of the Nashville office with writer-producer Billy Sherrill. Davis agreed to let Johnston continue to work, under the title "executive producer at large," with Cash and Dylan. "What choice did they have?" Johnston says. "Who else did they have who Cash and Dylan would work with?"

On the day after the Dylan session, Cash got a phone call from Don Davis, a music publisher and two-time husband of Anita Carter. Davis, who had earlier tipped him off to "Jackson," told Cash he had a song that would be a natural for him. It was written by *Playboy* cartoonist and songwriter Shel Silverstein, whose earlier parody, "25 Minutes to Go," was a highlight of the *Folsom* album.

Cash got a kick out of the zany tune about a father's odd way of teaching his son to stand up for himself, and he promised to record "A Boy Named Sue" as soon as he got back from the West Coast. But June placed a copy of Silverstein's song in a stack of material John was taking with him on the trip—on the outside chance he'd want to use it in the prison show.

III

San Quentin was just two days away when Cash met with the Granada TV representatives before a concert in San Diego, the second stop on the tour. Only vaguely aware of their plans for the documentary, Cash had been approaching San Quentin as just another show date, which meant his regular set list. When the Granada team of director Michael Darlow and producer Jo Durden-Smith asked him to write a song to commemorate the occasion, Cash was cool to the idea. Afterward, however, he began to think about the prison concert more seriously. Over the next forty-eight hours, he did what he did best—tried to find common ground with his audience by looking at the world through their eyes.

Because of his past San Quentin visits, Cash knew that the prison, just across the bay from San Francisco, was a much tougher environment than Folsom; it housed the state's only death row for men. Security would be far more intense. After the planning meeting, he started focusing on San Quentin's menacing reputation and he began to imagine the rage he sensed in the men—and the anger he sometimes felt in himself.

By the time he stepped on the stage on the night of February 24, he had written two songs. One was based on his arrest for public intoxication in Starkville, Mississippi, in May 1965; the other was a more important reflection on pent-up rage. He was again a man with a mission, and he did try to echo *Folsom* in one sense. He was brought a song by an inmate—a wistful tune titled "I Don't Know Where I'm Bound" by someone identified on the record only as T. Cuttie. It was an undistinguished number, yet Cash was seduced once again by the idea of redemption, and he vowed to find a place for it in the show.

Cash was still fiddling with the set order when Johnston told him not to worry about it and just concentrate on his performance. They could put together the album set list in the studio just as they had done with the *Folsom* album; the order he played the songs in didn't matter. Even as he was about to go onstage, nothing was set in concrete except that he wanted to bunch the new songs together near the end of the show.

"Hello, I'm Johnny Cash," he said to the 1,400 convicts, repeating what had become his standard greeting on tour. He opened with two of his favorites, "Big River" and "I Still Miss Someone," followed by "Wreck of the Old 97" and some other concert staples before getting to the first prison-related number, "Folsom Prison Blues."

Much to the delight of the crowd, he brought June onstage to do "Jackson" and "Darling Companion," a John Sebastian song they had learned from Ramblin' Jack Elliott. It was a half hour into the show when Cash played "I Don't Know Where I'm Bound" after announcing that the song had been written by a San Quentin inmate. The response was enthusiastic, but it didn't match the outpouring for "Greystone Chapel" at Folsom.

Cash then unveiled his two new songs. In "Starkville City Jail," he made fun of an overly aggressive police force, but "San Quentin" was his trump card.

"I was thinking about you guys yesterday," Cash told the convicts, suddenly serious. "I've been here three times before, and I think I understand a little how you feel about some things."

The inmates listened attentively.

"It's none of my business how you feel about some other things, and I don't give a damn about how you feel about some other things. I tried to put myself in your place, and this is how I think I'd feel about San Quentin."

Not knowing what to expect, the convicts were startled by the venom of the song's opening lines: *San Quentin, you've been livin' hell to me.*

The audience let loose a chilling roar of brotherhood.

> *You've hosted me since nineteen sixty-three.*
> *I've seen 'em come and go and I've seen 'em die*
> *And long ago I stopped askin' why,*
> *San Quentin, I hate every inch of you.*

Again, a monstrous howl.

> *You've cut me and you've scarred me thru an' thru.*
> *And I'll walk out a wiser, weaker man;*
> *Mister Congressman, why can't you understand?*

The number went on for nearly four minutes, and the tension in the room grew with each passing line. When Cash spat out "San Quentin may you rot and burn in hell," he could sense the crowd wanting more, and he played the song again, as Johnston had requested he do to make sure they had a solid version on tape.

Johnston was struck by the drama of the moment.

"All the guards were nervous. They thought there was going to be a riot." He says Cash felt an immense power when the prisoners got off their benches and, against show rules, stood on the tables and cheered. Adds Johnston, "He realized that all he had to say was,

'Let's go!' and there would have been a full-scale riot. He told me after, 'I was tempted.'"

Cash instead lightened the mood by playing "Wanted Man," a minor song he wrote with Bob Dylan that boasted of an outlaw's rambling ways, very much inspired by Hank Snow's "I've Been Everywhere." It even included a sly nod to being "sidetracked in Juárez."

Pleased with the two versions of "San Quentin," Cash took a breather while Carl Perkins entertained the crowd. During the break, he reached into his briefcase and pulled out the lyrics to Silverstein's "A Boy Named Sue." It was likely a spontaneous move, because no one in the band or on the Granada production team knew that he planned to do the song. After Perkins ended his song, Cash put the lyrics on a stand and asked the musicians to make up some music to accompany him.

It took a good thirty seconds for Perkins and the others to hook into a groove, but it finally came together deftly, and the San Quentin convicts began howling with laughter. Cash followed "Sue" with another twenty minutes of music, but he and Johnston both knew they had the heart of the album in the snarling, tightly woven "San Quentin" and this crazy novelty tune, "A Boy Named Sue."

As Cash headed on to the next tour stop, Johnston flew back to Nashville to begin putting the album together, and the Granada TV crew returned to London to work on the documentary. Everyone agreed on one thing: they had another winner.

IV

There was a fresh face on the California tour who brought a new level of professionalism to Cash's concert life. Lou Robin started producing jazz concerts while an undergraduate at Claremont Men's College near Los Angeles, then built one of the nation's most successful concert promotion companies in the 1960s with partner Allen Tinkley. They even did a date with the Beatles.

By the late 1960s, Robin and Tinkley had become increasingly exasperated by some of the "craziness" surrounding many of the rock acts, and they thought about expanding into the suddenly emerging field of country music. Barbara John, who did promotion for country radio stations in Southern California, suggested they do some shows with Cash. Robin was leery. What about all the drugs and the missed dates? She assured him that Cash had turned things around and arranged for Robin and Tinkley to meet with Holiff in July 1968. By the time they sat down at the Hollywood Roosevelt Hotel, the *Folsom* album had just taken off, and Robin felt he could not only expand Cash's bookings in the States but do good business in Europe and Australia as well.

To start, he asked Holiff to sell him a string of California and Nevada dates. If that worked out, he would think about doing all of Cash's shows. Holiff liked the idea of selling all the dates to a single promoter. He was tired of the tedious logistics of touring, haggling with individual promoters on Cash's fee for the night, and, most of all, the endless hassle of collecting money from promoters who tried to stiff or shortchange him. Plus, the arrangement would free him to do what he liked best—think about the big picture. Holiff sold Robin some West Coast shows starting the following February. The price was $5,000 a night.

Neither Robin nor Tinkley had ever seen Cash onstage. In fact, they hedged their bet by booking Marty Robbins as a supporting act on the tour to make sure they drew enough of an audience to earn back their guarantee. Typically, a show the size of Cash's would have to gross around $12,000 to $15,000 in ticket sales to cover the expenses of staging it—from hall rental, security, and sound equipment to advertising and the simple matter of printing the tickets. With the top tickets averaging around $3 at the time, it meant that their company, Artist Consultants, needed to draw at least four thousand people.

It was at San Quentin that Robin first saw Cash live, and he was dazzled by his charisma and command onstage. Robin also liked Cash personally. After all the drugs and irrational behavior Robin had seen on the rock circuit, he found Cash refreshingly warm and responsible. "He and June were both very nice, very appreciative," Robin says. The promoter was equally impressed four nights later when Cash drew twelve thousand fans to the Oakland Coliseum

Arena. By now, the *Folsom* album had been on the national charts for ten months, and his $5,000 fee proved to be a huge bargain.

To show good faith, Robin, a soft-spoken, unfailingly polite man, went backstage after the show and gave John and June a $5,000 bonus. "We thought it was right and maybe it would help build a relationship of trust," Robin says. "They were so touched they cried. They said there had been so many nights they were worried about just getting paid at all." This new relationship was off to a solid start.

The check took on even greater emotional significance an hour later when June's sister Helen learned that her teenaged son Kenny had been gravely injured in a car crash in Nashville. John and June used the bonus check to charter a plane to fly Helen home, though the boy died while the plane was still in the air. Cash was so touched by the gesture of the $5,000 check that he would still refer to it in interviews years later.

Cash returned to Nashville the first week in March and went straight to a Columbia studio to hear what Johnston had done with the San Quentin tapes. He was worried that the album might lack the urgency of the *Folsom* package, but he was delighted by what he heard. *Folsom* would remain closest to him because it was recorded first, but he felt the new album was every bit as dynamic, maybe even more so. Cash loved how Johnston kept both versions of "San Quentin" on the LP to underscore the volatility of the moment, and he was pleased by how well "A Boy Named Sue" had turned out.

Before heading home, he turned to Johnston and said, "Bob, I've got a problem with the TV show. If I can get Dylan, it'll be a hit, and if I can't, I don't think I even want to do it. Can you get him to go on the show?"

Johnston said he'd try.

When the producer phoned Dylan with the request, Dylan put him on hold and Johnston figured he was going to say no.

"That was the longest three or four minutes because I thought he was going to say, I've got a gig or I'm doing something, but he came back and said, 'Bob, I don't have anything to wear.' I said, 'God Almighty, what color do you want? What size do you wear?' I finally said, 'I'll take care of everything.' I ended up getting him a white suit that was too long and a black suit that was too short."

On March 12, Cash got more good news at the annual Grammy Awards ceremony when he was honored for best country vocal for "Folsom Prison Blues" and best liner notes for his introduction to the *Folsom* album.

Four days later, Cash taped the first of the TV shows—and there was worry within the Cash camp about how he would react to the pressure. "We had all seen him turn to the pills so often during moments of stress, and there was lots of stress on everybody when the show started, especially John," said Marshall Grant. "But he was straight as an arrow. He was the old John again and he looked great. We were all so proud of him."

V

Cash was the host, but it quickly became clear to him that creative matters, from the choice of guests to show format, were ruled by Screen Gems. Stan Jacobson, whom Cash had insisted the production company hire, was on board, but as a writer, not in one of the power positions of producer, director, or talent booker.

This was the age of variety shows in television; there were a dozen or so on the air at the time, including the Ed Sullivan, Glen Campbell, Jim Nabors, and Tom Jones programs. After the choice of host and format, the most important aspect of a series was the selection of guests. As the weakest network, ABC had to scramble for talent. Screen Gems faced the further problem of having to persuade guests to fly to Nashville, which was not a regular stop on the showbiz itinerary. Then there was the matter of Screen Gems wanting to select guests who would cross-promote other ABC shows or Screen Gems productions.

All these various requirements led at times to a crazy quilt of guests, much to the chagrin of Cash. The Screen Gems team tried to get off to a good start, at least with country audiences, by booking Glen Campbell and Jeannie C. Riley, whose calling card in 1968 was a huge country-pop hit called "Harper Valley PTA."

Coincidentally, it was profits from that single that largely made it possible for Shelby Singleton, a veteran record producer who released "Harper Valley PTA" on his Plantation label, to buy the rights to the historic Sun recordings from Sam Phillips for nearly a million dollars later that same year. Singleton knew that Cash was going to have a TV show, and he figured the exposure would reignite demand. And sure enough, two new greatest hits packages on Sun sold enough in three months for Singleton to earn back his entire investment.

The guest lists for the next few shows were more of a mixed bag. For every musical act that would have made sense to Cash (Gordon Lightfoot, Jerry Reed, Doug Kershaw, Linda Ronstadt), there was a series of actors (Dan Blocker, Eddie Albert, Doug McClure), comics (Fannie Flagg, Ron Carey, Charlie Callas), or teen pop acts (the Cowsills, Joey Scarbury). Jacobson tried to convey Cash's displeasure to executives on the show, but he too was basically an outsider that first season.

Cash was frustrated by his lack of input, but he kept looking forward to the Dylan episode, which would be the fifth show taped but the first to air. He thought that the power of that show would persuade Screen Gems to have more respect for his musical ideas. In a magazine interview at the time, Cash tried to be optimistic. "I never liked television, but now I have decided I am going to like it," he said. "I mean, if I'm going to have to do it every day, I might as well enjoy it. I don't like being so confined, but I like my guests, and it's my show, and it has to be good."

June's role in the TV series was minimal, but she attended every rehearsal and taping, chiefly to help support John in his run-ins with the production team and to offer suggestions. With such pretty young singers as Linda Ronstadt and Joni Mitchell guesting on the show, June wanted to keep an eye on her husband, too. When she noticed Ronstadt's skimpy, sexy attire, she even asked the show's wardrobe specialist to "dress her up a bit."

When Dylan showed up for the taping on May 1, he was as riddled with nerves as Cash. For all their acclaim and fame, these were both essentially shy, private men, another thing they had in common.

If they were nervous about going onstage to sing to adoring audiences, imagine how much more anxious they were stepping in front of cold, indifferent TV cameras, knowing that millions of people would be watching them. Cash tried to make the experience as easy as possible for Dylan, inviting him and his wife, Sara, to stay at his house. Cash had frequently invited some of Nashville's most promising songwriters to his house to spend the evening playing their new songs. He put together one such gathering in Dylan's honor. In the end, Cash was grateful that Dylan had agreed to appear on the show, and Dylan couldn't wait to get the whole thing over with.

Dylan had been to the downtown Ryman Auditorium before, but only as a fan, eager to check out the mother church of country music. The fact that Dylan had pretty much been out of the public eye since his 1966 motorcycle accident made him even more jittery about doing the show. And sure enough, his appearance was a magnet for some obsessive Dylan fans around the country, many of whom began lining up outside the Ryman hours before the taping. Backstage, Dylan kept his distance from other cast members and avoided the press. He was finally cornered by Red O'Donnell, a popular columnist for the *Nashville Banner*, but his answers were brief and unrevealing. Dylan seemed relieved when he could finally step onstage to perform two songs from *Nashville Skyline* before sitting down with Cash for a duet on "Girl from the North Country." Even together they looked uncomfortable. To make everything worse, the stone wall set looked a bit ridiculous. But the original set—a barnyard—had been worse. Dylan was so offended that he told Cash he couldn't sing in front of that, saying, "My fans would laugh me off the stage." Cash, through Jacobson, got that idea scrapped.

The audience gave Dylan a standing ovation and yelled for more after his numbers, with chants of "Bobby, Bobby." When Dylan didn't return to the stage, Jacobson found him in a Ryman office, sitting by himself, still edgy. "I wanted him to see the reaction," Jacobson says. "I told him, 'Bobby, take my hand, we're going back out.' He told me, 'No, we're not!' but I was finally able to convince him. I said, 'Yes, we are. They came to see you. They're standing for you. You owe it to them. They are your fans.' When he stepped back onstage, his fans went nuts. He was so relieved."

Aside from Dylan's part in the show, Cash was most proud of the segment in which he turned songs into mini-travelogues à la the *Ride This Train* album. Though he included an occasional hit in the segment, he mostly leaned toward the Old West or folk material, such as "Dark as a Dungeon," "The Legend of John Henry's Hammer," and "The Big Battle." Even here, he had to fight Screen Gems to make his vision of the segment a reality.

"When I signed on for the show, there was a segment called 'Cash Travels' that was going to be John's reflections on America using old stock footage," Jacobson says. "But I felt John deserved more. I suggested it should be today's look at yesterday and that we should shoot new footage. It was a whole different look. John loved the idea and wrote the 'Ride This Train' theme song in ten minutes." Cash was grateful and felt even more positive about Jacobson's role.

VI

With the all-important Dylan show in the can, Cash headed to Detroit for a May 4 concert co-starring Hank Williams Jr., who had come a long way since his teenage days of merely singing his daddy's songs each night. Hank Jr. wouldn't hit his commercial stride until the 1980s, but he was already starting to forge his own identity as an independent hell-raiser. The combination of the Hank Williams legacy and Cash's post-*Folsom* popularity resulted in the biggest box office single-day gross in country music up to that time: $93,000, more than half again the previous record of $59,000.

To promote the TV series, Cash did guest turns on the *Kraft Music Hall* and the *Glen Campbell Goodtime Hour.* Holiff also helped arrange for the documentary by Robert Elfstrom, *Johnny Cash: The Man, His World, His Music,* to make its debut on the public television outlet in New York City. Columbia did its part by releasing *Johnny Cash at San Quentin* to coincide with the June 7 series launch.

Early reviews were encouraging, singling out Cash himself for special praise. "After 15 years in show business, Johnny Cash is finally being discovered by network television," read the *Time* magazine review, which also praised the lack of showbiz clichés ("no Johnny Cash Dancers") and spoke to Cash's evolving image as a cultural icon, not just a country singer. "Cash and his songs are rooted in the basics of country life, the land, lost loves, wanderlust, the seasons, lonely trains hooting across the still prairie night, preachers, prison and Sweet Jesus and home sweet home."

The *Toronto Star,* too, stressed Cash's charm and authenticity: "Cash himself, with his lived-in face and take-it-or-leave-it manner, was an engagingly unpretentious host and a welcome relief from the endless ranks of Beautiful People who normally populate television....The wonder is not that Johnny Cash finally has made it to television, but that television took so long to find him." A Nashville TV critic declared it flatly "the best country music show ever offered on network television."

In the midst of all this, Cash couldn't help but allude in a Nashville newspaper interview to the continuing head-butting backstage. The issue this time wasn't guests but the show's locale. Most of the key staff people had come out from Los Angeles, and they weren't adjusting well to life in Nashville or the surprisingly primitive conditions in which they had to record the show. For all its history, the Ryman proved a torture chamber for the production heads and crew, from its lack of air conditioning to technical sound problems.

Cash drew a line in the sand in his interview. "I understand there's a movement under way to talk me into movin' the show back to California," he said. "But I'm not gonna do it. It wouldn't be the same show. That's a whole different way of life out there. That's not where I want to be. That's not what I want to be."

The only thing left was to wait for the ratings.

The first ones in, from the big cities, were dismal, but then viewership reports started coming in from rural areas, and they were sensational. Overall, the show was clearly a winner for ABC. Even a modest hit was cheered by the struggling network. The initial order of six shows was extended to fifteen. The guest list would continue to be uneven. There were some acts worthy of sharing the stage with Cash, including the country rock of Creedence Clearwater Revival and such country stars as Merle Haggard, Marty Robbins, Roger Miller, and Tom T. Hall. On the downside were artists with little or no relationship to Cash's music or ambitions, including Lynn Kellogg, Ed Ames, and Dale Robertson. Somewhere in the middle were the Monkees, another Screen Gems property.

Drawing millions of viewers each week, the TV show made Cash a hot property, and Columbia felt good about the chances of "A Boy Named Sue." It was a strange record, to be sure—edgy enough, with its references to all the "kicking and a' gouging in the mud and the blood and the beer," but also memorable enough with its humor and its feel-good lesson that it just might appeal to both the underground rock crowd who loved *Folsom* and to the mainstream television audience who enjoyed Cash the TV star.

And sure enough, the "Boy Named Sue" single, like the *Johnny Cash at San Quentin* album, was an immediate smash. The album would spend twenty weeks at number one on the country list and four weeks atop the pop list. "Sue" hit the singles charts three weeks later and went to number one in country and number two in pop. With his new Sun catalog, Singleton released old Cash material under various album themes, including *Get Rhythm, Story Songs of the Trains and Rivers,* and *The Singing Storyteller.* By the end of the year, Singleton had five of the Sun reissues on the pop and country charts. The man from Dyess was well on his way to being the biggest-selling record artist in America.

Cash continued to celebrate his success by reaching out to members of his family. Soon after the release of the *Folsom Prison* album he had purchased a house across the street from his in Hendersonville for his parents, and he would sit with his father whenever he was in town and watch the *CBS Evening News.* When he played the Hollywood Bowl in August 1969, he again tried to make peace with his nephew Damon Fielder. Again he sent a limousine driver to Oak View with a note: "I've told Mama Cash the truth about the Los Padres fire. Please come to my concert."

Damon, who hadn't seen his uncle in four years, accepted the apology. He got into the limousine and headed to Los Angeles. "The show was great and he was great when we got together after the show; the best thing was he wasn't on the drugs any longer. He was J.R. again."

In the midst of all this, Johnston kept reminding Cash about the danger of taking this success for granted; he needed to come up with strong new material to meet the high expectations. With his energy drained by the TV show, however, Cash found it difficult to do that. Fortunately there was a new crop of young songwriters in Nashville—and he finally realized that the best of them was virtually at his doorstep.

CHAPTER 21

KRIS KRISTOFFERSON, BILLY GRAHAM, AND ANITA CARTER

I

KRIS KRISTOFFERSON WAS ABOUT to accept a teaching position at West Point when the former Rhodes scholar took a two-week side trip to Nashville in the mid-1960s to see if anyone was interested in the songs he was writing. Through a friend, he had already received encouragement from Marijohn Wilkin, who co-wrote "Long Black Veil," one of the songs Cash sang at Folsom. She introduced Kris to publishers and took him to the Grand Ole Opry on a night when Cash was performing.

"To me, John was the most real thing that came out of that great bunch of people at Sun Records," Kristofferson says. "There was something awesome about him from the beginning, but especially in those days when he was so skinny and he walked around the stage like a wild animal. He was so wound up that he looked like he was going to explode any minute.

"But he also had something to say. It was Woody Guthrie, talking about humanity, human rights. He was someone who felt he could actually make the world better through his music, and I admired that. I told Marijohn that I had to meet him, and she brought him over and he shook my hand. It was electric. It transformed me.

Immediately, I knew where I wanted to be. As soon as I got my discharge [from the Army], I headed to Nashville."

It was quite a sacrifice for Kristofferson. He was under a lot of pressure to take the West Point assignment. Here was the quintessential All-American boy. Besides the Rhodes scholarship, he was a Golden Gloves boxer, the son of an Air Force major general, the winner of a prestigious fiction-writing contest. When he took a job as a studio assistant at Columbia—"janitor," he called it—just so he could be in a position to pitch songs to recording artists, his family pretty much disowned him, and his wife eventually filed for divorce. But Kristofferson didn't back down.

With his striking good looks and passion for music, he soon fell in with a group of Nashville songwriters and record producers. He'd sing his songs at the drop of the hat, hoping to find singers to record them. One source of frustration at Columbia was that he was warned his first day that he would be fired if he tried to lobby the artists; they were in the studio to work, not to be hassled. Kristofferson respected the rule. He was there in 1966 while Dylan recorded *Blonde on Blonde,* but never worked up the courage to say even one word to another of his heroes. It took an assist from mutual friend Jack Clement for Kristofferson to talk to Cash.

Soon after moving to Nashville, Kristofferson, who opposed the Vietnam War, wrote a song expressing a soldier's feelings about the war in the style of Dylan's talking blues numbers. He sang the song, "Talkin' Vietnam Blues," one night in a club that catered to music industry people. Clement liked it, and they became close. When Clement noticed a glum Kristofferson reading a letter a few days later, he asked if it was bad news. Indeed it was—one of an apparent series of letters from his mother, who was still trying to get Kristofferson to come to his senses and go back to West Point. He passed it along to Clement, who especially noticed the line that scolded him for idolizing someone who most people thought was just a drug addict.

Kristofferson forgot about the conversation until a few days later when he was working a Cash recording session. Cash walked up to him and said, "Always nice to get letters from home, isn't it, Kris?"

Even though that broke the ice, Kristofferson still didn't take advantage by slipping Cash tapes of his songs. In fact, he shooed away two other songwriters who snuck into the studio and tried to corner Cash. When a studio secretary heard of the incident, she thought that Kristofferson had been the one trying to pitch the songs and she barred him from working in the studio. He had to spend his entire shift in the basement erasing and filing old tapes.

"Somebody must have told John about it because he came down to the basement a few nights later to ask why I wasn't in the studio with him," Kris says. "I explained what happened and he said, 'Well, I'm not going to start the session until you come up.' So my boss brought a chair into the studio for me and I sat and listened to the session. The secretary gave me the nastiest look.

"But that's the kind of thing John would do all the time. I knew he had come down to the basement just to see me because there was no other reason for him to be there—and you've got to remember he was bouncing off the walls at the time. He was so pilled up. But even in that condition, he could reach out to people."

Cash became fond enough of Kristofferson to invite him to the house to sit in on the songwriter sessions he'd have in his living room, but he still didn't pick up on Kris's songs. "I just don't know what took me so long to really listen to what he was writing," Cash said later. "I can't imagine how many times he gave me a cassette of something he had just written, but I just hurled it into the lake with all the other tapes people had given me."

Even as other country singers began recording Kristofferson's songs, Cash still passed. This led the frustrated young songwriter to risk arrest by landing a helicopter on Cash's property one afternoon. It's such a great story that it has been repeated frequently, though usually enhanced to include the colorful image of Kris stepping from the helicopter with a beer in one hand and a cassette of "Sunday Mornin' Comin' Down" in the other—as a startled Cash looks on.

"I had to fly four hours a month as part of my National Guard service, and I thought it would be a good way to get John's attention," Kristofferson recalls. "But I didn't have a beer in one hand and a tape in the other. In fact, the song wasn't 'Sunday Mornin' Comin' Down.' And either John wasn't there or he was hiding in the house, because someone else came out of the house. I don't know if John ever even heard the tape. It was one of many."

The song that did catch Cash's attention, months after the helicopter incident, was "To Beat the Devil," a cautionary tale Kristofferson had written back in 1967 after passing Cash in the hall and seeing how messed up he was. "I thought he was his own worst enemy," he recalls. "Here was this man who worked so hard to get a message out to people, but I thought he was going to die in the process."

Cash didn't know "Devil" was about him, but he certainly identified with lines in the song contrasting the singer's idealism with his personal struggles:

And you still can hear me singin' to the people who don't listen,
to the things that I am sayin', prayin' someone's gonna hear.
And I guess I'll die explaining how the things that they complain about,
are things they could be changin', hoping someone's gonna care.

I was born a lonely singer, and I'm bound to die the same,
but I've got to feed the hunger in my soul.
And if I never have a nickel, I won't ever die ashamed,
'cause I don't believe that no-one wants to know.

It's odd that Cash returned to the song in 1969 at the height of his success, when it was clear his message was getting through to millions; it may just have reminded him of his earlier times. He recorded it on July 24, when he was in an especially good mood. He had performed at the Newport Folk Festival a few days earlier, where he was the prime attraction for the closing night's crowd of 7,500. Cash also had brought Kristofferson onstage in Newport to sing "Sunday Mornin' Comin' Down" and "Me and Bobby McGee."

The biggest news of the weekend, however, came from June.

Two months earlier, John had insisted after a romantic vacation in the Virgin Islands that he was sure June was pregnant—and that it was going to be a boy. June scoffed, because they had been trying for some time to have a baby, worried whether they could even conceive because of his extensive drug use and June's age. She was forty.

But a few weeks later she learned that his prediction was right. They even came up with a name: John Carter Cash. John was so certain it was going to be a boy, they didn't even think of a girl's name.

II

As soon as taping for the first season of shows ended, Cash turned his attention to recordings. It had been nearly a year since he had recorded a new album. "I felt there were a lot of people who only knew me from the prison album and the TV show," he said, "and I wanted to give them some music that meant a lot to me personally—a very personal album that kind of reflected my journey. I told Bob Johnston I wanted to introduce myself to these new fans and he said, 'That's great John, You should call it *Hello, I'm Johnny Cash,* and that's what we did. I was real proud of that record." The album's centerpiece was "To Beat the Devil."

The album, recorded mostly over four days in late August and early September, was one of Cash's most endearing works. *Hello, I'm Johnny Cash* was not as overtly ambitious as *Ride This Train* or as dynamic as *Folsom Prison,* but it came straight from the heart.

"Southwind," the opening tune, recaptured the joyful exclamation of the old *boom-chicka-boom* sound so well that it could have been recorded the same day as "Big River." Another song, "See Ruby Fall," was co-written with Roy Orbison after the two friends saw the words "See Ruby Falls" on a billboard promoting a tourist attraction in Tennessee and pictured a woman named Ruby falling off a barstool. It evolved into a song that, despite its novelty edge, captured perfectly the sentimental mood of honky-tonk heartache tunes. The record, too, was brightened by a vigorous piano arrangement reminiscent of "Home of the Blues" at Sun.

Cash celebrated his marriage with two songs, " 'Cause I Love You," a pledge of faithfulness that recalled "I Walk the Line" and was written in the Dylanesque style of "Understand Your Man," and the Tim Hardin ballad "If I Were a Carpenter," a Top 10 hit for

Bobby Darin in 1966. John and June sang it as a duet, apparently prompted by hearing Ramblin' Jack Elliott sing it on the TV show.

"Route No. 1, Box 144" was another Cash song with an especially strong autobiographical strain. Cash had been thinking about the song ever since visiting the military hospitals in Asia. He ended up with this tale of an "average good boy" who "grew up on a little farm just a couple of miles out of town." The only thing missing is the name Dyess. The young man marries his high school sweetheart and buys a farm of his own at Route No. 1, Box 144. With a baby on the way, the young farmer joins the Army. He's killed in battle and the body is returned home. The song ends with the town turning out to welcome him—another Cash commentary about how every life can matter.

> He never did great things to be remembered.
> He'd never been away from home before.
> But you'd thought he was president or something
> at Route 1, Box 144.

Cash then headed back on the road, where he found the crowds larger and more enthusiastic than ever. Instead of 3,000 to 5,000 fans, he was now pulling in 15,000 for two shows in San Antonio, breaking records at the New Mexico State Fair by drawing 48,000 fans over four days, and in Los Angeles he could have sold out two shows at the 18,000-seat Hollywood Bowl instead of the single scheduled date.

Things were going so well that Lou Robin and Allen Tinkley came up with a bold idea that gave even the normally ambitious Holiff pause: How about playing New York's 20,000-capacity Madison Square Garden? The 2,800-seat Carnegie Hall was one thing, but playing Madison Square Garden in a city that hadn't shown enough interest in country music even to have a country radio station would be something else entirely.

"Everyone said we were insane to put a country show in Madison Square Garden, but we knew he had gone beyond country music," Robin says. "Allen and I had done lots of shows in New York, including the Garden, and we knew the market. John was on every station by then, plus we put him in the round so we could advertise that every seat was a good seat. We finally talked Saul into it. He just said, 'Don't guess wrong!' So we booked the show for December fifth, and it sold out almost immediately."

III

The Johnny Cash Show had created such a buzz that ABC renewed it for 1970. Cash vowed to feature more country artists in the show when he spoke in October at a country music industry gathering in Nashville.

"There were some mistakes in my show this summer, partly my fault, partly ABC's, partly Screen Gems'," he said. "I was, as they say, not an established television star then. So the people in charge felt they should put guests from various fields of entertainment on every week. But the mail we received asked for more of my own people."

As the audience cheered, Cash pledged that during the new season "we're going to put more of the realism, truth, and down-to-earth feeling that is in country music into our show. We've already started lining up such guests as Merle Haggard, Charley Pride, as well as top new talent. We hope to present, with dignity, people like Roy Acuff, Ernest Tubb, Hank Snow. We feel country music has really come into its own, that it's the biggest thing in the world, and we're going to do our best for it."

The resentment over the non-country guests must not have been too great in Nashville, because that same week the Country Music Association awarded Cash five of the ten honors handed out at the group's annual ceremony. They were for entertainer of the year, best male vocalist, best album *(San Quentin)*, best single ("A Boy Named Sue"), and best group or duo (John and June).

Cash made more news when it was announced that he would play a Cherokee chief in a film, *The Trail of Tears*, for National Educational Television. Despite the disaster of *Five Minutes to Live*, Cash still thought he had potential as an actor. The film's director, Lane Slate, certainly built high expectations for him, making what is believed to be the first public reference to Cash as the heir to another cultural icon's role as a strong, silent American hero.

"He's got the same sort of power about him that John Wayne has," Slate said. "I don't know whether he'll ever be able to play anything but those strong parts, but Wayne has certainly been successful at it."

Cash had turned down at least six scripts before accepting *The Trail of Tears,* which also starred Joseph Cotton, Melvyn Douglas, and Jack Palance. The project appealed to Cash because it told of yet another shameless chapter in U.S.–Native American relations, this time the forced relocation in the 1830s of thousands of members of the Cherokee and other Native American nations from their lawful homes in the southeastern United States to reservations in Oklahoma. Thousands of the dislocated Cherokee alone died from disease or starvation during the trip.

Amid all this nonstop news, there was one occurrence during the fall of 1969 that the papers didn't cover. It was an event that could have destroyed Cash's new superstar status.

While in California, where John was to appear on another edition of the *Glen Campbell Goodtime Hour,* Cash apparently faced the biggest potential scandal since the days of Lorrie Collins and Billie Jean Horton.

According to speculation that would continue to circulate on a hush-hush basis within the deepest levels of the Cash camp for decades, June, by now five months pregnant, learned that John had had an affair. To make the report even more explosive, the talk went, the woman John had been intimate with was June's sister Anita.

Years later, Jimmy Tittle, a musician who was married to Cash's daughter Kathy, came across a song while organizing Cash's publishing company files. It was titled "Forbidden Fruit." When he mentioned the song to John, he was told that it was about Anita.

The only public reference to any Anita-John affair around that time would appear years later in the *National Enquirer,* in November 2003—after the death of all three principals. According to the scandal-minded publication, an "insider" reported that Anita, on her deathbed in 1999, asked for June's forgiveness for the affair.

If the speculation is true, the three were able to keep the news secret from most of the people in their inner circle.

But how could the marriage survive such a traumatic event?

The likely answer is that June was nothing if not a realist. Like most women who married country music stars at the time, she had seen enough backstage affairs to wipe away any sense of innocence about the future. When she said "I do," she was committing for life, as hard as that proved to be at times. The incident with Anita, if true, might have been more traumatic if John had an affair with someone other than her sister. In the fall of 1969, June may well have seen John's affair with Anita as a momentary relapse, not a sign that he wanted to end their marriage.

Cash, too, was aware of all the backstage temptations, and at the time of their marriage, he and June pledged to stick together as much as possible. John told his friend James Keach, "One of the things we talked about [before getting married], and one of her conditions and one that I wanted as well, was for us to stay side to side, work together, travel together."

After speculation arose regarding the Anita-John affair, some close to Cash saw June's suddenly increased role in the television series as a sign that he was trying to reassure her about their relationship. During the first season she'd kept a low profile. Before the start of the second season, however, Cash told producer Stan Jacobson that he wanted June to appear in every episode. In Jacobson's words, "It suddenly became the Johnny and June show." It was a partnership offstage and on.

IV

It was just weeks after this trauma that one of the world's most influential religious figures stepped into Cash's life, urging him to use his fame to inspire young people everywhere to turn to Christ. "When we were growing up, Billy Graham was the essence of true spirituality," says Cash's younger sister Joanne. "He was someone you never heard anything bad about. To Mama and Daddy, he was bigger than any singer on the radio. It meant the world to Johnny to be able to tell them that Billy Graham was coming to his house for dinner."

Days before the dinner, Cash's new star power was showcased on December 5, when he headlined the sold-out show at Madison Square Garden in New York, grossing $110,000, which was more than the Rolling Stones, Janis Joplin, or James Brown had registered at the arena. Reviews were even more glowing than at the Carnegie Hall date in 1968. In the *Post,* Alfred G. Aronowitz, a widely influential journalist in rock with ties to Dylan, focused on Cash's emerging role in bridging youthful liberal and older conservative factions in America.

"Johnny Cash knew how to talk to prisoners and to presidents," Aronowitz wrote. "He knew, as a matter of fact, how to talk to all America....Only Johnny knows how many times he's been shot down in his life, but he has kept picking himself up to become a folk figure so real, so heroic and so American that he could, as he did [at the Garden] endorse Richard M. Nixon's conduct of the Vietnam War and give a 'V' [peace] sign from the same stage."

Aronowitz looked at the seeming contradiction not as a weakness or hypocrisy but as the sign of a man struggling to understand the complexities of the times. He even pointed out how Cash, rather than duck the issue, raised the matter at the concert.

"I'll tell you exactly how I feel about it," he announced, regarding the war. "This past January, we brought our whole show over to the air base at Long Binh, and a reporter asked, 'That makes you a hawk, doesn't it?' And I said, 'No, that doesn't make me a hawk, but when you watch the helicopters bringing in the wounded, that might make you a dove with claws.'"

With his career expanding on all levels, Cash kept hearing he needed to build a business operation befitting a star of his level. He took the first step that month by buying the Plantation Dinner Theater in Hendersonville for $224,000, planning to turn it into a state-of-the-art recording studio facility. Not only would it give him a place to record less than five minutes from his house, but also he could make money by renting it to other musicians for their sessions. He would eventually house his publishing companies and a fan museum in the building, which he called the House of Cash.

*　　*　　*

As rewarding as the Madison Square Garden concert and the recording studio plans were for him, Cash was looking forward even more to sitting down with Billy Graham.

William Franklin "Billy" Graham Jr. was born in 1918, which made him fourteen years older than Cash, but they bonded like brothers. A native of Charlotte, North Carolina, Graham started actively pursuing the ministry as a teenager, and in 1947 he initiated a series of "Crusades" that grew from simple revival tents to fill arenas and stadiums around the world. By the time he contacted Cash, he was the most famous religious figure besides the pope.

He heard about Cash through his son Franklin, who suggested that Cash could attract millions of people to the Crusades, especially young people. Maria Beale Fletcher, a Nashville TV personality, agreed to introduce him to the singer, who was delighted to invite Graham and his wife, Ruth, to the house for dinner. During dinner, Graham asked John and June to take part in his Crusades, stressing the role Cash could play in spreading the word of Christ, a message that Cash embraced. Cash explained how fulfilled gospel music made him feel, that he had never been more inspired to write a song than when he wrote "He Turned the Water into Wine" during his trip to Israel. He also pointed out how warmly that song and "Were You There (When They Crucified My Lord)" had been received at Madison Square Garden.

Their first Crusade appearance came in May 1970 in Knoxville, with Cash singing before 62,000 worshipers at Newland Stadium on the campus of the University of Tennessee. He and June would eventually testify at nearly three dozen Crusades in front of nearly 2 million people. Cash and Graham grew close, frequently joining hands before the crowds at the Crusades, and also vacationing together.

"We both had a mutual faith in Christ and we also came from similar backgrounds, both of our families were southern farm families," says Graham. "But I also definitely saw the 'preacher' in Johnny. You heard it in his testimony and listened to it in his music. June encouraged that 'preacher' in him as well."

When Cash described himself as a "C+ Christian" at various

times in his life, most thought this American icon was just being humble. To those who'd been close to him at various points, it appeared he was being a bit generous with his evaluation. But there was no question Cash believed. He wasn't using his religion as commercial strategy; he carried his Bible with him everywhere, and he regularly read books to deepen his understanding of Judeo-Christian history.

The impact of Billy Graham's friendship and counsel was profound, which made it all the more difficult later when Cash would sometimes show up under the influence of pills at a Graham Crusade. It tore him apart to know that Graham would be looking at him and know that something was wrong, though Graham, in his forgiving way, never challenged Cash about it.

"Johnny Cash believed in the eternal hellfire and damnation," Bill Miller says. "He believed that if he died and he wasn't right with God that he would go to hell and he would experience the physical burning and gnashing of teeth. He never lost track of that and I think it scared him and tortured him...when he kept repeating the same sins over and over and kept asking for forgiveness. I think his [continued turning] to gospel music was his way of saying, 'God, I'm still here. I'm not perfect, but I want to be here with you.'"

As an adult looking back over his father's life, John Carter Cash, himself a devout Christian, was struck by the depth of his father's spiritual beliefs and the role of Graham, his grandfather Ezra, and his mother in reinforcing those feelings.

"Billy and my father maintained their friendship all through their lives," John Carter says. "When my father fell short, he could always reach out to Billy. Billy didn't judge my father; he was there as his friend unconditionally. Billy would lift him up, support him, and say, 'You can do this. Stand back up. You know who you are.' From that point on, Dad would tell you his purpose in life was to spread the word of Jesus Christ."

Three weeks after the dinner with Graham, Cash sat down at nine p.m. on New Year's Eve to write his second year-end reflection. As with the 1968 note, Cash was relentlessly upbeat: "This year, 1969, tops 1968 in every good way." In the six-page letter, he again focused almost exclusively on material accomplishments, something he would note and reject in his New Year's Eve letter two years later. He cited the massive album sales, the summer TV show ("a hit"), nice dinners at the house (with guests such as Bob Dylan, Joni Mitchell, and songwriter Mickey Newbury), the CMA awards ("all five"), the *Trail of Tears* film, the trips overseas ("What a night!!!!"), Billy Graham, and magazine profiles. He mentioned having given up cigarettes on Christmas Day, and then quickly asked himself, "(Can I tough it out????)." He also expressed thanks that his mother and father had moved to Hendersonville from California.

The only hint of disappointment was that his daughters weren't able to join him for Christmas. The sole trace of anger—"Bitter, Hateful"—was directed at Vivian, presumably because she wouldn't approve the trip.

In closing, he listed seven items under his "prospects for 1970," including the Billy Graham Crusades and the resumption of TV tapings.

Chief in his mind, however, was the item that topped the list: "Baby due March 10. Boy."

CHAPTER 22

"IT'S A BOY" AND THE WHITE HOUSE

I

"HELLO, I'M JOHN CARTER CASH'S DADDY."

When Cash opened his TV show with those words on March 15, 1970, his fans, now numbering in the millions, surely smiled, but they weren't surprised. Thanks to a burst of news reports, the first of more than two thousand floral bouquets began arriving at the small Madison Hospital within minutes of the announcement of the baby's birth on March 3. By the time the seven-pound, ten-ounce boy headed home six days later, he had received more than five thousand gifts.

"It's a boy, June . . . it's a boy," John said as soon as he was allowed to see his wife and his son. It seemed to June that the whole world was celebrating with them.

"I couldn't believe the flowers—they were everywhere, from the floor to the ceiling in that big hospital room and out in the hall, even at the nurses' station," she said. "And the letters and telegrams! From governors and the president and people all over the world—wiring and writing and calling to say how truly glad they were that John had a son."

When the family left the hospital, nearly one hundred patients and staff members gathered in the lobby with gifts, including a

$100 savings bond and a book of biblical stories. As news pho-
tographers captured the moment, Cash leaned over and playfully
grabbed one of his son's fingers. Then he wheeled June and John
Carter to his black Cadillac for the ten-minute ride home. They
hired one of the hospital nurses, Winifred Kelly, to be the boy's
nanny. She became part of what was a growing household staff that
included Peggy Knight, a friend of Maybelle's who was so close to
the Cashes she was often called "the third spouse," though there
was no sexual connection implied.

On the following morning, newspapers around the country, which
had printed photos of Cash in handcuffs in El Paso just five years earlier, now carried photos of a family man who was well on his way
to becoming a cultural icon. It was a remarkable transformation, in
fact, from even two years earlier, when Columbia Records had embel-
lished Cash's outlaw side in ads to build interest in the *Folsom* album.

In the ad that appeared in *Rolling Stone* in 1968, readers were
told: "The audience is convicts. They can't leave when the show's
over. Some of them know what it means when the songs talk about
killing a man. The atmosphere is electric....When you listen close,
you hear clanging doors, whistles, shouts. Responses that aren't the
same as yours. Because they're not walking around like you are.
You'll probably never really know what it's like. Johnny Cash does.
He's been inside prisons before. Not always on a visit."

Now, the Columbia ad in a *Billboard* magazine salute to Cash
conveyed a much different image.

"This man's place in American music has never really been occupied before," the ad copy declared.

> No musician has ever reached so deeply into the Amer-
> ican heart, and no musician has ever reached so many
> Americans. Last year alone, he sold more than six mil-
> lion records, more than anyone else has ever sold in a
> single year. And this year he is keeping up with that in-
> credible pace....
> He has consistently stood up for the underdog—for
> the American Indian, the prisoner, the poor, the young,

the individualist, the forgotten. And so doing he has struck a chord in all of us, a chord lost in the tumult and cynicism of the times. To hear Johnny Cash singing is to hear the song of freedom—a song imprisoned in our hearts. He sings for the prisoner in us all.

In an accompanying essay, *Billboard*'s respected editor Paul Ackerman called Cash a "great original."

"He is at once an underground hero and a favorite of the great mass of adult record buyers," wrote Ackerman. "His song material and style of performance cut across practically all key categories and appeal to all markets....He is the epitome of the music man who embraces realism and draws for his inspiration upon the inexhaustible accounts of his own and his fellow man's experience. The nation and its history are his reference books. The people are his audience."

Save for a word here and a hyperbole there, the characterizations were true. Cash was striking a unique chord with an inclusive but independent vision.

Rather than try to move toward mainstream pop in order to build an audience, Cash built the TV series—the sometimes hapless guests aside—around the songs and messages that he had been expressing ever since his Sun Records days. The signature *Ride This Train* album may have been largely ignored when it was released, but the songs and spirit of that album about the country's frontier heritage were now being heard and embraced in living rooms across America. To the millions actually seeing Cash for the first time, he came across as someone who reflected the country's roots and cherished values.

The timing of the TV show was crucial.

If Holiff had been lucky enough to talk CBS into a TV show even three years earlier, the Cash that America would have seen would have been a drug addict whose behavior was out of control most nights. In the ABC series, Cash was a man reborn. John Carter's birth assisted in that process in two ways. It presented Cash to the world as a family man, and it contributed greatly to his finally staying off drugs.

"That boy changed John's life," Grant said. "Over the years, John told many stories about 'quitting' drugs and his subsequent 'recovery.'...But the truth of the matter is that, except for a few clean and sober periods, Johnny Cash was never truly free of drugs from the late 1950s until the day his son was born."

II

When taping resumed for the TV show's second season, Cash was in a much stronger position than during the early episodes. Now that the program was a hit, ABC and Screen Gems had to keep the star at least reasonably happy. To that end, Stan Jacobson was named co-producer, which meant that Cash would have more say over choosing the guests. And sure enough, the second season, which ran on Wednesday nights from January 21 to May 13, relied much more heavily on Cash's country favorites, including Merle Haggard, Marty Robbins, and Loretta Lynn. Even the non-country guests, such as Ray Charles, Neil Diamond, and Tony Joe White, seemed more compatible. The bulk of the music, in fact, came from members of Cash's own troupe, including Perkins, the Statler Brothers, and Carter Family members. Most nights, too, the shows ended with a gospel song or an inspirational number.

Cash had long woven messages into his music, but he later credited Billy Graham with making him even more comfortable in that role. Over the next year or so, Cash introduced three songs that would go a long way in defining his public image. He sang the first one, "What Is Truth," on March 18, just two weeks after John Carter's birth. Cash had heard Merle Travis grumbling one day on the TV show's set about how he couldn't understand some of this new rock music, and as he often did, Cash tried to put himself in the place of the underdog, this time youth.

The country was still caught up in a severe generation gap, divided over everything from hair length to Vietnam. Still haunted by the wounded men he'd met on his trip to the Far East, Cash thought about the world his own son would someday encounter. As he sang the song on the show, he came as close to the role of a preacher as he had ever done. It was a less confrontational take on Dylan's defense of youth in "The Times They Are a-Changin'."

> *The old man turned off the radio,*
> *said, "Where did all of the old songs go?*
> *Kids sure play funny music these days,*
> *they play it in the strangest ways."*
>
> *Said, "It looks to me like they've all gone wild,*
> *it was peaceful back when I was a child."*
> *Well, man, could it be that the girls and the boys*
> *Are tryin' to be heard above your noise?*
>
> *And the lonely voice of youth cries,*
> *"What is truth?"*
>
> *A little boy of three sittin' on the floor*
> *looks up and says, "Daddy, what is war?"*
> *"Son, that's when people fight and die."*
> *A little boy of three says, "Daddy, why?"*
>
> *Young man of seventeen in Sunday school*
> *bein' taught the Golden Rule.*
> *And by the time another year has gone around,*
> *it may be his turn to lay his life down.*
>
> *Can you blame the voice of youth for askin',*
> *"What is truth?"*
>
> *Young man sittin' on the witness stand,*
> *The man with the Book says, "Raise your hand."*
> *"Repeat after me, I solemnly swear."*
> *The man looked down at his long hair.*
>
> *And although the young man solemnly swore,*
> *nobody seems to hear anymore.*

And it didn't really matter if the truth was there,
it was the cut of his clothes and the length of his hair.

And the lonely voice of youth cries,
"What is truth?"

The young girl dancin' to the latest beat
has found new ways to move her feet.
A young man speaking in the city square
is trying to tell somebody that he cares.

Yeah, the ones that you're callin' wild
are going to be the leaders in a little while.
This old world wakened to a new born day.
And I solemnly swear that it'll be that way.

You better help that voice of youth
Find what is truth?
And the lonely voice of youth cries,
"What is truth?"

Committed to the song, Cash showcased it again four weeks later. By then, Columbia had rushed it out as a single. The *Hello, I'm Johnny Cash* album had done well, though nothing close in sales to the prison albums, largely because it didn't produce a blockbuster single. Still, Cash regained enough pop airplay with "What Is Truth" to return to the Top 20 on the pop charts. Even more important, the song's TV exposure added immensely to Cash's growing role as a meaningful artist—though not everyone was pleased.

Whispers were being heard among country music circles in Nashville that all this success was going to his head. Just who did he think he was with this holier-than-thou attitude? Was he hosting a TV show or Sunday school? Instead of simply singing a gospel song at the end of the show, Cash twice devoted the "Ride This Train" segment to spiritual songs during March. Even network reps would soon begin to worry. They were starting to get feedback from affiliates that there was too much religion in the show.

*   *   *

President Richard M. Nixon didn't know much about country music, but he listened when Billy Graham spoke highly of Cash and his positive impact on the nation's youth. He invited Cash to perform some of his songs at the White House on April 17, 1970. Cash immediately passed the news along to his father, still anxious for the old man's approval.

Cash's decision to go to the White House was widely criticized by many of the young, liberal fans who had flocked to him after the *Folsom* album and his embrace of Dylan on the TV show. They despised Nixon, chiefly over the war in Vietnam, and they were disillusioned that their new hero was, to their minds, aiding and abetting the enemy on Pennsylvania Avenue. To Cash, his decision to go wasn't political. When he endorsed people, it was based more on friendship than on issues. He had never even voted. Cash would have been just as thrilled to get the invitation from a Democrat. It was the office of the presidency that he respected. He didn't weigh the impact of the move on what it would do to his image. Still, he didn't sacrifice his principles in the process, either. Along with the invitation, Cash received a list of songs the president would like to hear, and he sidestepped the list.

One song was "Okie from Muskogee," the hugely popular country hit by Merle Haggard which took a lighthearted slap at hippies and young protesters. Another was "Welfare Cadillac," a novelty country hit at the time. Written and recorded by Guy Drake, the song attacked a popular conservative target of the day: welfare fraud. The lyrics spoke about a man who used his welfare money to buy a Cadillac and then laughed at those who paid taxes.

When the president's request became public in mid-March, Herman Yeatman, the Tennessee welfare commissioner, wrote to Nixon protesting the idea of anyone singing "Welfare Cadillac" at the White House. He called the song an inaccurate depiction of welfare recipients. Sharing Yeatman's view, but not wanting to embarrass the president, Cash announced in response to press inquiries that he wasn't going to perform "Welfare Cadillac" because he didn't know the song and didn't have time to rehearse it. Don Reid of the Statler Brothers says the sole reason Cash refused to sing it was that he felt the song made fun of poor people. Cash wanted his performance to be inspiring, not political.

There were some 250 people, including many members of the country music industry, in the East Room of the White House when Nixon stepped to the microphone to introduce the evening's featured guest. Referring good-naturedly to the flap over "Welfare Cadillac," the president told the audience he had learned that no one tells Johnny Cash what to sing. "I understand he owns a Cadillac, but he won't sing about Cadillacs," he quipped.

When the laughter eased, the president addressed the role Cash was quickly assuming in pop culture.

"He was born in Arkansas and he now lives in Tennessee, but he belongs to America," Nixon said. "It's called country music and western music, but the truth is it's American music. It speaks in story about America in a way that speaks to all of us, north, east, west, and south."

Dispensing with the normal "Hello, I'm Johnny Cash" greeting, a deeply humbled Cash simply said "Thank you" to the president before launching into one of the songs Nixon had requested, "A Boy Named Sue." In view of his new son, he changed the song's final line to "And if I ever have a boy, I'm going to name him... John Carter Cash."

Dressed in the black frock coat and ruffled shirt that had become his signature attire on the TV show, he brought June onstage for "Darling Companion" and slipped in a medley of "I Walk the Line" and "Ring of Fire" later in the set. Mostly, Cash tailored the one-hour show with the same sensitivity and artistry he applied to the prison concerts. He felt as honored being invited to the White House as he had meeting Billy Graham, and he wanted to use the evening once again to testify to what he felt was important about music and himself.

"I was at such a high point in my career and there was so much to be thankful for—John Carter, June, the way God was coming back into my life," he told me. "I had been on television hundreds of times, but the White House was something different. I was thinking, 'If I die tomorrow, I want this show to define my goal as a songwriter and entertainer.'"

To the White House gathering he said, somewhat nervously, "I want to tell you a little bit about ourselves, about our background, where we came from, maybe why we're here. We hope to show you a little bit of the soul of the South." Cash then took the guests, including some Tennessee legislators and scores of Washington officials, back to Dyess with "Five Feet High and Rising" and "Pickin' Time" to explain his roots. Then, rather than trace his career through Sun Records and his hits, he spoke to his feelings about the country and its heritage—feelings that had led to many of the concept albums.

"This is the prettiest country in the world and I've been to a bunch of them and there ain't nothing like it anywhere," he said in a speech worthy of the best of Woody Guthrie or Pete Seeger. "With all these people we got in us from everywhere. Put them all together and get them to singing these songs and talking about all the things that had happened and the things that...It's even more beautiful." He then played a song that reflected that folklore tradition, "Wreck of the Old 97."

Warmed up, Cash mentioned how Billy Graham had told him that the country "needed some songs, some religious songs that said something to the people of today, especially the young people." He said the comments were a great inspiration to him and made him realize the huge platform he had in network TV.

After singing "Jesus Was a Carpenter," he introduced "What Is Truth" by saying he wanted to warn young people about the dangers of drugs, and that he realized he would be more effective if he could show young people he was on their side. "I wrote a poem for the youth of America," he said. "It was a twelve-verse poem, and we took four verses out and made a recording of it. It's on their side, which was the way I was feeling at the time. Maybe I was trying to be a kid again."

The lines about the injustices of war seemed pointed in the White House setting, but Cash softened the mood by saying respectfully that he hoped the president could bring the boys home as soon as possible. The applause was loud and long; once again Cash was being seen as "one of us." Cash devoted the rest of the set list to gospel tunes, ending with "The Old Account," a statement of joy at having one's sins washed away. It was another memorable example of Cash rising to the occasion with openness and heart.

Afterward, Nixon and his wife, Pat, gave John and June a two-hour tour of the White House, even encouraging Cash to lie down on the Lincoln bed. Nixon had offered to let John Carter stay in the Lincoln Bedroom during the performance, but the youngster remained at the hotel.

The president gladly obliged when Cash asked him to pose for a photograph with his seventy-two-year-old father. Marshall Grant later said that, for the first time, Ray Cash, a man not prone to show his emotions, actually looked proud of his son. Cash would write in his year-end letter that the White House performance was his "best concert to date. God surely with me."

The second defining song of the new season was Kristofferson's "Sunday Mornin' Comin' Down." Its message of loneliness and redemption seemed taken right from Cash's life, but Kristofferson didn't have the singer in mind when he wrote the song. "That was probably the most autobiographical song I'd written at the time," Kristofferson says. "I was thinking about losing my family and living in a condemned building in Nashville."

When he finished writing the song, Kristofferson's first choice to record it was Cash, but another successful Nashville recording artist, Ray Stevens, heard a demo tape of the song and was so moved by it that he gave him permission to record the song in late 1969. Cash finally began to think about recording the song after he heard Stevens's version. Still, he didn't commit to it for several more weeks.

"It didn't hit me until one day when I was at home and out by the lake and I realized how far I had come from the days when I felt like the man in the song...so empty and alone," he said. "All of a sudden the lines of the song started running through my head and I realized I could identify with every one of them. I was so caught up in the song I didn't even want to wait to go into the studio and record it. I wanted to do it as soon as possible on the TV show because Bob and I had been talking about taking some songs from the show and putting them into an album."

Here are the lyrics:

> Well I woke up Sunday morning,
> With no way to hold my head that didn't hurt.
> And the beer I had for breakfast wasn't bad,
> So I had one more for dessert.
> Then I fumbled through my closet for my clothes,
> And found my cleanest dirty shirt.
> An' I shaved my face and combed my hair,
> An' stumbled down the stairs to meet the day.
>
> I'd smoked my brain the night before,
> On cigarettes and songs I'd been pickin'.
> But I lit my first and watched a small kid,
> Cussin' at a can that he was kicking.
> Then I crossed the empty street,
> 'n caught the Sunday smell of someone fryin' chicken.
> And it took me back to somethin',
> That I'd lost somehow, somewhere along the way.
>
> On the Sunday morning sidewalk,
> Wishing, Lord, that I was stoned.
> 'Cos there's something in a Sunday,
> Makes a body feel alone.
> And there's nothin' short of dyin',
> Half as lonesome as the sound,
> On the sleepin' city sidewalks:
> Sunday mornin' comin' down.
>
> In the park I saw a daddy,
> With a laughin' little girl who he was swingin'.
> And I stopped beside a Sunday school,
> And listened to the song they were singin'.
> Then I headed back for home,
> And somewhere far away a lonely bell was ringin'.
> And it echoed through the canyons,
> Like the disappearing dreams of yesterday.

> *On the Sunday morning sidewalk,*
> *Wishing, Lord, that I was stoned.*
> *'Cos there's something in a Sunday,*
> *Makes a body feel alone.*
> *And there's nothin' short of dyin',*
> *Half as lonesome as the sound,*
> *On the sleepin' city sidewalks,*
> *Sunday mornin' comin' down.*

Cash first sang "Sunday Mornin' Comin' Down" during the "Ride This Train" sequence that aired February 25 and illustrated it with footage enacting some of the scenes from the lyrics. But Cash wasn't satisfied with that version, so he sang the song again on the April 8 show, this time with a more aggressive musical backing and a more convincing vocal. That version was included in the subsequent *Johnny Cash Show* album.

Kristofferson was at the rehearsal for that second show when he heard Cash sing "Sunday Mornin'" with the exact feeling Kris had when writing the song. When he went over to tell Cash how much he loved his vocal, John was huddling with an ABC rep who was trying to talk him into dropping the line "Wishing, Lord, that I was stoned" in favor of "Wishing, Lord, that I was home."

"He thought the original line would offend some viewers," Kristofferson says. "John turned and asked what I thought and I told him the line doesn't mean the same, but I said I knew how much the show meant to him and that I would understand if he felt he needed to change it.

"I didn't know what he was going to do until the taping. I was watching from the balcony of the Ryman, and he looked up at me just when he sang the line the way I wrote it, with 'stoned' in it. I was so proud of him. I could understand why people were starting to see him as the father of our country or something. He was a real hero."

Cash introduced the third signature song, "Man in Black," a year later in a show aimed at young people and featuring guests James

Taylor, Neil Young, and Joni Mitchell. In a sequence taped at Vanderbilt University, he met informally with students to answer questions on subjects ranging from drugs to Vietnam. Before the concert portion of the show was taped, Cash expanded upon his answers in a song, using his familiar black stage attire as a symbol to make the message more dramatic and personal.

Later, he was surprised when some critics accused him of being a fraud because the black clothing dated back to the Sun days and had nothing to do, really, with any social causes. "Of course," Cash said in return, "I'm a songwriter. I use my imagination. The important thing is the message of the song, not the imagery."

The song's lyrics go:

Well, you wonder why I always dress in black,
Why you never see bright colors on my back,
and why does my appearance seem to have a somber tone.
Well, there's a reason for the things that I have on,
I wear the black for the poor and the beaten down,
livin' in the hopeless hungry side of town;

I wear the black for the prisoner who has long paid for his crime,
but is there because he's a victim of the times.
I wear the black for those who've never read
Or listened to the words that Jesus said
about the road to happiness through love and charity.
Why, you'd think He's talkin' straight to you and me.

Ah, we're doin' mighty fine, I do suppose,
in our "streak of lightnin'" cars and fancy clothes,
But just so we're reminded of the ones who are held back,
up front there ought to be a man in black.

I wear it for the sick and lonely old,
for the reckless ones whose bad trip left them cold;
I wear the black in mournin' for the lives that could have been.
Each week we lose a hundred fine young men.
Ah, I wear it for the thousands who have died,

believin' that the Lord was on their side.
And I wear it for another hundred thousand who have died
believin' that we all were on their side.

Well, there's things that never will be right, I know
and things need changin' eve'ywhere you go.
But until we start to make a move to make a few things right,
you'll never see me wear a suit of white.
Oh, I'd love to wear a rainbow every day
and tell the world that ev'rything's OK.
But I'll try to carry off a little darkness on my back.
Till things are brighter, I'm the man in black.

Rather than release the live version, Cash went into the studio and recorded it again. For one of the few times in his career, he produced the session himself. The record proved as evocative in its gentle way as his Folsom tunes had been with their defiance. The record went on to get substantial pop and country airplay when released as a single, but its main impact was from his TV show. Within weeks, "Man in Black" joined "What Is Truth" and "Sunday Mornin' Comin' Down" as songs that largely established Cash as a symbol of American honor, compassion, and struggle.

The Vanderbilt episode was one of the high points in a series that spoke to young and old, urban and rural viewers at a time of great division in the country. Similarly, the series challenged racial boundaries in country music, which had embraced only one African American star in decades: Charlie Pride. Besides Pride, who was a repeat guest on the TV show, the program featured such black artists as Ray Charles, Stevie Wonder, O. C. Smith, and Odetta. Cash was especially proud of bringing Louis Armstrong onto the Ryman stage, where the jazz great had once been barred from performing because of his race. On the show, Armstrong re-created the trumpet solo he'd played on a Jimmie Rodgers recording of "Blue Yodel No. 9" in a 1930 session in Hollywood; Cash was thrilled to sing Rodgers's part. By celebrating that historic pairing, Cash wasn't just saluting his heroes; he was subtly underscoring his message of unity and tolerance.

III

Billy Graham and Richard Nixon weren't the only famous people interested in cultivating America's new hero. Bob Hope not only invited Cash to join him on his own TV show but also flew to Nashville to appear on Cash's program. Even Lester Maddox, the Georgia governor who was a leader in the Southern resistance to segregation, managed to share the stage with Cash at a concert for prisoners at the Municipal Auditorium in Atlanta. A special guest was Sheriff Ralph Jones, who three years earlier had given Cash the sobering lecture in his LaFayette jailhouse.

All the exposure finally led Gordon Jenkins, the arranger-composer who wrote "Crescent City Blues," to file suit in U.S. District Court in New York charging Cash with copyright infringement for using so much of "Crescent City Blues" when he wrote the lyrics of "Folsom Prison Blues." (Cash eventually paid Jenkins $75,000 to waive all future rights and royalties to the song.)

Even Hollywood came calling again. Cash recorded songs for two films, *I Walk the Line*, a drama starring Gregory Peck, and *Little Fauss and Big Halsy*, a comedy-drama featuring Robert Redford and Michael J. Pollard. He also put together modestly successful soundtrack albums to coincide with the release of both films. Neither album felt remotely inspired, except for "Flesh and Blood," one of Cash's most beautifully framed love songs. The track was released as a single and went to number one on the country charts.

Hollywood also reached out in another way. Still hopeful of a career in the movies, Cash signed to co-star with Kirk Douglas in *A Gunfight*, an eccentric western about two aging gunfighters who agree to sell tickets to a public showdown with the winner taking all. The most novel thing about the film, which was shot in New Mexico and Spain during the TV show's summer recess, is that it was financed by the Jicarilla Apaches of New Mexico.

"They said they wanted to support me [for what] I'd done with *Bitter Tears*," Cash said. "You see, the Americans gave them some of this dried-up old desert and what they did was strike oil on it. They had a lot of money lying around that they wanted to invest to make more money. They heard there was a movie possibility that I might be interested in."

Released in 1971, the film fared poorly at the box office, and critics were largely unimpressed. Mel Gussow of the *New York Times* was intrigued by the casting, though. "It is mostly the stars' presence that gives the movie authenticity—Douglas with his aging chin-dimple more and more resembling a bullet wound; Cash, his face corrugated, his voice rumbling and gravelly. They are a natural match: Douglas's grin hiding despair, Cash's frown concealing an inward ease."

On the recording front, there was so much public demand for Cash material that even the flimsy *World of Johnny Cash* album—a bargain-priced collection of old album tracks, none of them hits—was certified gold (500,000 sales). Cash's next album, *The Johnny Cash Show,* was drawn from the TV series performances, and on casual listening it seemed lazy by Cash's best standards. On reflection, the album was another daring step. Rather than showcase the TV show's most popular moments, it was built around the train segments that Cash felt so strongly about. After all those years, he was getting a second chance to expose that music to his new, larger audience. Thanks to the inclusion of "Sunday Mornin' Comin' Down," the album, too, went gold.

It was the last significant album of the Cash-Johnston partnership. Both men were vague about just what went wrong. Years later, Johnston says he went to London to record an album with Leonard Cohen, and by the time he got back to Nashville, both Dylan and Cash had moved on. "I don't know what happened," he continues. "He might have said, 'I don't want to work with Bob anymore.' I never heard anything from him.'"

Columbia's Clive Davis thinks that Cash grew disenchanted with Johnston's combative, anti–record company attitude. Johnston was still working with Cash in late 1970 when Davis flew to Nashville because of reports that the label's biggest star was unhappy with the way the company was treating him.

"Here was our biggest seller, and I was hearing that he was complaining we didn't promote or advertise his music enough," Davis says. "The fact was, we spent tremendous amounts of money to promote his music on every type of radio format and in all kinds of publications, including underground papers.

"I asked if he was really unhappy or was I getting bad information? I told him, 'We're behind you 100 percent in advertising and promotion.' He reacted with surprise and dismay, and he began to wonder how these misconceptions might have come about. He finally said the problem might be Johnston. Just before Christmas, Johnny notified me that he wouldn't be using Johnston again."

The TV show continued to be Cash's top priority, but the weekly schedule was far less demanding than his normal touring itinerary would have been. That allowed him to spend hours with John Carter, go fishing, work in his garden, and contribute to various philanthropic causes. "I have had two good years and I want to help people less fortunate than I," Cash said when asked by a reporter about his $10,000 gift to a thirty-five-year-old kidney patient in Nashville.

"It was typical of John," said Marshall Grant. "In that case, he read about the man in the paper, but he could just as easily have been driving along the highway and seen someone in trouble."

During the TV show run, anything Cash-related was news, especially in Nashville. The papers carried a steady stream of reports of Cash sightings and activities, whether it was two-month-old John Carter returning to Madison Hospital because of a cold or Cash serving as honorary "bell ringer" for the Tennessee Mental Health Association. Nashville readers also learned that a twenty-four-year-old man from nearby Smyrna, Tennessee, was arrested after sending Cash an extortion letter that threatened the safety of Cash and his family. The letter read, "Johnny Cash, if you want to keep making money and keep your family healthy, leave $200,000 in old bills in a plastic bag at I-24 and Old Hickory Boulevard Friday night."

Another consequence of Cash's new celebrity status was that tour buses, sometimes five at a time, lined up on the narrow road outside his house. They'd stop long enough for fans to take photos of the gate and even throw notes over the wall. In fact, there were now crowds everywhere he went.

In a notebook he carried around to jot down thoughts for songs he wrote, "Public life is unbelievable.... Being a 'star' means so many things and all of them opposite normalcy. If your face is familiar, you are stared at, pointed at, laughed at, whispered at, yelled at and followed. People say lots of things about you that they wouldn't say if they knew you heard. Everything you do well is taken for granted. Any mistake is a matter for great attention."

However uncomfortable the endless parade of fans sometimes made him feel, Cash appreciated the support and invariably went out of his way to be gracious. Rather than stay in the house, he would often go outside to shake hands with or sign autographs for the tour bus fans. Even on mornings when he'd be outside hoeing or tending to his grapevines, he would stop and chat with fans who drove by. Dr. Nat Winston believed that Cash's allegiance to fans went deeper than trying to thank them for their support. Like many in show business, the psychiatrist says, Cash had an enormous need for affirmation and adoration.

"One time we spent much of the day on a boat, fishing and relaxing, and John kept talking about how he needed to get away from everything, and he specifically mentioned the tour buses," Winston adds. "Well, when we got back to the house around six o'clock, there must have been ten or twelve buses lined up outside the gate, and he almost broke his leg trying to get out the car so he could race over to the fans. Whatever he said, he needed the adoration."

It wasn't only hard-core fans who wanted something from Cash. "Twenty state governors called me in the last year trying to get favors from me," he told Christopher S. Wren, in the first Cash biography. "People have called me from Washington asking me to use my name for something. They've put all this power in my hands. I keep searching for the wisdom, hoping I'll say the right thing and do the right thing."

For guidance, Cash continued to turn regularly to Billy Graham, whose constant message was that God had given Cash this power and that he should use it to tell people what God had done for him and what God could do for them. The words were reinforced by the feeling Cash got when he sang "What Is Truth" to sixty thousand people at his first Graham Crusade in Knoxville on May 24, 1970.

The adrenaline rush, he said, was even greater than at either of the prison shows.

After that Crusade appearance the evangelist told him, "God has given you your own pulpit. You can reach more people in one TV show than in fifty Crusades."

IV

Cash's escalating popularity made him feel invincible, and it was no surprise when ABC picked up the TV show for a third season. Yet there was trouble ahead. Almost immediately after the show returned to the air on September 23, viewership started to decline, though no one involved in the show could agree why.

In retrospect it is easy to see that the falloff could well have been due to circumstances beyond his reach. The public was tiring of the variety show format. Within nine months, nearly a dozen network variety shows would be canceled. In the final months of 1970, the arguments in executive offices from New York to Hollywood to Nashville over the reason for the drop in ratings ranged from the perennial matter of the wrong mix of guests to Cash's increasing emphasis on gospel music. Jacobson, who was in a key position to observe the ups and downs of the show's dynamics, eventually pointed to the religious factor. But his subtle warnings were overruled by other forces in Cash's life. The star received thousands of letters from fans and ministers around the country, all urging him to go beyond singing gospel songs to making a public declaration of faith.

Closer to home, June, too, was pushing for him to do the same thing. She even persuaded him to attend services from time to time at the neighborhood Baptist church. In a newspaper interview at the time, she said the country needed greater spiritual direction, telling the reporter, "If we don't have some kind of spiritual comeback, I think we're going to be in really bad trouble. Our morals are deteriorating to the point where people will just disintegrate."

The TV staff's grumbling about the gospel component made Cash even more aggressive on the issue. "John didn't like being told what to do," says Don Reid. "Nine times out of ten, when someone told John not to do something, he'd end up doing it. Plus, this was something deep in his heart."

The crisis came when Cash showed Jacobson a statement he planned to read on the show that would air November 18.

It read: "All my life I have believed that there are two powerful forces: the force of good and the force of evil, the force of right and the force of wrong, or, if you will, the force of God and the force of the devil. Well now, the force of God is naturally the Number One most powerful force, although the Number Two most powerful force, the devil, takes over every once in a while. And he can make it pretty rough on you when he tries to take over. I know.

"In my time, I fought him, I fought back, I clawed, I kicked him. When I didn't have the strength, I gnawed him. Well, here lately I think we've made the devil pretty mad because on our show we've been mentioning God's name. We've been talking about Jesus, Moses, Elijah the prophet, even Paul and Silas and John the Baptist. Well, this probably made the devil pretty mad alright, and he may be coming after me again, but I'll be ready for him. In the meantime, while he's coming, I'd like to get in more licks for Number One."

Jacobson found the statement unnecessarily strident and advised Cash not to use it, but Cash wouldn't listen. After the taping, Jacobson again suggested they cut the statement before the actual broadcast, but Cash was insistent. He told his closest ally on the show, "If you cut that out, I'll never talk to you again."

Years later, Jacobson stood by his position.

"There's no question it was a turning point," he says. "You could see it in the ratings. John had gone too far. I think he could have found a gentler way of doing the same thing, but he didn't see it that way."

As the ratings sagged, ABC and Screen Gems moved to reclaim control of the show. With it now apparent that variety shows were losing favor, Leonard Goldberg, vice president of programming for ABC, suggested that the music format be changed to a series of "theme" nights. Apparently Cash wasn't opposed, because he designed themes that fit with his general desires for the show. The December 23 episode, for instance, was turned into a Cash family Christmas show, complete with his mother at the piano during "Silent Night."

In his annual year-end letter, Cash was once again in an upbeat mood. "No year could possibly surpass this one for health, wealth, happiness, success, love, just sheer bliss in my marriage to June." Then he singled out John Carter: "Thank God for the sweetest blessing on earth....The whole country is raving about John Carter. The most famous baby in history. He's taking a nap now. Ready to walk. Just a couple of steps."

But he expressed more ambivalent feelings about the TV show. Describing the second season, he wrote: "A smash hit. Good shows this season. My best. Fan mail raves.... Proud of my show. Meaningful to people. Love doing it."

His tune changed sharply, though, when it came to the show's still unfolding third season. "Show still a hit. But since this makes 40 network shows, a little excitement is gone. Rating watchers are nervous. Start worrying."

He even asked himself whether he would continue to do a weekly TV show after the season ended, and he concluded:

"Doubtful.

"I don't care for the rating game.

"Must keep my performances honest.

"Must use meaningful guests.

"Don't really care.

"Will do what my heart and mind leads me to do."

V

Cash was able to follow his heart on the show as the new year, 1971, began. The January 20 and 27 tapings both saluted the history of country music, while the February 3 episode was devoted to the music of the Old West. The inspired show at Vanderbilt University was also his idea. When none of the themes attracted more viewers, ABC came up with its own themes, starting with a February 10 comedy special featuring such cornball country comedians as Archie Campbell, Junior Samples, Stringbean, and Homer and Jethro. "John was embarrassed by it," Jacobson says, and the two men balked when they were told to proceed with a circus theme.

"I mentioned the circus idea to John and he was furious," Jacobson continues. "He asked me, 'What do they want me to do? Sing 'I Walk the Line' while I'm holding a chimp'?"

Cash instructed Jacobson to tell ABC he wouldn't do the circus show. When Jacobson warned Cash that he, Jacobson, would probably be fired if Cash didn't cooperate, Cash told the co-producer, "Tell them if you go, I go." Relaying Cash's decision to the show's producer, Howard Cohen, Jacobson was given an hour to clear out his desk. "I warned them John said he wouldn't do the show without me," says Jacobson, "and Cohen said he'd talk to him."

Confident that Cash would back him up, Jacobson gave Cash's phone number to Cohen, and then he waited for a call from Cash or Cohen saying the circus idea was history. "It was Friday night, and when I didn't hear from anyone by 11:30, I knew it was all over," Jacobson adds. "Cohen had promised Cash the moon and he gave in."

In setting up the showdown, Jacobson made two mistakes. He failed to realize how much Cash hated confrontation—and he failed to realize how important that weekly national pulpit was to Cash. As much as he complained about it, Cash knew the value of the show in spreading his message.

Two nights later Jacobson went to see Cash. "We sat in the kitchen and had some coffee," Jacobson says. "It was just small talk. Neither of us mentioned the circus show. Finally, I got up and said, 'I understand,' and kissed him on the right cheek. Then I got into my car and drove home, crying all the way."

On the night of the circus taping, Jacobson stopped by to watch the end of the show in the mobile production room housed in a truck outside the Ryman. "I hadn't planned on going, but my curiosity got the best of me," he says. "When I got there, the show was just ending. John wasn't singing 'I Walk the Line,' but he was holding...a chimp."

*   *   *

Despite his preoccupation with the TV show, Cash had not forgotten about Glen Sherley, the San Quentin songwriter. Despite Marshall Grant's misgivings about the man, Cash believed in Sherley, his music, and his story. He saw a lot of himself in this son of Oklahoma farm workers, a man who had been in and out of prisons for years before he ever saw that Greystone Chapel in Folsom.

To Cash, Sherley, who was four years younger, was living proof of redemption, which is why he spent months lobbying California prison authorities to grant Sherley a parole. He even arranged for Billy Graham to phone Governor Ronald Reagan, urging that Sherley be given a second chance.

Though he had met the man for only a few minutes, Cash promised the parole authorities that he would personally provide Sherley with a job in Nashville. To demonstrate the point, Cash helped get one of Sherley's other songs, "Portrait of My Woman," to Eddy Arnold. Cash was probably as excited as Sherley when Arnold recorded it and the single became a modest hit. Thanks to that single and more Cash maneuvering, Mega Records, a small Nashville label, recorded a live album with Sherley in January 1971 at the California State Prison in Vacaville, where the songwriter had been reassigned. In a letter to Sherley days before the recording date, Cash mentioned that he and Graham were pulling for him: "We believe you are a man of destiny....The name Glen Sherley is to become a legend, a reminder to all men in prison that no matter how long, how...low they go, someone cares for them.... On with the show! Tear them up." It was signed "Your friend, Johnny Cash."

Before the album was released in May, John got the news that Sherley was being paroled on March 8. He arranged for Sherley to fly to Nashville. Cash told reporters at the airport that he and June were going to make Sherley a part of their show and sign him to their publishing company. Sherley then stepped into Cash's Cadillac and headed to the Cash family home, where he'd spend his first night of freedom in eleven years.

There was much to celebrate two weeks later as John and June flew to Australia for a tour beginning March 24. Besides the apparent redemption of Glen Sherley, they had just won another Grammy, this one for their duet on "If I Were a Carpenter," and Cash was more optimistic than ever about getting a fourth season after speaking to an ABC executive just before the flight.

It felt like a punch to the stomach hours later when Cash learned from a reporter upon landing at the airport that the show had been canceled. Forgetting all that was positive about the series, he would look back on it for years with bitterness: "I resented all the dehumanizing things that television does to you, the way it has of just sterilizing your head....Like all of a sudden I'm a machine and everybody is pushing buttons."

Lou Robin felt that Cash was worn out from the TV show. "He was tired of the grind, the compromises, and the weekend touring to help him meet his overhead," he recalls. Indeed, Cash could have made more money touring than he received for the TV show. That's why, after working all week on the show, he needed to do concerts on the weekends during the TV years to cover the cost of keeping his entire touring company—some twenty people—on the payroll.

"The advantage of the TV show was that it made him well known all over the world, which helped him sell more concert tickets and records—for a while," Robin says. "As concert promoters, Allen and I knew that somebody who was on TV every week would eventually start losing business. When you'd bring a show to town, fans would hear people say, 'We see him for free every week. Why should we pay to see him?' That wasn't the case just with John.

"In the early 1960s, we did a national tour with the cast of the *Beverly Hillbillies* TV show. At the time, it was the number-one show in every market, and all the people from the program were on tour. But the tour died. We ended up having to cancel several dates. It almost put us out of business."

From his desire that the program continue despite all those negatives, it's clear that what Cash really wanted was his massive platform. He was still getting letters from fans, many of them thanking Cash for his inspiration. This strengthened his sense of mission and purpose. Television had opened the door to a wider world for him. With the show gone, he and June turned to the only bigger picture they knew: the motion picture screen. They had been thinking about making a movie about the life of Christ ever since their first trip to Israel, and they decided this was the time.

Maybe, June suggested, the cancellation of the TV show was a blessing—a sign that it was time for them to take on the larger challenge. Cash spoke to Billy Graham, who encouraged him to proceed with the film. The evangelist told Cash that it could be his greatest gift to God.

PART
FOUR

Chapter 23

ISRAEL AND THE CALLING

I

The flight to Tel Aviv during the first week in November 1971 to begin filming his story of the life of Jesus gave Cash time to think about his future. He was glad to be doing concerts on a regular basis again; he felt that facing a live audience night after night would help motivate him to write new songs. From mid-March to the end of October, Cash had performed to nearly 400,000 people in sixty-one cities in the United States, Canada, Australia, and Europe.

"There were times in the 1960s when I was so far out of it that there was no real connection with the audience," Cash admitted. "But I felt a connection after I got sober and it meant the world to me. There were many nights when the response was so moving that I felt more excited than anyone in the audience. That told me I was on the right road."

Cash was also pleased with the new *Man in Black* album. Though it was not billed as a gospel collection, the material was chiefly religious; Billy Graham even lent his spoken voice to one of the tracks, "The Preacher Said, 'Jesus Said.'" He was in such good spirits that it didn't bother him when the album stalled at number fifty-six on the pop charts, the weakest showing of any LP since his superstar run began in 1968. After all, Billy Graham was telling him he was doing the Lord's work.

As for his film, Cash had considered various options: getting a major studio to bankroll it, hiring a veteran director, reaching out to a professional screenwriter. In the end, he decided to handle everything more informally. After all the compromises with ABC and Screen Gems, he wanted to finance it himself to avoid any outside interference. This film was going to be his vision.

As he headed to Tel Aviv, Cash was proceeding pretty much on faith alone. He had no formal script and only a vague outline in his mind. To assist him, Cash turned to two people he trusted: the Reverend Jimmie Snow, who had become as close to being his day-to-day pastor as anyone since Reverend Gressett, and Robert Elfstrom, who had directed the documentary about him.

Despite Cash's unease at attending church services because of the disruptions he caused, he enjoyed the friendship and spiritual support of pastors, and he had been looking for someone to fill that role ever since moving to Hendersonville. He had the bond with Billy Graham, but their schedules were hectic, leaving little time for them to get together except at the Crusades or on occasional vacation trips.

The Reverend Jimmie Snow became his point person.

As the son of Hank Snow, Jimmie grew up in country music and even spent a few years trying to follow in his father's footsteps. During that time, he succumbed to the same temptations that Cash experienced. "I had known Jimmie Snow since 1956 and had a lot of respect for him as a man," Cash remarked, adding, "I had seen him at his worst and he had seen me the same way."

Another thing Reverend Snow had going for him was that Cash was a big believer in signs from heaven. When Cash ran into the pastor during his drug relapse on the Far East tour, he saw Snow as one of those signs.

Still, it took several months before Cash would open up to him.

After the conversation at his house in 1969, when Cash asked Snow how he could get back in touch with his faith, he invited the minister to stop by the TV studio whenever he liked—and Reverend Snow was a regular at the Ryman, but he didn't press Cash.

After a few months Cash approached him, saying it was time they got together to resume their talk about God.

This time at the house, the reverend outlined a plan for Cash. "John would say things like, 'I'm not so bad,' and I'd say that anything we do in the negative is bad for us," Snow says. "I told him, 'The only thing that is going to give you strength is to give yourself totally and completely to God.'" Cash responded by dropping in on a Sunday service at Snow's Evangel Temple church, whose two hundred worshipers included many from country music, John's sister Joanne among them. At the minister's invitation, Cash picked up his guitar and sang a hymn called "My Prayer." Despite his feelings that day, Cash, with his busy schedule and a nagging hesitancy about fully committing himself, rarely made it back to Evangel Temple.

June's daughter Rosie was also a member of the congregation, and she sometimes talked her mother into going with her to the services, which mixed sermons with lots of singing by the church choir and members of the congregation. One Sunday in mid-April 1971, June heard an aspiring twenty-two-year-old songwriter named Larry Gatlin sing a gospel-tinged song called "Help Me," and she was deeply moved by the words and by the pure beauty of Gatlin's voice. She rushed home and said, "John, you've got to come hear this boy."

It was May 21 when John and June sat in a pew and listened to Gatlin's song, a sinner's prayer that reminded Cash of his own lost times in the 1960s.

As the service continued, Cash reflected on the pain he could have spared himself and others if he had asked for God's help earlier. When the pastor asked if anyone in the church wanted to step forward to make a spiritual commitment to Christ, Cash flashed back a quarter century to the day when he had made a similar public declaration in the Baptist church in Dyess. He realized it was time to do it again, aided now by a greater understanding of what that commitment meant.

Cash stepped from his pew and knelt at the altar. "I'm reaffirming my faith," he said. "I'll make the stand, and in case I've had any reservations up to now, I pledge that I'm going to try harder to live my life as God wants, and I'd like to ask for your prayers and the prayers of these people."

By then, June and members of his family had come up to the altar to stand next to him. John and June hugged, both of them in tears.

To Reverend Snow, Cash was a man wanting to pay back for all his blessings.

"He had all these dreams of things he wanted to do for God," he says. "We talked a lot about what he could do and he said, 'I would really like to make a movie about the life of Jesus. Would you be interested in helping me with that?"

On the drive home, Cash spoke to June, too, about the movie. He had already been working on some script ideas with Larry Murray, a writer from the TV show. Cash's vision of the film was an extension of the *Ride This Train* approach. He'd tell the story of Jesus through music and link the songs with his own narration. To illustrate the songs, the film would show Jesus's feet in various historical locations in Israel, from Jericho to the Jordan River.

One of the songs he now planned to use was Gatlin's "Help Me."

II

Robert Elfstrom was working on his boat at his lakefront vacation home in Maine when he got a phone call from Cash shortly after Labor Day 1971. The two had got along well during the nearly two years it took Elfstrom to film and then edit the documentary for National Educational Television (soon to become PBS). Cash was calling to invite Elfstrom to direct the gospel film.

"When I asked John what the film would be about, he said, 'Jesus,' and I remember saying 'Jesus who?' because the call caught me by surprise and I thought he might be talking about some rock performer with that name.

"John replied, 'Jesus *Christ!*'"

When Elfstrom, an agnostic, said he didn't know much about Jesus, Cash paid no attention. He simply asked Elfstrom to meet him a few days later in Oslo, where Cash was giving a concert. There was no way he was going to refuse. Like millions of fans, Elfstrom had fallen under Cash's spell.

In Oslo on September 12, Cash outlined his concept, and Elfstrom agreed to go to Israel with Murray in late October to start scouting locales. "We only had the vaguest idea of how we were going to tell the story, but I could feel his passion," Elfstrom says, "and I wanted to do what I could to help him even though I felt like I was probably the least qualified person on earth to direct a film like this. John didn't even know what he was going to do with the film, much less have a distributor. He just said, 'Let's make it the way I want to make it and you want to make it and then we'll see who wants it.'"

In the three years Elfstrom stood side by side with Cash during the making of first the documentary, then Cash's film, he came to admire him greatly.

"When I started working with John on the documentary, I was a clean slate," the director recalls. "I didn't know much about him and frankly didn't care. This was a job for me. But I started getting intrigued right away. There was magnetism about him that was apparent the first time I saw him in concert somewhere down South. He was electrifying, and the audience was captivated. Over time, I came to realize that onstage was where everything came together in his life, all that he had gone through back in Dyess and in the years in between. There was something in him that wanted to make his fans' lives seem significant and that they were worth something."

Elfstrom was equally fascinated watching Cash offstage. "He would be exhausted after the show some nights, but he was so gracious to fans in the dressing room," he says. "He would sign autographs or just answer their questions. He would never say no to anyone. It got to be so bad, from my point of view, that I didn't want to go to dinner with him because I knew people would come up and interrupt our meal. He would shake hands or just stand there patiently, sometimes for several minutes, while people struggled to get their little cameras to work."

Elfstrom found June equally appealing. "She was a queen, a real saint as far as I was concerned," he says. "They were completely in love. They had to be touching one another all the time, very childlike. If they were hugging and kissing, I would film them, and they would smile and giggle and be shy about it."

After a few months of filming, the producers of the documentary started asking Elfstrom if he had gotten any film of Cash talking about the drug years, but the director ignored them. "That wasn't what I wanted to do," he says. "I was into cinema verité. I wanted the reality that my camera was seeing in his world at the moment. I wasn't interested in that old sort of shotgun journalism. I didn't care about the music world or any drugs or promiscuity unless I came across it, and the only thing I saw him drink was a bottle of beer or a glass of wine. Drugs were simply not part of his life when I was with him. In the end, I wanted to show what I was seeing: John was a poet, an artist, and a wonderful, spiritual person."

In the documentary, Elfstrom followed Cash along the concert trail and into the studio, where the director came into contact with one of his own musical heroes, Bob Dylan. Though Dylan has tended to avoid cameras over the years, he had no objection when Cash brought Elfstrom along to film their duet of "Girl from the North Country."

"It was very informal," the director says. "You could tell they enjoyed each other's company. John even wanted Bob to buy property down there; he was going to sell him part of his property near the lake. But it never happened. The thing I remember from the session is that they forgot the words halfway through the song—I'm thinking Cash, actually—and they had to send someone out to get the lyrics."

III

John and June arrived in Israel on November 4 with a party of about thirty people, including John Carter and his nanny, and Larry Butler, a new staff producer at Columbia Records whom Cash had asked to produce the album soundtrack. They checked in to a hotel in Tiberias on the western shore of the Sea of Galilee. In their search for locales, Elfstrom and Murray felt that this area, about 120 miles north of Jerusalem, offered the best opportunities. Besides such historic sites as the Jordan River, it contained an abandoned Palestinian refugee village that was used by the crew to create a feeling of the Old Jerusalem.

"John put his whole heart into this film," Elfstrom says. "He was up with me at 3:30 in the morning, going out to various sites, and then he'd come to my room in his pajamas at night and we'd figure out the scene for the next day. Pretty early, we decided that we couldn't do a whole film just showing Jesus's feet in different locations. We needed to show more."

That decision led to their hiring actors to portray various people, including Roman soldiers and Jesus's disciples. Rather than professionals, they hired some of the long-haired hippies who were traveling through Israel at the time. They also turned to members of Cash's entourage—Holiff as the Roman-appointed high priest Caiaphas, Robin as a Roman soldier, Snow as Pontius Pilate, and Cash's sister Reba as the Virgin Mary. Elfstrom came up with the idea of June as Mary Magdalene. The chief casting problem was Jesus. John and June considered more than a dozen candidates but couldn't agree on one. Finally, they turned to Elfstrom, who with his long hair, beard, and soft good looks indeed seemed perfect for the role. Though he had no acting experience, Elfstrom was caught up in the spirit of the movie and said fine.

There was a sense of mission around the project, by now titled *The Gospel Road,* and Reverend Snow took advantage of the Jordan River to baptize John again—possibly as a blessing for the film itself.

By the time Cash headed home a few weeks later, there were a dozen or so scenes in the can, including the Last Supper and the Crucifixion. The latter was the film's most ambitious touch. "John came up with the idea of doing the crucifixion in lots of places to show that Christ died for people all over the world," Elfstrom says. "We ended up doing it once at Jericho in Israel, on the waterfront in Brooklyn Heights, on the Strip in Las Vegas, by the Hollywood sign in Los Angeles, and in Death Valley."

During the filming in the vast emptiness of Death Valley, a VW minivan filled with hippies drove up, and they stopped to watch. They got out, smoked some dope, and then returned to the van. As they sped off, the driver yelled, "Good luck with the resurrection!" The only witnesses to the Crucifixion at sunrise on the Las Vegas Strip were a huddle of drunks on the sidewalk.

At Jericho, a photographer from a Dutch publication came on the set just as a break was called. Elfstrom was already in place on the cross, his head covered by a crown of thorns. As he waited for action to resume, someone handed him a lit cigarette. The photographer immediately started shooting away. "John saw what was happening and he personally raced over to throw him off the set. He felt the photo was desecrating his Jesus."

Back in the States, John and June played a few concerts in the South before flying to Los Angeles to appear on Glen Campbell's TV show, where John was happy to see Nashville singer-songwriter Jerry Reed on the program too. Earlier in the year, Larry Butler had brought him a spiritually tinged Reed song, "A Thing Called Love"—and Cash grabbed hold of it. To flesh out the arrangement he envisioned, Cash brought Butler to the Evangel Temple to hear the church choir.

"I could tell he really wanted to use [the choir], but he left it totally up to me," Butler said. "He was man enough to let me do my job as producer. I remember us sitting in the church watching the choir with all these big hairdos, which were the thing back in the day. At one point John leans over to me and says, 'You know, they sure got a lotta hair in this choir.' I couldn't help but break out laughing."

Delighted with the final recording, which did feature the choir, Cash decided to release it in January as his next single. It went to number two in the country field but pretty much flopped on the pop charts. Still, the message—again—was something Cash believed in, and he was impressed enough by Butler for finding the song that he decided to make him his new producer.

While in Los Angeles, Cash finalized a contract that would take him back to Las Vegas for the first time in nearly a decade. Instead of playing one of the second-tier downtown hotels, he would be headlining at the town's biggest and most prestigious show-room—the same two-thousand-seat room at the hotel, by then renamed the Las Vegas Hilton, where Elvis Presley regularly head-lined.

It was hard to find entertainers with enough drawing power to fill the massive showroom twice a night, and Hilton executives had been trying to lure Cash for nearly a year, but he had bad memories of Las Vegas and didn't like the idea that he was encouraging his fans to gamble. David Victorson, the hotel's entertainment director, and Marty Klein, who was Cash's agent for television and other special appearances, worked out a deal that finally appealed to Cash. He would play the Hilton during Easter week. Cash would be bringing his religious message to the heart of America's so-called Sin City.

Though terms weren't publicly announced, he presumably got the Vegas superstar rate of $100,000 a week. The key for Cash was Klein's assurance that the Hilton would put no restrictions on his show. He was free to play as much gospel music as he wanted. Almost immediately, Cash began to design a special show for the occasion, just as he had done for Folsom and for the White House. As soon as he got back to his hotel, Cash phoned Billy Graham to tell him the news.

IV

Cash had begun recording the music for the *Gospel Road* soundtrack album in October 1971, but work started in earnest at a session in January 1972 when June laid down the vocal on "Follow Me," a John Denver ballad of devotion that was to be used in one of Mary Magdalene's scenes. Cash would go back into the studio with Larry Butler nearly a dozen more times over the next six months to record the instrumental segments as well as such songs as Gatlin's "Help Me," Kris Kristofferson's "Burden of Freedom," and Joe South's "Children." It was by far the most ambitious series of sessions that Cash had ever done. "John didn't do *The Gospel Road* because he wanted to be a movie star," Butler said. "He wanted to send a message through that movie; he wanted to tell what he thought really happened in the Holy Land." He brought that same drive into the studio.

Between sessions the Cash troupe went back on tour, drawing nearly 10,000 fans for a benefit in Nashville, 12,000 in Bloomington, Indiana, and 9,500 at Louisiana State University in Baton Rouge. He and June also did Reverend Snow a favor by guesting at the February 11 opening night of a new gospel show Snow would be hosting every Saturday night following the Grand Ole Opry. They also did a few dates in Europe before returning to the States to prepare for the important Las Vegas opening on March 30.

Despite the hotel's hard work in persuading Cash to play the main showroom, the Las Vegas Hilton booking was not considered a coup by rival hotel executives in town. Shows were designed to lure gamblers to the hotel casinos. The most prized entertainers were those, like Frank Sinatra at Caesars Palace or Dean Martin at the Riviera, who tended to draw high rollers. Country music bookings were usually limited to downtown hotels or, on rare occasion, the lounges of the more prestigious hotels on the Strip. Even if Cash could fill the huge showroom, many Vegas executives believed that the fans would just watch the show and then leave rather than spend hours at the dice or blackjack tables.

Representing Cash, Marty Klein stressed to the Hilton brass that Cash's audience ranged far wider than that for traditional country music. After all, he was selling more records than Elvis Presley and Barbra Streisand combined, both of whom had headlined the Hilton showroom. Klein, whose clients had also included Steve Martin and the team of Rowan and Martin, would prove a steady, wise voice for years in overseeing Cash's career in Vegas and in films. By the afternoon of the opening show, even some Hilton executives were expressing concern as they looked out the windows of the high-rise hotel and saw a sea of RVs in the parking lot. Weren't the Cash fans even going to stay at the hotel?

In his performance, Cash defied Vegas showroom clichés. He didn't open the show with a comedian (which even Elvis did), didn't feel compelled to use an orchestra (which Elvis also did), and ignored the mainstream hits that were considered essential in many showrooms around town (such as "The Impossible Dream" and "For Once in My Life").

The heart of the show was the gospel music he packed into the final third of the set, both familiar numbers, including "Peace in the Valley," and songs that would be featured in *The Gospel Road,* including "I See Men as Trees Walking." The evening's biggest surprise—and most controversial element—was the use of film slides from the movie projected on a screen during the final numbers.

For the finale, Cash sang the bright, optimistic, evangelical "A Thing Called Love" as he walked to the edge of the stage and shook hands with dozens of members of the audience. He then left the stage to another standing ovation. It was a bold and triumphant performance.

There were reports around town the next day that some members of the audience had complained about the show's heavy spiritual component—and even whispers that Hilton executives had gently asked Cash to tone things down. But the show continued through the week unchanged. In the end, everyone was happy. Campers or not, Cash fans did spend their money in the casino, though they favored slot machines over roulette wheels. Bottom line, the only thing the hotel execs wanted to know was when Cash could return.

For all the celebration in Nashville that Cash had opened the door for other elite country artists on the Strip, there was little attention given to another event in March that would have a profound impact on both the future of country music and Cash's place in it. If anything, the power brokers along Music Row considered the three-day Dripping Springs Reunion festival in the hill country near Austin, Texas, a black eye for country music. After all, the Woodstock-type show for country fans was a financial disaster.

The promoters needed to draw at least 25,000 fans a day to earn back their $250,000 investment, and their hearts sank when only 600 people showed up the first day at the 241-acre site. That was four people per acre. By Sunday the crowd had grown to 7,500, but it didn't help much. The three-day attendance was less than 20,000. The Nashville powers were not surprised. How did the promoters ever think they could draw 75,000 people with a show that headlined Willie Nelson and Waylon Jennings? Nelson hadn't had a Top 10 country hit in ten years, and Jennings, too, was an erratic seller.

Not that anyone in Nashville was rooting for the festival to succeed. Nelson had turned his back on the town after coming to feel that the executives at RCA Victor Records didn't understand how to market him, and they kept trying to change his singing style. ("What's with that odd, jazz-like phrasing?") He returned to his native Texas, where he put together a dance-minded show that combined honky-tonk and western swing, and found a receptive fan base wide enough that rednecks and longhairs were dancing side by side. Jennings, Cash's old roommate, was working more within the Nashville tradition, but he, too, was frustrated with the country music establishment and envied the freedom that he saw his pal enjoying.

While Jennings wasn't willing to give up his Nashville base, he was intrigued when he found that Willie's odd fan coalition responded strongly to his hard-edged honky-tonk-rock style. He was all for it when the promoters—noticing the success of Waylon and Willie in the Lone Star State—proposed the idea of a festival appealing to both country and rock fans. To fill out the bill, the promoters booked such mainstream country acts as Roy Acuff, Buck Owens, Bill Monroe, and Tex Ritter. But the emphasis was on this new, maverick strain of country music epitomized by Willie and Waylon.

That new movement was based on a foundation built largely by Cash, all the way down to the independent "outlaw" image created by his sixties lifestyle and Folsom attitude. Dylan, Haggard, and Kris Kristofferson, of course, all helped make country music much more acceptable in the rock community. The promoters behind the festival hadn't considered trying to book Cash because they figured he was far too big—and therefore costly—a star for them to afford.

The low turnout at Dripping Springs was eventually blamed on poor promotion. After spending their budget on talent and staging, the backers had hoped to spread the news by word-of-mouth, but it never happened. Even some Austin residents who attended the festival didn't even know about it until they happened to drive by the site that weekend.

As Cash hit the road again in April, he was drawing more people in just two shows—nearly ten thousand in Buffalo and just over fourteen thousand in the New York City area—than that whole Dripping Springs Reunion lineup. But momentum was beginning to shift in country music. During Willie's and Kris's sets especially, there were signs of an unlikely bonding taking place between country and rock fans over songs that spoke about yearning for individuality in a society that was encouraging ever greater conformity. While the only thing Nashville execs seemed to focus on was the poor attendance, those who'd performed at the festival, especially Nelson, saw it as a historic weekend, and he began talking almost immediately about staging what would become a series of Fourth of July picnics that would eventually draw ninety thousand fans a day. The festival also helped establish Austin as one of the nation's most important musical centers.

Within three years, Nelson, though just a year younger than Cash, and Jennings, just five years younger, would be considered by DJs and fans to be the rising "new" voices of country music. As unthinkable as it must have seemed in light of his Las Vegas and TV triumphs, Cash would have to battle the perception that he belonged to country music's past. In fact, the changing of the guard had already begun.

CHAPTER 24

THE GOSPEL ROAD AND A CHANGE OF MANAGERS

I

MARSHALL GRANT CONTINUED TO FOLLOW the music trade papers religiously, and he was taken aback when he picked up a copy of *Billboard* in January 1973. Where there had been as many as seven Cash albums on the weekly list of country best-sellers during the height of the TV show's run, there was now just one album on the list bearing the name Cash, and it was by John's younger brother Tommy— *The Best of Tommy Cash, Volume 1.* The drought reminded Grant of the dark days in the 1960s, when John's chart presence faded because he couldn't get it together for sessions. But Cash was now straight and going into the studio regularly with producer Larry Butler. So what was wrong?

The first place to look for an explanation was the music. The title song, "Man in Black," released back in the summer of 1971, was a signature-level work, but little else on the album had been worth a second listen. In hindsight, Cash should have paid attention to the warning signals when the album failed to stir much interest. With no defining mark aside from the religious undercurrent, *Man in Black* was the first of what would be a series of generic Johnny Cash albums.

Considering how plain and predictable the contents were, it

would have been altogether appropriate to think of it simply as Johnny Cash's "1971" album. In the same sense, *A Thing Called Love* was merely his "1972" album.

Cash was drawn to the spiritual tone of the title song, written by Jerry Reed, but Cash's version was overblown. In Reed's version, which appeared on a 1968 album, *Nashville Underground,* "A Thing Called Love" was an intimate parable, focusing more on Reed's vocal than on any instrumental flourishes. Cash's version shifted the tone of the song from the sound of the Nashville underground to the garishness of prime-time TV. From the opening assault by the Evangel Temple choir to the cascading strings, the embroidery stripped the songs of any hint of the personal. At his best, Cash spoke on a direct, one-to-one level to his audience, but now he seemed to be shouting out to the millions in the TV market.

Despite its radio-friendly arrangement, the "Love" single fell flat in its bid for pop airplay, as did Cash's version of a catchy but otherwise uneventful "Kate" by Marty Robbins. Both singles rose to number two on the country charts, but that was little consolation for the folks at Columbia Records, who continued to watch with dismay as Cash's sales shrank. Whereas the *Folsom Prison* album had stayed on the country charts for ninety-two weeks—nearly two straight years—the *Love* album fell off after just twenty-four.

But Cash wasn't even fazed. The cheering crowds who greeted him each night on the road were enough to encourage him. Plus, his artistic triumphs in the 1960s had led him to trust his own musical instincts; they would eventually, he believed, pull him through any sales slump. More important, there continued to be a gradual shift in Cash's personal agenda.

Ever since Dyess, three musical styles had formed a triangle of influences that framed his highly personalized brand of country and folk music: Jimmie Rodgers's tales of everyday life, the emotionalism of the blues, and gospel music. But the changes in his personal and professional life in the wake of *Folsom* and the TV show had made gospel music his major concern. He was slowly beginning to value the message in his music over the quality. His underlying question was: "Is this something people should hear?"

Gradually, his passion for music was shifting entirely toward his spiritual expressions—whether on screen or on record. Though he would never put it in such crass terms, secular music was ever so slowly becoming just his day job.

As Elfstrom stayed busy in New York editing the *Gospel Road* film through 1972, Cash continued between tours to work with Butler on the music for the soundtrack. Butler had become valuable enough as producer and tour pianist that Cash hired him away from Columbia to be general manager of the House of Cash studio. Johnny's relationship with Butler fell somewhere in between those he'd had with Don Law and with Bob Johnston. Like Law, Butler was wholly supportive of Cash's ideas, though he played a greater role than the Englishman had in shaping the musical arrangements in the studio. He didn't, however, follow Johnston's lead in pushing for the defiant edge that had defined Cash's most memorable music.

In between *Gospel Road* sessions, Cash and Butler also returned to a project Cash had begun shortly after his White House performance in 1970. During their conversation about the *Apollo 13* flight, the president had urged Cash to put some music on tape so astronauts could play it on a future space mission. Rather than use the Tennessee Three, Cash opted for a more personal approach when he went into the studio in December 1970. Accompanied only by Norman Blake on guitar, he recorded a few songs along with linking dialogue—a miniature version of *Ride This Train*. He turned to several songs he had previously recorded, including "Mister Garfield" and "Mean as Hell," to create a portrait of the American spirit. After a couple of days, Cash started thinking of the album in more ambitious terms—as something he would release on Columbia. This led him to set it aside until he could devote more time to it. Released in September 1972 under the weighty title *America: A 200-Year Salute in Story and Song*, the album generated some interest at Columbia headquarters. The hope was that it would tap into Cash's new role as a national icon, but the package didn't even match the chart success of *A Thing Called Love*. The LP was another sign of lax judgment—an unfocused and unfulfilling mix of history, folklore, commentary, and songs. The idea of tackling two hundred years of American history in less than thirty-five minutes was probably doomed from the start. Cash ended up jumping from a song about Paul Revere to one about heroes of the Alamo to a musical version of the Gettysburg Address to a reprise of his own song "The Big Battle."

When Cash started doing concept albums in the 1960s, there was a sense of daring and edge, a great young musician on a gallant quest to remain true to his artistic impulses. His choices were equally intuitive and painstakingly planned. Whatever the sales figures had been, the quality of the work was undeniable, and his artistry grew. He had proved himself time and again, never even considering making the compromises that might have brought him a mass audience for the concept albums sooner. In those ambitious works, Cash threw himself into his music because it was the only shelter from the emotional storm around him. The strength of those works empowered him with the self-assurance that is both essential and dangerous in an artist. When he was in a creative groove, there was no need for second-guessing. But the lack of critical reflection and outside input eventually catches up with even the greatest of artists. No one is invincible—not Elvis, not Sinatra, not Dylan, and not Johnny Cash.

That the *America* album was released at all suggests that nobody was protecting Cash from himself. Butler was too laid-back and deferential; no one at Columbia wanted to take on a legend despite the widespread misgivings about their star's direction, and Holiff, who should have been the last line of defense, had stopped confronting Cash altogether. Their relationship was hanging by a thread.

If Cash harbored private doubts about the state of his recordings, there continued to be plenty in his life to reassure him about the importance of his music. On June 19 he was cheered by 100,000 people when he was the featured performer at a Campus Crusade for Christ weekend in Dallas that was described by honorary chairman Billy Graham as a "religious Woodstock." Later that month he was awarded the Audie Murphy Patriotism Award at a Spirit of America festival in Decatur, Alabama. Most of all, Cash was getting ready to unveil his prized film.

* * *

The Gospel Road had its first public showing at the Tennessee theater in Nashville on October 23. "It's my life's proudest work," Cash told the motion picture editor of the *Nashville Tennessean* the day before the showing. "I want my friends to see the picture before I decide what to do with it." As expected of a hometown audience, the response was wildly enthusiastic. But there was still a lot of work for Cash to do. He had to find a distributor for the film so he could begin recouping his $200,000 outlay. He also had to put the finishing touches on the soundtrack album.

Because of his focus on the film project, Cash's secular career continued to take a secondary position, which led to the once unthinkable day in January 1973 when Grant couldn't find a Johnny Cash album anywhere on the country charts. For some time Cash had been displaced at the top of the charts by Charlie Pride, whose generally cheerful but otherwise unremarkable records were sculpted by none other than Jack Clement. Pride's albums didn't generate much attention in the pop field, but they topped the country charts for thirty-two weeks in a row in 1972.

Cash returned to the country charts in February with *Any Old Wind That Blows,* an album he had put together the previous fall, but it was another listless compilation that could be described simply as Cash's "1973" album. Nothing on the LP would become a permanent part of his repertoire.

Finally, the *Gospel Road* film was ready for its formal release.

With Holiff again on the sidelines, Lou Robin stepped forward. His corporate partner, Hal Landers, had talked 20th Century–Fox into paying Cash $200,000, the amount of his initial outlay, for the rights to distribute the movie. On February 14 the official premiere of *The Gospel Road* was held in Charlotte, North Carolina, with Billy Graham serving as honorary chairman. The following night, Cash showed the movie in Memphis, as close as practicable to Dyess. Again, understandably, the audiences loved the film.

When the album, a two-record set, was released two months later, Columbia took out a full-page ad in the music trades reprinting Cash's comment about its being his proudest work. Unlike the relatively aimless secular work he was doing, *Gospel Road* was inspired and uncompromising. He could have made it more accessible by limiting it to a one-record album built around the generally excellent songs, including the Statler Brothers' "Lord, Is It?" But Cash wasn't interested in shortcuts. Just as with *Bitter Tears* and *Ballads of the True West,* he wanted to tell his full story, and he didn't let anything stand in the way.

High principles aside, a double album containing mostly spoken dialogue was a hard sell, and the collection managed to get only to number twelve on the country charts while not registering in the Top 200 of the pop charts.

The film had even more trouble finding a broader audience. John waited anxiously for good news, but Fox wasn't able to supply any. The plan had been to release the film initially in the South, where the studio hoped it would create enough word-of-mouth to spark strong box office results. The studio would then slowly move the film into the rest of the country. But Fox found it couldn't even get bookings in the South for so heavily religious and unorthodox a movie. Billy Graham came to the rescue. His organization bought the rights from Fox to show the film for free in thousands of churches across the country. At least, Cash told himself, the film would be seen. That lifted his spirits enough for him to think about producing a second film, this one on the life of Saint Paul, but he eventually decided to write a book about the apostle instead.

With the album and film project complete, Cash took a pause. It felt as if a chapter in his life was over—the first chapter, he sometimes said. His long struggle had been rewarded. He had his family, his faith, his career. Once again he felt redeemed.

Even though Christopher S. Wren's biography of him had been in the stores for only two years, Cash wanted to write his own account, stressing the role of God in his life. It would be, in some ways, a companion piece to *The Gospel Road,* titled *Man in Black.* "You've told the world about your beliefs," Billy Graham said to him. "Now tell them about how those beliefs shaped your life."

II

Despite the near-constant volatility, the Cash-Holiff relationship endured in the 1960s because the two men needed each other. But that mutual need waned quickly in the 1970s. Thanks to Cash's superstardom, Holiff had made a fortune. But he was drained from the years of emotional combat. Also, as he told Lou Robin, he thought Cash's career had peaked and it was going to be downhill from then on. He feared that Cash would start popping pills again, and he couldn't imagine reliving that agony. At the same time, Cash saw that Robin, along with Marty Klein, was starting to do most of the work anyway, and Robin was a lot easier to deal with than Holiff. Everything didn't have to be a battle.

There was another problem for Holiff, a ticklish one revolving around Billy Graham and *The Gospel Road.*

The relationship between artists and managers is a delicate one, built around much the same kind of commitment and trust as a marriage. The only thing missing (usually) is sex. Artists want to feel that a manager cares about them as people, not just as cash cows, so any hint of distance or indifference can lead to a messy divorce. As much as John valued Saul, it was only a business relationship.

The seeds of the breakup began in the early 1970s, when John and June noticed that Saul wasn't showing up at the Billy Graham Crusades. When they asked him about it, Holiff said he needed to keep an eye on regular concerts to protect their interests. The Crusades were benefits put together by the Graham organization. He didn't feel a need to be there. The topic was dropped, but the Cashes were disappointed by his answer. They took it as a sign of a lack of interest.

Tensions between the two sides escalated when John and June began talking about *The Gospel Road.*

Holiff was cool to the project, pointing out that it'd be hard for Cash ever to recoup his money because of the difficulty of finding a mass audience for the film. When Cash mentioned his millions of record buyers and TV viewers, Holiff—reasonably—warned that he couldn't count on all those fans also wanting to see a gospel movie. Even though Holiff was on the set in Israel for part of the time, he still didn't embrace the project, causing Cash to turn to Robin to put together the logistics in the Holy Land.

The strain became so intense after the filming that Cash, at June's urging, confronted Holiff—not in person, as Cash hated face-to-face disagreements, but on the phone. In the conversation, taped by Holiff, Cash and his manager both sounded nervous; each was trying his best not to offend the other, but the edginess was apparent. After a discussion of their differing opinions of the prospects for *The Gospel Road,* they broached the subject of their own relationship.

"I'm one of the few people who [will] try to say to you exactly what they think without meaning to be harmful," Holiff told him. "I'm not trying to break things down. I'm just trying maybe to temper things a little bit by saying not exactly what people think you want to hear. I find a lot of people tell you exactly what you want to hear."

"I know that. I don't need that either."

"And that doesn't help."

"No, it doesn't."

The crisis was over for the moment, but the wound still wasn't healed. Everyone in the Cash entourage knew it was only a matter of time before Holiff would be out. In retrospect, they thought it was remarkable that the Cash-Holiff relationship lasted as long as it did.

The final showdown between the Cashes and Holiff occurred in July 1973 in the idyllic setting of Lake Tahoe, the second major gambling and entertainment center of Nevada. Soon after Cash's dramatic success at the Las Vegas Hilton, the Sahara Tahoe Corporation approached Cash's agents and offered the same $100,000-a-week contract. After his usual morning jog, Holiff was invited to have breakfast with the Cashes at the house on the lake supplied to entertainers by the hotel.

There aren't many more beautiful spots in the world, but the mood was anything but relaxed. As soon as Holiff sat down, June brought up the matter of the Billy Graham Crusades. Again Saul offered the defense of seeing no purpose in attending shows that he hadn't set up. According to Holiff, June lashed back with the charge that he was only interested in money. This time there was no turning back.

When the meeting ended, the nearly thirteen-year relationship was ended too.

Lou Robin learned from Cash a few days later that Holiff was out. He wasn't surprised. "John had been looking for the opportunity to get rid of Saul for a long time," he says. "Saul had done a lot for John. He saved his rear many times when John was out of control. He got him some good record deals and found promoters who would do the shows despite John's reputation for no-shows in the 1960s. But at some point he was just getting less and less interested. It got to where he was referring more and more to us, and John noticed that."

After a show two weeks later at Pine Knob in Michigan, Robin and partner Allen Tinkley made a pitch to John and June to take over the management duties. "We were in the limo with John and June, and we resolved everything by the time we got to the Detroit airport forty-five minutes later," Robin recalls. "It was easy because we had pretty much been acting as managers before that."

The news didn't become public until Holiff issued a press release on his Volatile Attractions, Ltd., stationery on October 27.

"After serving in the dual capacity of Johnny Cash's manager and agent for nearly thirteen years, Saul Holiff has announced his resignation, effective December 9, 1973," the statement began. "Holiff and Cash are parting on completely amicable terms after having shared, over the years, many ups and downs, and ultimately much good fortune together. Holiff's reasons for the severance are based mainly on the fact that he has a very young family that, due to prolonged absences from home owing to business and travel obligations, he has seldom had the opportunity to see their formative years. He hopes to spend a great deal more time with his family, and to reduce his active role in show business to one of semi-retirement."

The Canadian Jew and the fundamentalist Christian had struck many as an odd couple in Nashville, where signs of anti-Semitism were not uncommon. So there were inevitable whispers of anti-

Semitism in some industry quarters when the relationship started to crumble. But those whispers diminished when Cash turned to Robin, also Jewish, to manage him.

On November 3, *Record World,* one of *Billboard*'s rival music trades, reported the resignation and announced that Robin and Tinkley would continue to represent Cash for concerts and other personal appearances, while Marty Klein, of the Agency for the Performing Arts, would represent Cash for TV and movies.

But the news getting back to Holiff was that people connected to Cash were scoffing at the resignation story. The truth, they said, was that Holiff was fired. Furious, Holiff wrote a letter to Cash's sister Reba, who helped oversee the House of Cash operation. "I take umbrage at your spreading false information," he insisted. "As I am sure you know, I resigned of my own volition which, of course, was verified by Johnny's letter to me. It is unfair and unwarranted to give anyone an incorrect version."

About the break, Robin declares, "Bottom line, I think they got to a point where they had just had enough of each other."

In later years Cash was generous with his praise, frequently lauding Saul as the man who'd lifted his career aspirations. He and June would also invite him to Jamaica for a visit.

III

Cash's recording career continued on a downward spin. While he toured Europe, Australia, and the States in the closing months of 1973 and into 1974, Columbia continued to release albums, desperately hoping something would catch on. Unfortunately, the label wasn't given much to work with. As he often did when searching for a hit, Cash resorted to something that had worked for him before. In *Johnny Cash and His Woman,* he tried, among other things, to recapture the magic of "Jackson" by recording another Billy "Edd" Wheeler novelty titled "The Color of Love," but the song had neither the same humor nor the same drive. Similarly, the couple unsuccessfully aimed for the spirit and tone of "If I Were a Carpenter" with another Wheeler duet, "The Pine Tree."

After Butler resigned because he didn't think he was being paid fairly for his production duties, Cash caught everyone by surprise by re-teaming with Don Law. Once again Law simply nodded approvingly at every step in the process—though he would have better served his longtime friend by pointing out the freakish arrangement on another novelty, Chris Gantry's "Allegheny," that featured June squawking like an injured hawk. Grant thought it was downright embarrassing.

The record charts told Cash what Law wouldn't. *Johnny Cash and His Woman* gave Cash his poorest showing yet on the country charts. Released in December 1973, it stalled at number thirty-two. It was followed a few weeks later by a greatest hits package built around "Sunday Mornin' Comin' Down," and it did even worse, making it only to number thirty-five. Things didn't get any better in 1974 with a low-key collection of children's songs. Produced by Cash and former recording engineer Charlie Bragg, *The Johnny Cash Children's Album* was a pleasant enough piece of work, but it wasn't what Cash needed—an album strikingly original and purposeful enough for Cash to reclaim his position of leadership in country music.

The one bright spot during this time was a song Cash wrote in the "message" tradition of "What Is Truth" and "Man in Black." Like many Americans, Cash was troubled by much of what was happening politically in the country, including the Watergate scandal which forced Richard Nixon's resignation in 1974. Despite his public support of Nixon's policies, Cash quietly questioned the wisdom of the war. He wanted to reaffirm his faith in the country and the goodness of the American people. After weeks of reflection, he wrote "Ragged Old Flag."

> *On Flanders Field in World War I*
> *She got a big hole from a Bertha Gun.*
> *She turned blood red in World War II,*
> *She hung limp, and low, by the time it was through.*
> *She was in Korea and Vietnam,*
> *She went where she was sent by her Uncle Sam.*
> *Native Americans, brown, yellow and white*

All shed red blood for the Stars and Stripes.
In her own good land here she's been abused,
She's been burned, dishonored, denied and refused.
And the government for which she stands
Has been scandalized throughout the land.
And she's getting threadbare, and wearing thin,
But she's in good shape, for the shape she's in.
'Cause she's been through the fire before,
And I believe she can take a whole lot more.

Apart from his gospel songs, this was the first deeply felt spark from Cash in years, and the song quickly became a crowd favorite on tour. While considered too sentimental and jingoistic by many of the young rock fans who had turned away from him after the Nixon White House appearance, the recording was far less of a strident "love it or leave it" statement than his friend Merle Haggard's "Okie from Muskogee" and "Fightin' Side of Me."

If it had been released during the height of the TV show, "Ragged Old Flag" would most certainly have been a Top 5 country single. But times had changed, and it climbed only to number thirty-one. The accompanying album stopped at number sixteen.

The tunes on the *Ragged Old Flag* LP ranged from mediocre to good, but again there was nothing in them or in the arrangements to convince anyone that Johnny Cash had recaptured the magic—especially at a time when the Dripping Springs "outlaws" Willie Nelson and Waylon Jennings were finally being hailed as the new stars around Nashville. All Cash would have had to do was listen to Nelson's ambitious concept album *Phases and Stages* to see how far his own artistic standards had slipped.

Released by Atlantic Records two months before *Ragged Old Flag,* Nelson's album was a beautifully crafted account of the breakup of a marriage, with the man's story told on one side of the album and the woman's on the other. Like Cash's early concept albums, *Phases and Stages* was ahead of its time. It didn't do any better on the country charts than *Ragged Old Flag.* But Cash's own label, Columbia, saw the potential in what Nelson was doing. Within twelve months, Nelson, now signed by Columbia, returned with another concept album, *Red Headed Stranger,* that was so sparse and unorthodox in its storytelling that the label bosses wondered if they hadn't made a mistake. But the timing was perfect.

Not only had Nelson made a great album, but he had become a media favorite thanks to the outlaw movement, and the album was quickly embraced by DJs and the press alike. *Stranger* stayed on the country charts for two years, including five weeks at number one. At the same time, Cash's old roommate Waylon Jennings was regularly hitting number one on the country charts too. In fact, lots of names from Cash's past had number-one singles in 1974. In addition to Jennings, the list included his old Sun roster mate Charlie Rich, plus Hank Snow, Merle Haggard, Sonny James, and George Jones.

In the old days, one would like to think, Cash would have been motivated enough by all that competition to apply himself for months, if necessary, to reclaim his position as country music's greatest figure.

Instead, he continued to operate as if nothing were wrong. Without anyone to challenge him, he relied almost exclusively on his instincts and his cronies.

Just as he had gotten the idea for the children's album while fishing with his son, he decided that he wanted to make what was, in essence, a family album. In a series of sessions from January to mid-June 1974, Cash brought June, Rosanne, Carlene, and Rosie into the studio to join him on a wide range of tunes, including the Carter Family favorite "Keep on the Sunny Side," Cat Stevens's "Father and Son," and his own "Don't Take Your Guns to Town." Though the religious component in Cash's albums had been decreasing as he tried to put out more commercially palatable records, he saluted Christian evangelists in "Billy and Rex and Oral and Bob." Once again he co-produced most of the sessions with Charlie Bragg.

For the title tune of the album, he turned once again to Kris Kristofferson for "The Junkie and the Juicehead, Minus Me." He may have been slow to recognize Kristofferson's talent, but Cash by now had complete faith in it. He went around telling everyone how much he liked this new song, even though it was one of Kristofferson's weakest. The album dropped off the country charts after just four weeks. It was another embarrassment for Cash.

Columbia Records' patience finally ran out.

Charles Koppelman, national director of artists and repertoire for Columbia, called Cash to New York and gently told him that he was too great an artist to see his albums disappear from the charts as quickly as *Junkie* and *Ragged Old Flag*. Then Koppelman said he had an idea: Why not go into the studio with Gary Klein, a New York producer who had just made a smash hit called "Stop and Smell the Roses" with Mac Davis? Gary could work with Cash on picking songs and find the best studio musicians in the country to play on the tracks. All John would have to do was concentrate on his singing.

Rather than take Koppelman's suggestion as an attack on his artistic freedom, Cash was flattered by his interest. He returned to Nashville with high hopes. Others in Nashville, though, could see what was really happening. New York was taking over, and Music Row insiders didn't like it. If Klein could make Cash a hit all over again, other labels would also turn to their pop departments to help generate more sales from Nashville. All over town, country producers worried that their days were numbered.

Klein, however, was excited to be working with Cash. "Everybody knew a Johnny Cash record when they heard it," he says. "I felt honored to be working with him. But it was a very difficult project for me. His sound, style, and persona were so well established that it was intimidating. As it turned out, he made it easy. He was a pleasure to work with. He was always prepared and on time, always a gentleman."

The producer brought some excellent songs to the project, including "The Lady Came from Baltimore" and "Reason to Believe" by Tim Hardin, whose work Cash already knew because of "If I Were a Carpenter." Klein also brought Randy Newman's "My Old Kentucky Home (Turpentine and Dandelion Wine)" and the Band's "The Night They Drove Old Dixie Down." For his part, Cash threw into the mix such songs as his own "Lonesome to the Bone" and David Allan Coe's "Cocaine Carolina," a rowdy hell-raiser that could have been an album highlight in the irreverent contexts of either of the prison albums.

In interviews at the time Cash expressed optimism, singling out "The Lady Came from Baltimore" for special praise. That song was released as a single in December 1974, and Columbia's promotion team pushed it hard. The label was encouraged when it made number fourteen on the country charts, the best showing of any Cash single in two years. But that initial airplay didn't transfer into album sales. In fact, *John R. Cash* was the first top-level Cash album not to hit the country charts at all. The rejection may have been Nashville's way of saying to New York–based executives: Leave us alone. The album garnered little pop airplay or sales.

In the early weeks of 1975, Columbia and Cash both asked the same question: Now what?

What the record company still didn't understand was that Cash's focus was no longer on music. He and June had signed up the year before for a correspondence course on the Bible. For three years, at home and on tour, they would work on lessons they received from the Christian International School of Theology. Cash threw himself into his Bible study the way he'd once committed himself to making albums. He even told a few people that he might give up his career and become a full-time minister, but he quickly abandoned the idea—fearing, he said, that he would simply be a "celebrity preacher" who would attract people who wanted their photo taken with him rather than his spiritual counsel. Marshall Grant for one never took the idea seriously: "I think it was just another part of John finding a place for himself after the music started slipping away." Besides, June reminded him that he could reach far more people through his music than through any private ministry. But he didn't lose his thirst for the scriptures, especially the story of Saint Paul, a man "I couldn't get my mind off," said Cash.

As his record career continued to stumble, Cash's goal was to be the father he hadn't been in the 1960s.

Cash's struggle to regain the love and respect of his daughters was a lifelong one, as he documented in a series of letters to the girls, especially Rosanne. In May 1969, when he'd been feeling optimistic about the future, he wrote her: "Regardless of the mistakes your daddy has made in the past, the bad publicity I got, etc., please know that I'm above all that now. I really believe I've turned out to be a good man. I just wish I could spend more time with you girls. I miss you more than you know."

Fifteen years later he would still be trying to exorcise his guilt over abandoning his family: "I suppose I will always agonize over the fact that I split on you in 1967....Maybe it was a selfish quest, but it was a quest for self-survival."

CHAPTER 25

FAMILY MAN AND NATIONAL ICON

I

IN THE TWENTY YEARS SINCE he had cut his first record at Sun, Cash's résumé included some 1,800 concerts, nearly fifty albums, five movies, dozens of television shows, a divorce, and thousands of pills—and he was tired. After achieving superstardom and sobriety, Cash, at forty-three, looked forward in 1975 to the comforts of faith and family at least as much as new career horizons. Except for projects like *The Gospel Road,* he no longer approached every album with a sense of occasion.

"John kept writing songs or looking for songs—and he had hundreds to choose from because every young writer in Nashville dreamed of having Johnny Cash record his song," Marshall Grant recalled. "But everything was more casual."

When it was time to go into the studio, Cash would just bring in the last bunch of songs that had caught his ear. He didn't sit down and plan them. There wasn't a feeling of life and death about them anymore. He had other priorities.

Years later Cash told me he was lulled by his success in the 1960s and early 1970s into taking his music for granted. He felt he could devote most of his attention to his family and spreading God's word and still have plenty of time left over to make records. But suddenly, it seemed like everything dried up. By the time he realized what was happening, he didn't know what to do about it. Besides, he enjoyed those new priorities.

It was a slow transition in his life that began the day John Carter was born in 1970. The child instantly became the center of his and June's world. "He was like their dream come true," Carlene says. "Everything revolved around him. Rosie and I used to laugh about it, but we also kind of doted on him. It was fun having a little brother."

The couple put John Carter's crib in their bedroom and took him on the road with them, including a trip to Australia when he turned one year old. Besides bringing John Carter's nanny along on tour, Cash arranged for a bodyguard to stand outside the boy's hotel room door when John and June were doing their shows. It wasn't long, though, before they started taking him to the venues. When John Carter was barely old enough to walk, Cash would bring him onstage, eventually teaching him enough words to "Will the Circle Be Unbroken" for him to join the rest of the cast in singing it.

At the same time, Cash tried to rebuild a relationship with his daughters. In fact John's daughters, in various combinations, had been going on the road with him since the summer of 1968—when the demand for Cash's concerts was so great there was no way he could take six weeks off in the summer to be with them as he had in 1967. It was an eye-opening introduction to his professional world for the Cash daughters.

"He was a different person on the road," Kathy says. "He had his mind on his work. It was intimidating because he was the boss of all these people. You could tell he was glad we were there, but it was often, like, 'Be quiet.' He'd take a nap every day before the show. It was like we were on the bus and then in the hotels and back-stage waiting for him; it was just go, go, go. Then suddenly we'd be home, and it was fun again."

Rosanne remembers that period at the house vividly.

"We were all just so happy," she says. "He had gained weight and he looked so good and he seemed so happy. Sure, there were still problems of adjustment, but my main memory is joy. I had my dad back."

With his career going nonstop, Cash felt an increasing need to get away from the demands on him. He and June had been spending time at Eck and Maybelle's modest house in Port Richey, Florida, for years.

True to his enterprising nature, Eck Carter didn't just stumble upon the sleepy village north of Tampa. When he wanted a retirement home in the 1960s, he researched possible locations and found a magazine article that named Port Richey the ideal spot for value and lifestyle. Eck bought a bungalow on a river that fed into the Gulf of Mexico. John loved the fishing and the quiet,

At Port Richey, John and June became intrigued by an even more exotic vacation spot just a short flight away: the Caribbean.

"We went to the Virgin Islands," Carlene says. "It was our first time out of the country. We had incredible times. John would spend all day in his swim shorts, and we'd go fishing and snorkeling. We'd be there for a week one time, then ten days, then two weeks—and we went to different islands. St. John, then St. Thomas. They just loved the area, and they were always looking for new places, trying to get more seclusion, which is how they eventually got to Jamaica."

John and June made their first trip to Montego Bay in the early 1970s, and Jamaica became their new vacation spot of choice. The moment Cash spotted Cinnamon Hill, an eighteenth-century plantation house nestled 280 feet above the sea, he felt much the same attraction that he had for the Hendersonville house. When he and June learned it had been built by the great-grandfather of one of their favorite poets, Elizabeth Barrett Browning, they felt even more attached to the grounds. There was something about the bright evening sky, he said, that reminded him of the stars at night in Dyess on his walks to town when he was a boy.

John W. Rollins, a wealthy American businessman, had bought the old place and was planning to renovate it. But Cash's charm worked again, and Rollins, a onetime lieutenant governor of Delaware, soon sold him the house.. The Cashes would try to spend at least part of the year—often the Christmas holidays—at Cinnamon Hill for the rest of their lives. The Rollins family would remain good friends.

Wanting a place closer to home, Cash also bought a one-hundred-acre farm named Bon Aqua about an hour from Hendersonville. He frequently went there by himself for a day or two to unwind after a tour. Because John and June were together almost constantly on the road, they welcomed occasional breaks from each other during their time off. While John went to Bon Aqua, where he loved to trim his grapevines or just walk the grounds, June enjoyed going to New York for a weekend of often lavish shopping. (A favorite joke among the Cash inner circle was that "she had a black belt in shopping.")

II

As his fame continued to grow, Cash found there were more demands on his time than just touring and recording, many of them attached to his new role as a national icon. Cash felt it was his responsibility to use his money and fame to help others, however costly or time-consuming. His support for causes close to his heart sometimes led him into strange alliances. Besides sharing the stage with segregationist Lester Maddox for prison reform in 1970, he joined Texas billionaire and future third-party presidential candidate H. Ross Perot at a press conference the same year to build a grass-roots movement to help free American prisoners of war in North Vietnam.

Another demand on his time came from financial advisers and accountants who encouraged him to invest his money. He didn't feel comfortable making business decisions, but he had seen how his country music heroes and peers had often ended up broke because they hadn't handled their money wisely. In 1970 he paid just under $1 million for 146 acres of undeveloped property that stretched from Gallatin Road, Hendersonville's main street, the equivalent of several city blocks, to his property by the lake. His immediate goal was to preserve the natural tree-lined state of the property, but he didn't rule out its eventual use for commercial purposes.

It was a big deal in town in 1972 when he finally opened his recording studio at the House of Cash, but it did not, as hoped, jump-start his recording output.

All too often Cash's busy schedule wore him out mentally and physically, causing him to enter the studio unprepared.

"John would come in, pick up his guitar, sit down on a stool, and literally start trying to write songs," Grant said. "Sometimes we'd stay for several days but accomplish nothing. Oh, we'd record something, but it was usually thrown together with no thought or arrangement."

In that busy summer of 1972, Cash also took time away from his weeks with the girls to become one of the first musicians of the rock era to use his celebrity to lobby Congress. Most of his contemporaries felt uncomfortable stepping into the political arena, but Cash knew the media attention and, he hoped, the public pressure that could accompany his visit.

On July 27 he appeared with Glen Sherley and Harlan Sanders, another songwriter who had done time in Folsom, before a U.S. Senate judiciary subcommittee hearing on a prison and parole reform bill that had been introduced at Cash's urging by Tennessee Republican William Brock. As expected, Cash was mobbed by autograph seekers in the Senate Office Building corridors, and his testimony was widely reported.

"I've seen things that would chill the blood of the average citizen," Cash told the senators, then gave some examples of prison brutality that had come to his attention, including the case of a fifteen-year-old boy who was dying in an Arkansas prison after being raped by older prisoners, and of a young man who hanged himself after being stripped of his clothing as punishment. "Prisoners have to be treated as human beings. If they're not, when they're turned out, they're not going to act like human beings." In his turn at the microphone, Sherley pushed for laws that kept young first-time offenders from being incarcerated and for better ways to deal with hardened criminals.

Afterward, Cash generated additional publicity for his cause by meeting with President Nixon. When asked by the press if he would support the president's reelection campaign, Cash remained loyal despite his misgivings about the war. "If he asked me, I would," he said. "The dignity of the office should be upheld and respected by all citizens, and I will do anything I can for him. President Nixon has done a lot for peace." According to Cash's nephew Roy, who served in Vietnam, "he was opposed to the Vietnam War, but he was not a draft-card-burner kind of protester."

While Cash continued to advocate for prison reform, he was increasingly having doubts about Sherley. Things had gone well at first. Sherley joined Cash on tour, and he married a House of Cash employee, Nicki Robbins, at Cash's home in December 1971. Cash even arranged for Sherley's two sons from his first marriage to be flown in for the ceremony. But by the time of the Senate hearing, Sherley was showing signs of instability, and his songwriting was so weak that some in the Cash camp, including Grant, began to question whether Sherley had actually even written the song Cash sang during the Folsom concert, "Greystone Chapel."

One story widely circulated among Cash's inner circle was that Harlan Sanders, who was at Folsom at the same time as Sherley, wrote the song and Sherley, in effect, stole it. According to one version of the story, when Sanders learned that Cash was going to record it, Sherley promised to give Sanders the royalties.

"Glen was with us for about eight months when John started getting songs from Sanders, and they were good, a lot better than anything Glen had given us," said Larry Butler. "One day John walked in and said, 'I think we got the wrong man out of jail.'"

The Cash party became further disillusioned with Sherley after a few months on tour. "I think that because Glen had spent so much of his life in prison, he felt out of place and was very insecure on the outside," Grant said. "You couldn't get Glen into bed at night, and you couldn't get him out of bed in the morning, which began to be a problem because of our busy travel schedule."

The breaking point was when Sherley, apparently angered by being ordered around, looked Grant in the eye and said, "I'd like to take a knife...and just cut you all to hell. It's not because I don't love you, because I do. But that's just the type of person I am. I'd rather kill you than talk to you."

When Grant relayed his concern to Cash, Sherley was dropped from the tour. He returned to California, where he ended up working on a cattle ranch. Apart from the Cash connection, his country music legacy was limited to his name appearing in stories over the years with those of Cash, Merle Haggard, and David Allan Cole whenever roundups were written about country stars who had done jail time. On May 11, 1978, at his brother's home near Salinas, Sherley—the man who provided the feel-good heart of the Folsom concert—committed suicide with a gunshot to the head. Cash was rattled. He continued to support prison reform, but he stopped using Sherley as an example of redemption. In his 1993 autobiography, he didn't mention Sherley's name.

That didn't mean Cash lost his empathy for prisoners. In January 1997 he would phone Gary Gilmore the night before he became the first person executed in the United States in a decade. Gilmore's case gained worldwide attention because Gilmore, who was sentenced to death after killing two people in Utah, demanded the state carry out the execution rather than use legal maneuvering to prevent it. In *Shot in the Heart,* a gripping, award-winning book about his brother and his family, Mikal Gilmore said Cash was Gary's "biggest hero" and that Gary told him about the phone call from Cash: "When I picked up the phone," I said, 'Is this the real Johnny Cash?' and he said, 'Yes, it is.' And I said: 'Well, this is the real Gary Gilmore.'"

III

Despite family obligations, charity projects, awards dinners, Billy Graham Crusades, and endless touring eating up 90 percent of his time, Cash still found opportunities to keep his hand in acting and television, including a guest star role in an episode of the popular TV detective series *Columbo* in 1973 and a documentary about the history of American railroads in 1974. He was also beginning to outline his novel about Saint Paul. But the most dramatic moment of 1974 revolved, once more, around John Carter—only this time it was a moment of terrifying fear.

It was Labor Day, and Cash felt especially drained. He canceled a TV appearance and headed to Bon Aqua with June. Soon after arriving, he got a phone call: John Carter had had an accident and was in Madison Hospital.

John and June backstage in Anaheim, California, a year after their marriage in
March 1968. (© Dan Poush)

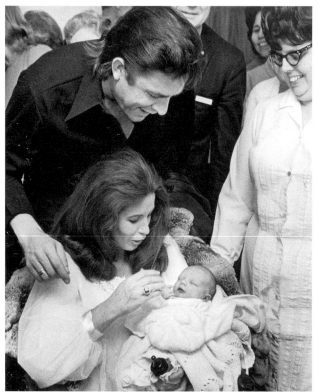

John and June at the hospital with John Carter in 1970. (Sony Music Entertainment)

June, Anita, John Carter, and John during an appearance on the television show *This Is Your Life,* which was taped in Nashville in early 1971. (Sony Music Entertainment)

With the superstardom gained after the Folsom album, Cash turned increasingly to the Bible and used his popularity to express his faith through his music and ABC television show. (Sony Music Entertainment)

At Rosanne's 1979 wedding to singer-songwriter Rodney Crowell, Cash poses with daughters, from left, Rosanne, Tara, Cindy, and Kathy. (Rosanne Cash collection)

Cash with manager Lou Robin and his wife, Karen, during a fifties-themed party in the 1970s. (Lou Robin collection)

John and June share the stage with Billy and Ruth Graham at one of the many Graham Crusade concerts in the 1970s. (Courtesy Billy Graham Evangelistic Association. Used with permission. All rights reserved)

One side of John and June in a playful photo shoot in 1980. (Marty Stuart collection)

The other side of John and June at the 1980 photo shoot. (Marty Stuart collection)

Cash with John Carter and a flock of kids in the mid-1970s. (Sony Music Entertainment)

Rosanne Cash comforts her father during a family gathering for June's birthday in 2001. (©Annie Leibovitz)

John and June at the same family reunion in 2001. (©Annie Leibovitz)

Cash during a break in the filming of the profoundly moving *Hurt* video in the Hendersonville house in fall 2002. (Mark Romanek)

John Carter Cash is at his father's side as he celebrates June's birthday in her hometown in Virginia just weeks after her death in 2003. It was his next-to-last public performance. (© 2003 Daniel Coston)

John with Rick Rubin in the producer's house during the final stages of recording the album *The Man Comes Around* in 2002. (© Martyn Atkins)

John's sister Reba had taken John Carter and seven other young-sters for a ride through the woods near Cash's house. The front wheels of her Jeep hit some loose gravel on the road on the way back to the lakefront house, and the vehicle flipped over, hurling the children to the ground. A Grand Ole Opry tour bus had been following the Jeep; the driver and other passengers turned the Jeep right-side up and freed the children, who were then rushed to the hospital.

John and June sped to the hospital, praying every mile of the frantic hour-and-a-half journey. It was, he said later, the most fright-ening ninety minutes of his life. June was near hysteria by the time they parked the car and joined John's parents in the emergency room.

"Where's my boy?" Cash shouted. "Which room is John Carter in?"

When he couldn't seem to get an answer, he and June became even more desperate.

Finally, they learned that John Carter had just left in an ambu-lance for Vanderbilt Children's Hospital, thirty minutes away in Nashville. Cash's knees were trembling. He was too afraid even to ask about his son's condition.

John's and June's worst fears were relieved when they got to Van-derbilt and heard John Carter's cry. Not only was he alive, but also the injury wasn't as severe as feared, just a mild concussion and slight skull fracture. He needed to be kept in intensive care a couple of days, just for a precaution, but they were assured that everything would be fine.

Cash used the next few days to think once more about his fast pace.

"I must slow down," he wrote later. "I must keep priorities in or-der. I must weed out the commitments I make that are not a part of what I feel He really wants me to do."

In relating the hospital experience years later, Cash valued one other moment. He learned that his daughters Rosanne and Kathy had spent the whole first night in the hospital waiting room. On the last night of John Carter's hospital stay, Cash was thinking about all his children and wrote a song titled "My Children Walk in Truth."

He wanted to record the song, and he might have done just that a decade earlier, but now he was second-guessing himself more and more. He wouldn't record "My Children Walk in Truth" for nearly a decade. And for all his promises about a slower pace, Cash continued to push himself to the limit in every area of his life except recording.

IV

It was only natural that as the oldest Cash daughter, Rosanne was the first to move to Hendersonville to live with her father. It was the week she graduated from high school in 1973, and she immediately went on the road with him. Watching her father onstage and learning to play the guitar, Rosanne quickly developed an interest in songwriting. When Cash was off the road, Rosanne reverted to being a teenager.

"We were still trying to get to know each other, and he kept encouraging me in different directions," she says. "That was him in a nutshell. He was always so expansive. He would never tell you that you were wrong. He treated you with real respect and let you make up your mind. He'd never lecture you."

Even when Rosanne and Rosie got into trouble after borrowing their dad's vintage Chevy, he didn't scold.

"We went someplace and got drunk with a bunch of people and somebody puked in the car," Rosanne says. "We got home real late and we planned to get up early, like six a.m., and clean it before Dad got up and saw it. Of course we sleep until eight, and by the time we get outside, Dad has seen it and has had someone take the car somewhere to get it cleaned.

"We were supposed to go with him to Bon Aqua that day, and he has Rosie and me ride with him in his regular car, which was a Mercedes or something. No one says a word about what happened to the Chevy. Finally, Dad pulls up to an ice cream stand and buys us ice creams. He gives them to us, but still doesn't say a word—all the way to the farm, which is more than an hour.

"Finally, we get to Bon Aqua and he sits down on the front step and pats on the step; he wants us to sit with him. After all this time, he says very calmly, 'You have a choice. You can stay at home and do drugs or you can go on the road with me, see the world, and make a lot of money.' I was so touched that I started crying. I was already on the road, but he was going to make us choose. That's what he always tried to teach us: 'Everyone has a choice in life. It's up to you to make the right one.'"

Rosanne treasured those years with her father, but she finally decided she had to begin building her own identity. After three years she moved to London, where, thanks to her dad's connections, she got an entry-level job at CBS Records. Within six months, she felt that she was just spinning her wheels, and she headed back to Nashville to attend Vanderbilt University and start working on her career as a songwriter. She was the only one of Vivian's daughters to think seriously about the music business, though June's daughter Carlene pursued a similar path.

By then, Kathy had also moved to Hendersonville and begun working with a cadre of her relatives in the museum souvenir shop housed in the House of Cash complex. Cindy was the third daughter to head south, but it took a while. She was married right after high school and had a baby, but the marriage lasted less than two years. Cash offered to take care of all her bills if she wanted to go to college, which she did. After about a year, Cash called her and said, "I think it's my turn." When asked what he meant, he replied, "I think it's my turn to have you live near me."

Cash sent plane tickets for Cindy and the baby, and had a moving van transport her belongings to Hendersonville, where he had already rented an apartment for them near his house. Cindy got a barber's license and started cutting hair in a shop on Music Row. When her dad began spreading the word about her, even onstage, fans would show up to take her photo at the shop. It made her feel uncomfortable, and she quit. Cash then hired her to do hair and makeup on the tour.

After studying acting in Los Angeles, Cash's youngest daughter, Tara, moved to Nashville in her early twenties with an eye on modeling and acting. Cash got her some bit parts, but she eventually went to work in the production office and found she enjoyed being behind the camera more than in front of it.

Cash's generosity wasn't limited to his children. "From the time I was a child," says his niece Kelly Hancock, "I remember the love that radiated from John. He was always doing for others, usually without any fanfare or recognition, for he preferred it that way."

The temporary takeover of Cash's career by Columbia with the Klein album served as a wake-up call. Within weeks of its release, he told Grant, "I don't even consider that 'my' album." Redirecting his attention to music, Cash scheduled more formal recording sessions in 1975—thirty-six in all—than he had done the two previous years combined (thirty-one).

During this period, he fulfilled a long-standing pledge to produce an album for June. They went into the studio on January 31 to begin work on the collection, which consisted chiefly of songs June had written with John or various other family members, including Maybelle, Helen, Carlene, and Rosie. While on breaks from the road, they went back into the studio twice in February and once in March to finish the project, which Columbia agreed to release.

The label was hoping that the album, *Appalachian Pride,* would benefit from the Cash connection, but the execs were kidding themselves; Cash's fan base wasn't even buying *his* albums at this point. *Billboard* didn't bother reviewing June's album, and few were surprised when it tanked.

In returning to the studio the first week in May to work on his own music, Cash quickly realized that his skills were rusty and his confidence was low. Unable to write anything substantial himself, he continued to turn to others. He wanted to find the kind of song that would define him, something with character and a point of view. He found it in a song by Guy Clark, one of the many young folk- and country-flavored writers with a strong literary bent coming out of Texas. The song, "Texas 1947," touched on many of the familiar themes in Cash's music, including railroads, small towns, big dreams, and final chances.

Two weeks after finishing another engagement at the Las Vegas Hilton, he and the Tennessee Three devoted an entire session on May 6 to the song. He wasn't fully pleased, and after a Billy Graham Crusade appearance on May 12 in Jackson, Mississippi, he went back into the studio with a couple of other musicians to redo his vocal. He had to record it a third time before he was satisfied.

By now Cash was thinking about an album, but not one of his formal concept works. He was too concerned with trying to regain his confidence to attempt something so grand. Unfortunately, he wasn't able to come up with more songs of "Texas 1947" quality. The most telling moment on the album would be Cash's own "Down at Dripping Springs," in which he acknowledged the rising Willie and Waylon outlaw movement that he had helped inspire but of which he was not even remotely a part. Despite the box office disaster of the inaugural Dripping Springs festival in 1972, Nelson put on a one-day festival at the same spot in 1973 and, thanks to word-of-mouth about the first festival, and better promotion, drew forty thousand fans. The news spread through Nashville that something was happening with this outlaw movement. Waylon was red-hot on the charts, and Willie was heating up.

It would have been ideal for Cash to step in and take his rightful place at the forefront of this exciting movement. And he might have pulled it off if he had been able to write a compelling song—something even half as striking as "Luckenbach, Texas (Back to the Basics of Love)," the anthem that Bobby Emmons and Chips Moman would write in 1977 for Jennings. But Cash wasn't able to deliver one. From the lyrics of "Down at Dripping Springs," it wasn't even clear if he was truly saluting the outlaw movement in the song or subtly trying to remind country fans that he was the godfather of the whole thing. Even Larry Gatlin, who was mentioned in the song, couldn't figure out what Cash was trying to say.

For all his hopes that this would be the album to bring him back, Cash had trouble deciding on a title for it. He thought about *Texas 1947*, but he wanted to do something to involve John Carter in it the way he had Rosanne, Carlene, and Rosie in the *Juicehead* album. An idea came to him one day when he was walking through his vegetable garden with his son. He'd call the album *Look at Them Beans*—after a Joe Tex novelty number he had recorded—and use a photo of him and John Carter frolicking in the field. To make it more of a family affair, June wrote the liner notes.

Cash wanted to release "Texas 1947" as the first single, but he went along when Columbia execs advised him that "Look at Them Beans" had more potential. When that single stalled at number seventeen that summer, the label followed with the Guy Clark song, but there was no momentum. Retailers and DJs had already given up on the album.

By contrast, the outlaws were picking up even more speed. At the same week in November that "Texas 1947" entered the country charts at number ninety, Jennings's "Are You Sure Hank Done It This Way" was number one. Nelson's "Blue Eyes Crying in the Rain" was in its fourth month on the charts.

In his uncertainty, Cash told himself it was time to try another live album—after all, he had done well with them before. Rather than a prison album this time, he wanted to record one of his shows in Europe, where audiences continued to be amazingly responsive, buying nearly a third of all Cash albums sold. Columbia liked the idea.

For the new album, Cash chose London Palladium, one of England's most celebrated venues. Besides the Tennessee Three, he was joined onstage at various points by June, the Carter Family, and Rosanne, plus Jerry Hensley on guitar and Larry McCoy on piano for two shows on September 21, 1975.

The idea was to cover the various high points in Cash's career, and the set list rambled all over the place, from Bob Dylan's "Don't Think Twice, It's All Right" to Kristofferson's "Me and Bobby McGee" all the way back to "Hey, Porter." But the song that held Cash's attention that day was one he had written three months earlier in New York City. It was a flimsy novelty about a bum who sees a strawberry cake at a fancy banquet in a hotel. Feeling he deserves a piece of that cake after all his earlier years of hard work, the bum grabs a slice and races away, enjoying every bite.

As he often had in the past, Cash relied on his instincts. He felt that the song spoke to the resilience of the workingman and to the principle of fairness. Maybe so, but the song had no charm or punch.

He decided to make it the title track and put two photos of himself on the back of the album eating strawberry cake.

* * *

Released in early 1976, the album made the charts only briefly. With no game plan, Cash went into the studio with producers Charlie Bragg and Don Davis to work on the next album. In Grant's words, "We were just plodding along," until Davis gave Cash a tape of a quirky novelty song about an auto factory worker who falls in love with the fancy cars he's making and, knowing he could never afford to buy one, starts stealing one piece of the car at a time from the factory until he has enough parts at home to build one of the cars for himself.

It seemed like just the kind of poor-man-wins-out tale that Cash would have liked, but he put down the guitar after running through it once and told everybody he was going to go pick up John Carter at school. Grant stopped Cash and told him he thought the song sounded like a hit; he at least ought to give it a try. Cash countered by saying that Marshall liked the song only because he used to be a car mechanic himself. Still, he did record a quick version of "One Piece at a Time" that afternoon.

Someone on the Columbia promotion staff heard the recording and played it for some DJs, then went back to Cash with good news. Everyone was flipping over the record. Cash agreed to release it as a single, but he didn't have much faith in it. In his liner notes for the *One Piece at a Time* album, he seemed to be saying he was just spinning his wheels, wondering if anyone cared about his music anymore. As the single started climbing the chart in the spring, Cash crisscrossed the country on tour. He returned to Nashville just in time to learn that the record was number one on the country charts. It was his biggest hit since "What Is Truth."

As much as he rejected chart success as a measure of his work, Cash couldn't help but be excited when "One Piece at a Time" hit the public nerve that he'd been hoping to strike with "Strawberry Cake." "He was ecstatic, like a kid," Rosanne recalls. "He felt so invigorated."

Cash knew he had been lucky. He hadn't written the song, and he almost hadn't even recorded it. Worse, he still didn't have any ideas about what to do next. He wanted to take time off to focus on music, but he didn't want to cut back on the amount of time he was spending with his family or decrease his charitable work or stop doing his Crusade appearances. The only thing left was to reduce his concert schedule, but that wasn't really an option. His living expenses had expanded greatly during the superstar years, partly because he loaded his payroll with family members, aides, and household staff.

Then, when the record royalties tailed off rapidly in the 1970s, Cash refused to make cuts in his payroll, which was why he needed all those concert dates to keep afloat. Despite the $100,000 paydays at Madison Square Garden and the Las Vegas Hilton, his grosses by 1975 were more commonly in the $10,000-to-$20,000 range. He felt like he was on a treadmill—and it would be a long time before he got off.

Despite John's good behavior during the early years of the 1970s, the adults in Cash's inner circle lived with the fear that it was just a matter of time before he would succumb once more to amphetamines—and they were seeing warning signs of that relapse as early as 1975. "John's behavior started becoming increasingly erratic," Marshall Grant said. "He wasn't missing shows like before, but he would go through periods where he was moody and distant. The pressures were building up, and they just overwhelmed him."

In the old days, Grant was close enough to Cash to go to him with his concerns, but the men had grown apart, and he didn't want to risk alienating his boss even more. "Besides, John would have just brushed me off," Grant said. "He had a way of just slamming the door on unpleasant topics."

The gradual separation dated back to the late 1960s, when Cash began to feel that Grant was being condescending when confronting him regarding drugs. Cash appreciated all that Grant did as his lieutenant on the road, but he thought that the group's success was going to Grant's head, giving him a self-assurance that was grating. Whenever Grant would brush aside Cash's requests or rebuke him in public, Cash took it as a sign of disrespect. Lou Robin noticed the pair's tense moments and envisioned a blowup ahead.

Robin was more concerned with Cash's conduct. He had heard all the war stories from the 1960s and he, too, noticed that Cash was starting to act strange, and was sometimes unreachable for days at a time between tours. "There were some days when he was just irrational," Robin says, pointing to the *Strawberry Cake* album as an example. "As time went on, you could see it in the shows. He did them by rote a lot of nights when he was on pills. I'd make sure he didn't do interviews because we didn't want people seeing him in that condition. But all this was gradual. It didn't really get bad until the late 1970s."

Robin often went to June for insight. "I'd say, 'What do we do about this or that,' and June would say, 'It's him. Not much we can do about it until something disastrous happens.'" Robin's wife, Karen, who became close to June during the hours together on the road, believed that Cash's slide from sobriety started with wine. "He knew the horrors of the pills and he really tried to avoid them, so he found another escape," she says. "He really got into it, learning about wine and building this big [collection]. It doesn't matter if it's alcohol or amphetamines when you have an addictive personality, and eventually he couldn't resist the pills any longer."

CHAPTER 26

LOSING THE MUSE

I

THE MAN IN BLACK WAS such a beloved figure as the decade passed the halfway mark that it was hard for outsiders—or even some insiders—to imagine that anything essential was missing in his life. But there was. The all-important affirmation that the music had brought him had slipped away. "The biggest problem," Grant insisted, "was we weren't making good records."

How far had he fallen in terms of sales?

Between the day in 1971 when the TV show went off the air to the end of 1976, Conway Twitty, Merle Haggard, Charley Pride, Loretta Lynn, Sonny James, Charlie Rich, Tammy Wynette, Dolly Parton, Ronnie Milsap, George Jones, and Don Williams all had at least five number-one singles each—a collective eighty-two singles at the top of the charts. Cash had just "One Piece at a Time."

Desperate to gain his creative momentum, Cash worked hard on the *Last Gunfighter Ballad* album in July 1976. He spent more time than usual thinking about what songs he wanted to include on the album, and that reflection led back to his childhood days and the sentimental Gene Autry hit he listened to countless times on the family radio: "That Silver-Haired Daddy of Mine."

Not everything that found its way onto the album worked, but there was energy in most of the tracks and a conviction in Cash's voice that made the album one of his best of the 1970s. In addition to the title tune by Guy Clark, Cash's own "Ridin' on the Cotton Belt" was an ode to watching his daddy ride the rails which felt true, and there was an undeniable tenderness in "Cindy, I Love You," a song he wrote for his daughter's eighteenth birthday.

"We were in the green room at the Merv Griffin TV show and Dad asked me what I wanted for my birthday, which was coming up, and I told him I'd love a song," Cindy says. "He said, 'That's easy,' and he went away for about ten minutes. Then he came back and said, 'Do you want your birthday present early?' There were about twenty people in the room, and there wasn't a dry eye when he finished. It was so lovely. In fact, I was a little disappointed when I heard the record itself, because there were all these other voices on it. I liked it better when it was just him singing to me."

The album's defining moment was "Far Side Banks of Jordan," a beautiful, spiritual-tinged love song that he learned from the Oak Ridge Boys, who had replaced the Statler Brothers as part of the touring troupe. Written by Terry Smith, a Nashville schoolteacher and part-time songwriter, the song told of a husband and wife being reunited in heaven. Cash had recorded the song by himself nearly a year earlier, but it wasn't until he turned it into a duet with June that it caught fire. The magical part was when June sang about promising that if she died first, she'd wait for him on the far-side banks of Jordan—all the more powerful because no one expected June would die before John.

Of the sessions Grant recalled, "Maybe he was just feeling good after 'One Piece at a Time,' but you could see the difference. He didn't look lost. He was there before some of the musicians and eager to get started on the next song."

But Cash's next album was a disaster creatively—revealing his difficulties, amid the pills and other priorities—in maintaining a strong creative focus.

Even before the *Last Gunfighter* album was released in February 1977, Cash was thinking about a follow-up. It wasn't lost on him that Willie Nelson and Merle Haggard had both just released hit concept albums (the spiritual-edged LP *The Troublemaker* and *My*

Love Affair with Trains, respectively). Maybe it was time for him to do another one. As he crossed the country on tour in the fall of 1976, he thought about his nonstop lifestyle and imagined it would be a good theme to use to connect another series of stories about people and places around the country. In quiet moments on the road, he began sketching out ideas for the album that he'd call *The Rambler.*

As in the sixties, he would link the eight tunes with dialogue, this time between the Rambler (played by Cash) and the Fisherman (played by Jack Routh, who was married to Carlene from 1974 to 1977).

He had only three of the songs in the can before breaking for a nine-day tour of the Northeast and Canada. Things progressed smoothly until the troupe got to New Haven. Grant, who had been pleased with how well John was performing on the tour, found an incoherent Cash that afternoon in the dressing room.

"Why, John?" Grant asked, in a rare confrontation. "You've had all these good years. You've got the world by the tail. You're the man in country music. You have a great family, a great wife. You've got everything a man could possibly dream of. Why have you turned your back on them?"

Grant said Cash sarcastically replied, in effect, "Mind your own business." A few hours later, Grant was disheartened when Cash stepped into the spotlight and turned toward him. Cash was in even worse shape than he had been earlier in the day. But as Grant had seen so many times before, however, Cash's blurry state didn't keep him from putting on an entertaining show.

"No one in the audience—or in the cast and crew, for that matter—noticed anything unusual about John that night," Grant said. "No one but June. She looked so sad onstage, and her eyes said it all. She and I looked across the set at each other, each of us silently asking the other, *Are we going to go through this again? Is this what's going to happen?*"

As Cash returned to the studio in February and March for more work on *The Rambler,* the sales verdict was in on *The Last Gunfighter Ballad,* and once again, the news was not good. Despite the album's rewarding moments, the LP did as poorly as *Look at Them Beans* and *Strawberry Cake.* The *One Piece at a Time* album had been an exception, not a turnaround commercially. *The Rambler* again pointed out the price Cash was paying for not having a strong producer. The dialogues between songs were clumsy—truly rambling sketches that bordered on condescending in their clichéd homespun philosophy. Worse, the songs felt superficial. Cash wasn't writing about love or pain or loneliness or adventure with the fierce, sometimes helpless resolve of his best years. Even the arrangements on the album felt stock, with one echoing the bass-heavy outlaw sound associated with Waylon Jennings. The whole thing felt like a crass product.

The Rambler was another failure when it was released that summer, which must have been confusing to Cash. He'd made a terrific album in *Last Gunfighter* and a poor one in *The Rambler,* and they both fared almost identically on the charts. *Gunfighter* spent seven weeks on the charts, peaking at twenty-eight, and *Rambler* remained on the charts for eight weeks, reaching number thirty-one. It didn't seem to matter what he did.

Depressed, he didn't go back into the studio for another six months.

It was during this break from recording that Cash learned that Elvis Presley had died of a heart attack on August 16 in Memphis at the age of forty-two. "June and I loved and admired Elvis Presley," he told the press. "He was the king of us all in country, rock, folk, and rhythm and blues. I never knew an entertainer who had his personal magnetism and charisma. The women loved him and the men couldn't stop watching him."

In the weeks that followed, Cash thought a lot about Elvis. Some of his deeper feelings came out in an interview. "I always felt bad," he said, "that he got so popular and so sought after that he had to close his world around him and exclude so many people. So, I have to say the Elvis Presley that died, I didn't know him very well."

True enough; Cash had lost touch with Elvis. He had never really gotten over his suspicions about Elvis and June, but the main thing that haunted him in the summer of 1977 was the question of their legacies. It wasn't so much a matter of who had the most success or impact as it was a question of whether they had both squandered their talent. Cash had watched with everyone else as Elvis became a bloated and lazy performer, sometimes moving about the stage in a dazed, drugged fog—and the image hit too close to home. It saddened him to see Elvis go out so badly. He wondered about his own future.

Far from the musical spotlight, Cash found a new cause. His fascination with Saint Paul increased dramatically when he read *The Life and Epistles of St. Paul* by W. J. Conybeare and J. S. Howson as part of the final reading list for his Bible course. In hours he might have devoted to his music in the past, he now read profusely, especially enamored with such works as *The Apostle,* a 1943 novel by Sholem Asch based on the life of Saint Paul, and an acclaimed 1972 biography, also called *The Apostle,* by John Pollock, a Cambridge-educated clergyman who was also Billy Graham's authorized biographer.

Cash spent hours roaming through bookstores, including his favorite, Foyle's, in London, looking for more books or articles on Saint Paul. Among books he pointed to favorably was Frederic William Farrar's two-volume set, *The Life and Work of St. Paul.* He frequently turned, too, to the hundreds of books, many of them about religious subjects, which he had inherited following Ezra's death in 1975.

To learn more about Paul and Jewish laws, Cash asked Karen Robin, a convert to Judaism, for assistance. "We used to go to religious bookstores and I would pick out books for him that I thought he should read, about the religious laws and why Paul did certain things," she says. "On the road to Damascus, Paul became a follower of Jesus. John identified with that conversion and wanted something like that to happen to him. And in the writing of the book he came to a better understanding of himself."

Cash slowly began to think of the apostle as a hero—intrigued by this highly educated Jew's transformation from a fierce persecutor of Christians to the most famous of Jesus's followers. He first thought of writing a formal biography but worried that he wasn't a good enough biblical scholar and decided to write Paul's story as a novel.

"He was invincible," Cash later wrote about his subject. "He made it his life's mission to conquer and convert the idolatrous, pagan world over to Jesus Christ. And he did everything he planned that he lived long enough to do. He smiled at his persecutions. He was beaten with rods, with the lash, with stones; he was insulted, attacked by mobs, and imprisoned; his own people hated him. Yet he said, because of Jesus Christ, he had learned to be content in whatever state he was!"

II

Hearing about Cash's recording hiatus, Larry Butler felt that his friend could use some help in the studio. An easygoing guy, Butler had recovered from the frustration of not being paid normal producer rates for his work with Cash. (He claimed he was underpaid by a "low six figure" amount.) He genuinely liked Cash, and he was looking for a challenge.

In their time apart, Butler had taken over as head of the Nashville division of United Artists, where he signed Crystal Gayle and Dottie West, before starting his own production company. His biggest coup was getting Kenny Rogers to sign with UA and concentrate on country music after his modest success with the pop-rock group the First Edition. Like so many of the top male country stars, Rogers, who was six years younger than Cash, didn't write songs. But Butler didn't see that as an issue; he'd find hits for the Texan.

Butler's faith in Rogers paid off in the early months of 1977 with Rogers's version of "Lucille," a devilishly catchy Roger Bowling–Hal Bynum barroom tale about a hardworking family man pining for a woman who's walked out on him and their kids at an already low point in their lives. The single went to number one on the country charts and number four on the pop charts, but those numbers don't begin to reflect its impact. It seemed as if country and pop radio stations were playing "Lucille" nonstop, thanks to the sentimental story and an infectious chorus that was hard to shake.

As the weeks went on, Butler kept thinking that "Lucille," with its underdog viewpoint and unchecked emotion, would have been a good choice for Cash. "It was what country music storytelling was all about," Butler said. "I don't know if his version would have been as big as Kenny's, but it made me think about John, and so I just called him. I thought maybe I could find another big song for him. He was as nice as could be on the phone. It was as if nothing had ever happened. We decided that day to get back together."

Four weeks after Elvis's death, Cash and Butler began work on a new album in Nashville. The material was a mix of Cash songs and tunes Butler had found. The producer sympathized with Cash's decline on the charts. "With some artists, all they want to talk about is 'Will this song be a hit?' They'd record anything if they thought it would sell," Butler said. "But John wasn't like that. His writing was a little off by this time, but he still was not one to jump on a bandwagon with a bunch of people because this would give you a number-one record. If he didn't believe in something...he wouldn't do it—and that's what I loved about him."

During this period Butler realized that Cash's creative instincts were being drained by his hectic schedule.

"I could see that John was getting worn down by all the touring and other obligations," Butler recalled. "I'm sure he would rather have spent the time working on his songwriting, but that's a star's life, and maybe after all these years, he didn't have that much to say as a writer. It happens to everyone at some point. The question is whether you can ever regain that touch, and I'm sure John spent a lot of time thinking about that."

Butler noticed a difference between Cash's attitude toward his own songs on the new album and the pair's early albums together. "Before, he would come in with his songs and get right to work on them," he said. "Now, it was more like, 'Here's something I wrote. What do you think?' The desire was there, but some of the confidence was gone."

By most standards, *I Would Like to See You Again* was one of Cash's best albums of the 1970s—in a class with *Hello, I'm Johnny Cash* and *The Last Gunfighter Ballad,* and probably more overtly commercial than either. The high points included the title song as well as "There Ain't No Good Chain Gang," an explosive, outlaw-rich duet with Waylon Jennings, and "Who Is Gene Autry," a song

Cash wrote to explain to his son his childhood love for Autry and other cowboy movie stars. Cash sounded as if he was enjoying himself again in the studio.

Butler knew from the moment he finished the "Chain Gang" track that the song was going to be the first single from the album. In his eagerness for a hit, however, he put too much radio-friendly embroidery on the title track to make it feel like vintage Cash.

Cash devoted most of November to shows in Europe and the Midwest before filming *Thaddeus Rose and Eddie,* a TV buddy movie for CBS co-starring Bo Hopkins and featuring June and Diane Ladd. In an Associated Press review that ran when the film aired the following February, Jerry Buck urged viewers not to miss it. Calling it a "diamond in the rough," Buck said the film "will remind you of 'Marty,' brought up to date and set down in Texas."

This gave the Cashes much to look forward to as they headed to Jamaica in December. John Carter was nearing seven, and he remembers his father on those mostly carefree days at Cinnamon Hill. "He would do a lot of writing down there," Cash's son recalls. "He would get up, have breakfast, and then go out on the back porch, and he would either write or he would just spend time in prayer. After that he'd rest for a while or go off and spend time outdoors. Then he wrote again at night. He loved writing, whether it was a song or a story or just thoughts about his life or his faith."

Cash was in Las Vegas at a Billy Graham Crusade when the new single was released the first week in February. Feedback from radio was quick and positive: the "Chain Gang" single had entered the *Billboard* country charts. It would eventually climb to number twelve, his best showing—aside from the gimmicky "One Piece at a Time"—since "Any Old Wind That Blows" in 1972. The album followed early in April, and while sales were promising, they weren't spectacular. "Even if it didn't do all that we wanted, I think it caused a lot of good buzz among radio programmers and around Nashville," Butler said. "I'd like to think it sort of made John viable again, which meant we were in perfect shape to make another advance with the next album. John went off to Europe on tour and I started looking for some more songs."

* * *

Cash enjoyed playing before new audiences, and Lou Robin was always looking to brighten the itinerary. His coup on the April 1978 European swing was to book a series of concerts in Prague, where Cash recorded a live album—a retrospective of sorts featuring such favorites as "Big River," "Ring of Fire," and "I Still Miss Someone." The album was released to good response in Czechoslovakia and throughout Europe.

While Cash then toured the States during May, Butler kept looking for material, but it was tricky because he was also looking for songs for Kenny Rogers, who'd just scored his third number-one country single. If he found a great song, which one would he give it to? Butler was faced with that dilemma when he heard Don Schlitz's song "The Gambler," a very catchy number about lessons in life. If Butler hadn't been working with Rogers, he might have thought of Cash. But either because he felt that Rogers's voice fit the song better or simply because Rogers was the hotter artist, Butler recorded the song with him, and he loved the result—only to learn that higher-ups at United Artists were cool toward it. "I told several people at UA that this could be a major record for Kenny," said Butler, "but they didn't agree with me and I took it to John." Cash had already recorded a few tracks for the new album before going into the studio with Butler on July 6, 1978, to record "The Gambler." Butler was surprised by two things. First, Cash was spacey during the session, and second, he showed no interest in the Schlitz song. Marshall Grant later pointed to that session as the moment when Cash's pill use again became alarming. "He had been keeping things pretty much under control," said Grant, "but he just seemed to cave in."

Everyone in the studio thought "The Gambler" sounded more like a hit than anything they had recorded in ages, but Cash had trouble getting it on tape. "He kept going into the bathroom, and every time he'd come out, he would be a little higher," Grant recalled. Finally, Cash uncharacteristically started arguing with Butler about the song and the arrangement. Given Cash's dislike of the song, Butler quickly sent word to UA that he had also recorded the song with Cash, implying that the label had better hurry up and release the Rogers version before Cash could have a hit with it.

While UA weighed the future of "The Gambler," Butler continued to work with Cash through August on their album, Cash's mood shifting greatly from session to session. It was around this time that Jack Clement gave Cash a song, "Gone Girl," which Cash wanted to use as the title song of the album.

Cash felt safe and entertained when he was around his old Sun friend. He also felt that Jack had good karma. He seemed to be reaching for that karma when Clement played the same guitar on "Gone Girl" that he'd used on "Big River." While some tracks turned out well, especially a version of the Rolling Stones' "No Expectations" and Cash's own "I Will Rock and Roll with You," it wasn't enough. Many of Cash's vocals sounded listless and tired, leaving the tracks flat. The most obvious example is "The Gambler," which offered none of the carny salesmanship of Kenny Rogers's version.

Caught under Clement's spell, Cash wanted "Gone Girl" to be the first single and then be followed at some point with "I Will Rock and Roll with You." There was no sign that he was counting on "The Gambler" as a single.

But Cash was angered when Rogers released "The Gambler" and it started streaking up the charts.

John felt that Butler had sold him out, according to Robin. "Once he recorded the song with John, Butler shouldn't have let UA release the Rogers record. That's the agreement you have in the studio. If Kenny was going to release it, there's no reason Butler should have even brought it to John."

"I was the culprit," Butler acknowledges. "I was the bad guy with John, but I believed in the song. Kenny did want to put it out."

Meanwhile, for all Cash's faith in "Gone Girl," the single went only to number forty-four on the country charts. "I Will Rock and Roll with You" did a little better, but that was nothing next to "The Gambler," which won a Grammy for Rogers as country song of the year.

The touring schedule was especially intense following the "Gone Girl" sessions, with Cash sometimes doing two shows a day to pick up extra money. Oddly, he did little to curb his expensive lifestyle.

At one point during the "Gone Girl" sessions, he decided to take everybody in the band and their wives to Israel so they could visit the Holy Land—and he wanted all thirty or so people to fly first class and stay in the best hotels.

"On one hand, he was out there working as much as he could to meet his large payroll," said Marshall Grant. "On the other, he was spending more money—even if it was out of the goodness of his heart."

It was a pattern of spending and giving that John Carter saw often as a teenager.

"My parents were always big spenders," he once remarked, pointing to the time when his mother paid $12,000 for a leather handbag in an exclusive New York City shop. Each of their vacation homes—from the New York apartment to the estate in Jamaica—was filled with "massive pieces of furniture, side tables, dressers, and cabinets, each overloaded with Mom's things. She owned more sets of fine china than most people could use in a lifetime." June also loved collecting rarities and antiques. "She had hundreds of pieces of Wedgwood crystal and various patterns of Spode china, antique Chinese pottery, and hand-painted and unique stoneware."

At the same time, he added, they were never slow to give—from their pocketbooks or their hearts.

"On a New York street, I was with Mom when a homeless lady asked for money....[June] reached into her pocketbook and pulled out a $100 bill....She was always giving spontaneously, and she gave most of all to her family."

Cash appreciated expensive things, but he would have been happy in the quiet of the farm or the Port Richey house. June was the one who wanted the finer things—and John felt she deserved them. Besides, it wasn't the luxuries that caused Cash to struggle with finances much of his life; it was the large payroll. From the final "Gone Girl" session on August 29 to the end of the year, he did thirty shows in nineteen cities, and there would have been more except for the break he took to tape another Christmas TV special—and the week of cancellations after the death of Maybelle Carter on October 23.

Death seemed to be all around him—from Elvis to Glen Sherley to Eck, and now Maybelle, whom he had come to depend on as much as his own mother. As he headed into the final weeks of the year, Cash was at his lowest emotional point, career-wise, since the 1960s.

In the brief amount of time he did have at home, he spent a lot of it with his mother and speaking on the phone with Billy Graham. Cash had given his life to Christ, and he tried to spread the word in his music.

What had he done wrong?

CHAPTER 27

THE PILLS RETURN AND ALL HELL BREAKS LOOSE

I

JOHN CARTER CASH KNEW ABOUT PILLS. One of his earliest memories on tour was the medicine bag that his mother carried from town to town. "My mother and aunts had enough over-the-counter and prescription pills to fix any given ailment," he said. "Everyone's big black bag was filled to the top, hard to close because of the plethora of bottles crammed inside. It was a standing joke about the road group: everyone was always looking for the perfect pill, the one that would fix everything at once."

Carlene agreed, calling the medicine bag an old Carter Family tradition. "When I began to travel, I got myself one. Everyone had a pill to mend everything. If you were constipated, there was a pill for that. If you were in pain, there was a pill for that. Long drive? Sleepy? There was a pill in the medicine bag to keep you awake. Exhausted and still couldn't sleep? There was a pill for that, too."

Like almost everyone in country music, June took her share of pep pills in the 1950s and 1960s, but no one paid much attention—especially in contrast to the rampaging Cash. Well, almost no one. In her memoir, Vivian Cash wrote that her daughters found June's actions strange during their early visits to Hendersonville.

"They described her as arriving at the breakfast table, incoherent and confused, eyebrow pencil scrawled over her forehead, and clearly not 'right.' And as the years went by, they would tell me of June passing out or fainting from taking too many pills...or saying things that didn't make sense—like the time she was certain she had zebras in her head. The girls would come home and laugh about it, but it wasn't funny to me."

Whatever June's pill intake was in the 1960s, it pretty much dwindled to nothing, along with John's, in the early 1970s. As June approached fifty, however, she felt old and "busted down." Despite being enough of a realist to know that nothing is guaranteed, she still couldn't help believe that her and John's blessings—highest among them John Carter and their devotion to Christ—wouldn't give them at least a few years of peace. She had fought so hard and so long to provide a future for her two daughters and to keep John healthy and content.

Just when it looked as if everything was comfortably in place, June realized that John had fallen back into bad habits—not just pills but also, she suspected, infidelity. Unlike in the 1960s, when she'd gone to war over his drug use, she was more cautious this time. She, too, began increasingly to reach into her medicine bag for pills to calm her. When Marshall Grant and Lou Robin came to her for help in getting John straight, June remembered the explosive breakups and long periods of separation in the 1960s and realized that she couldn't stand that kind of pain again. For better or worse—and she put it in exactly those terms at times—she was still Mrs. Johnny Cash. She didn't want to risk losing her family and her identity.

When times seemed darkest, John and June found a shared strength in their faith, especially when they would appear in the Billy Graham Crusades and at concerts sponsored by other evangelical figures. It wasn't surprising, then, in the closing weeks of 1978 that Cash thought it was time to do another gospel album. It would be his most ambitious album since *The Gospel Road.*

Cash was sensitive to the complaints that he wasn't simply singing gospel music, like other country music stars, but was alienating part of his audience by aggressively proselytizing.

"All I was trying to do in those records was express my faith in the hope it might provide inspiration to others," Cash said late in his life. "God looked through a lot of sins to find the goodness in my heart and he could do the same for others. If someone was looking for hope, I was trying to offer it. I never meant to say to anyone that my way was right and their way was wrong. That was not my role."

In a letter to Rosanne at the time, he spoke about his declining popularity, but voiced no regrets. "I did a lot of things in the last few years that turned a lot of my country fans off. But I expected it. (1) I wrote a book (and I'm writing another one). (2) We made a movie. (3) I made public professions of faith in God thru Jesus Christ. Boy, that one really turned a lot of people off, which thrills me to death. (You aren't a good Christian unless you suffer.)"

As he imagined it, the new album would be another two-record set of spiritual songs, and he'd bring together June, Anita, Helen, and Rosanne, plus his old standby Jack Clement. He knew Columbia might balk, so he wasn't thrown off stride when the label showed no interest. He had another plan ready.

"We asked Columbia if they would let him record it for another label, and the company had no objection—as long as it didn't interfere with John giving them another, non-gospel album soon," Lou Robin says. "That's when we signed a small deal with a new label in town, Cachet."

To make sure no one would think he was leaving Columbia, Cash quickly announced that he was set to begin recording another Columbia album in February—an album that would mark Cash's twenty-fifth anniversary in the music business. Hence the title, *Silver*.

Knowing that he would be concentrating on the gospel album, he needed a strong producer to work with him on the *Silver* collection, and he turned to Brian Ahern, who had produced several of Emmylou Harris's excellent early albums. Cash knew that Ahern, who also worked with Anne Murray and had a reputation as notoriously independent, was no label stooge. He could count on Ahern to represent him at meetings with the label. Cash hated business meetings—and he understood that any meeting with a record company executive was business. "I'd sit through those meetings and

I'd forget I was even in the music business. I felt I was in the selling business."

He specifically never wanted to sit through another meeting like the one in the early 1970s when he was focusing on gospel music. As he related the story, a label exec told Cash he should "stop going to church and go back to prisons." It may have been a joke, but Cash never forgot.

The gospel album became even more poignant and personal for him when Sara Carter, the last surviving member of the original Carter Family, died on January 8 at her home in Northern California. She was eighty.

When he went into the studio in Nashville in mid-January, he knew what song he wanted to record first for the gospel album— "This Train Is Bound for Glory," a rousing song popularized in the 1930s by Sister Rosetta Tharpe, his longtime favorite. In fact, Cash would often describe her as his favorite singer—not favorite gospel singer, but favorite singer period. Her style was remarkably close to the flamboyance and spirit of rock.

To give a black gospel feel to the session, Cash brought in a mostly female vocal group, the Twenty-First-Century Singers, from Tennessee State University. Over the next couple of days he recorded two other tunes written by or associated with Tharpe. The edgy mix of sacred and sensual in Tharpe's music made him think briefly about devoting half of the album to her songs, or maybe even to use the entire album to showcase black gospel music. In the end, though, he wanted to include too many of his own songs to make either approach viable.

He wished he could have devoted all his time to it, but there were always other commitments. After five nights on tour in Florida, on February 8, 1979, Cash returned to Jack Clement's studio in Nashville to spend two days adding musical touches to the gospel tracks. Three days later, the musicians were again in Clement's studio, only this time it was to work with Ahern on *Silver.* Switching back and forth between albums, the musicians sometimes found it hard to keep track of which album they were working on. At one point he had them recording for both the gospel album and the Ahern album on the same day.

While Cash was obsessed with the gospel tracks, the Ahern music could have suffered from a lack of energy, but the pills and Ahern's strong will prevented it. The album's songs were largely supplied by such Cash favorites as Billy Joe Shaver, Guy Clark, and Clement, and Ahern supplied him with some of the most dynamic musical foundations that Cash had enjoyed in years—musical backing that drew attention away from the damage the pills were doing to Cash's voice. John even did one track with his old friend George Jones. The album sounded contemporary and sharp.

From the start, Ahern envisioned the centerpiece to be "Ghost Riders in the Sky," a mystical Old West tale that had been a rumbling pop smash for both Vaughn Monroe and Peggy Lee in 1949. And Cash gave it his all.

After a few dates in the Midwest, he returned to Clement's studio—this time for two quick days with Ahern, before sneaking in a day at the Columbia studio for the gospel album. This pace was enough to try anyone's nerves, but Cash's rapidly increasing drug use made it all the more stressful for Marshall and June.

Out of the blue, Cash informed Grant of new travel instructions: He wanted a suite with separate bedrooms for him and June. "I don't know if he was nervous about us finding the drugs again or if he just needed more time by himself," Grant said.

June tried to put a positive spin on it, explaining that she liked to watch TV at night, while John enjoyed reading or working on his songs. Privately, she felt deeply vulnerable and turned to the Mayo Clinic in Rochester, Minnesota, for help in combating the constant anxiety. "Over the years, she and John had been treated at the clinic for various illnesses," Grant said. "One of the doctors there who understood both of them pretty well told June, 'Your biggest problem is being the wife of Johnny Cash. You'll have to do something about that before we can do anything for you.'"

The line sounded eerily similar to what Vivian Cash's doctor had warned a decade earlier.

Grant's own unease was relieved when he learned that John wanted Marshall to sing with him on one of the songs for the gospel album, "I Was There When It Happened," the song they had worked up for their Sun audition. It would be the first time Marshall's voice was featured so prominently on one of their records. As he thought back on the gesture years later, he couldn't decide whether John was thanking him for all the good times or if he was saying good-bye.

Everyone, especially Cash, got a brief reprieve from all the anxiety on a twelve-day European tour in March. The affection shown by the crowds helped reduce some of Cash's stress. He was especially beloved in Ireland, where his song "Forty Shades of Green" had become something of a national anthem. There was so much respect for Cash in Northern Ireland that battling factions in the ongoing Catholic-Protestant conflict called a truce to allow his performance in a Belfast church to proceed. Leaders of the opposing factions even sat across the aisle from each other. Cash learned just how temporary the truce was the next afternoon when a currency exchange booth was blown up just hours after he passed by it.

"Ghost Riders in the Sky" became a solid hit on country radio, eventually going to number two on the charts. But once again it was a false alarm; the single didn't trigger any rush to buy the *Silver* album. There may have been a moral tucked into the lyrics, but the record's appeal lay in its production values. It didn't speak to any of Cash's emotional strong points. To the record buyers he was trying to reengage, the reaction to the record was likely "*So what.*"

II

Descending deeper into pills, June was on edge as the band headed to Cleveland in late July 1979 for a three-day engagement at the Front Row Theater. By then, June and John's old friend Jan Howard had joined the tour as part of the Carter Family. June knew that John and Jan had a close relationship dating all the way back to the 1960s, probably (most thought) an affair at some point. There was enough talk about the two that some people thought that Jan was another of the women Cash might have proposed to instead of June. Like Billie Jean, Jan was pretty, outspoken, and fun to be around. Plus, she had gone through an enormous amount of pain; one of her sons, Jimmy, was killed in Vietnam, and a second, David, took his own life. It was easy for John to feel protective of her.

For her part, Jan acknowledged spending lots of time with John, but she denied a sexual relationship. "I loved him," she says. "But I didn't love him like that." She tells how John would often call—frequently to ask her to go fishing—when he was trying to get away from being Johnny Cash. "He just needed to escape from everything around him for a while," she adds.

The incident in Cleveland started out simply enough. Onstage during the final show of the engagement, Cash paused after a song, looked over at Jan, and said in a way that June—in her anxious state—took as highly suggestive, "That's just about the prettiest dress I've ever seen, Jan."

Alone in her adjoining hotel room that night, June couldn't sleep; she couldn't erase her suspicions about John and Jan from her mind. Around two a.m. she noticed that one of the lines on her phone was lit up. She didn't want to pick up and risk having John hear the click, but she wanted to know who he was talking to at that hour. She went into the sitting room that connected their separate bedrooms.

Finally, she took a chance and ever so slowly picked up the phone. It was Jan, and June didn't like what she was hearing. The term that later circulated through the Cash camp was "phone sex."

June spent the rest of the night debating what to do. Should she be the good soldier again and proceed to Omaha, the next stop on the tour, or should she send a message to John by returning home to Hendersonville? Sometime after dawn, she walked across the sitting room and knocked on John's door and, without asking for an explanation, gave him an ultimatum.

"If Jan goes to Omaha, then I go home, and that's just all there is to it," she told him. "I'll take John Carter and go home, and it's over."

Cash called Marshall and told him that he had to see Jan. When Grant informed him that she was already on the way to the airport with the rest of the band, Cash insisted, "I've got to talk to her right away."

Sensing the urgency, Grant drove to the airport, where he found Jan handing her ticket to the gate agent. He led her to a phone booth and put her on the line with Cash. As soon as she said hello, Grant wrote in his memoir, "there was a god-awful quietness, and the look on her face was just terrible." He said Jan listened without saying a word for maybe five minutes, then dropped the phone and let out a bloodcurdling scream that could be heard all over the airport.

With her demand met, June was at John's side onstage that night, the start of a six-day run, as if nothing had happened, but there was more drama ahead.

Cash went to Lou Robin's room and said he was going to fire Helen and Anita. He wasn't even asking Robin to fire them; he was going to do it himself. But first he picked up a bottle of wine that happened to be in the room. He drank it in one furious gulp. Then he went across the hall and fired his sisters-in-law.

The Carters became hysterical, especially June, who was sprawled across Helen's bed in a dead faint when Grant entered the room. He tried wiping her head with a cold washcloth, but it didn't help. Helen wanted to call an ambulance, but Marshall worried that it might lead to bad publicity. Instead, he called John, who had apparently gone to his room after the firing. Seeing June lying there passed out, Cash yelled at her and slapped her on both cheeks, trying to revive her. When that didn't wake her, Helen started screaming again, "She's dying, she's dying." Cash told Helen that everything would be fine and left the room.

Eventually, June got up and was so hurt by John's action that she decided to fly home that minute.

"I was in the lobby that night and there's June with a suitcase, headed out the front door," Robin says. "It was midnight and I asked where she was going and she said, 'I'm leaving. John just fired my sisters...I'm going to the airport.' But I told her there were no flights at this hour and I talked her into [staying at] at the hotel."

Figuring she didn't want to go back to John's room, Robin called Goldie Adcock, the wardrobe lady, and asked her to let June stay with her.

When Marshall went to John's suite the next morning, however, he was shocked to find them together again. "It was like the worst of the sixties again," he said. "You never knew what to expect."

Pushing June through the airport in a wheelchair later that day, Grant knew the crisis hadn't passed. June looked defeated. "She had nothing," he later said. "Her family had been fired from the show, she was a physical wreck, and now there was no way to reconcile the problems we had. It was a terrible situation."

Meanwhile, Jan Howard was sufficiently shaken and depressed that she checked into a Nashville hospital for two weeks. "There were rumors everywhere about me and John, and no matter what I said, people believed them," she says. "I even heard things like the reason I was in the hospital was that I was having an abortion."

Johnny Western, who kept in touch with Cash, was approached after the Cleveland episode by someone who identified himself as a writer for the *National Enquirer* and offered him $2,500 to confirm that John and Jan were having "this big, torrid affair." Concerned about a scandal, Western immediately phoned Lou Robin, who said he'd get the message to Cash.

"As it turned out, the article never ran, and I saw John shortly after that," Western says. "He came over to me and said, 'I want to thank you for calling Lou on that deal with Jan Howard, but, you know, you were getting screwed. The *National Enquirer* offered Reba five thousand.' He had this kind of smile on his face. In his mind, it was over and done."

When Western heard that June was still by John's side when the tour resumed four weeks later in Dubuque, Iowa, he assumed the crisis was over. But June was apparently just biding her time.

There were practical career considerations holding John and June together. They both believed their relationship—the hard times and the good—was part of their appeal. Older fans, they thought, came out to concerts or tuned in to the TV specials not just to hear John's music but to see *them.* There were lots of singing duos over the years who could lay claim to the title of King and Queen of Country Music—including some who had more hit singles, notably George Jones and Tammy Wynette, and Conway Twitty and Loretta Lynn. But none was as warmly embraced as John and June. To millions, their personal redemption was living affirmation of Cash's music and themes. It wasn't just the music that was inspiring; the couple was inspiring together. June, fans believed, was one of John's blessings, and John was repaying her with his love and devotion.

Beyond the risk of destroying all that, June believed that John still loved her. And there was John Carter. She was clinging to any reason she could find to stay married, but in the end she no longer had the strength. One week after the tour's final show, on December 19 in Las Vegas, June flew to London—alone. A few days later, she asked an attorney to draw up divorce papers.

"She was really messed up," says Carlene, who was married at the time to British rock musician Nick Lowe and in the early stages of her own recording career. "She had lost her self-esteem. She spent a few weeks with us, and we all tried to help her feel better about herself again. Kris [Kristofferson] came to see her, and he told her how beautiful she was and that she'd get past all this. I tried to be neutral. I didn't encourage her to leave [Cash], but I also told her that if she wasn't happy, she should do something [about it].

"I kept saying, 'Mama, why are you so scared to leave him if you are so unhappy?' and she said, 'I'm afraid that I won't have John Carter.' I tried to tell her the court would never take her son away from her, but I finally began to realize that she was just flashing her wings a little bit, like, 'I'm going to show him. I can live a life without him.' She was trying to shock him."

After three weeks, June moved to the upscale Dorchester Hotel, and Cash flew to London in hopes of wooing her back. "I could see he was devastated too, and he wanted her back, but it wasn't going to be easy," Carlene says. "It was really a tough time for both of them. The pills were the big problem. John wasn't perfect. He would go off the handle and say things he didn't mean to say, including some very hurtful things. But he wasn't mean-spirited. He had a good heart. He couldn't have done something as cruel as fire the Carter Family if he wasn't on pills."

Cash was contrite enough during the London meeting that June relented; neither was willing to test life without the other. John and

June were holding hands and singing "Jackson" again when their tour kicked off February 1 in St. Petersburg, Florida.

To Grant, it still felt like walking through a minefield. Beyond the fragile relationship between John and June, and Cash's reliance on his pills, Cash was rarely speaking to him anymore. As the tour moved through Fort Myers, Jacksonville, and Fort Lauderdale, Grant wondered who would last longer in Cash's circle, June or him.

Through all the domestic turmoil, Cash looked forward to the release of the gospel album, now a two-record set titled *A Believer Sings the Truth*. His writing continued to be uneven; the imagery of Jesus as "The Greatest Cowboy of Them All" was especially strained. But the passion of the Sister Rosetta Tharpe numbers and the immediacy and verve of other tracks were reminiscent of Cash's Sun days.

The wild card was Cachet Records. The label started off aggressively, taking out a full-page ad in the trades which quoted Cash as saying, "This is the album I've wanted to do all my professional life." What Cash soon learned was that Cachet wasn't able to follow through financially. The album sold around thirty thousand copies and then hit a wall, Robin believes, because of lack of distribution. In lieu of back royalties, the label gave Cash the remaining twenty thousand copies from its warehouse. Cash tried to distribute the album himself, but there wasn't much market for it, so boxes full of the LP sat in a back room at the House of Cash for years. To help Cash recover some of his production costs, Robin eventually talked Columbia into releasing a single-album version of *A Believer,* but sales were again minimal.

III

Cash and Grant were still barely speaking in the early months of 1980. The end came suddenly in a pair of incidents, both of which might simply have been dismissed in calmer times as a case of frayed road nerves. But pills and the strife with June had left Cash feeling edgy and defensive.

The first involved Cash's desire to perform the Rodney Crowell song "Bull Rider" from the *Silver* album. Cash was scheduled to play a rodeo, and he thought the song would be a natural. But when Cash asked Marshall to get the guys together so they could rehearse it, Grant brushed him off.

"I kept asking him to rehearse the song and he'd just say he didn't have time," Cash recalled later. "I would probably have looked past it if he just refused once, but I kept after him and he just wouldn't listen to me. I was going through a lot at the time, and this was one of many things that made me think that Marshall didn't care about me any longer. I didn't think I could work with him anymore."

The second incident occurred on Cash's bus during a California tour in February. Cash was as bad at reading maps as at driving a car, but he was looking over a map this day, trying to help the bus driver find an unfamiliar city. Grant, who knew virtually every back road in America because of his years on the road, saw John fumbling with the map and he said something to the effect of "Give me that. You don't know how to read a map!" Cash felt humiliated.

When the tour ended, he decided to fire Marshall.

From his apartment in New York, he phoned his secretary, Irene Gibbs, and dictated a letter to Marshall. He told her to sign it and send it.

As soon as he saw the registered letter, which arrived during the first week in March, Grant knew his twenty-five years with Cash had come to an end. He wasn't surprised, knowing how irrational Cash had become again. He wasn't even surprised that Cash didn't tell him the news in person, because he knew how John hated personal confrontation. That didn't ease the hurt.

In his 2006 memoir, Grant said he thought about including a copy of the letter in the book but decided against it. "Let's just say that I know it was the drugs talking, and John said things in that letter that he later regretted."

Two days after the letter arrived, Carl Perkins stopped by Grant's house to offer support and to pass on some troubling news. Earlier in the day Perkins had also dropped by to see W. S. Holland, who told him he heard Marshall had been fired because he'd been caught stealing a million dollars through kickbacks and other schemes while handling travel arrangements and band purchases.

The news made Grant physically ill, and he called friends in the Cash organization. Yes, they confirmed, that's what Cash was telling people—though Cash denied it years later. "I fired Marshall because our relationship had just broken down," he said.

As days went by, Grant felt increasingly bitter—not so much about Cash's charges of theft, because he didn't think anyone believed them, but about the way Cash had "stolen me and Luther blind" over the years to support his drug habit. He was referring to Cash's abandoning the agreement the three had made at Sun Records to share revenue equally. Grant decided to sue his old friend.

Cash didn't waste any time in getting back on the road after firing Grant. Within days he was onstage with Joe Allen, one of Nashville's most respected bass players, standing in Grant's place. It was now an eight-piece band. After years with a compact unit, Cash had slowly been expanding the group ever since he'd had the TV show. The changes began with a series of piano players, including Butler, who joined Grant, Wootton, and Holland. Then a third guitarist, Jerry Hensley, came aboard in 1974. Two horn players, Bob Lewin and Jack Hale Jr., became regulars in 1978. All of these changes made Cash and Robin decide it was time for a new name. They came up with the Great Eighties Eight.

Between tours, Cash was in and out of the studio early in 1980 working on a new album, *Rockabilly Blues,* but he lacked vocal authority, and his four new songs were again subpar.

But there was more working against *Rockabilly Blues* than its unevenness. Everyone's attention in Nashville in the summer of 1980 was on the phenomenal country and pop reaction to an album that had been released in May: the soundtrack to the film *Urban Cowboy.* The movie, which starred John Travolta and Debra Winger, did for country music what *Saturday Night Fever* did for disco—it took the music into the pop mainstream. Suddenly, people who had never shown any interest in country music were buying cowboy boots and heading for the local honky-tonk to ride the mechanical bulls.

It was the biggest thing to hit Nashville since Willie, Waylon, and the outlaw movement, and record companies went all-out to try to produce more records that could jump on the pop-flavored *Urban Cowboy* bandwagon. Given all the excitement, who was going to pay attention to what was, for all practical purposes, just another Johnny Cash album?

During a tour break soon after firing Grant, John and June headed for the peaceful surroundings of Cinnamon Hill. John Carter described Jamaica as a way for his parents to "regain their center" and "renew their focus." June loved the estate and its grounds every bit much as John. She'd sometimes dance in the yard, singing or whistling to the hundreds of birds gathered there; she claimed to have a name for every one of them.

The atmosphere on this trip, however, was grim. Their future together was still on the line. Even if she had lived too long with Cash's addiction for her truly to believe that things would get better, she had to hear him pledge his love and his devotion. She wanted contrition.

For much of the week, John Carter was witness to their shouting matches. Things got so heated one evening that Cash asked his son to leave the room. John Carter tried to listen through the thick stucco walls, but he couldn't make out the words. He felt as if his world was coming to an end when his father suddenly opened the door and invited the trembling boy to rejoin them.

"Son," he recalls his dad saying. "We have something tell you."

Braced for the worst, John Carter heard his mother shout, "We're going to get married again!"

The three hugged one another long and hard.

On the next afternoon, John Carter—wearing a brand-new suit for the occasion—watched his parents stand in front of a pastor from Mount Zion Church near Montego Bay to renew their wedding vows. The youngster's world was "one again." His parents' struggles, he believed, were over. Looking back on that day years later, John Carter would shrug at how innocent he was.

There was another major piece of good news for Cash, as he continued to tour the big cities and small towns across the country, stopping only to tape an appearance on the Mike Douglas TV show or record another Christmas album. During the annual Country Music Association TV show in October, Johnny Cash was introduced as the newest member of the Country Music Hall of Fame. To celebrate, June surprised John with a brand-new Mercedes-Benz.

Much was made in the weeks after the announcement by both the media and Cash loyalists about the fact that he, at forty-eight, was the youngest living inductee of the Hall of Fame, an impressive honor considering that membership was usually given to artists who were far past their prime. Yet the honor was tempered by that very fact, for many in Nashville considered Cash to be just that—well past his prime. Among those along Music Row too young to know much about Cash's pre-*Folsom* days, it wasn't uncommon to hear variations on the sentiment, "I didn't know he was only forty-eight. It seems like he's been around forever."

CHAPTER 28

NO ONE'S LISTENING

I

MARTY STUART WAS A NEW BREED of cat in Johnny Cash's world, someone with more of a love of country music history and an authenticity more in line with Cash's own feelings than anyone who worked regularly with him—and yet still young and brash enough to tell his hero when he felt Cash was wrong. This last quality may have been Stuart's greatest contribution to Cash artistically. For most stars, even great ones like Cash, there is a thin line between support and disloyalty. They say they want to hear the truth, but they invariably gravitate toward those who offer only good news and turn a blind eye to personal vices.

"One thing I noticed the first time I worked with John was he was surrounded by sycophants," says producer Brian Ahern. "Nobody ever said boo to him. After we did *Silver,* I vowed to myself to get him out of Nashville if we ever did another album together. But Marty was different. Marty would speak up."

To many around Cash, Stuart, at twenty-one, came across as just a wide-eyed, starstruck kid who adored him. "To me, *Johnny Cash at Folsom Prison* stands out as the most landmark, groundbreaking country album since the days of Jimmie Rodgers," Stuart says. To him, Cash "was a man on a mission; someone coming up from the ashes, drawing on the sum total of everything he did from 1955 to 1968—the songwriting creativity, the search for songs, the years of touring. It was the perfect country record and it blows my mind that it was done before noon."

Stuart grew up looking for the same spark in country singers that Cash always sought. "Our county fair in Philadelphia, Mississippi, brought entertainers to town every year, and I developed a pretty good radar for who was the real thing and who was just going through the motions by the time I was seven, eight, nine years old," says Stuart. "My heroes were a lot of the same people as Johnny Cash's."

The first time Stuart saw Cash in concert was in Jackson, Mississippi, in 1970. "The TV show was real hot and he filled up the Coliseum," Stuart recalls. "All I remember is the stage went black and he simply walked out and said, 'Hello, I'm Johnny Cash.' The place went nuts. The next thing I knew I was standing right in front of the stage, looking up at him. I don't even remember leaving my seat, but there I was. There was a fire in him onstage that made you feel he wanted to make a difference in people's lives, and I was hooked. From that moment, I knew this is what I wanted to do with my life. I didn't have a choice." After spending years apprenticing on mandolin and other string instruments with Lester Flatt and Doc Watson, Stuart was in Nashville in 1980 trying to figure out his next step when he learned that a buddy of his was making a guitar for Cash. As enterprising as he was talented, Stuart talked his pal into letting him tag along when he delivered the guitar to Cash at Clement's studio in Nashville. They hit it off.

A few weeks later, Cash had Wootton track Stuart down to ask if he'd like to sit in with the band at a show in Iowa. Stuart, who happened to be only a hundred miles away, jumped into a rental car and joined Cash onstage for a matinee performance. He already knew all the songs by heart. After the concert, Cash asked Stuart, "Do you want to go to work for me?"

Even though working with Cash was a dream come true, Stuart realized over the next few weeks that he felt a little deflated.

"Johnny Cash and the Tennessee Three were my Beatles," says Stuart. "I knew every record they did, and I was a little torn to see what he had become. I was hoping to work with the guy who was at Folsom Prison and who did the benefits for the Indians, but I found myself in the middle of this kind of big family show. It wasn't as rock 'n' roll as I thought it would be. It wasn't as edgy. It was closer to something like Lawrence Welk. I felt he was a little lost in his world. There was so much dragging him down. He had a lifestyle that was huge. He and June had houses upon houses; they had kids upon kids; employees upon employees; it was really a cumbersome lifestyle. I kept looking for a way to talk to him about all this."

Stuart found his opportunity a short time later when Cash casually asked if he was enjoying himself on the road. He was surprised when the young man replied with a mere "Pretty much." He asked the newcomer to sit with him and explain himself. Stuart knew this was his chance, and he didn't back down.

"I could tell he was really interested," says Stuart. "I told him not to get me wrong. I loved his music and I was glad to be in the band; it was more money than I'd ever made. But I also said the music wasn't lean and mean the way I thought it would be.

"I think he sensed in me a fighting partner. He wasn't content being let out to pasture. He didn't want to just be a senior-citizen flag-waver. I believe he wanted to be a rock star again. He wanted to get back where he started, and I wanted to go there with him."

Rick Blackburn, who had taken over as head of Columbia's Nashville country operation in 1980, also struck up a key relationship with Cash. He spoke frankly about the challenge of selling records, something Cash appreciated; for once, Cash felt that a record company executive was truly on his side. And he was grateful when Blackburn signed Rosanne to a contract.

"The thing I tried to stress with John was that there were factors working against him and a lot of artists of his age," said Blackburn, a former country DJ whose background in the music business was in marketing and promotion. "Outside of the *Urban Cowboy* thing, country music wasn't selling. You could have a number-one country single and it'd only mean twenty-five thousand albums. Country had to find a whole new audience, and that meant young people, because that was the big, untapped audience.

"We'd spend hours thinking about ways to try to sell records to that audience—and don't let anyone tell you John didn't care about sales at this point in his life. He never gave up his vision as an artist; he made the records he wanted to make. But when he had a new record out, he would call every Monday morning so I could update him on the latest sales figures. He was still huge—he was playing Las Vegas and all—but he wanted to be on the charts again. He wanted to reach young people. He wanted to be relevant."

After recording a Christmas album in August, Cash guested the following month with Emmylou Harris and Levon Helm on *The Legend of Jesse James,* a concept album designed by English songwriter Paul Kennerly that won considerable critical acclaim but sold only modestly.

He then turned to Jack Clement once more to help him on a pair of sessions in September designed to provide music for another CBS television film, *The Pride of Jesse Hallam,* in which he would also act. Cash always felt safe in Clement's reassuring hands. "Jack has stood by me through everything, especially when life hasn't been too inspiring," Cash said. "Day or night, whatever my condition. I've always found a refuge in his presence."

For Cash, the films offered a break from the endless one-nighters. Even if his performances tended to be wooden, he enjoyed the challenge of acting, and he tried to find roles that were as inspiring as his music. In *Hallam,* he played an illiterate farmer who teaches himself to read and write so he can better raise his children after his wife dies. Cash was heartened when CBS received thousands of letters from people who had struggled with illiteracy; it reminded him of the outpouring of gratitude from fans after the *Holy Land* album and the *Gospel Road* film.

Two days after the Clement session, on September 5, Cash went into Columbia Records' studio with superstar producer Billy Sherrill, who had co-written a story song, "The Baron," that the Columbia execs thought might work for Cash. In truth, Sherrill, who had never paid much attention to Cash when he ran Columbia's Nashville office, might have preferred to give the song to a hotter artist, but Blackburn helped steer him to Cash. Country DJs welcomed anything by Sherrill with open arms. Cash went along with the project despite his resentment of the producer's earlier coldness. Except for those few days in the studio, Cash spent most of the year on tour, including nearly two weeks in Australia in June and a week in England in October. He also found time to make Billy Graham Crusade appearances in Calgary and Houston.

Meanwhile, Grant continued to mull over his next step. He met with his attorneys and began organizing old financial statements to try to build a case that Cash had reneged on his partnership promise. Grant finally decided to file the suit the week after Christmas; he chose that time, he said, to minimize embarrassing publicity, figuring people would be busy with their holiday festivities.

In an action filed in U.S. District Court, Grant asked for $2.6 million in lost wages and damages resulting from alleged slanderous statements.

Cash was angered and told his attorneys to fight the case to the end. He couldn't believe the relationship had come to this.

To Grant's mind, he wasn't suing his old friend J.R., he was suing a drug addict.

The case was eventually settled without going to trial. Under the terms of the agreement, neither party was supposed to reveal the details. But within hours, the word around Nashville was that Cash had paid Grant just under $1 million. The two old friends wouldn't have a meaningful conversation for more than a decade. Prompted by Grant's suit, children of Luther Perkins, too, sued Cash, but their case was settled for a much smaller sum.

II

Cash went into the studio with Clement in late January 1981 to work on tracks for an album titled *The Adventures of Johnny Cash.* But those sessions were halted in mid-March when Sherrill needed Cash to record enough songs to fill an album built around "The Baron," which was taking off on country radio—more, quite likely, because of Sherrill's name than any sudden renewed interest in Cash. They cut the additional tracks in three days, using songs mostly selected by Sherrill. Cash brought Stuart along, even letting him arrange one old folk tune that the guitarist had suggested, "Hey, Hey Train." It proved to be the most satisfying track on the LP.

Even though "The Baron" went to number ten on the country charts, it was a record, much like Cash's "Ghost Riders in the Sky," that didn't excite old Cash fans or attract new ones. The story song—about a pool shark being confronted by a young man who turns out to be his son—may have struck Sherrill as another "Boy Named Sue." For most listeners, however, the song merely echoed the feel-good storytelling success of "Lucille" and "The Gambler," and left Cash sounding like he was recycling Kenny Rogers. The album performed only marginally better than *Silver,* though the title song did lead to a 1984 TV movie, *The Baron and the Kid,* with Cash in the title role.

Meanwhile Cash was off to Europe in late April. He was joined onstage in Stuttgart by Carl Perkins and Jerry Lee Lewis, who did enough songs together for Columbia to release a live album titled *The Survivors* a year later. It was a modest attempt to capture the freewheeling spirit of the "Million Dollar Quartet" session, which was attracting lots of media attention since bootleg copies were beginning to circulate around this time. As on that celebrated 1956 day at Sun Records, Lewis, Perkins, and Cash sang songs associated with them and some gospel favorites as well. The problem with the set was that it didn't include Elvis. It wouldn't do any better than Cash's other recent albums.

What fascinated Marty Stuart, who was touring Europe with Cash for the first time that April, wasn't that reunion but Cash's energy and attitude on the whole tour. He believed that John, given the right circumstances, could be relevant again in the studio.

"All of a sudden he was a rock star again," Stuart remembers. "He brought a higher level of energy and confidence to the European shows. People always talked about how he prowled the stage with the electricity of a panther in the 1960s, but this was the first time I saw it, and it was great being onstage with him."

By the end of the year he had done nearly one hundred concerts, a half-dozen TV shows, several benefits, and two Billy Graham Crusades, as well as joined Luciano Pavarotti, Itzhak Perlman, and

Lena Horne in performing before President and Mrs. Reagan at Ford's Theatre in Washington, D.C.

On the home front, John and June had come a long way toward repairing their marriage since renewing their vows, and they returned to Jamaica for Christmas. To celebrate, they invited John's sister Reba and her husband to join them—along with one of John Carter's school chums. When they sat down for a dinner of roast turkey, rice and beans, and fried plantains on December 23, the family felt especially grateful. They were all at the dinner table when three men with nylon stockings over their heads burst into the room, one of them shouting, "Someone is going to die here tonight!" One was carrying a hatchet, another had a dagger, and the third waved a pistol. Apparently mistaking the school friend for John Carter, one of the intruders grabbed the boy and demanded $3 million or they'd kill him, John Carter remembered. Cash in retrospect put the amount at $1 million, but everyone agreed that the ordeal lasted four hours as the robbers ransacked the house, looking for money and jewels.

Satisfied they had everything of value, the men locked Cash and the rest, including the boys, in the basement and fled. Cash and Reba's husband broke down the door and phoned the police, who quickly captured one of the robbers. He was subsequently killed when he tried to escape. The others were caught a few weeks later during another robbery, and they too were killed while reportedly trying to escape from prison. Cash described the Jamaican police as "action-oriented."

Reba was so shaken by the experience that she vowed she would never return to Jamaica, but Cash told reporters that Cinnamon Hill was his home and he would always come back to it

In his unrelenting empathy for the underdog, though, he felt guilty about the "desperate young men" who had threatened his family, possibly to feed their own. "I felt I knew those boys," he wrote in his 1997 autobiography. "We had a kinship, they and I. I know how they thought, I knew how they needed. They were like me."

Despite Cash's lack of chart success, in the late 1970s and beyond Lou Robin did such a shrewd job in maintaining a high profile for him on tour and on television that few outside Music Row noticed how little he mattered commercially in a country music recording world where such artists as Alabama, Kenny Rogers, Dolly Parton, and Willie Nelson were each topping the album charts for ten weeks or more at a stretch. The *Adventures* album never even charted. Still, Cash hosted *Saturday Night Live* in April, where he was a good sport about his image. In one skit, he fulfilled a death-row prisoner's final request by singing "99,999 Bottles of Beer on the Wall." In a second, the Man in Black let two women test themselves for dandruff by shaking their hair over his black clothing. But, significantly, he didn't perform any of his new songs. The show's viewers were treated to "I Walk the Line," "Folsom Prison Blues," "Ring of Fire," and "Sunday Mornin' Comin' Down."

Around this time, William S. Paley, chief executive of CBS, the parent company of Columbia Records, was encouraging his top executives, including Rick Blackburn, to attend Harvard Business School workshops for at least one week a year. At one of the sessions, Blackburn became intrigued by the ways companies were using research to pretest consumer interest in their new products. Once back home, he contacted a Columbia University professor, Sidney Furst, who had a national reputation for such testing, notably with Pringles potato chips.

It is a long way from potato chips to country albums, but Blackburn wanted to know which recording artists interested young country fans. He believed that the information could help him concentrate his energy and promotion money on those artists who stood a chance of picking up young fans. In Furst's report, the artists preferred by these potential buyers were rated "new and contemporary"; the artists generating little or no interest were rated "old and traditional."

Cash had turned fifty. To young buyers, he was considered old and traditional—which meant he was essentially irrelevant to them. Many of his generation were equally dismissed, including George Jones and Loretta Lynn. By contrast, the study found high interest in artists the buyers considered young and contemporary—a group that included the not-so-young Willie

Nelson and Waylon Jennings, because of their ties to the outlaw movement. Among others registering high with the panelists: Rosanne Cash.

"I went over the findings very carefully with John," said Blackburn, "because I wanted him to know what he was up against. I explained things like why other artists would be getting more promotion money. I said, 'John, if I had my choice of having a hit with anybody on the label, it'd be you, but there is nothing I can do for you as long as the numbers are the way they are.' The thing I remember is he was so gracious about it. He said he understood. He said he'd like to reach that younger audience, but he wasn't going to change his music to do so. I knew that was going to make it hard for John ever to be a big seller again, but I respected his integrity as an artist."

Cash didn't know how to proceed. He had Stuart telling him he had lost his edge, and he had Blackburn telling him record buyers didn't care about him. With no plan, he turned once again to a personal passion—an acoustic gospel album produced by Stuart.

Cash got the idea for the gospel album when he and Stuart visited Luther Perkins's grave in Hendersonville on Luther's birthday, January 8, 1982. Perkins was almost as much a hero to Stuart as Cash. "Bob Wootton did a great job, but Luther was an irreplaceable part of J.R.'s sound," says Stuart, one of the few in the Cash entourage who usually referred to him as J.R. "The two were soul mates. J.R. gained something just knowing Luther was by his side in the studio. I've often wondered about how things might have turned out if Luther hadn't died."

The trip to Luther's grave at Hendersonville Memorial Gardens had become an annual ritual for Cash and Stuart. They called it "Luther Day," and they'd spend hours figuring out what pill Luther might have wanted that year. They'd end the visit by placing a cigarette and one of those very pills on Luther's headstone. "I treasured those visits because it offered a great look into the wonderfully sick and twisted humor that was the hallmark of the old band," Stuart says. "J.R. would even begin the visits by jumping all over Luther for resting while the rest of us were out there busting our tails to make a living."

During that 1982 graveyard visit, Cash said he'd like to do the gospel record with Stuart. After they spoke about the idea for a few minutes, Cash turned toward Luther's grave and said, "If L.M. don't speak up and disagree, we'll call it a done deal."

Not unexpectedly, Columbia had no interest in another Cash gospel album until a gospel music executive named Ken Harding agreed to establish a subsidiary label for Columbia specializing in gospel music. He'd call it Priority Records, and Cash's album would be its first release. With that set, Cash and Stuart began work on the album in May. The project was such a labor of love for Cash that he seemed to prolong it purposefully. Then again, the slow pace (the album wasn't finished until December) may have been due to Cash's heavy drug use.

The first session offered a window into Cash's erratic studio behavior at the time. He showed up wearing brown knee-high boots, only to look down and declare there was no way that he—the Man in Black—should be recording in brown boots. While the musicians watched, he sat on the studio floor and carefully painted the boots black. Then he learned that Julie Andrews was recording in the studio down the hall, and he went in and asked her if she'd like to do a duet. She agreed, and they recorded a song ("Love Me Tender," as Stuart recalls). After all this delay, Cash started recording the gospel album. With just two songs done, he announced he was going out to get some milk and cheese. He promised to be right back.

The next Stuart saw of Cash was on the TV news later that night.

Cash bought the milk and cheese, then he apparently headed home. On the way, his car got stranded in a ditch in a field. He spun his wheels until the grass caught fire and burned up the car, the silver Mercedes that June had given him the night of his Country Music Hall of Fame induction. After watching all this unfold on television, Stuart phoned Cash to see if he was okay. Cash assured him that he was fine: "The car was a total loss, but the milk and the cheese were delicious!"

Once again, Cash took a break from music that summer to star in a TV movie. *Murder in Coweta County,* co-starring Andy Griffith, was a drama based on a struggle for justice in rural Georgia in the late 1940s. Cash's acting was self-conscious, as usual, but the film—in which Cash played a county sheriff who brings a wealthy landowner to justice after he kills a farm worker—again spoke to Cash's belief in good triumphing over evil.

Ever since Cash initiated the policy of separate bedrooms on tour, John Carter slept in his own bed in his father's room when he joined his parents on the road. This gave him a frightening front-row look at his father on pills. On several occasions, John Carter was alarmed when Cash's labored breathing would suddenly stop for long periods of time. The boy wanted to run to his mother's room for help, but he was worried that it could lead to more arguments. So he lay awake in his bed praying that his father would be all right.

Cash was in such bad shape one night during the filming of *Coweta County* that John Carter, who was now twelve, couldn't hold himself back. He rushed to his mother for help.

"Dad's not breathing!"

June went to John's room and shook him, but there was no response.

"We have to get him into the tub," she said. Together, she and John Carter pulled him from the bed and dragged him into the bathroom, where they dumped him in the tub and turned on the shower so the cold water would startle him awake. It worked.

Looking into his father's drained face, John Carter screamed, "I can't take it anymore! You have to stop the pills, Dad! You have to stop!"

Recounting the scene in *Anchored in Love,* his 2007 book about his mother, John Carter wrote, "My father never hit me, but I had never talked to him this way either. This was the one time he came close to lashing out at me. His dark, flat eyes flashed, and he clinched his huge fist."

Cash didn't go further than that, but his son would always look back on the night as a turning point in their relationship.

There would still be good times when Cash would set aside drugs and actually be a dad. In late August 1983, for instance, Cash took John Carter and June on a five-day fishing and rafting trip through remote stretches of Alaska, and it was such a wonderful memory that John Carter devoted seven pages to it in his book. June took ten pages to describe the week in her own 1987 memoir, *From the Heart*.

Summarizing the experience, John Carter wrote, "When we left the wilderness, Dad was clear eyed and strong, and Mom was the same joyful and supportive mother I had known all my life....There was still hope for the future of our family. And for a short period, I was as happy as I had ever been."

But those memories were the exception in what was an especially turbulent year. His recollections of the Alaska trip are surrounded by accounts of heartbreak. The juxtaposition of the good times and bad indicate how fragile and unpredictable life could be around Cash. An event early in the year seemed to set the tone—an accident that Cash often cited as a turning point in his fight against drugs, and a renewed dependency that led to thoughts of suicide.

Cash loved animals and was so fascinated by the forms and characteristics of different species that he gradually built an informal animal compound on a large piece of vacant land across the street from his house in Hendersonville; its occupants ranged from zebra and wild boar to ostriches and scores of birds. The property also included a petting zoo of sorts for John Carter.

Cash was hospitalized early in 1983 for pneumonia, and when he got home, he decided to visit the animals, even though the temperature was freezing. As he was walking through the woods, an ostrich jumped onto the trail in front of him and hissed menacingly. Cash waited until the ostrich left the trail, and then he continued his walk. When he returned minutes later, the ostrich again blocked his path, but Cash, who had picked up a formidable six-foot branch on his walk, wanted to show the creature who was boss.

When the ostrich made a move toward him, Cash, possibly feeling the effects of medication, swung the stick, but he missed. The ostrich leaped into the air and landed on Cash's chest. The blow broke two of Cash's ribs, and the bird's claw ripped him open down to his belt. Cash staggered backward and broke three more ribs falling on a rock. As the ostrich stood poised for another attack, Cash swung the piece of wood again, causing the animal to flee. Cash went back to the hospital, where he was stitched up, but the ribs still hurt. For relief, he upped his intake of pills, pretty much giving up any attempt to combat the recurring addiction.

"Justification ceased to be relevant after that," Cash wrote in his second autobiography. "Once the pain subsided completely, I knew I was taking [the pills] because I liked the way they made me feel. And while that troubled my conscience, it didn't trouble it enough to keep me from going down that old addictive road again."

Cash found himself making the rounds of various doctors once more, gathering enough pills to support his habit. When his excessive consumption upset his digestive system, he began drinking wine to calm his stomach. Soon, he was again going through periods when he was out of control.

"I was up and running, strung out, slowed down, sped up, turned around, hung on the hook, having a ball, living in hell," he wrote. "Before long I began to get the impression that I was in trouble—I had bleeding ulcers, for one thing—but I kept going anyway. The idea of taking things to their logical conclusion, just drugging and drinking until I slipped all the way out of this world, began to dance quietly around the back of my mind."

He described that frightening feeling as "weirdly comforting."

III

Back on tour, Lou Robin was surprised a few weeks after the ostrich attack to see Cash one afternoon in the lobby of the hotel where they were staying in Augsburg, West Germany. Cash invariably took long afternoon naps, and when Robin questioned him, Cash simply said he couldn't sleep—and Robin could tell from Cash's nervous, jittery state that he was high. Cash had been on pills pretty heavily much of the year, causing Robin to cancel one show in Beckley, West Virginia, and leading an exhausted Cash to check in to the Nashville hospital again with pneumonia.

Through it all, Robin had noticed that Cash was savvy enough to keep out of the public's sight on days when he reached for the pills too often. That's what troubled Robin this day. If Cash was this badly strung out in the afternoon, what would he be like that evening when he performed live on *Wetten, dass?*, a hugely popular German TV show?

When Robin mentioned the show, Cash replied, "I'm thinking about ending my song tonight by bending down and thanking the audience—the way Elvis used to do. What do you think?"

Robin thought it was a horrible idea, but he was even more concerned about the risk of a meltdown in front of the show's 30 million viewers. Robin offered to cancel, but Cash wanted to go ahead.

"The strange thing is John loved going to Europe because he thought he would be free to take all the drugs he wanted without his family and the Music Row crowd watching his every move," Robin says. "What he didn't understand was that he was under more scrutiny in Europe, not less, because he was still such a big star. The press was everywhere."

Watching him onstage that night, Robin worried about the impact the performance would have on ticket sales for the upcoming two-week tour. Cash was sweating profusely and stumbling his way through a song.

The worst moment came at the end, when Cash was kneeling before the crowd. As he stood up, he lost his balance and had to grab the microphone stand to steady himself.

Newspaper headlines the next day pulled no punches. Declared one front-page report, "Johnny Cash Sick or Drunk on TV Guest Appearance."

The impact was immediate.

"We went on to do the dates, but business fell way off," Robin says. "We may have even had to cancel a few shows. It was the nightmare of all nightmares."

Wanting a strong hand in the studio, Cash teamed up with Brian Ahern again in April 1983. As he had promised himself after their first album together, Ahern took a stronger stand, recording in Los Angeles with his own handpicked band, which included the increasingly omnipresent Stuart, who that year became the latest in Cash's growing list of musician sons-in-law when he married Cindy. They would be together five years. Out of respect, Ahern listened to a half dozen of Cash's latest songs, but nothing came close to catching his ear; the songs seemed bland, in some cases only half-finished. Some of those songs would actually turn up on subsequent Cash albums, but Ahern didn't want any part of them.

For years Cash's chief problem as a writer was his failure to move forward. He had plenty of raw material available if he'd just look at the complexity of his life and the world around him, but he continued to focus on the ideas and imagery that had worked for him before.

Instead of telling Cash he didn't like the songs, Ahern turned to material from a writer who was all about moving forward: Bruce Springsteen.

It takes courage and immense creative drive to search constantly for revealing new songs and themes. Springsteen proved a master at always demanding more of himself. Even before his breakthrough hit "Born to Run" in 1975, Springsteen had already realized this important rule.

"The writing is more difficult now," Bruce said in 1974. "I got a lot of things out in that first album. In the new songs, I started slowly to find out who I am and where I want to be. It was like coming out of the shadow of various influences and trying to be me. You have to let out more of yourself all the time. You strip off the first layer, then the second, then the third. It gets harder because it's more personal."

The songs Ahern played for Cash were "Johnny 99" and "Highway Patrolman" from Springsteen's 1982 album *Nebraska,* where he chronicled with gripping starkness the way hardships, economic and social, can drive people to desperate means.

"Cash was familiar with Springsteen, and he seemed vaguely familiar with 'Johnny 99,' but he certainly hadn't thought about recording it," Ahern says. "When the songs finished, all I said was that we had made some inroads on the last album and that we needed to keep cracking the whip. I think it was clear to him that I was saying his songs weren't good enough, and there was this long pause. I was thinking he might fire me, but I was willing to take that chance. I'd rather be fired than put out a bad record."

Finally Cash signaled his approval, and he didn't mention his own songs again. They decided to call the album *Johnny 99*. Cash loved the Springsteen songs for much the same reason he so admired Dylan's songs: their daring, compassion, and commentary. He also enjoyed being back in the creative center of pop and rock, the music of young America. Rick Blackburn hoped *Johnny 99* would appeal to those coveted young record buyers, thus putting Cash into the "new and contemporary" mainstream.

Hopes were raised even higher when pop and rock reviewers, some of whom hadn't paid attention to a Cash album in years, praised the collection. The biggest hurdle was country radio. Feedback was discouraging. Most DJs didn't see "Johnny 99" or "Highway Patrolman" as country records.

To play it safe, Columbia released Cash's remake of an old George Jones hit, "I'm Ragged but I'm Right," as the first single in September. It was a flop. Finally, the label decided to give "Johnny 99" a try, but it didn't fare any better. As the country promotion department had predicted, country radio ignored it. The album never had a chance in the marketplace.

In retrospect, all the parties may have been overly optimistic. You couldn't have been any hotter than Springsteen in 1983. He was, in many ways, the rock 'n' roll equivalent of Johnny Cash, not just a record maker but a heroic figure whose music and image reflected many of the traditional values of America. Even so, rock radio shied away from the downbeat *Nebraska*. Whereas Springsteen's last three albums had sold a total of 14 million copies, *Nebraska* struggled to reach the 1 million mark.

IV

Cash had certainly been there, and for years longer than Springsteen. As 1983 progressed, those closest to him noticed that he was gradually falling deeper and deeper into depression. No one felt it more acutely than John Carter. Speaking of the period he says,

"My parents were tender and wonderful people, but it got to a point when my dad was no longer there for me."

Cash's son remembers coming home from school one day and finding his dad in "an almost trancelike state, as though he were asleep but somehow still functioning: Slurred, low speech; blood-shot eyes; a head that drooped." Cash, his son said, had stashes of drugs everywhere, and he was becoming increasingly "volatile and unavailable."

Once again, the addiction reached a crisis point in Europe. Cash was in bad shape, and the shows in November reflected it. One morning John Carter woke up to find the hotel room he shared with his father littered with wine bottles his dad had taken from the minibar and consumed during the night.

Near the end of the English dates, John and June were staying at a hotel in Nottingham that had lovely old wooden paneling. Cash was so wasted that he began hallucinating about a Murphy bed stored in one of the walls. Despite June's assurances there was no bed in the wall, Cash started ripping at the paneling with his bare hands with such force that the wood began to splinter. One of the pieces got lodged in his right hand, causing it to bleed and become infected, swelling to almost twice its normal size. When reporters noticed it, Cash told them he had been bitten by a poisonous spider.

Watching all this, June again decided she had had enough—both the drugs and the recurring periods of emotional distance between them. After the final show of the tour, she told John she was going to stay with Carlene and husband Nick Lowe in London. Wasted, Cash could barely understand what she was saying. On the way to the airport the next morning he kept asking, "Where's June?"

Back in Nashville, he checked in to the Baptist Hospital, where the doctors realized that the hand was the least of Cash's problems. He had a bleeding ulcer and other ailments. Doctors ended up re-moving his spleen and several feet of intestine. Lou Robin was so concerned he phoned June in London and urged her to return. "John may be dying," he said.

To make matters worse, Cash was anything but a model patient. His daughter Kathy got a call from him early one evening, asking her to bring him a six-pack of beer and some pills. When she refused, he said angrily: "Did you say no to your dad?" Kathy explained, "Because you're in the hospital, you've had surgery, you don't need beer, and you don't need pills. They're giving you what you need." He said, "Piss on you, then. I'll call someone else." And he hung up.

That other call must have worked, because by the next day he'd accumulated a considerable amount of Percodan and amphetamines. He even managed to smuggle Valium into intensive care with him, stuffing it under the bandages that covered his stomach.

When he started fading in and out of consciousness two days later, the hospital team feared for his life until Cash, in a moment of consciousness, directed nurses to the drugs under the bandages. Sure enough, half of the Valium had dissolved and found its way into Cash's body through his wound. This was on top of the morphine the doctors had already given him.

Cash's hallucinations caused him to be so unruly during the hospital stay that the only visitor allowed was June, except for one time when Carrie demanded to see her son. Cash remembered awaking at one point to feel his mother's hand on his forehead and to hear her plead for his life: "Lord, you took one of my boys and if you're going to take this one, he's yours to take, but I ask you, let him live and teach him to serve you better. Surely, you have work for him to do."

As he slowly began to recover, the family was told that he needed psychological help to survive. Through the hospital, the family contacted the Betty Ford Center, a heralded new alcohol and drug addiction treatment facility in the celebrity-rich Palm Springs area a couple of hours east of Los Angeles. Co-founded just a year earlier by the former first lady, who suffered from alcohol addiction, the clinic housed around a hundred inpatients at a time. To convince Cash to check into Betty Ford, the family staged an intervention.

Among those confronting Cash in a hospital meeting room were June, John Carter, other family members, and friends. The session was led by a specialist from the hospital. As Cash looked on, the guests sat around him in a circle.

"Every one of them had written out something they wanted me to know about my behavior toward them," Cash recalled, complaints ranging from lying and neglect to scores of broken promises about curbing his drug use. Of them all, he said, John Carter's note hit hardest. The teenager reminded him of the horrible embarrassment he felt whenever his father, under the influence, stumbled around the farmhouse at Bon Aqua in front of the boy's school friends. As John Carter started reading the note, John reached out and hugged him tightly.

Cash was in no mood to resist. He looked at everyone around him and said softly, "I want to go. I want some help."

PART
FIVE

Chapter 29

AT BETTY FORD AND DROPPED BY COLUMBIA RECORDS

I

FOUR DAYS BEFORE CHRISTMAS 1983, John and Michelle Rollins, neighbors in Jamaica, flew John in their private jet to Palm Springs, where he was taken to the Betty Ford Center's drug rehabilitation clinic. In Nashville, Reba announced his treatment, explaining he wanted to guard against any recurrence of his drug problems. While continuing to be treated for his stomach condition, Cash met with his counselor and attended group lectures on addiction; one of the talks, most days, was given by Betty Ford herself. He was one of several celebrities at the center at that time, the most prominent being Elizabeth Taylor. During their frequent talks, Cash and Taylor discovered they were born only one day apart in 1932 (she liked to point out she was twenty-four hours younger). They exchanged birthday cards for years.

Bill Miller visited him at Betty Ford and found him surprisingly upbeat. "I think he was relieved in a way," Miller says. "He had chosen to go in and say, 'I realize I have a problem and I am committing myself to this program,' which made the fans able to think, 'That's cool,' rather than see him stumbling onstage or crashing a car or some other ugly stuff." Cash was also visited by Gene Autry, Kristofferson, and Lou Robin, among others.

During many restful hours, Cash resumed work on his novel about Saint Paul and wrote letters of apology to his children and others. Kathy Cash recalls the tenderness of his words. "I was so mad about what he had done to me on the phone that I didn't even go to Betty Ford, which made me feel bad because I got this letter saying he was sorry and that he loved me," she says. "I cried when I read it."

In a January 17 letter to Rosanne, Cash said he was looking forward to having June visit him, but he knew she was going to be wary. Kristofferson says June told him that she was thinking of leaving. "I said, 'June, that's like telling me there's no Santa Claus.'"

When June finally came with John Carter, Cash ran to his son and gave him a hug that lifted the boy off the ground. "The light was back in his eyes," John Carter remembered. "He seemed brand-new."

June held back for a few seconds before finally reaching out to hold John's face in both hands as she told him she loved him. In her journal that week she wrote, "I can love John for the man he is inside. I can accept him whether he is stoned or not. What matters is that I keep my heart close to God. Jesus will keep me safe."

Kristofferson said he got a telegram from June telling him not to worry: There still is a Santa Claus.

After forty-three days, Johnny Cash was home. And in his regained clarity, Cash saw the trouble some of his children were going through, including Cindy, who was battling her own drug problem. "He came to my house one day and had tears in his eyes," Cindy says. "It was the first time I ever saw my dad cry. He goes, 'I came over here, Cindy, because I cannot watch you die.' I asked him what he was talking about, and those tears just started coming down his face. He told me, 'You need help. Your plane leaves at three o'clock this afternoon for Loma Linda Hospital in California.' And I was on the plane. I was there for three months."

After more rest, Cash headed to Des Moines on March 27 for the first stop of an eight-city tour. Fifteen days later he went back into the studio for his first significant session in twelve months.

Hopeful for a breakthrough, Blackburn again paired him with

producer Billy Sherrill, even though their first teaming hadn't clicked. Sherrill had another song that Columbia execs, in their desperation, thought might finally turn things around for Cash—a goofy novelty titled "The Chicken in Black" that featured Cash as the main character. Written by Nashville songwriter Gary Gentry, "Chicken" told the story of Johnny Cash needing a brain transplant because his old brain just wore out.

In the song, Cash heads to New York City, where a transplant specialist tells him he's in luck—a bank robber has just been killed and his brain is available. Cash is soon back in Nashville, and everything is just fine until he steps onstage at the Grand Ole Opry. Halfway through "I Walk the Line," he suddenly stops singing and demands that everyone in the audience stick up their hands and give him their money and their valuables.

Panicked, Cash calls the specialist to ask for his old brain, but he learns it has been put into a chicken that is already causing a sensation by singing Cash's songs in auditoriums and at fairs all around the country. The Chicken in Black, as the bird is billed, has even signed a ten-year recording contract. Meanwhile, Cash is reduced to walking the streets of Nashville, telling people to stick their hands up. The record ends with Cash repeating the signature humming phrase from "I Walk the Line."

Given his past success with novelties, Cash may have figured he had another hit. He also may have imagined that the self-mocking might combat charges among some country music observers after *Man in Black* and the Billy Graham Crusades that Cash had become pious and self-important. The record would show everybody that he could laugh at himself.

Talking to the media just before "The Chicken in Black"—or "Brain Transfusion," as it was originally called—was released in July, Cash, as usual, was upbeat. "I did a session last week that I feel really good about," he told me. "I recorded a thing that everybody thinks could be a good record, a thing called 'Brain Transfusion,' and I'm probably going to be doing it on the road."

Because Sherrill was involved and because they hoped there might be a groundswell of support for Cash among country fans after his Betty Ford Clinic stay, Columbia ordered a video to accompany the record's release. In the video Cash assumed the role of a chicken, dressed in a bright yellow and blue outfit in the style of a comic book superhero.

Rosanne was heartbroken. She called it the "nadir" of his 1980s decline. "There was an undercurrent of desperation in it. It was painful," she says. Waylon told Cash he looked like a buffoon in the chicken costume. Hearing this reaction, Cash suddenly turned against the project. He later said that "The Chicken in Black" was the only thing he ever recorded that he flat-out hated. About the video he added, "It was godawful."

Even though the record was moving up the lower rungs of the country chart in the summer of 1984, Cash demanded that Columbia reclaim not only the video from TV stations but also unsold copies of the single from stores. Needless to say, he stopped performing the song live, which set up a perfect gag for the tour crew.

"John liked to know from time to time what the audience wanted to hear, so we would hand out cards at some shows asking fans to write down any requests," Lou Robin says. "One night we took the cards and wrote 'Chicken in Black' on every one of them and gave them to John. He looked so puzzled that we finally had to let him in on the joke."

Columbia executives didn't find anything funny in Cash's reversal. If he hadn't made such a fuss over it, the song might have become a hit, they told themselves. As it was, it stayed on the country charts eleven weeks. Amid bad feelings, the Cash-Sherrill album was shelved. The incident further fueled Cash's disillusionment; he blamed the record label for getting him into what he called the whole "fiasco."

"There were times when I didn't care," he later said of this period. "It was, like, complete apathy from the record company, and I guess I got that way too." But it was not the end of the line for Cash and Blackburn. They still clung to the hope that something could turn their luck around.

"Chicken in Black" aside, Cash appeared to be in reasonably good spirits as he remained on tour pretty much through the summer and fall of 1984, including a successful trip to Europe in early

November. He had already begun work on a new album with Chips Moman, one of the record business's hippest producers and songwriters. He'd overseen Elvis Presley's landmark 1968 recording sessions in Memphis, which had resulted in Elvis's strongest singles in years, including "Suspicious Minds."

At the end of the European concert dates, Cash headed to Montreux, Switzerland, to tape his annual TV Christmas special. He was looking forward to the week because his guests were going to be Jennings, Kristofferson, and Nelson, a sort of summit meeting between Cash and the outlaw movement he'd helped inspire. After tapings each evening, the foursome would gather in a suite at the hotel and take turns singing songs. In contrast to his close relationship with Jennings and Kristofferson, Cash barely knew Nelson, but they took advantage of the gatherings to correct that.

Moman, who had also produced Nelson's last two albums, flew in to see how his new musical buddies were getting along, and he enjoyed the vibe in the songfests. Late one evening the four started joking around about making a record together, and Moman took it from there.

Within days, John, Willie, Waylon, and Kris were in a Nashville studio with Moman, trying out some material. During the session, Marty Stuart, who played guitar and mandolin on the date, remembered a mystical Jimmy Webb song called "Highwayman" that had four distinct verses, which, divided up, would be perfect for the quartet's voices and personas.

From the first playback there was magic in their collective voices. With Moman's encouragement, the group, which they called The Highwaymen, assembled some other songs that spoke to the nostalgic appeal of these four veteran talents coming together. After hearing a couple of others, including "The Last Cowboy Song," written by Ed Bruce and Ron Petersen, and Guy Clark's "Desperadoes Waiting for a Train," Blackburn felt he had the makings of a classic.

Released in late May 1985, just days after Cash went back to Baptist Hospital to have doctors remove some adhesions and scar tissue that had formed after his stomach operation, the album was an immediate winner.

Blackburn hoped that Cash's contributions to the collection

would finally connect him with the contemporary country audience. Of the four Highwaymen, Nelson was by far the hottest record seller at the time; Jennings was second. Blackburn looked forward to testing Cash's next solo album.

Meanwhile, Cash returned to acting. He signed to play the role of John Brown in the TV miniseries *North and South.* Filming was scheduled for late June, just before The Highwaymen made their first public appearance, in the rain, at Nelson's annual July 4 picnic at Southpark Meadows near Austin.

The album had gone to number one on the country charts by the time The Highwaymen were onstage again two months later before eighty thousand people at the first annual Farm Aid benefit concert at the University of Illinois. The benefit was designed to raise funds for and public recognition of family farmers who were struggling to pay their mortgages. Because Kristofferson wasn't able to be there, Glen Campbell, who had recorded the original version of "Highwayman" years before, took his place. The album would stay on the country charts for sixty-six weeks, more than Cash's previous sixteen albums combined.

With interest stirred, The Highwaymen signed to star in a made-for-TV version of John Ford's *Stagecoach,* the classic 1939 western that made John Wayne a star. In the film, Kristofferson would play Wayne's part as the Ringo Kid, Nelson took the role of celebrated gambler-gunfighter Doc Holliday, Cash was cast as the marshal, and Jennings portrayed another gambler. Others in the cast included June Carter and Jennings's wife, Jessi Colter. Cash and Kristofferson also starred in another made-for-TV film, *The Last Days of Frank and Jesse James.* Both were embarrassing to everyone, it seems, except the principals. They approached the whole thing as a lark.

Oddly, the group didn't consider following the album with a tour. "No one thought of the Highwayman album as anything more than a one-time thing," Lou Robin says. "Everyone had his own band and his own tour lined up months in advance. Which musicians would they use? What songs would they do? The idea of dropping everything else and touring just seemed too complicated."

*   *   *

Blackburn's hope that all those *Highwayman* buyers would pick up Cash's next album wasn't realized. In the fall, *Rainbow,* the LP Cash had started with Moman before The Highwaymen project, came and went without a trace. There were a few strong songs in it, including Kris Kristofferson's "Here Comes That Rainbow" and John Fogerty's "Have You Ever Seen the Rain?" but the arrangements and vocals were strangely pedestrian. To judge from the tone of the liner notes, Cash had been skeptical all along about any Highwaymen coattails.

"I don't think about sales and promotion when I record a song," he wrote. "I don't record songs to do family or friends a favor. I don't record a song because I publish it. I record a song because I love it and let it become part of me. And even a blind pig gets a grain of corn once in a while. So who know, maybe it'll sell hundreds."

Still, Blackburn continued to believe in Cash, and he okayed a reteaming of Cash and Jennings with Moman, tucking the sessions in between tours. Cash also agreed to be the subject of a celebrity roast to raise money for the Jewish National Fund in Memphis. The roasters included Jennings, Blackburn, Sam Phillips, and Moman.

During that fall of 1985, Moman got involved in a campaign in Memphis to salute the city's rich musical heritage. As part of the project he proposed an album toasting the city's Sun Records history. He quickly enlisted Cash, Carl Perkins, Roy Orbison, and Jerry Lee Lewis to perform on the album *Class of '55.*

"When J.R., Jerry, Carl, Roy, and Chips walked into a press conference at the Peabody Hotel, the place exploded," Marty Stuart recalls. "There was five minutes of applause, hollering, and tears. Sam Phillips and Cowboy [Jack Clement] were also there. It was wonderful to see all those characters back on Union Avenue. If the music on the record matched the electricity surrounding the event, it would have been a second coming."

The music didn't come close to matching it except when the foursome was joined by guests John Fogerty, the Judds, and Rick Nelson on a rollicking seven-minute version of Fogerty's "Big Train (from Memphis)," a salute to Elvis Presley that appeared on Fogerty's *Centerfield* album earlier that year. Most of the remaining songs were marginal, and the singing was lazy.

Moman couldn't find a label that was interested in releasing the album. Finally Mercury got involved because one of Johnny Cash's biggest fans in the music business, Steve Popovich, had recently taken over as head of Nashville operations for Mercury Records, a division of PolyGram.

"I'm not embarrassed to say I was in awe of John since the first time I saw him in concert," said Popovich, whose father was a Pennsylvania coal miner. "He had such charisma onstage and I believed what he was saying in the songs like 'Man in Black.' He stood up for people like my dad and everyone else from that coal mining town."

When Popovich, who'd worked with Cash at Columbia, learned that Moman had this new album, he wanted to be involved. Popovich felt it would go a long way toward putting his stamp on Mercury. He was thrilled when he brought the four artists onstage at Nashville's annual Fun Fair music showcase and "the place went wild."

Unfortunately, Moman failed to obtain permission from Columbia to use Cash on the album. "Chips had gotten money to make the album from Federal Express, whose headquarters are in Memphis," says Lou Robin. "When Rick [Blackburn] heard about it, he was furious. He demanded Chips pay him $100,000 to keep John's voice on the record—and Chips had to come up with the money."

It was probably the easiest money Columbia ever made off Cash during the 1980s.

II

Cash continued to work on his book, but he was having trouble with the climactic scene on the Damascus road when Jesus, following a bolt of blinding light from the heavens, spoke to Paul, who then underwent his conversion. Cash had trouble relating to the "heaven-and-earth connection" Paul experienced—as symbolized by the blinding light. He finally found his answer at Christmas, just two days after his father died from complications of Parkinson's disease.

Ray Cash, at eighty-eight, had been ill for much of 1985. His eyesight was failing, and he spent most of the time in bed. On occasion, family members would gather around his bed and sing some of Carrie's favorite hymns.

It was an especially difficult time for John. He still harbored resentment over the way his father had treated him when he was growing up in Dyess and how Ray had continued to withhold his approval. At the same time, he felt guilty for not being able to brush these feelings aside and care more about the man. When he wrote his second autobiography a decade later, Cash still had ambivalent feelings. There were times when he couldn't relate to his father, but there were other times when he felt they were kindred spirits.

"In some ways my father is an enigma to me," he wrote. "His presence in my memory is awesome, yet it's fleeting, something I can turn my back on and even, sometimes, laugh about. On stage the other night, I decided to do 'These Hands' and said, 'I'll dedicate this song to my mother and father, who worked so hard to put me through school and encouraged me to go out and sing.'

"Right then I felt my father's presence beside me protesting, 'I didn't encourage you!' He was right, of course—his attitude had always been, 'You won't amount to a hill of beans. Forget about that guitar'—and I almost laughed out loud right there in front of everybody."

In the most telling revelation, Cash admitted that he no longer thought much about his father, didn't even visit his grave, though he would drive past the cemetery almost every day he was home. At the same time, he called Ray Cash "the most interesting specter in my memories, looming around in there saying, 'Figure me out, son.'"

At the funeral parlor on Christmas Day, Cash was touched to see his father "so handsome in that fine blue suit and burgundy tie." After months of suffering, Cash told himself, his father at last was at peace. He then dropped his mother off at her house, where scores of family and friends were waiting, and he headed home to change into more comfortable clothes.

When he opened his closet door, he saw a box of fireworks he had bought months earlier. Knowing how much his father loved fireworks, he had planned to set them off on his parents' front lawn

Christmas night so his father could see them from the window. He took the box back to his parents' house and stood in the yard, setting off the wide array of skyrockets, Roman candles, and sparklers. Afterward, he went inside the house and kissed his mother good night.

Cash was drained. Back home, he went straight to bed and soon found himself dreaming of his father. As he later described the dream, Cash was back on his parents' lawn when a long, bright silver car came over the hill and stopped about fifty feet in front of him. When the left rear door opened, Ray Cash stepped out and walked toward his son. His father reached out his hand, and a "long row of light streamed up from the ground" between them. "The stream of light between us widened, grew in brilliance and became an unbreachable gulf."

Then suddenly both the light and his father were gone.

Cash got up and paced the floor for hours, thinking about the light in the dream and slowly visualized more clearly Saint Paul's experience on the Damascus road. Almost immediately, he resumed work on the novel. When he finished it, he wrote on the first page of the manuscript:

This book is dedicated to my father, Ray Cash
1897–1985, veteran of World War II
Discharge: Honorable. Conduct: Good.

Mark Stielper, a Maryland businessman and lifelong fan, had crossed paths with Cash in the early 1980s and he enjoyed numerous conversations with John about Saint Paul. Stielper, who had once considered entering the priesthood, not only shared Cash's fascination with biblical history, but he developed an encyclopedic knowledge and abiding passion about John's life and career.

"We bonded over [Saint] Peter and [Saint] Paul," remembers Stielper. "I don't think we spoke a word about his music for a long time. I later went on an educational archaeological dig to Rome. When I returned and met up with him at Cinnamon Hill, he told me that one of his greatest unfulfilled dreams was going on a dig in Jerusalem."

Though twenty-five years younger than Cash, the tall, soft-spoken, but opinionated Stielper evolved quickly into a valued confidant who was independent enough—he wasn't on the payroll—to speak frankly when he felt the need. As years went by, he came to be seen within the Cash camp as the family historian, building a massive library of Cash's correspondence and personal effects. He also developed a strong rapport with John Carter Cash and others in the singer's inner circle.

When the book was finished, Cash was "very satisfied," Stielper says. "It was almost like writing an autobiography; that's how much he identified with Paul. The book wasn't written in a vacuum. Of course, this was also a time of great unhappiness and drama in his life, particularly with his ill health and the realization that, commercially, he wasn't going to scale those late-1960s heights again."

Cash's pace was hectic in the early months of 1986. He spent much of January in Arizona and Mexico filming *Stagecoach*. On February 25, Jimmy Webb's "Highwayman" won a Grammy for best country song, though The Highwaymen themselves lost in the country group vocal category to the Judds' "Why Not Me." He did have something to cheer about, however: Rosanne won in the female country vocal category for her recording of "I Don't Know Why You Don't Want Me."

To promote the publication of *Man in White,* Cash attended a booksellers convention, but it didn't stir interest. Sales were minimal. Like Dylan, Cash didn't like dwelling on the past. As soon as the book was done, he was ready to move on. "After he was finished with the promoting and the tours and the book conventions," Stielper says, "I never heard him mention *Man in White* again."

Around this time, three of Cash's albums hit the stores: *Heroes,* the collection with Jennings; *Class of '55;* and *Believe in Him,* the gospel album he made with Stuart in 1982. Original plans to release *Believe* on Priority Records ended when the label folded a week before the album was to have hit the stores in 1984. It took two years for Robin to find it a new home on the Christian music label Word.

The three albums were an uneven bunch. *Class of '55* was a mess. Moman helped Cash and Jennings find a strong common ground in *Heroes* that reflected the wistful nature of the two road warriors looking back over the glory days. The title song, written by Jennifer Kimball and Tim Kimmel, was intended as a salute to the cowboy movie stars Cash and Jennings watched as children (one of those stars, whip-wielding Lash LaRue, even appeared with them on the back cover). But a listener couldn't help but imagine the song also applying to the old country music heroes, especially when Cash sang, "Heroes, so good to know / So hard to find, sad when they go."

The most engaging of the albums was the long-delayed *Believe in Him*. In the sessions, Stuart surrounded Cash with the energy and spirit of the Sun Records days. In fact, their version of "Belshazzar" was far more colorful than the one he had recorded on Sun. The duet with Jessi Colter on the traditional spiritual "The Old Rugged Cross" was another standout. Cash's own songs, including "One of These Days I'm Going to Sit Down and Talk to Paul," were also stirring.

Good or bad, the albums were all commercial disappointments. *Believe in Him* didn't chart at all. Five weeks after the albums hit the stores, things got even worse.

III

Robert K. Oermann, the respected country music columnist for the *Nashville Tennessean,* often dropped in on Music Row power brokers for informal talks to keep up with the latest developments in the business. During a visit with Rick Blackburn on July 14, Oermann was surprised when the label head spoke frankly about the difficult time he had gone through in reshaping the roster to meet what he felt were changing tastes in country music. Discussing longtime Columbia artists whose contracts weren't likely to be renewed, he mentioned Cash. Later in the conversation, he called the roster reduction "the hardest decision I've had to make in my life."

When Oermann got back to the newspaper office, he kept thinking about what was obviously an important story. Because the Cash comment had been off the record, Oermann phoned Blackburn's office, hoping to get permission to print the scoop. But Blackburn was on his way to California on business and couldn't be reached. Oermann then phoned Lou Robin, who confirmed that Cash's contract with Columbia had run out.

The Tennessean ran the story on July 16 under the headline "'Man in Black' without a Label." It read in part:

"Johnny Cash is without a country music record label.

"The Country Music Hall of Fame member who is arguably the most legendary star in country music has been with Columbia Records since 1958, but sources at the company say his contract will not be renewed.

"Columbia/Epic/CBS Nashville head Rick Blackburn would say only that, 'This is the hardest decision that I've ever had to make in my life.'

"Others on Music Row say that Cash's contract was allowed to expire...because Cash has not had a solo Top 10 hit since 1981's 'The Baron.'

"'We don't know where we'll be going,' said Cash's manager Lou Robin yesterday during a telephone conversation. 'Other people are talking to us. There's a lot of places, where they're interested in somebody like Johnny Cash.'"

The news was the talk of the industry, prompting a wave of anti-Blackburn sentiment. How could Columbia drop the man who, in effect, had been synonymous with the label for three decades—the man who had made the company millions? Dwight Yoakam, one of country's most promising newcomers at the time, led the charge: "The man's been there 30 fuckin' years making them money....He built the building."

No one was hit harder by the article than Blackburn, who was angry, and Cash, who was humiliated.

When Oermann finally reached both parties, Blackburn accused the reporter of having "ambushed" him, and Cash was upset that Blackburn had made the decision public before telling him.

Oermann wrote a column on July 21 in which he apologized to both Blackburn and Cash for not having handled the story differently. The headline read "Reporter's Aim Was in Wrong Direction." While stressing that the report was accurate, Oermann said he regretted using the off-the-record Blackburn quote and for not holding the exclusive an extra day to make sure he had comments from both men.

"Rick and Johnny were/are friends," he wrote, "and in my haste I hurt that friendship with a story. Now comes the ironic part: Rick Blackburn has always talked straight to me. He's never hidden from me or any other press person. And on Music Row he's a guy who stands out with a lot of personal integrity. I think the story made him look like he might not have those qualities. Fortunately, reporters get another day to set the record straight. And today's that day for me.

"I am sorry for the way the story was written, sorry for the damage to the friendship between Rick and Johnny. I can't be sorry for reporting news. That's my job. I certainly wish Johnny Cash well on what is bound to be an exciting new chapter in his illustrious recording career. He will doubtless find continued success, more hits and lots of publicity at his new label. During his musical career, he's been a model of ethics, of honesty."

Unknown to Oermann, Blackburn had still hoped to re-sign Cash; he knew as well as anyone what Cash meant to the label, but he had heard through the grapevine that Cash had been offered $1 million to sign with Mercury.

"I got the impression that anything less than $1 million would be insulting, and I knew there was no way we could approach that figure," Blackburn said years later. "But I hadn't given up. I was planning to meet with John as soon as he got back to Nashville. If we still couldn't work anything out, I'd at least let John make the announcement, which would have been easier on him. But once that story ran, there was no turning back."

As soon as Oermann's article appeared, Popovich—whose boss, Dick Asher, was also a former Columbia executive and a Cash fan—went to Cash's office at the House of Cash to meet with his old friend. "He was down, almost in shock, and I wanted to help rebuild his ego and self-pride," Popovich said. "We talked about working together during the old days at Columbia and I told him I wanted to work with him again. I said, 'Unlike new acts, you are already pre-sold to millions of people around the world. That makes you a dangerous artist with the right song and right producer.'"

There was no $1 million offer, nothing even close. The Mercury deal was such a modest one that it would have been unthinkable during Cash's glory years at Columbia, but Robin and Cash weren't in a position to demand more. In fact, they felt fortunate to find anyone to sign him. During the search for a new label, Cash went around to one major company and actually auditioned as he had for Sam Phillips long ago. He played guitar and sang some of his new songs. The label head never even got back to him.

Five weeks after Oermann's Columbia bombshell, the *Tennessean* reported the move to Mercury.

"I feel great," Cash told Oermann in his usual upbeat way of talking about his latest recording. "I'm so happy. This did wonders for my little ego." Cash added that he'd spent the night before at his farm in Bon Aqua, thinking about the move. "Then Thursday morning I went to CBS [Columbia] and told the folks there of my decision. We had a big hug and a few tears." Then he walked across the street to pose for photos with Popovich, who had gained a reputation as an artist-friendly executive for his work at CBS with such figures as Cash, Bruce Springsteen, and Cheap Trick. He was best known for his development of Meat Loaf while founder and president of Cleveland International Records.

"It's a great honor to be working once again with Johnny. I love the man," Popovich said. "At CBS we enjoyed much success. The world is waiting for more great Johnny Cash music."

Looking back years later, Popovich recalled how nervous Cash was that day in the office; he had even brought Waylon Jennings along for support.

Rival labels shook their heads over Mercury's decision to sign Cash.

"I can't overemphasize the odds against him," Popovich said years later. "I was on a panel at a country music convention shortly after we signed John and someone in the audience asked, 'Why did you sign Johnny Cash? Don't you think he's had his better days?' I looked at him and said, 'I've got news for you, young man. If Johnny Cash is over, country music is over.'"

CHAPTER 30

THE BEGINNING OF THE MERCURY ERA AND HEART SURGERY

I

CASH MAY HAVE HAD A NEW LABEL, but he didn't have a plan.

It was a reminder that even our greatest artists can lose their way. Some never recover their creative instincts and drive, but the strongest fight boldly and courageously, and often reconnect with their art. But it's never easy—and Cash showed neither boldness nor courage in the fall of 1986.

At a time when he should have realized he was making a last stand in Nashville, Cash timidly turned to the usual suspects when he went into the studio on September 3 to make his Mercury debut. His good-time buddy Jack Clement, who hadn't given Cash a significant hit since "The One on the Right Is on the Left" in 1966, would be his producer. The songs were from, among others, old regulars Guy Clark and Merle Travis, the musicians were mostly from his band, and the Carter Sisters—the wounds of the Cleveland breakup mended—were always ready to step forward with more backing vocals. No one approached the album as if Cash's music was a problem in need of fixing. Everyone around him blamed Columbia, the DJs, and the fickle fans for his career slump.

Looking at most of the late seventies and eighties albums, Cash supporters could point correctly to one or two tracks per album that were good enough to have been monster hits in earlier days, but those days were gone. The truth was this: For the rest of his life, Cash was going to have to fight for everything he got. None of the awards he continued to receive were going to cause people to buy albums.

Yet Cash kept on telling himself it was just a matter of time before all was well. He had seen many artists go through dry spells, notably Dylan, only to rebound. What he failed to notice was that Dylan didn't feel the need to crank out an album every few months; he waited until he had something to say. He also failed to see that Dylan didn't keep chasing after another "Blowin' in the Wind" or "Highway 61 Revisited." Following his motorcycle-related absence from the scene in the late 1960s, Dylan went in a softer but challenging new direction with "John Wesley Harding" and followed that with a country-edged album.

Then in 1975 Dylan changed directions again with the ballad-heavy look at romantic wreckage in *Blood on the Tracks,* only to return four years later with the fire-and-brimstone gospel of *Slow Train Coming.* Indeed, he changed paths so fast in search of new musical ideas that he often left his fans scratching their heads—or booing. About the latter, Dylan quipped, "You can't worry about things like that. Miles Davis has been booed. Hank Williams was booed. Stravinsky was booed. You're nobody if you don't get booed sometime."

Cash often quoted his friend's line "He not busy being born is busy dying," but he didn't apply that principle to his music.

The first Mercury album, *Johnny Cash Is Coming to Town,* did have a welcome sense of energy and drive, but at its core it was as generic as many of the LPs Cash had made at Columbia. The standout track was the Bobby Braddock–Charlie Williams song "The Night Hank Williams Came to Town"—one of those tunes that would probably have been a smash in earlier times. Cash loved the sentiments of the song, which were wrapped in an infectious sing-along arrangement, because it reminded him of the time the Louvin Brothers came to Dyess.

Cash included another song with a similar message about the

uplifting power of music: James Talley's "W. Lee Daniel (and the Light Crust Dough Boys)." Cash had listened to Daniel's western swing band (Bob Wills was an early member) on the radio in Dyess, and he loved Talley's ode to it.

If Cash had been more on top of his game, he would have realized he had a theme in those two songs and searched for others that spoke to the power of live music to enchant. Instead, he surrounded them with tunes that not only had no connection but were rarely more than passable, or were even annoying—such as Guy Clark's toast to a tractor, "Heavy Metal (Don't Mean Rock and Roll to Me)."

This wasn't an album that was going to reestablish Cash in the best of times, much less when Nashville was viewing his Mercury project with skepticism. Jack Clement later acknowledged there was no guiding purpose during the sessions. "I felt like he was a little bit bewildered and confused at that point. He didn't know exactly what to do, so we would try a bunch of different things."

Cash, in turn, may have felt let down. After all, Clement could have stepped in to provide a direction, and he certainly should have erased some of the album's cluttered arrangements. Marty Stuart, always trying to get Cash back to the basics of *boom-chicka-boom,* returned to the studio some nights after hours to create his own versions of several of the tracks, removing what he felt were excessive touches. He played his remakes for Cash, but Cash was too loyal to Clement even to hint at a change in approach. Work continued through February as Cash and Clement, in their search for something that felt right, recorded enough songs for two albums.

When Cash handed in the debut, Popovich was in a position to advise him gently to rethink parts of the album, but the big-hearted executive respected Cash too much to cast any doubts. He wanted to build Cash's confidence, not shatter it. Popovich realized that the album was dead in the water in March 1987, as soon as he heard country radio's cool response to the "Hank Williams" single. If country DJs were already thinking Cash's days as a radio star were long over, Columbia's decision to drop him made him seem more dated than ever. No one wanted to play a has-been. "I thought we had some good stuff," Popovich said. "The world just wasn't waiting."

Not everyone was so generous. In a humiliating review, *USA To-*

day called *Johnny Cash Is Coming to Town* one of the year's ten worst albums.

Cash's creative lethargy wasn't the only factor when it came to understanding the challenges of a stalled career. The problems ran deeper than the demanding tour schedule, the weeks wasted on the made-for-TV movies, the drugs, or the mounting fiscal responsibilities. By the spring of 1987, the years of abusing his body had left him worn down. He was fifty-five going on seventy-five, and for the rest of his life he'd have to battle another unforgiving enemy: his declining health and the accompanying pain.

II

There's no way you could look at those album covers from the 1960s and not realize that Johnny Cash was one sick puppy, but by the mid-1980s his addiction was becoming a secondary problem. Those close to Cash on the road knew within six months of Betty Ford that Cash was again taking pills; they could see it mostly in his sometimes careless or distant performances. But he wasn't out of control—nothing close to the old ODs. He'd suddenly be his old self, then slip back into mild pill use for another six months or so. The real fear was his deteriorating health.

That fear was heightened when Cash suddenly stopped singing during the second song at a Saturday night concert May 16, 1987, at Lincoln High School in Council Bluffs, Iowa. He tried to say something to the audience, but his speech was slurred and he appeared ill and shaky. June rushed in from the wings and escorted John backstage, where he was then transported to Mercy Hospital.

A backstage photo of the moment showed a dazed, frightened man. He was treated for stress and exhaustion as well as an irregular heartbeat. As news spread across the country, the hospital was flooded with calls, cards, and flowers for its famous patient. On Sunday he flew home. The show was his thirty-seventh of the year. After some rest, he resumed touring on June 13 in North Platte, Nebraska. He insisted he felt fine. He'd do seventy-seven more shows, including a tour of Europe, before the end of the year.

Taking a break from touring in early November, Cash attended a meeting of the Hendersonville Regional Planning Commission to request the rezoning of ninety-five of the acres he had purchased near his house on Old Hickory Lake. In his most ambitious investment move to that point, he planned to build 219 houses, priced between $75,000 and $175,000, and to use part of the land for a commercial strip.

Counting on his goodwill in the community to sway the commissioners, Cash was deeply disappointed when more than thirty landowners from the area showed up to protest his plan. They maintained that the proposed 1,300-square-foot houses weren't compatible with the larger, more expensive homes in the area. In the end, the commissioners denied the request.

Following a week of shows later in November, Cash called it quits on touring for the year. He planned to devote December to recording and rest in Jamaica. On December 2, 3, and 10, he went into the studio to finish work on an album featuring new versions of his old hits. The collection, for which recording had started in the fall, was originally to be released only in Europe, but it was issued in the United States the following year in conjunction with an exhibit on Cash at the Country Music Hall of Fame.

Twenty-four hours after finishing that project, Cash and Clement resumed work on the second Mercury album. They had several tracks left over from the first album, but they wanted to see if they could come up with some stronger tunes. Again, Cash and Clement had no direction in mind. After one day's work, they took a break, and Cash headed to Jamaica for the holidays. When they resumed recording on January 8, 1988, they were still haphazardly accumulating tracks.

After a break for a press conference at which Cash made his first endorsement in a presidential race (supporting Democrat Al Gore Jr.), he and Clement finally came up with a concept—or at least a strategy—for the album, and it made sense. If country DJs weren't interested in a Johnny Cash album, maybe they'd play the record if he were teamed with a "hot" artist. What about a duet with Hank Williams Jr., who was red-hot, registering seven number-one singles in the 1980s, two in 1986 alone? What about one with

Paul McCartney, whom John had met in Jamaica? What about—get this—a duet with Rosanne Cash? That would bring more than the human interest angle of father and daughter; Rosanne was almost as hot as Hank Jr., with five number-one singles in the 1980s and two Top 5 singles in 1986. In fact, her version of her dad's song "Tennessee Flat-Top Box" had just gone to number one.

Popovich loved the idea, especially the Hank Jr. track, a spiritually tinged feel-good song by Jennifer Pierce called "That Old Wheel." He told everyone at PolyGram in New York that he had a smash. He also thought that a remake of "Ballad of a Teenage Queen," featuring both Rosanne and the Everly Brothers, could be huge. He had hoped the McCartney duet could be the third single, but "New Moon over Jamaica," a song written by Cash, McCartney, and Tom T. Hall while sitting on Cash's porch at Cinnamon Hill one night, was so devoid of character that not even Popovich on his most enthusiastic day could muster much praise for it. Even if it wasn't a single, he figured the McCartney name would still lure buyers. The eventual album, titled *Water from the Wells of Home*, would also feature duets with Hall, Waylon, June, John Carter, Emmylou Harris, and Glen Campbell.

In late March, the Country Music Hall of Fame in Nashville unveiled its two-thousand-square-foot Cash exhibit, the most elaborate salute to an artist in the museum's twenty-year history. Cash attended a private preview, then left for a brief engagement in Las Vegas, during which he experienced hoarseness onstage. He had canceled three shows earlier in the month in the Midwest for the same reason. He was now concerned enough to check in to the Eisenhower Medical Center in Palm Springs on March 30 to have tests done for laryngitis and bronchitis. The doctors found nothing serious and advised him simply to rest his voice. But Cash had more concert obligations. Within a week he was back onstage in the Midwest, where he did four shows before heading to Europe for more dates. He also agreed to play frontier hero Davy Crockett in a multi-part TV tale that would air as part of NBC's *Magical World of Disney* series.

Making no effort to rest his voice, Cash found another project that appealed to his missionary role: he'd record the entire New

King James version of the New Testament for a cassette package marketed by Thomas Nelson, a gospel-oriented media company in Nashville. Work began on September 13 and continued, off and on, for nearly a year. "To turn the written word into the spoken word has long been my dream," he wrote in the liner notes that accompanied the nineteen-hour package. "But little did I dream that speaking the New Testament aloud in its entirety would so much further enrich my spiritual life."

September was also when Mercury released "That Old Wheel" as a single, hoping to build interest in the forthcoming album. But even Hank Williams's presence couldn't push it any higher than number twenty-one on the country chart. That was better than any Cash single in nine years, not counting The Highwaymen teaming, but not enough to turn the album into a winner. The CD fared even more poorly than *Johnny Cash Is Coming to Town*.

As Cash thought about his next recording move, he felt abandoned. His "angels" at Mercury—Asher and Popovich—had both left the label.

"I felt bad about leaving John, but my mother was dying, plus Dick Asher wasn't at the company any longer and the people in New York just didn't get what I was trying to do," Popovich said. "A lot of people worked really hard to help John turn things around, but we just couldn't do it."

III

The headline on a story in the *Nashville Tennessean* on Wednesday, December 14, 1988, seemed straightforward enough: "Cash Enters Hospital for Regular Checkup." But there was apprehension in country music circles. Roy Orbison had died of a heart attack at fifty-two just five days earlier, and Jennings, fifty-one, had undergone a triple bypass heart operation at the same Baptist Hospital the day before Cash's physical. Before meeting with his doctor, Cash visited his old roommate in intensive care. Jennings told Cash that being in a hospital can be a great leveler. "When they get you up to walk you, you can hardly stand up, and they put that little gown on you," Jennings said. "You're about halfway down the hall, and you feel the draft from behind. You know you ain't got no back, and you got no shorts on, and people are looking at your ass. That superstar shit goes right out the window." Twenty-four hours later, Cash learned he would also be having heart surgery.

The two-and-a-half-hour procedure on December 19, which used blood vessels from Cash's chest and leg to bypass two diseased coronary arteries, went well. Doctors found that there was approximately a 90 percent blockage at the critical point where the two arteries come together to provide the blood supply for the heart's primary pumping chamber. There was no evidence of actual damage to the heart.

Talking to reporters, cardiologist Dr. Charles E. Mayes said that Cash's stressful lifestyle likely contributed to his problems, and he warned that his famous patient needed to change that lifestyle in the future, including stopping smoking, exercising more, and eating fewer fatty foods. The forecast was that Cash, after ten to twelve days at the hospital, should be able to return to the concert trail by February.

Cash enjoyed spending time in the hospital with Waylon; the two had become especially close in recent years. They had even talked for a while about joining an investment group that wanted to build a $30 million hotel and commercial complex on Music Row, but their interest was fleeting. In the days after the surgery, there was renewed worry when Cash developed a serious case of pneumonia. During this time he had a vision, he later related, that he was in heaven and at peace. When he awoke, he was so upset to have been brought abruptly back to earth that he thrashed around the room, pulling tubes out of his arm and even wrestling with members of the hospital staff. An article in the *Nashville Banner* suggested that doctors might have been to blame for overmedicating him.

Whatever the cause, Cash was all smiles when he left the hospital on January 3. "I'm fifty-six now and I never want to go through this again," he told reporters. He called the stay a "great, soul-searching experience" and pledged to follow the doctors' advice about a change of lifestyle. "No cigarettes—I can never have another cigarette."

June, wearing a fox fur hat and full-length mink coat, offered a gentle word of caution—and realism—when she spoke to the writers. She said Cash was "committed to life," but she didn't know if he was capable of the kind of change the doctors wanted. "I've never seen anybody keep Johnny Cash to anything," she said knowingly. Indeed, Cash had sneaked a cigarette a half hour before going into the operating room.

At a press conference after the operation, his doctor said, "Most patients are not brave enough to smoke thirty minutes before surgery."

Even before the operations, Cash and Jennings had been talking with Nelson, Kristofferson, and producer Moman about a long-overdue Highwaymen follow-up album. But the second album didn't live up to the standards of the first one. "As an album, it could have used a little more time spent on it," Jennings said in retrospect. "We ran in and out too quick, and we didn't have that one great song. It's hard to find material that goes over with four people, each with strong, let-it-all-hang-out opinions."

One important person missing from the sessions was Marty Stuart. He and Cindy had divorced in 1988, and Cash, to show support for his daughter, severed ties with Stuart for a while. Eventually, however, he would welcome him back into his life—just as he did other ex-sons-in-law, including Rodney Crowell and Nick Lowe.

After the Highwaymen sessions, Cash was honored in Nashville by B'nai B'rith's Anti-Defamation League for humanitarian service. Rosanne was one of the speakers. "You sparked something in me," she told her father. "It was tolerance. And that's what I loved about you."

Cash continued to ease into touring, heading to Europe for a three-week stretch that began April 26 in Cork, Ireland. The shows were a struggle because Cash had trouble breathing. He finally entered the American Hospital in Paris for treatment of what was announced publicly as a pulled leg ligament. Privately, doctors told Cash he had a potentially serious condition and strongly advised him to cancel the show that night.

"They told them he was risking his life if he did the show before taking tests to find out the exact nature of the problem," Lou Robin says. "But John insisted on doing the show anyway, and to show the doctors, he did a longer show than usual. After it was over, I drove him back to the hospital so they could take the tests."

Back home in the States with an apparently clean bill of health, Cash became only the second country artist honored by the Songwriters Guild of America. Among the speakers at the two-hour tribute on June 28 was Sam Phillips, who told the Nashville gathering, "I was wrong as much as I was right. But...I was right to keep listening to Johnny Cash."

Cash was grateful to be among such other Guild honorees over the years as Johnny Mercer and Sammy Cahn, and he charmed the crowd by telling about his feelings while riding to the tribute with June in her new Rolls-Royce. He told her, "You know, [it's] great to get the roses while you're still alive."

Accepting the honor, he said, "Of all the awards, this is the one. It's for writing songs. I've found that songs are our children, an extension of ourselves....It's what's most important to me."

On top of that award, Cash was delighted to learn that a group of maverick U.S. and mostly British musicians—including Pete Shelley of the Buzzcocks, and Marc Almond of Soft Cell—had recorded a tribute album featuring some of his biggest hits, including "I Walk the Line" and "A Boy Named Sue." The collection—whose title, 'Til Things Are Brighter, was taken from "Man in Black"—raised funds to fight AIDS. In Buck Hogarth's liner notes, Cash was saluted for speaking out "for the little man."

His next Mercury album, Boom Chicka Boom, would be just another lost Johnny Cash album. It never made the charts.

On the road meanwhile, Cash continued to face health issues. In late August he canceled three performances in Oregon and Washington because of bronchitis and a respiratory infection. Once again Cash found himself turning increasingly to pain pills. Rather than hide it, he shared the information with his doctors, who advised him to return to rehab.

In September 1989, June flew to California to visit her daughter Rosie, who had checked in to the Betty Ford Center to deal with her own drug use. She arrived only to discover that Rosie had unexpectedly left. Apparently she had taken another patient's credit card and bought a ticket home.

June was planning to head back home herself, but in their meetings with her to discuss Rosie's situation, the Ford staff recognized that June, too, had an addiction problem and needed counseling. They talked her into taking an outpatient course. "They made her think the program was to help her better understand Rosie's addiction," says Kti Jensen, a masseuse and nutritionist who was brought in to help treat June. "That was the only thing they could do. She was too deep in denial to admit she had a problem. Under the outpatient program, she didn't even have to check in to Betty Ford. She stayed at a nearby hotel." June and John liked Kti so much they hired her to work with them full-time.

Finally deciding to follow his doctors' advice about more rehab treatment, Cash entered the Cumberland Heights Alcohol and Drug Treatment Center in Nashville as soon as his tour ended in mid-November. Talking to reporters at the end of his Cumberland stay, he described the course as "an in-depth look at yourself." He added, "You study the history of your chemical abuse and learn to look for the danger signs of a relapse."

Inadvertently, he mentioned in the interview that June had been at Betty Ford—the first public hint that Mrs. Johnny Cash might have a drug problem too. In the interview, Cash stressed that she was there only for a six-week codependency course, not for an addiction problem. He explained that she had a painful herniated disc that required medication, but he said he never saw her take drugs unless she was in intense pain. Yet he left the door slightly open with his added remarks: "Her use has certainly never caused a problem in our relationship....If she does have a problem, it will be for her to say."

After the Cumberland stay, John and June spent the holidays in Jamaica, where, as usual, the drug use waned after rehab visits. John pondered his next move. Without Asher and Popovich, he felt like an orphan at his label. He would re-team with Jack Clement to make a fourth album, but he had few hopes for it. For all practical purposes, Cash believed his recording career was over. Except on oldies stations, he was no longer a singer on the radio.

There was one bright spot. Lou Robin met with the representatives of Nelson, Jennings, and Kristofferson to finalize a Highway-men tour. The goal was to promote the upcoming album, but Robin and the others also wanted to give the musicians the chance to feel a certain thrill once again: walking onstage to the wild cheers of ten to twenty thousand fans in arenas across the country.

IV

Seeing The Highwaymen onstage at the Rosemont Horizon Arena outside Chicago on May 6, 1990, made the audience feel as if they were looking at a living Mount Rushmore of country music. Among them, these familiar faces and voices had made it through a collective twelve marriages, 115-plus years on the road, and untold bottles of whiskey and pills as they spread their tales of restless ideals and troubled times.

The show itself was put together expertly. Rather than focus on tunes from the two Highwaymen albums, the quartet gave the audience a survey of their signature solo songs. Wisely, they all spent the entire two hours onstage, playing one another's tunes. It was a marvelous piece of country music history.

Despite the ticket sales, rave reviews, and adoring fans, the country music establishment was skeptical. Record company executives, radio program directors, and journalists around the country didn't see the shows as a commercial rebirth as much as a last hurrah. They were quick to note that the individual Highwaymen could once headline arenas by themselves, but now they had to join together to do so.

Despite the warmth of the audiences, The Highwaymen themselves guarded against reading too much into the shows. Even Nelson by now was finding it hard to come up with Top 10 country hits. Was their era of country music over?

In his hotel room two days later in Minneapolis, Cash was still thinking about his place in the new world of country music. He had spent the morning with a word processor rather than a guitar, and was about 120 pages into an early draft of his second autobiography. "I love that thing," he told me. "I wrote my other two books by hand and it was like carving in stone."

On the state of country music, he was less upbeat. "I wonder what would happen if I were starting out today in the music business," he said, a protein drink by his side. "I think the only job I'd be able to get would be singing in a coffeehouse somewhere because that's where I could sing songs that mattered to me. I sure couldn't get into singing most of the things you hear on the radio."

Cash was too proud a man to spend much time complaining about a swollen left jaw that was causing him such pain that he had to hold an icepack to it as he spoke during the interview. He just said it was the result of some dental work he'd had done before the start of the tour; it'd be better soon. But in fact, the jaw pain would haunt Cash for the rest of his life.

What had happened was that within days after a routine visit to the dentist in New York in January 1990 to have an abscessed tooth removed, Cash developed a cyst between the gum and his jaw, requiring surgery to cut into his mouth and scrape the cyst from the jawbone. The operation apparently weakened the jaw and caused even more agony. He was in such pain during a TV taping at the Grand Ole Opry on February 7 that he'd needed to use an icepack in between taping segments. After three hours he couldn't take it anymore, and he had to bow out of the show. June stepped in for him as co-host with Barbara Mandrell.

Despite more visits to the dentist, Cash found no escape from the suffering, and he had to cancel some concert dates in late February. But he was determined to keep his commitments to The Highwaymen—even after the pain intensified during a steak dinner a week before the opening date. Though he wouldn't know it for several weeks, the jaw was broken. The left side of his face was so swollen during the tour that a camera crew, which was shooting documentary footage, was instructed to shoot Cash only from the right side. He made it through the dates, but even his gritty resolve wasn't up to pressing on. He was unable to continue on the two-week European leg of the tour, causing the dates to be postponed.

Cash kept on thinking for years that he was just one doctor's visit or operation away from an end to his pain, but Lou Robin saw the operations fail time and again over the next few years—he estimated sixteen operations in all. "The pain was monstrous and it didn't let up," Mark Stielper says. "Such unending agony totally consumes one's life. It overwhelms everything else. But he couldn't do like the rest of us and go to bed. His was a public life. He wasn't a complainer, didn't make a point of airing all his ills in the marketplace. It would gall me when people would write that 'Johnny Cash looks like he's on drugs again' or complain because there wasn't a new record out or such. He was desperately trying to simply function day to day, to stay alive."

David Ferguson, who was Jack Clement's engineer, remembers meeting Cash when he stopped by Clement's studio one day. A Nashville native with an easygoing demeanor, Ferguson had been a Cash fan since childhood.

"I had heard Jack might be working on an album with John, but I was still surprised when he walked in unannounced one day," says Ferguson, who would be at the singer's side in the studio for most of the rest of Cash's life. "He was looking for Jack, but Jack was out somewhere, and John just made himself at home. I was so nervous meeting my hero, but he was as nice as he could be...no airs about him, plus he was so funny.

"At one point, he looks over and sees this expensive exercise bike that some salesman had talked Jack into buying even though everyone knew Jack was too lazy ever to get on it.... John finally turns to me and says, 'Well, who is Jack going to pay to ride that thing for him?'"

Ferguson also recalls darker times with Cash. He had visited Cash in Baptist Hospital after the heart surgery and pneumonia at the end of 1989. "I walked in and he was in there all alone, sitting in a wheelchair and looking so bad that I started crying. I had to leave the room. I felt so sorry for him. He was so sick."

A year later, after a European tour in December 1990, Cash stopped by Clement's office and Ferguson could tell he was hurting. He told Clement and Ferguson about how hard he had fought to get off the pills and then this jaw thing happened and now he couldn't help himself; he was back on the pain pills.

Ferguson wasn't prepared for what happened next. This time his hero was the one who cried.

CHAPTER 31

BRANSON, THE ROCK AND ROLL HALL OF FAME, AND U2

I

CASH WAS HONORED BY THE record industry again with a Living Legend Award—for ongoing contributions and influence in the recording field—during the Grammy ceremony in Los Angeles on February 21, 1991, but the affair left him melancholy. What "ongoing contributions"? If he was a legend, why was his career in such bad shape? The evening's other recipients—Aretha Franklin, Billy Joel, and Quincy Jones—were still going strong. The only future he saw for himself was more of the aches and pains that were coming at a distressing pace. Instead of the kick he used to get from the road, he longed more and more for the quiet comforts of home—reading his books, tending to his garden, and spending quality time with his family. In other words, retirement.

Retirement was a foreign concept to country singers; most of them kept performing the old hits as long as they could walk—or even be wheeled—onstage. Roy Acuff, the Grand Ole Opry patriarch, set the standard. When the singer's wife, Mildred, died in the 1980s, the Opry was all he had left; he moved into a house on the Opry grounds and kept taking his turn at the microphone, singing "Great Speckled Bird" or "Wabash Cannonball" whenever his health permitted. Acuff was eighty-seven the night Cash got the Grammy award.

Before his mounting health problems, Cash had assumed that he too would always keep performing, but no longer. Still, he couldn't figure out a way to retire; he had too many financial obligations. When Mark Stielper asked Cash about it, he said, "They won't let me retire." "They" were all those in the family, household, and band who depended on him for their income, a number that at any given time in the 1980s and 1990s ranged from thirty to forty. "Financially, he couldn't [retire]," Stielper says. "He needed advance money from the next tour to pay the bills from the last one."

And then there was more bad news from Mercury. Cash's fourth album for the label, *The Mystery of Life,* was another commercial failure. Once again, Cash blamed the label for a lack of interest in him. He insisted for years that the label had pressed only five hundred copies of the album. It was another of his exaggerations, but the underlying point was accurate. He wouldn't make another album for Mercury, which suited the label just fine.

Cash suffered the hardest blow on May 11 when his mother died of cancer at the age of eighty-one. In contrast to the ambiguity he felt after his father's death, Cash had always looked upon his mother as an unending source of inspiration and love. He had been pleased in the late 1980s when she suggested he open a museum and souvenir shop near the house, and he watched proudly as she greeted fans. Even after her death, Cash felt her presence. Whenever he was honored or otherwise felt blessed, he imagined her sharing the moment with him. At the same time, her death left him feeling increasing vulnerable. "Closing my mother's coffin was the hardest thing I've ever had to do," Cash told Ralph Emery, the Nashville TV version of Larry King.

Three days after the funeral at the First Baptist Church in Hendersonville, Cash felt the shadow of death again: eight members of Reba McEntire's band were killed when their chartered plane crashed into the side of a mountain near San Diego. The tragedy reminded him of all the other country entertainers who had been killed in plane crashes—including Patsy Cline—as well as the close calls he had had in the air. Cash was forced to think about his own mortality even more when, at McEntire's request, he delivered the eulogy at the funeral for the band members.

One positive thing about this season of darkness—which had begun with his heart surgery in 1988—was a deepening of his need and love for his wife. The illnesses and pills had pretty much erased his lingering sexual urges, leaving the infidelities a thing of the past. He was grateful to June for the way she had stayed by his side through all the tough times, and he felt increasingly responsible for her as she underwent trials of her own. June sensed this change in him, and she too felt closer and more devoted.

Until country music set up shop along the Highway 76 strip in the small town of Branson in the Missouri Ozarks, the community's only claim to pop culture fame was that it was part of the character Jed Clampett's old stomping grounds in the TV series *Beverly Hillbillies*. The show's creator, Paul Henning, spent time in Branson as a boy, and the town was mentioned—along with several other Ozark towns—in the show's early episodes outlining Clampett's past.

Branson's identity became tied to country music through a series of events in the 1980s. Developers saw country music as a way to lure tourists. First, the Roy Clark Celebrity Theatre opened early in the decade and served as a showcase for name entertainers. By the start of the 1990s, other country stars, including Mel Tillis, Ray Stevens, and Mickey Gilley, opened theaters, and millions of tourists a year were streaming into the entertainment center. To performers, Branson offered a place to perform without having to travel hundreds of miles between shows.

Cash was intrigued when a Southern California investor, David Green, approached him with a plan not only to build a 2,500-seat theater for him but also to construct a $35 million entertainment complex called Cash Country. Best of all, Cash didn't have to put any of his own money into the eighty-acre project, which would include an amusement park, go-car track, and souvenir shop. He'd get a royalty for the use of his name. Branson also promised an easier lifestyle. "The idea was to cut down on the road," Lou Robin says.

Not everybody thought it was a good move. Most contemporary country best-sellers looked at the city the way rock artists in the seventies and eighties looked at Las Vegas showrooms: it was decidedly unhip. "It was impulse," Rosanne says of the project. "Like

'Strawberry Cake' and 'The Baron,' like 'Chicken in Black.' All impulse....He was floundering a bit; there was something desperate about it and confused. He was trying to find his center. I think he realized that. I have a letter from him where he asks me to come and play at his theater in Branson, and I remember when I got it, I just kind of groaned, 'How long is this going to last?'"

Despite Cash's reservations, the appeal was too strong; he was in. With his star aboard, Green held a press conference in Branson on April 30 to announce the project, and construction began six months later.

"David Green made it all sound so perfect," Stielper says. "John and June could come off the road—a lot of expenses saved—and settle into Branson, in his own theater, where the people would come to him. At that point in his life—the Mercury relationship was dead, he was hemorrhaging money—it was too good to be true. And it was."

With the opening of the theater set for spring of 1992, Cash continued to tour steadily in 1991. He spent most of May in Australia with The Highwaymen, then a week in June with the group in Las Vegas. After more than fifty shows on his own, including some in Europe, he re-teamed with The Highwaymen in November in the States. The only recording was for a Christmas album, which was released by Delta Records after Mercury passed. He and June spent the holidays in Jamaica, where he enjoyed many fun-filled hours on the golf course driving range—not swinging a club but driving a golf cart around at high speed while John Rollins's son Ted leaned out of the cart and tried to grab golf balls off the ground. "It was best played when the driving range was active," Rollins says. "We called the game 'ball busters,' and we both thought it should be an Olympic sport."

II

Cash welcomed in 1992 with another major award. In an emotional ceremony on January 15 at the Waldorf Astoria hotel in New York City, he was inducted into the Rock and Roll Hall of Fame. Introducing Cash, Lyle Lovett praised his music for helping show the world what happens when "rural sensibilities and values mix with an urban environment."

For his part, Cash was on edge. He had never considered himself a true rock 'n' roller, and he worried that performers who were closer to the rock tradition would resent his inclusion. Indeed, there was some public questioning of Cash's credentials—enough for music journalist Karen Schoemer to write a stirring defense in the *New York Times:* "Mr. Cash's voice has a somber, bracing dignity that seems willing to bend or flinch for no one. His songs take their imagery from American mythos: train wheels, state lines, prison walls, barroom brawls, cotton fields, rivers and floods as great as those that swept the Bible. His characters...live by a rigid code of ethics that harks back to the Old West, yet Mr. Cash gives them all a resonance that speaks to the rebellious spirit rock cherishes so dearly. Man in Black, outlaw of justice, friend to the downtrodden, Mr. Cash has always been poised on the cusp between right and wrong, shadow and light; he walks the line between country sincerity and rock and roll autonomy."

To his relief, Cash found none of that questioning among the musicians and guests at the ceremony. He was touched by the warmth backstage of such major players as Keith Richards, John Fogerty, and record producer Phil Spector. Cash had spent the previous night working on a speech but ended up speaking extemporaneously. Rather than reflect on his own accomplishments, he thanked people who had helped him—especially Sam Phillips and Jack Clement. But he devoted most of his time, his voice quivering with emotion in places, expressing gratitude to the artists who had influenced him, country figures such as Hank Williams and the Carter Family, as well as blues and gospel artists, notably Sister Rosetta Tharpe. He also praised Alan Lomax's field recordings in the 1930s and 1940s, saying, "I listened to those by the hour and by the day, and the week, and the month."

On the day after the ceremony, Cash relaxed in his hotel suite, taking phone calls from well-wishers, including Bob Dylan, and joking with family members, including Rosanne, whose favorite moment was when her father joined a line of celebrated rock guitarists on a freewheeling version of Jimi Hendrix's "Purple Haze."

"That was the most psychedelic experience of my life," Rosanne said, laughing so hard that she doubled up in the chair. "I mean, I'm the kid who wore a black armband to school the day Hendrix died...so the last thing I ever thought I would see was my daddy on a stage playing acoustic guitar on 'Purple Haze.'"

Cash laughed along. "I got the biggest kick out of it [the jam] when Keith Richards saw that I was watching Fogerty to get the keys we were supposed to be playing and Keith leaned over and said, 'Thank God you're watching him, because I sure don't know what the hell I'm doing either.'

"But you know what really blew me away? I was standing at the urinal in the rest room before the dinner and I heard this voice behind me singing 'Loading Coal,' which is probably one of the most obscure songs I ever recorded [from the *Ride This Train* album]. I wondered who in the world could be singing that song, and when I looked around, I saw Keith, and he had this big smile on his face. So I turned around and we sang the chorus together. That's when I guess I knew everything was going to be okay."

This was one time when Cash was not making up a story. Keith Richards once described himself as a Johnny Cash freak—to the point of paying him this remarkable compliment: "As far as early rock 'n' roll goes, if someone came up to me and for some reason they could only get a collection of one person's music, I'd say 'Chuck Berry is important, but, man, you've got to get the Cash.'"

Cash was only a month away from turning sixty, but he was feeling briefly renewed. After two nights performing at the Trump Castle Hotel and Casino in Atlantic City, he and June headed back to Israel to film an Easter TV special for the Nashville Network. When the cable channel eventually passed on the project, Cash and aides redesigned the footage into a forty-five-minute home video titled *Return to the Promised Land,* which was released in the fall of 1993 by Billy Graham's World Wide Pictures. It was finally time for Branson.

Most of the complex in Branson was still in the early stages of construction, but the Johnny Cash Theater itself was scheduled to open on May 15, even though it looked far from finished when Cash did a national TV interview early that month with Larry King. Cash had been increasingly dubious about the project as he learned of various setbacks in construction. Still, he was prepared to fulfill his contract.

Under his deal with Green, Cash would perform ninety-four dates between May and December, sometimes a matinee as well as an evening show. He was guaranteed $30,000 per day and 35 percent of box office grosses if receipts totaled $65,000 for the day. The main lure continued to be the break from highways and airports. Cash planned to be joined onstage in Branson by June, the Carter Family, John Carter Cash, and a four-piece band that included W. S. Holland.

Because Cash wouldn't be appearing there full-time, Green asked Lou Robin to book some other acts to fill in the vacant nights. Among those Robin signed were Wayne Newton, who had been a huge draw for years in Las Vegas and was a real coup for upstart Branson, as well as magician David Copperfield, rock veterans the Everly Brothers, and such country stars as Eddie Rabbitt and Crystal Gayle. But it was all for nothing. The theater wasn't ready by May 15 or July 15. In August, Green threw in the towel and filed for Chapter 11 bankruptcy.

The news jolted Cash. He worried that his reputation would take another hit, because many people in Nashville, not realizing he hadn't actually invested in the project, would see Cash Country as his failure. He also felt bad for the workmen and suppliers who hadn't been fully paid. Even before the official bankruptcy, Cash was angry—doubly so because he had been seduced into what he had come to see as a demeaning career move. In a May 30 letter to Marty Stuart, he took a slap at the pandering entertainers and undemanding audiences he saw in the tourist center: "If he (or she) is an entertainer each show should be opened with the line—'Good evening. Elvis will be out a little later.'"

With his plans suddenly up in the air, Cash headed to New York in mid-October to appear on *Late Night with David Letterman* and then pay tribute to Bob Dylan during a televised thirtieth-anniversary salute to the singer before sixteen thousand people at Madison Square Garden. During the show, whose cast also included Tom Petty, Eric Clapton, and Dylan, John and June sang "It Ain't Me, Babe" to a warm response.

Then, unexpectedly, Branson came calling for a second time. A federal bankruptcy judge approved Green's $4.1 million sale of the property in November to Branson-based developers, who announced they hoped to begin hosting shows at the theater the following spring. Jim Thomas, one of the new buyers, had doubted that Cash would want to perform at the theater because of his hard feelings from the Cash Country experience. But he was wrong. Cash still needed the money, and his body was pleading for a break from the road. As Cash continued to tour on his own and with The Highwaymen, Lou Robin worked out a deal for him to play the newly renamed venue which was now set to open in the spring of 1993: the Wayne Newton Theatre.

What proved to be the most important thirty-day stretch in Cash's career since Folsom began in early February 1993 with an encounter in Dublin with the Irish band U2 and ended with his meeting an admiring record producer in California.

Cash had first met Bono in the late 1980s when Jack Clement brought Bono and bassist Adam Clayton by Cash's house for dinner. In most cases when Cash met with admiring young rock musicians, including the Beatles in San Francisco in the 1960s, the visits were pleasant, but little more than that. It was different with U2, especially the group's young lead singer. A bit like Cash himself, Bono was at once respectful and rebellious.

Cash had liked the way this articulate and entertaining young man was interested not just in music but in history and spirituality. Cash ended up talking about Saint Paul with Bono that night at dinner and gave him a signed copy of *Man in White*. The pair even tried writing a song together, titled "Ellis Island," though they never finished it. Cash enjoyed it when Bono good-naturedly challenged his claim that he was descended from Scottish royalty, insisting instead that Cash was Irish. Recalling the meeting years later, Bono says, "I told him there was this large Cash family in Ireland and they all looked exactly like him."

The Irishman's favorite moment came at dinner. "We were all holding hands around the table and Johnny said the most beautiful, most poetic grace you've ever heard. Then he leaned over to me with this devilish look in his eye and said, 'But I sure miss the drugs.' It was that contradiction that I admired about his music as well. It was hard and it was caring, it was about sinful behavior and devotion."

Bono and Clayton had such a great time that the band paid homage to Cash in their *Rattle and Hum* album package with a huge photo of them in the Sun studio just beneath a framed photo of Phillips and Cash.

In the early weeks of 1993, Bono was working on a song, originally called "The Pilgrim," for the band's upcoming *Zooropa* album. The narrative was inspired by a character in the Book of Ecclesiastes—specifically a sinner's lonely, tortured search for wisdom and faith. To freshen the story, Bono gave it a futuristic spin. The band had the melody down, but Bono wasn't pleased with the words or his vocal. When he heard about Cash's upcoming concert date in Dublin, he realized the song would be perfect for Cash. Changing the title to "The Wanderlust" and then "The Wanderer," Bono wrote the final version of the tune with Cash in mind.

On the day of Cash's Dublin show in February, Bono invited him to join U2 in the studio to record the song. He was flattered but anxious. It had been three years since he'd had a meaningful solo recording session, and here he was with the biggest rock band in the world. To make him even more unsettled, the band's swirling, highly layered techno-ish sound was a long way from *boom-chicka-boom*. Was he really right for this song? Was the band just trying to be nice and help him gain some attention?

As soon as Cash read the lyrics, however, he began to feel at ease. Talking about the song later, he said, "It's the search for three important things: God, that woman, and myself." He delivered each line with a conviction and empathy that rivaled his performance on "Sunday Mornin' Comin' Down." These weren't his words, but they were his story:

I went out walking through streets paved with gold
Lifted some stones, saw the skin and bones
Of a city without a soul
I went out walking under an atomic sky

Where the ground won't turn and the rain it burns
Like the tears when I said goodbye.

Yeah, I went with nothing, nothing but the thought of you.
I went wandering.

I went drifting through the capitals of tin
Where men can't walk or freely talk
And sons turn their fathers in.
I stopped outside a church house
Where the citizens like to sit.
They say they want the kingdom
But they don't want God in it.

I went out riding down that old eight-lane
I passed by a thousand signs looking for my own name.
I went with nothing but the thought you'd be there too
Looking for you.

I went out there in search of experience
To taste and to touch and to feel as much
As a man can before he repents.

I went out searching, looking for one good man
A spirit who would not bend or break
Who would sit at his father's right hand.
I went out walking with a bible and a gun
The word of God lay heavy on my heart
I was sure I was the one.

Now Jesus, don't you wait up, Jesus, I'll be home soon.
Yeah, I went out for the papers, told her I'd be back by noon.
Yeah, I left with nothing but the thought you'd be there too
Looking for you.

Yeah I went with nothing, nothing but the thought of you.
I went wandering.

Bono has frequently said there's a moment during the band's best nights onstage when the feeling in the venue is so joyful that it's as if God is walking through the room. Bono and Cash both felt that spirit during this session.

"To me, Johnny Cash—with all his contradictions—was a quintessential character of the scriptures, or at least the characters in the Bible that interested me," Bono says. "I remember at Trinity College [in Dublin] when someone put out a pamphlet pointing out how flawed all the people in the Bible were....David was an adulterer, Moses was a murderer, Jacob was a cheater. These were some wild blokes. Well, one day someone put out the same pamphlet, but wrote on it something like 'That's why I'm a believer. If God had time for these flawed characters, then God has time for me.' And I think Johnny and I shared that view."

At the Dublin concert, Cash brought Bono, The Edge, and Larry Mullen on stage that night to sing "Big River" with him.

Despite the excitement of the session, Cash left Dublin in much the same melancholy mood that followed the Grammy Award ceremony. The brilliance of the song made him feel all the more uncertain about his place in the music world. He couldn't even imagine U2 actually putting the track on the album, and he thought about calling Bono to say he'd understand if the band wanted to redo it with Bono's voice. But Bono beat him to the punch. He called to assure Cash that the song was going to be on the album. "I felt like it was a real connection, a very spiritual thing," Cash said of his work with U2. "These guys are really spiritual people. I also loved the way they reached millions of people with their message."

Heading back to the States, Cash tried to prepare mentally for what he expected to be the last chapter of his musical career: his Branson debut in May. But first he had some more tour dates, starting with a couple of routine club stops in California—the Great American Music Hall in San Francisco on February 26 and the Rhythm Café in Santa Ana the following day. For someone used to playing 18,000-seat arenas in both regions, the size of the clubs—about 550 seats each—was too significant to ignore. But Santa Ana was where he met Rick Rubin.

CHAPTER 32

RICK RUBIN

I

THE ONLY CHILD OF AN upper-middle-class family from Long Island, New York, Rick Rubin grew up on hard rock and punk, but his entry into the record business was via hip-hop, a genre he became obsessed with while a pre-med student at New York University in the late 1970s. He especially loved the way DJs in clubs came up with dynamic sounds by "scratching"—rapidly twisting and turning vinyl recordings on spinning turntables. When he noticed that rap recordings lacked that club energy because producers used real musicians instead of turntable DJs, Rubin began making records in his NYU dorm room employing "scratching" and other bits of turntable wizardry. The difference was immense.

After gaining attention around New York City when the first record he produced was a huge club hit, he teamed with a bright young entrepreneur named Russell Simmons to start Def Jam Recordings, which they would build into the Motown of hip-hop. At Def Jam, Rubin produced such hit acts as the socially conscious Public Enemy and rap 'n' punk rockers the Beastie Boys. In the early 1990s, wanting to expand his musical terrain, he moved to Los Angeles, where he won even more success and acclaim working with rock and heavy-metal acts, including the Red Hot Chili

Peppers, Slayer, and Tom Petty and the Heartbreakers. By his late twenties he was being hailed as his generation's Phil Spector.

The path to Cash grew out of a desire to set new challenges for himself. Instead of working just with youngish rockers, he wanted to connect with someone who was "great and important, but who wasn't doing their best work. I wanted to see if I could help them do great work again."

Cash was skeptical when Lou Robin told him a rap producer wanted to make a record with him, but he figured, what the heck. He invited Rubin to come to the show at the Rhythm Café, about an hour's drive south of L.A. When the burly young man with the long, unruly beard and gentle, Zen-like manner walked into the dressing room, Cash didn't know what to make of him. Cash later described his first impression of Rubin as "the ultimate hippie, bald on top, but with hair down over his shoulders, a beard that looked as if it had never been trimmed and clothes that would have done a wino proud."

Rubin was a man of as few words as Cash, which meant there wasn't a lot said that night. Robin remembers them sitting on a couch, just staring at each other for several minutes. June thought the idea of John working with a heavy-metal producer was absurd, but Cash sensed an independence in Rubin that he liked. Besides, there were no other options. He thought his record career was over. He agreed to get together with Rubin to see what they could come up with.

Thanks to Mercury's lack of interest in Cash, who still owed the label one more album, Rubin was easily able to work out a deal. He paid Mercury a modest royalty on Cash's future album sales and got the rights to sign Cash to his American Recordings label. "More than anything, I got the feeling that he was curious about why I would want to work with him," Rubin says. "My first challenge was to rebuild his confidence."

"I'd love to hear some of your favorite songs."

Those were Rubin's first words to Cash when they sat down in the producer's spacious home high above the celebrated Sunset Strip in Los Angeles on May 17, 1993, to begin exploring the process of making an album together. It was just two weeks before Cash's debut in Branson.

Normally, Rubin would spend lots of time talking to acts he was working with for the first time, trying to learn about them so he could better understand their music. With the reserved, soft-spoken Cash, Rubin realized he needed to reverse the process; he would learn about Cash the person through his music. Wanting to keep things informal, Rubin didn't even turn on the recording equipment when he asked Cash to sing some of his favorite songs. Accompanying himself on acoustic guitar, Cash responded with all kinds of tunes—cowboy songs, train songs, gospel songs, heart-break songs, funny songs.

On their second night together, Cash went into a number that caught Rubin's attention. The producer didn't know if it was a song or a poem; he just knew it was the kind of strong personal state-ment he associated with Cash's best work in the 1950s and 1960s. He reached over and turned on the recording equipment and asked Cash to repeat the number. To Rubin's mind, he wasn't recording songs for a record, just assembling ideas. The song was "Bury Me Not on the Lone Prairie," a popular nineteenth-century folk song that Cash learned as a boy in Dyess and included in the *Ballads of the True West* album. But it wasn't the song that intrigued Rubin so much as the two-minute recitation that preceded it, a personal statement of faith.

"It got back to the sort of mystical root of who Johnny Cash is," Rubin says. "It was something that sounded like it was coming from someplace deep inside of him. It was epic, and that's what Johnny was to me—epic."

The recitation, in fact, was a poem, "A Cowboy's Prayer," written in the 1920s by Charles Badger Clark, who was the first poet laureate of South Dakota. The words summarized Cash's own feelings about finding his greatest connection with God outside church walls.

When he finished the number again, Cash paused, then started it a third time, perhaps feeling he could do a better version of it. Ap-parently satisfied, he went on to "Just the Other Side of Nowhere," a song from one of the first demo tapes Kris Kristofferson had ever given him. Again, Rubin cheered him on.

Warmed by Rubin's show of enthusiasm, Cash then did something that surprised even him. He started singing a song he had written four years earlier but refused to record because he was too protective of it; he didn't want it wasted on a Mercury album that no one would hear. The song, "Drive On," was an evocative look at buddies from Vietnam and the emotional scars of that war. Again Rubin was intrigued. Cash later explained that the song was "really a piece of history." The lines, including the "drive on" exhortation, came right out of the mouths of troops, and he wanted the song to demonstrate their resilience and resolve. "It wasn't pro-war or antiwar or anything else," Cash said. "It's just pro-people." The song also echoed the "Sail on!" optimism of the Joaquin Miller poem he'd loved as a boy.

It was the next song Cash played that night, however, that proved to be the breakthrough in the pair's relationship: "Delia's Gone."

Looking back at those early meetings, Cash often drew a parallel between Rubin's patient manner and Sam Phillips's similar approach in the studio. As he told music writer Sylvie Simmons, "Sam Phillips put me in front of that microphone at Sun Records in 1955 for the first time and said, 'Let's hear what you've got. Sing your heart out,' and I'd sing one or two and he'd say, 'Sing another one, let's hear one more.'"

The even more remarkable parallel, Cash would come to understand, was between what Rubin did for him in those Sunset Strip get-togethers and what Phillips did with a fledgling Elvis Presley in 1954. When Elvis sat down with Phillips, he needed direction—he needed an outside listener to point out where his strengths lay. During Presley's first recording session, Phillips gave it to him by declaring after the impromptu version of "That's All Right," "That's it."

Though Rubin had never heard it before, "Delia's Gone" was the old folk-blues song that Cash had rewritten in the 1960s into his own statement about violence and remorse. By singling the song out, Rubin was saying, in essence, "That's it." It went:

> *Delia, oh, Delia Delia all my life*
> *If I hadn't have shot poor Delia*

I'd have had her for my wife
Delia's gone, one more round Delia's gone.

I went up to Memphis
And I met Delia there
Found her in her parlor
And I tied her to her chair
Delia's gone, one more round Delia's gone.

She was low down and trifling
And she was cold and mean
Kind of evil make me want to
Grab my sub machine
Delia's gone, one more round Delia's gone.

First time I shot her
I shot her in the side
Hard to watch her suffer
But with the second shot she died
Delia's gone, one more round Delia's gone.

But jailer, oh, jailer
Jailer, I can't sleep
'Cause all around my bedside
I hear the patter of Delia's feet
Delia's gone, one more round Delia's gone.

So if your woman's devilish
You can let her run
Or you can bring her down and do her
Like Delia got done
Delia's gone, one more round Delia's gone.

This was the tough, hard-edged side of Cash that Rubin wanted to hear, the side he felt had largely been missing from Cash's recordings since he became a symbol of American goodness and family in the 1970s. What Cash had lost during that period was the confidence and inner drive to continue pushing musical and cultural boundaries. Rubin's goal was to help Cash regain his confidence in ways that would brush away all those years of uneven, sometimes indifferent recordings—almost as if Cash had never lost track of the bold, maverick tradition of his best fifties and sixties recordings. Rubin didn't want to take Cash back to the earlier decades, but he did want to see what kind of music Cash, at sixty-one, would make if he could recapture the spirit of the singer-songwriter who first electrified the pop world at Folsom Prison.

"I'm talking about the original Johnny Cash who loomed large and was surrounded by all this darkness, yet who still had vulnerability," Rubin says. "I wanted, if you will, to take him back to the 'I shot a man in Reno just to watch him die' Man in Black, and 'Delia's Gone' did it perfectly. He kills the girl, and then is remorseful. I loved how the brutal act was followed by this haunted life. I was trying to get him to go from all these years of thinking his best stuff was behind him and just phoning in records to thinking we could make his best albums ever. I don't know if he really believed that, but he was willing to give it a try."

Not only was Rubin surprised by how good a song "Drive On" was, but he was even more impressed by "Like a Soldier," another song Cash wrote during the Mercury period but kept to himself until he felt he was in good hands. In it, Cash used the image of a duty-bound military survivor to describe his own struggles and the prospects for a blessing of salvation. In some ways it was a sequel to Kristofferson's song "The Pilgrim, Chapter 33," with its Cash-inspired lines about "a walkin' contradiction partly truth and partly fiction / Taking every wrong direction on his lonely way back home." In "Like a Soldier," Cash was back home and looking back over his journey.

The lyrics of the graceful song go in part:

> *Like a soldier getting over the war*
> *Like a young man getting over his crazy days*
> *Like a bandit getting over his lawless ways*
> *Every day is better than before*
> *I'm like a soldier getting over the war*

There were nights I don't remember
And there's pain that I've forgotten
Other things I choose not to recall
There are faces that come to me
In my darkest secret memory
Faces that I wish would not come back at all

But in my dreams' parade of lovers
From the other times and places
There's not one that matters now, no matter who
I'm just thankful for the journey
And that I've survived the battles
And that my spoils of victory are you.

Rubin was amazed by what he was hearing. This was even more than he had imagined. Almost immediately, he began thinking about ways to enhance the impact of the songs by applying more musical shading, but he wasn't ready to bring musicians in yet. He wanted more of the pure Cash. Things were going so well that Rubin began suggesting a few songs for Cash, notably "Thirteen," a tale of bad luck and hard times written for Cash by heavy-metal rocker Glenn Danzig, and "Down There by the Train," a story of sin and salvation by Tom Waits.

"I wasn't trying to look for songs that would 'connect' Johnny to a younger audience," Rubin says. "I was just trying to find songs that really made sense for his voice. By that I don't mean baritone. I mean resonate with his character so he could sing the words and have them feel like he wrote them."

After three days they had nearly three dozen songs on tape. Rubin was ecstatic. And as he left for Branson, Cash was cautiously optimistic.

II

Going from Rubin's living room to the Wayne Newton Theatre in Branson was a case of culture shock in the extreme. Cash wasn't even able to enjoy the luster of playing in his own theater, as he had earlier envisioned. All the attention in the venue was focused on Newton. When the theater opened in early May, the newspaper account told it all: "If anyone still doubted that Branson had hit the big time, they needed only to be on hand last weekend when a glowing spaceship arrived amid blasts of smoke and streams of laser lights. In a stage show the likes of which this southwest Missouri town has never seen, the King of Las Vegas took his place on his own Ozarks throne."

A concluding paragraph underscored Cash's secondary role: "When [Newton's] away from Branson for short stints back in Las Vegas this summer, Johnny Cash will fill in."

Things were worse than Cash imagined when he opened his first two-week engagement on May 31. The atmosphere was touristy, leading him to wonder if the audience even cared about the music. Most of the crowd were bus tour groups who were simply attending shows that the tour organizers had lined up for them. They expected to be led backstage after the show for autographs, pictures, and chit-chat, things that Cash might have enjoyed at one time in his career but not now that his health was such an issue.

Kathy Cash operated a souvenir shop in Branson at the time. "Dad hated the whole retirement aura of Branson," she recalls. "One day he said, 'Do you know the difference between *Jurassic Park* and Branson? Blue hair.'"

As the word got out that Cash wasn't going to be available for all the gladhanding, attendance at his shows slowly decreased. Paid attendance the second week, for instance, ranged from 907 to 2,084. His guarantee was down $10,000 from the 1991 pact and the number of days was cut to forty.

Two weeks after the Branson engagement, Cash was back in Rubin's living room offering new versions of songs from the May sessions as well as recording additional ones. Rubin continued to tape his vocals to help him decide which songs might work best together on an album.

Part of Rubin's genius was that he didn't simply portray Cash as a rebel. He wanted to break through the public image of Cash as a superhero by capturing his human side—the struggle and the pain and the grit. Says Rubin, "When I asked artists what they admired about him, that's what they often mentioned—that vulnerable, hurt aspect, the man who wouldn't give up."

Rubin especially liked Cash's rendition of Danzig's "Thirteen," and he asked Cash to open the new session by redoing the song, this time accompanied on guitar by Danzig himself. Pleased with the result, Rubin began thinking the tune could sound great on the album alongside "Delia's Gone."

Cash's hopes for the coming album continued to rise, while many of those around him tried to caution him against putting too much faith in this "bearded hippie." They didn't want to see Cash set himself up for another painful fall.

Tom Petty, whose new album, *Wildflowers,* was being produced by Rubin concurrently, was confident that Cash was in good hands. A fan ever since buying the *Folsom Prison* album as a teenager and seeing Cash weekly on the ABC show, Petty admired him for his socially conscious music and for bringing so many cool guests on the show. "He wrote about real things and America in a way that didn't feel phony to me," says Petty.

Like so many, Petty lost track of Cash for years—remembering only one album from the 1970s and 1980s: the dreadful *Look at Them Beans.* After playing it, he asked himself, "'God, what's happened to him?' It was obvious he was kinda lost," recalls Petty, "but I still admired him for what he had done earlier."

When Rubin mentioned to Petty early in 1993 that he was thinking about working with Cash, Petty urged him on. "Rick was just over the moon about working with Johnny. I don't know if any record meant more to him than Johnny's."

Two days after returning to Branson on July 6, there was another death in Cash's circle—his older brother Roy, who had been second only to his mother in encouraging him to become a singer. John and June attended the funeral in Memphis. He at first declined when his nephew Roy Jr. asked him to deliver the eulogy. "Oh, Roy, I don't know if I can do that," Cash objected. "I may come apart." But he eventually relented, and he expressed his love for his brother. He was most moved that day when Roy Jr.'s daughter Kellye, Miss America 1987, sang the closing hymn, "I Bowed on My Knees and Cried Holy." A few days later, Cash called her to say he'd had no "real peace in Roy's passing and the funeral until I heard you sing that piece of music, and I now know that Roy is in heaven."

There was still more reason for Cash to despair. He wasn't the only one relying on pills to keep him going. Both June and John Carter were struggling against growing addiction problems.

John Carter, in his early twenties, had checked in to rehab units in 1991 and 1992, but he was showing signs of deepening depression. His world turned infinitely darker in 1993 when he found his mother passed out on the floor in Branson. He rushed to her side, flashing on all the times when he had feared for his father's life in similar situations. "Mom!" he shouted, "Wake up! Please, Mom."

If what happened next hadn't been so tragic, he wrote later, it would have been almost comical. "She rolled over, her long hair splayed over her face, opened her eyes, and focused on me deliberately. 'I am awake,' she answered calmly. 'I was in meditation.'"

It was John Carter's introduction to his mother's addiction, and it terrified him. Just as drugs stole his father from him in the 1980s, he feared addiction might now take his mother away.

In *Anchored in Love* he wrote: "For so long Mom had obsessed over the addictions of her husband, her daughters and her son. Next she moved into denial. Then came the time, I believe, when she had simply had enough, when the struggle with the addicts in her life overcame her strength and resolve. With no better way of describing it, I think the cumulative mental, physical and emotional pain combined in such a way that the drug use eventually seemed OK to her.

"She would never have acknowledged that she too was an addict. I believe she always had the illusion of control, as though the drugs were her friends, her helpers. I think she thought of herself as the master, not the slave, of the pills she took. After all, she never got angry, fell down or picked a fight with her loved ones when she was under the influence of narcotics. She simply stopped speaking in full sentences and went off into her own world. Her mind was not the same."

With all this heartache around Cash, music once again became his chief escape and hope, a way to rally against the tensions and pressures—physical, emotional, and financial—in his life. Though he still drew upon his faith, he was finally back to a place where he was looking to music for self-affirmation. Through every concert and every bus ride and every sleepless night, he longed for the day when he would go back to Rubin's living room and sing his heart out.

III

When recording resumed July 21, Cash was unusually productive. Over three days he sang more than two dozen songs, including two more that had been suggested by Rubin: Neil Young's "Heart of Gold" and Leonard Cohen's "Bird on The Wire." He also played a new one of his own, "Redemption," a solemn tale of the liberating power of the blood of Jesus.

As Cash headed back on the road for most of August, Rubin brought in some musicians to explore dressing up some of the tracks—guitarist Mike Campbell from Tom Petty and the Heartbreakers, and bassist Flea and drummer Chad Smith, both from the Chili Peppers. To experiment further, he later went through the songs again with the Red Devils, a blues-rock band that was generating a lot of excitement on the L.A. club scene.

One song Cash recorded during this period was "Devil's Right Hand" by an acclaimed young singer-songwriter in Cash's own maverick country-rock tradition. Steve Earle was one of scores of musicians who would name Cash's TV show as a major influence. "That show was my main cultural touchstone," Earle says. "Where else could I see Bob Dylan, Neil Young, and Derek and the Dominos alongside Roger Miller and Merle Haggard? The show made me feel that having long hair and wearing cowboy boots in Texas wasn't so weird after all." (When Earle spent two months in jail for cocaine and weapons possession in 1994, he remembers fondly that Cash was one of only three musicians who wrote him a note. The others were Emmylou Harris and Waylon Jennings.)

After weeks of experimenting, Rubin decided that less was more; he favored the intimacy of the solo recordings. In fact, he would use those living room vocals for the record. "I didn't want anything to distract from Johnny," Rubin recalls. "I wanted his presence to fill the record." With the format resolved, Rubin felt it was time for the next step. He wanted Cash to perform the songs live, so he booked the hip Viper Room on the Sunset Strip for the night of December 3.

He chose the Viper Room, which was partly owned by Johnny Depp, because it was small; Cash's appearance there would be more of an exclusive event than if he had played one of the bigger mainstream clubs, such as the Troubadour or the Roxy. Mainly, however, Rubin had Cash's needs more in mind than the audience's. He wanted to introduce John to the role of facing an audience alone.

"That was an enormous leap—to go from the safety onstage or in the studio of singing with a band behind you to just facing an audience with your own guitar," Rubin says. "Once we decided that we were going to make it a solo acoustic album, I noticed a change in him when he was just singing in my living room. Before, he had been relaxed and singing in a very personal, intimate way. But suddenly he changed. He began *performing* the songs, and it wasn't the same.

"What I was looking for was a direct transmission from his heart, and we had that at first. There was even a point—and we have it on tape—where I am saying to him between songs, 'Can we try to do it a little more personal?' and he understood, because he says to himself, 'Get off the stage, Cash.'"

For Rubin, the Viper Room show was part of the process of getting Cash comfortable singing the songs by himself. He figured once Cash got over the anxiety of singing in front of an audience—and he was terrified that night—it would be easier for him to sing when he returned to the informality of Rubin's living room.

Cash had his usual second thoughts about the whole approach. To try the solo role on someone whose judgment he trusted, he sang several of the songs he was planning to sing at the Viper Room for Marty Stuart in Nashville. "I could tell he had done this for four or five other people, looking for [affirmation]," Stuart says. "I told him, 'I can't see nothing wrong with this; this is as pure as it gets.

I think it resets country music's clock. It absolutely takes it back to a new beginning, setting it up for the twenty-first century. In some way, it can parallel what the Carter Family and Jimmie Rodgers did at Bristol.' I said, 'Country music needs that, and in broader terms, American music could use it too.'"

At the Viper, where Cash was introduced by Depp, the tastemaker audience—including Sean Penn and members of the Chili Peppers—was enthralled. Rubin sensed a buzz starting even before Cash concluded his ninety-minute set with renditions of some of his early hits. "Cash was nervous, but the show was a triumph," Petty recalls. "Johnny was so happy. He felt like he was starting to matter again." (Depp was Cash's first choice when asked who he would like to see portray him in any future movie.) To follow up quickly, Rubin took Cash back into his living room three more times that week to make the final series of recordings—and sure enough, Cash was looser. The Viper Room experience had made him more comfortable singing on his own. On the first night, Cash even played Rick another of his unrecorded songs, "Let the Train Whistle Blow," a bittersweet farewell that combined warmth, independence, and bravado.

After those sessions, Rubin and Cash picked thirteen songs for the album, and Rubin then listened to all the various solo versions to pick the most evocative take on each song. Most of the final choices, as it turned out, dated back to the original living room sessions in May. Cash was pleased with the decision to make the album barebones. He told Rubin he had been thinking about a solo acoustic album for years; he even had a title, *Late and Alone*. Rubin preferred *American Recordings*. He felt it better fit Cash's classic status in American popular music, and, of course, it was the title of Rubin's record label. With the content settled during the early days of 1994, Rubin and his staff focused on marketing.

He got an unexpected assist when U2's *Zooropa* became not only an international best-seller that stayed on the U.S. sales charts for forty weeks but also a huge critical success, thanks in part to "The Wanderer."

Writing in *Rolling Stone,* Anthony DeCurtis couldn't have given more glowing praise to the collaboration: "It's a wildly audacious

move that could so easily have proved a pathetic embarrassment—U2 overreaching for significance again—but it works brilliantly. Speak-singing with all the authority of an Old Testament
prophet, Cash movingly serves as a link to a lost world of moral
surety, literally replacing the various corrupted and confused personas Bono...had occupied in the course of the album. Cash's
'Wanderer' is no less lost than the album's other dead souls, but his
yearning to be found and redeemed sets him apart."

Cash didn't know what to expect in the weeks before *American
Recordings* was released in May 1994. He even mailed advance
copies to a few people whose judgment he valued, asking the
straightforward question "What do you think my fans will think of
this?" He was encouraged by the responses. At the same time, an
equally anxious Rubin was heartened when his marketing and publicity teams reported they were finding lots of interest in the project.
He was overjoyed the day he got an early copy of *Rolling Stone's* review of *American Recordings*.

The write-up wasn't just a rave; it was a game changer in every
sense for Cash and Rubin. Not only did the magazine give the album the coveted lead review space, but it was paired with a review
of an album by another American musical landmark, Frank Sinatra. To make things even better, Anthony DeCurtis gave the Sinatra
album high praise, calling it the "finest available glimpse of the
singer onstage: easy, affable and in command," but went on to say
the Cash album was "an even more crowning achievement."

He called the album at once "monumental and viscerally intimate, fiercely true to the legend of Johnny Cash and entirely contemporary." And DeCurtis was just warming up. He maintained
that Cash's voice sounded better than it had in more than forty
years, and his singing reflected "a control reminiscent of Heming-
way's writing. Not a feeling is flaunted, not a jot of sentimentality is
permitted, but every quaver, every shift in volume, every catch in a
line resonates like a private apocalypse."

Cash read the review time and again, trying to convince himself
that his years in musical exile were over. It was, to his knowledge,
the first time in two decades that *Rolling Stone* had even bothered

to review one of his albums. Over the next few weeks, he read scores of raves in other publications as well. "It's been ages since anyone of Cash's stature bared himself so completely—and successfully—as the Man in Black does on his first album for Rick Rubin's record label," Randy Lewis wrote in the *Los Angeles Times*. "With just his own unmistakably craggy voice and acoustic-guitar accompaniment, Cash has collected 13 songs that peer into the dark corners of the American soul. In that respect, it's akin to Clint Eastwood's 'Unforgiven,' both in its valedictory, folklore-rich tone and in its wealth of characters who embody good and evil in varying proportions. A milestone work for this legendary singer."

Though he wanted desperately for all his albums and artists to succeed, Rubin had developed a special fondness for Cash, and he dearly wanted him to regain the respect and attention he deserved. He also felt a responsibility: he had led Cash into this new, unknown territory.

To spread the word, Cash did a show and delivered the keynote address at the annual South by Southwest music festival in Austin, Texas, a prestigious showcase for vital new music. Knowing the importance of video in reaching record buyers, Rubin showcased Cash in a stark black-and-white video of "Delia's Gone" in which Cash tossed dirt over the murdered Delia's face as she lay in her open grave. MTV objected to some of the imagery in the video, which was directed by Anton Corbin, the Dutch photographer who had shot U2's *Joshua Tree* album cover. Corbin defended his work, calling the video's message "anti-violence."

The resulting controversy delighted Rubin, who wanted to position Cash on the cutting edge of contemporary music. "From the beginning of rock 'n' roll there's always been a stark figure that never really fits," he told *Rolling Stone*. "He's still the quintessential outsider. In the hip-hop world you see all these bad boy artists who are juggling being on MTV and running from the law. Johnny was the originator of that."

To further emphasize that maverick image, Rubin selected a photo for the album cover that showed a menacing Cash, wearing a full-length preacher's coat and standing in the wilderness holding onto his guitar case with two dogs at his side. It was an image reminiscent of Robert Mitchum in the role of the crazed preacher in the film *The Night of the Hunter.* "They did the photo shoot while Johnny was on tour in Australia, and the idea was just to show him with his guitar," Rubin says. "This stark image fit the mood of the album, but the whole thing about the dogs was an accident. John thought it was great—the fact that one was black and one was white. To him, it was the idea of sin and redemption."

By most standards, the album was only a modest success. It's easy to see why the country music establishment—including country radio—would turn a cold shoulder. Here was an "outsider," Rick Rubin, stepping in and tampering with a Nashville artist. Plus, they maintained, this wasn't even a country record. Cash was doing songs by a heavy-metal rocker and Tom Waits, for goodness' sake. And finally, country radio had already turned Cash out to pasture; there was no reason to backtrack now.

Even so, *American Recordings* made it to the middle of the country charts, likely propelled by old fans intrigued by all the media praise. But the real audience for the album proved to be the young, adventurous wing of the rock 'n' roll market. The album sold nearly 80,000 copies in its first two months—a figure the *New York Times* called disappointing. But it was a victory for Rubin and Cash. The CD sold more copies than any Cash album since *Man in Black* in 1971. By the end of the year, the figure had reached nearly 150,000.

More important to Rubin, the album's impact on critics and tastemakers laid a foundation. "I felt as if we were starting from scratch and introducing a new recording artist," Rubin says. "By those standards, the album was a huge success."

For Cash, making music was once again a consuming force in his life. He was no longer, as he had for years, leaving everything to chance. He felt relevant.

"I was worried that I had blown everything by not treating my music seriously enough for all those years," Cash told me. "I was even starting to think that no one would care about it after I was gone. But Rick made me think I might have a legacy after all...and even add to it. I vowed not to let it slip away again."

Cash's daughter Rosanne looked at the new relationship in even more dramatic terms. "Rick came along at exactly the right time," she says. "Before Rick, Dad was depressed, discouraged. It was a powerful thing that happened between them, and Dad was completely revitalized and back to his old enthusiastic self. I think Rick saved his life at that moment. Well, maybe 'saved his life' is too strong, but...maybe not."

CHAPTER 33

THE END OF THE CONCERT TRAIL AND STRUGGLING WITH PHYSICAL PAIN

I

CASH'S CREATIVE RESURGENCE with *American Recordings* should have led to a victory lap—and a few shows served as just that, starting with an invitation-only industry audience at Fez Café, an intimate music club in New York City. It was three days before the release of the album in April, but the buzz was already strong. Cash was as nervous as his friend Mark Stielper had ever seen him. "He thought they would laugh at him," says Stielper. "Instead, he was a god...and he was astonished."

After years on the family circuit, Cash was self-conscious about playing to young rock audiences. "I feel a little pressure with this new surge, this new promotion," he told me at the time. "It's like 'the old rebel is back,' and what do I have to rebel about? There's nothing right now, and it makes me feel like I'm playing a role, but that's what show business is about. The important thing is I enjoy being out there again."

To relate better to this new audience, Cash spent time familiarizing himself with some of the best young bands, especially Nirvana and its gifted leader Kurt Cobain, who spoke about youthful insecurities with such sensitivity and insight that he was widely hailed as the John Lennon of his generation. Cash identified strongly with the young man from Seattle, not just his struggle with drugs and early poverty, but also the fact that Cobain felt he didn't deserve the adoration of fans around the world.

This was on Cash's mind in the days after Cobain killed himself on April 5. "I can understand why Cobain felt that way, but he wasn't justified in thinking he was a fraud," Cash told me. "He was successful because he was speaking honestly from his gut, but we all worry about whether we deserve the attention. In the early years, I felt guilty about it all. I had come from this real poor background and I didn't feel like I deserved all this money and attention. I kept thinking, 'I'm not what they think I am. I don't have all the answers. I'm not magic.' But then you grow with it and you learn that it really doesn't matter what other people think of you. You're just one human being, and you're doing the best you can. But it's not easy. It almost destroyed me, too."

The high point of Cash's reconnection with the adventurous wing of the young rock world came when he appeared before more than fifty thousand fans on June 26 at one of England's most popular outdoor festivals, Glastonbury. The safe thing would have been for him to perform on one of the festival's secondary stages, but he agreed to test himself on the main stage. Sharing the bill with such established stars as Peter Gabriel and such upcoming ones as Radiohead and Rage Against the Machine, Cash—backed this time by his band, including John Carter on rhythm guitar—was again embraced by the audience during a set with a solo stint featuring four songs from the new album, including "Delia's Gone" and "Let the Train Whistle Blow."

Interviewed backstage for a TV broadcast, Cash was asked, "How does it feel to be cool again?"

Cash chuckled and acknowledged it felt great.

The audience looked so young to him when he walked onstage, he told the interviewer, he thought of saying, "Hello, grandchildren," but the young faces mainly reminded him of the days when he and Elvis did shows together. "Feels like déjà vu," he said. "No time has passed; it feels like that sometimes, no time has passed."

British critics were as enthusiastic over the "new" Johnny Cash as their U.S. counterparts. Writing in *New Musical Express,* England's most influential music weekly, Paul Moody declared, "Here's a man so capable of putting on a show that we simply fall into the palm of his hand and let him take control...it's a legend come to life before our eyes." The rival *Melody Maker* agreed: Cash was "absolutely brilliant."

Rubin and Lou Robin had hoped to follow Glastonbury with a main stage appearance two months later in the States before hundreds of thousands of fans at the twenty-fifth-anniversary salute to the granddaddy of all rock festivals, Woodstock. Other main stage acts ranged from Bob Dylan to one of the decade's most dynamic young bands, Nine Inch Nails, featuring Trent Reznor, a favorite of Rubin's. But Robin backed off when Woodstock organizers offered Cash only a spot on a secondary stage at the upstate New York affair. This disappointment was largely behind the scenes. To the public, Johnny Cash was back in a big way.

It was difficult for Cash to bounce back and forth between the acclaimed, spirit-raising gigs and the regular old concert trail, where a few young fans would show up, drawn by the new album, but most just wanted the old favorites. The mood of those shows was backward-looking, and Cash's performances were inconsistent.

Rubin pushed strongly for Cash to invest in his future by devoting more time to shows with the cutting-edge sensibilities of *American Recordings,* but the traditional dates were more lucrative, and June too preferred that approach. There was also resistance from musicians in the Cash camp to anything associated with Rubin because he hadn't used them on the recordings.

"I could tell from day one that Rick Rubin didn't like me or the Johnny Cash band," W. S. Holland says. "I don't think any diehard Johnny Cash fans would pick those [Rubin albums] over the things he did earlier." Others in the entourage felt that Rubin must dislike June Carter, because she didn't appear on the records or onstage at the Viper Room or other club dates.

While Rubin did want his own musicians who would be comfortable moving from country to supercharged rock, he says the situation with June "was not about excluding her, but about playing to his [Cash's] strength."

*　　*　　*

Four weeks after the release of *American Recordings,* Cash was back in Branson, where things were worse than ever. After a bitter public dispute—and subsequent lawsuit—with Wayne Newton, the developers stripped Newton's name from the theater and announced plans to sell it. Until a buyer was found, the owners would continue presenting shows, including Cash, in the renamed Shenandoah South Theatre. The problem, Lou Robin says, was that the owners didn't aggressively promote the shows or court the all-important tour bus group business.

By the second engagement, which ran July 26 to August 13, Cash was doing matinee performances in the 2,500-seat theater for as few as 181 customers and evening shows for fewer than 300. The total attendance for the first week was 3,838. It didn't help that Cash's health was continuing to decline. He'd spend much of his day in bed, trying to save his strength for the shows.

Still, there were special moments—including a return to Carnegie Hall on September 14, where Rosanne joined him onstage for a duet of "I Still Miss Someone." It was a moment of healing for both of them, a break from the years of guilt on his part and resentment on hers. "As we sang together," Rosanne said later, "all the old pain dissolved and the old longing to connect was completely satisfied under the lights and the safety of a few thousand people who loved us, thus achieving something I'd been trying to get since I was six years old. It was truly magic for both of us."

On that high note, Cash was soon in San Francisco, where he headlined at one of the nation's most important rock showcases, the Fillmore West. Then it was back to Branson on October 6 for another unbearable ten days. Later in the month Cash taped his second guest appearance on the network TV drama *Dr. Quinn, Medicine Woman,* the story of a female doctor in the post–Civil War West; the Cashes would become close friends with Jane Seymour, the show's star, and her husband, James Keach. While gathering information about Cash's life for a film he wanted to make, Keach developed a strong point of view regarding his subject. "I think most artists suffer," he says. "They feel 'less than' in some way or another. That's what their writing is all about; they're searching. John was a very shy, humble man who was searching for God and himself."

Cash also performed with Billy Graham at a Crusade in Atlanta and met up with The Highwaymen in Los Angeles to begin work on the group's third album. Although the second album hadn't done as well as the first, the group continued to do occasional tours, and they wanted a new album to promote those dates. After a week of recording, Cash headed back to Branson for the last time.

Cash's final Shenandoah South gig was supposed to have run from November 10 until December 8, except for a few days off, but he walked offstage for the last time Saturday night, November 19. He couldn't take it anymore. He told Robin to cancel the rest of the engagement. "I have no plans to come back at all," he said two days later in an interview with a Springfield, Missouri, newspaper.

That Branson show turned out to be Cash's final concert performance anywhere for the year. He wanted to relax and to think about what was closer to his heart: the songs for his next album. He got added stimulus when *American Recordings* was honored as the best contemporary folk album of the year at the Grammy ceremony on March 1, 1995, especially on a night when his old friend Dylan's *World Gone Wrong* was voted the best traditional folk album. He liked the company he was keeping again.

The truth, however, is that the Grammy was less important to him than seeing his son's friends all of a sudden growing more interested in him. That was a big deal. Says Rubin, "that's what really excited him. He felt like an artist again."

II

There was never a doubt that Cash and Rubin would do a follow-up album, but they did need to deal with the question of format. With the success of the debut CD, the conventional choice would have been to come back quickly with another collection in the same solo acoustic style. Cash certainly had a world of fruitful material to draw from. One thing that impressed Rubin and Petty was Cash's extraordinary knowledge of songs in various genres, from country and blues to gospel and folk. It reminded Petty of the equally astounding musical knowledge of another legendary music figure he worked with extensively in the late 1980s: Bob Dylan.

"They both know hundreds of songs," Petty says. "If you're sitting around picking or playing music for fun, they will go through tunes as far back as sea chanteys and Scottish folk songs and hymns and deep into the blues. It just boggled my mind how many songs each of them could play at will. I can only imagine what it was like when they got together. Bob and I had many talks about how much he looked up to Johnny, how he felt he was the genuine article. That might have been where I really got into John's Sun stuff. Bob just loved it. The same with Johnny. He adored Bob. It really was like they were brothers or something."

Rubin, however, didn't want another acoustic album. He envisioned John working with a band this time, and Cash was all for it. He even had a band in mind: "How about Tom's band?" Rubin called Petty, but he didn't want just Tom's band, the Heartbreakers. He also wanted Tom, not only for his musicianship, but for his spirit; he knew how much Cash liked him.

"Rick calls me at home and said he's going to make an electric record with Johnny and that Johnny wants to use my band," Petty says. "Rick also wanted me to play bass because Howie [Heartbreaker bassist Howie Epstein, who had been going with June's daughter Carlene for years] was not in great condition. I said, 'When do we start?'"

When work on the second album began in Los Angeles, Rubin noticed two major changes in Cash. "The great thing was John's confidence was back," Rubin says. "He was full of ideas. But I also noticed he was beginning to have some serious health issues. I had seen an occasional hint of it before, but it was far more apparent on the second album. There were times when he just had to stop recording and take a rest. I could see something was wrong." One mounting problem, especially troublesome for a singer, was asthma.

"John's health problems did accelerate, and [it] probably seemed to Rick that it all happened at once, but the damaged facial nerve was excruciating from 1995 on, and the pain was constant," says Mark Stielper. "He could barely exist, which just makes the work he produced so much more compelling,"

Marty Stuart was also struck by Cash's fragile state. Ever since his move into a solo career and subsequent divorce from Cindy in 1988, Stuart hadn't seen much of Cash, but the rapport was still strong when they met, quite by surprise, on a flight to Los Angeles. By the time the plane landed, Cash had enlisted Stuart to play on the Rubin sessions. Stuart loved the first album—"It was pretty brilliant...the whole idea of a boy and his guitar sitting there, the right choice of songs"—but he wasn't totally surprised by the album's quality. He always believed that Cash could someday reclaim his early greatness.

"The guy I saw in the Rubin sessions was a guy who was given a second chance, or maybe the third chance in his career, and he recognized the moment and took advantage of it," he says. "His artistry was firing again. But I also saw old age and sickness finding its mark and putting a cloud over the proceedings, and it broke my heart. Some days were better than others at the session. I know he was using the pills again, but I would have taken whatever I needed, too, to reduce the pain. He was pretty good most of the time at covering it up, but there were times when he just couldn't go any more, and he'd say, 'I'll deal with this tomorrow.'"

Even after they agreed on the concept for the second album, Cash figured he and Rubin would revisit some of the many songs they had left over from the earlier sessions, but Rubin wanted to start fresh.

"Johnny liked the first album when we finished it, but I don't think he was convinced that anyone else would care," Rubin says. "But the reaction to him—again from young people, especially—brought a new excitement as we went into the second record, and I wanted to use that excitement to come up with new ideas. I figured the material left over from the first album would eventually find its way into an album, but not yet.

"My goal was still to get him to be the best artist he could be again, to make him believe that we were going to make the best album he had ever made. That was a mind-blowing idea to him because he really believed his Sun Records and the early Columbia albums were his best work, that nothing came close to that. I kept saying, 'Okay, but let's do something better than that. That was a hard hurdle to get over. It took time, but I think he eventually did start believing in it."

Before the first session, the pair exchanged notes and tapes for weeks while searching for new tunes, and they had a bevy of choices. Petty had observed their enthusiasm for finding songs during the making of the first album. Rubin and Petty went out to dinner one night with Cash, and he played old Hank Williams radio broadcasts while they were in the car. "Johnny would go on and on about how much he loved this song or that one and Rick kept saying, 'Write it down, write it down,' so they wouldn't forget to try it."

By the time the sessions started, Cash and Rubin had a pretty good idea of what numbers they wanted to record. "Some songs were obvious, but the more we did together, the more I realized what a great interpreter Johnny was, and I looked for things that would be a real stretch," Rubin says. Though Cash's own suggestions had been the heart of the first album, he was eager for more of Rubin's suggestions. During that first session Cash smiled and told Petty, "I want to make a record that will offend Johnny Cash fans."

Once Cash and Rubin agreed on a song, they'd play a recording of it for the musicians. Then the musicians would gather in a circle and work for a half hour or so on an arrangement, with Cash singing along. Then they'd begin recording, usually wrapping up the song within two or three takes.

"Those were wonderful sessions," Petty says. "Everything was so loose and natural. If I happened to be fooling around on the organ, Rick might hear something and say, 'Keep doing that on the next song.' That even happened when we played this old country song, 'Kneeling Drunkard's Plea.' I barely know how to play the organ, but Rick liked something and he said, 'Play some churchy thing,' and I just kind of went into this sound and it ended up on the record."

The album's musical backing proved revelatory, providing explosiveness on the upbeat tracks that made you wonder what Cash might have sounded like in the 1970s and 1980s if he'd had a driven, world-class band behind him. "Country Boy," a song of his from the 1950s, rocked with the stinging force of the Allman Brothers, or maybe even Dylan's *Highway 61 Revisited* days. For many longtime Cash fans, the music was breathtaking. It's no wonder Cash's vocals felt inspired.

As the sessions proceeded, Petty questioned some of Rubin's choices, including "Rusty Cage," a howling expression of personal affirmation written by Soundgarden's Chris Cornell, who stood with Kurt Cobain as one of the leaders of the grunge movement in rock. Even Cash wondered about Rubin's judgment as he listened to the dark, relentless drone of the Soundgarden recording in which Cornell's words were largely reduced to an inaudible scream. "That song was the point where I thought Rick had lost his mind," Petty says later. "When he played it, I thought there's no way in the world we are going to be able to make that work. I said, 'Rick, this isn't going to work.' But Rick got a guitar player and played 'Rusty Cage' the way he imagined Cash's record would sound."

Seeing that Cash still wasn't sold, Rubin, who had no experience as a singer, sang the lyrics so Cash could better envision the final recording. "If Johnny felt the words were right—that they were a story he could tell—I figured we could figure out a way to support those words musically, and 'Rusty Cage' was an example of that," Rubin says. "When Johnny actually heard the words, he was down with it."

No one was more pleased with the recording than Cornell, a longtime Cash fan. "I was simply knocked over that Johnny Cash would record a song that I wrote," he said. "I remember when my brother brought home *At San Quentin* when I was nine. We listened to it over and over for about a year. Short of the Beatles covering a song that I wrote, it was the biggest fan experience I've ever had."

But one Rubin song that no one accepted was the unlikely choice of an old Robert Palmer pop-rock tune, "Addicted to Love." Though Cash good-naturedly attempted a vocal, there was so much ridicule from Petty and the others that Rubin quietly put the track on the shelf.

* * *

As the recording continued off and on into 1996, Cash was steadily crisscrossing the country doing the old songs—from the Primadonna Casino just outside Las Vegas and the Silver Star Casino in Philadelphia, Mississippi, one week to the University of Michigan and the Sheraton Hotel ballroom in Honolulu, Hawaii, another week. Then it was back into the studio, where, in addition to Petty and Stuart, he was backed by Heartbreakers guitarist Mike Campbell, keyboardist Benmont Tench, and drummer Steve Ferrone.

When the sessions ended, Rubin and Cash picked fourteen songs from the thirty or so they'd recorded and decided to title the album *Unchained,* after one of the songs. The tune, an expression of Christian humility and gratitude, was by Jude Johnstone, a little-known Nashville songwriter who was friends with Cash's daughter Kathy. Cash loved the theme, and Rubin thought the title fit the spirit of Cash's renewed artistry and image. In the cover photo by Andrew Earl, Cash looked less theatrical than on the first record; dressed in his usual black, he stands by a weathered old barn, his hair almost totally gray rather than dyed black. This photo didn't telegraph "outlaw" so much as "seasoned old musician." Additional photos inside the album booklet showed Cash looking every bit his sixty-six years—and then some.

Beyond Beck's "Rowboat" and the Cornell number, most of the remaining songs were old Cash favorites. They ranged from the Hawaiian-flavored ballad "The One Rose," which he first heard on a Jimmie Rodgers record, to "I've Been Everywhere," the Hank Snow hit. Cash's only new composition was "Meet Me in Heaven," which was inspired by the inscription on his brother Jack's gravestone.

One of the collection's strongest tunes was the title track from *Southern Accents,* Florida native Petty's 1985 concept album about growing up in the South. Near the end of the sessions, Cash thanked Petty for his work on the album and apologized for not having recorded any of Petty's tunes. When he asked Petty which one he should add, Petty told Cash he didn't need to do that—he already had plenty of good songs. Overhearing the conversation, Rubin suggested "Southern Accents" and talked an embarrassed Petty into singing it. Cash was hooked on the opening lines:

> *There's a southern accent, where I come from*
> *The young 'uns call it country*
> *The yankees call it dumb.*

At the end of the song, Petty remembers with a smile, "Johnny looked at me and said, 'I've got to record that. It's better than 'Dixie.'"

While he waited for the release of the album in November, Cash was back on the road, this time a mix of prestigious locales, including the Greek Theatre in Los Angeles and the Fillmore West again in San Francisco, and lots of less glamorous meat-and-potatoes venues in secondary markets. During the shows, Cash's health problems continued to mount.

On December 7 Cash, though suffering from the flu, was feted in Washington, D.C., at the Kennedy Center Honors along with four others—playwright Edward Albee, jazz saxophonist Benny Carter, actor Jack Lemmon, and dancer Maria Tallchief. "To say the least, it's been a good party and a long ride," Cash told a *New York Times* reporter.

By that time *Unchained* had entered the pop charts, but its showing was disappointing. It stayed on the key *Billboard* pop chart only two weeks, peaking at number 170. After two months, sales were less than for *American Recordings* for the same period. One reason was that most of the music press largely passed on the album, partly because they had seen the earlier album as part of a larger human interest story. *American Recordings* had also given a lot of young music writers an excuse to write about someone who was an early hero for many of them. In some ways, they felt that they had already given Cash his due.

The fact that the first album wasn't a big commercial hit also made media exposure for the second album less likely. There, too, was disagreement over the music itself among the few critics who did review *Unchained,* even though it was, in many ways, a more personal and affecting collection. Rubin wasn't discouraged; he viewed *Unchained* as simply the second step in a building process. He continued to believe the best was yet to come.

Cash was back on the concert trail in 1997. He spent most of April in Europe, and then returned to the States, where on May 12 in New York he taped an episode of VH1's *Storyteller* series with Willie Nelson. On the show, they sang some songs and talked about their experiences. Rather than use the platform to showcase his current work, Cash sang only "Drive On" and "Unchained" from the two Rubin albums. He and Nelson focused mainly on vintage material, from Nelson's "On the Road Again" to Cash's "Don't Take Your Guns to Town." After more U.S. dates in May and June, Cash toured Europe again in July, rightfully took it easy during most of August, and then went back out on the road, touring in a big way in September and October, playing such varied spots as the House of Blues in West Hollywood, the Mid-South Fair in Memphis, and the University of New Mexico.

One of those dates—October 4 at the House of Blues—proved to be a godsend for June. Vicky Hamilton, a young record executive and talent manager who had played a key role in the development of the flamboyant glam-rock bands Mötley Crüe and Guns N' Roses, told Rubin backstage how much she enjoyed June's moments in a lively guest spot. She was especially moved by the couple's duet on "Far Side Banks of Jordan" and loved the way June literally kicked John in the butt during a vigorous rendition of "Jackson." Rubin told Hamilton that she ought to make a record with June. Hamilton's reaction: no way. She didn't know anything about country music except what she had heard as a child in Charleston, West Virginia. But Rubin kept pressing her. "You'd be perfect, you're a coal miner's daughter," he said. "Go talk to her." Hamilton was intrigued, but also intimidated. She knew enough about country music to realize that John and June were icons, and she did little more than nod hello as she and June passed on the stairs. Later that night, Rubin told June about the conversation and gave her Hamilton's number.

June wasted no time. Early the following morning, she phoned Hamilton's office at Vapor Records, an upstart label owned by Neil Young and Elliot Roberts. "When I got in, there was this note from June in my inbox," Hamilton says. "It read, 'Rick Rubin says you need to make my record. Call me back. June Carter.'" Hamilton still thought the idea was crazy, but she returned the call out of courtesy.

"June was determined," she says. "We got together at the Four Seasons, where she and John were staying, and she was so excited about making a record that I got swept up in it and I started thinking it might work. I'd help her find a label deal and a producer. I liked her right away and wanted to help her."

Meanwhile, Cash continued to struggle physically, causing June to worry most nights whether they'd make it through the show. His failing eyesight made it difficult for him even to make his way from the dressing room to the stage; the stage crew put fluorescent tape on the floor to help guide him. Lou Robin watched carefully for any sign he'd have to cancel the next group of dates. By now, John was openly talking about retirement, though the earliest target date anyone recalls him mentioning was sometime in 2000. Holland, his longtime drummer, figured the end was going to come much sooner, and he warned other members of the band and crew to think about lining up another job—just in case. "It wasn't the kind of thing you're never ready for," Holland says. "But I wouldn't have been surprised if John had to stop at any point."

That point finally arrived the night of October 25, 1997, at the Whiting Auditorium in Flint, Michigan—just about as routine a stop on the tour trail as you could imagine.

III

Cash had been playing Flint since the 1960s, but this was the first time he had played the two-thousand-seat home of the Flint Symphony Orchestra. It was the same week Cash's second autobiography was published, and he and June were scheduled to fly to New York the following day to kick off a brief book promotion tour.

Val Awad, the production manager for the Whiting, sensed something was wrong as soon as she saw Cash backstage. "It wasn't drink, it wasn't drugs, it was something else," she said. "I thought maybe Alzheimer's; I didn't know."

As soon as Cash walked onstage, several members of the audience, too, felt the same concern.

After a few numbers, Cash dropped his guitar pick and nearly tumbled onto the floor when he bent over to pick it up. "As Johnny began to stagger, we, as nurses, instinctively started to stand up to go to his aid as he looked like he could fall," said Marie Macaulay, an RN who was sitting with some co-workers near the stage.

Cash, however, was able to straighten up with the help of a bandmate. Embarrassed, he decided to share with the audience a secret he had been carrying for months. He told the crowd he had Parkinson's disease, which ran in his family. He'd noticed he was having impaired balance, difficulty concentrating, and occasional slurred speech, classic symptoms.

Mistaking the statement for a joke, several in the audience laughed.

"It ain't funny," Cash replied sharply before he caught himself. "It's all right," he told the audience. "I refuse to give it some ground in my life."

Cash didn't want to leave the stage, though band members were ready to help lead him to the dressing room. He ran through several more songs, including "Rusty Cage" and "Delia's Gone," as well as old favorites such as "Get Rhythm" and the ever-present "I Walk the Line."

His daughter Cindy watched it all from the edge of the stage, and she rushed to his side once he did finally head for the dressing room. "When he left the stage, he told me to please help him walk," she says. "I didn't think about this maybe being his last show; I just didn't want him to fall. I could see that he was dizzy and he was starting to panic. It was heartbreaking."

CHAPTER 34

A HERO AGAIN

I

JOHNNY CASH PROCEEDED TO NEW YORK, as planned, for the TV show appearance but canceled the rest of the book tour and returned home to Hendersonville to meet with a team of doctors. Lou Robin issued a press release saying that Cash was indeed suffering from Parkinson's disease and needed to cancel all public appearances indefinitely. "He's faced a lot of challenges in his life," Robin wrote. "He thrives on challenges. Johnny feels confident that once the disease is medically stabilized, he will soon resume his normal schedule." A week later the diagnosis was changed to Shy-Drager syndrome, a harsher disease that also attacks the nervous system. He was told he had eighteen months to live.

Within days, Cash was back in Baptist Hospital with double pneumonia and other ailments. The treatment included the use of a ventilator to clear Cash's lungs, and ultimately an induced coma. Rumors circulated through the Nashville music industry that he was dying. His family and friends gathered around him. Cash remembered regaining consciousness well enough on occasion to hear the dire talk around him, though he still couldn't communicate. On one occasion he awoke to find his old friend Merle Haggard cradling him in his arms. On another he heard his doctor speaking to God. "She told God that she and medicine had done all they could, it was in His hands now." She spent the whole night praying.

Watching all this for more than a week, June sent word out on the Internet that fans should pray for John. He was now, she too felt, totally in God's hands. The following morning, Cash not only had come out of the coma but was sitting up in bed drinking coffee. He and June maintained that his recovery was due to divine intervention.

The experience had a profound impact on Cash's children. Hours before he awakened, Rosanne poured her heart out to him in a four-page letter: "In these 10 days, I have learned more than I thought possible about love and the resources of the human spirit and the fragility of us all. Dad, you were so sweet laying in your bed. It was an opportunity to be close to you in a way I've never known before. All pretense, any issues, defenses, resentments, fear, expectations, everything just fell away like cardboard and there you were, your pure essence, and there I was in awe and appreciation....All else was burned away in these 10 days. It was an honor to be able to just give love to you—to wipe your forehead, stretch your hands and feet, hold your hand and pray for you."

Rosanne closed the lengthy letter with these words: "I love you so much, dad—nothing else is real. Please forgive me for the way I've hurt you, separated myself from you and withdrawn. I am so deeply grateful and proud that you are my father."

The letter meant the world to Cash, who just months earlier had pleaded—once again—in a note to Rosanne for her and his other daughters for them to stop blaming him for the early years of neglect. In the letter, written at the Cinnamon Hill house on Christmas Eve 1996, he wrote: "I believe I'm still being paid back—out of a lot of resentment for leaving you girls 29 years ago. I believe I have never been forgiven for the neglect, emotional abuse and abandonment. I believe I'm somehow expected to 'make up' for it, which is impossible. For me, it was a matter of survival. When God gave me a son, I vowed not to make the same mistake again and I didn't."

Then to correct the impression he'd given that he loved his

son more than his daughters, Cash added: "When the lady at the…Kennedy Center asked for a list of people I wanted invited, your name was first on the list, followed by your sisters and John Carter, 5th [the order of his children's birth]. My brothers and sisters and co-workers came last."

Over the next few months, Cash put on a brave front. He told friends and loved ones that he simply refused to accept the Shy-Drager diagnosis and that he looked forward to getting back into the studio. But he was still in constant pain and kept worrying how, without any tour income, he was going to be able to go on supporting all those people who depended on him. He also wanted to simplify his life.

He had put the House of Cash building, which included his museum, up for sale in 1989 for $795,000, but no buyer emerged. In explaining Cash's decision at the time to try to sell, his brother Tommy, who had become a real-estate agent and was handling the property, said, "I'm not going to get into why he has decided to cut down generally all the unnecessary expense in his life and his career, but he is in the process of doing that. He is putting out many, many, many dollars for things that could be cut back on, and this is just one thing they're considering doing."

He was now thinking about a new sales push. In putting the property back on the market, Cash was selling not only the museum building (now for $1.2 million), but also an old railroad depot which John and June had moved from Madison to their property to display June's antiques ($75,000), the lot on which the museum and depot both sat ($250,000), and two seven-acre-plus lots adjoining the property ($1.8 million).

The year-end balance sheet from one of the years after Flint showed his net income at well under $100,000. Even at the end of his life, Cash's assets—aside from property and future royalties—were accounted in the low seven figures, far less than is generally assumed for a star of his stature.

Unchained won a Grammy for best country album in February 1998—over bigger sellers by artists such as Alan Jackson, Patty

Loveless, George Strait, and Dwight Yoakam. This was even sweeter than the contemporary folk Grammy. The album had been up against the best that Nashville could produce, and Cash had won. Rubin was especially delighted. He took Nashville's indifference to the albums personally. After that Grammy, he bought a full-page ad in the March 14 issue of *Billboard* magazine literally giving the finger to those professionals who had turned their backs on Cash and continued to ignore him.

The $20,000 ad was dominated by a striking photo that Jim Marshall, a noted rock photographer who had also been at Folsom, had taken of a snarling Cash flashing his middle finger at the camera the day of the 1969 concert at San Quentin. Lou Robin says Cash was "fed up" with the TV crew following him everywhere he went and he decided to send them a message. In the ad, which Rubin showed Cash before submitting it to the trade publication, the text read, "American Recordings and Johnny Cash would like to acknowledge the Nashville music establishment and country radio for your support."

Cash was uneasy about the ad. Before agreeing to it, he phoned Billy Graham. "He didn't tell me what to do or not to do, just that he wouldn't judge me either way," Cash said. "After my talk with him, I prayed about it and called Rick back. I gave him the go-ahead."

The ad was cheered and jeered in Nashville—tacked up on scores of record company bulletin boards by young Turks who also resented the conservative ways of most of the city's record labels, but criticized, too, as a crude West Coast record industry gimmick. Asked about the ad, Rubin told *USA Today,* "We hope it will open the eyes of the country community and hopefully they'll say, 'The guy did win...and he's making records considered the best in country and maybe we should readdress the situation.'"

Willie Nelson, who cut out the ad and hung it on the wall of his tour bus, told the same paper, "John speaks for all of us."

No longer having to spend weeks on the road, Cash spent most of the summer and fall of 1998 putting together songs for the new album and visiting his doctors. He and June also worried about the failing health of others around them. Both of June's sisters were seriously ill. Helen had been hospitalized for months with various stomach problems. She passed away on June 2.

All this brought John and June closer together. As their world shrank, their love deepened. They were enjoying the kind of relationship he had dreamed about in the Air Force and his fans had imagined they were living all along. To Cash, their love was another sign of redemption. He was also thrilled that June was getting the chance to make an album again.

"The love affair between them was never stronger than those last years," says Kelly Hancock, Cash's niece. "June told me one day that nobody truly knew the depth of her love for John, and I must agree."

II

Vicky Hamilton, who at forty-one was experienced at pitching new bands to record labels, didn't think she'd have any trouble finding a label that wanted to work with someone as celebrated as June Carter, but she was turned down by everyone she contacted in Los Angeles and in Nashville. Nobody wanted to sign a nearly seventy-year-old woman. After several months, Hamilton realized there was only one person in the record business who wanted to be involved with a June Carter Cash album—Hamilton herself. "I was astonished and pissed," she says. "I never had the idea of starting my own record label, but I did it out of anger that the industry would not support someone as iconic as June Carter Cash."

Even then, Hamilton couldn't find a deal. Thinking it'd be easy to get a major label at least to go into a joint venture on an album, Hamilton formed her own label, Small Hairy Dog, and returned to established labels, but she was again rebuffed. Finally, in the summer of 1998, she worked out a deal with tiny Risk Records, an indie label in Los Angeles, which put up $35,000.

Much like Rubin with Cash, Hamilton prepared for the album by asking June to send her tapes of songs she'd like to record. The song Hamilton focused on was "Far Side Banks of Jordan." Hamilton had heard the Cashes sing it at the House of Blues, where there wasn't a dry eye in the place, she says, including hers.

Of the forty or so songs Carter sent Hamilton, there were old songs—"Ring of Fire" and "Will the Circle Be Unbroken"—as well as new compositions, notably "I Used to Be Somebody." This last, with references to palling around with James Dean during her acting days and hanging out with Elvis Presley on the concert trail, came across to some listeners as a somewhat bittersweet reflection on what might have been if she hadn't given up acting and other solo career dreams for Cash.

But Hamilton says she perceived no sense of regret or thwarted ambition when she spoke to June about the song. "Oddly enough, I never got the feeling the album was so much about her," she adds. "We had a lot of fun making it, but I got the feeling she did it because that's what he [John] really wanted. He was so supportive, so proud of her. To my mind, they were truly soul mates. They had a closeness that I've only seen a couple of times in my life. It was a great love story."

John Carter said that his mother was the "director, the bandleader, the vocalist, and the cheerleader" during the recording sessions in the fall of 1998. "Spontaneity was the order of the day," he recalled. "You never knew exactly what was going to happen or how the sound would actually come together."

Early in the process, June named the album *Press On,* a statement of resolve from "Diamonds in the Rough," a Carter Family song. Over the weeks of recording, June was joined by Cash, Marty Stuart, Norman Blake, and champion fiddler Laura Weber (who would become John Carter's second wife). It was a warm family affair.

The sessions were understandably emotional for John Carter. Years later he would speak in detail about watching his parents seated so close together their heads nearly touched as they put their hearts into the lyrics on "Far Side Banks of Jordan." The scene was dear to him for another reason. It was the last time, he says, he saw them both strong together. For the rest of their lives, one or the other would be ravaged by illness.

Like everyone else around the couple, John Carter imagined that his father would pass first. Yet years later, listening again and again to that day's recording, he points to a "sadness and conviction" in his mother's voice that made him wonder whether she didn't believe that she might be the first to go. The album would be released the following April.

That April was also noteworthy when Cash was saluted in a TV special taped in New York City for the cable channel TNT's *Master Series*. In the days leading up to the show at the Hammerstein Ballroom, the question was whether Cash, who had just celebrated his sixty-seventh birthday, would be well enough to attend. It had been nearly two years since the final concert in Flint, and he had spent two weeks in serious condition in Baptist Hospital the past October with pneumonia.

Lots of his friends were represented in the telecast. Dylan, U2, and Springsteen checked in with videotaped performances: U2 with a reggae-flavored version of "Don't Take Your Love to Town," Dylan with "Train of Love," and Springsteen with "Give My Love to Rose." Among those on hand in person, Kristofferson sang "The Ballad of Ira Hayes," Lyle Lovett delivered "Tennessee Flat-Top Box," and rapper Wyclef Jean performed "Delia's Gone."

Finally, Cash appeared onstage to a grand ovation. Marshall Grant, setting aside the bitterness of the lawsuit, stood by his side as Cash sang "Folsom Prison Blues" and "I Walk the Line." During the final number, June and the rest of the old cast joined him. The show was widely reviewed, providing additional steam to Cash's revived career.

Because Cash wasn't strong enough to travel to Los Angeles regularly for recording sessions for the third album, Rubin arranged for engineer David Ferguson to set up some recording equipment in a cabin on Cash's Hendersonville property. In the liner notes for what would become *American III: Solitary Man,* Cash described the relaxed atmosphere that surrounded the sessions, which started just weeks after the TNT special.

"I began the album…in the cabin, in the middle of a 50-acre compound surrounded by cedar trees, deer, goats and peacocks," Cash wrote. "The window unit air conditioner doesn't work anymore. We had buffalo, and every time it came on, they rammed it with their horns. Sometimes we have to stop tape for a thunderstorm. We play back the songs and the mockingbirds sing along with it."

But that tranquil scene couldn't obscure the physical struggle involved in making the album. Last-minute cancellations were becoming increasingly frequent. "It was a hard one because Johnny was sick and he was trying to get himself out of pain," David Ferguson says. "I'd get a call the day before he wanted to record, and a lot of times I'd get a call the next morning saying he wasn't up to it so we'd cancel the session. As time went on, it got to where we were canceling sessions 60 to 80 percent of the time."

On those days when Cash made it to the cabin, his work ethic was strong. He'd often work for an hour, take a break for something to eat, and work another hour. "There was never anything wrong with his mind," Ferguson says. "It was just his energy level.

"Sometimes the pain would be so bad that he would just stay in the house, but sooner or later, he'd be back in front of the microphone singing. It was literally day by day. None of us knew how long it was going to keep going, but no one wanted to stop—most of all Johnny."

Cash tried to block out his pain and worry by constantly searching his memory for old songs that still spoke to him, be they spirituals or something with a wry philosophical edge such as "Nobody," a 1920s number he first heard on a Bing Crosby record. He was attracted to the song, which was co-written by vaudevillian Bert Williams, for its "sad sack" humor. Cash conveyed the wistfulness so deftly that Ferguson thought he had written it. Cash did write another of the songs, one he first recorded in the 1970s but reprised for this album—"Country Trash," a playful look at Cash's own Arkansas roots, a backwoods connection that had once embarrassed him but eventually became a source of inspiration and even pride.

When Ferguson had a few tracks done, he sent them to Rubin, who discussed them on the phone with Cash. Rubin didn't like everything he heard. Sometimes the vocal was weak; other times the song didn't add anything to what fans already knew about Cash. At the same time, Rubin marveled at the best of the recordings. He couldn't believe that this great artist had been exiled by the music business for all those years. Meanwhile, he too continued searching for songs for Cash, listening to dozens of albums. Periodically he would burn a CD of ten to twenty of his favorite songs to get Cash's reaction.

A week after the first round of Hendersonville recording sessions ended on May 21, John and June were at the Troubadour, a club within walking distance of the Viper Room in West Hollywood, to celebrate the release of June's new album. Backed by a four-piece band that included John Carter on guitar, she delivered affectionate versions of various songs from the collection.

But there was no doubt the central theme of the evening was her life with John—from the early "Ring of Fire," delivered in the gentler acoustic style of the Carter Family, to Cash's joining her for "Far Side Banks of Jordan" and their most famous duet number, "Jackson."

Upstairs in the club dressing room, Cash beamed as well-wishers congratulated his wife. Seven months later they would both have even more reason to cheer, when *Press On* won a Grammy in the same category that Cash's *American Recordings* had earlier—best contemporary folk recording.

Yet these moments of celebration were becoming fewer and fewer. Cash looked frail at the Troubadour. He had to sit on a couch backstage and couldn't get more than a few words out without having to pause to regain his breath.

On top of their own illnesses, John's and June's spirits were further dampened because Anita was dying. She had suffered from rheumatoid arthritis for years, even going to Mexico in hopes of finding a miracle treatment. By the time of the Troubadour date, her liver and kidneys were failing. John and June took her into their home, where she finally died on July 29. She was sixty-six. In a period of thirteen months, June had lost both her sisters. "That hit her very, very hard," Rosanne says. "She rebounded after Helen's death and was her old self fairly soon, but I don't think she ever got over Anita's death. It was a terrible blow."

Then in October, Cash was rushed to the hospital, where he was listed in serious condition with pneumonia. As he spent several more days in a coma, rumors again swept through Music Row that Johnny Cash was dying. Yet he was soon sufficiently recovered to go to Jamaica to recuperate. While there, however, he had a relapse and had to be flown back to Baptist Hospital.

One good piece of news came out of these hospital stays: Cash learned from his doctors that he did not have Shy-Drager syndrome after all. "I think they had to change their minds because if I did have Shy-Drager I'd be dead by now," Cash said later. The doctors now said he was suffering from autonomic neuropathy, which covered a wide range of nervous system disorders. It didn't matter much to Cash; he still felt terribly ill.

Rubin was in Los Angeles through most of 1999, working with a variety of rock acts, but that didn't prevent him from looking for more songs to challenge Cash. After "Rusty Cage," he knew that the musical style of the song didn't matter as long as Cash could identify with the lyrics, so he spent hours at home at night listening to album after album by punk and post-punk groups as well as by such mainstream acts as Neil Diamond and Simon & Garfunkel. He also kept his ears open when he went to concerts, and he knew he had the perfect song the night he heard "The Mercy Seat" by Nick Cave, a lanky Australian known for delivering gothic tales of darkness and salvation with a frightening, typhoon-like intensity. Rick had been a Cave fan for years, and he had heard "The Mercy Seat" on an earlier Cave album, but it didn't hit him until he heard it live.

He was struck by the duality of the song—a seemingly defiant man in the electric chair reflecting on a gracious God on his throne. It was tailor-made for Cash, but Rubin knew it was going to be a difficult choice. One thing in his favor was John's fondness for prison songs. What he didn't know was that the Cave song would remind Cash of the chill that had come over him when he walked by the electric chair during a tour of the grounds the day he did a show at Tennessee State Prison in Nashville.

When Rubin played "The Mercy Seat" for Cash in April 2000 in Hendersonville, Cash felt intimidated by the complexity of the story. They cut a version of it, but agreed to wait until Cash was in Los Angeles again to finish it.

Meanwhile, Rubin had several other songs that would end up on the pair's third album, including Neil Diamond's "Solitary Man," Tom Paxton's "The Last Thing on My Mind," and Tom Petty's "I Won't Back Down." In some ways the Petty song seemed too obvious—Cash proclaiming his own independent spirit via a song that had been a huge hit in 1989. But part of Rubin's strength as a producer was the ability simply to focus on what worked—"what would be great," as he put it.

Unlike most record executives, he didn't think of chart position when asked to name his favorite recordings. Like Cash, Rubin wanted hits, but he didn't measure the greatness of a song or an album by numbers. That's how Rubin could come up with an obscure Beck song ("Rowboat") to open the second album and a hit Petty song ("I Won't Back Down") to open the third. He was focused on what was appropriate. About "I Won't Back Down" Rubin says, "It's a powerful lyric, and it served as a good organizing principle for Johnny. Hearing Johnny sing it in his weakened state was really a statement of what he's all about. We didn't do it just because people would recognize the song quickly. Tom just loved it. He felt Johnny did a better job on it than he did."

During Rubin's two weeks in Nashville, Cash recorded eleven songs, ranging from a sweet hymn—"Wayfaring Stranger," which he first heard on the radio in Dyess—to a nineteenth-century folk song, "Mary of the Wild Moor," which he learned from the Louvin Brothers, to a new Cash composition, "Before My Time," a love song with the simplicity and appeal of some of the early Sun hits:

> *I know that hearts were loving*
> *Long before I was here*
> *And I'm not the first to ever cry*
> *In my bed or in my beer*
> *There were songs before there was radio*
> *Of love that stays and love that goes*
> *They were writing melancholy tunes*
> *And tearful words that rhyme*
> *Before my time*
> *Before my time…*

But what the old time masters had
Is what I feel for you
Love is love and doesn't change
In a century or two
If some way they had seen and knew
How it would be for me and you
They'd wish for love like yours
And they would wish for love like mine
Before my time
Before my time.

Rubin returned to Los Angeles deeply pleased. Despite the health problems, Cash was expanding again as an artist. He was sifting through both his memory bank of songs and his personal experiences to see which tunes still spoke to him and what new ones he could create. After writing two autobiographies, he now wanted to tell his story through his music: a musical and personal self-portrait.

"It was like that time at the White House with Nixon," Cash told me. "If these were going to be my last recordings, I wanted them to tell a little bit of a road map, so to speak, about who I was as a musician and as a man. I've been really conscious about handing something down."

III

When Cash finally was able to travel to Los Angeles, Ferguson accompanied him. Cash was feeling good, but he worried about capturing the nuances of the Nick Cave song. "I went to his room at the Four Seasons," Ferguson says. "He said, 'Man, I've got this "Mercy Seat" song hanging over my head. It's a great song, but I am worried sick about it. I don't know if I can do it right.'"

Cash indeed had a hard time capturing the dark, conflicting strains in the song, but he kept at it. "He worked and worked on it," Ferguson notes. "But that's one of the things I admired about Johnny. He had a work ethic better than anybody you've ever met.

If he was drawn to a song, he wouldn't give up until he got it right."

In the end, Cash became as enamored with "The Mercy Seat" as Rubin was, and he wanted to open the album with it, but Rubin was afraid that the track would be too powerful and make the rest of the album feel anticlimactic. Rubin believed it was best to open with the more accessible "I Won't Back Down" and "Solitary Man." He had always liked Diamond's own hit 1966 version, but he felt Cash could bring an interesting maturity to the lyrics—and Cash again came through. Whereas Diamond's single drew most of its effect from the lilting guitar intro and the infectious sing-along charm, Cash made the words the central attraction. They agreed *Solitary Man* should be the album title.

Yet the first eye-opener on the album was the song Rubin and Cash placed fourth—U2's "One." Cash had wanted to record another U2 song ever since "The Wanderer," and Rubin agreed this would be the ideal choice. Though Bono had written the lyric to underscore the differences among people, Cash saw it as a love song, and Bono marveled over the interpretation Cash brought to his words.

In assembling the album tracks, Rubin followed "One" with the lighthearted "Nobody" before setting up "The Mercy Seat" with "I See a Darkness," written by another of Rubin's underground rock favorites, Will Oldham, who frequently recorded under the pseudonym Bonnie Prince Billy. It was a profoundly moving sequence.

No one—not even Sam Phillips—had understood the depth and range of Cash's artistry or worked as hard at keeping Cash focused on his strengths as Rubin. It was the equivalent of Martin Scorsese and Robert De Niro teaming on such landmark films as *Raging Bull* and *Taxi Driver*, where the director and actor seem interlocked. To make it work, the director—or producer—needs to partner with a great talent and then find the ideal showcase for him.

What especially enriched the Rubin-Cash relationship was that for every song from Rubin that stretched Cash's creative reach, Cash's choices brought a warm, often disarming touch to the proceedings. Thus Rubin was able to follow "The Mercy Seat" with a series of selections, some of which Cash had written (including

"Before My Time" and "Country Trash"), that gave the CD an unde-niably personal stamp.

For all the months spent recording vocals and adding instrumen-tal touches, the new album felt remarkably effortless. To point out that these albums were part of an ongoing creative journey, Ru-bin used the word "American" from the first album—*American III: Solitary Man*.

The media were back on board in the months leading up to its release in October 2000. The two Grammy wins and the lingering impact of the first two albums were more than enough to convince editors and writers that Cash and Rubin were making amazing strides. But Cash also benefited strongly from a three-CD package that had been released the previous May by Columbia in association with American Recordings. The set was built around three themes, with one disc devoted to each: *Love God Murder.* The liner notes were written by June, Bono, and film director Quentin Tarantino, respectively.

Cash personally chose the selections, which stretched across his entire career, and he made some inspired pairings, among them, following "Folsom Prison Blues" with "Delia's Gone" and "Don't Take Your Love to Town" with "Highway Patrolman" on the "Mur-der" package, and "I Still Miss Someone" with "The One Rose" on the *Love* disc. It was a spectacular showcase that documented the imagination and range of Cash's musical catalog—all the more impressive because knowledgeable Cash followers knew there was enough compelling work left over to fill another set.

Adding the stamp of approval of a new generation of rock lead-ers, Bono wrote, "Empathy and grace are written in his face, etched into his voice . . . [and] so are the years in the wilderness."

Cash's longtime booster *Rolling Stone* checked in with a lengthy profile the week the album was released. Anthony DeCurtis, who had given *American Recordings* a rave review, found Cash "expan-sive, good-humored and, above all, indomitable" during an after-noon interview in the living room of the house in Hendersonville. But DeCurtis noted there were also moments when Cash would "put his hands over his eyes and rub them, as if in pain."

Still, Cash's outlook was positive as he spoke about his relationship with his new musical partner. "From the first day...we trusted each other to be honest," he said of Rubin. "I said, 'I'm gonna sing you a song and if you don't like it, you tell me. And if you got a song that you like and I don't, you've got to listen to me. I can't sing it if I don't like it.' But he has come up with some really fine songs, and he has never pushed anything on me. We get along beautifully."

He was even more eloquent talking about June and their future. "There's unconditional love there," he said. "You hear that phrase a lot, but it's real with me and her. She loves me in spite of everything, in spite of myself....She has always been there with her love, and it has certainly made me forget the pain for a long time, many times. When it gets dark, and everybody's gone home, and the lights are turned off, it's just me and her."

American III: Solitary Man was the first of the Rubin-produced albums to crack the Top 100 pop chart, thanks to sales of nearly ninety thousand in its first two months in the stores—almost 50 percent more than *Unchained.*

Nothing, however, was coming easily. While in Jamaica for the holiday season, Cash went through another siege of pneumonia that was serious enough for him to return to the Baptist Hospital in Nashville. He was still too weak to travel to Los Angeles for the Grammy Awards ceremony on February 21, so he watched on television as he was honored for best male country vocal for his performance of the song "Solitary Man."

Cash and Rubin approached the fourth album with high hopes. They had gotten past the novelty aspect of an odd couple making music together and now had the public's attention—and they wanted desperately to deliver something lasting. Rubin began to look for a song even more challenging than "The Mercy Seat." Cash wanted to write something epic—a final statement, a work that would define his spiritual beliefs.

"I know everyone will say I've got to be out of my skull, but I feel like my recording career has just begun," Cash told a reporter. "You know, my dreams and ambitions after all these years are pretty much the same as they were at the beginning. I still just want to make records and sing on the radio. After I finally got on the radio I just wanted to make better records and that's still what I want to do."

Cash was finally back in touch with the standards that had once defined his best songwriting—from Jimmie Rodgers to Merle Travis on. At the same time, he held on to his spiritual inspiration. In a very real sense his musical vision was complete.

CHAPTER 35

"THE MAN COMES AROUND" AND "HURT"

I

ONE SONG HAD BEEN HAUNTING Cash for years, and it was back on his mind in the early weeks of 2001. He had started laying down tracks for the new album the previous fall, just three months after finishing *Solitary Man*. "That's the way we worked," Ferguson says. "We just kept recording. There were no big breaks between albums." During the September and November sessions in Hendersonville, Cash recorded more than twelve songs, including Bruce Springsteen's feverish "I'm on Fire" and Fred Neil's "Everybody's Talkin'," the wistful song from the film *Midnight Cowboy*. But none of them would make the fourth album. Cash and Rubin were just marking time. They both feared that Cash had enough strength for only one more album, and they were both searching for one song that would serve as their pinnacle accomplishment.

Up most mornings by five, Cash would shower, have breakfast, and take in the news on CNN before settling in a chair, either in his upstairs office or in the house's massive round room below. He'd invariably think about that new song—one largely inspired by U2's, "The Wanderer." Cash loved the way Bono took a story from the scriptures and turned it into a parable that spoke to contemporary music fans. Cash wanted to write a "modern gospel" song that would speak to the young fans who had begun listening to him.

Cash had been talking to Rubin about recording two gospel albums—a collection of hymns he'd learned as a child and a set of black gospel tunes he also prized, but Rubin kept advising him to wait. The producer wanted to establish Cash's relevance with modern audiences before releasing something as specialized as a gospel album. But John wasn't thinking about a gospel album now. He wanted this "modern gospel" song for his next general album. He traced its genesis to a dream he had on the same 1993 European tour when he recorded "The Wanderer." John Carter believes that the vision occurred in Germany, just days before Dublin. "He came to me and said he had the strangest dream about visiting Queen Elizabeth in Buckingham Palace," he recalled.

As Cash told it, he walked into a room and found the queen sitting on the floor knitting and laughing. She looked up and declared, "Johnny Cash, you're just like a thorn tree in a whirlwind." The image stuck with Cash, though he had no idea where it was from until, he claimed, he came across a reference in the Old Testament. Soon after, he began thinking of using the line in a story—a poem perhaps—and he continued to seek out accompanying images in the scriptures. He eventually changed his plan from a story to a song, but the idea lingered in his mind for years until he thought of writing it in the style of "The Wanderer."

Looking forward to his fourth album, he began to think of the new song as the ultimate statement he was seeking. In the final weeks of 2000, Cash wrote verse after verse, day after day. It was his overriding passion for months. As with Folsom and San Quentin, he was trying to seize the big moment.

When John Carter walked into his father's office to hear the song for the first time, early in 2001, he noticed some twenty sheets of paper on the desk containing forty or so alternative verses of the song, now titled "The Man Comes Around." The expression of salvation was as uncompromising as Bob Dylan's "Gotta Serve Somebody" from his spiritual-driven *Slow Train Coming* album from 1979, which Cash greatly admired. John had even recorded

"Gotta Serve Somebody" during the previous fall's sessions in the cabin and included a lighthearted reference to it in one of the early versions of his new song. In that verse he substituted "But you gotta know it'll be written down / when the man comes around" for Dylan's "But you're gonna have to serve somebody":

> You can be first on the draw
> You can kill your mother in law
> You can steal some of the pilgrims' mackinaw
> But you gotta know it'll be written down
> When the man comes around.

Though the lyrics didn't mention Jesus's name or the words "judgment day," it was about Christ's second coming and the final judgment, the fundamental tenet of his faith. In the series of verses, Cash cited other images from the Bible, including the "whirlwind in the thorn tree" and "the virgins are all trimming their wicks." It was more overtly spiritual than U2's "The Wanderer," but just as majestic and bold.

> There's a man going around taking names
> And he decides who to free and who to blame
> Everybody won't be treated all the same
> There'll be a golden ladder reaching down
> When the man comes around
>
> The hairs on your arm will stand up
> At the terror in each sip and in each sup
> Will you partake of that last offered cup?
> Or disappear into the potter's ground
> When the man comes around
>
> Hear the trumpets, hear the pipers
> One hundred million angels singing
> Multitudes are marching to the big kettledrum
> Voices calling, voices crying
> Some are born and some are dying

It's alpha and omega's kingdom come
And the whirlwind is in the thorn tree
The virgins are all trimming their wicks
The whirlwind is in the thorn tree
It's hard for thee to kick against the pricks
Till Armageddon no shalam, no shalom
Then the father hen will call his chickens home
The wise man will bow down before the throne
And at his feet they'll cast their golden crowns
When the man comes around

Whoever is unjust let him be unjust still
Whoever is righteous let him be righteous still
Whoever is filthy let him be filthy still
Listen to the words long written down
When the man comes around

Hear the trumpets, hear the pipers
One hundred million angels singing
Multitudes are marching to the big kettledrum
Voices calling and voices crying
Some are born and some are dying
It's alpha and omega's kingdom come
And the whirlwind is in the thorn tree
The virgins are all trimming their wicks
The whirlwind is in the thorn tree
It's hard for thee to kick against the pricks
In measured hundred weight and penny pound
When the man comes around.

A musician himself, John Carter tried to be honest when he was asked his opinion of his father's songs, and this time he raved. When he wondered about the phrase "virgins trimming their wicks," Cash reached for the Bible that was always on his desk and quoted Matthew 25, the parable of the ten virgins. As much as John Carter liked what he'd heard, Cash continued to work on the song, constantly revising lines. John Carter remembers his father asking him one day as he was working on the song, "So, the word 'shalom' is Hebrew for peace. What is the word in Arabic?"

John Carter told him "shalam."

"He wanted the song to be universal," his son says. "He knew the answer. I think he was just sort of checking again to see what I thought. He really was borderline obsessed with writing that song. It was the most important thing he had written, maybe ever, and he just loved it."

While Cash was crafting "The Man Comes Around," Rubin was haunted by another song. The producer had long been a fan of Trent Reznor, the young rock auteur whose dark, controversial music combined the seductive songwriting craft of Nirvana, the gear-grinding howl of industrial rock, and the raw, unsettling language of William Burroughs.

"I am the pusher, I am the whore...I am the need you have for more," Reznor taunted in one of the songs on *The Downward Spiral,* a 1994 album that employed shocking nihilistic and decadent images, but was at its core an anguished cry for something to believe in during a time when such traditional support systems as religion and family had failed for so many. It was one of the darkest rock collections to crack the Top 10 album charts in America.

Though Rubin didn't produce records by Nine Inch Nails, the group name under which Reznor worked, he was close to the singer-songwriter, calling him the most exciting musician of his generation: "His whole vision blows me away." Rubin especially liked "Hurt," a song that expressed soul-robbing alienation in such a masterly way that Reznor used it to end most of his concerts. "Hurt" was a leap for Cash, Rubin knew, but he felt that Cash was capable of delivering a chilling interpretation.

"I realized at one point while looking for songs," recalls Rubin, "that I really hadn't looked at post-punk music, so I listened to Depeche Mode and found 'Personal Jesus.' I didn't even know if it was a pro- or anti-Jesus song, but I could imagine him singing it.

"I also listened to a lot of REM. I'm sure I sent Johnny 'Losing My Religion,' though I didn't think he'd want to sing that. I also sent 'Everybody Hurts.' I even thought about sending him a Radiohead song, 'Creep.' But 'Hurt' stood above everything. To me, it was a song about an older person reflecting on their life with remorse. It was so heartbreaking."

When Rubin assembled his next CD of songs for Cash to consider, he put "Hurt" first and was disappointed during their next phone conversation when Cash didn't mention the song. Undeterred, Rubin made another CD and again led it with "Hurt." There was still no response from Cash. Rubin again put "Hurt" at the top of the next sampler CD. He went one step further this time, including a note telling Cash how strongly he felt about the song and urging him to read the lyrics carefully.

The song's opening verse and chorus go:

> *I hurt myself today*
> *To see if I still feel*
> *I focus on the pain*
> *The only thing that's real*
> *The needle tears a hole*
> *The old familiar sting*
> *Try to kill it all away*
> *But I remember everything*
>
> *[Chorus]*
> *What have I become*
> *My sweetest friend*
> *Everyone I know goes away*
> *In the end*
> *And you could have it all*
> *My empire of dirt*
> *I will let you down*
> *I will make you hurt.*

Cash felt the power of the words, but he still didn't know if he could make them his own. He didn't want to disappoint Rubin, however, so the next time they spoke on the phone he said, "Okay, let's do it."

*   *   *

Although Cash and Rubin continued to march toward what would be cornerstone moments in their working relationship, it wasn't nonstop—especially on Cash's part. There was a break while John and June spent much of the first quarter of 2001 in Jamaica. Even back in Hendersonville, recording was periodic. He made it to the cabin only about one day a week, and even then his output was hampered by his limited lung power.

It isn't uncommon for recording artists to sing several takes of a song and then have an engineer or producer splice together parts of each to create the final product. Rubin and Ferguson had been doing that to a limited extent since the second album, but the need for it had increased dramatically. By the start of the fourth album, Ferguson was splicing John's vocals together phrase by phrase in some cases. The idea wasn't to camouflage Cash's declining vocal power but rather to build the most compelling emotional portrait possible. "I looked at all these albums from a documentary standpoint," Rubin says. "If the frailty of the voice matched the frailty of the lyrics, that was all the better. If he had the right song, the weakness of his voice became a strength."

Cash wasn't up for a formal recording session until March 13, when he recorded the old Marty Robbins gunfighter ballad "Big Iron." The next day he was finally comfortable enough with "The Man Comes Around" to record it. Still wanting to tinker with the lyrics, he recorded it again on March 28 and again the day after. Everyone in the studio shared his passion for the song. Stuart even went to his warehouse after Cash sang the song for him to get the famed Fender Esquire guitar that Luther Perkins had played on the Sun sessions. It was, in a way, Stuart's attempt to reconnect Cash with Luther. "I remember I had my eyes closed through the whole song," Stuart says. "I just kept telling myself, 'Don't blow it. This is history.' I felt it was like going back fifty years and shaking hands with the Tennessee Two sonically. It was just magical."

As summer approached, progress on the album slowed while Cash began spending more time in his room at Baptist Hospital than at home. His eyesight was so bad that John Carter had been forced to print out the lyrics to "The Man Comes Around" in large eighteen-point type for him. Cash also had trouble playing guitar on the sessions because he had lost much of the feeling in his fingers. His feet were so sore that he had to wear large, specially made shoes that greatly limited his mobility. For anyone just stepping into the cabin studio, it would have seemed impossible that this man was actually making an album—much less some of his greatest music ever.

Rosanne was anxious enough about her father's condition to fly from her home in New York to Nashville to see him in July. "There were so many hospital visits by that time in his life that they tend to blur together," she says. "But that was one of the worst. He was there for two weeks, and I slept in another hospital room to be near him."

Then everything took an unexpected turn. While all the attention was on John, June contracted pneumonia and checked in to Baptist Hospital in August, sharing an adjoining suite with John, as they had done many times before at the medical facility. Doctors found that June had heart problems sufficiently serious for them to install a pacemaker immediately. No sooner were John and June back home when Cash had to reenter Baptist Hospital with a series of liver and kidney problems. He was attached to a dialysis machine. Once again, the family thought the end was near. His weight dropped by some fifty pounds, to its lowest point since the pill-popping pre-*Folsom* days.

Somehow, in between all these crises, Cash managed to record more songs for the fourth album. He had a particularly good three-day stretch during which he recorded "The Man Comes Around" for the fourth time. It was his last recording session for the year.

When Rubin got a copy of "The Man Comes Around," he wasn't any more knocked out by it than Cash had initially been by "Hurt." The two songs that would do so much to cement Cash's legacy in the twenty-first century could both easily have been set aside if either man hadn't valued the other's opinion so strongly. If the demo of "The Man Comes Around" had been from someone other than Cash, for instance, Rubin likely would have passed on it. But he gave special attention to any new Cash composition. "The versions of the songs he sent me rarely ended up sounding like the way they did on the final album," Rubin says. "When he recorded in Nashville, more often than not it was really just to get his vocal performance. We would then take the vocal track and make a new instrumental track to go around it. We would sometimes make the song faster, sometimes slower. That was the biggest change. It wasn't ever with the words; it was the rhythms."

In between other recording projects over the next few weeks, Rubin looked at "The Man Comes Around" from different angles—"unlocking the code" is how he describes it. "When we finally got the right feel for it, the track was fantastic. I loved it." Rubin replaced the original gentle country-styled backing with a more tense and stark futuristic sound and added slightly distorted bits of narration at the beginning and end for even more character and color. Cash was thrilled with the new version.

Finally it was time to turn their attention to "Hurt." Because of Cash's condition and the complexity of the song, Rubin wanted to wait until Cash came to California to record it, which meant he had to wait until the new year. John and June once again headed to Jamaica for the holidays. While there, they learned that Waylon Jennings, who had long suffered from a diabetes-related disease, had to have his left foot amputated.

When he heard of the operation, John phoned Waylon in Phoenix, where he and Jessi had moved, and the pair agreed to get together in the new year. They ended the conversation by both saying "I love you." But Cash and Jennings never kept that date. On February 13, 2002, Jennings died in his sleep.

Two weeks later Cash celebrated his seventieth birthday and wondered about his own future. Increasingly, one verse in "Hurt" was meaning more and more to him:

> *What have I become?*
> *My sweetest friend*
> *Everyone I know*
> *Goes away in the end.*

Rubin and Cash were accumulating a lot of strong tracks for the new album, including versions of Depeche Mode's "Personal

Jesus," Sting's "I Hung My Head," Cash's early "Give My Love to Rose," and the traditional Irish ballad "Danny Boy," which was recorded in a church with an organ accompaniment. But Rubin's focus remained on "Hurt." Reznor had written the song in a fit of depression over his heroin addiction, but Cash came to see it as a deeply personal reflection on the struggle in life against false values and spiritual compromise. In March he learned that President George W. Bush was going to present him with the National Medal of Arts at a ceremony in April at Constitution Hall in Washington, D.C. Cash appreciated it, but it was his trip to California that meant most to him.

The "Hurt" sessions went spectacularly, and Rubin positioned the album, which was titled *The Man Comes Around,* for release in November to take advantage of the holiday season, which accounts for more than a quarter of the year's album sales. To promote the album, he wanted a video, Cash's first since "Delia's Gone." His first choice for a director was Mark Romanek, a Chicago native who had directed acclaimed music videos for Nine Inch Nails, Michael Jackson, and David Bowie. Romanek had been lobbying Rubin to let him make a Cash video ever since the first album. As much as he loved "Hurt," however, Rubin didn't force the song on Romanek, believing that people do their best work when they are passionate about something. He invited Romanek to his house in mid-September 2002 and played three tracks for him to choose from: "The Man Comes Around," "Danny Boy," and "Hurt." Rubin would have gone along with whatever song Romanek wanted.

As soon as he heard "Hurt," Romanek had his pick. "Holy crap," he thought. "This is great."

Though the budget for "Hurt" was, at around $100,000 to $150,000, minuscule next to the $1 million or more budgets Romanek was used to working with, he was ecstatic. "The truth is, I would have done a video of Johnny singing 'Happy Birthday,'" he says. "I wanted to work with him so much. But 'Hurt' was something more. It was so powerful. I definitely had chills listening to the song."

Romanek suggested early November in Los Angeles as a possible shooting date, which would enable Rubin to distribute the video by the end of the year.

Over the next few days, Romanek put a CD of "Hurt" on his music system and pushed the "repeat" feature. "It felt like I listened to it a million times, hoping for an idea for the video to do the music justice," he says. "I began thinking of something I had always wanted to do—a rip-off of a Samuel Beckett play called *Krapp's Last Tape*, where a person was dwarfed by this pile of crap they had accumulated during their life. I began thinking of a very stylized video. I was going to have Johnny sitting in a chair with a microphone singing the song and there was going to be literally a mountain of stuff piled up behind him. I wanted it to look like crap, just...objects from his past."

Romanek's concept for the video was highly theatrical, with Cash singing the song alone on a stage. As the video unfolded, actors in work clothes would walk onstage and start taking all the stuff away, so that at the end of the video, Cash would be sitting on a bare stage with just a spotlight on him. To create further interest, Romanek planned to have celebrities doing cameos as the workmen; two he had in mind were Beck and Johnny Depp. The whole thing would be shot on a soundstage.

Plans were far along when Romanek got an urgent phone call from Rubin on October 16—a Wednesday night. "Johnny's taken a turn for the worse," Romanek was told. "He's planning to go to Jamaica earlier than planned. There's no way he can jump on a plane and come to L.A. to do this. You've got to go to Nashville tomorrow because they're leaving Monday."

II

The turn in Cash's health caught everyone by surprise. John and June had seemed to be going through a good spell for much of the spring and summer of 2002. He had resumed recording songs for the next album in April, reprising his earlier version of the Rolling Stones' "No Expectations" as well as his version of the Eagles' "Desperado" and his own 1970s excursion into honky-tonk heartbreak, "Tear-Stained Letter." In July, August, and September, he added eighteen more tracks, ranging from Stephen Foster's "Beautiful

Dreamer" and Ian Tyson's "Four Strong Winds" to Curtis Mayfield's "People Get Ready" and Sister Rosetta Tharpe's "This Train." The last two were for the long-awaited black gospel set.

At the same time, June started work in midsummer on another solo album, this time produced by John Carter for Dualtone Records, a new indie label in Nashville that focused on singer-songwriters and the country music tradition. She wanted to salute her Carter Family legacy by recording songs she had heard as a child—"Keep on the Sunny Side," "Church in the Wildwood/Lonesome Valley," and "Wildwood Flower" the best known of them. To help his mother select the songs, John Carter listened to every studio recording the Carter Family had ever made.

To give the project even more of a family vibe, it was mostly recorded in the cabin in Maces Springs, Virginia, where June was raised. The couple had bought the cabin in the 1980s and loved spending time there because the phone rarely rang. John Carter's wife, Laura, played guitar and fiddle and sang on various tracks, and a slew of other family members made cameos, including Cash, Carlene Carter and her daughter Tiffany Anastasia, Anita Carter's daughter Lorrie Carter Bennett, and Joe Carter, the son of A.P. and Sara. The only disconcerting note was renewed worry over June's health. June had ballooned to nearly two hundred pounds. To spare her embarrassment, John Carter used a drawing of his mother rather than a new photograph on the cover of the album.

Cash, meanwhile, continued to pile up honors. On September 13 he was feeling well enough to accept the free speech award at the first annual Americana Music Awards ceremony in Nashville. In presenting the award, John Seigenthaler, the former editor of the *Nashville Tennessean* and a longtime friend, saluted Cash's history of standing up for "the poor and oppressed, including prisoners and Native Americans."

Referring to the September 11 terrorist attacks the year before, Seigenthaler said, "At a time of tragedy and terror and civil strife and danger, he knows that we must reach beyond the bombs and the barriers to embrace Christian, Jew, and Muslim as one. This 'Man in Black' is a symbol of rebellion against those whose minds are closed to other ideas." Cash then recited the lyrics to "Ragged

Old Flag," updating the song by including references to Desert Storm and Afghanistan.

Two weeks later Cash was saluted again by the release of two tribute albums. The more ambitious one, *Kindred Spirits,* was produced by Marty Stuart and featured such guests as Bob Dylan ("Train of Love"), Bruce Springsteen ("Give My Love to Rose"), and Steve Earle ("Hardin Wouldn't Run"). A second album, *Dressed in Black: A Tribute to Johnny Cash,* featured such artists as Raul Malo ("Guess Things Happen That Way") and James Intveld ("Folsom Prison Blues").

John and June also made a rare appearance in late September at the weekly Saturday night barn dance sponsored in Maces Springs by descendants of the Carter family. Admission at the one-thousand-capacity building was just $4 for adults, and the seating was first come, first served, in the room's eccentric mix of old school bus seats, church pews, and movie theater chairs. It was the most informal setting in which you'd ever expect to find a country music superstar.

Word had spread through the county that Cash was going to appear that evening and the overflow crowd greeted him with an explosion of cheers when he took the stage.

Things started off well as Cash, backed by a local three-piece group, opened with "Folsom Prison Blues" and followed with "Sunday Mornin' Comin' Down," but his shortness of breath showed in places on "Suppertime." Most of the fans were too excited to notice when he missed an occasional word, but June quickly rushed to his side at the end of the piece, allowing him to sit and rest while she sang a few numbers. After a couple of minutes Cash was back at the microphone, and the crowd again roared.

Following the brief set, the Cashes took seats in the audience to watch the other performers, but they were rushed by fans eager for autographs or just the chance to shake their hands. Overwhelmed, John and June retreated backstage, where several admirers stepped forward to help steady him when he headed down the steps on the way back to his car. Moments later, he and June were sitting in their robes in the nearby cabin. June was eating corn bread and milk, and John had milk and cookies on a tray in front of him.

Though this was more than a month before the release of *The Man Comes Around,* Cash was already looking forward to the next album he wanted to make, the collection of black gospel tunes. Earlier in the day he'd played for me a tape of some rough vocals of the songs he was thinking about including in the collection. When the tape ended, he picked up an acoustic guitar and sang a few more songs in a similar style—without any of the pauses he usually needed during conversation.

But the shakiness of his performance at the barn dance that evening brought out a vulnerability that he hadn't shown when singing the gospel songs. Back in the small house's living room, he told me he'd feared that his recording days were over when he finished *The Man Comes Around.* In fact, he had designed the last track as a farewell—a group sing-along version of "We'll Meet Again," a sweet, optimistic song that had become a virtual anthem for soldiers during World War II, especially in England, thanks to a recording by Vera Lynn. Cash, however, had first heard the song on an Ink Spots recording. It became a special favorite of his after he heard it again in Stanley Kubrick's political satire *Dr. Strangelove.*

"The last album was so hard for everybody, not just me," he told me. "They had to do so much to fix my vocals because I had to keep stopping during the songs to rest and get back my breath. I'm getting good write-ups and I'm proud of the albums, but they're not really selling all that much—compared to the other acts that Rick works with. So I felt I was overstaying my welcome with Rick.

"I had just finished my last vocal for the record and I shook hands with Rick and I said, 'It's been fun.' I think it was my way of saying I understood if he wanted to call it quits. But he immediately asked what I wanted to do next. I mentioned the black gospel album and then I mentioned an album of songs that would show my musical roots, and Rick said, 'Let's do them both.' I was dumbfounded. It was just what I wanted to hear. I had thought I might finally be at the point where I would only be singing for myself. I'm a lucky man."

It was the second time that day Cash had mentioned the word "lucky."

Earlier he'd told me a conversation he had in 1970 with Michael Nesmith of the Monkees. Cash had given Nesmith a tour of his house after the group appeared on his TV show. "We were standing outside looking at the house and Michael said, 'I'm glad for you. Shame you can't keep it.'

"I asked what he was talking about, and he said, 'We can't keep things like that in this business. My bet is you'll lose this place and this woman because this business is awfully rough and you're as vulnerable as anybody else.'"

After a brief pause, Cash continued the story.

"I knew what Michael was saying, but I told him I'd take that bet, and you know what? I won. I guess I'm one of the lucky ones." June stood up and kissed her husband on the forehead and went to bed, but John still wanted to talk.

Haltingly for the next forty-five minutes, when his breath didn't desert him, he told me about personal things, especially some regrets—not being a better father to his daughters, not being a better husband to June in the early days, not being a better Christian, and not being a more dedicated musician.

As time went on, the breaks to catch his breath became more frequent. Still, Cash wasn't finished.

"I needed help…"

He paused.

"…to make that last record, and I'm not just talking about Rick and the others."

He paused.

"I called upon Jesus. He stood with me. I can never praise Him enough for all his blessings."

Cash again had to pause.

"But I tried to praise Him with 'The Man Comes Around.' If someone is still listening to my music fifty years from now…"

He paused, then repeated, "…if someone is listening at all, I hope they're listening to that song."

III

Romanek took a red-eye flight to Nashville on October 18 to begin work on the "Hurt" video. Accompanied by his producer Aaris McGarry and cinematographer Jean-Yves Escoffer, they were met early the next morning by Cash in the Hendersonville house's library. Romanek was saddened to see Cash surrounded by a massive wall of books he was no longer able to read. Though weak, Cash was gracious and took the three men upstairs to meet June, who was resting in bed.

There wasn't time to arrange to shoot the video on a local soundstage, so Romanek looked around the house for an appropriate setting. He decided on the living room, where Cash could sit at the piano. "I don't remember him being associated with the piano, so I thought that would be more interesting than having him with a guitar," the director recalls. "We could then shoot him somewhere else in the room with the guitar and at the dining table—and that was the only affectation that we put into the video. It seemed weird for him to be sitting at a bare table, so we set up this sort of banquet at the table."

As Romanek and team spent the rest of the day assembling a local crew and ordering lighting and other equipment, he was troubled by one thing. "I didn't know if the scenes in the house were going to be enough to make a three-and-a-half-minute video," he says. "When I spoke to Rick that night on the phone, I told him my concerns, and Rick suggested we check out the House of Cash museum." The museum had been closed for some time and it was in a state of disrepair.

The combination of Cash's health and the museum's shabby appearance gave Romanek pause. "I found myself struggling with how to do this," he says. "Do I try to glamorize everything and put a scrim over the lens and use lighting tracks you might do with an aging woman who is vain—or do I show it the way it is? My instinct—because it was Johnny Cash—was that we had to be very truthful and show how he looks because it's wrong—especially for this song—to try to prettify the whole thing. Finally I decided that the only thing to do was to be honest. I realized, 'This is Johnny Cash. I should do the bold thing, not the safe thing.'"

Cash allowed Romanek to shoot the museum and had no prob-lem with his showing the broken records and places where the ceiling had recently caved in from the rain. A woman from Cash's housekeeping staff came in at one point and offered to clean things up, but Romanek gently shooed her away. He wanted everything the way it was, dust and all. The only "prop" he added to the mu-seum was a "Closed to the Public" sign on the front door; the museum was closed, but Romanek wanted to make the point more clearly. The museum scenes—including stacks of video and film archives in the basement—were meant to help add contrast to the performance scenes, which were all filmed in the house.

At one point in the shooting, June walked from her bedroom to the stairs and looked down at her husband, who was lip-synching to the instrumental track of "Hurt." When Romanek noticed her, he was struck by the anxious, loving look on her face, and he asked if she would mind being in the video. After putting on some makeup, she returned to the stairs and the cameras again rolled. Her loving but highly anxious expression was an unexpected highlight of the eventual video. Because Cash had trouble lip-synching, the shoot went slowly. He did two or three takes by the piano, two or three more near some Frederic Remington paintings, a take or two by the stairs, and finally the climactic banquet scene.

Romanek's idea was for Cash to sing right into the lens for added impact, but Cash, because of his limited sight, couldn't locate the lens; the problem was solved when a tiny flashing light was placed next to the lens. Just before the final take, the director approached Cash with a suggestion: "This is the last thing we are going to shoot, so if you want to do something crazy, go for it—if you want to sweep the food off the table, this is the time. Let's be bold.' He said, 'I think I've got something, Mark.' And that's when he poured the wine onto the table. It was totally him, and that turned out to be one of my favorite moments in the video."

Back in Los Angeles, Romanek and his team went through the footage and found some haunting material, but they still weren't sure it was enough to hold someone's interest for an entire video. It wasn't until they interspersed shots from the archives of the younger, charismatic Cash with the Hendersonville footage that the video came to life. This took longer than expected, but Rubin was patient.

"It was that juxtaposition that gave the video its power," Romanek says. "It's the shocking contrast of a man in his prime smacked one frame right up against someone who is coming toward the end of his life. It's a shocking dose of everyone's mortality. Plus the song made an equation that was way beyond the sum of its parts."

When the team, including editor Robert Duffy, was finished, a copy of the video was sent to Rubin. Two hours later, Rubin was on the phone. "He said, 'Wow,' but it wasn't a good 'wow,'" Romanek remembers. "It was kind of like, 'I'm upset by this—emotionally upset. It's obviously very powerful, but I don't know if it's good or bad.'"

Ultimately, Rubin knew the decision to release the video rested with Cash, and he sent him a copy without comment. When Cash phoned, he wanted to know how Rubin felt about it, and the producer said he had been troubled at first but had grown to believe it was a marvelous piece of art, especially Cash's performance and such scenes as the spilling of the wine at the dinner table.

In turn, Cash told Rubin that he was disturbed watching it and needed time to think it over; his tone led Rubin to believe he was leaning against releasing the video.

When Cash showed the video to people around him, several, including June, advised him not to allow the video to be released. She felt his fans might believe he was destitute. But Rosanne, among others, argued strongly in favor of it. "Dad showed me the video in his office at the house and I cried all the way through it," she says. "I told him, 'You have to put it out. It's so unflinching and brave and that's what you are.' I was tremendously proud of him. I thought it was enormously courageous. It was a work of art, excruciatingly truthful. I thought, 'How could that be wrong in any way?'"

After a few days, Cash phoned Rubin with an answer. "I remember sitting in my car in Santa Monica, looking at the ocean while talking to Johnny, having a feeling that nobody's ever going to see this video," Rubin says. "I thought for sure he was going to say no, but he decided it should be seen."

Rubin immediately phoned Romanek, who had been aware of the dissension in Cash's camp. "It was a nail-biting week," the director says. "It seemed like it could go either way. I knew we were treading this line which some might see as disrespectful or some kind of premature eulogy, which was not what I was trying to do. I didn't pick that song. He picked the song. If he had sung 'These Are a Few of My Favorite Things,' it would have been a lighter video."

For Cash, the decision was a striking example of his courage as an artist; in the end, he saw it as part of his artistic journey. Where *Folsom* showed a young man full of energy and creative fire, "Hurt" showed a man—the same man—nearing the end of his life, struggling to maintain both his health and his faith.

Though thrilled by Cash's decision, Romanek wondered if youth-oriented MTV or any other TV music outlet would even show the video. "Videos were aimed at sixteen-year-olds mostly," the director relates. "I kept thinking, 'He's a senior citizen. Nobody is going to show this.'"

As feared, the "Hurt" video was largely ignored in the weeks after the album was released, and few music writers made special mention of the "Hurt" track; perhaps the song was too closely identified with Reznor for them to pay much attention. Similarly, little was said about the other two major rock covers, "Personal Jesus" and "In My Life." In fact, one reason why critical reaction was mixed was that many critics thought Cash spent too much time doing remakes of overly familiar songs, including "Bridge over Troubled Water," which had been a massive hit for both Simon & Garfunkel and Aretha Franklin, and "The First Time Ever I Saw Your Face," which was strongly identified with Roberta Flack.

When the reviews came out in November, two themes were common: a widespread suspicion that this would be Cash's final album and special praise for the title track. In England, *Mojo* magazine declared, "If this is Cash's last album, then what a magnificent way he has chosen to say goodbye." England's *Uncut* found it to be "probably the most consistent of the Rubin-produced albums."

Even in a *Rolling Stone* preview of the album three months before its release, the focus was on "The Man Comes Around." While the article mentioned "Hurt" and the other cuts in passing, it contained this quote by Marty Stuart about "The Man Comes Around": "It's the most strangely marvelous, wonderful, gothic, mysterious, Christian thing that only God and Johnny Cash could create together."

Pitchfork, a fiercely independent Internet publication known for championing innovation and daring, especially in young indie rock, made the strongest case for the album's title track: "The Cash-penned 'The Man Comes Around' is an epic tale of apocalypse, interpreting Revelations with uplifting exuberance. Restraint, resignation, and a hope of peace pervade the prophetic imagery. Truly, the subdued fury and beauty of this track reduces everything that follows. The immediate question posed is: if this man can still write and perform works of this caliber, why is he resorting to the words and music of others?"

The *Village Voice*'s Robert Christgau, one of the nation's most probing and influential rock critics, also singled out "The Man Comes Around," writing, "First and best comes the newly written title tune, a look at death as cold as 'Under Ben Bulben.'" The *Los Angeles Times* called the song "a judgment-day tale as stark as anything else Cash has written."

With the expectation level that had been raised by *American III: Solitary Man* and the heavy press attention, *The Man Comes Around* got off to the fastest sales start of any of the Rubin-produced albums. After two months, sales had reached nearly 120,000 copies. But then, in the absence of a hit single or video, sales dropped after Christmas to just 6,000 a week—and stayed at or below that level through January.

Rubin saw the "Hurt" video as his last chance to recapture the public's attention. Knowing that MTV and other primary video music channels took their lead in programming from what radio was playing, on January 14 he took a copy of the video to Kevin Weatherly, the general manager of KROQ-FM in Los Angeles. If the influential station played the record, Rubin knew other stations around the country would follow, and that would make MTV at least consider showing it.

Weatherly, a master at spotting potential hits, was touched by the video and played the record immediately on the station. He wanted to test it on his young rock audience. The radio request lines lit up. Rubin was thrilled. As expected, MTV followed the station's lead, and the response was impressive enough for the channel to keep showing the video.

In Nashville, CMT's editorial director, Chet Flippo, praised the video: "Music videos come and go, but the stunning video for Johnny Cash's Hurt is one that will endure for a long, long time. Visually arresting, artistically captivating, emotionally devastating—it's the kind of drama to which great music videos aspire. It's a gripping testimony to Cash's career and to the magnitude of his stature both as an artist and a man. Along the way, it graphically demonstrates his elevation to worldwide icon."

This video-driven excitement spread to the retail music world. The album sales, which had totaled only 6,800 copies the week ending February 2, suddenly leaped to 13,300 the following week, according to Nielsen SoundScan. It then jumped to 18,100 the following week, then 21,000, before hitting a peak of 26,500 the week ending March 9. By the end of June, sales for *The Man Comes Around* were over 400,000. It was on its way to becoming the first Cash solo album since *San Quentin* to top the 1 million sales mark.

But the impact of the video went far deeper than sales. For millions of young music fans, Cash became as beloved and respected a figure as he had been in the days of his prison albums and his TV show. His legacy was stronger than ever. His old drummer W. S. Holland was amazed by the resurgence. "It sounds odd just saying it, but you know Johnny Cash may be remembered someday more for that video than any of his records."

The video exposure also redirected attention to Cash's recording of "Hurt." Seeing him sing the song made it easier for young rock fans to notice the changes he'd made in the original—not just altering the line "I wear this crown of shit" to "I wear this crown of thorns," but the way he had made the song into a parable. In its first decade the album eventually sold nearly 2 million copies in the United States alone. No one seemed more moved than the song's writer, Trent Reznor, who admitted he had mixed feelings about Cash's recording such a personal song. After seeing the video, however, he was so touched he cried. "It really, really made sense, and

I thought what a powerful piece of art," he said. "I never got to meet Johnny, but I'm happy I contributed the way I did. It felt like a warm hug."

When most people watched the "Hurt" video the first few times, their attention was directed solely at Cash, who seemed on the edge of death as he sat at the piano and dinner table with trembling hands and a nearly vacant stare. Even when one finally started paying attention to June on the stairs, the sadness and uncertainty on her face appeared to be a reflection of the prospect of facing life without him.

What neither Rubin nor Romanek knew at the time was that June's anxiety and anguish were the result of news she'd received from her doctor the day before. She had a serious leak in a heart valve.

Because of all the time she had spent in hospitals, June dreaded going back. She told several close friends that she'd had a premonition of dying if she ever did. The news of another operation was akin to a death sentence. As she stood on the stairs in such despair, she was likely thinking not so much what she would do without John as what John would do without her.

CHAPTER 36

THE FINAL DAYS

I

RATHER THAN AGGRESSIVELY ADDRESS her own deteriorating condition, June spent the final months of her life trying to ease her husband's burdens. She asked, "What can I do for you, John?" so often that it became a mantra. She wasn't alone. Everyone around the couple focused, as they had for years, on his endless needs. Anyway, June and her sisters had all had reputations as hypochondriacs; they seemed to be in a continual contest to prove who had the worst ailment.

"June fell through the cracks," says Mark Stielper. "I do not believe that she purposely didn't take care of herself. It's just that all eyes—including hers—were elsewhere. We all thought her maladies were, in comparison, minor, and that it was a case of 'June being June,' i.e., being dramatic."

Cash knew about his wife's heart valve problem, but he didn't press her about getting it taken care of; he thought of her as invincible. Meanwhile, he wanted to get back into the studio to finish recording the gospel album he had started the previous summer. For much of the time, though, he seemed to be barely hanging on. When he and June got back from Jamaica just after Christmas, he went into Baptist Hospital for an operation to deal with an ulcer on his foot. He was released just after New Year's, but returned to the hospital almost immediately after a fall at the house. He remained there for three weeks. No sooner had he gotten back home than he fell again and reentered the hospital, and was there the day the "Hurt" video aired on January 31, 2003.

But to everyone's surprise, he found the strength to resume work on the album for two days the first week in March. Because he was having an elevator installed in his house, he and June had moved across the street to the smaller single-story house where his parents had lived during their final years. Ferguson set up recording equipment there, and Cash recorded four songs, including "God's Gonna Cut You Down," an old spiritual which warned that all sinners eventually have to answer to God, and Kristofferson's "Jesus Was a Capricorn."

Progress was stopped on March 15 when he was rushed back to the hospital, where he was placed on a ventilator again. June canceled her plans to fly to Spokane to appear on a bill with George Jones, a rare performance she had been eagerly anticipating. With family gathered around, Cash again rallied and was cheered by all the awards coming his way. The country music world had finally embraced him again. CMT, the country music cable channel, named an award after him, the Johnny Cash Visionary Award, designed to recognize "extraordinary musical vision, innovative and groundbreaking music videos and pioneering initiatives in entertainment." Cash didn't dwell on how Nashville had resisted almost all of his own "pioneering initiatives." He was grateful for the recognition.

On March 28 in a CMT special, Cash was named one of the most important male artists in the history of country music. Watching the telecast from Cash's hospital room, Mark Stielper figured either Cash or Hank Williams would end up at number one. And his prediction of a two-man race looked likely as the countdown ran through the heart of the list.

Resting in bed, Cash heard many of his heroes and contemporaries named: Gene Autry was number thirty-eight, his beloved Jimmie Rodgers number thirty-three, Elvis Presley number fifteen, Merle Haggard number six, Waylon Jennings number five, Willie

Nelson number four, and George Jones number three. That left just Williams and Cash.

Stielper let out a victory yelp when Hank Williams's photo came up on the screen, tipping off his selection as number two, making Cash number one.

Johnny Cash's legacy had not just been restored by this latest series of albums; it had been enhanced.

"Well," he joked, "if I'm that important, I better get out of this bed and get back to work."

Cash's sister Louise died a week after the telecast, but he was still too weak to attend her funeral. Similarly, Cash had to watch from home on April 7 when he was honored with a special achievement award during CMT's new Flameworthy Video Music Awards ceremony. Though visibly ill herself, June accepted the award for him.

Rick Rubin, who watched the telecast with Cash at the house, was worried about his friend's continued deterioration. A few months earlier Rubin had told Cash about Dr. Gene Scott, a controversial TV evangelist in Los Angeles whose sermons came across as a wildly colorful mix of profound biblical scholarship and semicrazed ranting. What had particularly interested Rubin was Scott's claim that he had defeated prostate cancer without surgery by taking communion daily. Cash was intrigued by the account. When Rubin, who was born into a Jewish family but never actively practiced the religion, mentioned he had never taken communion, Cash said they should do it together sometime.

During the Flameworthy telecast, Cash recalled the conversation and led Rubin through a brief ceremony. Cash spoke a few words and then both men shared some crackers and grape juice, in lieu of the wafer and wine. Eager to do everything he could to help Cash battle his health problems, Rubin suggested they continue the practice daily over the phone. Cash would go through the actual ceremony, while Rubin would just visualize the taking of the wafer and wine. They would share communion in that way almost every day for the rest of Cash's life.

*   *   *

The end for June came quickly.

There was no way to ignore her needs on April 11, when she was finding it difficult even to breathe. She was taken to Baptist Hospital and placed in the intensive care unit, where she told visitors that she didn't have long to live. Like John, however, she was strong, and her doctors allowed her to go home after a few days while they planned her treatment.

Trying to tell himself that things would be okay, Cash went into the studio a few days later to record "Help Me," the Larry Gatlin song that Cash had first heard in Reverend Jimmie Snow's church. In one of his most memorable vocal performances, Cash conveyed the tenderness of the song in every line, struggling all the time to find enough breath to keep going.

> *I never thought I needed help before,*
> *I thought that I could do things by myself.*
> *Now I know I just can't take it anymore.*
> *With a humble heart, on bended knee,*
> *I'm beggin' You, please, for help.*

Hearing the recording for the first time in California, Rubin was moved. "I couldn't believe how great the record was," he says. "It was so heartfelt. It was less a 'song' than someone spilling his guts. I kept thinking, 'I can't believe I'm hearing this.' It was one of the most chilling moments I ever had listening to music."

Cash wanted to continue recording after the "Help Me" session, but his energy gave out the second day and he had to quit early.

On Monday, April 28, June suffered another setback.

As it happened, John Carter arrived at the house just in time to see his mother being helped into her Lincoln Town Car for a trip to the hospital. As the vehicle passed him on the way out of the driveway, June was so weak that she could only mouth the words, "I love you."

On Wednesday, May 7, doctors proceeded with the heart valve replacement and told the family that the operation went well. John Carter visited June in the coronary care unit, but she couldn't speak because her mouth was covered by an oxygen mask. She smiled faintly and reached out to hold her son's hand. John Carter tried to assure her that she'd be fine, but something in her eyes told him she didn't believe him—as if she was saying, "No, son, I won't be leaving here alive."

In the early morning hours of May 9, June suffered a coronary arrest. Her heart stopped for several minutes, perhaps as many as fifteen. She sank into a coma and was placed on life support. Then she was declared brain dead. John Carter entered her room to find his dad already there, sitting on a chair next to June.

II

As John's and June's children came together at the hospital, June still on life support, there was a sense of genuine grief. Rather than resenting June for the breakup of their parents' marriage, John's daughters had grown to appreciate what she meant to their father.

"I hate what happened to my mother, but I came to see over the years that Dad had a friend, a lover, and they grew closer and closer the older they got," Cindy says. "It was a wonderful love story."

Mark Stielper agrees. "John and June did have a happy ending to their love story," he says. "Each doted on the other as they closed out the world around them and quietly allowed peace to reign. I heard John say to her many times 'We saw it all, didn't we, baby.' Whereas at one time he meant that ruefully, it became a valedictory."

It had been a hard few weeks for Rosanne—the death of her aunt Louise adding to worry about John and June. During this period she wrote a song, "Black Cadillac," that she later described as a "postcard from the future." The song was triggered by Louise's death, but she came to realize it was actually about her father. Key lines go:

> *Now it's a lonely world*
> *Guess it always was*
> *Minus you and minus blood*
> *My blood.*

Though June's neurologist told Cash that there was no way his wife was "coming back from this," he refused to accept it. Rosanne and the others took turns wheeling him into June's room several times a day so he could sit with her.

After much urging from the children, Cash accepted the inevitable; he allowed the doctors to take June off life support. But that wasn't the end.

To add to the heartache, June's pacemaker kept her heart beating for another three days. That may have been the hardest period, John Carter says. "We stayed there, praying and hoping. But we knew she was already gone." The final days were "beyond terrible," Rosanne says. "It made me go home and rewrite my living will afterward."

As they waited for the end, John, the children, and friends, including Ted Rollins, sang hymns. Recalls Rollins, "It was very emotional and peaceful at the same time. It was unbelievable to be a part of that...and [hear him] say his good-byes and gently touching her and saying how much he loved her."

On Thursday, May 15, at 5:04 p.m., as Cash and the others sang "Oh Come, Angel Band," June Carter Cash died. She was seventy-three.

Rubin spoke to Cash at the hospital by phone shortly afterward and found him shattered. "He talked about all the pain he had gone through in his life, but nothing to compare with this," the producer says. "I didn't know if he was going to make it past this. I'm not talking about making more records; I'm talking about his life."

Trying to find some way to give Cash hope, Rubin asked, "Do you think you can find anywhere in you the faith to get through this?"

There was something about the word "faith" that changed Cash's demeanor, Rubin says. In a loud, clear, strong voice, Cash said, "My faith is unshakable!"

"It was like a whole other Johnny Cash again," Rubin adds. "I suddenly felt everything was going to be all right."

The news announcement noted that the funeral—set for two p.m. Sunday the eighteenth at the First Baptist Church of Hendersonville—would be private. But Cash wanted to open the service to the public, and Lou Robin sent out a statement: "Thanks to June's friends, fans and loved ones for the outpouring of love at this terrible time. I love you all."

Knowing how much his mother loved flowers, John Carter suggested the funeral notice read, "In lieu of donations, send flowers."

When Sunday arrived, more than 1,500 mourners watched as Cash was rolled into the church in his wheelchair. For most of the mourners, it was the first time they had seen him in that condition.

Rosanne led a parade of speakers. "My daddy has lost his dearest companion...and his soul mate. If being a wife were a corporation, June would have been a CEO. It was her most treasured role." Rosanne humorously recalled the time June picked up the phone and had the "nicest" half-hour phone conversation with someone, only to say afterward that the caller had dialed the wrong number. The incident symbolized to Rosanne June's generosity and upbeat spirit. John's oldest daughter also said she loved June for the way she'd accepted all of her children without ever using the term "stepdaughter." "She always said, 'I have seven children.'" Music was provided by a variety of artists, including Emmylou Harris, the Gatlin Brothers, Sheryl Crow, and some of the Carter clan members.

Cash was helped to his feet and led to the side of the casket, where he leaned over to say good-bye.

Music would again be his refuge. On the drive home, Cash turned to John Carter and said, in a weak, raspy voice, "I don't know about you, but I have to get to work. I have to get into the studio."

Afterward at the lake house property, Cash gathered with his children, grandchildren, and a few close friends at the bell garden, a rock and concrete structure housing some thirty brass bells. After Cash said a prayer, the mourners, in keeping with a family tradition, rang the bells seventy-three times, for each of June's years. The sound could be heard for miles.

III

Within the week, Cash insisted on going back to work, recording a track for a Carter Family tribute album that John Carter was producing. They had already chosen the song, "I Found You among the Roses," making it all the more emotional for everyone in the room when Cash sang the song's opening line, *Once again dear it's rose time, it's June time.*

John Carter marveled at how his father found the strength to sing the song; he was convinced that Jesus was by his father's side that day. "I don't think it occurred to him at that moment what was going on, but he later realized how sad it was and he said he didn't want that song to be on the record," John Carter says. "It was just too close to home." He respected his father's wishes and left the song off the album.

"There was so much sadness there," his son adds. "He came to me at one point and said, 'Love with everything you have because it all passes like the blink of an eye.'"

The atmosphere around the house after June's death bordered on panic. His children were familiar with tales of how the death of one spouse often leads to the death of the other—a new fear in addition to Cash's long trail of illnesses and hospital vigils.

At her dad's insistence, Cindy had proceeded with longtime plans to marry fiancé Eddie Panetta in California even though it meant missing June's funeral. Following the wedding, Cindy and her new husband left for Mississippi, where they planned to live. But she was so concerned about her father's health that, with her husband's encouragement, she went to Hendersonville to see him. She ended up staying there for months.

By now the elevator had been installed, which Cash used to get from his bedroom to the kitchen and den, but he spent most of his time in his small office, even sleeping there on a special hospital bed. Though he had never been fond of long phone conversations, he was now talking frequently on the phone to old friends.

The saddest part of each day was evening.

"We were sitting in his office one day when the sun was going down and it was getting dark outside," Cindy says. "He told me, 'I always get frightened when the sun goes down.' It was because he couldn't see anymore. I asked him one time to look at me and tell me what he saw. I said, 'What part of me can you see?'

"He said, 'I see a light around you showing me the shape of you.'"

When Cindy realized her father couldn't see her face, she broke down.

Cindy spent many hours reading to him from his favorite books, which he had moved to a nearby shelf. She'd also wheel him outside every day and let him feel the breeze and listen to the birds chattering, especially crows. "He loved being outdoors," Cindy says. "He once told me he even thought God spoke to him through crows."

One day, Cash asked his daughter to drive him to the cemetery to visit June's grave.

Standing over her marker, he started sobbing again. "I'm coming, baby."

Kathy, who was living in Nashville, also spent numerous days at the house, and Rosanne and Tara flew in for visits when they could.

In the midst of all this, a storm was brewing between some of the children and their parents' longtime staff, especially Peggy Knight, who had been John and June's aide-de-camp for decades.

As John Carter spent more time with his father, he began to feel the staff was putting up a wall between him and his dad, ignoring family wishes. Even before his mother's death, he'd been made to feel increasingly unwelcome by the staff. As the discomfort increased after June's death, John Carter and Cindy expressed to their father their concerns about Knight and the others. The issue added to what was already an unbearable tension at the house by the lake.

Cash resumed work on the next Rubin-produced album the same week as he contributed to his son's Carter Family tribute. Over the next few days he recorded such material as Merle Travis's "Dark as a Dungeon" and the Carter Family favorite "You're Gonna Miss Me When I'm Gone" and an old spiritual "There Ain't No Grave (Gonna Hold My Body Down)."

The sessions were slow, but Cash was in good hands. Ferguson and John Carter recognized that every line out of Cash's mouth was a piece of history worth preserving whatever the time and cost. They felt they literally had John's life in their hands; they were sure the recording was keeping him alive.

After a short break, Ferguson was back at the house the first week in June when old friend Jack Clement stopped by. During the session John suddenly said to Clement, "Cowboy, let's cut 'Aloha,'" referring to "Aloha 'Oe," an old Hawaiian song of farewell that the pair had been singing together for fun for some thirty years. Clement was game and even played Hawaiian-style slide guitar. Rubin immediately thought of it for the end track of Cash's next album, much as "We'll Meet Again" closed *The Man Comes Around.*

On June 12, for reasons since forgotten, Ferguson set up some equipment next door in Marty Stuart's house so Cash could record Gordon Lightfoot's "If You Could Read My Mind." During the session, Rubin called with one of the few suggestions that Cash rejected out of hand: the Frank Sinatra hit "My Way." Cash wasn't a Sinatra fan, and he found the statement of personal independence grating. Stuart and the others at the session cheered his decision. It would be the last session for a month.

John went to June's hometown in Virginia later in the month to celebrate her birthday by performing at a barn dance. While seated in a chair, he spoke to the audience in a weak, barely audible voice, "I don't know hardly what to say tonight about being up here. The pain is so severe there is no way of describing it. It really hurts." Two weeks later John was back on the same stage, somehow finding the strength to do seven songs.

Shortly after he returned to Hendersonville, he heard from Vivian, who was in town and wanted to drop by to get his blessings for a book project. Cash was happy to see her, and they had a pleasant visit. Vivian wanted to write a memoir that would tell some of their story, mainly through the mass of letters they exchanged during the Air Force years.

Cash was supportive. "I've been thinking about that for the past couple of years," he said. "I think it's a great idea."

Vivian, in her book, said she'd told Johnny that their story might help other women who were going through the same kinds of trouble they had. "I so much want for good to come out of those darkest hours," she wrote. But she'd warned him, "Some of your fans might be upset by hearing the details of our divorce and what happened." She quotes his answer: "Like I said, all my fans will read it. They'll love it. It's time." It was the last time she would see him.

Out in California, Rubin continued to look forward to his daily phone visits with John. He was thinking less and less about finding new songs and more about figuring out how to help him.

IV

For some time Rubin had been working with Phil Maffetone, a nationally known author and practitioner in the fields of nutrition, exercise, sports medicine, and biofeedback techniques. His patients had included figures from the worlds of sports, business, and music—from Tom Seaver and Mario Andretti to James Taylor and the Red Hot Chili Peppers. He had left his practice in 2002 to become a songwriter, which is how he met Rubin. In exchange for his helping Rubin learn more about fitness and nutrition, Rubin helped Maffetone with his music. About a month after June's funeral, he told Maffetone and Cash about each other and the pair agreed to meet.

Before flying to Nashville to assess Cash's condition, Maffetone had what he describes as "a troubling" phone conversation with John's primary physician, Dr. Terri Jerkins. He introduced himself and asked about the medicines Cash was taking. The answer startled Maffetone. Cash was on around thirty medications.

"I can't imagine that many unless someone's in a first-aid state and they're in the hospital, hanging on for their life," he says. "But that's temporary, not a regular basis for months and years. While I'm on the phone, I'm writing this down and I'm thinking, 'This medicine is clashing with that and that is clashing with another one'; it was a train wreck."

Maffetone arrived at the house on July 8, a Tuesday, and met with Cash in his office, where he was still confined to a wheelchair, a respirator by his side. Cash looked more helpless than he had just months before in the "Hurt" video.

John was cordial, but, just as he had been when he'd met Rubin for the first time, he was passive, not sure that he could be helped. Billy Graham had been urging him to go to the Mayo Clinic, but Cash didn't have the strength even to consider it. Rubin had sent others to talk to him—"holistic types," some in Cash's camp called them—but Cash hadn't connected with any of them. It was only out of courtesy to Rubin that he agreed to meet with one more outsider.

Maffetone was surprised to find Cash wearing heavy shoes—"big enough to wear in battle"—and leg braces even though he was in a wheelchair.

"Why are you wearing these things when you're not even walking?" Maffetone asked Cash, who had no answer.

Maffetone told Cash that he wanted to work with him in many areas, including diet, exercise, and brain function. But first he wanted to get him out of the wheelchair, partly as a way of rebuilding John's confidence.

"The first thing we want to do," he told him, "is take those things off and get you moving."

"I can't do that," John replied.

"Yes, you can...one step at a time."

Maffetone told Cash the reason he couldn't stand up was that his muscles had been turned off. He needed to reestablish communication between the muscles and the brain, which Maffetone would try to do by massaging the muscles involved.

When Maffetone again asked Cash to take off the shoes and braces, John didn't respond.

"It was one of those nervous, quiet moments," Maffetone recalls. "So I bent down and took off the shoes and then the braces and he was still silent. I said, 'Now we're going to do some biofeedback so you can stand up.'"

It took a long time, possibly two hours, before Maffetone had Cash's muscles sufficiently stimulated for him to repeat his request for John to stand up.

Maffetone sensed that Cash was getting annoyed; it was humiliating for him to be helpless and to be told to do something he didn't think was possible. But finally, with Maffetone's help, he did stand, if shakily.

"I put my hand on his arm, but I offered no support. He really was standing on his own," Maffetone says. "He looked around, even though he couldn't see, and he said, 'Wow.' Then I asked him if he was comfortable enough to take a few steps, and he wasn't. Then I asked him to lift his leg like he was going to take a step and put it forward, and he said, 'I don't know if I can do that.' But he did lift it and he started to move it forward, though he kind of stumbled around."

Maffetone told John to sit back down so he could work on muscles that enabled the foot to move up and down.

"When John got back up, we went through the same thing again—lifting one leg, then the other—and he ended up taking several steps."

The next day Cash greeted Maffetone with good news: for the first time in ages, he had been able to shower while standing and without fatigue. As they worked together, Cash took as many as fifteen to twenty steps and even sat on an exercise bike, pushing the pedals for approximately a minute.

For the first time in a month, Cash felt strong enough to record a song the next day, July 11, and again on July 14, the day Maffetone returned to his home in Florida. He left John with a list of exercises to help improve his eyesight and restore feeling in his fingers, perhaps even enabling him to play the guitar again, which in turn could lead him to resume another lost skill, songwriting. He promised to be back in a week.

It was during this period that Tara flew to Nashville for three days and spent virtually every waking minute with her dad. She was saddened seeing him in such immense pain, yet she treasured the closeness. Tara had brought a tape recorder, and she turned it on when she tried to lift his spirits by playing a kind of musical word-association game with him, throwing out a word—"bird"—to see if he could sing a song with the word in it, in that case "Bird on The Wire."

The exercise went on for several minutes.

"Dad, do you know a fishing song?" Tara asked, and Cash responded by singing, "Gone fishing, there's a sign up on the door, gone fishing, ain't a workin' no more"—"Gone Fishin'," which he had learned from a Bing Crosby–Louis Armstrong recording while he was in the Air Force.

When he finished, Tara challenged him with "blueberries."

This time he was stumped, so Tara came up with "cabin."

That was easy (the spiritual "Lord, Build Me a Cabin in Gloryland," which he learned from a Bill Monroe recording), but "frog" and "bush" eluded him.

Cash did, however, come up with songs for "rock" (the spiritual "Oh, Mary, Don't You Weep"), "walk" (not "I Walk the Line," but the gospel number "He Walks with Me in the Garden"), "knife" ("Wolverton Mountain," from his Louisiana Hayride days), and "fountain" (the spiritual "There's a Fountain Filled with Blood").

At one point he said, "I'm winning, Tara," and his daughter answered, "I know you are" and immediately stumped him again with "garden hose."

"He loved the game," Tara says. "He was such a walking encyclopedia musically."

Tara watched her father go through the exercises with Maffetone, which gave her hope, but her memory of that visit would be mostly one of heartache at seeing her father so frail.

On the day she left, Tara and her father had breakfast. When they were finished, they stood. Tara hugged him and started to cry. Her father knew exactly what she was thinking and tried to comfort her. "This isn't the last time you're going to see me, baby." But Tara knew it was. "It was just excruciating. He was so sad."

Continuing to feel that the household staff was not operating in their father's best interests, John Carter and Cindy urged Cash to fire Peggy Knight, but he resisted. Kathy was neutral. She had issues with Knight and the staff, but she felt the timing was bad; their absence would make her father feel even more alone.

On the morning of July 20, John Carter and Cindy went to their father's office in another attempt to persuade him to take action.

"Dad, there is something Cindy and I want to talk to you about," John Carter said.

"Wait!" Cash responded. "First there is something I want to tell you. I'm going to fire Peggy Knight in the morning."

The next day Cindy listened as her father addressed his longtime housekeeper in his office.

"Peggy, sit down," he said. "I'm sorry, but you have disrespected my children, my family, and myself. You're fired."

Knight protested, but Cash wouldn't reconsider.

The following weeks were a time of upheaval.

"Peggy's departure ushered in a period of uncertainty and more unhappiness," according to Mark Stielper, "as other longtime staff followed her, to be replaced by an ever-changing lineup of nurses and caretakers unknown to Cash, who greatly missed the comfort of routine and familiarity, and who was then obliged to endure the indignities that came with strangers tending to his most intimate needs." Quoting from "Hurt," he added, "'Everyone I know goes away in the end' had been prophetic."

Maffetone returned to Hendersonville on the day after the firing and found Cash making continued progress. "When I walked into the room, he was on his exercise bike," he says. "When he saw me, he said, 'Dr. Phil, look at this.'" Cash had also begun regaining some of his eyesight and some feeling in his fingers.

To encourage him even more, Maffetone placed a guitar on Cash's lap and told him, "It won't be long before you're strumming again." Cash looked up and smiled. He was starting to believe he could get better. He even sang a new song he was writing—a train song, good-natured enough to include a mocking reference to his struggle with asthma. He even called it "Asthma Coming Down Like the 309." It was only half-finished—he would eventually retitle it "Like the 309"—but Cash was finally feeling good about himself again.

The worst times continued to be in the evening, when Cash felt most alone and anxious about the new nurses and caretakers who had entered his life.

Kathy went to his office one night and found him cowering in his chair.

Referring to the new nurse, he told his daughter, "That girl is sitting right outside my office. She never leaves," continuing, "She keeps asking me if I need something. I don't know her. I can't even see her."

"He was freaked out," Kathy says. "It's like all of a sudden he's got all these people in there that he doesn't know and he was scared; he was alone in the house with them at night, so he would ask me if I'd spend the night with him, so I'd sleep on the couch outside

Dad's office or in [one of the bedrooms] and the nurse would be on the couch. I told her to come get me if he hollers because I didn't want just anybody walking in on him at night."

Some nights Kathy would sit with her father and read him a story. When she thought he had dozed off on one visit, she eased out of her chair and almost got to the door, when she heard a weak voice say, "Where do you think you're going? Tell me a story."

Trying to lighten the mood, she says, she replied, "'Once upon a time there was a little daddy that would not go to sleep,' and I would tell this whole big story about this dad and this daughter, and he laughed so hard. We ended up staying awake for another hour and a half."

As painful as life was, Cash continued to gain strength. He recorded a song on July 31 during Maffetone's third visit. Maffetone was impressed by engineer Ferguson's patience with Cash, who could often get out only a few words at a time before pausing, but he kept at it until they had a usable version.

During each of his visits, Maffetone continued to stress the need to reduce Cash's medications, but making progress was hard. John Carter, Rosanne, and Kathy agreed with him to varying extents, but they knew their dad liked his doctor and, as with Peggy Knight, would resist breaking ties with her.

Before going into the studio again at the end of July, Cash learned that his mentor, Sam Phillips, had died in Memphis. It meant almost all the original Sun gang was gone now. Elvis had died in 1977, Roy Orbison in 1988, Charlie Rich in 1995, and Carl Perkins in 1998. As he thought about it, he realized many of those he knew at Columbia Records had also died—Don Law, Johnny Horton, Marty Robbins, and Lefty Frizzell. Throw in Hank Snow, Tex Ritter, Merle Travis, Ernest Tubb, Webb Pierce, Patsy Cline, Roger Miller, Conway Twitty, Sister Rosetta Tharpe, Chet Atkins, and Waylon. It was easy to be maudlin. But the only real sign that Cash was losing his will to live was when he would mention June's name and start sobbing.

Most days he looked forward to recording another song—even if he usually had to acknowledge quickly that he didn't feel up to it after all. On July 31 he did record "Here Comes the Boy," a song he had written years earlier. Ever since finishing "The Man Comes Around," Cash was no longer looking to make a big statement. The only songs that seemed truly to move him were the gospel tunes.

Maffetone checked back in on August 15 and was pleased to learn that Cash was feeling well enough to think about attending the MTV Video Music Awards ceremony on the twenty-eighth in New York, where the "Hurt" video was up for six awards, including video of the year. He was excited about the ceremony because he was proud of "Hurt," and he knew the show spoke to young music fans. His competition for video of the year would come from the rap, R&B, and dance fields—Missy Elliott, Eminem, 50 Cent, and Justin Timberlake—and he was further thrilled when the initial industry buzz suggested "Hurt" was the probable winner in the top category.

Cash was also talking about flying to Los Angeles in early September to do some recording with Rubin. He was feeling well enough to be looking forward to one of his favorite pastimes: simply going to the local Walmart, where he loved getting into a motorized cart and roaming through the aisles, stopping frequently to talk to shoppers or store employees who recognized him—and most of them did.

Rosanne visited her dad a few days before the awards show with her son Jake, and she shared her father's excitement over the MTV event. While at the house, she spent hours watching CNN with her dad or reading to him, from both the Bible and the poetry of Will Carleton.

On August 21, the day after Maffetone left for Florida, Cash recorded "Like the 309," according to records filed with the American Federation of Musicians Local 257 in Nashville. It was the last song he would record for the Rubin albums. But later that day he recorded one more song—a version of "Engine 143" for the Carter Family tribute album that his son was producing.

Years later John Carter would point out how fitting it was that the last words of the song, which was about a railroad engineer killed in a crash, were the final ones Johnny Cash ever recorded: *Nearer, my God, to Thee.*

V

Shortly before Cash was to leave for New York, Lou Robin learned from a member of the MTV staff that Cash wasn't going to win any of the major awards at the Music Video show, the producers just wanted him to sit in the audience and take a bow. Cash was too weak for such a gesture and the trip was canceled. Plans to go to California were also dropped.

On August 26—two days before the telecast—Cash complained of stomach pains, and he was rushed back to Baptist Hospital, where he was treated for pancreatitis. He did not watch the MTV show.

Cash wasn't alone in feeling that "Hurt" had been unfairly short-changed.

"This is a travesty. I demand a recount," Memphis native Justin Timberlake told millions of MTV viewers when he accepted his award for best male video, one of the categories in which "Hurt" was nominated. "My grandfather raised me on Johnny Cash. I'm from Tennessee and I think he deserves this more than any of us in here tonight. So I guess in some cool way I share this award with him. He deserves a round of applause." The audience roared its agreement.

News of Cash's hospitalization alarmed Maffetone because Cash seemed to end up with more medicines each time he checked in. He kept in touch with Cash by phone, noticing a gradual decline in his vocal strength. Once again the family was on alert. Still, they had gone through this so many times that it was hard to believe their dad wouldn't rally again. And he was allowed to return home on Wednesday, September 10.

"I talked to him the day he got out and said, 'Dad, you went into a tunnel,' and he said, 'I sure did,'" Rosanne says. "I remember it feeling like an abyss, that hospital visit. I couldn't speak to him, that was part of it. I'm not sure why; maybe he was on a ventilator again. I was scared to death. I thought that was it."

On Thursday morning Maffetone found Cash slumped in his wheelchair, hardly able to move. Virtually all the progress of the pre-vious weeks had been lost. Cash's oxygen levels were dangerously low, and his blood sugar levels were also down. Maffetone estimates that Cash was then on close to forty different medications.

Maffetone tried to work on Cash's leg and foot muscles in hopes of getting him walking again, but it exhausted Cash, and they agreed to take a break. Shortly after noon, Maffetone was relaxing in John's office, his hand on Cash's shoulder as a sign of support. Cash turned around and looked him straight in the eyes. This was strange because Cash's limited eyesight usually forced him to search around before he could focus on a person's face, but this time it was as if his vision was suddenly perfect again.

"It's time," Cash said.

Maffetone felt a chill pass in the room when he heard those words; he had heard them before from patients who were about to die.

"All I knew was that we needed to get him to a hospital. This was an emergency," he says.

Maffetone watched as Cash was wheeled to the ambulance.

It was a horrible sight.

Cash's stomach had shut down.

John Carter, who was in the cabin setting up equipment in case his father felt up to recording, made it to the house just as the paramedics were strapping Cash onto a stand-up stretcher. As the ambulance left for Baptist Hospital, phone calls were made to Cash's children. Lou Robin was alerted in California. He took a midnight flight.

John Carter followed the ambulance to the hospital, where Dr. Jerkins told him that his dad might not make it this time. He stayed by his father's side in the emergency room and then in the intensive care unit. Kathy and Rosanne joined him, along with other family members, including Cash's brother Tommy and sister Joanne.

Shortly after midnight, Friday, September 12, most of the group left, planning to return in the morning after getting some sleep. Rosanne and Kathy settled in a room across the hall from the intensive care unit, while John Carter went upstairs to the suite the hospital kept for his dad and tried to get some sleep.

Kathy was startled to overhear a nurse telling someone on the phone, "We're losing him; his vitals are dropping."

Kathy, Rosanne, and John Carter rushed to their father's side, and Cash opened his eyes.

"I thought for a split second maybe he'd be okay, but the look in his eyes told me different," Kathy says. "He looked frantic, like he wanted to talk, but couldn't with the tube down his throat. I told him how much I loved him. I told him he was the best daddy I could have ever had, and if he was tired of his pain and sadness, it was okay to go on. We'd all be okay."

At one a.m. J.R. Cash closed his eyes for the last time.

Moments later a nurse leaned over and clipped locks of his gray hair, one for each of his children.

Epilogue

NASHVILLE, Tenn. (AP) Johnny Cash, a towering musical figure whose rough, unsteady voice championed the downtrodden and reached across generations with songs like "Ring of Fire," "I Walk the Line" and "Folsom Prison Blues," died Friday. He was 71.

WITHIN HOURS OF LEARNING about his friend's death, Bob Dylan wrote these words: "Johnny was and is the North Star; you could guide your ship by him—the greatest of the greats, then and now."

Dylan's words came in response to a request from *Rolling Stone*, and they were the first in a series of tributes that appeared in the magazine's October 16, 2003, issue—and Cash could not have asked for a finer voice. His admiration for Dylan was deep and lasting—the recognition of a standard of artistry that, along with Jimmie Rodgers's, forever inspired him.

In an essay as eloquent as his best songs, Dylan went on to say of Cash: "He is what the land and the country are all about, the heart and soul of it personified and what it means to be here; and he said it all in plain English. I think we can have recollections of him, but we can't define him any more than we can define a fountain of truth. If we want to know what it means to be mortal, we need look no further than the Man in Black. Blessed with a profound imagination, he used the gift to express all the various lost causes of the human soul. This is a miraculous and humbling thing. Listen to him, and he always brings you to your senses. He rises high above all, and he'll never die or be forgotten, even by persons not born yet—especially those persons—and that is forever."

Cash also would have been pleased with the voices of the others who shared their feelings with *Rolling Stone* readers.

One of them, Merle Haggard, addressed Cash's life of physical pain in moving, personal terms: "Johnny Cash lived in constant, serious pain. On a scale of one to 10, it was somewhere around an eight for the last eight years of his life. He dealt himself some terrible years when he didn't do the right things. He didn't eat right, so his bones got brittle, his jaw broke during some dental surgery and it never healed. He lives as an example of a man in pain, going from one stage of bad health to another, but he held his head up the whole way. He was like Abraham or Moses—one of the great men who will ever grace the earth. There will never be another Man in Black."

In another tribute, Bono addressed Cash's universality: "Every man could relate to him. But nobody could be him. To be that extraordinary and that ordinary was his real gift. That and his humor and bare-boned honesty....I think he was a very godly man, but you had the sense that he spent his time in the desert. And that just made you like him more. It gave his songs some dust. And that voice was definitely locusts and honey. As for 'Hurt,' it's perhaps the best video ever made."

It wasn't just music magazines that saluted Cash.

Time magazine, whose covers had served as a road map of who and what was important in life and culture for generations, marked the passing of only one individual on its cover in all of 2003—Johnny Cash. The words next to a stark photo of the elderly Cash on the September 22 cover read simply, "Johnny Cash 1932–2003." Inside, an essay by *Time* film writer Richard Corliss recounted the darkness and light in Cash's life.

He wrote: "Rarely before Cash had a singer taken vocal pain—not the adolescent shriek of most rock singers, but the abiding ache of a veteran victim—and made it so audible, so immediate, so dark and deep. Rarely, before or since, has a voice also shown the grit to express, endure and outlive that misery. His songs played like confessions on a deathbed or death row, but he delivered them with the plangent stoicism of a world-class poker player dealt a bum hand.

"That—and his determination to transcend or ignore musical genres—made Cash's death...an event that provoked a serious sense of loss among people of all ages. Children of the '50s remember the startle of his first eminence; the one Southern star who was not a rebellious kid but a grownup with cavernous eyes and a voice to match. Kids of the '60s recall his pop hits, the TV show he was host of for two years and the easy alliances he formed with musicians beyond country's borders. The X and next generations know his old songs as if they were standards, and his boldly simple later work—especially 'Hurt'—as emblems of moral and musical purity, an antidote to the glitz and aggression of teen icons. Cash made patriarchal integrity cool."

It was bright and warm in Hendersonville on the morning of Monday, September 15, when Cash fans, family members, and friends gathered at the First Baptist Church for a two-hour service that was by turns solemn and cheerful—and laced with music. The casket was adorned with an intricate wreath with roses, figs, potatoes, and cotton on the twig within its weave, a nod to the early days in Dyess.

The ceremony was preceded by gentle piano versions of spirituals, including the Carter Family standard "Will the Circle Be Unbroken." Larry Gatlin led the mourners in singing "Oh Come, Angel Band." Emmylou Harris and Sheryl Crow teamed on the hymn "The Old Rugged Cross" and Bob Dylan's "Every Grain of Sand."

Cash's own voice—that unmistakable, unvarnished baritone—filled the church during a video montage that showed scenes of him through the years, including his TV duet with Dylan and an early version of "I Walk the Line" when the eyes of the darkly handsome young man flashed with vitality. In the narrative, Cash was heard saying he was neither preacher nor prophet, only a "singer of songs."

Rosanne spoke movingly about the loss of her father. She said people had approached her to say they couldn't "imagine a world without Johnny Cash." Her reply was that she couldn't begin to imagine a world "without Daddy."

After the service, Cash was laid in the ground alongside June's burial place at Hendersonville Memory Gardens cemetery just off Johnny Cash Parkway. Nearby graves held John's parents, June's mother and sisters, and Luther Perkins.

The wording on John's tombstone came from Psalm 19:14. It read: "Let the words of my mouth, and the meditation of my heart, be acceptable in thy sight, O Lord, my strength, and my redeemer."

June's marker carried these words from Psalm 103: "Bless the Lord, O my soul: and all that is within me, bless his holy name."

A few feet behind their graves, a bench was later placed linking them even more closely. The words facing their graves read:

CASH —— CARTER
I Walk the Line
—
Wildwood Flower

Following the burial, Cash's son and daughters said a final, private farewell. They rolled his wheelchair, in which he had spent so many anguished hours, from the house to the bluff overlooking Old Hickory Lake. John Carter then picked it up and hurled it into the water below. Cindy, Rosanne, and Tara looked back on the moment as profoundly sad. Kathy found it so painful to part with any piece of her father that she stayed back at the house. John Carter considered the moment liberating—a way of striking back at the menacing symbol of his father's cruel captivity. He says, "Dad would have loved it."

For someone who had worried through much of the 1980s that he had thrown away his legacy, Cash would have been thrilled to see how his music continued to be embraced by fans old and new in the years after his death. As often happens when major recording artists die, there was a big upswing in Cash's record sales in late

2003, but, unlike with most stars, his music didn't then fade from public consciousness. He continued to be heard in TV commercials and film soundtracks.

The most dramatic surge of attention was stirred by director James Mangold's 2005 film *Walk the Line,* starring Joaquin Phoenix as Cash and Reese Witherspoon as June. The movie took in $120 million at the box office in the United States and another $67 million around the world. It brought in an additional $125 million in DVD sales in the States alone. The film earned five Academy Award nominations, including a best actress Oscar for Witherspoon. Thanks to the film, a soundtrack album and a Cash retrospective album both became million-copy sellers. When Cash's fifth Rick Rubin album, the posthumous *American V: A Hundred Highways,* was released in the summer of 2006, it entered the U.S. sales charts at number one. "Hurt," meanwhile, was widely acclaimed as the best music video ever made. Johnny Cash was more beloved than ever.

In the years after Cash's death, those close to him asked themselves if John—tired of the pain and eager to be reunited with June and his other loved ones—simply gave up on life. Phil Maffetone continues to maintain that Cash did not have to die in 2003, that he could have lived several more productive years if his medication had been brought under control. At the time, he wanted to write an essay about how Cash's death was symptomatic of a dangerous, growing tendency in the medical profession to overmedicate, but the family had gone through enough heartache. Besides, some suggested, it was possible that their father's physical issues, after years of hard living, were more severe than any of them realized. Cash's physician, Dr. Terri Jerkins, said in 2012 that she could not discuss the specifics of Cash's treatment because of confidentiality laws.

Most of the daughters felt that their father was ready to die. "He seemed more vulnerable than any other time I'd ever seen him," Tara says. "He was lonely and afraid. Life had thrown him a huge curveball when June died. He was lost." Cindy agrees. "I think June dying was his way of saying, 'Okay, I've spent my time in hell, I'm going to heaven.'"

Kathy, too, feels that her dad was tired of being sick and lonely. "He hated being dependent on people to help him with everything, and I think he was just ready to go. We had a long discussion about death about two months before he died. He said he couldn't wait to be out of pain, see everyone, and finally see Jesus. He said, 'Baby, this body is so tired and sick. I'm ready to move on. I know all my children will be okay.' We also talked about Jack and how often Jack visited him in 'dreams.' He told me about some of the conversations they had and that he had progressively aged and was always two and a half years older than Dad. He told me Jack had a white beard and a head of white hair. He said, 'I've missed him every day of my life, but being able to see and talk to him in dreams has helped the pain immensely.'"

As for Rosanne, after endlessly weighing the possibilities, she says only, "I don't know. I don't know."

John Carter, however, is convinced that his dad didn't give up on life after June died.

"Music was his refuge, his only outlet," he says. "Dad couldn't see, he couldn't read anymore, and his wife was gone, but he didn't just lay down. We have to realize that some of the greatest work in the *American* series was done after my mother was gone. So did he die with a broken heart? Absolutely. But did it kill him? I don't believe so. His spirit did not stop. His body gave up. I firmly believe that if his body hadn't given up, he'd still be here making music now.

"Everyone carries burdens around with them. I believe the thing about Dad that people find so easy to relate to is that he was willing to expose his most cumbersome burdens, his most consuming darknesses. He wasn't afraid to go through the fire and say, 'I fell down. I've made mistakes. I'm weak. I *hurt.*' But in doing so, he gained some sort of defining strength. Every moment of darkness enabled him to better see the light. Perhaps, at the end of each life, there is a balance of this darkness and light. To me, as far as my father's life, the light wins—hands down. His most enduring legacy is that this message continues to spread."

Acknowledgments

My journey on the book began in early 2009, soon after Lou Robin's reply to my question about how much of the Johnny Cash story had been told. Lou, who managed Cash for more than a quarter century, said, "Only about twenty percent." True enough. During nearly four years of research and writing, I found that John's life was more far complex than I had imagined, and some of the more troubling discoveries caused me to question just how much the public needs to know about an artist. In those moments, I ultimately relied on Cash's own words. Time and again he said he wanted people to know his entire story—especially the dark, guilt-ridden, hopeless moments—because he believed in redemption and he wanted others to realize that they too could be redeemed regardless of how badly they had stumbled. This full disclosure was a goal that John didn't always live up to in his own autobiographies because, he said, he didn't want to hurt those close to him. But he wanted, without reserve, the complete story to come out eventually.

Because it was the music that drew us all to Johnny Cash, my primary focus in this book is on his artistry, initially the question of how someone from a cotton patch in Arkansas could develop such a deep sense of compassion and purpose in his music. But in time the exploration expanded to reflect on how hard he had to struggle to maintain his artistry amid a torrent of personal problems and career pressures.

The first I want to thank are John's children—John Carter Cash, Rosanne Cash, Kathy Cash, Cindy Cash, and Tara Cash, as well as June's daughter Carlene Carter. Though concerns were sometimes expressed when uncomfortable topics came up, the consensus was that they, too, felt the full story should be told. As well as sitting down for repeated interviews, John Carter, Rosanne, Kathy, Cindy, and Carlene patiently answered e-mails that numbered in the hundreds. Rosanne provided particularly invaluable counsel. I was in touch with Tara only via e-mail, but she too was wonderfully supportive. Other Cash relatives who contributed to this portrait were Lorrie Bennett, Joanne Cash Yates, Roy Cash Jr., Damon Fielder, Tommy Cash, and Kelly Hancock. Thanks also to Cathy Sullivan and Terri Dunn for graciously allowing the use of various Cash documents. And Shari Wied of Hal Leonard Corporation.

There is another layer of people who gave so generously of their time out of love and respect for Cash that I think of them as part of his extended family. Chief among them, Johnny Western, Kris and Lisa Kristofferson, David Ferguson, Bill Miller, James Keach, Don and Harold Reid, Marty Stuart, Larry Gatlin, and Kti Jensen.

Lou Robin was instrumental throughout, not only sharing hundreds of pages of documents outlining Cash's years on the road, but also putting me in contact with key players. He and his wife, Karen, were always ready to talk about their years with John and June. It must have been a sometimes difficult role for Lou, because one of his chief duties for years was protecting Cash's image; but he recognized the importance of telling all of John's story so that we might better understand the man and his art—both what Cash overcame and what he accomplished.

For contributing insights and experiences and/or helpful letters and other documents, I am also grateful to Brian Ahern, Gene Beley, Rick Blackburn, Bono, James and Louise Burton, Larry Butler, Geoffrey Cannon, Jack Clement, Larry Collins, Lorrie Collins, Jessi Colter, Tom Cording, Jonathan Cott, Clive Davis, Steve Earle, Robert Elfstrom, Ralph Emery, Colin Escott, Sylvia Flye, Dr. Billy Graham, Marshall Grant, Peter Guralnick, Merle Haggard, Tom T. and Dixie Hall, Vicky Hamilton, A. J. Henson, Everett Henson, Jonathan Holiff, W. S. Holland, Billie Jean Horton, Jan Howard, J. E. Huff, Bob Johnston, Rich Kienz, Peter Lewry, Bob Mahaffey and other Air Force buddies, James Mangold, Mac McBride, David McGee, Edwin "Rip" Nix, Robert K. Oermann, Tom Petty, Larry Porter, Chuck Riley, Mark Romanek, John Singleton, Reverend Jimmie Snow, Robert Sullivan, Jimmy Tittle, Kevin Weatherly, Richard Weize, Johnny Wessler, and Dr. Nat Winston. I'd also like to thank those who helped provide access to key interview subjects and materials: Heidi-Ellen Robinson, Paul McGuinness, Larry Jenkins, Tony Dimitriades, Jim Guerinot, Jeff Rosen, Tresa Redburn, Maria-Elena Orbea, Cindy Hively, and Renee White. Also, thanks to the research staffs at public libraries in Memphis and Nashville, Tennessee; West Helena, Arkansas; Los Angeles and Ventura, California; and London, England. Also, Nashville Local 257 of the American Federation of Musicians. In addition, I am forever grateful for the encouragement and friendship of all my colleagues over the years at the *Los Angeles Times,* from Charles Champlin to Dean Baquet, but particularly Bret Israel and Donna Frazier Glynn, who were consistent supporters throughout the writing of the book.

Let me also thank my agent, Luke Janklow, who brings an overriding sense of passion and imagination to every aspect of developing, selling, and protecting a writer's idea. Little, Brown and Company is an author's dream. I am indebted foremost to John Parsley, my editor, for his belief in the project and his steady, reassuring nurturing of it, from the initial outline to the finished manuscript. My gratitude also extends to Michael Pietsch, Reagan Arthur, Malin von-Euler Hogan, Elizabeth Garriga, Peggy Freudenthal, Marian Parker, Amanda Brown, and Amanda Lang. Finally, Chris Nolan and Amanda Heller.

My deepest appreciation to Rick Rubin, who cares so profoundly about Johnny Cash that he not only agreed to spend dozens of hours recounting the American Recordings years, but also read parts of the manuscript for accuracy and to trigger his recollection of additional details.

I am also indebted to the person who accompanied me every step of the way. Mark Stielper evolved from a boyhood fan of John and June into a confidant and, eventually, the family historian. He is working on his own book, an imaginative work built around Cash's TV show—a project that made the countless hours he spent answering my questions all the more generous. There were times when he told me things that he has been saving for years, and I appreciate his trust and friendship. We didn't always interpret events in the Cashes' lives the same way, but Mark kept me focused on telling John's real story rather than simply the accepted "fairy tale," as he often put it.

Next, let me thank my immediate family. The list stretches from my parents, Alice Marie and John, through my first wife, Ruthann Snijders, and her husband, Dutch, on to our children, Kathy Morris and Rob Hilburn, our son-in-law Ronald Morris and daughter-in-law Sarah Coley-Hilburn, and to our four grandchildren, Christopher Morris and Lindsey Morris, Genevieve Hilburn and Grant Hilburn.

I am also blessed by the way my wife, Kathi, has shown the same affection to all of my family that she has given to her own children, Keith Bond and Kate Bond. Kathi read every stage of the manuscript, not only correcting errors but asking questions that made the book better.

Guide to Recordings and DVDs

Johnny Cash's music was featured on more than one hundred albums—spread (primarily) across four record labels—and recycled on hundreds of compilations around the world during his near-fifty-year career, so it can be daunting to decide just where to start exploring his music. This guide is designed to assist in that search—both for those interested in his entire body of work and for those wishing to focus on a particular period. Several of the albums are now out of print, but all can still be found in new or guaranteed used editions.

I. The Original Recordings

An Introduction Package

The Legend (Hip-o). Though disappointingly thin on the Columbia Records period, this twenty-one-song retrospective includes such essential tracks as "Hey, Porter" and "I Walk the Line" from the Sun Records days and the breakthrough U2 collaboration ("The Wanderer"). It ends with selections from the Rick Rubin productions, including the seminal "Hurt" and "The Man Comes Around."

Sun Years

The emphasis at Sun was on singles rather than albums, which make Cash's "best of" compilations on Sun more important than the original Sun albums. Those singles represent some of his most dynamic works. The best combine a dazzling burst of artistic awakening, reflecting both a rich sense of imagery and deeply authentic vocals.

Johnny Cash: The Sun Years (Sun/Rhino). If you aren't familiar with the Sun recordings, this eighteen-song overview is a good starting point. It contains the original version of "Folsom Prison Blues" as well as such other essential tracks as "Big River" and "Give My Love to Rose."

Johnny Cash: The Complete Sun Recordings, 1955–1958 (Time Life). If you are drawn to the Sun period, this three-disc box set gives you everything Cash recorded with Sam Phillips and Jack Clement in the 1950s as well as a few demos and a forty-page booklet. New copies of the album can be pricey, but used copies often go for little more than the single-disc Rhino package.

Columbia Years

This is where Cash's creative vision was honed. One reason he left Sun was for the artistic control that Columbia promised, and that freedom was a missed blessing. Without a strong guiding hand in the production booth during his early years at Columbia, Cash stumbled a lot as he tried to plot his musical course. He was at his weakest when he was aiming for a hit, at his strongest when following his creative instincts and imagination in a series of concept albums that were more ambitious and purposeful than anything else country music had seen.

Johnny Cash: The Complete Columbia Album Collection (Columbia Legacy). The sixty-three-disc box includes everything (for good and bad) that Cash released on Columbia Records during his lifetime, including the Highwaymen albums. Warning: The CDs vary greatly in quality, with the best being those released in the 1960s and early 1970s. The set devotes two discs to various singles that didn't originally appear on albums as well as guest appearances on albums from other artists (among them Bob Dylan and Willie Nelson). Finally, there's one disc devoted to highlights from the Sun era.

Johnny Cash the Legend (Columbia Legacy). Released in a limited twenty-thousand-copy edition in 2005, this lavishly designed package features 104 songs—the vast majority from the Columbia years—on four discs. It also includes a bonus CD that includes Cash's first radio show on KWEM in Memphis in 1955 and a bonus DVD taken from a CBS television special in 1980.

Johnny Cash: Love God Murder (Columbia Legacy, American

Recordings). Don't turn here if you're looking for the hits. It is, instead, a personal look by Cash at three dominant themes in his music. Liner notes by June Carter Cash, Bono, and Quentin Tarantino.

The best of the individual albums. Look, where possible, for deluxe or anniversary editions of the albums because they'll usually contain bonus features; the Folsom and San Quentin collections are prime examples.

Ride This Train. The first, great concept album—Cash's first step toward an examination of America's roots and character (1960).

Blood, Sweat and Tears. An engaging mix of folk and country (1963).

Bitter Tears: Ballads of the American Indian. Reflections on the struggle of Native Americans (1964).

Johnny Cash Sings the Ballads of the True West. Two-disc expansion of the theme outlined in *Ride This Train* (1965).

Johnny Cash at Folsom Prison. Breathtaking display of artistry and dynamics (1968).

The Holy Land. Fiercely independent statement of faith (1969).

Johnny Cash at San Quentin. Striking examples of rage and rebellion (1969).

Hello, I'm Johnny Cash. Winning mix of themes and musical styles. One of Cash's most consistent and intimate non-concept recordings (1970).

Gospel Road. Ride This Train meets *The Holy Land.* Highlight: "He Turned the Water into Wine" (1973).

Johnny 99. Bold attempt to reestablish his relevance in pop culture. Built around Bruce Springsteen's title tune and "Highway Patrolman" (1983).

Mercury Years

This was a bleak period. After being dropped by Columbia Records, Cash signed with Mercury in 1986 and went into the studio with little confidence or game plan. The first album—*Johnny Cash Is Coming to Town*—had flickers of promise, notably "The Night Hank Williams Came to Town" and "W. Lee O'Daniel and the Light

Crust Dough Boys" (neither of which he wrote), but not enough to recapture the attention of country music DJs or fans. When the album flopped, Cash's confidence sank further—and the subsequent Mercury releases showed it. No Mercury album is essential listening.

American Recordings Years

The albums with producer Rick Rubin not only made Cash relevant again, but also cemented his musical legacy. Start with the acoustic *American Recordings,* the first of the albums, and *American IV: The Man Comes Around,* which contains "Hurt" and the epic title track. I would then quickly proceed to all the other albums, which document the Rubin-Cash relationship and give you a sense of an artist coming to grips with his mortality: *Unchained, American III: Solitary Man, American V: A Hundred Highways, American VI: Ain't No Grave,* and the splendid five-disc *Unearthed.*

II. THE VALUABLE EXTRAS

With most recording artists, any exploration of their music can be easily satisfied by sticking to the original releases, but they are just the starting point with Cash. There is an endless amount of information and pleasure to be gained by looking at the back pages of Cash's work—and various record companies have produced collections that allow us to virtually step inside the recording studio and witness his creative growth.

Bear Family Box Sets

Johnny Cash: The Man in Black, 1954–1958 (Bear Family). This German label is testimony to one man's vision and passion: Richard Weize, who started Bear Family Records in the mid-1970s to salute his favorite artists—not just with traditional "best of" packages, but with lavish box sets, often containing five to ten discs, as well as richly illustrated oversized booklets or sometimes hardback books. This five-disc set takes us through the Sun years and into the first few Columbia sessions. We hear, for instance, Cash's first try at "Folsom Prison Blues" during a session on March 22, 1955, then we hear him record "Folsom Prison Blues" again four months later, this time nailing it. Excellent liner notes by Sun historian and author Colin Escott detail each session, including which musicians sat in.

Johnny Cash: The Man in Black, 1959–62 (Bear Family). The journey continues, offering a fascinating account of Cash's sometimes clumsy attempt to define his artistic course.

Johnny Cash: The Man in Black, 1963–69 Plus (Bear Family). The beat goes on, though the six-disc set, for contractual reasons, doesn't include the Folsom concert or the Dylan-Cash recording session of February 18, 1969.

Johnny Cash: Come Along and Ride This Train (Bear Family). The focus in this four-disc collection is on Cash, the auteur, by offering the early concept albums, including *Ride This Train* and *Blood, Sweat and Tears.*

Johnny Cash: The Outtakes (Bear Family). This three-disc package takes us into some of the key Sun Records sessions more deeply than the other sets listed. We hear not just one version of "Folsom Prison Blues" from March 1955 but four. To illustrate Weize's desire for completeness, we also hear eleven takes—including three false starts— on the relatively unimportant "Don't Make Me Go." Not for everyone, but I found it a delight.

Columbia Legacy "Bootleg" Series

Johnny Cash: Personal File (Columbia Legacy). Especially interesting for those who enjoyed Cash's first acoustic album with Rick Rubin, the songs on this two-disc package were recorded by Cash, accompanied only by his own acoustic guitar, mostly in 1973. You won't find hits, but it offers a revealing look at Cash's private musical exploration at the time—a heavy emphasis on gospel.

Johnny Cash: Bootleg II, From Memphis to Hollywood (Columbia Legacy). The treat here is the tape of Cash's first radio show from 1955—which aired just before Sun released "Hey, Porter" (the same show featured on the *Johnny Cash the Legend* package). It also includes some early demos and various selections from the 1960s, including Cash's failed attempt to come up with a title song for the James Bond film *Thunderball.*

Johnny Cash: Bootleg III, Live around the World (Columbia Legacy). The concert high points: the Newport Folk Festival in 1964, Vietnam in 1969, and the White House in 1970.

Johnny Cash: Bootleg IV, The Soul of Truth (Columbia Legacy). This two-disc document takes us beyond the celebrated *Gospel Road* and *Holy Land* albums to provide a deeper look at Cash's gospel leanings. The music, from the mid-1970s to the early 1980s, includes several tracks that were previously unreleased.

Real Bootleg Album

The Dylan-Cash Sessions. This album has been released under various titles in bootleg form, but never officially by Columbia. It's delightful hearing Cash and Dylan have so much fun as they trade lead vocals on songs associated with both artists and such wild cards as tunes written or recorded by Elvis Presley, Carl Perkins, and Jimmie Rodgers.

Roots Collections

These albums contain key versions of songs that became identified with Cash as well as some recordings that helped shape his musical tastes.

Deep Roots of Johnny Cash (Bear Family). The selections range from Merle Travis's "Dark as a Dungeon" and Tex Ritter's "Sam Hall" to Bing Crosby's "Galway Bay" and Jimmie Rodgers's "The One Rose."

Johnny Cash: Roots and Branches (Hip-O Chronicles). An essential collection because it contains Gordon Jenkins's original recording of "Crescent City Blues," the song that inspired "Folsom Prison Blues." Other musts: Sister Rosetta Tharpe's "Strange Things Happening Every Day," Anita Carter's "(Love's) Ring of Fire," and Peter LaFarge's "Ballad of Ira Hayes."

III. DVDs

Johnny Cash at Town Hall Party (Bear Family). Cash and the Tennessee Two do guest sets in the late 1950s during two episodes of Town Hall Party, a weekly TV show broadcast live from a Los Angeles–area ballroom. Songs include "I Walk the Line," "Don't Take

Your Guns to Town," and "Folsom Prison Blues"—topped off by a zany impersonation of Elvis Presley.

Five Minutes to Live (Bear Family's And More Bears subsidiary). This "crime thriller" was supposed to be Cash's step into a film career, but it's fascinating only in the sense of showing how far wrong something can go.

Johnny Cash: The Man, His World, His Music (can be found from various companies). This documentary by Robert Elfstrom was put together in the months after the Folsom Prison concert in 1968, just as Cash was beginning to taste the superstardom ahead.

The Gospel Road (20th Century–Fox). Cash co-wrote, starred in, and financed this ambitious movie as personal testimony to his Christian faith.

The Best of the Johnny Cash TV Show, 1969–1971 (CMV Columbia Legacy). Contains sixty-six performances from the flawed but also uniquely inspiring ABC series that helped define Cash's superstar image and showcased some of the era's top country and rock talent. Among the guests: Bob Dylan, Neil Young, Merle Haggard, and Derek and the Dominos.

Hurt (American Recordings/Lost Highway). The classic music video directed by Mark Romanek.

R.H.

SOURCE NOTES

As the pop music editor and critic for the *Los Angeles Times* from 1970 to 2005, I interviewed Johnny Cash and June Carter Cash numerous times, stretching from backstage at the Long Beach Municipal Auditorium in 1967 (freelancing) and the landmark Folsom Prison concert in 1968 to the Highwaymen tour in the 1990s on to a day at June's childhood home in Maces Springs, Virginia, in 2002. I also did an extensive interview with John in 1973 for *Rolling Stone*. While at the *Times*, I interviewed Bob Dylan, Sam Phillips, Saul Holiff, Waylon Jennings, Scotty Moore, Knox Phillips, Willie Nelson, and Keith Richards—and drew upon those interviews at various points in this book. All the interviews listed below were conducted in person and/or by e-mail from early 2009 until the end of 2012. In almost every case, the e-mails were follow-ups to in-person interviews. In the text I've used "told me" only for Johnny Cash. In case of direct quotes from people still living, I've used "says." I have used "said" for direct quotes from someone who has died or for quotes from other sources.

Here is the list of sources drawn upon during the writing of the book.

INTERVIEWS

Brian Ahern, Norm Bale, Gene Beley, Lorrie Bennett, Rick Blackburn, Bono, James Burton, Louise Burton, Larry Butler, Geoffrey Cannon, Carlene Carter, Cindy Cash, Joanne Cash, John Carter Cash, Kathy Cash, Rosanne Cash, Roy Cash Jr., Tara Cash, Tommy Cash, Jack Clement, Larry Collins, Lorrie Collins, Rich Collins, Jessi Colter, Lou Copits, Robert Crick, Clive Davis, Steve Earle, Robert Elfstom, Ramblin' Jack Elliott, Ralph Emery, Red Ernst, Colin Escott, Jerry Farwell, David Ferguson, Damon Fielder, Sylvia Flye, Dale Franklin, Larry Gatlin, Marshall Grant, Robert Greenwalt, Merle Haggard, Dixie Hall, Tom T. Hall, Vicky Hamilton, Kelly Hancock, William Harrell, A. J. Henson, Everett Henson, Jonathan Holiff, W. S. Holland, Billie Jean Horton, Jan Howard, J. E. Huff, Kti Jensen, Bob Johnston, Kris Kristofferson, Lisa Kristofferson, Peter Lewry, Jim Marshall, Mac McBride, Aris McGarry, David McGee, Bob Mehaffey, Alan Messer, Bill Miller, Bob Moodie, Rip Nix, Robert K. Oermann, Henry Palma, Ben Perea, Margie Perkins, Tom Petty, Steve Popovich, Al Qualls, Don Reid, Harold Reid, Orville (Wayne) Rigdon, Chuck Riley, Lou Robin, Karen Robin, Ted Rollins, Mark Romanek, Rick Rubin, Pat Shields, John Singleton, Shelby Singleton,

Rev. Jimmie Snow, Gayle Stelter, Mark Stielper, Marty Stuart, Robert Sullivan, Larry Tart, Al Thurston, Jimmy Tittle, Harry Yates, Tom Youngworth, Kevin Weatherly, Johnny Wessler, Johnny Western, Dr. Nat Winston.

James Keach's taped conversations with Cash in connection with the film *Walk the Line*. Also director James Mangold's tapes.

Lyrics, letters, and other assorted writings shared by Cindy Cash, John Carter Cash, Kathy Cash, Rosanne Cash, Tara Cash, Jonathan Holiff, Kris Kristofferson, Lou Robin, Mark Stielper, Marty Stuart, and Johnny Western.

Interviews conducted with Roy Cash Jr., David Ferguson, Marshall Grant, and Michael Streissguth for a 2008 American Masters documentary about Cash. Morgan Neville, producer-director.

Books—General

Note: I've listed below, in parenthesis, the chapters that the following volumes were especially helpful for.

Barker, Hugh, and Yuval Taylor. *Faking It: The Quest for Authenticity in Popular Music*. New York: Norton, 2007. (Chapter 1.)

Berry, Chuck. *The Autobiography*. New York: Harmony, 1987.

Brown, Maxine. *Looking Back to See: A Country Music Memoir*. Fayetteville: University of Arkansas Press, 2005.

Burke, Ken, and Dan Griffin. *The Blue Moon Boys: The Story of Elvis Presley's Band*. Chicago: Chicago Review Press, 2006. (Chapters 3–6.)

Cantor, Louis. *Dewey and Elvis*. Urbana: University of Illinois Press, 2005. (Chapters 3–6.)

Cash, John Carter. *Anchored in Love*. Nashville: Thomas Nelson, 2007. (Chapters 12–14, 21–22, 26–28, 30–34, 36.)

———. *House of Cash: The Legacies of My Father, Johnny Cash*. San Rafael, Calif.: Insight Editions, 2012.

Cash, Johnny. *Man in Black*. Grand Rapids: Zondervan Press, 1975. (Chapters 1–20, 22–23, 35.)

———. *Man in White*. Nashville: Thomas Nelson, 2006. (Chapters 24, 26.)

———, with Patrick Carr. *Cash: The Autobiography*. New York: Harper San Francisco, 1997. (Chapters 2–35.)

Cash, June Carter. *Among My Klediments*. Grand Rapids: Zondervan, 1979.

———. *From the Heart*. New York: Prentice Hall, 1987. (Chapters 28, 30, 35.)

Cash, Rosanne. *Composed: A Memoir*. New York: Viking, 2010. (Chapters 11–14, 19, 22–23, 36.)

Cash, Vivian, with Ann Sharpsteen. *I Walked the Line: My Life with Johnny*. New York: Scribner, 2007. (Chapters 2–6, 8–18, 20, 36.)

Christgau, Robert. *Christgau's Record Guide: Rock Albums of the '70s*. New York: Ticknor & Fields, 1981.

Cohn, Nik. *Rock from the Beginning*. New York: Pocket Books, 1970.

Cooper, Daniel. *Lefty Frizzell: The Honky-Tonk Life of Country Music's Greatest Singer*. Boston: Little, Brown, 1995.

Cott, Jonathan, ed. *Bob Dylan: The Essential Interviews*. New York: Wenner Books, 2006.

D'Ambrosio, Antonio. *A Heartbeat and a Guitar: Johnny Cash and the Making of Bitter Tears*. New York: Nation Books, 2009. (Chapters 13–15.)

Davis, Clive, with James Willwerth. *Clive: Inside the Record Business*. New York: William Morrow, 1975. (Chapters 18–22.)

Davis, Skeeter. *Bus Fare to Kentucky: The Autobiography of Skeeter Davis*. New York: Birch Lane Press, 1993.

Diekman, Diane. *The Faron Young Story: Live Fast, Love Hard*. Urbana: University of Illinois Press, 2007.

———. *Twentieth Century Drifter: The Life of Marty Robbins*. Music in American Life. Urbana: University of Illinois Press, 2012.

Dylan, Bob. *Chronicles*. Vol. 1. New York: Simon & Schuster, 2004.

Escott, Colin, and Kira Florita. *Hank Williams: Snapshots from the Lost Highway*. Cambridge, Mass.: Da Capo, 2001.

———, and Martin Hawkins. *Good Rockin' Tonight: Sun Records and the Birth of Rock and Roll*. New York: St. Martin's Press, 1991. (Chapters 4–6.)

———, with George Merritt and William MacEwen. *Hank Williams: The Biography*. New York: Back Bay Books, 2004.

Gilmore, Mikal. *Shot in the Heart*. New York: Anchor Books, 1995. (Chapter 25.)

Gordon, Robert. *It Came from Memphis*. Boston: Faber and Faber, 1995.

Grant, Marshall, with Curtis Zar. *I Was There When It Happened: My Life with Johnny Cash*. Nashville: Cumberland House, 2006. (Chapters 3–11, 13–15, 17–28.)

Green, Douglas B. *Singing in the Saddle: The History of the Singing Cowboy*. Nashville: Country Music Foundation Press and Vanderbilt University Press, 2002.

Guralnick, Peter. *Careless Love: The Unmasking of Elvis Presley*. New York: Little, Brown, 1999.

———. *Feel Like Going Home: Portraits in Blues and Rock 'n' Roll*. New York: Back Bay Books, 1999.

———. *Last Train to Memphis: The Rise of Elvis Presley*. New York: Little, Brown, 1994. (Chapters 3–6.)

———. *Lost Highway*. New York: Vantage, 1982.

Haggard, Merle, with Tom Carter. *My House of Memories for the Record*. New York: Cliff Street Books, 1999.

———, with Peggy Russell. *Sing Me Back Home: My Life*. New York: Times Books, 1981.

Halberstam, David. *The Fifties*. New York: Villard, 1993.

Hemphill, Paul. *The Nashville Sound: Bright Lights and Country Music*. New York: Simon and Schuster, 1970.

Heylin, Clinton. *Bob Dylan: A Life in Stolen Moments*. New York: Schrimer Books, 1996.

Hopkins, Jerry. *Elvis*. New York: Simon and Schuster, 1971.

Horstman, Dorothy. *Sing Your Heart Out Country Boy*. Nashville: Country Music Foundation Press, 1996.

Howard, Jan. *Sunshine and Shadows.* New York: Richardson and Steinman, 1987.

Jennings, Waylon, with Lenny Kaye. *Waylon: An Autobiography.* New York: Warner Books, 1996. (Chapter 17.)

Jones, George, with Tom Carter. *I Lived to Tell All.* New York: Villard, 1996. (Chapter 13.)

Jones, Margaret. *Patsy: The Life and Times of Patsy Cline.* New York: Harper Collins, 1994.

Kaplan, James. *Frank: The Voice.* New York: Doubleday, 2010.

Klein, George, with Chuck Crisafulli. *Elvis: My Best Man.* New York: Three Rivers Press, 2010.

Kleist, Reinhard. *Johnny Cash: I See a Darkness.* New York: Abrams ComicArts, 2007.

Knight, Peggy. *Cooking in the House of Cash.* Nashville: Premium Press, 2004.

———. *My 33 Years Inside the House of Cash.* Nashville: Premium Press, 2004.

Laird, Tracey E. W. *Louisiana Hayride: Radio and Roots Along the Red River.* New York: Oxford University Press, 2005. (Chapter 5.)

Landau, Jon. *It's Too Late to Stop Now: A Rock and Roll Journal.* San Francisco: Straight Arrow Books, 1972.

Lewis, Myra, with Murray Silver. *Great Balls of Fire: The Uncensored Story of Jerry Lee Lewis.* New York: William Morrow, 1982. (Chapter 6.)

Logan, Horace, with Bill Sloan. *Elvis, Hank, and Me: Making Musical History on the Louisiana Hayride.* New York: St. Martin's Press, 1998. (Chapters 5–6.)

Louvin, Charlie, with Benjamin Whitmer. *Satan Is Real.* New York: It Books, 2012. (Chapter 1.)

Malone, Bill C. *Country Music USA.* Austin: University of Texas Press, 1985.

———. *Don't Get Above Your Raisin': Country Music and the Southern Working Class.* Urbana: University of Illinois Press, 2002.

———. *Southern Music American Music.* Lexington: University Press of Kentucky, 1979.

Marcus, Greil. *Mystery Train.* New York: E. P. Dutton, 1982.

Miller, Stephen. *Johnny Cash: The Life of an American Icon.* London: Omnibus Press, 2003. (Chapters 1, 4–5.)

Moore, Scotty, with James Dickerson. *That's Alright, Elvis.* New York: Schirmer Books, 1997. (Chapters 3–6.)

Nassour, Ellis. *Honky-Tonk Angel: The Intimate Story of Patsy Cline.* Chicago: Chicago Review Press, 2008. (Chapter 12.)

Nelson, Willie, with Bud Shrake. *Willie: An Autobiography.* New York: Simon and Schuster, 1988.

Patoski, Joe Nick. *Willie Nelson: An Epic Life.* New York: Little, Brown, 2008.

Perkins, Carl, and David McGee. *Go, Cat, Go! The Life and Times of Carl Perkins.* New York: Hyperion, 1996. (Chapters 3–7, 18–20, 22–24.)

Pleasants, Henry. *The Great American Popular Singers.* New York: Simon & Schuster, 1985.

Richards, Keith, with James Fox. *Life*. New York: Little, Brown, 2010.

Rijff, Ger, comp. *Long Lonely Highway: A 1950s Elvis Scrapbook*. Ann Arbor: Pierian Press, 1987.

Sanjek, Russell. *Pennies from Heaven: The American Popular Music Business in the Twentieth Century*. New York: Da Capo Press, 1996.

Scaduto, Anthony. *Bob Dylan: An Intimate Biography*. New York: Grosset & Dunlap, 1971.

Selvin, Joel. *Ricky Nelson: Idol for a Generation*. Chicago: Contemporary, 1990.

Shelton, Robert. *No Direction Home: The Life and Music of Bob Dylan*. New York: Ballantine Books, 1986.

Silverman, Jonathan. *Johnny Cash and American Culture: Nine Choices*. Amherst: University of Massachusetts Press, 2010.

Sisk, Eileen. *Buck Owens: The Biography*. Chicago: Chicago Review Press, 2010.

Streissguth, Michael. *Johnny Cash: The Biography*. Cambridge, Mass.: Da Capo, 2006. (Chapters 1–20, 22, 24, 26–27.)

———. *Johnny Cash at Folsom Prison: The Making of a Masterpiece*. Cambridge, Mass.: Da Capo, 2004.

Style, Lyle E. *Ain't Got No Cigarettes: Memories of Music Legend Roger Miller*. Winnipeg: Great Plains Publications, 2005. (Chapters 13–14.)

Tart, Larry. *Freedom through Vigilance: History of U.S. Air Force Security Service*. Vol. 2. West Conshohocken, Pa.: Infinity Publishing, 2010. (Chapter 2.)

Thomson, Graeme. *The Resurrection of Johnny Cash*. London: Jawbone Press, 2011. (Chapters 31–34.)

Tosches, Nick. *Country: Living Legends and Dying Metaphors in America's Biggest Music*. New York: Scribners, 1985. (Chapter 8.)

———. *Hellfire: The Jerry Lee Lewis Story*. New York: Dell Trade Paperback, 1982.

Tost, Tony. *American Recordings*. New York: Continuum, 2011. (Chapter 34.)

Turner, Steve. *The Man Called Cash: The Life, Love, and Faith of an American Legend*. Nashville: W Publishing Group, 2004. (Chapters 1–5, 7–15, 17–27, 29, 35–36.)

Urbanski, Dave. *The Man Comes Around: The Spiritual Journey of Johnny Cash*. Lake Mary, Fla.: Relevant Books, 2003. (Chapter 1.)

Wald, Elijah. *Escaping the Delta: Robert Johnson and the Invention of the Blues*. New York: Amistad, 2004.

Wald, Gayle F. *Shout, Sister, Shout: The Untold Story of Rock-and-Roll Trailblazer Sister Rosetta Tharpe*. Boston: Beacon Press, 2007.

Weissman, Dick. *Which Side Are You On?* New York: Continuum, 2005.

West, Red, Sonny West, and Dave Hebler with Steve Dunleavy. *Elvis: What Happened?* New York: Ballantine Books, 1977.

Whiteside, Jonny. *Ramblin' Rose: The Life and Career of Rose Maddox*. Nashville: Country Music Foundation Press and Vanderbilt University Press, 1997. (Chapter 6.)

Wren, Christopher. *Winners Got Scars Too: The Life and Legends of Johnny*

Cash. New York: Dial Press, 1971. (Chapters 1–7, 9–15, 17–22.)

Zwonitzer, Mark, and Charles Hirshberg. *Will You Miss Me When I'm Gone? The Carter Family and Their Legacy in American Music.* New York: Simon and Schuster, 2002. (Chapters 11–12.)

BOOKS—COLLECTIONS

Cash by the Editors of Rolling Stone. New York: Crown, 2004. Especially: Rosanne Cash, "My Dad Johnny Cash"; Anthony DeCurtis, "Johnny Cash Won't Back Down"; Jason Fine, "Home Sweet Home: In the Studio with Johnny Cash"; David Fricke, "The *Rolling Stone* Interview with Rick Rubin"; Mikal Gilmore, "The Man in Black"; Ralph Gleason, "Johnny Cash Meets Richard Nixon"; Steve Pond, "Broken Down in Branson"; and Steve Pond, "The *Rolling Stone* Interview: Johnny Cash."

I Still Miss Someone. Compiled by Hugh Waddell. Nashville: Cumberland House, 2004.

Johnny Cash and Philosophy: The Burning Ring of Truth. Edited by John Huss and David Werther. Chicago: Open Court, 2008.

Ring of Fire: The Johnny Cash Reader. Edited by Michael Streissguth. Cambridge, Mass.: DaCapo, 2002.

BOOKS—PHOTO HISTORIES

Cash, Cindy. *The Cash Family Scrapbook.* New York: Crown Trade Paperbacks, 1997.

Miller, Bill. *Cash: An American Man.* New York: Pocket Books, 2004.

BOOKS—REFERENCE

Brackett, Nathan, with Christian Hoard, eds. *The New Rolling Stone Album Guide.* New York: Fireside, 2004.

Gentry, Robert. *The Louisiana Hayride: The Glory Years. Vol. 1. 1948–55.* Many, La: Gentry, 1998. Includes ads for every Louisiana Hayride show as well as some newspaper articles about them.

———. *The Louisiana Hayride: The Glory Years.* Vol. 2. *1956–60.* Many, La.: Gentry, 1998.

Gordon, Robert. *The King on the Road: Elvis Live on Tour 1954 to 1977.* New York: St. Martin's Griffin, 1996.

Gray, Michael, and Roger Osborne. *The Elvis Atlas: A Journey through Elvis Presley's America.* New York: Henry Holt, 1996.

Guralnick, Peter, and Ernest Jorgensen. *Elvis Day by Day: The Definitive Record of His Life and Music.* New York: Ballantine Books, 1999.

Lewry, Peter. *I've Been Everywhere: A Johnny Cash Chronicle.* London: Helter Skelter, 2001.

Smith, John L. *The Johnny Cash Discography.* Westport, Conn.: Greenwood Press, 1985.

———. *The Johnny Cash Discography, 1984–1993.* Westport, Conn.: Greenwood Press, 1994.

Whitburn, Joel. *The Billboard Albums*. Menomonee Falls, Wis.: Record Research, 2006.

——. *Pop Memories, 1890–1954: The History of American Popular Music*. Menomonee Falls, Wis.: Record Research, 1986.

——. *Top Country Albums, 1964–2007*. Menomonee Falls, Wis.: Record Research, 2008.

——. *Top Country Songs, 1944–2005*. Menomonee Falls, Wis.: Record Research, 2005.

——. *Top Pop Singles*. Menomonee Falls, Wis.: Record Research, 2009.

——. *Top R&B Albums, 1965–1998*. Menomonee Falls, Wis.: Record Research, 1999.

——. *Top R&B/Hip-Hop Singles, 1942 to 2004*. Menomonee Falls, Wis.: Record Research, 2004.

BOOKLETS—FROM ALBUM BOX SETS

These sets provide detailed recording session information, including personnel, as well as lengthy and insightful essays about the various stages of Cash's career at Columbia and Sun in the 1950s and 1960s.

Johnny Cash: The Man in Black, 1954–1958. Bear Family Records, 1990. Essay by Colin Escott. 5 CDs.

Johnny Cash: The Man in Black, 1959–1962. Bear Family Records, 1991. Essay by Colin Escott. 5 CDs.

Johnny Cash: The Man in Black, 1963–69 Plus. Bear Family Records, 1995. Essay by Colin Escott. 6 CDs.

Johnny Cash: Come Along and Ride This Train. Bear Family Records, 1991. Essay by Bob Allen. 4 CDs.

Cash: Unearthed. American Recordings, 2003. Text by Sylvie Simmons. 5 CDs.

PROFILES AND ESSAYS

Ackerman, Paul, and staff. "Cash—Past and Present Together." *Billboard* salute, May 23, 1970.

Braun, Saul. "Good Ole Boy." *Playboy*, November 1970.

Carr, Patrick. "The Big Thumb." *Country Music*, 1997.

Cooper, Peter, and staff. "Goodbye Mr. Cash." *Nashville Tennessean*, September 13, 2003.

Corliss, Richard. "The Man in Black." *Time*, September 22, 2003.

Cusic, Don, and Jennifer Bohler. "Johnny Cash–*Cash Box*–Silver Salute." *Cash Box*, 1980.

Davis, Frances. "God's Lonely Man." *Atlantic*, March 2006.

Dearmore, Tom. "First Angry Man of Country Singers." *New York Times Sunday Magazine*, September 21, 1969.

Flanagan, Bill. "Johnny Cash, American." *Musician*, May 1988.

Guralnick, Peter. "John R. Cash: I Will Rock 'n' Roll with You (If I Have To)." *Country Music*, July–August 1980. (Chapters 1–6.)

Kamp, David. "American Communion." *Vanity Fair,* October 2006.

LaFarge, Peter. "Johnny Cash." *Sing Out!* May 1965.

Linderman, Larry. "*Penthouse* Interview: Johnny Cash." *Penthouse,* August 1975.

Martin, Gavin. "Out of the Black." *New Musical Express,* May 30, 1987.

Oermann, Robert K. "Superstar Cash Still Speaks for the Heart of America." *Nashville Tennessean,* April 26, 1987.

Orr, Jay. "The Man Is Back." *Nashville Tennessean,* April 17, 1999.

Tosches, Nick. "Chordless in Gaza: The Second Coming of John R. Cash." *Journal of Country Music* 17 (1995).

Wells, Steven. "Old, Gifted, and Black." *New Musical Express,* April 27, 1991.

Wenner, Jann. "Country Tradition Goes to Heart of Dylan Songs." *Rolling Stone,* May 25, 1968.

PERIODICALS

Of the countless newspapers and magazines that reported on Johnny Cash, the ones that I went back to repeatedly were the *Nashville Tennessean,* the *Nashville Banner,* the *Memphis Press Scimitar, Billboard, Rolling Stone,* the *Los Angeles Times,* the *New York Times* and the scores of small-town papers whose pages can be found in the Access Newspaper Archives link on the Los Angeles Public Library website. Articles of special interest are cited in the chapter listings that follow.

CHAPTER 1

Interviews

Joanne Cash, Johnny Cash, Kathy Cash, Rosanne Cash, Roy Cash Jr., Tommy Cash, Damon Fielder, A. J. Henson, Everett Henson, J. E. Huff, James Keach.

Websites

Myfamily.com (a website run by Everett Henson devoted to the history of the Dyess colony).

Additional sources

"American Recordings" liner notes by Johnny Cash. Contained in the album *American Recordings,* American Recordings record label, 1994.

"Dyess Colony Redevelopment Master Plan," prepared by John Milner Associates, West Chester, Pa., April 2010.

"The Founding of Dyess Colony" by Pat Pittman. *Arkansas Historical Quarterly,* Winter 1970.

"President's Visit Opens Centennial Celebration," an account of Eleanor Roosevelt's trip to Dyess in 1936, available through the Old State House Museum in Little Rock, Ark.

"Trouble in Paradise: Dyess Colony and Arkansas Politics" by Donald Holley. *Arkansas Historical Quarterly,* Autumn 1973.

Recordings

Deep Roots of Johnny Cash. Bear Family Records, 2006. Most of the twenty-four songs on this CD, including Jimmie Rodgers's "The One Rose" and Vernon Dalhart's "The Engineer's Dying Child," offer a sample of the music that influenced Johnny Cash as a boy in Dyess.

The Singing Brakeman: 1927–1933, Jimmie Rodgers. Bear Family. Cash's main inspiration saluted in a six-disc box set. Includes "Hobo Bill's Last Ride."

CHAPTER 2

Background

Marty Stuart believes that Cash wrote "Folsom Prison Blues" in Germany because he heard an early version of a tape that was made on the tape recorder Cash bought in Germany. But Marshall Grant disputed that view. He said Cash didn't write the song until well after he returned to the States. He speculated that the tape was made in Memphis.

Interviews

Johnny Cash, Rich Collins, Red Ernst, Jerry Farwell, Sylvia Flye, William Harrell, James Keach, Bob Mehaffey, Bob Moodie, Ben Perea, Orville (Wayne) Rigdon, Chuck Riley, Gayle Stelter, Larry Tart, Al Thurston.

Recordings

"Crescent City Blues" can be heard on Gordon Jenkins's concept album *Seven Dreams,* a single CD which has been re-released by Basta Records. It is also on *Johnny Cash: Roots and Rivers,* a single CD on Hip-O.

Websites

http://6912th.org/cashpage.htm (a site that focuses on Johnny Cash's 6912th Radio Mobile Squadron, which was stationed in Landsberg, Germany).

CHAPTER 3

Background

One of the haziest parts of the Johnny Cash story is how he got to Sun Records. He told at least five different versions, and none fully squared with anything Marshall Grant recounted. To make matters worse, the numbering system at Sun Records proved to be notoriously unreliable in chronicling the company's early recording history. Because tape was expensive, Sam Phillips would often tape over something if he wasn't planning to release it, and he would often combine tracks from various tapes onto a single tape so he could reuse the others. In the latter process, he would sometimes end up with tunes from a Cash session and, say, a Charlie Rich session or a totally unrelated radio commercial on a single tape.

To retrace the steps, I met with Grant and went over the early days in Memphis week by week, matching his earlier recollections with everything else we could find about those months in late 1954 and early 1955. During the interview, Marshall's account often differed from what both he and John had written. He showed no reluctance to revise his timetable, however, and we came up with a schedule of events that he felt confident was "ninety-nine percent" correct.

Interviews

Joanne Cash, Johnny Cash, Roy Cash Jr., Tommy Cash, Damon Fielder, Marshall Grant, Scotty Moore, Knox Phillips, Sam Phillips, Mark Stielper.

Articles, Essays, and Reviews

Gilmore, Mikal. "The Man in Black." In *Cash by the Editors of Rolling Stone.*

Recordings

Phillips, Dewey, *Red, Hot and Blue.* Memphis Archives Records. These radio broadcasts offer a colorful glimpse of the DJ who was stirring things up in Memphis in the mid-1950s. Cash named his first Sun Records single after the title of Phillips's radio show.

"The Sun Collection," various artists. Rhino. This 1994 CD box set offers a comprehensive summary of the musical world Cash stepped into in 1954 and helped expand.

CHAPTER 4

Interviews

Johnny Cash, Roy Cash Jr., Colin Escott, Dale Franklin, Marshall Grant, David McGee, Knox Phillips, Sam Phillips.

Articles, Essays, and Reviews

Gilmore, Mikal. "The Man in Black." In *Cash by the Editors of Rolling Stone.*

CHAPTER 5

Interviews

James Burton, Louise Burton, Johnny Cash, Kathy Cash, Roy Cash Jr., Larry Collins, Lorrie Collins, Billie Jean Horton, Barbara King, Claude King, David McGee, Sam Phillips, Mark Stielper.

Articles, Essays, and Reviews

Gilmore, Mikal. "The Man in Black." In *Cash by the Editors of Rolling Stone.*

Gleason, Ralph J. "It Looks As If Elvis Has a Rival—From Arkansas." *San Francisco Chronicle,* December 16, 1956.

Green, Ben A. "Johnny Cash Achieves 'Life's Ambition.'" *Nashville Banner,* July 14, 1956.

Recordings

Johnny Cash: From Memphis to Hollywood. Columbia Legacy, 2011. This two-disc package contains the first Cash broadcast on KWEM in Memphis as well as a sample of early demos that Cash did at Sun—including "I Walk the Line," "Get Rhythm," and "Country Boy."

Chapter 6
Background

When was "I Walk the Line" written? Many articles about Cash point to the November 19, 1955, show in Gladewater, Texas, but that date goes against much that Cash said and virtually everything Grant said about the song. (We won't even get into Vivian's claim that he wrote the song while they were driving in the car one day; most likely he was simply singing the song to her for the first time.)

In his first autobiography in 1975, Cash said he wrote the song after his first Hayride appearance in Shreveport, which would have made the song's birthday December 3, 1955. In his second autobiography, he placed the song in 1956, when he was "having a hard time resisting the temptation to be unfaithful to [Vivian] back in Memphis." He goes on: "I put those feelings into the beginning of a song and sang the first two verses for Carl Perkins backstage before a show." If the Gladewater location holds, the date would most likely have been February 12, 1956, because Cash and Perkins had played the Louisiana Hayride the night before.

When I asked Marshall Grant about the song just weeks before his death in 2011, he wasn't buying any of Cash's recollections. He said Cash heard him doing some slow, repetitive bass runs while warming up before an afternoon show in Longview, Texas, during the spring of 1956. "John told me to play the run again and he started humming along—just the way he did on the record—and he came out with the opening line 'I keep a close watch on this heart of mine,' then he stopped and said, 'Whatever you do, Marshall, don't forget that run.' That night in the car, John wrote 'I Walk the Line,' and Sam recorded it as soon as we got back to Memphis." If Grant is correct the song was probably written after Louisiana Hayride appearances on March 24 or 31. What is certain is Cash recording "I Walk the Line" on April 2, 1956, in Memphis.

Interviews

Norm Bale, James Burton, Louise Burton, Johnny Cash, Roy Cash Jr., Jack Clement, Larry Collins, Lorrie Collins, Sylvia Flye, Marshall Grant, Billie Jean Horton, David McGee, Sam Phillips, Johnny Wessler.

Articles, Essays, and Reviews

Gilmore, Mikal. "The Man in Black." In *Cash by the Editors of Rolling Stone.*
Smith, Leo. "Foster Park, R.I.P." *Los Angeles Times,* September 10, 1992.

Recordings

The Big "D" Jamboree Love, vols. 1 and 2. Dragon Street Records, 2000. More than fifty recordings from the stage of the Big "D" Jamboree in Dallas in the late 1950s. Includes three numbers by Johnny Cash and five by Carl Perkins.

Folk Songs of the Hills, Merle Travis. Capitol Records, 1947.

Johnny Cash: Live Recordings from the Louisiana Hayride. Louisiana Hayride Series, Scena Records, 2003. Contains sixteen songs performed during Louisiana Hayride appearances.

CHAPTER 7
Interviews

Carlene Carter, Johnny Cash, Rosanne Cash, Roy Cash Jr., Jack Clement, Larry Collins, Lorrie Collins, Sylvia Flye, Marshall Grant, James Keach, Sam Phillips, Johnny Western.

Articles, Essays, and Reviews

Gilmore, Mikal. "The Man in Black." In *Cash by the Editors of Rolling Stone.*

Johnson, Robert. "Gleason Signs Cash for 10 Guest Spots." *Memphis Press Scimitar,* January 7, 1957.

CHAPTER 8
Interviews

Johnny Cash, Rosanne Cash, Jack Clement, Larry Collins, Lorrie Collins, Sylvia Flye, Marshall Grant, Merle Haggard, W. S. Holland, Billie Jean Horton, Sam Phillips, Johnny Western.

Articles, Essays, and Reviews

Johnson, Robert. "Johnny Cash Moving to Hollywood." *Memphis Press Scimitar,* August 5, 1958.

Recordings

The Collins Kids at Town Hall Party. Bear Family, 2002. Larry and Lorrie Collins at Town Hall Party in Compton, Calif. (DVD).

Johnny Cash at Town Hall Party, 1958–1959. Bear Family, 2002. Cash at the Town Hall Party show in Compton, Calif. (DVD).

CHAPTER 9
Interviews

Johnny Cash, Kathy Cash, Larry Collins, Lorrie Collins, Sylvia Flye, Marshall Grant, Merle Haggard, Saul Holiff, Billie Jean Horton, Mac McBride.

Articles, Essays, and Reviews

Anderson, Pat. "Friend's Death Saddens Opry Homecoming." *Nashville Tennessean,* November 6, 1960.

"Events and Discoveries." *Sports Illustrated,* June 15, 1959. Cash's racetrack visit with Silky Sullivan.

CHAPTER 10
Interviews

Johnny Cash, Roy Cash Jr., Larry Collins, Lorrie Collins, Damon Fielder, Sylvia Flye, Marshall Grant, W. S. Holland, Saul Holiff, Billie Jean Horton, Margie Perkins, Johnny Western.

Recordings

Five Minutes to Live, a film starring Johnny Cash. Bear Family/And More Bears, 2004 (DVD).

Chapter 11
Interviews
Johnny Cash, June Carter Cash, Larry Collins, Lorrie Collins, Damon Fielder, Marshall Grant, Jonathan Holiff, W. S. Holland, Mac McBride, Mark Stielper, Johnny Western.

Chapter 12
Interviews
John Carter Cash, Johnny Cash, June Carter Cash, Sylvia Flye, Marshall Grant, Billie Jean Horton, Rip Nix, Mark Stielper.
Recordings
In the Shadow of Clinch Mountain, Bear Family. Carter Family. A twelve-disc history of Carter Family recordings.

Chapter 13
Interviews
Johnny Cash, Dixie Hall, Tom T. Hall, Saul Holiff, Harlan Howard, Johnny Western.

Chapter 14
Interviews
Johnny Cash, June Carter Cash, Kathy Cash, Rosanne Cash, Jack Clement, Damon Fielder, Sylvia Flye, Mark Stielper, Johnny Western.

Chapter 15
Interviews
Johnny Cash, Roy Cash Jr., Marshall Grant, Mark Stielper, Johnny Western.
Recordings
Cash's long-unreleased version of "Thunderball" is available on *Johnny Cash: From Memphis to Hollywood Bootleg II.* Columbia Legacy. The two-disc set also includes the song from the film *Five Minutes to Live.*

Johnny Cash: Roots and Rivers, various artists. Hip-O. Anita Carter's recording of "(Love's) Ring of Fire" is one of sixteen tracks on this collection of early versions of songs identified with Cash. Also includes Peter La Farge's "The Ballad of Ira Hayes," the Kingston Trio's "Jackson," Gordon Jenkins's "Crescent City Blues," and Jimmie Davis's "I Was There When It Happened."

Johnny Cash Live Around the World Bootleg III. Columbia Legacy. This two-disc CD features the Newport Folk Festival concert.

Chapter 16
Interviews
Johnny Cash, Kathy Cash, Rosanne Cash, Jack Clement, Damon Fielder, Sylvia Flye, Marshall Grant, Johnny Western.
Articles, Essays, and Reviews
Hurst, Jack. "Cash Plans $25 Million Suit against the Klan." *Nashville Tennessean,* February 4, 1966.
"Judge Lenient with Cash, Could Have Gotten a Year." UPI, March 9, 1956.
"Pill Smuggling Laid to Johnny Cash." *Nashville Tennessee,* October 6, 1956.

Chapter 17
Background
Jonathan Holiff was estranged from his father at a young age, but he became so consumed by his father's history after Saul's death in 2005 that he spent years piecing his father's story together. The search was inspired when, shortly after Saul's death, Jonathan discovered a treasure trove of letters, home movies, tapes, and other artifacts in a storage locker his father had kept for years in Nanaimo, British Columbia, where the elder Holiff lived his final years. Jonathan used the material as the basis of a documentary film, *My Father and the Man in Black,* which began a run of film festivals in 2012.

Because of his difficult relationship with his father, Jonathan came to the project as a "hostile witness," and despite the empathy he felt after learning about his father's deep depression and insecurity, he remained an objective observer—not at all self-conscious about describing his father as "controlling, emotionally abusive, and neglectful on the home front." In the film Jonathan does achieve some closure after finding audiotapes in which Saul reflects on his life and children.
Interviews
Johnny Cash, Kathy Cash, Clive Davis, Jonathan Holiff, Bob Johnston, Don Reid, Harold Reid, Mark Stielper.
Video
Pete Seeger's Rainbow Quest—Johnny Cash and Roscoe Holcomb. Shanachie, 2005 (DVD).

Chapter 18
Interviews
Johnny Cash, Kathy Cash, Rosanne Cash, Tommy Cash, Clive Davis, Marshall Grant, Bob Johnston, Bill Miller, Don Reid, Harold Reid, Mark Stielper, Dr. Nat Winston.
Articles, Essays, and Reviews
"Johnny Cash's Wife Granted Divorce." Associated Press, December 23, 1967.

Chapter 19

Interviews

Gene Beley, Carlene Carter, John Carter Cash, Johnny Cash, Clive Davis, Marshall Grant, Stan Jacobson, Bob Johnston, Don and Harold Reid, Rev. Jimmie Snow.

Recordings

Johnny Cash at Folsom Prison, Legacy Edition. Columbia / Legacy, 2005. Contains the complete two concerts.

Articles, Essays, and Reviews

"Cash, June. 'Walk the Line' in Kentucky." *Nashville Tennessean,* March 2, 1968.

Shelton, Robert. "Johnny Cash Stirs New York Hearts." *New York Times,* December 8, 1968.

Chapter 20

Interviews

Geoffrey Cannon, Johnny Cash, Clive Davis, Stan Jacobson, Bob Johnston, Jim Marshall, Mark Stielper.

Articles, Essays, and Reviews

Gleason, Ralph J. "Johnny Cash at San Quentin." *Rolling Stone,* May 31, 1969.

"Graham Breaks Bread with Balladeer Cash." *Nashville Tennessean,* December 8, 1969.

Satterfield, Lawayne. "Johnny Cash Story Told in New Film." *Nashville Banner,* September 13, 1969.

Sawyer, Kathy. "Johnny Cash Show to Be More Country." *Nashville Tennessean,* October 19, 1969.

Thomas, Patrick. "Cash and Dylan Tape TV Number in Nashville." *Rolling Stone,* May 31, 1969.

Chapter 21

Interviews

Joanne Cash, John Carter Cash, Johnny Cash, Kathy Cash, Rosanne Cash, Jack Clement, Billy Graham, Marshall Grant, Stan Jacobson, Bob Johnston, Kris Kristofferson, Bill Miller, Lou Robin, Mark Stielper, Jimmy Tittle, Nat Winston.

Chapter 22

Interviews

Johnny Cash, Clive Davis, Marshall Grant, Stan Jacobson, Bob Johnston, Kris Kristofferson, Lou Robin.

CHAPTER 23
Interviews
Larry Butler, Johnny Cash, Larry Gatlin, Kris Kristofferson, Don Reid, Harold Reid, Rev. Jimmie Snow.

CHAPTER 24
Interviews
Larry Butler, Johnny Cash, Bob Elfstrom, Marshall Grant, Jonathan Holiff, Gary Klein, Kris Kristofferson, Lou Robin, Rev. Jimmie Snow.
Articles, Essays, and Reviews
O'Donnell, Red. "Cash's 'Gospel Road' Opens." *Nashville Banner,* October 23, 1972.

CHAPTER 25
Interviews
Larry Butler, Carlene Carter, Kathy Cash, Rosanne Cash, Marshall Grant, Jonathan Holiff, Karen Robin, Lou Robin.

CHAPTER 26
Interviews
Larry Butler, Carlene Carter, Cindy Cash, John Carter Cash, Johnny Cash, Jack Clement, Marshall Grant, Lou Robin, Karen Robin.

CHAPTER 27
Interviews
Brian Ahern, Carlene Carter, John Carter Cash, Marshall Grant, Jan Howard, David McGee, Lou Robin, Mark Stielper, Johnny Western.

CHAPTER 28
Interviews
Brian Ahern, Rick Blackburn, John Carter Cash, Kathy Cash, Lou Robin, Marty Stuart.
Articles, Essays, and Reviews
O'Shaughnessy, Anne. "Johnny Cash Sued by Former Associates." *Memphis Press Scimitar,* June 23, 1981.

CHAPTER 29
Interviews
Rick Blackburn, Cindy Cash, John Carter Cash, Johnny Cash, Rosanne Cash, Kris Kristofferson, Bill Miller, Robert K. Oermann, Steve Popovich, Mark Stielper, Marty Stuart.

Articles, Essays, and Reviews

Oermann, Robert K. "'Man in Black' without a Label." *Nashville Tennessean,* July 16, 1986.

———. "Reporter's Aim Was in Wrong Direction." *Nashville Tennessean,* July 21, 1986.

CHAPTER 30

Interviews

Johnny Cash, Jack Clement, David Ferguson, Kti Jensen, Kris Kristofferson, Steve Popovich, Lou Robin, Marty Stuart.

Articles, Essays, and Reviews

"Cash Critical, but Stable after By-Pass Surgery." *Nashville Banner,* December 20, 1988.

Graham, Rex. "Cash Vows Lifestyle Change Following Hospital Release." *Nashville Banner,* January 3, 1989.

CHAPTER 31

Interviews

Bono, Johnny Cash, Rosanne Cash, Lou Robin, Ted Rollins, Rick Rubin, Mark Stielper, Marty Stuart.

Articles, Essays, and Reviews

Appleton, Charlie. "Missouri Town Gets Johnny Cash Park." *Nashville Banner,* April 30, 1991.

Pond, Steve. "Broken Down in Branson." In *Cash by the Editors of Rolling Stone.*

CHAPTER 32

Interviews

Carlene Carter, John Carter Cash, Johnny Cash, Kathy Cash, Rosanne Cash, Tom Petty, Lou Robin, Rick Rubin, Mark Stielper, Tom Petty, Johnny Western.

Articles, Essays, and Reviews

Pond, Steve. "Broken Down in Branson." In *Johnny Cash by the Editors of Rolling Stone.*

CHAPTER 33

Interviews

Cindy Cash, Johnny Cash, David Ferguson, W. S. Holland, James Keach, Tom Petty, Lou Robin, Rick Rubin, Marty Stuart, Jimmy Tittle.

Articles, Essays, and Reviews

Sylvester, Ron. "'Man in Black' Charges Out of Branson Shows." *Springfield (Mo.) News-Leader,* November 22, 1986.

Chapter 34
Interviews
Bono, John Carter Cash, Johnny Cash, June Carter Cash, David Ferguson, Merle Haggard, Vicky Hamilton, Lou Robin, Rick Rubin.
Articles, Essays, and Reviews
DeCurtis, Anthony. "Johnny Cash Won't Back Down." In *Johnny Cash by the Editors of Rolling Stone.*

Chapter 35
Interviews
John Carter Cash, Johnny Cash, June Carter Cash, Rosanne Cash, David Ferguson, Vicky Hamilton, Aris McGarry, Mark Romanek, Rick Rubin, Marty Stuart, Kevin Weatherly.
Articles, Essays, and Reviews
Fine, Jason. "Home Sweet Home: In the Studio with Johnny Cash." In *Johnny Cash by the Editors of Rolling Stone.*

Chapter 36
Interviews
Cindy Cash, John Carter Cash, Johnny Cash, June Carter Cash, Kathy Cash, Rosanne Cash, Tara Cash, David Ferguson, Kti Jensen, Dr. Terri Jerkins, Phil Maffetone, Karen Robin, Lou Robin, Ted Rollins, Rick Rubin, Mark Stielper, Marty Stuart.

INDEX